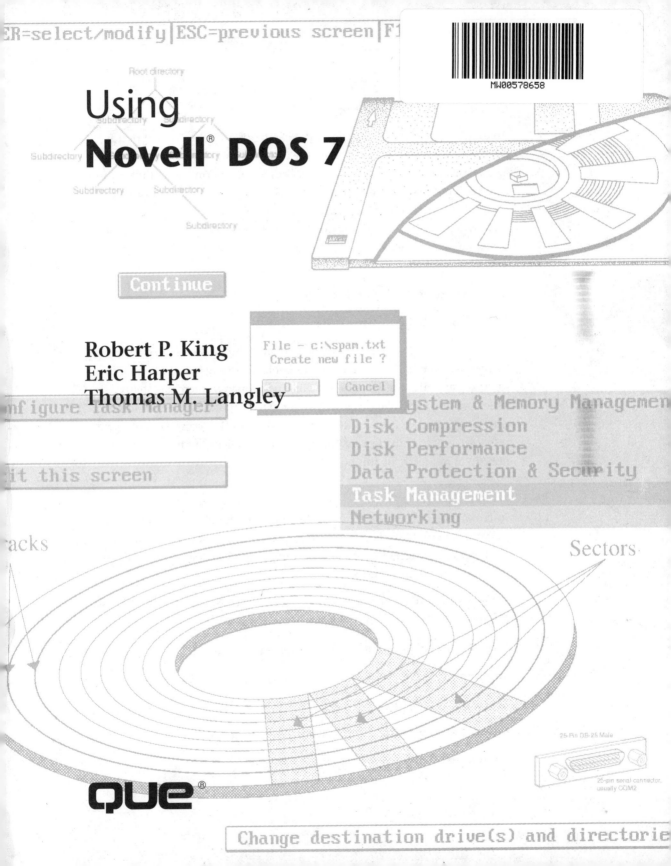

ER=select/modify ESC=previous screen F1

Using
Novell® DOS 7

Continue

Robert P. King
Eric Harper
Thomas M. Langley

File – c:\spam.txt
Create new file ?

O   Cancel

nfigure Task Manager

it this screen

ystem & Memory Management
Disk Compression
Disk Performance
Data Protection & Security
Task Management
Networking

acks   Sectors

que®

Change destination drive(s) and directorie

Using Novell DOS 7

Copyright© 1994 by Que® Corporation

Library of Congress Catalog No.: 93-86413

ISBN: 1-56529-104-2

96 95 94   6 5 4 3 2 1

Interpretation of the printing code: the rightmost double-digit number is the year of the book's printing; the rightmost single-digit number, the number of the book's printing. For example, a printing code of 94-1 shows that the first printing of the book occurred in 1994.

Screen reproductions in this book were created with Collage Plus and Collage Complete for DOS from Inner Media, Inc., Hollis, NH.

Using Novell DOS 7 is based on Novell DOS 7.

Publisher: David P. Ewing

Director of Publishing: Michael Miller

Director of Acquisitions and Editing: Corinne Walls

Marketing Manager: Ray Robinson

Dedication

To Pat, whom I never stopped loving.

Robert P. King

These chapters are dedicated to the memory of George L. Reese, my friend and companion, and to these people who helped me and cared for me during this past year:

Morgan Hamilton, my friend, how can I say thank you to someone who was there through the rough times, stood by me while I worked through my grief, and helped me get on with my life?

To my family, their love has kept me sane.

Christine and Janet, you were there when I needed you.

To Jim and David, kindred souls, we travel a common road, sharing the same pain, the same joy.

My friends at MCC, thank you for welcoming me home.

To the nurses and caregivers at the Medical College of Virginia, we really tried to win.

And finally to the people at Project Inform who relentlessly work for the day when no one else will die from AIDS.

Thomas M. Langley

Credits

Publishing Manager
Brad R. Koch

Acquisitions Editors
Angela J. Lee
Thomas F. Godfrey III

Product Directors
Robin Drake
Timothy S. Stanley

Production Editor
Virginia Noble

Editors
Lori Cates
Susan Shaw Dunn
C. Kazim Haidri
Patrick Kanouse
Heather Kaufman
Phil Kitchel
Susan Ross Moore
Linda Seifert

Technical Editors
Michael Watson
Rosemary Colonna

Figure Specialist
Wilfred R. Thebodeau

Book Designer
Amy Peppler-Adams

Cover Designer
Dan Armstrong

Production Team
Gary Adair
Angela Bannan
Paula Carroll
Karen Dodson
Rich Evers
Bob LaRoche
Joy Dean Lee
Linda Quigley
Michelle Self
Marc Shecter
Amy L. Steed

Indexer
Johnna VanHoose

Editorial Assistant
Michelle Williams

Composed in *Goudy* and *MCPdigital* by
Que Corporation

About the Authors

Robert P. King is an independent computer consultant servicing small business clients, with a specialty in multiuser systems and providing custom software to them. Besides providing ad hoc support to his own clients, he provides support as an independent sysop on Novell's desktop products support forum, NDESKTOP, on CompuServe. Mr. King received a B.A. from St. John Vianney Seminary and an M.A. from Villanova University. He was a contributing author of Que's *Using DR DOS 6.0* and *Using MS-DOS 6.0*, Special Edition.

Eric Harper is a reviews editor for *LAN Times* magazine. He works in the *LAN Times* Testing Center in Provo, Utah, evaluating and writing about Windows, Windows NT, DOS, UNIX, and Network Management products. Before starting at *LAN Times*, Mr. Harper worked for Novell Technical Support and has done private consulting. He received a B.A. degree from Brigham Young University. His other writing experience includes projects for New Riders Publishing, Brady Publishing, and Sams Publishing.

Thomas M. Langley is no stranger to personal computers. He began working with microprocessors when Intel introduced the 4004 and has since worked with nearly every device Intel has manufactured. A native of New Jersey, Tom moved to Richmond, Virginia, where he began designing microprocessor software in earnest when Digital Research introduced CP/M 1.4. He continually strives to find new ways to put computers to work both at home and in business. As a technical support engineer for NationsBanc Services Company, Tom has had the opportunity to create PC-based systems that interact with the huge information processing environment that exists within that company's corporate enterprise. Besides involvement with computers, he is an avid gardener, amateur musician, and human rights activist. Tom is an active member of the Metropolitan Community Church of Richmond, where he volunteers as caregiver for persons with AIDS and HIV infection.

Acknowledgments

The editorial staff would like to thank Michael Watson for his tremendous efforts in ensuring the technical quality of this book. His expertise and generous contributions are greatly appreciated.

Trademarks

Contents at a Glance

Contents at a Glance

Advanced Techniques

Command Reference

Maximizing Your System

Appendixes

Using the Network

Contents

12 Backup Utilities   307

V Device Utilities   329

13 Controlling System Devices   331

14 Managing the Display and Keyboard   373

VI System Security Utilities   401

15 System Security   403

16 Virus Protection   423

IX Using the Network   561

23 Introduction to Networking   563

24 Network Maintenance   589

Introduction

When personal computers were first invented almost 20 years ago, there was no such thing as a common operating system. Each computer manufacturer supplied either no operating system or a very rudimentary one. Then a young man by the name of Gary Kildall wrote CP/M (Control Program for Microcomputers) and founded Digital Research, Inc. to manufacture and distribute an operating system that could be used for most of these new machines. This enabled software designers and programmers to produce applications that ran on most microcomputers as long as they ran CP/M.

When IBM decided that the fast-growing small-computer industry was the place to be and introduced its PC, the company licensed an operating system supplied by Microsoft, but written by a small Seattle programming shop and based on CP/M. Although Microsoft and IBM gained control of the personal computer market (away from CP/M machines), Digital Research stayed as an important player in the industry, with its technical expertise in operating systems.

Digital Research's engineers continued to advance operating system technology with their Concurrent DOS and then MULTIUSER DOS, along with industrial-strength operating systems such as FlexOS, on which most major point-of-sale systems are based. In the late 1980s, Digital Research decided to get back as a major player in single-user operating systems for PCs. Microsoft had developed MS-DOS as far as Version 4, which was something of a disaster. Moreover, Microsoft had announced that it did not think PC operating systems should stay with DOS and had decided to move to Windows. Digital Research saw an opportunity with so many millions of DOS-based machines and so many thousands of software programs that run on DOS. Moreover, what Microsoft envisioned required much more in the way of hardware resources than most people had.

Thus, in 1990, Digital Research introduced DR DOS 5, compatible with MS-DOS, but much enhanced. DRI then continued in DOS technology ahead of Microsoft with DR DOS 6, which, according to most objective experts, ran Windows better than MS-DOS, as well as provided new features and utilities that many people once purchased from third-party sources. We were off to what some like to call "the DOS Wars." A year after DR DOS 5, Microsoft changed its mind about advancing DOS and issued MS-DOS 5. A few months later, DRI released DR DOS 6. Over a year and a half later, Microsoft tried to catch up again with MS-DOS 6.

About two years ago, Novell, Inc. purchased Digital Research and created Desktop Systems Group (NDSG). This move made DR DOS a part of one of the largest personal computer companies and gave Novell the DOS capability to merge with its premier network capability.

Novell DOS 7, the successor to DR DOS 6, is the prime offering of the merged technologies and companies. This new DOS takes personal computer technology to new heights. There are so many new technologies, enhancements, and improvements, as you will see in Chapter 2, that *Using Novell DOS 7* is indispensable in learning all about what you now can accomplish with this new version. *Using Novell DOS 7* will help you learn more about these features and become more proficient with the system. You will find that *Using Novell DOS 7* provides the information you need in a way that makes learning about Novell DOS 7 the pleasure that it should be.

Who Should Read This Book?

Using Novell DOS 7 was written with you in mind. You purchased Novell DOS 7 to get the best possible performance out of your computer, and this book was written to help you achieve that goal.

The book is both a tutorial and a reference work. As a tutorial, it enables the beginning user to come up to speed with the operating system. As a reference, it provides in-depth information that experienced Novell/DR DOS

users will find helpful. The book is divided into logical parts that make referencing information easy. If you are an intermediate user, you'll appreciate
not only the reference value of this book but also the clear, concise information and advice that appears throughout its pages.

What Hardware Do You Need?

To use Novell DOS 7, you need an IBM PC- or PS/2-compatible with at least
512K of RAM, two floppy disk drives, and a monochrome monitor. However,
to get the most out of the operating system, your computer should include a
hard disk, at least 1M of RAM (more memory is better with an 80286 or
higher processor), and one of the following:

- 8088 or 8086 CPU with expanded memory specification 4.0

- 80286 CPU with a NeAT, LeAP, or SCAT chipset

- 80386, 80486, or Pentium family of CPU

If you have at least two computers available, you can also interconnect the
machines with the built-in network. If you use a mouse (some people love
them, but others hate them), many of the utilities now use a full-screen mode
with which you can use a mouse, although it is not necessary to use one, of
course.

Chapter 4, "Installing Novell DOS 7," provides a detailed explanation of the
hardware requirements for each of the major features of Novell DOS, as well
as how to install or revise your setup for these features.

What Does This Book Include?

Using Novell DOS 7 covers as much information as possible about Novell DOS
7, including the DOS kernel, the built-in network, the enhanced utilities, and
other extensions. However, one item is not really discussed at all: NETWARS,
a game that can be played over the built-in network or on a stand-alone computer. Those of you who are enthralled with games probably need no help.
And those of you who do not appreciate these diversions probably don't
want to waste time on NETWARS anyway.

Some minor items are not covered as completely as possible. One is DEBUG, the program debugger. While the discussion of DEBUG in Appendix D does list the commands and how to start and exit the debugger, there is no discussion of how to debug programs. That really is more for a programmer's course. Magazines often offer small utilities you can create by using DEBUG, so this appendix can be of help there.

Appendixes B and C provide information on installing Windows 3.1 and GeoWorks Ensemble 2.0 under Novell DOS 7. However, because of scope and space limitations, no information is included that shows you how to use Windows 3.1 or GeoWorks. For more information on using Windows, see Que's *Using Windows 3.1*, Special Edition.

Otherwise, you will find that all facets of Novell DOS 7 are thoroughly discussed, from installation and use, with explanations and examples, to a quick reference for command formats.

One more thing. Although *Using Novell DOS 7* teaches you how to connect to a NetWare 2.x, 3.x, or 4.x network, the book does not show you how to use those networks. If you are able to add your computer as a workstation on one of these systems, you should contact the network administrator for information about your network.

The Details of This Book

Take a quick look at the organization of this book. You'll notice that it is laid out in order from easy to difficult topics, making learning for the beginner a snap. The book is also divided into logical pieces, making reference easy. For example, if you have questions about Novell DOS 7 memory management, you can look at Chapter 22, "Optimizing Memory."

Overall, the book is divided into 10 parts, containing 24 chapters and a comprehensive Command Reference (Part X), as well as helpful appendixes.

Part I: Novell DOS Basics. Part I is an introduction to the computer and Novell DOS. If you are a beginner with computers and operating systems, this part provides the foundation you need. More experienced users can get an overview of all the improvements and additions to DOS. For everyone, there is a discussion of the evolution of DOS and the rationale for Novell DOS 7.

Chapter 1, "Understanding DOS," provides information about the concept and history of DOS, as well as the development of Novell DOS. You also learn about the components of the computer and how Novell DOS functions with each component.

Chapter 2, "What's New in Novell DOS 7?" describes the new features that have been added to Novell DOS in its progression from DR DOS 6, along with other changes made in Version 7, including prior commands that have been enhanced.

Chapter 3, "Getting Help with DOSBook," shows you the on-line documentation and how to use it and the reference screen for each Novell command. You learn also in this chapter about the way to issue commands to DOS at the command line.

Part II: Setting Up Your System. Your great adventure with Novell DOS begins with the installation. This part of the book leads you through the major parts of the operating system, the hardware requirements for installing the major features, and the actual installation. This includes what you need for networking your computer and for other hardware devices that can be attached.

Chapter 4, "Installing Novell DOS 7," assists you in determining the optimum setup for your computer and its components, based on the features you want to use. Install puts Novell DOS on your computer; Setup lets you change your configuration when you change your system components or change your mind about the features you want to use.

Chapter 5, "Installing the Network," leads you into the world of networking with the installation of the Desktop Server and the Universal Client. Desktop Server gives you a peer-to-peer network as part of Novell DOS; Universal Client enables you to connect to this peer-to-peer network and to full NetWare systems.

Part III: Files and Directories. The real importance of an operating system is its capability to track the location of files. You interact with the operating system with commands that enable you to manage the files you create, and to organize and store the files in directories.

Chapter 6, "Understanding File Storage," teaches you some fundamental concepts: drive and disk structures, DOS directories, paths, DOS files and their attributes, and the use of wild cards.

Chapter 7, "Managing Files and Directories," instructs you in the powerful techniques of creating, deleting, renaming, and changing directories. Directories provide the basis for organizing files on a disk. You also learn the file management commands: copying, moving, deleting, comparing, and listing files and their contents.

Part IV: Disk and File Management. The acronym DOS stands for *disk operating system* and indicates the importance of your disk subsystem to your computer. Novell DOS includes all the tools you need to work effectively with your hard disk: preparing it for use, duplicating disks, checking its integrity, and improving its capacity and performance.

Chapter 8, "Preparing Disks," shows you all the utilities you need to begin using a disk. Included in this chapter are formatting a disk and preparing it for booting. You also learn how to unformat a disk formatted by mistake.

Chapter 9, "Copying and Comparing Disks," examines the DISKCOPY and DISKCOMP commands. These commands enable you to back up floppy disks and ensure that the copy routines are performed successfully.

Chapter 10, "Undeleting Files," helps you overcome problems caused by accidentally erasing files that really shouldn't have been erased.

Chapter 11, "Disk Optimization Utilities," introduces you to several powerful disk utilities that come with Novell DOS. Using these utilities enables you to check the status of and possibly repair errors on your computer's disk subsystem, increase the storage capacity of your disk, and increase your disk's performance.

Chapter 12, "Backup Utilities," teaches you how to make fast and easy backups of your important information regularly. Don't miss this most important chapter. It could save you more than the cost of your computer.

Part V: Device Utilities. An operating system manages more than just the disk. Novell DOS also gives you the ability to manage other devices attached to your computer, such as your video display and your printer and other ports. The two chapters in this part show you how to manage these devices.

Chapter 13, "Controlling System Devices," shows you how to manage your printer, print in PostScript from DOS, set up printer ports, and transfer files between computers without a network. Included in this chapter is the SHARE utility for disk management.

Chapter 14, "Managing the Display and Keyboard," continues with the theme of devices. In particular, this chapter focuses on the utilities of Novell DOS that manage the keyboard and video display.

Part VI: System Security Utilities. No matter how careful you are, you always need to plan security. Files can be accidentally deleted by you or others. Furthermore, certain files and disks may contain sensitive information others should not access. Then, of course, there is the issue of virus infection. This part of the book deals with all these issues, on and off the network.

Chapter 15, "System Security," steps you through the commands that enable you to keep others off your system entirely, or out of specific directories and files on your disks.

Chapter 16, "Virus Protection," leads you through protecting your system from the modern scourge of computers: the virus.

Part VII: Advanced Techniques. Although Novell DOS is a standard operating system with standard procedures, it isn't so structured that you cannot customize it. Part VII shows you how to customize Novell DOS to your liking and how to use powerful features of Novell DOS.

Chapter 17, "Using the Novell DOS Text Editor," provides you with a tutorial for using the text editor that accompanies Novell DOS. The editor enables you to create files to customize Novell DOS, as well as create memos and other little notes when you do not need a full-featured word processor.

Chapter 18, "Configuring Your System," helps you work with the powerful and very flexible CONFIG.SYS file used by DOS to configure itself for your computer, its resources, and the features you want to use.

Chapter 19, "Using Batch Files," teaches you what a batch file is, how to create a batch file, and the special commands that you use with a batch file to automate normally tedious operating system tasks and produce some nice effects for your own system.

Chapter 20, "Using HISTORY and DOSKEY," gives you a complete tour of one of the neat features of Novell DOS. With HISTORY and DOSKEY, you can drastically reduce the number of keystrokes required for repetitive tasks.

Part VIII: Maximizing Your System. One thing that Novell DOS enables you to do exceptionally well is to manage memory and provide that memory for use by other programs. Part VIII teaches you how to use Novell DOS memory management, as well as how to manage multiple programs.

Chapter 21, "Multitasking and Task Switching," steps you through task management. Task Manager enables you to open more than one program at a time, both in a task-swapping mode and as a true multitasker. Then, by using a key combination, you can switch between programs that are open.

Chapter 22, "Optimizing Memory," guides you through the powerful memory management features of Novell DOS. You learn how to load Novell DOS and other programs into areas of memory that your computer could not normally access.

Part IX: Using the Network. This part of *Using Novell DOS 7* explores the peer-to-peer network built into Novell DOS. You can also connect to larger, full-service NetWare networks while maintaining your own system.

Chapter 23, "Introduction to Networking," shows you how to install a sample network, from the planning stage to network startup.

Chapter 24, "Network Maintenance," shows you how to tune the network for best performance, how to use the Novell DOS 7 network utilities, and how to use network diagnostics.

Part X: Command Reference. The comprehensive Command Reference contains the Novell DOS 7 commands, shown with syntax, applicable rules, and examples where needed. You can use this part both as a reference when you have problems and as a source of practical advice and tips during "browsing sessions." In all, the Command Reference is a complete, easy-to-use, quickly accessed resource on the proper use of Novell DOS commands.

Appendixes. Appendix A, "Internationalizing Your System," describes features for using Novell DOS in connection with foreign countries. This appendix shows you how to use special characters from the keyboard and place them on the display.

Appendix B, "Installing and Using Windows 3.1," helps you get Novell DOS 7 ready to run the Windows 3.1 operating environment. Also discussed are the considerations for running Windows 3.1 under Task Manager, as a task swapper and a multitasker, as well as without Task Manager.

Appendix C, "Installing and Using GeoWorks," helps you get Novell DOS 7 ready to run the GEOS operating environment. Also discussed are the steps for using Task Manager and GeoWorks together.

Appendix D, "Using DEBUG," provides information about the program debugger. This program is designed for people who are comfortable with machine language programming.

Conventions Used in This Book

Certain conventions are used in *Using Novell DOS 7* to help you learn the techniques described in the text. The following sections describe these conventions.

Special Formats. Words printed in uppercase include DOS commands (CHKDSK) and file names (EXAMPLE.DOC). Special enhancements include those shown in the following table:

Enhancement	Meaning
italic	New terms or phrases when they are defined
boldface	Information you are asked to type
special typeface	Direct quotations of words that appear on-screen or in a figure

Note

This paragraph format indicates additional information that may help you avoid problems or that should be considered when you use the described features.

Caution

This paragraph format warns you about hazardous procedures (for example, activities that delete files).

In addition, tips appear in the margin to suggest easier or alternative methods of executing a procedure, or to offer shortcuts to simplify or accelerate the processes described in the text.

Keys and Key Combinations. In most cases, keys in this book are represented as they appear on the keyboard. The arrow keys are represented by name (for example, "the up-arrow key"). The Print Screen key is abbreviated PrtSc, Page Up is PgUp, Insert is Ins, and so on. On your keyboard, these key names may be spelled out or abbreviated differently.

Note that throughout the text, the term *Enter* is used instead of *Return* for the Enter key. Note also that "enter **DIR**" means that you should type the command name DIR and then press Enter.

Uppercase letters are usually used in the examples for what you type, but you can type commands in either uppercase or lowercase letters—unless specifically noted, as in ANSI.SYS escape sequences where case can be important.

Syntax Lines and Command Examples. The command conventions used in this book have been established to help you learn to use commands quickly and easily. All syntax lines appear in a `special typeface`. The notation for issuing commands and running programs appears, in fullest form, in lines like the following:

```
CHKDSK drive:path\filename.ext switches
```

Command names appear in **boldface**. To activate the command in the preceding example, you *must* type the word **CHKDSK**. Any literal text that you type in a syntax line is shown in uppercase letters. Any text that you replace with other text (variable text) is shown in lowercase letters.

Not all parts of a syntax line are essential in all cases for the command to work. Any parameters that you see in **boldface**, besides the command name, are commonly used with the command but may not be required. In many cases, if you do not include these items, DOS uses the item's default value or setting, or the current directory or drive.

Portions of a syntax line that appear in *italic* are placeholders (variables). A *placeholder* holds the place for an actual name or value that you type when you issue the command. In other words, you don't type the word *filename*; you replace *filename* with the actual name of a file.

For some commands, you can enter one of two or more parameters, but you cannot enter more than one at a time. In such cases, the choices are shown separated by a vertical bar (|). For example, the BREAK command syntax is BREAK ON | OFF, meaning that you must enter the command as either BREAK ON or BREAK OFF.

Whenever you include a file name on a command line, you must provide a full path specification if the file is not located in the current path. If the command is in a different directory, you must specify the path.

Examples accompany the explanations of most commands and appear also in the special typeface. Presentations of command prompts and responses are indented. On occasion, the entire prompt or the text to be typed at the prompt cannot fit on one line of the printed page in this book. In such cases, the continued portion of the line is indented further.

A Few Last Words

Que's authors strive to make the best book possible, which means that they are concerned about meeting your needs. Que wants you to be successful with Novell DOS 7 and the book. Was this book useful? Did it help you better understand and operate your computer? Have you any suggestions? Are there topics Que should include? Should some topics be excluded? Please share your thoughts with Que. Write a note and send it to the following address:

Que Corporation
201 West 103rd Street
Indianapolis, IN 46290
Attn: Product Development

Please enjoy this book. Use it. Wear it out. Be successful in using Novell DOS 7.

Part I

Novell DOS Basics

Continue

1 Understanding DOS

2 What's New in Novell DOS 7?

3 Using DOSBook

Root directory

Subdirectory   Subdirectory

Subdirectory   Subdirectory   Subdirectory   Subdirectory

Subdirectory   Subdirectory

Subdirectory

Continue

File - c:\spam.txt
Create new file ?

0   ►   Cancel

nfigure Task Manager

xit this screen

ystem & Memory Managemen
Disk Compression
Disk Performance
Data Protection & Security
Task Management
Networking

racks

Sectors

25-Pin DB-25 Male

25-pin serial connector,
usually COM2

Change destination drive(s) and directorie

Chapter 1

Understanding DOS

Your computer consists of various hardware components: a central processing unit, memory, video screen, keyboard, floppy or hard disk drive (or both), possibly a printer or two, and maybe even a mouse, CD-ROM drive, scanner, or other devices. Your computer consists also of an *operating system* that ties the hardware together and lets your software use the various devices without having to know how specifically to control them. When you want to print something to your printer, for example, you just tell your operating system (DOS) to print the data. DOS knows how to interact with your printer and produce the "hard copy." Without the aid of the operating system, you might have to perform quite a few steps just to tell your computer to print a document.

This chapter explores the following topics:

- DOS concepts

- How DOS works with your computer

- How DOS evolved

- The new road taken by Novell DOS 7

Basic DOS Concepts

Novell DOS 7 is an operating system. An *operating system* processes your instructions and allocates the resources for the work you want to do. The operating system frees you from worrying about the technical details. If Novell DOS is doing its job, you don't need to know a lot about computers to be productive. However, understanding the way Novell DOS interacts with your computer may help you understand the way you can interact with Novell

DOS. This knowledge can help you decide how to configure Novell DOS to get the most out of your particular system, as well as help you utilize the advanced features of Novell DOS 7.

Hardware Platforms

Novell DOS can be used with all computers based on Intel's 8086 micropro-cessor family. That family includes 8086, 8088, 80286, 386, i486, 586 (Pentium), and compatible microprocessors, and encompasses IBM PCs and compatibles and PS/2s and compatibles. The hardware platform is further defined by the amount of system memory, the control components, and the circuits, as well as by the peripheral devices you attached to the system components.

Hardware Variations and Limitations. Basically, all computers with micro-processors in the 8086 family process information the same way. The differ-ences among them are how much information they can process and how fast. The 586 family is the most powerful; the 8086/8088 is the least power-ful.

The number of memory addresses that an 8086 or 8088 CPU can directly access is 1M (1 megabyte, or 1,024 kilobytes). The more powerful processors in the family can address more memory, but to ensure compatibility with all CPUs in the 8086 family, Novell DOS uses the 1M address range. One of the benefits of using Novell DOS 7, however, is that it can enable your CPU to take advantage of all available memory.

Depending on the hardware and software device drivers installed on your computer, as well as the amount of memory, Novell DOS can be configured to free up *conventional memory*—the first 640K of RAM—thereby increasing the speed and responsiveness of your hardware and software.

Novell DOS 7 is compatible with the *extended memory specification (XMS)*, a protocol that provides a standard interface to upper, high, and extended memory. It also has two device drivers that support the LIM *expanded memory specification (EMS)*.

In addition, Novell DOS 7 includes a DPMI (DOS Protected Mode Interface) server that allows one or more programs to use the protected mode capability of 386 and higher processors and to use the memory above the 1M boundary of non-DPMI software. Novell DOS 7 includes also a DPMS (DOS Protected Mode Services) capability for TSRs and system device drivers to use DPMI services. This is a new technology provided by Novell, which results in larger conventional memory limits.

To some extent, the type of hardware platform you use will dictate the way you can use Novell DOS. If your hardware is limited, Novell DOS will be limited. For instance, some features, such as advanced memory management, are limited by the power of the microprocessor, the amount of installed memory and, in some cases, the availability of add-on boards. Furthermore, some of Novell DOS 7's disk management features apply only to hard disk storage.

Chapter 4, "Installing Novell DOS 7," helps you maximize your Novell DOS installation on your system. You can also read Chapter 22, "Optimizing Memory," for everything you need to know about using the memory in your specific computer.

8088 and 8086. Despite the inherent speed-and-power limitations of the 8086 and 8088 microprocessors, Novell DOS 7 can help you optimize their performance. You can use Novell DOS to free up some conventional memory by using more *upper memory*—the remaining RAM from 640K to 1M.

With LIM 4.0 EMS hardware and software device drivers, you can use Novell DOS 7's HIMEM.SYS memory management driver to load the operating system kernel into upper memory, freeing conventional memory for applications.

80286. You can also use a LIM 4.0 EMS device driver on a 286-based computer to load TSRs (terminate-and-stay-resident programs), device drivers, and the Novell DOS system kernel into upper memory. If your computer has *extended memory* (the memory installed above 1M), you can use the memory manager HIMEM.SYS to relocate the Novell DOS operating system kernel to high memory, the first 16K of extended memory. In addition, you can access up to 15M of extended memory on 80286-based computers by using XMS. And DPMS client TSRs and device drivers can be located in the extended memory area (above 1M).

80386, 80486, and 80586. On 80386-, 80486-, and 80586-based computers, the Novell DOS EMM386.SYS device driver lets you use LIM 4.0 expanded memory without any add-on cards. You can relocate the Novell DOS operating system kernel to upper or high memory, and you can use upper memory for TSRs, device drivers, and operating system data structures. You can access up to 1000M of extended memory on 386-, 486-, and 586-based computers by using XMS. DPMI and DPMS client applications, TSRs, and device drivers are also able to use the extended memory on these machines.

Devices. *Devices* are the peripheral hardware components attached to your computer system. They provide input into the computer, receive output from the computer, or both. For instance, most systems include devices such as a printer, disk drives, a keyboard, and a display monitor. Some systems include other devices, such as a mouse, a modem, a CD-ROM drive, a plotter, a scanner, or a tape drive.

The devices are attached to your computer mechanically, perhaps connected by cable, or inserted internally into a circuit board slot. They are controlled by the computer's *basic input/output system (BIOS)*, a set of low-level programmed routines that provides an interface between the hardware and software. Novell DOS organizes your devices into a productive computing environment.

Understanding Device Drivers. Novell DOS contains the software instructions that let you, your computer, and your peripheral devices communicate. Because each device is different, Novell DOS depends on device drivers to interact with each device. *Device drivers* are software programs loaded in addition to the operating system for the purpose of managing the devices. If Novell DOS lacked device drivers, it couldn't communicate with the various device types available for each different computer system.

Device drivers for the keyboard, display, disk drives, printer, and auxiliary devices, called *resident drivers*, are automatically loaded when you start Novell DOS. Additional device drivers, called *installable device drivers*, come with Novell DOS; you can install them when you need them. Load drivers only for the devices you use.

Two basic kinds of device drivers are available. *Character device drivers* control devices that manipulate data one character at a time, such as printers and keyboards. *Block device drivers* control devices that manipulate large blocks of data at one time, such as disk drives.

Optimizing Storage. Disk drives require specific instructions to be useful. Novell DOS communicates with the disk drives through a *disk controller*. DOS tells the device driver what to do, and the device driver tells the controller. The controller accesses the disk and returns the required information to the device driver.

Novell DOS works hard to optimize your storage devices for better organization and quicker access. It has a disk optimizer utility that changes the arrangement of data on the disk so that Novell DOS can find the data faster.
Novell DOS lets you convert your disk drives into Stacker compression drives,
so that data is automatically compressed when you write to the drive and
decompressed when you read from the drive. Novell DOS supports hard disk
partitions up to 2G (*gigabytes*—billions of characters) in size. You can use the
DRIVPARM command to set physical characteristics for a specified disk drive,
or add logical drives. You can use the NWCACHE command to reduce the
time it takes to access files on a hard disk by telling Novell DOS to remember
the most used data on the disk.

Managing Printing. To control printer devices, Novell DOS uses device
drivers that call the name of the port where the device is attached. For instance, if the printer is attached to parallel port 1, Novell DOS names it LPT1.
Any command issued to LPT1 affects that printer.

You can use Novell DOS to redirect output to a printer device and to print
text files in the *background* while you continue working with your PC. You
can use it to print a graphics display onto an IBM-compatible graphics
printer. Code page switching enables you to change between character sets
so that you can print documents in different languages.

Controlling the Display. Novell DOS manages your video display according
to the type of display adapter you have. For instance, you may have a monochrome adapter (MDA), a color graphics adapter (CGA), an enhanced graphics adapter (EGA), or a video graphics array (VGA) adapter.

The ANSI.SYS device driver provides options for programs that need to
move the cursor, alter the screen display, or assign keyboard usage. The
DISPLAY.SYS driver enables code page switching for EGA and VGA displays.

Managing Connectivity. Novell DOS enables you to connect your computer
to other computers. It is totally integrated with the resources for a peer-to-
peer network that lets you share hardware and software resources with other
computers, and the capability to connect as a network client to other networks—NetWare 2.x, 3.x, and 4.x systems—so that you can share their resources.

The Novell DOS Desktop Server provides the means to be the server for a local network without having to dedicate a computer to be a file server. The Novell DOS Universal Client provides the capability to connect to a Desktop Server or a full NetWare network. All you have to do is add a network card and use cable to connect your computer to another computer.

You can use the Novell DOS FILELINK utility to send or receive files over a serial or parallel port cable connected to another computer, without having to use floppy disk drives to transfer data from one system to the other.

Novell DOS 7 Components

The role of an operating system is very complex, encompassing such varied tasks as file maintenance, memory management, data storage and retrieval, system connectivity, system and data security, and application launching. To ensure that every operating system function is accomplished quickly and efficiently, Novell DOS is made up of a series of software-based modules. The modules come on several floppy disks. The exact number of disks depends on the specific disk format used: 5 1/4-inch or 3 1/2-inch floppies, and double or high density. When you install Novell DOS, you set configurations and copy the system files from the floppies onto your hard disk, or even onto floppy disks if you want.

Together, the modules control the operating functions of your PC. They make sure that the computer understands the commands you enter and that each task is accomplished quickly and efficiently. Independently, each module serves a unique role.

Some parts of Novell DOS you may never know. These include the operating system program routines and data tables that make up the very core of Novell DOS, called the *kernel*. These routines let Novell DOS interact with the PC's basic input/output system (BIOS).

The *command processor* is the Novell DOS module that interprets your instructions and sends them on to the kernel for execution. It also provides the *user interface* (the Novell DOS prompt). The user interface is the part you use to input commands to the command processor. The user interface is the part of Novell DOS you'll use all the time. Figure 1.1 shows the flow among the different components of Novell DOS.

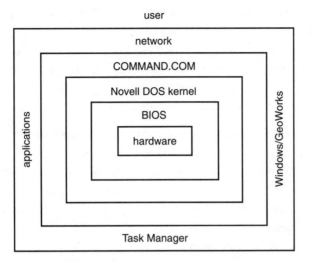

Fig. 1.1
A diagram of
Novell DOS 7
components.

Novell DOS Basics

You can add an operating environment on top of Novell DOS and the
COMMAND.COM command processor so that you don't have to work directly with the command interpreter. Two popular environments are Windows and GeoWorks. Novell has announced that it is working with Apple
Computer to provide a user interface for its customers, but no time frame has
been announced. Currently, Novell DOS 7 does not include a shell or a visual
or graphic user interface.

Using the Command Line. Traditionally, character-based programs like
Novell DOS use a command-line interface. Novell DOS displays a *prompt* on-
screen that means it is waiting for instructions. You use the keyboard to type
commands, which are displayed on-screen. When you press the Enter key, the
command is entered into COMMAND.COM, the Novell DOS command processor. The information you type beginning at the Novell DOS prompt and
ending with the Enter key is the *command line*. The typical command line
prompt looks like this:

```
C:\>
```

The commands used to communicate with Novell DOS are similar to the
commands used with other versions of DOS. People who use a keyboard often and people who are experienced DOS users should be comfortable typing
commands at the command line.

Understanding the Command Processor. The command line is your gateway to COMMAND.COM, the Novell DOS command processor. COMMAND.COM is a program loaded into memory each time you start Novell DOS. When you want your PC to perform a task, such as copying a file or displaying a directory, COMMAND.COM interprets the commands you issue at the interface level so that the Novell DOS kernel can process them.

COMMAND.COM has two parts. The *resident part* remains in memory as long as Novell DOS is running, and the *transient part* is stored on disk. COMMAND.COM executes internal commands directly. When you issue external commands, COMMAND.COM loads the appropriate program files from disk into memory and then executes the command. It loads and executes batch files and applications programs, as well as provides utilities and commands for keeping your files and disks organized.

Working with the Novell DOS Kernel. The Novell DOS kernel is a core file of instructions and routines that performs most of the operating system services you rely on. For instance, the kernel manages your files and disks, allocates memory, accesses device drivers, and handles character input and output. The kernel provides a uniform layer of services to all the programs that use Novell DOS.

Novell DOS accesses the kernel each time you issue a command through the command processor. The kernel, stored on the Novell DOS boot disk, is a hidden file that is loaded into memory each time you boot your computer. Novell DOS 7 has the capability of loading its kernel into upper or high memory, thereby freeing up more conventional memory for application use.

The kernel is built on the PC's BIOS, a series of routines used to communicate directly with the hardware. The BIOS routines are written specifically for controlling the basic elements of the PC hardware, so Novell DOS lets the BIOS handle the details of getting the hardware to accomplish the task at hand. While the BIOS takes care of the hardware, the kernel can make sure that commands received from COMMAND.COM are processed.

Note

BIOS routines are stored in read-only memory (ROM). Each version of Novell DOS can include new BIOS extensions that adapt the BIOS routines for new hardware or software features.

Using the Utility Programs. Novell DOS 7's built-in set of utility programs is arguably what differentiates it from other PC operating systems. Although most operating systems use utilities accessed through external commands to perform more complex tasks, the utilities included with Novell DOS 7 provide a level of hardware and software management that previously could be obtained only by using various add-on packages.

The Novell DOS utilities are stored as files and are executed by using the command processor. Each utility provides a unique function. Some of the utilities provide sophisticated disk management functions, such as caching and data compression. Other utilities provide security features that let you limit access to files as well as to the computer as a whole. A multitasker/task switcher, called Task Manager, allows you to work with several applications at a time; and, of course, there is the built-in network with its components. In addition, Fastback Express provides advanced backup and restore capabilities, and the Search & Destroy virus scanner provides added protection to your system.

Caution

The Novell DOS 7 utilities are written specifically for Novell DOS 7. They take into consideration the precise way the command processor communicates with the kernel and the way the kernel communicates with device drivers and the BIOS. These utilities make use of some of Novell DOS 7's special features, such as memory management, not available in earlier versions of the product or in other DOS products. For these reasons, utilities written for other versions of DR/Novell DOS or for other DOS products may not work correctly with Novell DOS 7.

The Novell DOS utilities are provided for your convenience. You can use them to optimize your computer system for your own needs. Some of them you'll use every day, for such operations as copying, erasing, or editing files. Some you may never use, or you may not be able to use given the limitations of your hardware (disk caching, for example). As you learn more about configuring and optimizing your system, you can choose the utilities that will help you get the most from your computer system.

Understanding the Evolution of DOS

When microcomputers were first introduced in the mid-1970s, each manufacturer provided either a proprietary operating system or none at all. Digital Research, Inc. then produced CP/M, which provided a common interface to any hardware platform for which CP/M was configured either by DRI or the manufacturer. Except for the processor, the hardware was not common. Although some of these early computers were rather powerful for their time, portability, connectivity, and the transfer of data remained a problem.

DOS—The Early Years

Then in 1981, IBM introduced the PC and led the way into standardized hardware. DOS became the standard operating system for personal computers. Standardization, connectivity, and file transfers with the use of common DOS floppy disks solved many problems. Over the next 10 years, DOS basically evolved only enough to handle hardware improvements. For example, DOS 3 allowed hard disk sizes up to 32M, and DOS 3.1 added file sharing in response to the rise of computer networks. DOS 3.3 allowed multiple partitions of 32M. COMPAQ's OEM version of MS-DOS, numbered 3.31, increased partition size to 512M. Digital Research's DR DOS 3.31, introduced in 1988, was compatible with COMPAQ 3.31.

In the meantime, applications began to appear with more features, demanding more memory. Networks, including peer-to-peer systems, became more prevalent and demanded memory resources. User interfaces, device drivers, and TSR (terminate-and-stay-resident) programs appeared with more frequency and, again, demanded additional memory.

The introduction of the 80286 processor with its ability to address more memory really didn't help the 640K conventional memory barrier. The advent of the 386 processor did offer possibilities with its memory-paging capabilities, but there was no clear-cut way for programs and utilities to access the added memory. Some makers of major applications developed their own way of addressing higher, upper, and extended memory. Even third-party companies introduced memory managers that optimized memory to increase conventional memory for application software.

DOS Version 5.0—Expanding Conventional Memory

For DOS, it was Digital Research that led the way in 1990 with DR DOS 5.0 to move at least parts of the operating system into the mostly unused memory areas between 640K and 1M of RAM, freeing conventional memory for applications. This version of DOS also was notable because it provided for the first time an interactive DOS installation and setup utility, provided enhanced DOS utilities, and also for the first time offered the public the opportunity to purchase DOS at retail to upgrade the existing DOS on their machines. Microsoft, a year later, followed suit with similar features in MS-DOS 5.0.

If you had an 8086 or 80286 machine with expanded (EMS or LIM 4.0) hardware-supported memory, or you had an advanced-chip 80286 machine or an 80386 memory-paging computer, you were able to use DR DOS 5.0 to substantially increase available conventional memory by moving large portions of DOS, device drivers, and TSRs into upper memory. Users with networked computers really appreciated the room made for application software that was becoming more sophisticated and requiring more memory.

The memory area between 640K and 1M was left by the PC designers for use by the video and disk controller. There was actually little use by anything else until memory management. Most of the 384K was free and provided an ideal place for loading parts of DOS and device drivers, as well as other TSRs.

DR DOS 5.0 also included a disk cache to assist with system speed, among other improvements.

DOS Version 6.0—Expanding Disk Storage

As the 1980s turned into the 1990s, users demanded more of their computers; they added more software to their systems, and the newer software became easier to use and offered additional features. All of this placed storage demands on computers. Hard disks were just too small to hold all that people demanded of them. One of the new software programs that people started to use was Windows, a graphic user interface that sits on DOS and provides services to users. Windows and applications that are written for Windows demand lots of disk storage.

Then, of course, came the increased use of laptop and notebook computers. The physical size of these machines required hard disks of limited capacity.

In August of 1991, Digital Research again led the way with the next generation of DOS, Version 6.0, including disk management utilities that offered dynamic disk compression. This new technology, available only for a short time by buying an add-on package from another company, now was integrated with DOS. In March of 1993, MS-DOS 6.0 was introduced with disk compression included.

Disk compression drivers sit in memory and act between the operating system and application software and the disk controllers. When files or any data is to be written to disk, the disk compression utility applies an algorithm to eliminate empty space and duplicate characters in the data, making the file take less space than it would uncompressed. When DOS or any program requests a disk read, the compression utility restores the data to its full original size in memory for either DOS or the application to use. Depending on what is compressed, there may be little or no storage savings or as much as a 16-to-1 savings. In normal usage, most users experience about a 2-to-1 savings. Thus, a 40M disk can store approximately 80M of programs and data.

At first glance, some people might think that this compressing and decompressing of data would slow down the computer. In actual practice, this is really not the case. All the work is done in RAM, which is extremely fast, and the little time lost there is made up by having to access the disk for only about half the time it would otherwise take.

Incidentally, it was during the summer of 1991 that Novell, Inc. purchased Digital Research, Inc. and made it the centerpiece of the new Novell Desktop Systems Group (NDSG). In 1992, Novell also started to bundle DR DOS with its peer-to-peer network, NetWare Lite.

Novell DOS 7.0—Advancing DOS Technology

One of the major points of each generation of DOS has been the downward compatibility. You did not have to upgrade your system or purchase new software to use the new version of DOS, although perhaps to gain the advantages of some of the new features, you may have upgraded your computer hardware. At least your applications did not cease to be useful.

DOS has been such a functional environment and very viable for millions of users and tens of thousands of software programs that Novell has pledged itself to continue this functionality and viability. DR DOS 5.0 introduced memory management, and DR DOS 6.0 introduced disk management. Yet, some problems continue for users. For example, disk compression, although it greatly expands disk storage, uses about 40-50K of RAM.

Novell DOS 7.0, therefore, has been released to enhance DOS not only to solve the remaining problems but also to advance DOS to new levels. Novell has even created new technology for DOS 7.0 with DOS Protected Mode Services (DPMS). DPMS is an API (Application Programming Interface) that allows software developers to write device drivers and TSRs that can load into memory above 1M and leave upper memory for other things, thus maximizing conventional memory. DPMS is able to work on any machine with an 80286 or higher processor and with any version of DOS.

In addition, Novell DOS 7 includes preemptive multitasking, which allows a machine with an 80386 or higher processor to run more than one application at the same time and easily switch between them. When a task is switched to the background, it keeps running. Thus, printing and posting or calculations can be performed in the background while the operator works on something else.

Novell also has built a peer-to-peer network into Novell DOS 7. This means that any computer with Novell DOS 7 can share its resources with any other connected computer, share the resources of another computer as a client, and become a client of a NetWare system.

See Chapter 2, "What's New in Novell DOS 7?" for a complete list of the new technologies, enhancements, and improvements to DOS.

From Here...

This chapter gave you an overview of the tools that Novell DOS uses to manage your computer system. Understanding the way Novell DOS interacts with your PC helps you understand how to use Novell DOS efficiently. For specific details on using Novell DOS to enhance your computer, see the following chapters:

- Chapter 2, "What's New in Novell DOS 7?" describes the improvements and technology advancements of Novell DOS 7.

- Chapter 4, "Installing Novell DOS 7," helps you through the installation process for your new operating system.

- Chapter 5, "Installing the Network," guides you through the installation process for the Novell DOS network.

Chapter 2

What's New in Novell DOS 7?

Novell DOS 7 isn't just an upgrade to DR DOS 6, a mere tweaking or the adding of a utility or two. Novell DOS 7 is a real advancement in DOS technology. Novell, Inc. not only has made a real commitment to the viability and advancement of DOS, but also has followed through on its promise. DOS has reached a whole new level. Those programmers at Novell have been busy.

In this chapter, you learn about the new technology and the new features of Novell DOS 7, including the integration of networking with DOS. You also read about the other many improvements, including full-screen DOS and Windows editions of many utilities.

This chapter covers the following topics:

- DPMI and DPMS

- Multitasking

- Stacker disk compression

- Integrated networking

New Features

The new or advanced technologies introduced with Novell DOS 7 include DOS Protected Mode Interface (DPMI), DOS Protected Mode Services (DPMS), preemptive multitasking, automatic disk compression, CD-ROM support, and integrated networking. Whereas DOS 5 was known for the introduction of memory management, and DOS 6 for the introduction of disk compression,

DOS 7 is the generation of DOS known for multitasking and the integration of network architecture.

But many power users will be more interested in DPMS because it provides more conventional memory for RAM-hungry application software, while still loading a slew of device drivers, network drivers, and TSRs (terminate-and-stay-resident programs).

DPMI and DPMS

For an understanding of the memory problems of the PC and of the importance of DPMS, perhaps it is best to start with the basic memory architecture of the personal computer and then review what happened to memory and DOS.

When the designers of the PC laid out system memory, they were working with a processor that addressed 1M of RAM. So they split memory into *conventional* or *lower memory* (the first 640K) and *upper memory* (from 640K to 1M). The 384K of upper memory was reserved for system ROM and device RAM, such as video and disk controller memory. The lower 640K had to hold the operating system, device and network drivers, and TSRs, as well as provide memory for application software (see fig. 2.1).

With the introduction of DR DOS 5.0 and memory management, conventional memory was regained by placing sizable portions of DOS and device drivers, as well as some TSRs, into upper and high memory. Because of the sparse capabilities of the 8086 and some 80286 processor chips, you could do this on only those machines where you added to your system expanded memory that conformed to the LIM (Lotus-Intel-Microsoft) specification 4.0. If your 80286 system included a Chips & Technologies NEat or other enhanced chip set, or if you had a 386 or higher processor, you were able to take advantage of this memory management. Figure 2.2 shows what happened to conventional memory when parts of DOS and other items are moved above 640K.

Novell DOS Basics

Fig. 2.1
PC memory
architecture.

```
1M ─────┐
        │  ROM BIOS
        │                      ⎫
        │                      ⎬ upper memory
        │                      ⎭
        │  video RAM
640K ───┤
        │  conventional        ⎫
        │  memory              ⎬ free
        │  for applications    ⎭
        │  mouse, etc.
        │  TSRs
        │  device drivers
        │  operating system
        └──────────────────
```

In the meantime, along came the proliferation of disk compression and its inclusion in DOS 6.0 in response to space demands by larger application software and the use of Windows and Windows applications. Disk compression takes about 40-50K of memory. Even with memory management, much of this winds up in conventional memory. Adding to the demand for memory was the widespread acceptance of disk cache devices (first included with DR DOS 5.0) for beefing up system speed.

Fig. 2.2
PC memory
architecture with
memory manage-
ment.

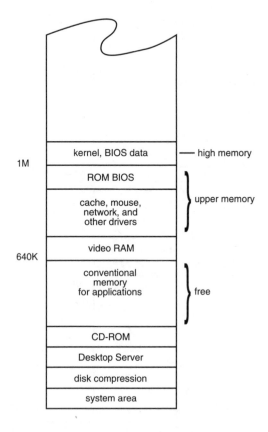

DPMI (DOS Protected Mode Interface). Over the last several years, DOS
extender schemes have been introduced for use with application software.
These schemes provided programs a way of using the extended memory over
1M, placing the 386 and higher processors in protected mode so that this
memory was available as if it were part of the lower 640K conventional
memory. DPMI (DOS Protected Mode Interface) has become the scheme of
choice to access extended memory.

Novell DOS 7 now includes a DPMI server for 80386 and higher processor
machines. DPMI client applications (those that include DPMI services but
without the DPMI server) are supported, and multiple DPMI clients are supported under the multitasker.

DPMS (DOS Protected Mode Services). There were no such means for device drivers and TSRs to do the same thing (access extended memory). Thus, Novell determined that by providing DPMS (DOS Protected Mode Services), users could move disk compression drivers, network drivers, TSRs, CD-ROM extensions, disk cache, and other device drivers to extended memory above 1M.

DPMS is what is called an *API (Application Programming Interface)*. Novell has made this API available to software developers. Drivers and other TSRs that are created with it will run with other versions of DOS, including previous versions of DR DOS, MS-DOS, and PC DOS. Such programs can run on 80286 and higher processor machines. The only requirement is that there be more than 1M of RAM in the computer. DPMS also works with Windows. Figure 2.3 shows what happens with memory as a result of the introduction of DPMS.

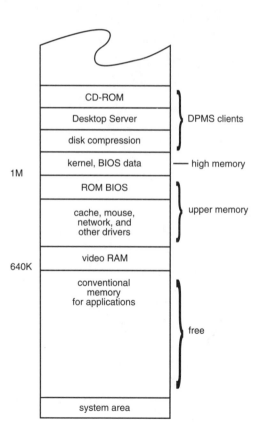

Fig. 2.3
PC memory architecture with memory management and DPMS.

DPMS has two parts to it: the *DPMS server* and the *DPMS client*. The DPMS server is a disk file named DPMS.EXE, installed in the root directory of the boot drive when Novell DOS 7 is installed or distributed by software developers with their products. The DPMS client is the device driver or TSR developed with the API. When DPMS clients are to be used, the Novell DOS Install utility places the DPMS.EXE server command in the CONFIG.SYS or DCONFIG.SYS file.

Novell DOS 7 includes several DPMS client device drivers: NWCACHE, the disk cache; STACKER.BIN, the disk compression driver; SERVER, the network Desktop Server; and NWCDEX, the CD-ROM extension. These drivers use very little conventional or upper memory. The result for users is that conventional memory is available for larger and more sophisticated applications, and users can still avail themselves of these advanced functions on their systems.

> **Note**
>
> NWCDEX is the Novell DOS CD-ROM extension, which is a DPMS client, and replaces MSCDEX 2.2 so that you can use your CD-ROM drive and still retain conventional memory for your applications.

Multitasking

As personal computers have become more prevalent and users have added application software to their systems, the cry came for a means to increase productivity. The way many people work is that they use several applications constantly—perhaps a word processing program, a database, electronic mail, and electronic spreadsheets. Even in order-entry departments, people often need access so that they can work with orders and inventory status as well as customer accounts.

What usually happens is that when you have to work like this, you jump back and forth through system menus—loading one program, doing some work, returning to the menu and loading another program, doing some more work, returning to the system menu, and so on.

DR DOS 5.0 provided a task switcher, as did MS-DOS 5.0 (although the latter would run from only the DOS Shell), but task switching suspends execution of programs when they are switched to the background. Programs can run only in the foreground under task switchers. Task switching is an improvement over single-tasking, but leaves something to be desired. It is certainly advantageous to have applications in background continue printing, processing, communicating, or doing whatever they are supposed to do.

Novell DOS 7 introduces a very powerful preemptive multitasker, called Task Manager. With Task Manager, you can easily and instantaneously switch between several DOS applications without having to exit one program and load another. You can take advantage of this feature if your system is based on an 80386 or higher processor and you have at least 2M of RAM, although 4M or more provide support for more DOS sessions. Each DOS session acts as the host for a single task and application. You don't need to purchase special multitasking software for Task Manager. Windows runs under the multitasker. Graphics applications under Task Manager aren't suspended when switched to background.

What *preemptive* means is that a running program can be interrupted by another task that has a higher priority. The multitasking API provides the means for software developers to set task priorities for efficient use of system resources. The API includes functions for interprocess communications, program execution control, and shared memory.

The multitasking feature of Novell DOS 7 makes you more efficient and lets you use your computer to its fullest. The computer continues application processing while you go on to other tasks. Novell has also announced that the multitasker allows developers to "...use Novell DOS 7 as a platform for numerous application areas that require multitasking. These include monitoring and process control environments."

If you do not have an 80386 or higher processor, or if do not have enough memory to operate Task Manager as a multitasker, you can still use the task-switching capability of Task Manager. As you read earlier, though, tasks in background are suspended. Programs actually continue running only when they are in foreground (on the video screen).

Enhanced Disk Compression

DR DOS 6.0 was notable for its inclusion of SuperStor disk compression. Although SuperStor was not a full-fledged utility package as if purchased as an add-on to your system, it was quite an improvement and was fully optimized to work with (and was integrated with) DR DOS. Novell has provided a major upgrade to this disk compression. Stacker disk compression, Version 3.1, from Stac Electronics has been included with Novell DOS 7.

Consisting of a full suite of utilities both for the DOS environment and for the Windows environment, Stacker is loaded by a special driver immediately after the operating system is loaded when you boot your computer, and does not need to be loaded from the CONFIG.SYS or DCONFIG.SYS file. This is a powerful enhancement, especially with the CONFIG.SYS and DCONFIG.SYS menuing and bypassing features. In addition, the Stacker driver has been made a DPMS client. Disk compression no longer needs to take 40-50K of memory below the 1M memory area, fighting for space with other device drivers, TSRs, and network drivers.

The features included in the Stacker suite are the capabilities to dynamically resize compressed volumes; to remove compression entirely without erasing all files (only those that exceed the normal noncompressed drive size need to be removed); to compress floppy disks; to use compressed floppies in computers that do not have Stacker disk compression installed; and to include complete compressed disk defragmentation and repair utilities. Included also is a disk compression preview utility so that you can see the effect of compression before you actually take the step.

> **Note**
>
> If you already have disk compression installed on your system—such as DoubleSpace, SuperStor, or an earlier version of Stacker—Novell DOS 7 will upgrade your system for you to the current Stacker version. Chapter 4, "Installing Novell DOS 7," shows you how to have Setup perform the conversion for you.

Networking

One of the most important advancements in DOS technology with Novell DOS 7 is the integration of networking with DOS. There are several parts to this architecture:

- The Desktop Server allows your computer to share resources with other computers running Novell DOS 7.

- Universal Client services connect your computer as a client with other computers running the Desktop Server.

- Universal Client services enable your computer to connect to NetWare 2.x, 3.x, and 4.0 networks.

- Novell DOS 7 is the perfect DOS environment for computers attached as clients in NetWare systems.

As computers have expanded throughout the workplace and even with multiple systems in the home, keyboard time has become a bottleneck for access to applications and data. Network computing can solve this problem as applications, data, and other resources such as printers are made available across the network to others who need access. Many small businesses, workgroups, home users, and others entering the world of networking are often disenchanted, however, with the high cost of full-fledged networks and their requirement for a full-time file server.

Peer-to-peer networking is a cost-efficient method of entering the world of networks. There is no need for a dedicated file server. Any workstation on the network can share its resources with any other. Novell DOS 7 thus provides a simple, efficient, reliable, and cost-effective network. Small businesses, workgroups, and first-time network users will find this an ideal solution for their needs.

Peer-to-Peer Networking and NetWare Compatibility. The desktop networking technology of Novell DOS 7 is fully compatible and integrated with the NetWare environment, and you can use the same network adapter cards and drivers in the peer-to-peer environment.

> **Note**
>
> To attach your Novell DOS 7 computer to a NetWare network, you must use a compatible network interface card. The complete list of available network adapters is provided in the network setup screen in the Install/Setup utility for Novell DOS. You can also refer to Chapter 5, "Installing the Network," in this book for more on network cards and cabling.

The Novell DOS Universal Client is a network redirector that provides your computer access to resources on any NetWare network file server or Desktop Server—through a single common interface. This is a boon to users who need to access enterprise-wide networks as well as local workgroup systems.

> **Note**
>
> To assist with network management, the network configuration utilities, the administration utilities, the workgroup diagnostics, and the industry standard SNMP network-management agent are all included. Except for SNMP, all have both DOS and Windows environment versions.

Security. In addition to file and directory passwording and to the DOS security provided by DR DOS 6.0 for stand-alone system login, Novell DOS 7's networking environment includes security extensions to match the security of NetWare networks. The owner or system administrator can limit access to resources and even restrict access within certain hours. A single login procedure can provide access to both your local computer and the network.

Enhanced Commands

In addition to the new technology and major enhancements to DOS, Novell DOS 7 provides a myriad of other improvements and utility upgrades, including the following items (other enhancements may be discussed elsewhere in this book):

- You may have noticed that when you opened your Novell DOS 7 package, you did not receive a full manual. The folks at Novell have decided that much of what they once documented in their system manuals can be provided on-line. Thus, they greatly improved DOSBook, the Novell DOS 7 on-line documentation. With the multitasker (or task switcher), you can access DOSBook and keep it running without interfering with your current application.

    DOSBook includes all normal documentation and two search engines, as well as access through the table of contents and the DOSBook index. You can search by entering one of the following at the DOS prompt:

    HELP *keyword*

    DOSBOOK *keyword*

    The first search engine places you at the first, or closest, match of the command or keyword you typed. The second search engine allows you to type any keyword anywhere within DOSBook and also be placed at the match or closest match in the index.

    Refer to the next chapter, "Getting Help with DOSBook," for a discussion of the use of DOSBook.

- DOSBook includes a complete listing of error messages, including general conditions that can cause problems, as well as methods for handling and preventing them.

■ Starting with DR DOS 5.0, you can use a configuration file named DCONFIG.SYS in place of the more customary CONFIG.SYS file name. Both are valid. But as with DR DOS, Novell DOS 7 prefers DCONFIG.SYS and uses this file if both files are present in the root directory of your boot drive. You can chain from the one file to the other if you like. However, Novell DOS does include an enhanced CONFIG.SYS or DCONFIG.SYS file and batch file processing. More exotic prompt statements are available to you with the new *system information variables*. Enhanced menus can be written in the configuration files and batch files for supporting various boot and environmental schemes.

■ You can change the boot process by pressing the F5 or F8 key at boot time. If you press the F5 key when Starting DOS... is displayed on-screen, Novell DOS completely bypasses the CONFIG.SYS or DCONFIG.SYS file and the AUTOEXEC.BAT file during the boot process. (The Stacker driver is still loaded so that compressed drives can be used.) The use of either function key can help if you modify the configuration files and there is a problem with your new setup, or you want to boot cleanly to use a disk utility, for example. (Some disk utilities want all device drivers and TSRs removed from memory in order to work properly.)

   If you press the F8 key when Starting DOS... is displayed on-screen, Novell DOS does process the CONFIG.SYS or DCONFIG.SYS file and the AUTOEXEC.BAT file, but stops at each command or statement and asks you whether the command should be executed.

■ You now have an improved Install/Setup utility for installing any possible configuration, even code page switching, without having to use an editor. This utility enables you to check your configuration, previewing the changes to the configuration files before actually committing to them.

■ Fifth Generation's Fastback Express file backup and restore utility for both DOS and Windows environments is included with Novell DOS 7 for data safety.

■ Fifth Generation's Search & Destroy antivirus utility, which can be run as a TSR or stand-alone program in both the DOS and Windows environments, is included with Novell DOS 7 for system safety.

- Support for Microsoft Windows' permanent swap file on a compressed drive has been added to Novell DOS 7.

- NWCACHE, an advanced disk cache, compatible with NetWare, replaces SuperPC-Kwik, which was distributed with DR DOS 6.

- To further DOS compatibility standards, Novell has changed the names of several Novell DOS utilities from earlier usage in DR DOS, but they still retain their technical and feature superiority. These include EDIT, changed from Editor, and DEBUG, changed from SID86. The Novell DOS DEBUG utility is also a superset of the same commands in the Microsoft version of the utility. This will be helpful to those users who like to take advantage of DEBUG scripts provided in some popular computer magazines.

- Novell DOS 7 now includes a new SETVER command for those new applications that require the features of more recent versions of DOS.

- Several utilities—including UNDELETE, EDIT, FILELINK, and DOSBOOK—now have the same full-screen interface with pull-down menus and mouse support.

- The HISTORY feature, pioneered with DR DOS 5.0, has been enhanced in Novell DOS 7 with a DOSKEY macro capability.

- The FILELINK utility not only has been enhanced with a full-screen interface that can be used along with the earlier command-line version, but also can now connect with another computer through a parallel port.

In addition to the preceding items, a number of existing DOS utilities have been enhanced with additional options. For example, the CHKDSK command has been expanded to check not only standard DOS disks and floppy disks but also Stacker compressed drives.

From Here...

Wow! You have just read quite a list. Novell DOS 7 is a major advancement in DOS technology. It includes DPMI, DPMS, enhanced memory management, preemptive multitasking, enhanced security, a suite of protected mode drivers, improved disk compression, integrated networking support, and peer-to-peer networking, just to mention a few highlights.

The following chapters help you to get started in installing Novell DOS 7 with its network and learning how to use the on-line documentation:

- Chapter 3, "Getting Help with DOSBook," teaches you how to use Novell DOS 7's computerized reference material.

- Chapter 4, "Installing Novell DOS 7," helps you through the installation process for your new operating system.

- Chapter 5, "Installing the Network," guides you through the installation process for the Novell DOS network.

In the next chapter, you can begin your great adventure by learning to work with the on-line documentation, DOSBook.

Novell DOS Basics

Chapter 3

Getting Help with DOSBook

Over the past decade, as software, including DOS, has become more sophisticated with more and more features, documentation has become more and more important. In the early days, a simple manual was all that was needed to run a lot of software. Then manuals grew larger, and the information contained in them was harder to access. Meanwhile, software developers started to provide help within their programs so that when you needed some specific information to assist you with what you were attempting to do, you could often press F1 or some other key for that information.

Also over the years, book publishers, like Que, began to provide documentation to users who were befuddled by what is usually a terse explanation of commands and features. These publishers provided books on software and other computer-related subjects, like *Using Novell DOS 7*, that are easy to use with step-by-step instructions and useful hints and cautions, yet are complete. Many of these books are for beginners and experienced users alike.

There are times, however, when on-line documentation is helpful. You know how to do what you want. You just need a refresher on a specific command or command switch. Novell DOS 7 includes a full reference manual on-line, called *DOSBook*. Read this chapter to learn about DOSBook and how to use it.

In this chapter, you learn how to do the following:

- Access DOSBook

- Search for a command or topic

- Navigate DOSBook

- Print a DOSBook section or chapter

Accessing DOSBook

DOSBOOK.EXE is the external file for the Novell DOS on-line documentation. The Install utility places the file in the \NWDOS subdirectory. Assuming
that you have not changed the system path, you can access DOSBook from
any DOS prompt on your system. For more information on system paths,
refer to the section "Understanding PATHS" in Chapter 6, "Understanding
File Storage."

DOSBook is a full-screen utility, with pull-down menus and mouse support,
and is very easy to use. To access DOSBook, simply enter the following command at the command prompt:

```
DOSBOOK
```

The opening or welcome screen, shown in figure 3.1, is displayed on your
system. This screen shows the five major sections of DOSBook:

- Introduction to Novell DOS 7.

- Configuring Novell DOS.

- The list and explanation of Novell DOS 7 commands.

- Table of contents for DOSBook. You can access any reference you need
  from this section.

- Index for DOSBook. You can access any reference also from this section.

Although not shown on the opening screen, a glossary (dictionary of terms)
is also included in DOSBook. You access the glossary by holding down the Alt
key and then pressing the letter G (Alt-G).

To access any of the sections of DOSBook listed in the opening screen, you
can use the Tab key to move the highlight bar to the title of each section, and
press Enter when the correct section is selected. You can hold down the Shift
key and at the same time press the Tab key to move backward through the
title list. Using a mouse, you can move the mouse pointer to the title of the
section you want to select, and click the left button.

You use the same procedure throughout DOSBook. Use the Tab key (and the
Shift-Tab key combination) to move to the next highlighted word on-screen;
then press Enter. You can also use the mouse to point to the next highlighted

word, and click the left mouse button. On color monitors, the highlighted keywords are displayed in red. On monochrome monitors, keywords are underlined.

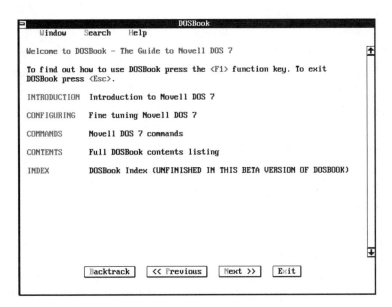

Fig. 3.1
The DOSBook opening screen.

Novell DOS Basics

Using the Search Engine

Two versions of a search engine are built into DOSBook. The first is available from the DOS prompt. With this version, you can use either the word *HELP* or the command *DOSBOOK*, followed by the keyword for which you are looking. The format is

> **DOSBOOK** *keyword*

or

> **HELP** *keyword*

When DOSBook loads in response to either of these formats for the search engine, the DOSBook index is displayed with the highlight bar placed at the matching entry for your keyword, or if there is no exact match, at the closest match found. Figure 3.2 shows the result of the search using the keyword *format*. That is where the highlight bar is displayed.

Fig. 3.2
Result of a
keyword search.

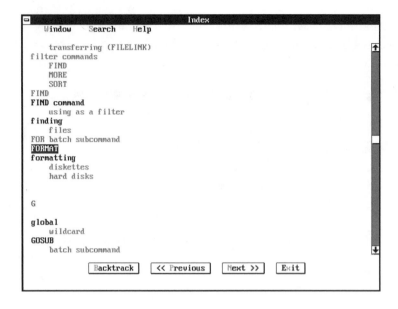

The second version of the search engine is within DOSBook itself. Whenever you are in any part of DOSBook, including within the help system but not within the pull-down menus, you can perform a search on any keyword by merely typing the word. As soon as you begin typing the keyword, the Index Search dialog box is displayed in the center of the screen, as is shown in figure 3.3.

Fig. 3.3
The Index Search
dialog box for
keyword entry.

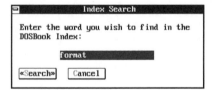

You can also perform a manual search by proceeding to the table of contents and selecting an entry, or by proceeding to the index and selecting an entry. You access the table of contents by holding down the Alt key and then pressing the letter C (Alt-C). You access the index by pressing Alt-I. Either command places the highlight bar at the beginning of either the table of contents or the index.

From that point, use the Tab key to move from section heading or keyword to section heading or keyword. When the Tab key highlights the last entry displayed on-screen, the next page of the listing is displayed, starting with half the previous page at the top (before the next entry) so that you can see exactly where you are in the list. The PgUp (PageUp) and PgDn (PageDown) keys move you from page to page within the table of contents and the index. After you have highlighted your choice, press Enter for DOSBook to display the documentation on your selection.

When you are within the reference text, you can use the PgUp or PgDn key to move within the section so that you can read the entire text for your selection. Figure 3.4 shows the reference text for the Novell DOS FILELINK command.

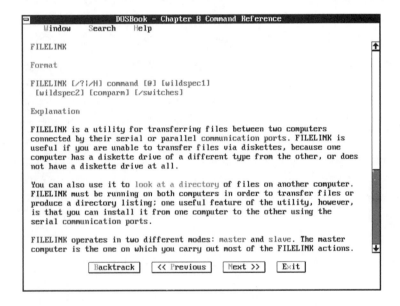

Fig. 3.4
DOSBook reference text for the FILELINK command.

DOSBook also has a continue-search function for use after you have located text on your specified keyword. Just press the F3 key. A dialog box appears that shows the section numbers being incremented as the search is made for the next occurrence of your keyword (see fig. 3.5). If the next occurrence is found rather quickly, this dialog box may not be displayed as the next text reference is displayed. You can continue pressing F3 to see all references matching your specification. The search may continue through the index and the glossary sections. When the end of DOSBook is reached, the search continues from the beginning of the reference utility.

Fig. 3.5
The DOSBook F3
continue-search
function.

```
Searching section 00169. Press <Esc> to stop.
```

Using Other Features of DOSBook

DOSBook contains what is referred to as *hypertext*. Throughout the entire documentation are highlighted words. These hypertext *links* indicate that there are further references to those keywords in other sections of DOSBook. Use the Tab key to move the highlight to any of these hypertext links, and press Enter to see the next reference. If you have a color monitor, hypertext keywords are displayed in red. On monochrome monitors, these keywords are underlined. If you use a mouse, place the mouse pointer on the highlighted keyword and click the left mouse button.

There are also glossary keywords throughout DOSBook. These keywords are displayed in blue-green on color monitors. You can discern no difference in glossary keywords on monochrome monitors, until you use the Tab key and highlight one of the keywords. They are not underlined as are hypertext keywords. When you highlight one of the glossary words and press Enter, a glossary pop-up box is displayed to define the term. The pop-up box disappears after a few seconds, unless you hold down the Enter key. If you use a mouse, place the mouse pointer on the highlighted keyword and click the left mouse button. Hold down the button to keep the glossary box displayed.

In addition to using the features mentioned, you can print any section or chapter of DOSBook to a printer or disk file. To take advantage of this feature, you need to access the Window pull-down menu. Do this by pressing Alt-W, or placing the mouse pointer on the menu title and clicking the left mouse button. DOSBook displays the Window menu shown in figure 3.6.

As you can see, the first selection on this menu and the one highlighted automatically when you open the menu is Print Section. There is no shortcut key for this option. Just highlight the option and press Enter. If there is a highlighted character in the selection, you can just press that key. Figure 3.7 shows the Print dialog box that appears on-screen.

If you just want to print to your regular printer, press the Enter key. The PRN entry is for the normal or default printer. If your printer is attached to a port other than LPT1 and no MODE command is in effect to redirect printer output to the proper printer port, you can enter the port designation in place of PRN. Just use the Backspace key to remove PRN and type COM1:, COM2:, COM3:,

COM4:, **LPT1:**, **LPT2:**, or **LPT3:**. Read more about redirecting printer output and the MODE command in Chapter 13, "Controlling System Devices."

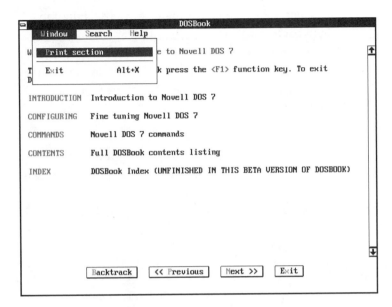

Fig. 3.6
The DOSBook Window pull-down menu.

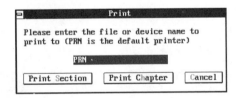

Fig. 3.7
The DOSBook Print dialog box.

If, instead, you want to send the documentation to a disk file, use the Backspace key to remove the printer entry (PRN), and type the name of the file you want to use for the DOSBook output. You can specify the full path and name (drive, directory, and the file name and file extension) if you don't want to use the current directory. For instance, if you are printing the documentation for the FILELINK command and saving the file in the C:\DOCS subdirectory, you use the following specification:

```
C:\DOCS\FILELINK.DOC
```

After you have accepted the output destination, either a printer or a disk file, press the Tab key. The Print Section button is highlighted. A section or page of DOSBook is a part of the documentation covering a specific topic. For example, for the topic FILELINK, the section covers two pages on your display

Tip
Generally, a section of DOSBook is what is displayed between the PgUp and PgDn keys on any topic or reference.

in the DOSBook command reference on that topic. If you want to output the current section of DOSBook, press Enter.

You can output a complete chapter of DOSBook by pressing the Tab key to move the highlight bar to the Print Chapter button and then pressing Enter. Alternatively, you can place the mouse pointer on this button and click. A chapter of DOSBook encompasses a group of sections, just as in a regular book. With regard to FILELINK, for example, the chapter refers to the entire Chapter 8 Command Reference of DOSBook, as shown on the top line of the DOSBook screen.

After you make your selection and press Enter, the documentation is sent to either the printer or the disk file, as you specified. When the printing is finished, the Print dialog box is removed from the screen. If you want to abort the printing process, you can either press the Esc key or click the Cancel button in the Print dialog box, or you can use the Tab key to highlight the button and then press Enter.

To return to the opening screen of DOSBook, you can press the Esc key anywhere within DOSBook, unless you are already at the opening screen. Pressing the Esc key at the opening screen exits DOSBook and returns you to the Novell DOS prompt. You can also press Alt-X from anywhere within DOSBook to return to the DOS prompt, including from within the help system and from the pull-down menus.

> **Note**
>
> If you are using Task Manager, as either a multitasker or a task switcher, you can set one of the sessions or tasks for DOSBook so that it is always available to you at the touch of a key. To learn how to do this, read Chapter 21, "Multitasking and Task Switching."

You can also use a mouse to move within DOSBook. You can click the menu selections and the navigation buttons, as well as the hypertext links. Referring to figure 3.6, notice the scroll bar on the right side of the reference text. If there is a slider displayed within the scroll bar, the slider shows the position of the current material displayed within the current section. You can use the mouse to scroll the text up or down by clicking on the up or down arrow at the top and bottom of the scroll bar, or by dragging the scroll bar slider. You drag an item with the mouse by placing the mouse pointer on the item, pressing and holding down the left mouse button, moving the pointer and the item to the new location, and then releasing the mouse button.

You can also see in figure 3.6 the menu bar at the top of the screen and the access buttons at the bottom. In the next section of this chapter, you learn about all the navigating tools you can use to get the most out of DOSBook.

Navigating DOSBook

As mentioned, the DOSBook screen is divided into three parts. The menu bar is at the top, the text section is in the middle, and the navigation buttons are at the bottom. The mouse scroll bar is at the right of the text portion of the screen.

Accessing the Menus

There are two ways to access the pull-down menus at the top of the screen. Using your mouse, move the mouse pointer to one of the three menu titles. Then click the mouse. The menu drops down. To select one of the other menus while a menu is open, place the mouse pointer on the title of the other menu, and click the left mouse button. To exit any of the menus, move the mouse pointer out of the area of the open menu and click the left mouse button.

Using the keyboard, press the Alt key and simultaneously press the first character of the menu title, as in Alt-W, Alt-S, and Alt-H. (The first letter of the menu title is also highlighted.) The menu drops down. To move to a menu to the left or the right of an open menu, press the left-arrow key or the right-arrow key. To exit from a menu, press the Esc key.

As shown in the Search menu displayed in figure 3.8, each of the three menus has several options. You can select any of the options from within the open menu in one of three ways: using the up- or down-arrow key to move the highlight bar to your selection and then pressing Enter, typing the highlighted letter of the selection, or pressing the shortcut key if one is displayed to the right of the selection. If you are using a mouse, you can place the mouse pointer on the option and click the left button.

You can also bypass the menus and use the specific shortcut key for the menu selection. Without accessing the menu, simply press the shortcut key. In the Search menu shown in figure 3.8, for example, the option Repeat Last Text Search shows the F3 key. After you have entered a keyword by typing it, you can find the next occurrence of the keyword by pressing F3.

Novell DOS Basics

Fig. 3.8
The DOSBook
Search menu.

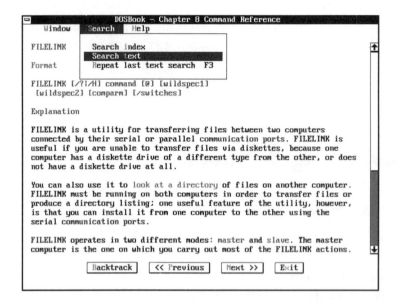

> **Note**
>
> If there is no shortcut key shown in the pull-down menu for the action you want to
> take, you must execute the command from the menu.

Table 3.1 lists the menu options for DOSBook.

	Table 3.1 Menu Options for DOSBook		
Menu	**Command and Description**	**Key to Press**	**Shortcut**
Window	*Print Section*. Prints the currently displayed section or the current chapter of DOSBook.	P	
Window	*Exit*. Returns you to the DOS prompt. This is also a navigation command button.	X	Alt-X
Search	*Search Index*. Displays the Search dialog box in which you type the keyword you want to find. The result of the search is displayed in the DOSBook index.	I	

Menu	Command and Description	Key to Press	Shortcut
Search	*Search Text.* Displays the Search dialog box in which you type the keyword you want to find. The search starts with the currently displayed screen and continues from there if the keyword is not found.	T	
Search	*Repeat Last Text Search.* After the keyword has been found,continues the search for the next occurrence of the last keyword you typed in the Search dialog box.	R	F3
Help	*Help for DOSBook.* Accesses the DOSBook help system, which shows you how to use and navigate DOSBook.	H	F1
Help	*Contents.* Accesses the DOSBook table of contents.	C	Alt-C
Help	*Glossary.* Accesses the DOSBook glossary (dictionary of important terms).	G	Alt-G
Help	*Index.* Accesses the DOSBook index.	I	Alt-I
Help	*Backtrack* (a navigation button). Takes you back through the screens of text, the contents, the glossary, and the index that you have referenced.	B	Alt-B
Help	*Next* (a navigation button).Lets you flip forward through DOSBook to the next section in the utility.	N	Alt-N
Help	*Previous* (a navigation button).Lets you flip backward through DOSBook to the previous section in the utility.	P	Alt-P
Help	*About.* Displays the DOSBook utility name, version, and copyright information in a note box in the center of the screen. Press the Enter key or click the OK button to exit from the note box.		

Using the Navigation Buttons

As you learned earlier, four *navigation buttons* are at the bottom of the DOSBook screen. These buttons assist you in moving within the on-line documentation. You can access these buttons with the keyboard or mouse. To use the keyboard, hold down the Alt key and press the highlighted letter; for example, press Alt-B to backtrack through the material you have previously displayed on-screen in the current session of DOSBook.

Table 3.2 lists the buttons and their shortcut keys, along with an explanation of the actions associated with each of the navigation buttons.

Table 3.2 DOSBook Navigation Buttons		
Button	**Shortcut**	**Action**
Backtrack	Alt-B	Moves backward through previous pages of the documentation displayed in the current DOSBook session.
<< Previous	Alt-P	Flips backward through the documentation. This is the same as moving backward through the pages of a book.
Next >>	Alt-N	Flips forward through the documentation. This is the same as moving forward through the pages of a book.
Exit	Alt-X	Exits DOSBook. Clicking this button or pressing Alt-X returns you to the DOS prompt.

You can scroll through the reference text by using the up- and down-arrow keys or the scroll bar. Pressing the PgUp, PgDn, Home, and End keys moves you through the text. Table 3.3 lists the various keys you can use to move throughout the displayed text.

Table 3.3 DOSBook Text Movement Keys	
Key(s)	**Action**
PgUp	Scrolls forward through the current section of DOSBook.
PgDn	Scrolls backward through the current section of DOSBook.
Home	Moves the cursor to the top of the screen.
End	Moves the cursor to the bottom of the screen.
Ctrl-Home	Moves the cursor to the beginning of the current page or section.
Ctrl-End	Moves the cursor to the end of the current page or section.
Tab	Moves the cursor/highlight bar forward to the next keyword. Red keywords are hypertext links for further reference on the subject; blue-green keywords are hypertext links for displaying the glossary definition pop-up box for the keyword. Press Enter to see the reference or definition.

Key(s)	Action
Shift-Tab	Moves the cursor/highlight bar backward to the previous keyword. Press Enter to see the reference or definition.
Esc	Returns to the DOSBook opening (welcome) screen if it is not displayed; if the opening screen is displayed, returns to the DOS prompt.

From Here...

In this chapter, you learned about DOSBook, the on-line documentation that is part of Novell DOS 7. You learned also how to find any topic in DOSBook by using the powerful search engine—just type the keyword you are seeking, and DOSBook does the work. You can also navigate through the reference material by using the pull-down menus and the navigation buttons, as well as the table of contents and index. You can use the keyboard or mouse to work within the utility.

Now move to the next chapter, where you learn to install Novell DOS 7 and become familiar with various configurations established with the Install/ Setup utility.

I

Novell DOS Basics

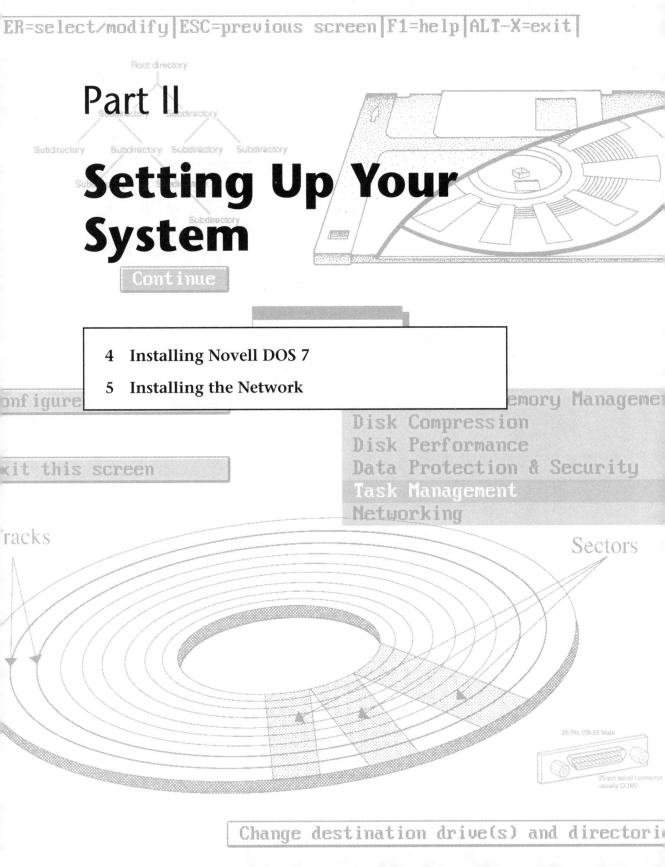

Part II

Setting Up Your System

Continue

4 **Installing Novell DOS 7**

5 **Installing the Network**

Root directory

Subdirectory Subdirectory

Subdirectory Subdirectory Subdirectory Subdirectory

Subdirectory Subdirectory

Subdirectory

Continue

File - c:\spam.txt
Create new file ?

OK   Cancel

nfigure Task Manager

ystem & Memory Managemen
Disk Compression
Disk Performance
Data Protection & Security
Task Management
Networking

it this screen

acks

Sectors

25-Pin DB-25 Male

25-pin serial connector,
usually COM2

Change destination drive(s) and directorie

Chapter 4

Installing Novell DOS 7

The first step in taking advantage of Novell DOS 7's new technology, features, and improvements is installing the operating system. In this chapter, you learn what the hardware requirements are for installing Novell DOS 7 and using the various features. You learn how to reconfigure and change the features on your system, using the postinstallation version of INSTALL.EXE, renamed SETUP.EXE. You learn how to install or use certain devices, such as the SETVER command, a mouse, a CD-ROM drive, and the PostScript driver. Finally, you learn how to uninstall Novell DOS 7.

Because of the uniqueness of networking, the installation of the Novell DOS 7 network components is covered in Chapter 5, "Installing the Network."

This chapter covers the following topics:

- Hardware requirements for Novell DOS 7

- Hardware requirements for multitasking

- Hardware requirements for networking

- Installing Novell DOS 7

- Using the Setup utility

- Installing other devices

- Uninstalling Novell DOS 7

Novell DOS 7 Hardware Requirements

The first hardware requirement for installing Novell DOS 7 is that you have an IBM or IBM-compatible personal computer running an 8086, 8088, or higher microprocessor (80286, 80386, 486, Pentium, or compatible) and that the computer is capable of running DOS. This may seem rather obvious, but some companies have manufactured computers that supposedly are IBM-compatible but really are not, and some computers are less compatible than others.

Several other hardware requirements exist. Your computer must have a hard disk, with at least 5.6M of free space on it. If you have a very early PC that has less than a 10M (10 million character) hard disk, you have a problem. Actually, you can install the operating system, but there will be little or no room for anything else. Your computer must also include a floppy disk drive—either a 5 1/4-inch drive with a capacity of 1.2M (high density), or a 3 1/2-inch drive with a capacity of 720K (double density) or 1.44M (high density).

Although you can make a Novell DOS bootable floppy disk at installation time, it is a bare-minimum DOS boot disk, which cannot have the major features of Novell DOS on it.

There is no requirement that some version of DOS already be installed on your computer. You can install Novell DOS 7 on a brand new computer, on a computer in which the existing hard disk has been wiped clean, or on an active DOS computer. If the computer has a version of DOS currently installed, Novell DOS 7 replaces that version but saves the original version by default, in case you want to restore it later.

You do not have to boot with the INSTALL disk (the first disk) to install Novell DOS, unless there is no DOS at all on your system. Computers with no existing DOS boot from floppy drive A. If you have no existing DOS and your Novell DOS disks aren't the right size or capacity for drive A, you must exchange the disks for the right size and capacity before you can load Novell DOS. If you have an existing version of DOS, you can install Novell DOS from drive B, as long as the drive size and capacity match the floppy disks in your Novell DOS 7 package.

Note

Currently, distribution packages of Novell DOS 7 include either 1.2M 5 1/4-inch disks or 1.44M 3 1/2-inch disks, and the contents are marked on the package. If you require either 360K 5 1/4-inch double-density disks or 720K 3 1/2-inch double-density disks, you must request from Novell the disks in that size. Novell's phone number is 1-800-NETWARE (follow the directions to direct your call to the proper area).

Memory requirements start with 512K of RAM, although if your computer has only 640K of memory or less, you gain the added functionality of only some of the Novell DOS 7 commands. You can start to gain advantages with at least 1M of RAM, but more is better, especially if you have a computer with an 80286 or higher microprocessor.

In the next several sections of this chapter, you learn about the hardware components that your computer must contain so that you can use the main features of Novell DOS. If you are not sure about what is contained within your specific machine, check the documentation (your sales slip often lists all major components) or contact your dealer for assistance. If all else fails, the Install/Setup utility provides default settings for your computer, determined from its reading of your system. After installation, there is a command you can issue to DOS that displays some components of your system (SETUP/ ADVISE).

Task-Switching Requirements

Task switching is the capability, provided by the Novell DOS utility called Task Manager, to load more than one application program at a time and switch between them. You can do this instead of having to exit a program and load another one to switch from one application to another. This feature makes you more productive by saving time.

With task switching, each loaded program or command environment is re-ferred to as a *task*, and any program that you can see displayed on the screen is in the *foreground*. All loaded programs that are not displayed on the screen are in the *background*. Background tasks, when switched off the screen, are saved either to RAM or to the hard disk in a special swap file if there is not enough RAM.

Tasks in the background do not run. They are suspended while switched out. This action is similar to placing a bookmark in a book when you put it down for a period of time. When you pick up the book again, you reopen the book at the bookmark and continue where you left off. Task Manager saves the program being placed in the background with a similar method, retaining your place in the program until you switch it back to the foreground and the program resumes running.

You can install Task Manager as a task switcher on any computer that can run Novell DOS 7. That includes 8088, 8086, 80286, and 80386 or higher microprocessors or compatibles. You don't even need lots of memory (RAM), because the task switcher uses disk space when there is no RAM available for swapping out background tasks.

You may have a computer with an 80386 or higher microprocessor and 4M of RAM and want to run lots of tasks simultaneously. You can use the multitasker to switch between tasks (see the next section, "Multitasking Requirements," for more details). However, you are limited in the number of tasks that can run under the multitasker, which is based on the amount of RAM in your computer. With only 4M of RAM, the maximum is 3 DOS sessions. Even with only 1M of RAM, you can run up to 20 simultaneous tasks under the task switcher. Of course, when tasks are switched to the background under the task switcher, they are suspended. Only the foreground task is actually running.

Refer to Chapter 21, "Multitasking and Task Switching," for a discussion of the installation and use of Task Manager as a task switcher.

Multitasking Requirements

Multitasking works similarly to task switching; however, with the multitasker, loaded tasks that are in the background do not stop running. With the multitasker, any program that you can see displayed on the screen is in the foreground. All loaded programs, or tasks, that are not displayed on the screen are in the background. Background tasks, when switched off the screen, however, are not suspended. They keep running. Thus, you can start one application posting transactions, switch to another application and start it printing, and then switch to a third program and continue working without having to wait for the other processes to finish.

Using Task Manager as a multitasker requires a computer with an 80386 or higher processor and a minimum of 2M of RAM, although to create multiple tasks, you do need to have 4M of memory in your computer. With multitasking, each running application or command environment is referred to as a *DOS session*. This term is very descriptive of what is happening to your computer with multitasking.

When you watch channel 3 on television, channels 6, 10, 12, and so on, are still televising. You are not, however, watching them (unless you have the screen-on-screen feature on your set). When you change to channel 6 to watch another program, channel 3 keeps airing. With multitasking, the 80386 or higher microprocessor is placed in protective mode, and sections of memory are set up as if they were individual DOS PCs, all sharing the same keyboard and monitor. When you switch DOS sessions, you are changing channels to watch (work with) another program (DOS session).

> **Note**
>
> Even though you may have a computer with an 80386 or higher microprocessor, if you do not have at least 4M of RAM installed in your machine, use Task Manager as a task switcher. If you do have 4M of RAM or more, install Task Manager as a multitasker.

Refer to Chapter 21, "Multitasking and Task Switching," for a complete understanding of the installation and use of Task Manager as a multitasker.

Networking Requirements

Networking is the term used in computing when two or more computers are connected so that the resources of one or more of the computers can be shared by the other computers. There are basically two types of networks: central-server-based networks and peer-to-peer networks.

With central-server-based networks, at least one file server provides the resources and runs the network. Computers are connected to the file server as workstations by network interface cards and the appropriate cabling. When a workstation sends a request to the server for an application and data files, the server transmits the application and the data through the cabling to the workstation where they are loaded into memory and executed.

Peer-to-peer networks consist of two or more connected computers where any station can supply resources to any other. There is no need for a dedicated file server, and any device connected to any station can be made available to any other station. Peer-to-peer networks also are interconnected with cables attached to network interface cards installed in each computer on the network.

Novell DOS 7 includes complete peer-to-peer network software, consisting of a Desktop Server and Universal Client. In a peer-to-peer network, you can install your computer as a desktop server, a client, or both. The desktop server provides resources to the network. The client requests resources from the server.

With the Universal Client software in Novell DOS, you can also be a workstation on a central-server-based network (NetWare 2.x, 3.x, or 4.x).

II

Setting Up Your System

> **Note**
>
> Novell, Inc. also sells a peer-to-peer network product without DOS, called Personal NetWare. This is the same network software delivered with Novell DOS 7. Personal NetWare is positioned as a stand-alone network for installation on computers that are not using Novell DOS, and is the replacement for the prior Novell peer-to-peer network known as NetWare Lite. Thus, your Novell DOS 7 networking software allows you to connect your machine as a desktop server, a client, or both to a Personal NetWare network.

The hardware requirements for networking your computer with Novell DOS 7 start with at least one other computer running Novell DOS Desktop Server, Universal Client, or Personal NetWare, or having access to a NetWare server-based network (Version 2.x, 3.x, or 4.x). You also need to purchase or have access to a network interface card (NIC) and the appropriate cabling.

Three major types of network cards exist: ARCnet, Ethernet, and Token-Ring. Each one denotes a different method for the transmission of information across the network and a different wiring scheme. There are many opinions as to which type is the best to use, but it is not in the scope of this book to discuss that issue here. If you are connecting to an existing network, see the network administrator for the NIC and cabling you must use for that specific network. If you are establishing a new network, see your dealer for various options and pricing.

In any case, Novell DOS 7 and its network components can support many types of NICs. Table 4.1 lists the cards for which drivers are supplied (as of the writing of this book). The Setup Network screen for the network card lists all current cards that were distributed with your copy of Novell DOS. Refer to the next section on using the Setup utility and selecting the NIC.

Table 4.1 Novell DOS 7 Network Card Selections

Manufacturer	Card
3Com	3C1100 3 Station Ethernet
3Com	3C501 EtherLink
3Com	3C503 EtherLink II
3Com	3C503 EtherLink II TP

Manufacturer	Card
3Com	3C503 EtherLink II/16
3Com	3C503 EtherLink II/16 TP
3Com	3C505 EtherLink+
3Com	3C523 EtherLink/MC
3Com	3C523 EtherLink/MC TP
Ansel	M1500
Ansel	M2100
Cabletron Systems	Ethernet E20
Cabletron Systems	Ethernet E21
Cabletron Systems	Ethernet EHUB
Cabletron Systems	Ethernet E3010
Cabletron Systems	Ethernet E3010-X
Cabletron Systems	Ethernet E3020
Cabletron Systems	Ethernet E3020-X
Cabletron Systems	Ethernet E3030
Cabletron Systems	Ethernet E3030-X
Cabletron Systems	Ethernet E3040
Cabletron Systems	Ethernet E3040-X
Cabletron Systems	Ethernet E31
Cabletron Systems	Ethernet E31-X
Cabletron Systems	Token-Ring T20
Cabletron Systems	Token-Ring T30
EXOS	105
EXOS	235T
Hewlett-Packard	MC Adapter 16
Hewlett-Packard	MC Adapter 8/16/16+

II

Setting Up Your System

(continues)

Table 4.1 Continued	
Manufacturer	**Card**
IBM	FDDI DOS ODI LAN driver for NetWare
IBM	PS/2 Ethernet Adapter
IBM	Token-Ring 16/4 Credit Card Adapter
IBM	Token-Ring Network 16/4 Adapter/A
IBM	Token-Ring Network Adapter II & 16/4 Adapter
IBM	Token-Ring Network Adapter/A
Intel	EtherExpress32
Intel	EtherExpress ISA Family
Intel	EtherExpress MCA Family
Intel	593
Intel	596
NCR	WaveLAN
Novell	Ethernet NE1500T
Novell	Ethernet NE2100
Novell	Ethernet NE3200
Novell	NTR2000 Token-Ring Adapter
Novell	RX-Net & RX-Net II
Novell	RX-Net/2
Novell/Eagle	NE/2
Novell/Eagle	NE1000
Novell/Eagle	NE2-32
Novell/Eagle	NE2000
Novell/Excelan	EXOS 205T Ethernet
Novell/Excelan	EXOS 215 Ethernet
Novell/Excelan	LANZENET Ethernet
Racal-Datacom	ES3210 ODI MLID

Manufacturer	Card
Racal-Datacom	InterLan AT/XT ODI MLID
Racal-Datacom	NI5210 ODI MLID
Racal-Datacom	NI6510 ODI MLID
Racal-Datacom	NI9210 ODI MLID
SMC	EtherCard PLUS Family Adapter
SMC	PC130/130E/270E ODI Driver
SMC	PC500WS/550WS (short or long card) ODI Driver
SMC	PC600WS/650WS ODI Driver
SMC	PS110/210/310 PS/2 ODI Driver
SMC	Token-Ring Elite Family Adapter
Thomas-Conrad	TC3042 TCNS 8-Bit Adapter
Thomas-Conrad	TC3045 TCNS 16-Bit Adapter
Thomas-Conrad	TC3046 TCNS MC Adapter
Thomas-Conrad	TC3047 TCNS EISA Adapter
Thomas-Conrad	TC4035/TC4045 Adapter
Thomas-Conrad	TC4046 Adapter
Thomas-Conrad	TC5045 Ethernet Adapter
Thomas-Conrad	TC5046 Ethernet Adapter, 16-Bit
Thomas-Conrad	TC5046 Ethernet Adapter, 32-Bit
Thomas-Conrad	TC6x42 ARCnet 8-Bit Adapter
Thomas-Conrad	TC6x45 ARCnet 16-Bit Adapter
Thomas-Conrad	TC6x46 ARCnet MC Adapter
Ungermann-Bass	NIUpc
Ungermann-Bass	NIUpc/EOTP
Ungermann-Bass	NIUps
Ungermann-Bass	Personal NIU

II

Setting Up Your System

(continues)

Table 4.1 Continued	
Manufacturer	**Card**
Ungermann-Bass	Personal NIU/ex
Wearnes	2107C
Wearnes	2110T
Xircom	Credit Card Ethernet Adapter
Zenith Data Systems	NE2000 Module

As mentioned, more cards may be supported in your Novell DOS 7 package. For the current list, check the Setup, Networking, and Primary Network Interface Card configuration. You may be able to use another network card, but the driver must be supplied with the card by the manufacturer, and an OEM Supplied Driver selected from the installation list in Setup. You must make sure that the card and driver work with Desktop Server.

The last hardware requirement for installing a network on your Novell DOS 7 system is a cable. You need the correct cable for the network interface card you selected.

> **Note**
>
> Make sure that you determine any other hardware requirements for the type of network interface protocol you are installing. For example, if you use ARCnet cards, you need to use a connecting device called a *hub*. An Ethernet card using coaxial cable requires T-connectors and terminating resistors. Your network administrator or dealer can assist you with any such requirements.

Using the Install/Setup Utility

Before you start the actual installation of Novell DOS 7, you should take several safety precautions for your system and data. Because installing a new operating system can be likened to major surgery on your computer, you should first make a complete backup of all program and data files. Nothing should go wrong, but you never know when someone might plow into a utility pole and cut off power, or some other minor catastrophe interrupts the process. Use whatever is your normal backup software to protect your applications and data.

Second, you should not install any new software from the distribution disks. Use the DISKCOPY command to make copies of the original disks and then install from the working copy. (See Chapter 9, "Copying and Comparing Disks," for details on using DISKCOPY.)

Tip
The DISKCOPY command works only if you have an existing version of DOS on your computer.

If you are installing Novell DOS over another version of DOS, the default is for Install to preserve that other version. Thus, you can later uninstall Novell DOS and restore your other version. If you want, you can change this installation default and not save the existing version of DOS.

Preparing for Installation

Before you start to make disk copies of the Novell DOS disks, make sure that they are write-protected so that you do not accidentally erase them. If you are using 5 1/4-inch floppies, use a write-protect tab (little black tapes that come with disks) and cover the square notch on the right side of the floppy, toward the top. If the disks you received from Novell do not have this notch, you do not need to write-protect them; they already are. If you are using 3 1/2-inch disks, turn each floppy over and make sure that the square slide on the top left of the disk is pushed toward the top, so that the hole is open. If the disk has a square hole without a slide on the right side of the back, it is a high-density indicator hole and should not be covered.

The next step is to decide how and where to install Novell DOS. Consider the following:

- If you are using a computer that already has DOS installed on it, turn on your system. Novell DOS 7 should be installed using your current operating system, especially if you have installed disk compression on your hard disk.

- If your Novell DOS disks fit in drive A of your computer, insert the INSTALL disk (the first disk) in drive A. If the disks fit in drive B, insert the INSTALL disk (again, the first disk) in drive B.

- Check the amount of disk space on your hard disk. If you are installing only basic Novell DOS, you need 5.6M of free space. If you want to install the Novell DOS Window utilities, you need an additional 1.6M of free space, for 7.2M total. If you want to install the Novell DOS network components, you also need another 5M of free disk space. For all three parts, you must have approximately 12.2M free. Note that the three major components do not have to be on the same drive. You can place DOS on drive C, and the network on drive D, for example.

Using the Install Utility

If your system already has a version of DOS on it, insert the working copy of the INSTALL disk (the first disk) in the correct floppy drive and log onto that drive. To do this, enter **A:** if the drive is A:, or **B:** if the drive is B:. At the A:> prompt, then enter the following:

    INSTALL

If this is a new installation (not over a preexisting version of DOS), just insert the disk in drive A and turn on your computer. The installation program automatically starts with the booting process.

If you are installing on a new or clean hard disk, Novell DOS first notifies you that you must prepare the hard disk with FDISK. Refer to Chapter 8, "Preparing Disks," for more on this process. The installation process is halted while this preparation procedure is carried out. You must create at least one partition for drive C, but you may create extended partitions for other logical drives (D:, E:, and so on), as long as you have room. Simply tell FDISK the size in megabytes of each partition. Once FDISK sets up the logical drive, it automatically formats the drive. When you complete this operation, press Esc; your system reboots and the installation procedure starts over, but this time with a hard disk ready for it.

The installation procedure begins with the copying of the Install/Setup utility (which comes in two files) and the FORMAT utility to the hard disk. The opening screen is then displayed (see fig. 4.1).

Notice that the top line of the screen shows the name of the utility and the bottom line shows the navigation keys you can use within the utility. When more than one action button or selection box is on-screen, use the Tab key, the up- or down-arrow key, or the mouse to move between the buttons or boxes. After you select the button or box you want, press Enter to continue (or just click the item with the mouse). This basic screen format is the one for all Novell DOS utilities that use a full-screen type interface.

Making a Bootable Floppy Disk. If you want to make a bootable floppy disk, you can do so right now. Otherwise, you have to wait until after you install Novell DOS 7. Choose Generate a Bootable Floppy Disk. Install responds with a message telling you of your selection and requesting that you insert a blank disk in the floppy drive, after which you press Enter. (To skip this process and return to the opening screen, press Esc.) After Install completes the format, it copies the correct files to the new floppy, after requesting that you switch back to the installation disk so that Install can read the files before writing them to the new disk.

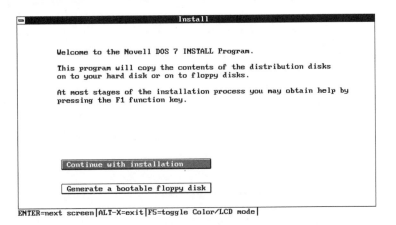

Fig. 4.1
The Novell DOS 7
Install opening
screen.

Note

You should be aware that the process of making a bootable floppy disk does not place the entire operating system on the hard disk, nor does it make the floppy able necessarily to access all of your hard disk, especially if your hard disk has been compressed or requires special drivers. You may have to add files or change the configuration files on the floppy to work with your hard disk after booting on the new floppy.

Usually, you install Novell DOS 7 on your hard disk, so choose Continue with Installation.

Registering the Software

Install now requires that you enter your registration information, as shown in figure 4.2. Enter your own name, your company name, and the serial number for your copy of Novell DOS 7. You must enter your name and the serial number, which is printed on the INSTALL disk (the first disk). You can, however, skip the company name.

The highlight appears on the Name entry line, with the cursor at the first position. Just type your name. You can use all uppercase, both upper- and lowercase, or all lowercase. Install then displays a data entry box, with your characters showing as you type them. You can also press Enter and, after the data entry box is displayed, start typing your name. When you finish with your name, press Enter or click OK. You can also press Esc or click Cancel to return to the registration screen.

Fig. 4.2
The Novell DOS 7 product registration screen.

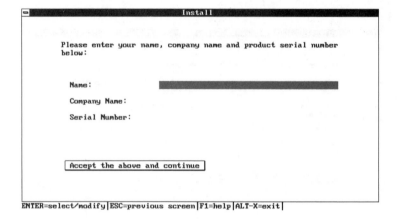

Follow the same procedure for your company name, if you want to enter that. To skip the company name, tab down to the Serial Number entry line. Follow the same procedure as for your name. Make certain that you copy the serial number as printed on the first disk of your Novell DOS 7 set. If you do not enter your name or the product serial number, Install displays an error box informing you that You must enter your name and product serial number. You cannot continue the installation without this step. After you are finished, press Enter.

Checking for Viruses. You can now have Novell DOS check your system for any virus that might have infected your system. If you have never done this before, or have not checked your system in a long time, it is a good idea to take this step at this time although it is not a default. Novell DOS 7 includes Fifth Generation's Search & Destroy (SDScan) antivirus utility, which will be placed on your system.

Choose Perform Virus Scan from the next screen that appears. Your video screen clears briefly while Search & Destroy loads. You are led to an operations screen, as shown in figure 4.3. Press Enter to start the scan. SDScan displays the letter for each drive as it scans the drive, as well as the name of each file scanned.

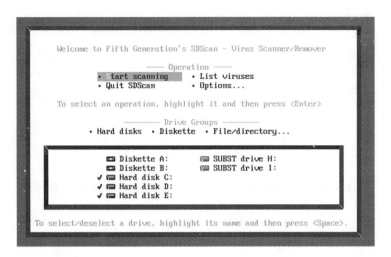

Fig. 4.3
The SDScan
operations screen.

If you watch the files carefully, you may see that only executable files (COM
and EXE), along with archived or packed files (ARC, LHA, and ZIP), are actually searched for viruses. Some large archived files may cause the scanner
problems because of the way the files are produced. In this case, you may see
an error warning that the scanner ran out of memory while checking one of
these files. Press Enter to skip the current archived file that is causing the
error message.

If you want, you can change the default settings for SDScan. Refer to Chapter
16, "Virus Protection," for directions. However, for the purpose of the installation, the default settings are fine.

When the scan is finished, choose Quit SDScan in the operations screen. The
Install utility switches to the screen for the next configuration issue—keyboard type.

Specifying the Keyboard Type. At this point, assuming that most people
who are reading this book are in the United States or are using a U.S. keyboard, you should accept the default keyboard selection by choosing Accept
the Above and Continue. If you do want to change the keyboard, select the
Keyboard Type entry line and press Enter. A scrollable list of all allowable
keyboard drivers appears. Choose the driver you want; then press Enter.
Install removes the keyboard list and displays your selection. Use Tab to
change the selection. Choose Accept the Above and Continue.

> **Note**
>
> If you booted with the Novell DOS INSTALL disk, Install now attempts to load the
> selected keyboard driver. When you finish the installation and reboot your system,
> the selected keyboard driver is in effect.

Selecting the Components to Install. Install now displays the software
installation screen, as shown in figure 4.4.

Fig. 4.4
The Novell DOS 7
software installa-
tion screen.

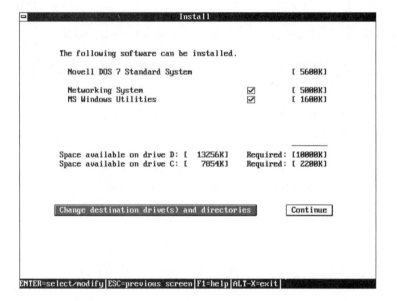

When the Novell DOS 7 installation program first loads, it scans your system
to determine your system components and to see whether Windows is on the
system, as well as how much disk space is available. The results affect the
current screen (refer to fig. 4.4).

As you can see, the standard Novell DOS 7 system takes 5600K (5.6M). The
default installation procedure is to install the network, which requires another 5000K (5M). If Windows was not installed on your system, the MS
Windows Utilities option is not checkmarked for installation. Install then
displays the total current installation space requirements and the space
available.

To change the components to be installed, select Networking System or
MS Windows Utilities. Choose Change Destination Drive(s) and Directories
if you want (and have) other drives available.

Selecting Locations for Files. Install next displays a screen for you to change the locations of the DOS system files, DOS utility files, and network files. Select the appropriate line for your changes. A data entry screen appears. Make the appropriate changes and press Enter. You can also press Esc or click Cancel to return to the location screen without making any changes.

When you finish setting the locations of the Novell DOS files, choose Accept the Above and Continue. With your changes made, the software installation screen is redisplayed and may look similar to the screen shown in figure 4.5.

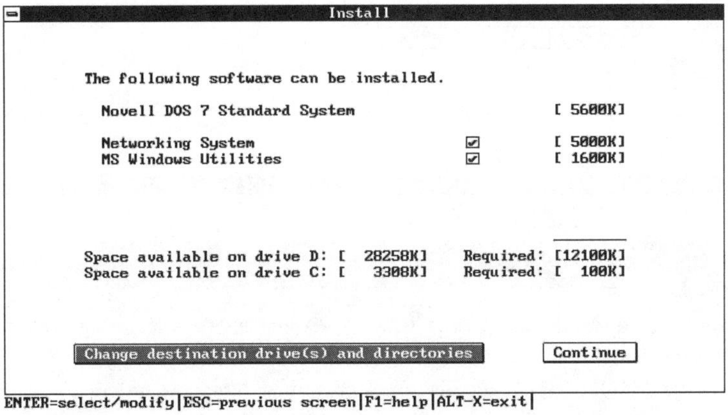

Fig. 4.5
The Novell DOS 7 software installation screen after changes.

Installing the Files. As you can see in figure 4.5, the Windows utilities are going to be installed, along with the standard system and the network. However, all files except the system boot files are to be stored on drive D, which has sufficient space on the computer in this example.

At this point, choose Continue. Install now requests confirmation to proceed with the installation, or you can change the installation settings. For now, accept the default settings and press Enter.

Install then requests a second confirmation, displaying the software destinations and several other configuration items (see fig. 4.6).

If you want to make further changes, press the Esc key to return to the previous screen, and go ahead and make the changes. If not, choose Start Installation and press Enter. After Install copies all the files to your hard disk, you can always go back and fine-tune your installation.

Fig. 4.6

The Novell DOS 7 installation confirmation screen.

```
┌─────────────────────────────────────────────────────────────┐
│ ▭                          Install                            │
├───────────────────────────────────────────────────────────── │
│                                                               │
│     The installation will now begin.                          │
│                                                               │
│        System files will be copied to      C:\               │
│        Utility files will be copied to     D:\NWDOS          │
│        NetWare files will be copied to     D:\NWCLIENT       │
│        MS Windows files will be copied to C:\WINDOWS         │
│                                                               │
│        Memory manager will be              Novell DOS EMM386.EXE │
│        Disk Cache will be                  Novell DOS NWCACHE.EXE │
│                                                               │
│     If you select to proceed now, you will be unable to interrupt │
│     the installation process.                                 │
│                                                               │
│          ┌────────────────────────────┐                      │
│          │  Start Installation        │                      │
│          └────────────────────────────┘                      │
│                                                               │
│          ┌────────────────────────────┐                      │
│          │ Go back to previous screen │                      │
│          └────────────────────────────┘                      │
│                                                               │
├───────────────────────────────────────────────────────────── │
│ ENTER=select/modify│ESC=previous screen│F1=help│ALT-X=exit │  │
└─────────────────────────────────────────────────────────────┘
```

> **Note**
>
> Except for changing the selection to install the networking software or the Windows utilities, or changing the destination location for the files, you probably will want to accept the default configuration determined by Install. After your system is rebooted with Novell DOS 7, use Setup to make other changes if you like.

If you want to make changes, refer to the section "Using the Setup Utility" later in this chapter to understand the various configuration issues and the modifications you can make.

Install begins by creating, if necessary, the directory structures for what is to be installed, and then proceeds to copy the files. As each disk is read, the utility requests that you remove the current disk and insert the next disk.

> **Caution**
>
> Make certain that you insert the correct disk. Install does not ask for the number of the disk in the set, but for the number of the disk as named on the label. For example, the name on the second disk in the set is UTILITIES 1. Depending on the software selections you are installing, Install may request a disk out of numbered sequence.

When Install finishes copying all the files to your hard disk, it displays Install's final screen (see fig. 4.7). You have the option of viewing the README file, which is the latest word on any changes to Novell DOS since the documentation was finalized, as well as any special notes of which you should be aware. You can also view the new CONFIG.SYS or AUTOEXEC.BAT file created in the installation process.

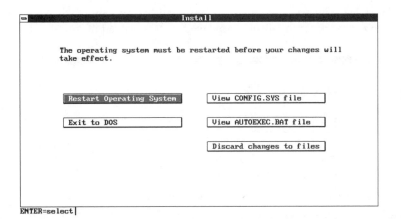

Fig. 4.7
The Novell DOS 7
Install final screen.

II

Setting Up Your System

Note

Use the View CONFIG.SYS File or View AUTOEXEC.BAT File button to preview your new system configuration. You can then go back and make changes before ending the Install utility.

The button at the bottom right of the final screen allows you to abort the installation, even at this point. Choose Discard Charges to Files to do so.

For your new installation to take effect, you must reboot your computer. Remove the final disk from the floppy drive. Choose Restart Operating System. A dialog box prompts you to remove all floppy disks and run the Setup utility after Novell DOS 7 loads. The system reboots with Novell DOS 7.

Using the Setup Utility

The Install and Setup utilities for Novell DOS 7 are really the same utility. During the installation procedure, the program is not only copied to the hard disk but also renamed as SETUP.EXE. The setup files, along with the rest of the Novell DOS 7 utilities, are normally placed in the \NWDOS subdirectory. The system path is also set or modified to include this directory, unless you manually changed the path list. You can read more on system paths by referring to Chapter 6, "Understanding File Storage."

Use the Setup utility to change your system configuration, install Stacker disk compression (including conversion from SuperStor or DoubleSpace compression, if necessary), configure your network, and make other changes. These topics are discussed in later sections of this chapter.

To start the Setup utility, enter the following at the DOS prompt:

    SETUP

Novell DOS responds by opening the screen shown in figure 4.8. Notice that the title at the top of the display now reads Setup instead of Install.

Fig. 4.8

The Novell DOS 7 Setup opening screen.

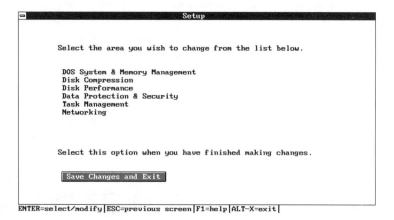

```
┌────────────────────────────────────────────────────────────┐
│■                          Setup                              │
├──────────────────────────────────────────────────────────────
│                                                              │
│     Select the area you wish to change from the list below.  │
│                                                              │
│        DOS System & Memory Management                        │
│        Disk Compression                                      │
│        Disk Performance                                      │
│        Data Protection & Security                            │
│        Task Management                                       │
│        Networking                                            │
│                                                              │
│                                                              │
│     Select this option when you have finished making changes.│
│                                                              │
│        ┌─────────────────────────┐                          │
│        │ Save Changes and Exit   │                          │
│        └─────────────────────────┘                          │
│                                                              │
└────────────────────────────────────────────────────────────┘
 ENTER=select/modify│ESC=previous screen│F1=help│ALT-X=exit│
```

The system areas listed in the middle of the screen represent the configuration items available for your modification. To access an item, use either the keyboard or the mouse.

Note that if you press the Esc key while in Setup, the previous screen is redisplayed. Pressing the F1 key provides you with on-line help for the selected item currently displayed. Alt-X lets you exit from Setup, after confirming that you want to exit to DOS.

The next sections discuss the configuration areas listed in figure 4.8.

Configuring DOS System and Memory Management. The first option, DOS System & Memory Management, pertains to the following items:

■ *Memory Manager.* Includes EMM386.EXE, the memory manager for computers with 386 and higher microprocessors; HIMEM.SYS, the memory manager for 80286 computers (as well as 8088 and 8086 computers with LIM 4.0 memory); the loading of DPMS software; and the location in RAM of Novell DOS itself.

- *Country and Keyboard.* Includes the handlers and drivers for supported country codes, keyboard nationalities, and keyboard types. Refer to Appendix A, "Internationalizing Your System," for more on these handlers and the available country and keyboard codes.

- *DOS System Parameters.* Includes the setting of system paths, environment parameters, keyboard HISTORY, disk parameters (buffers, files, and FCBs), PROMPT command formats, and directory locations for temporary and initialization files.

- *Optional DOS Device Drivers and Utilities.* Includes extended support for displays (ANSI.SYS and GRAFTABL), file fastopen support, file-sharing support, and code page switching.

- *Global Color Set.* Establishes the screen colors (on color monitors) for Novell DOS's full-screen utilities.

The Setup screen for DOS System & Memory Management is similar to the screen shown in figure 4.8 but contains the configuration areas described in the preceding list.

Memory Manager Options. When you select this area, the screen shown in figure 4.9 is displayed. The Novell DOS 7 Install utility determined the best memory manager for your system, based on its analysis of your computer and its resources. If you have a 386 or higher microprocessor, a check mark appears in the box next to i386/486/586 Memory Manager. If you have an 80286 processor, the 80286 Memory Manager box is checked.

To add or remove a check mark, move to the box and press Enter or the space bar. When an option contains a small box with a down arrow at the right, a selection list is available for that option. To access the list, choose the option, select your choice from the list, and press Enter. The option then displays your choice.

> **Caution**
>
> Although Setup may allow you to checkmark both memory managers, do not do so. You can load and use only one memory manager at a time.

For understanding DPMS (DOS Protected Mode Services), see Chapter 2, "What's New in Novell DOS 7?" If your computer contains more than 1M of

RAM, Install may have checkmarked this box. The bottom line on memory options refers to the location of DOS itself in memory: whether the DOS kernel and data structures should be loaded into lower (conventional) memory, upper memory, or high memory. You can read more about memory by turning to Chapter 22, "Optimizing Memory."

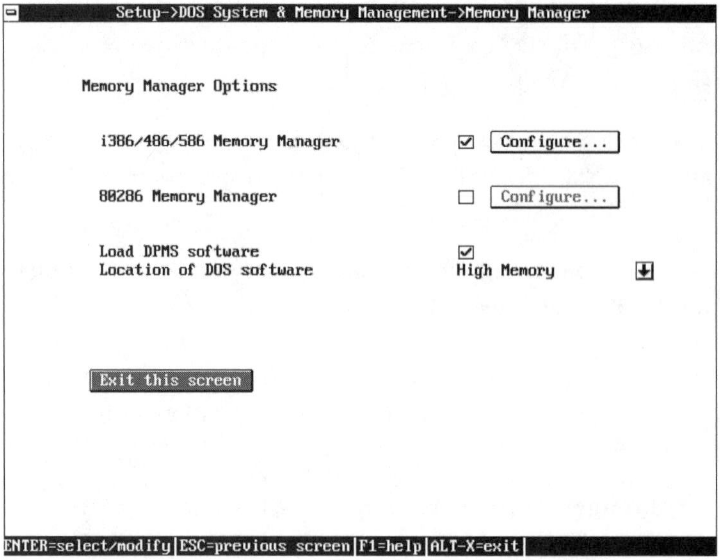

Fig. 4.9
The Setup memory manager options.

```
┌──────────────────────────────────────────────────────────────┐
│ ■   Setup->DOS System & Memory Management->Memory Manager      │
│                                                                │
│                                                                │
│      Memory Manager Options                                    │
│                                                                │
│          i386/486/586 Memory Manager      ☑  ┌─────────────┐   │
│                                               │ Configure...│   │
│                                               └─────────────┘   │
│          80286 Memory Manager             ☐  ┌─────────────┐   │
│                                               │ Configure...│   │
│                                               └─────────────┘   │
│          Load DPMS software               ☑                    │
│          Location of DOS software         High Memory     ⬇   │
│                                                                │
│                                                                │
│                                                                │
│          ┌──────────────────┐                                  │
│          │ Exit this screen │                                  │
│          └──────────────────┘                                  │
│                                                                │
│                                                                │
│                                                                │
│                                                                │
│                                                                │
└──────────────────────────────────────────────────────────────┘
 ENTER=select/modify│ESC=previous screen│F1=help│ALT-X=exit│
```

If Install (or you) chose the 386 or higher memory manager (EMM386.EXE), choose the Configure button for the 386 memory manager. The screen shown in figure 4.10 is displayed.

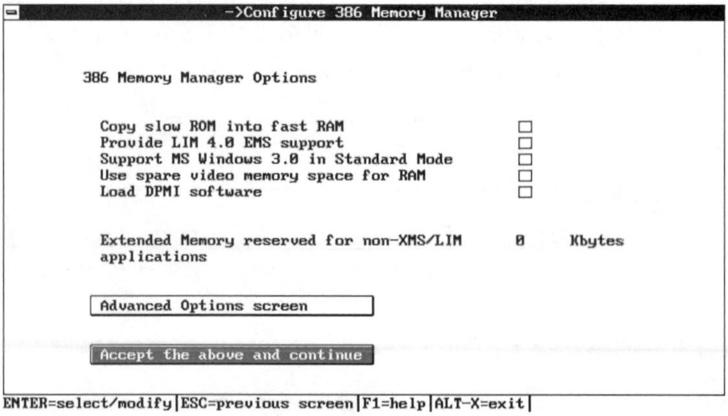

Fig. 4.10
Configuring the 386 memory manager.

```
┌──────────────────────────────────────────────────────────────┐
│ ■               ->Configure 386 Memory Manager                 │
│                                                                │
│                                                                │
│        386 Memory Manager Options                              │
│                                                                │
│          Copy slow ROM into fast RAM              ☐            │
│          Provide LIM 4.0 EMS support              ☐            │
│          Support MS Windows 3.0 in Standard Mode  ☐            │
│          Use spare video memory space for RAM     ☐            │
│          Load DPMI software                       ☐            │
│                                                                │
│          Extended Memory reserved for non-XMS/LIM  0   Kbytes  │
│          applications                                          │
│                                                                │
│          ┌──────────────────────────┐                         │
│          │ Advanced Options screen  │                         │
│          └──────────────────────────┘                         │
│          ┌────────────────────────────────┐                   │
│          │ Accept the above and continue  │                   │
│          └────────────────────────────────┘                   │
│                                                                │
└──────────────────────────────────────────────────────────────┘
 ENTER=select/modify│ESC=previous screen│F1=help│ALT-X=exit│
```

All PCs contain information built into the hardware on programmed chips called ROM (read-only memory). This "firmware" enables the hardware to operate together and even to load DOS. The operating system has to access ROM firmware in order to utilize the hardware, but this process is relatively slow. Using the EMM386.EXE memory manager, or even some memory managers from third-party companies, you can transfer the ROM firmware into RAM or extended memory. This greatly accelerates the accessing of ROM information. The downside is that it may take precious extended memory. Thus, you have to decide whether you want to copy slow ROM into fast RAM. It may just be a trial-and-error process if you have a lot of use for your extended memory.

Another option here is whether you want EMM396.EXE to provide LIM 4.0 EMS (expanded memory) support. Unless you have specific applications that require it, you may not need to activate this option. Novell DOS uses extended memory to provide the emulation for expanded memory.

The third option in this area is to notify Setup whether you require support for Microsoft Windows Version 3.0, which you use in standard mode (this option is for 80286 machines or for 386 machines with less than 2M of RAM). Note that this option does not refer to Microsoft Windows Version 3.1.

Your computer sets aside a block of memory just above lower memory for use by your video adapter. If you have a nongraphics monitor or do not use graphics application software, you can increase the amount of lower memory available for applications. Choose Use Spare Video Memory Space for RAM to use this video memory. This can be as much as 64K.

The next configuration option is Load DPMI Software, which enables Novell DOS to provide DPMI services to applications that require these services from the operating system. Note that some applications that use DPMI can supply their own support if necessary, but not all of them can.

You can also specify the amount of extended memory to reserve for use by application software that requires extended memory but does not work with XMS (extended memory specification) or LIM expanded memory. Programs that are able to use XMS or LIM memory cannot access this reserved memory. Unless you have documentation that tells you to provide this memory, you can leave this value at 0.

Finally, an Advanced Options Screen button enables you to view a table showing the current availability of upper memory.

Caution

If you access the Advanced Options screen, do not change anything unless you are experienced in handling upper memory. You could very easily make some changes that cause your system to lock up during the boot.

To return to the Memory Manager Options screen, choose Accept the Above and Continue; then press Enter. If you use the Esc key to exit from this screen, the changes you made are not retained.

If you chose to use the 80286 memory manager (HIMEM.SYS), you can, at the Memory Manager Options screen, choose the Configure button for the 286 memory manager. The only option here is one for using spare video memory for lower memory. There is also an Advanced Options Screen button that displays a table showing the current availability of upper memory. As with the 386 Memory Manager Advanced Options screen, if you access this screen, do not change anything unless you are experienced in handling upper memory. You could very easily make some changes that cause your system to lock up during the boot. Choose Exit This Screen and press Enter to return to the DOS System & Memory Management screen.

Note

If you ever do establish a configuration that locks up your computer on booting, you can bypass the configuration files and fix the problem. When the boot occurs, you can see the message Starting DOS.... While this message is on-screen and nothing else follows it, you can press the F5 key. Novell DOS 7 continues to boot after you press F5, but bypasses the CONFIG.SYS and AUTOEXEC.BAT files. You can read more about these files in Chapter 18, "Configuring Your System."

Country and Keyboard Options. When you choose Country and Keyboard, each of the options has a list from which you can make your selection. Choose an option to access its list. After you decide on your choice, press Enter to return to the options screen. Choose Exit This Screen.

You can learn more about the Novell DOS handlers for country and keyboard nationalities by reading Appendix A, "Internationalizing Your System."

DOS System Parameters. When you select DOS System Parameters from Setup's DOS System & Management screen, another configuration area list is presented. It contains a number of options for you to consider. The first is System PATH. If you need to learn about the system path, read Chapter 6, "Understanding File Storage." When you select this area, you are presented with either a blank line or a line displaying the current PATH statement. If you want to modify the path, choose the line. A data entry box is displayed. When you complete your entry, press Enter to return to the PATH screen, and choose Accept the Above and Continue.

The next area of DOS System Parameters is Environment Parameters. When you select this area, you are presented with several settings:

- *BREAK (on/off).* If this is set to on, you can interrupt applications at any time by pressing Ctrl-Break. Use this setting very carefully because, in the wrong place, you can damage data files.

- *LASTDRIVE (A-Z).* This setting allows you to reserve drive letters for use with such devices as SUBST and ASSIGN. Networks use drive letters starting with the letter following the LASTDRIVE. Every allowed drive letter takes 80 bytes of memory.

- *VERIFY (on/off).* If this is set to on, DOS checks that all disk writes are made correctly. This added operation slows down your system but reduces the chance of not finding disk problems until too late.

- *Environment Size (128-32751).* This value tells DOS the amount of memory to reserve for environment data, such as PATH. You can see the amount established by looking at the SHELL statement in your CONFIG.SYS or DCONFIG.SYS file, following the /E: parameter. Normally, the values should be 512 to 1024 for most circumstances.

After you make your selections, choose Accept the Above and Continue.

The next option, Configure Keyboard HISTORY, lets you recall previously typed commands at the DOS prompt with the press of a key or two. You can store approximately 10 commands, depending on length, for every 256 bytes of memory. If you are accustomed to working at the DOS prompt, you will probably find HISTORY a very helpful device. However, if you are accustomed to working through system menus or some user interface (such as Windows or GeoWorks), you can save the memory and not activate HISTORY.

II

Setting Up Your System

The first choice is to turn HISTORY on or off. The second is to establish the size of the keyboard HISTORY buffer. The third is to determine whether the operating mode of HISTORY is Insert or Overwrite when you perform command-line editing. If you turn Insert on, characters to the right of the cursor are moved to the right when you type new characters on the recalled command line. If you turn Insert off, you overwrite characters to the right of the cursor when you edit the command line.

When you are finished with this option, choose Accept the Above and Continue.

With the Disk Parameters option, you can make the settings for various disk I/O parameters:

- *BUFFERS (3-99).* DOS uses memory to store data when it reads from and writes to disk. Generally, the more buffers specified, the faster your system performs read and write operations. However, each disk buffer requires 528 bytes of RAM, and there is a point of diminishing return. For a system of only 640K total memory, 15 is the optimum. Novell suggests setting buffers at 3 when you use a cache.

- *FILES (5-255).* DOS requires a table (or list) of open files— files that are in use. The number specified here tells DOS how big the list should be, the number of files, and thus, how much memory to reserve for this table. The default is 20, but some applications require more. For Windows 3.1, use 60 files as a minimum.

- *File Control Blocks, or FCBs (0-255).* Some older software uses FCB calls to open files instead of using the customary file handle calls. The default setting is 4,4 if you need them at all. Each FCB requires 50 bytes of memory. For minimum memory use, try FCBS=1,1.

When you are finished, choose Accept the Above and Continue.

The PROMPT Command option enables you to customize the PROMPT display on your system and display various information every time you return to DOS. The data entry screen for this option provides a list of preprogrammed selections and a line that allows you to design your own.

For a thorough discussion of the PROMPT command, refer to Chapter 14, "Managing the Display and Keyboard." That chapter provides some helpful examples.

Choose Accept the Above and Continue when you are finished with this option.

The last option, Directories for Temporary and Initialization Files, enables you to specify the location directories for Novell DOS's temporary and initialization files. The environment variable TEMP is set to the value entered here. The default is C:\TEMP. The DOS configuration files (those with the extension INI) are usually placed in the \NWDOS directory. You can change the location if you like.

Choose Accept the Above and Continue. Then choose Exit This Screen to return to the DOS System & Memory Management screen.

Optional DOS Device Drivers and Utilities. Figure 4.11 shows the optional operating system devices and support utilities that you can tell Novell DOS to load on your system. The first is for extended support using the ANSI.SYS driver. Some programs require that ANSI.SYS be loaded in your CONFIG.SYS or DCONFIG.SYS file so that they can properly control your video screen.

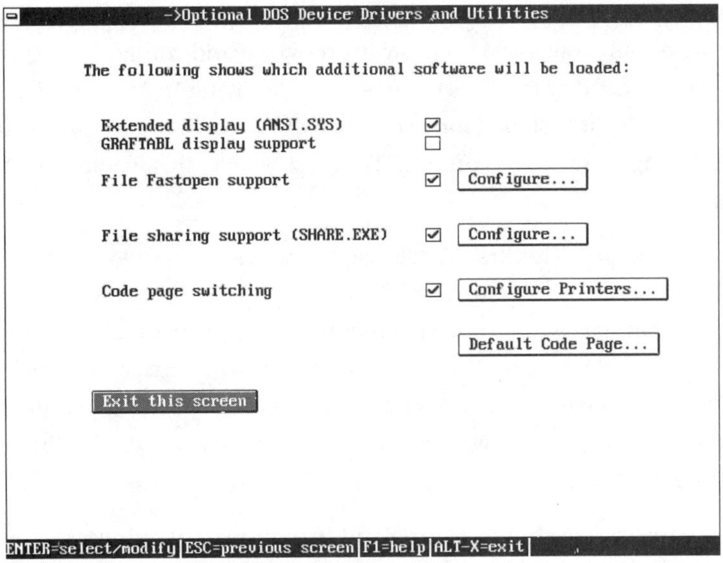

```
┌─────────────────────────────────────────────────────────┐
│ □            ->Optional DOS Device Drivers and Utilities │
│                                                          │
│      The following shows which additional software will be loaded: │
│                                                          │
│        Extended display (ANSI.SYS)        ☑             │
│        GRAFTABL display support           ☐             │
│                                                          │
│        File Fastopen support              ☑  [ Configure... ] │
│                                                          │
│        File sharing support (SHARE.EXE)   ☑  [ Configure... ] │
│                                                          │
│        Code page switching                ☑  [ Configure Printers... ] │
│                                                          │
│                                              [ Default Code Page... ] │
│                                                          │
│        [ Exit this screen ]                              │
│                                                          │
│ ENTER=select/modify│ESC=previous screen│F1=help│ALT-X=exit│ │
└─────────────────────────────────────────────────────────┘
```

Fig. 4.11
The optional DOS Device Drivers and Utilities screen.

The GRAFTABL Display Support option works only on CGA (Color Graphics Adapter) monitors for displaying international characters. If you do not change your country code, you do not need this driver. Read more about country codes in Appendix A, "Internationalizing Your System."

Fastopen is a device whereby a special disk cache is established just for the directory tables of frequently used files. If you are installing NWCACHE or some other cache, it is best not to activate the File Fastopen Support option.

The range is from 128 to 32768. The default 512 is sufficient for most systems. Also be aware that each entry requires 2 bytes of memory.

The File Sharing Support (SHARE.EXE) option is required when you can run more than one program on your system at the same time, or when other systems can access your files on a network. If you install Task Manager as either a task switcher or a multitasker, or you install the network on your system, SHARE must be loaded. If a check mark appears beside the File Sharing Support (SHARE.EXE) option, you can then select the Configure button for this option and specify the number of concurrent (simultaneous) file locks, with a range of 20 to 1024. Each file lock takes 16 bytes of memory. The second value is for specifying the amount of space allocated for file-sharing data.

The term *code page switching* refers to switching alphabetic character tables on your system so that national language and custom support can be used on your system for a country other than that for which your machine was built. If you tell the Install/Setup utility to activate code page switching, you can select the default code page from the list provided and configure your printer if it has the capability to change character tables. Refer to Appendix A, "Internationalizing Your System," for a complete discussion of code page switching, including a list of such printers. For most people, this feature is not necessary.

Global Color Set. This area allows you to set the colors used by Setup, EDIT, and the other full-screen utilities of Novell DOS 7. This is one area where you can have some fun experimenting with the various color sets preprogrammed by Novell. Choose Selected Global Color Set, and the available list is displayed for you. If you do not have a color screen, you must use either Mono or LCD; otherwise, try them all and see what you like best for your system.

Setup allows you to select a color set and then displays your selection on the example screen. If you don't like your choice, just reactivate the list and make another choice. When you are satisfied, choose Accept the Above and Continue.

You have now finished with the DOS System & Memory Management area. Choose Exit This Screen.

Configuring Disk Compression. Novell DOS 7 includes Stacker Version 3.1, the disk compression utility from Stac Electronics. It includes all utilities for the creating of compressed hard and floppy disks, the repair and optimization of compressed drives, and the in-place resizing and removal of the disk compression.

Before proceeding, you should understand what disk compression is. The following section describes the process of disk compression and the products available for compressing your data.

What Is Disk Compression? In DOS, files are stored on disk exactly as they are written or created. Especially with word processing and data files, there is a lot of empty space. For example, most databases allow 30 to 40 characters for your name, yet the names of most people are closer to 20 characters in length. The remaining allowable space is kept, however. This is a common approach for a very high percentage of files on most systems. In addition, many duplicate characters are present.

Disk compression is a series of algorithms that reduce file contents to the smallest possible size by removing empty spaces and duplications, which are replaced with keys indicating what is condensed. When the files are decompressed, the compression algorithms are reversed, and the keys are interpreted, resulting in the restoration of the files to their original size and contents.

Amazingly, some files can be reduced by a factor of 16 to 1; other files, particularly executable program files, can hardly be condensed at all, having a compression ratio of 1 to 1. On most systems, the overall average of file compression works out to be about 2 to 1. This means that files taking up 4M of disk space can be compressed and stored in only about 2M of disk space. This effectively doubles the capacity of your hard drive.

The basic scheme of disk compression is to take a normal drive, create a very huge file, and treat this file as if it were an actual, logical disk drive. The new compressed drive then receives a drive letter, usually the next available one after the last existing drive. The compression drivers then exchange or swap the drive letters so that the compressed drive receives the letter designation of the original, uncompressed drive, and vice versa. See Chapter 11, "Disk Optimization Utilities," for further information about disk compression.

Considerations for Disk Compression. There are several considerations you may want to make before installing disk compression. First of all, you should be aware that your system does require a noncompressed portion of the boot drive. The disk compression drivers and the boot files must be able to be read before disk compression can take effect.

Second, some programs that write to and read from disk by directly accessing the disk, thus bypassing the operating system and the drivers, cannot work with disk compression. Usually, Windows swap files cannot be stored on compressed drives. However, Novell DOS 7 includes a utility for Windows that allows the Windows permanent swap file to be placed on a Stacker compressed drive.

In any case, you should not compress your entire hard disk. In fact, Novell DOS 7 does not allow you to do so. It automatically allows enough space for the requisite boot files. If you have only one hard disk, the recommendation is that you leave approximately 10 percent of the drive capacity as noncompressed. If you have more than one hard disk, an obvious choice may be to compress one disk and not the other. Of course, you could compress part of the first disk and also the entire second disk.

Note
When you select Disk Compression, Setup informs you that you can now reboot your computer so that you can disable any software which may interfere with the stacking process. This specifically applies to any device drivers, TSRs (terminate-and-stay-resident programs), or disk cache utilities that can affect writing to the disk. Task Manager is a device that must be removed. NWCACHE, by default, has write-delay caching turned off, so there is no effect with it. If in doubt, reboot your computer and check your CONFIG.SYS or DCONFIG.SYS file and your AUTOEXEC.BAT file for any other drivers you might want to disable until the compression is installed or converted.

Several scenarios are possible on your system when you select Disk Compression from Setup's main area list. The following paragraphs describe these possibilities.

Caution
You cannot change the disk compression on your system, or you will not be able to uninstall Novell DOS.

Compressing an Uncompressed Disk. You have no disk compression on your system at all. This gives you a very simple choice to make: to install Stacker or not to install it. When you choose to install disk compression, Setup analyzes the disk structure of your system and displays the drives available for you to compress. To install disk compression, simply select the drive from the available drive list displayed by Setup.

Setup then analyzes the drive to make sure that there is sufficient space for the installation. If the drive is too full, Setup notifies you of the fact and requests that you remove enough files to create the space needed so that it can do its conversion work.

When the conversion is complete, Setup notifies you that it is going to reboot your system so that the new Stacker drivers installed on your system can be loaded. Press Enter to reboot.

Updating a Disk Compressed with Stacker 3.1. You have Stacker 3.1 disk compression installed on your system. This is the same version as that supplied with Novell DOS 7. When you select disk compression configuration, Setup displays the status of your current drives. You can add any noncompressed drives to your compressed list and fine-tune your current Stacker drives.

Updating a Disk Compressed with Earlier Versions of Stacker. If you have a version of Stacker disk compression earlier than 3.1 installed on your system, the Novell DOS 7 Install utility provided your system with the 3.1 Stacker driver that is loaded before the CONFIG.SYS or DCONFIG.SYS file and that can process your older-version compressed drives. When you select disk compression configuration, Setup displays the status of your current drives. You can add any noncompressed drives to your compressed list, but you can also fine-tune your current Stacker drives, which you should do. The Stacker 3.1 compression algorithms are more efficient than the older ones. You can increase your compression ratios with the new version and, thus, increase available disk space.

Converting from SuperStor. You have SuperStor disk compression installed on your system. When you select Disk Compression, Setup tells you that it can convert from SuperStor to the newer, more powerful Stacker compression. Go ahead and do it. It does not take long, and because the Stacker driver loads before the CONFIG.SYS or DCONFIG.SYS file, as well as loads above the 1M RAM area because it is a DPMS driver, you can increase lower memory significantly.

On completion of the conversion, Setup notifies you that it is going to reboot your system so that the new Stacker drivers installed on your system can be loaded. Press Enter to reboot.

Converting from DoubleSpace. You have DoubleSpace disk compression installed on your system. The same thing applies with DoubleSpace as with SuperStor. Setup can convert your disk compression to the more powerful Stacker 3.1 as well as increase your lower memory.

On completion of the conversion, Setup notifies you that it is going to reboot your system so that the new Stacker drivers installed on your system can be loaded. Press Enter to reboot.

Configuring Disk Performance. The third menu option for configuration is Disk Performance. When you select this option, Setup displays a screen with two options: VDISK.SYS (for a RAM disk) and NWCACHE (a disk cache).

One of the slowest parts of your computer is a disk drive, which is a mechanical device. You can configure in your system a much faster disk drive with no moving parts, called a *RAM disk*. This device consists entirely of memory and, thus, is sometimes referred to as a *memory disk* or *virtual disk*. To create such a disk, you set aside part of the random-access memory in your system, using the device driver VDISK.SYS.

The advantage of using a RAM disk is that any program or data files are accessed extremely fast, as there are no mechanical parts slowing down the process. Using a RAM disk has a disadvantage, though. When you turn off or reboot your computer, the virtual drive and its contents are lost, as memory is erased. Therefore, when you load VDISK, you have to copy the files you want stored on the RAM disk to it; and before you turn off your system or reboot it, you have to copy the files back or lose them.

Another device provided with Novell DOS 7 to speed up your hard disk is called a *cache.* This is a utility that stores in memory the most recently used disk data so that when it is needed again, the disk does not have to be accessed, thereby speeding up performance. NWCACHE.EXE is the name of the utility that provides this feature.

A disk cache works because there actually is a high degree of repetition in accessing data on disk drives. A correctly installed disk cache can reduce disk access by as much as 80 to 90 percent, or even more.

NWCACHE is a DPMS utility, meaning that if you enable the DPMS driver, the utility is loaded into extended memory, above 1M. This helps you maintain a large lower memory area for running your applications. You can learn more about NWCACHE by reading Chapter 11, "Disk Optimization Utilities."

The configuration screen lists the two utilities with check boxes and configure buttons. When you place a check mark in the first box, the configure button is enabled.

Configuring the RAM Disk. VDISK.SYS has four configuration parameters: the disk size, the sector size, the maximum number of files that can be stored on the RAM drive, and the type of memory to be used.

You can use lower memory, extended memory, or expanded memory for the RAM drive. Lower memory is automatically used if your computer has no extended or expanded memory. You can read more about the various types of memory in Chapter 22, "Optimizing Memory."

First, you can tell Setup the amount of memory to use for the RAM disk. The disk size is entered in K (thousands of bytes). For lower memory, the range you can enter is from 1K to 256K. The default is 64K if you have no other type of memory. If you use extended memory, you can have a RAM disk with as much extended memory as your system can use. If you use expanded memory, you can have a RAM drive as large as 32M, if your system has that much memory. VDISK will use all available extended or expanded memory as a default. Of course, for extended and expanded memory, you must use a memory manager that controls the type of memory you want to use, such as EMM386.EXE or HIMEM.SYS.

The second parameter for VDISK.SYS is the sector size, or the allocation unit for files. The allowable values are 128 bytes, 256 bytes, and 512 bytes. The smaller the number, the more efficient the use of the disk space. The default is 128 bytes.

Next, you can tell VDISK the maximum number of files that can be stored on the RAM disk's root directory. The range is from 2 to 512, with a default of 64 files.

The last parameter is for the type of memory you want to use for the RAM disk. If you use expanded memory, the /X switch is appended to the command line for loading VDISK.SYS. If you use extended memory, the switch is /E:*n*. If entered, *n* specifies the number of sectors that can be transferred between lower and extended memory. The range is from 1 to 8 sectors, with 8 as the default.

Setup places the command to load VDISK.SYS in the CONFIG.SYS or DCONFIG.SYS file, after the memory manager, but before any other device that can use extended memory. Setup also uses the DEVICEHIGH command. If you modify the command yourself, you can use DEVICE or HIDEVICE. Removing the /E or /X switch forces the RAM disk into lower memory.

When you have entered (or agree with) the parameters for VDISK, select Accept the Above and Continue to return to the Disk Performance configuration screen. There you can proceed to select and configure the disk cache.

Configuring the Disk Cache. The disk cache has four configuration parameters: the maximum cache size, the minimum cache size, whether to allow for write delays, and whether to allow for memory lending.

The maximum cache size is the amount of memory the cache uses to store disk data. Unless you specify a maximum, or the cache cannot allocate the specified amount, NWCACHE tries to use all available extended or expanded memory by default, with a maximum of 7670K.

The minimum cache size is the amount of memory that the cache retains if it lends memory to applications. The difference between the maximum and minimum cache size is what is available for lending to requesting programs, if lending is enabled. The default is based on the amount of memory in your computer. Table 11.3 in Chapter 11 lists the default minimum cache sizes.

Write delays are the part of the cache that can hold disk-write requests in memory until the cache can consolidate several disk writes, thereby saving disk access time and increasing performance. The default in Setup is not to enable this feature, because a problem such as a power failure can result in the loss of data. When write delay is not enabled, the cache is said to be *write through*, meaning that when a disk write is requested, it is performed without any delay. This is a conservative setting, and most users may want to enable write delays.

The fourth parameter for you to consider is whether NWCACHE should enable the lending of memory to an application that requests it. The default setting is ON. This allows the cache to have as much memory as possible to improve disk performance, but to make some of the memory available to an application temporarily. Lending is done only up to the difference between the maximum and minimum cache sizes. Ensure that lending is enabled when using Microsoft Windows.

When you have entered (or agree with) the parameters for NWCACHE, select Accept the Above and Continue to return to the Disk Performance configuration screen. Choosing Exit This Screen returns you to the main configuration screen for Setup.

Configuring Data Protection and Security. The next area for configuration on the Setup main screen is Data Protection & Security. When you choose this option, the screen shown in figure 4.12 is displayed.

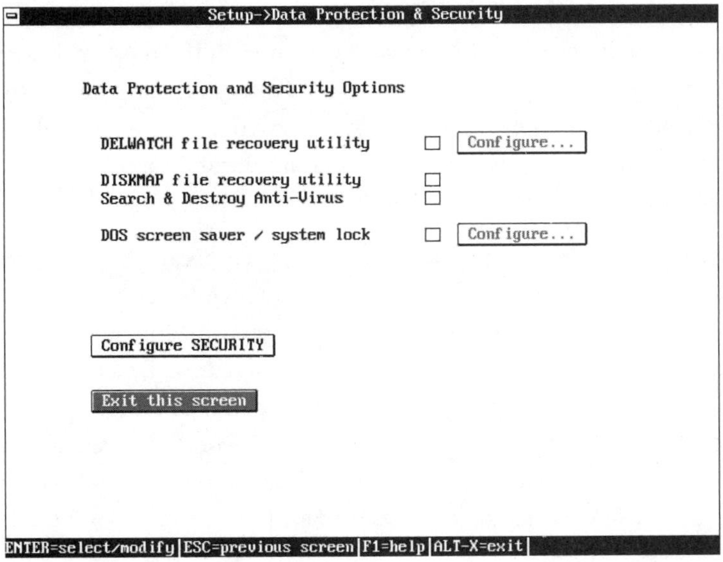

Fig. 4.12
The Data Protection & Security screen.

As you can see in this figure, there are four check boxes for activating specific security measures provided with Novell DOS 7. When you select DELWATCH File Recovery Utility or DOS Screen Saver/System Lock, additional buttons are activated for configuring these options. Here are descriptions of the options available in this screen:

- DELWATCH is a file recovery utility. When you erase any file, DELWATCH retains the information on the file and does not allow DOS to make the space available for other files. Thus, if you erase any file accidentally, you can easily recover it without damage by using another Novell DOS utility, UNDELETE. You can tell Setup how many files DELWATCH can preserve. When the maximum number is reached, the oldest file is truly erased whenever a new file is added to the protected list. DELWATCH can also save files with the same name in the same directory. You tell the difference by the date and time stamp on the file. Besides all that, you can specify the type of files to be saved or the type of files not to be saved. Refer to Chapter 10, "Undeleting Files," for more on DELWATCH and UNDELETE.

- DISKMAP is a companion utility to DELWATCH. It prepares a map of your hard disk every time you boot your system or rerun the utility. DISKMAP assists UNDELETE in recovering erased files. Refer to Chapter 10, "Undeleting Files," for more on DISKMAP.

- SDScan, the Search & Destroy Antivirus scanning utility from Fifth Generation Systems, protects your system from the modern scourge of computer viruses. SDScan can be loaded into your boot files, so that whenever you boot your system, it checks your system. You can also run SDScan manually whenever you want. Read Chapter 16, "Virus Protection," for more on this utility.

- LOCK is the DOS and Windows utility for temporarily locking your system, protecting it from unauthorized use while you are away. This utility is also a DOS screen-saver utility. You can configure the DOS screen saver as a TSR to take effect when there is no keyboard or mouse activity for the specified period. You can specify the number of minutes or the number of seconds for the inactivity period. You can also access LOCK as a stand-alone program from the DOS prompt, without it being a TSR. Refer to Chapter 15, " System Security," for more on LOCK.

The final option in this area is the Configure SECURITY button. When you choose Configure SECURITY, the screen shown in figure 4.13 is displayed.

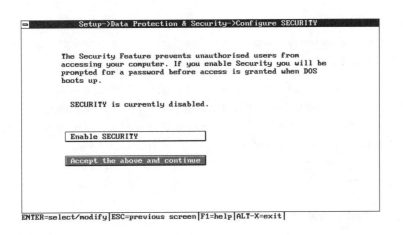

Fig. 4.13
The Configure
SECURITY screen.

Here you can enable and disable system login security. After you have enabled security, no one can get into your system without the correct password.
You cannot remove the security without the master password. You cannot
even boot on a floppy disk from another operating system, so make sure that
you protect and remember your passwords when you enable security.

For a thorough understanding of login security and the selection and use of
passwords, read Chapter 15, "System Security."

Configuring Task Management. This configuration area allows you to tell
Setup to install Task Manager on your system. As you read at the beginning
of this chapter, there are two modes of operation for Task Manager: task
switching and multitasking. When you select Task Management, Setup displays the Task Manager Options screen. Choose one of the operating modes.
You cannot select both modes.

If you select the multitasker, you can proceed to Configure Task Manager by
selecting that option. The multitasker configuration screen appears on your
monitor, as shown in figure 4.14.

You access the Task Manager menu by pressing a hot-key combination. The
default combination is Ctrl-Esc. Very few software programs use these keys in
combination. However, if necessary, Setup allows you to change the hot keys.
You use a Shift key and a main key. The first two options on this screen let
you select, from lists, the keys you can use.

Foreground/Background Ratio refers to the amount of processor time given to
foreground DOS sessions as compared to background sessions. The range for
the time-slice (tick) value is from 1 to 20. The default value is 5, which gives

II

Setting Up Your System

the best overall performance for most users. This means that the program which you are actively working on in the foreground gets five processor ticks for every tick given to each background program.

Multitasking programs that require or are capable of using extended memory (XMS) or expanded memory (LIM) are supported by Task Manager. You can enter a value from 0 to 8192 (kilobytes) per DOS session that can access this memory. This memory is not allocated, just available to fill any request. Be sure that this setting does not exceed the available amount of memory on your system.

Fig. 4.14

The screen for configuring Task Manager as a multitasker.

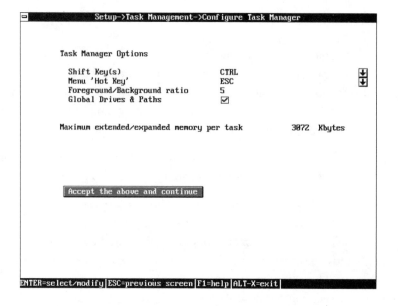

```
┌─┐                Setup->Task Management->Configure Task Manager
├─┘
│
│     Task Manager Options
│
│        Shift Key(s)                        CTRL                        ▼
│        Menu 'Hot Key'                      ESC                         ▼
│        Foreground/Background ratio         5
│        Global Drives & Paths               ☑
│
│     Maximum extended/expanded memory per task        3072  Kbytes
│
│
│
│        ┌──────────────────────────────────┐
│        │  Accept the above and continue   │
│        └──────────────────────────────────┘
│
│
│
│
│
ENTER=select/modify│ESC=previous screen│F1=help│ALT-X=exit│
```

If you select the task switcher, you can proceed to Configure Task Manager by selecting that option. The task switcher configuration screen appears, as shown in figure 4.15.

You access the Task Manager menu with a hot-key combination, usually Ctrl-Esc. You can change either or both of these keys, using the lists accessed when you select either of the top two options on this screen.

Because the task switcher saves background tasks to a disk file, there has to be a location for this file. On this screen, you can specify that location or accept the default subdirectory, \NWDOS\TMP.

You can control other parameters too. The first is for the amount of XMS extended memory Task Manager can use for task switching. When this memory is exhausted, Novell DOS uses a swap file on disk. Using extended memory provides the fastest response. If your system has LIM or expanded (EMS) memory, you can use this memory for Task Manager. Although using this memory is a little slower than using extended memory, it is still faster than a swap file. If you specify Task Manager to use LIM memory and then exhaust this memory, Task Manager uses a swap file (sometimes referred to as virtual memory) on disk. If you need a refresher on the various types of memory in your computer, refer to Chapter 22, "Optimizing Memory."

Fig. 4.15
The screen for configuring Task Manager as a task switcher.

The last option you can select is for the amount of expanded memory that each task uses if any program requests the use of such memory. With expanded memory limited on a per-task basis, if several programs that loaded at the same time request expanded memory, all can get their share. Otherwise, the program that loaded first may use all of expanded memory.

Configuring Networking. The last option on the Setup main screen is Networking. If you decide to install Novell DOS 7 networking components, several scenarios are possible:

■ The original Install procedure copied the Novell DOS network files to your hard disk. Now you can proceed to configuring the network.

■ Install did not copy the network files to your hard disk, or if they were copied, you erased them. When you select Networking and the files are not on your hard disk, Setup knows this and instructs you to insert the floppy disks from your Novell DOS 7 distribution set into the correct drive and then proceeds to copy the files at this time. You can proceed to configuring the network.

■ You have already installed the network for Novell DOS 7 but want to modify the configuration. You can proceed to reconfiguring the network.

■ You already have installed NetWare Lite and want to upgrade to the Novell DOS 7 peer-to-peer network. Chapter 5, "Installing the Network," shows you how to do this.

Because of the nature of this subject, Chapter 5 continues with a full discussion on installing the network and the various installation and configuration issues.

Saving the Configuration. When you finish with the main configuration areas of the Setup utility, choose Save Changes and Exit. Setup proceeds to update your configuration files and displays a message box informing you that Setup is complete. Choose OK to continue. The screen shown in figure 4.16 then appears.

Fig. 4.16
Setup's final screen after configuration.

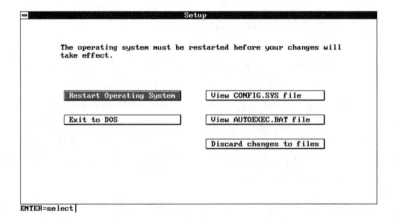

Normally, this screen contains five buttons. If, however, you ran Setup but did not make any changes to the CONFIG.SYS, DCONFIG.SYS, or AUTOEXEC.BAT files or use Alt-X to abort the utility, only one button is displayed: Exit to DOS. Here are descriptions of the five options in this screen:

■ *Restart Operating System.* This causes your system to reboot. Any changes made to the configuration files cannot take effect until there is a reboot.

■ *Exit to DOS.* This returns you to the Novell DOS prompt without rebooting. Remember that the changes you made cannot take effect until you reboot your system. However, this step may be necessary if you disabled utilities, device drivers, or TSRs to run Setup.

■ *View CONFIG.SYS File.* This enables you to preview the changes made to your CONFIG.SYS file by using the Setup file viewer, as shown in figure 4.17. The file viewer is not an editor. You can only look at the file; you cannot make any changes. If the displayed file is longer than the viewing area allows, use the up- and down-arrow keys or the PgUp and PgDn keys to scroll through the file so that you can view all of it. Press Esc to return to Setup's final screen.

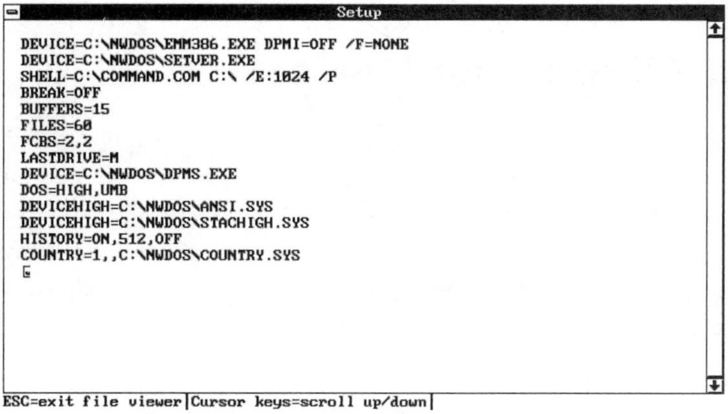

```
=                              Setup                              ↑
  DEVICE=C:\NWDOS\EMM386.EXE DPMI=OFF /F=NONE
  DEVICE=C:\NWDOS\SETVER.EXE
  SHELL=C:\COMMAND.COM C:\ /E:1024 /P
  BREAK=OFF
  BUFFERS=15
  FILES=60
  FCBS=2,2
  LASTDRIVE=M
  DEVICE=C:\NWDOS\DPMS.EXE
  DOS=HIGH,UMB
  DEVICEHIGH=C:\NWDOS\ANSI.SYS
  DEVICEHIGH=C:\NWDOS\STACHIGH.SYS
  HISTORY=ON,512,OFF
  COUNTRY=1,,C:\NWDOS\COUNTRY.SYS
  ▪
                                                                  ↓
ESC=exit file viewer|Cursor keys=scroll up/down|
```

Fig. 4.17
Using the Setup file viewer with the CONFIG.SYS file.

■ *View AUTOEXEC.BAT File.* This option is the same as the one for viewing the CONFIG.SYS file, except that you can choose this option to view the AUTOEXEC.BAT file.

■ *Discard Charges to Files.* If, after you configure your system and view the boot files, you decide that you don't want to make the changes, you can choose this option. The original CONFIG.SYS and AUTOEXEC.BAT files are restored. The configuration changes you made during the current session of Setup are discarded.

II

Setting Up Your System

> ### Note
>
> You can use Setup to make changes to an item, such as Task Manager, by modifying the initialization file, such as TASKMGR.INI, rather than the CONFIG.SYS, DCONFIG.SYS, or AUTOEXEC.BAT file. In this case, you cannot discard your changes with the Discard Changes to Files button. You must rerun the Setup utility and modify the Task Manager parameters. You can also use a text editor to change TASKMGR.INI directly, but unless you really know what you are doing, this is not recommended.

One further note is needed on Setup's final screen. You cannot use the Esc key to return to the configuration main menu. You must exit the utility and rerun Setup.

Installing Other Devices

Several devices are provided with NOVELL DOS 7 that are not installed for you. You have to do that yourself, using EDIT or some other text editor, so that you can modify the CONFIG.SYS, DCONFIG.SYS, or AUTOEXEC.BAT file. You also have to do this installing if you are using a mouse with your system and need to load the mouse driver. Novell DOS does not provide a mouse driver.

Installing SCRIPT

If you have a printer that uses the PostScript printing language, but the application software you are using cannot output to the PostScript printer, you get what is called "garbage" instead of recognizable information—that is, unless your printer is capable of changing printing modes and you go through the bother of changing the mode. Novell DOS 7 includes a PostScript driver. This device driver lets you print in PostScript format from many DOS applications and from DOS itself. SCRIPT intercepts printer output and translates the data with the information the PostScript printer can understand and use. For details on using SCRIPT, see Chapter 13, "Controlling System Devices."

Installing the CD-ROM Driver

If you do not have a CD-ROM installed in your computer system, or you did not install the DPMS server with the Novell DOS 7 Install or Setup utility, you can skip this section.

Novell DOS 7 includes a driver called NWCDEX.EXE to replace the
MSCDEX.EXE CD-ROM driver, Version 2.1 or 2.2. NWCDEX is a DPMS client
utility. This means that the CD-ROM driver is placed in extended memory,
above the 1M area, thus saving lower memory.

If you have a CD-ROM drive installed in your computer system, you are most
likely using a driver called MSCDEX.EXE. If you are not familiar with this,
check your AUTOEXEC.BAT file or the batch file that loads your CD-ROM
driver. You are looking for a command that starts with MSCDEX.EXE
/D:MSD001. (There is probably more to the line.)

Once you find the command for MSCDEX, all you have to do is change the
name of the CD-ROM driver to NWCDEX—note that you are changing MS to
NW—and then save the file. You do not have to make any other changes to
the command statement.

The following switches are available for NWCDEX:

/D:*drivername*   This is the name of the CD-ROM driver. This normally is distributed with the drive itself and is required.

/E   If you do not have DPMS installed, you can use this switch to make use of expanded memory (LIM/EMS).

/K   This switch tells NWCDEX to look for the supplementary volume descriptor. This is used with Kanji, a Japanese dialect.

/L:*drive*   This switch specifies the drive letter. You do not need this switch unless the drive letter interferes with network drive letters, as the driver normally uses the first unused drive.

/M:*value*   This option tells NWCDEX the number of buffers to allocate for the CD-ROM data. The default is 14.

/N   This switch tells NWCDEX not to use DPMS, which is the default if the DPMS server is available.

Installing the Mouse

When you installed your mouse, chances are that there was an installation
program for the device that placed the mouse driver on your hard disk

Tip
Novell DOS does not include a mouse driver.

II
Setting Up Your System

Tip
Verify the name of your mouse driver before adding mouse commands.

(probably in a directory called \MOUSE) and placed the mouse driver in your CONFIG.SYS or AUTOEXEC.BAT file.

When you installed Novell DOS 7, the mouse driver line in either file should not have been touched by Install, or later if you ran the Setup utility. If, because you created new boot files for your system, the mouse driver command was not included, you need to add the command to your CONFIG.SYS or DCONFIG.SYS file or to your AUTOEXEC.BAT file. The command in either DCONFIG.SYS or CONFIG.SYS is

```
DEVICE=C:\MOUSE\MOUSE.SYS
```

You can also use the DEVICEHIGH= command if you have any upper memory available, thus saving lower memory.

The command you use in AUTOEXEC.BAT is

```
C:\MOUSE\MOUSE
```

Make sure that you use the correct drive letter, directory name, and device file name if they are not exactly as given in these examples.

Note

If you look in your original CONFIG.SYS and AUTOEXEC.BAT files and cannot find any command or device statement for a mouse, do not worry. Some software programs, such as GeoWorks and Windows, have their own mouse drivers built in, and you may not need to use a separate mouse driver in either of the boot files.

Using VER and SETVER

One of the installation issues with software and operating systems is the version of DOS you are using. If you enter **VER** at the DOS prompt, you receive the message that the current operating system is Novell DOS 7. If you use the command **SET** at the DOS prompt, the system variable OS is displayed as OS=NWDOS, and the system variable VER is displayed as VER=7. In addition, Novell DOS 7, in response to internal requests by other software as to the version of DOS, replies that it is DOS 6. This means that Novell DOS 7 reports itself as being compatible with MS-DOS 6.

Novell DOS 7 also includes a utility automatically placed in your CONFIG.SYS or DCONFIG.SYS file to provide an expected DOS version number to software that may refuse to run unless it receives that expected answer. Some software programs internally seek a version number from DOS. The programs usually do this because they use certain services found only in that version. The problem is that most later versions of DOS also include those services, so SETVER is the utility that can return a special version number to a program. If the subject program is included in the SETVER program list, the program can run under the current version.

The Novell DOS 7 Install utility placed the correct SETVER command in your CONFIG.SYS or DCONFIG.SYS file, as

```
DEVICE=C:\NWDOS\SETVER.EXE
```

The line in your file may be different if the location of your DOS files is different.

If you want to see the list of programs with their special version numbers, enter the following at the DOS prompt:

```
SETVER /P
```

The /P switch tells SETVER to display only one screenful of data at a time, pausing so that you can read the list. The original list distributed with Novell DOS 7 is longer than one screenful. SETVER then displays the current list of software and the associated DOS version numbers that it has been told to provide. The first entry reads as `Global version 6.00`, meaning the DOS version number provided unless the requesting program is in the following list.

The list then consists of two columns: the first is the name of the program file (name and extension), and second is the DOS version number.

You can modify the version table maintained by SETVER. To do this, make sure that you know the correct DOS version required by the software. Then enter the following command at the DOS prompt:

```
SETVER path filename.ext n.nn
```

If the location of the file for SETVER—SETVER.EXE—is not in the system path, you must include the location of SETVER.EXE. This is normally C:\NWDOS. You must include as the *filename.ext* the complete name and extension of the program with which you are concerned. You must also include the version number in the format *n.nn*, such as 3.30. When you finish making any entries to SETVER, you can see your entries by entering **SETVER** **/P**. For the new entries to take effect the next time you run the listed software, you must reboot your computer.

You can modify an existing entry in the SETVER version table by entering the existing program name but with a different version number. You can delete an existing entry in the SETVER version table by entering the full program name and adding the /DELETE switch, without any version number. Whenever you use the SETVER command for adding new programs, modifying program entries, or deleting entries, SETVER displays a message screen, as shown in figure 4.18.

Fig. 4.18

The Novell DOS
SETVER message
screen.

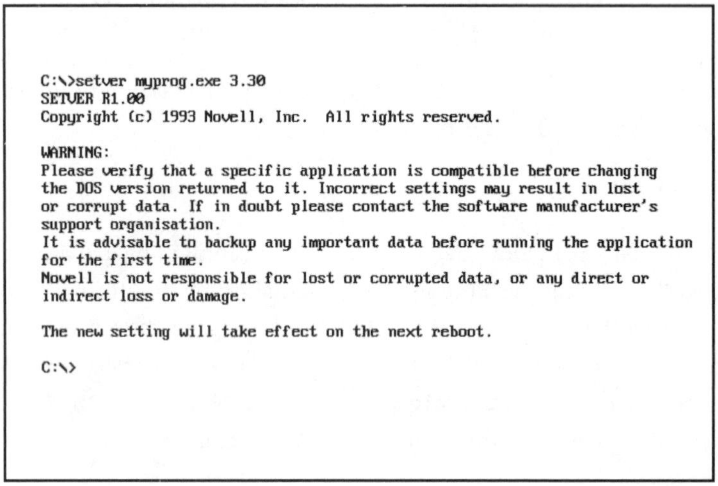

```
C:\>setver myprog.exe 3.30
SETVER R1.00
Copyright (c) 1993 Novell, Inc.  All rights reserved.

WARNING:
Please verify that a specific application is compatible before changing
the DOS version returned to it. Incorrect settings may result in lost
or corrupt data. If in doubt please contact the software manufacturer's
support organisation.
It is advisable to backup any important data before running the application
for the first time.
Novell is not responsible for lost or corrupted data, or any direct or
indirect loss or damage.

The new setting will take effect on the next reboot.

C:\>
```

If you like, you can prevent the display of this message screen. Simply add the /QUIET switch to the end of your normal SETVER command line.

> **Note**
>
> Just because you add a version number to the SETVER version list for a specific program, the program may not necessarily run under the version of the operating system. You must make sure that the program is compatible.

Uninstalling Novell DOS 7

Included with Novell DOS 7 is a utility called UNINSTAL that is used to uninstall Novell DOS 7, should you ever want to do this.

When you installed Novell DOS 7, and the prior version of DOS was retained on your system, Install preserved a copy of your original boot track on your hard disk, along with the boot and configuration files and any other file required to operate the old DOS, as well as a special system file telling Install what it did. Install renamed the retained files, prefacing them with @ and changing the file extension to UI, and then hid these files. You cannot see these files in the root directory on your hard disk with the normal DOS DIR command. You are able to see them with the Novell DOS XDIR command. Do not erase these files if you want to uninstall Novell DOS later.

Be aware of the following points:

- First, there must have been an existing operating system on your computer before you installed Novell DOS 7.

- Second, the Install utility must have saved the prior version of DOS on your system. By default, this is what Install does. However, you are able to change the default and tell Install not to save the old operating system.

- Third, you cannot have converted your system's disk compression to Stacker, unless you were already using Stacker, and you cannot have installed disk compression.

- Finally, once you uninstall Novell DOS 7, the only way you can reinstall the operating system is to use the distribution disks or their working copy. The uninstall process deletes the Novell DOS files.

Tip
If you think you might return to an earlier DOS version, don't rely on the UNINSTAL utility only. Make a backup before installing Novell DOS.

Before you uninstall Novell DOS, make sure that you have a backup of your system. If you made one before you installed Novell DOS and it is not an old backup, it may be sufficient.

To start the utility, enter the following at the DOS prompt:

```
UNINSTAL
```

Novell DOS responds by displaying the information shown in figure 4.19.

II

Setting Up Your System

Fig. 4.19

The Novell DOS
UNINSTAL utility.

```
C:\>uninstal
UNINSTAL R2.00  Novell DOS Un-Install Utility.
Copyright (c) 1991,1993 Novell, Inc.  All rights reserved.

Reading Uninstall data file.

You have selected to uninstall Novell DOS.
Are you sure you want to continue ? (Y/N)
```

You must now confirm that you want to continue. If you want to continue, press Y. If you do not want to continue, press N.

If you answered yes, the utility proceeds to remove the Novell DOS 7 files and restore the prior DOS files it preserved on your hard disk. The process does not take long, but do not interrupt it. If you answered no, you return to the DOS prompt.

If you tell UNINSTAL to restore your prior version of DOS, but it cannot find the special files it used to preserve your old DOS, you receive the message One or more of the files required by UNINSTAL are missing. UNINSTAL is therefore unable to proceed. You return to the DOS prompt and must reinstall the other version of DOS.

If the prior version of DOS was saved and the disk compression device was converted to Stacker 3.1 with Novell DOS 7, UNINSTAL notifies you that it cannot proceed, as shown in figure 4.20.

Fig. 4.20

UNINSTAL cannot
execute because of
compression
conversion.

```
C:\>uninstal
UNINSTAL R2.00  Novell DOS Un-Install Utility.
Copyright (c) 1991,1993 Novell, Inc.  All rights reserved.

Reading Uninstall data file.

The compression status of drive C: has changed since Novell DOS was
installed. Uninstallation is no longer possible. Enter UNINSTAL /C to
discard your old operating system.

C:\>
```

Most people may want to execute the Novell DOS 7 UNINSTAL utility on one occasion. That is with the /C switch:

```
UNINSTAL /C
```

This option for UNINSTAL tells the utility to remove the old operating system files preserved in the installation process. Of course, once you execute this option, you can no longer uninstall Novell DOS 7.

From Here...

In this chapter, you learned the hardware requirements for installing Novell DOS 7 and its major components. You learned also how to install Novell DOS and how to use the Setup utility to complete your system's configuration. Now you may want to turn to the following chapters:

- Chapter 5, "Installing the Network," guides you through the installation process for the Novell DOS 7 network.

- Chapter 10, "Undeleting Files," provides more on DISKMAP, DELWATCH, and UNDELETE.

- Chapter 15, "System Security," explains LOCK and login security.

II

Setting Up Your System

Chapter 5

Installing the Network

As you read in Chapter 4, Novell DOS 7 contains the components of a peer-to-peer network: the Desktop Server and the Universal Client software. With this software on a group of Novell DOS 7 networked computers, you can share your computer's resources with other users; share the resources of another computer; or connect to an existing NetWare network, running NetWare Version 2.x, 3.x, or 4.x. You can also connect to a desktop server and a NetWare system at the same time. This chapter explains how to install the network and configure your system as a server, client, or server-client.

In this chapter, you learn also how to upgrade your system to the Novell DOS 7 desktop server peer-to-peer network from the earlier NetWare Lite product from Novell.

Before installing the network, you must first install the hardware required for the network. Refer to the preceding chapter, "Installing Novell DOS 7," for the hardware requirements. Then follow the appropriate steps described in this chapter to install the network setup for your particular configuration.

This chapter covers the following topics:

- Installing the network interface card
- Connecting the network cables
- Installing the network software
- Configuring and activating the network
- Upgrading from NetWare Lite

Installing and Configuring the Network Equipment

If you are connecting to a NetWare network, a Novell DOS peer-to-peer network that uses network interface cards, or a Novell Personal NetWare peer-to-peer network that uses network interface cards, you need to install the network board. As a general rule, you must use the same type of card and cabling throughout the network.

Following the documentation that came with your *network interface card (NIC)*, you configure the card by setting values that define the board for use with your computer. You must provide values for the following items:

- The *interrupt request line (IRQ)*, which is what the NIC uses to signal the computer's processor. The IRQ must be unique.

- The base *input/output port (I/O port)*, which is the conduit for data transfer between the NIC and the computer. The I/O port must be unique.

- The *base memory address*, which is the starting location in memory that the NIC uses to store data to be shared over the network with other computers. Some NIC models do not require this address. If your network adapter does require the base memory address, you may be able to use D800, which is available on many systems.

Table 5.1 lists some IRQs and the devices that normally use them. You may want to check your system documentation or local dealer to learn which IRQs are available on your system. Software utilities, such as CHECKIT, can display the devices and the IRQ numbers actually used in your system. Select a line number that is available. If you do not have the listed device in your system, the IRQ line is probably available.

Table 5.1 Common IRQ Lines and Associated Devices	
IRQ	**Device**
0	Timer output
1	Keyboard
2	EGA/VGA
3	COM2:

IRQ	Device
4	COM1:
5	LPT2:
6	Floppy disk
7	LPT1:
8	Real-time clock
9	Available
10	Available
11	Available
12	Available
13	Coprocessor
14	Hard disk
15	Available

Table 5.2 lists some I/O ports and the devices that normally use them. Again, you may want to check your system documentation or local dealer to learn which ports are available on your system. Select an I/O port that is available. If you do not have the listed device in your system, the port is probably available.

Table 5.2 Common I/O Ports and Associated Devices

I/O Port	Device
1F0	AT disk controller
200-20F	Game controller/joystick
220	Novell network keycard
240	Available
260 (278-27F)	LPT2
280	LCD on Wyse 2108 PC
2A0	Available

(continues)

Table 5.2 Continued	
I/O Port	**Device**
2C0	Available
2E0 (2E1)	COM4: GPIB-Adapter 0
	COM2: Data acquisition
300	Available
320	XT hard disk interface
340	Available
360 (378-37F)	LPT1:
380 (380-38C)	SLDC/Sec Bi-Sync interface
3A0 (3A0-3A9)	Primary Bi-Sync interface
(3B0-3BB)	Monochrome display control
3C0 (3C0-3CF)	EGA display control
(3D0-3DF)	CGA display control
3E0 (3E8-3EF)	COM3:
(3F0-3F7)	Disk controller
(3F8-3FF)	COM1:

Tip

Be sure to record the settings you provide for each NIC. When you configure the network software, you are required to provide this information.

You also may have to set a unique station number on the NIC. Refer to the adapter's documentation.

Connecting the Cables

Connect the computers to be networked with the correct cable, depending on the NIC selected. You may have to provide other hardware, such as a hub, depending on the connectivity protocol and format. Check the NIC documentation for the correct cable to use.

Installing the Network Software

The default option for Install is to include copying the network software to your hard disk. You may or may not have done this with the installation of

Novell DOS 7. If you did not change this option and the files were copied at installation, you can skip this section and move to the next section, "Configuring and Activating the Network."

If you did not copy the network files at installation, you must copy those files, using Setup. You cannot just use the DOS COPY command, because some of the files are packed and have to be restored to full size and possibly renamed, and the files have to be placed in the proper locations. At the DOS prompt, enter **SETUP** to display Setup's main menu. Use the Tab key or the up- or down-arrow key to move the highlight bar to the Networking option; then press Enter. You can also use your mouse to click this option.

If Install did not copy the network files, Setup detects this and provides the message The network software is not installed on your system. Use the Tab key or the up-arrow key to highlight the Install Network Software button. Setup then requests the locations for the floppy drive from which it will copy the files, as well as the destination drive and directory for the files, as shown in figure 5.1.

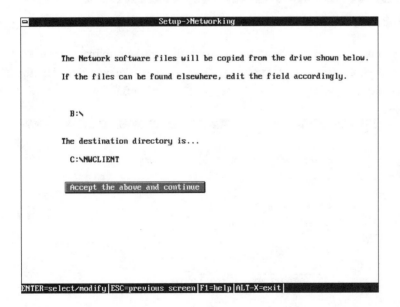

Fig. 5.1

The Setup screen for copying network files.

Make sure that you change the A: in the source drive data-entry line if the floppy drive for your Novell DOS installation disks is not drive A. Move the highlight bar to the top line and press Enter. Use the Del key to erase the current drive letter, which is probably A:. Then just type **B:** or whatever is the correct location of the installation files, and press Enter. Use the Tab key or the down-arrow key to move the highlight bar to the data entry line for the destination directory. Unless you have reason to do so, do not change the directory from \NWCLIENT. Just tab down again to the Accept the Above and Continue button and press Enter.

The Setup screen then changes and displays a percentage bar across the top, and a file-listing window at the bottom. You are requested to insert the correct floppy disk in the designated source drive. Be sure to follow the disk title and number as displayed in the dialog box. Insert each floppy as requested and then press Enter.

When Setup finishes copying the network files, it displays a dialog box informing you of that fact. Press Enter or click OK to continue. Setup then continues to the networking configuration screen, as described in the next section.

Configuring and Activating the Network

If you did not have to copy the network files, start Setup by entering **SETUP** at the DOS prompt. From Setup's main menu, choose Networking. The first network configuration screen appears, as shown in figure 5.2.

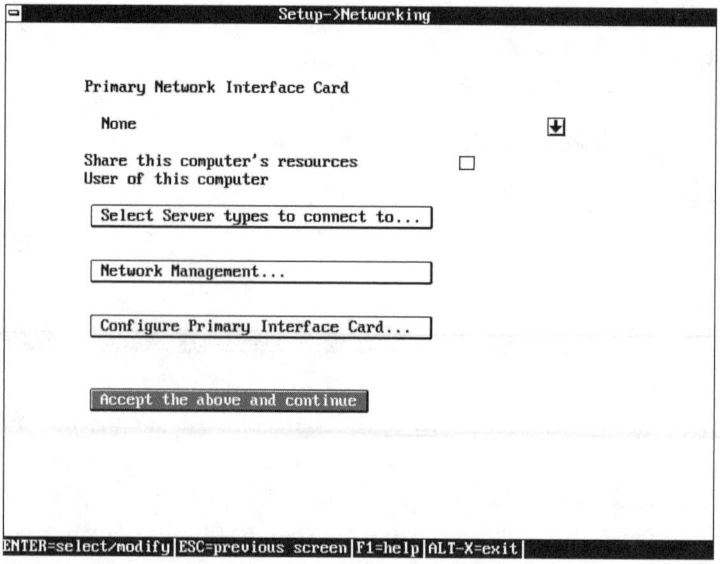

Fig. 5.2
Setup's network configuration screen #1.

If your computer is already part of a network, Setup may detect the type of network interface card (NIC) and then display its name on the top data-entry line. If what is displayed is not correct or if your computer is not already part of a network, you must tell Setup what card you have installed. You cannot configure the network with the `Interface Card` line reading as `None`. You can also select OEM Supplied Driver if you have a NIC that is not on the list. In this case, you must use the driver that came with the card.

After you highlight the NIC you installed in your system, press Enter to make your selection. When you press Enter, the NIC list is removed from the display, and your selection is placed on the data entry line. You then answer five items—or leave them as defaulted by Install/Setup. Use the Tab key or the up- or down-arrow key to move the highlight bar to any of these items.

The first item is a check box asking whether you want to share your computer's resources—that is, to be a desktop server on a peer-to-peer network. Press the space bar or the Enter key to place a check mark in this box if you want your computer to share its resources. If you don't want your computer to be a server and a check mark is present, press the space bar or Enter to remove the check mark.

Every computer in a network is known to the network by a unique name. The next item is for the entry of the name of the user of the computer. This name is used whether the computer is a server or just a client in the network. Highlight the data entry box and type the name, a maximum of 10 characters with no spaces. If you checked the box for the computer to share its resources, Setup adds the characters `_PC` to the name you enter.

The third item is for selecting server types to which you can connect. Highlight this item and press Enter. The second Network configuration screen is displayed, as shown in figure 5.3.

II

Setting Up Your System

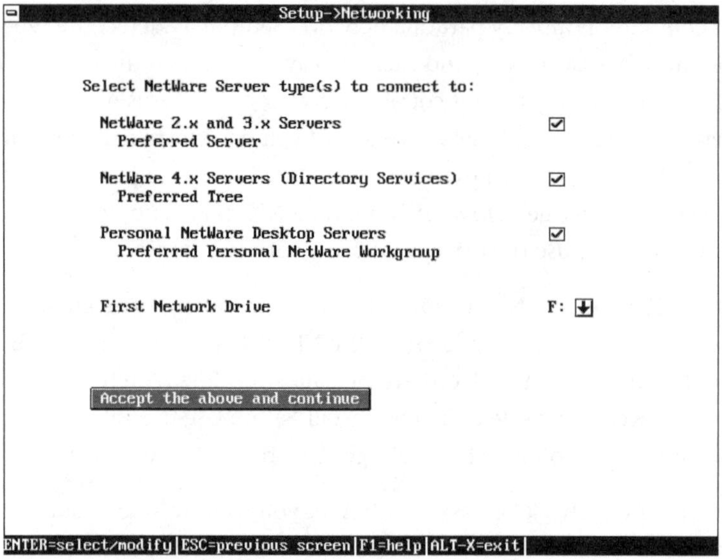

Fig. 5.3
Setup network
configuration
screen #2.

```
┌─────────────────────────────────────────────────────────────┐
│ □                    Setup->Networking                        │
│                                                               │
│                                                               │
│        Select NetWare Server type(s) to connect to:           │
│                                                               │
│            NetWare 2.x and 3.x Servers              ☑         │
│               Preferred Server                                │
│                                                               │
│            NetWare 4.x Servers (Directory Services)  ☑        │
│               Preferred Tree                                  │
│                                                               │
│            Personal NetWare Desktop Servers          ☑        │
│               Preferred Personal NetWare Workgroup            │
│                                                               │
│            First Network Drive                    F: ⬇        │
│                                                               │
│                                                               │
│                                                               │
│           ┌─────────────────────────────┐                    │
│           │ Accept the above and continue │                   │
│           └─────────────────────────────┘                    │
│                                                               │
│                                                               │
│                                                               │
│                                                               │
│ ENTER=select/modify│ESC=previous screen│F1=help│ALT-X=exit│   │
└─────────────────────────────────────────────────────────────┘
```

Tip
Because each of
the network driv-
ers takes up
memory, do not
activate more than
you actually
require.

The top part of this screen requests that you indicate to which type of network servers you are connecting your computer: NetWare 2.x and 3.x Servers, NetWare 4.x Servers, or Personal NetWare Desktop Servers. You can connect your computer to one or more of the various servers. Depending on the check marks you place here, Setup configures the network to load the appropriate drivers. If you do not want your computer to have access to the server of a NetWare network, remove the check mark next to the network type.

Below the boxes is a data entry line for you to enter the name of the primary or default server to which you want to attach your computer. If you enter the name of a server here, the login procedure for the network attempts to connect you to that server. To type the server name, first highlight the data line next to Preferred Server, Preferred Tree, or Preferred Personal NetWare Workgroup. Press Enter, and Setup displays a data entry box. Type the name, up to 15 alphanumeric characters with no spaces, and press Enter. You can use Esc to abort the data entry box.

Note

If your computer is the only desktop server in your Novell DOS network, you do not need to have access to another server or workgroup.

> **Note**
>
> Each network server to which you want to connect your computer must provide
> access rights for your use.

The last item on this second configuration screen lets you determine the first
network drive letter. Ordinarily, the first network drive letter starts at F:. The
drive letters before that, A: through E:, are for your local drives and are not
made part of the network unless they are mapped as such on your computer
configured as a server. Network drives are not available until you log onto the
network and use the drive for logging onto it. You can change the drive letter, but be careful, especially if you are connecting to an existing network.
This data entry line also has a windowed list of drive letters (A: through Z:).

When you are finished with the configuration items on this screen, choose
the Accept the Above and Continue button. Setup again displays the first of
the networking configuration screens so that you can continue with the Network Management option. When you choose this button, the third network
configuration screen is displayed, as shown in figure 5.4.

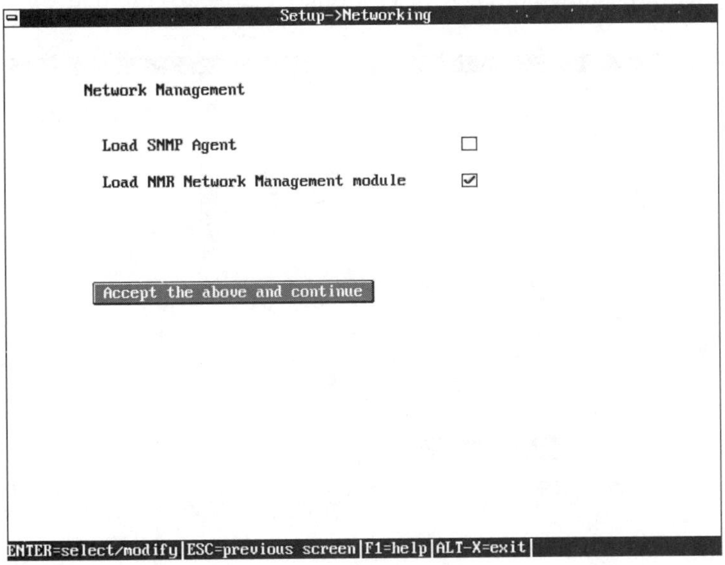

Fig. 5.4
Setup's network
configuration
screen #3.

This part of the network configuration offers two items. The first item for you to consider is whether to load the Simple Network Management Protocol (SNMP) module as part of your network configuration. The SNMP agent enables network management communications and other services to be provided on your network. Unless you are a network administrator, unless the computer being configured is a server, and unless you have access to the industry-standard network management software from Novell or other companies, follow the default setting of off (no check mark in the box). For a small peer-to-peer network, do not load this module.

The second check box is for loading the Novell Management Resources (NMR) network management module. This allows your computer to provide information to network management software. If you are installing a small peer-to-peer network, you can remove the check mark if you want, even though the default for Setup is to include the module.

When you are finished with the configuration items on this screen, choose the Accept the Above and Continue button. Setup again displays the first of the networking configuration screens, enabling you to continue with the Configure Primary Interface Card option. When you choose this button, the fourth network configuration screen is displayed, as shown in figure 5.5.

Fig. 5.5
Setup's network configuration screen #4.

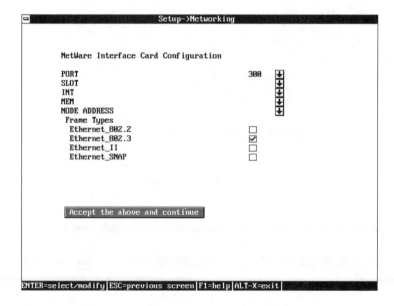

The use of one of the many standard network interface cards causes Setup to display a screen similar to that shown in figure 5.5. The settings are for those items that you used to configure the NIC when you installed it, and presumably wrote down for entry now. Note the following descriptions of these items:

- *The I/O port of your board.* The I/O port is usually set between 200H and 400H. Check your NIC documentation for the default setting of that adapter.

- *The slot number in your computer where you installed the NIC.* This entry should be used for MCA (Micro Channel Adapter) computers. Otherwise, unless you have an older-style network adapter, you do not need to enter any value here.

- *The INT or unique interrupt level for the board.* This is the same as the IRQ number.

- *The MEM or memory base address used for transferring data to and from the network.* The base address is usually between C0000H and F0000H. Some boards do not require this address. Check your NIC documentation.

- *The node address—a unique number for every computer attached to the network.* For your peer-to-peer network, you do not need this number. But if you are attaching to a NetWare server-based network, make sure that every computer uses a different node number.

- *The media frame type.* This is the protocol for the type of packets and the headers (information) to use for sending data across the network. Follow the default built into Setup if you are not sure, or check the NIC documentation.

To make changes, use the Tab key or the up- or down-arrow key to move the highlight to the individual entry lines, and then press Enter. Or you can click the line where you want to change a setting. When you open a selection list (a list is available if a down arrow is displayed), use the up- or down- arrow key to highlight your choice. Then press Enter.

After you finish configuring the network, choose Accept the Above and Continue. Setup then returns you to the main menu. At this point, the highlight bar is on the Save Changes and Exit button. Press Enter or click the button.

Setup then makes any necessary changes to your CONFIG.SYS or DCONFIG.SYS file and saves it. Your old CONFIG.SYS or DCONFIG.SYS file is preserved with the extension BAK. The same occurs with the AUTOEXEC.BAT file. A line is also added to this file so that whenever you boot your system, you are asked whether you want to Load Network Software (Y/N)?

Setup also enables the driver and other software and files that match the settings you entered earlier for the network, including NET.CFG and STARTNET.BAT. If the NIC driver is not on your hard disk, Setup asks you to insert the correct installation disk, and you have the opportunity of telling the utility what floppy drive or other drive you are using for those disks. If your computer was already connected to a network, Setup replaces the appropriate network files with the versions that come with Novell DOS 7. You can watch the progress of Setup as it performs its task to prepare the correct drivers and files. When Setup is finished, a dialog box is displayed in the center of the video screen to inform you of this fact. Press Enter or click OK to continue.

At this point, the network software is installed on your system, and you have established your computer as a desktop server or a client in a network. The final Setup screen is shown in figure 5.6.

Fig. 5.6
Setup's final
screen.

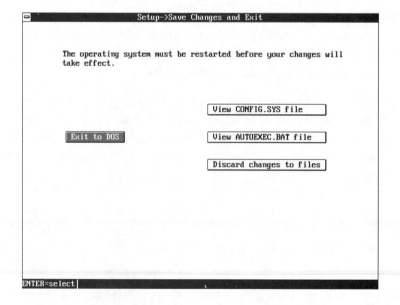

Press Enter or click the highlighted button to return to DOS. You need to reboot your computer before your changes in Setup can take effect. When your system reboots, you are asked whether you want to load the network. If you answer N, you can always start the network at a later point by entering the following command at the DOS prompt:

```
STARTNET
```

Note that you cannot load the network after you have loaded Task Manager. If you want to use Task Manager, load the network first.

Now you must allocate resources, establish accounts, and set passwords on your network, as described in the next section.

Allocating Resources and Setting Up User Accounts

If you are establishing a server, you will want to allocate resources that you can share over the network, and establish user accounts for others to control access to those resources.

If you are configuring your computer only as a client, obtain a user account from the administrator of the network to which you are connecting your computer.

Upgrading from NetWare Lite

If your system is already connected to a NetWare Lite peer-to-peer network, you can upgrade your system to the Novell DOS 7 peer-to-peer network. A utility is provided that transfers the major components to the new network: the NetWare Lite server, the user accounts, the shared resources, and the current rights. The old network passwords are not able to be moved because of the problem caused by encryption. You will have to enter new passwords for the new network yourself.

The steps for upgrading are rather simple:

1. You must first install the Novell DOS 7 network, as discussed earlier. After rebooting your system, start the new network desktop server.

2. Log into the workgroup as supervisor and assign the desktop server to a workgroup. Be sure to use a name containing as many as 15 alphanumeric characters and with no spaces.

3. At the Novell DOS prompt, enter

   ```
   NLMIGRAT
   ```

   The utility then reads the NetWare Lite settings information and provides the information to the new network: server names and settings, user names and accounts, allocated resources, and access rights for printers and directories.

4. After NLMIGRAT finishes its work, which does not take a long time, you must reboot your computer and answer Y (yes) to the question about starting the network. You can now log into the workgroup.

From Here...

In this chapter, you learned how to install your computer adapter card and how to use Setup to install the network software, in case you did not do so at installation of Novell DOS 7. You learned also how to configure the network for your system.

For more information, refer to the following chapters:

- Chapter 4, "Installing Novell DOS 7," provides instructions on installing the operating system.

- Appendix B, "Installing and Using Windows 3.1," provides information on installing Windows after installing the network, and on installing the network if Windows is already on your system.

- Chapter 6, "Understanding File Storage," shows you how to start working with Novell DOS.

Part III

Files and Directories

Continue

onfigure

Disk Compression
Disk Performance
Data Protection & Security
Task Management
Networking

emory Managemen

xit this screen

racks

Sectors

Change destination drive(s) and directorie

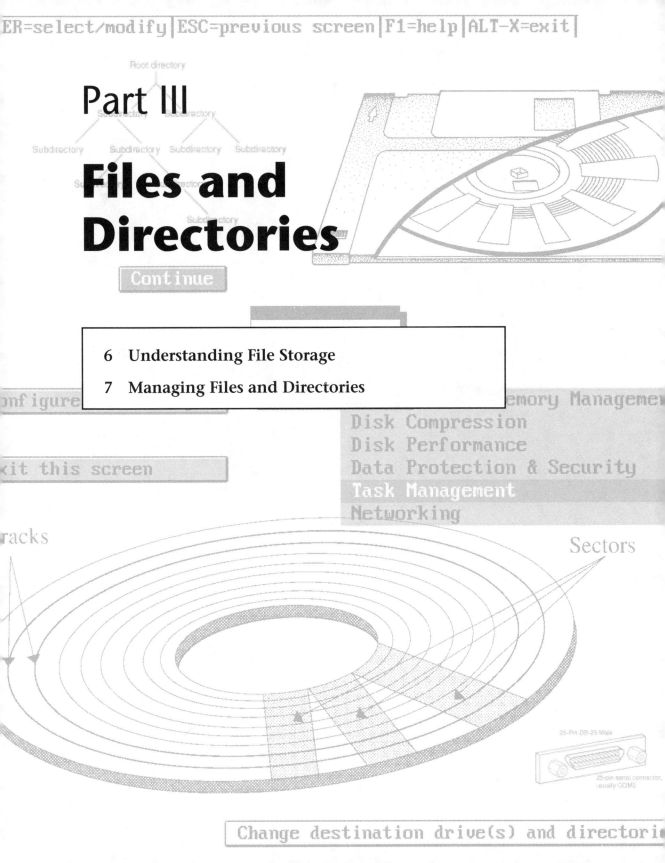

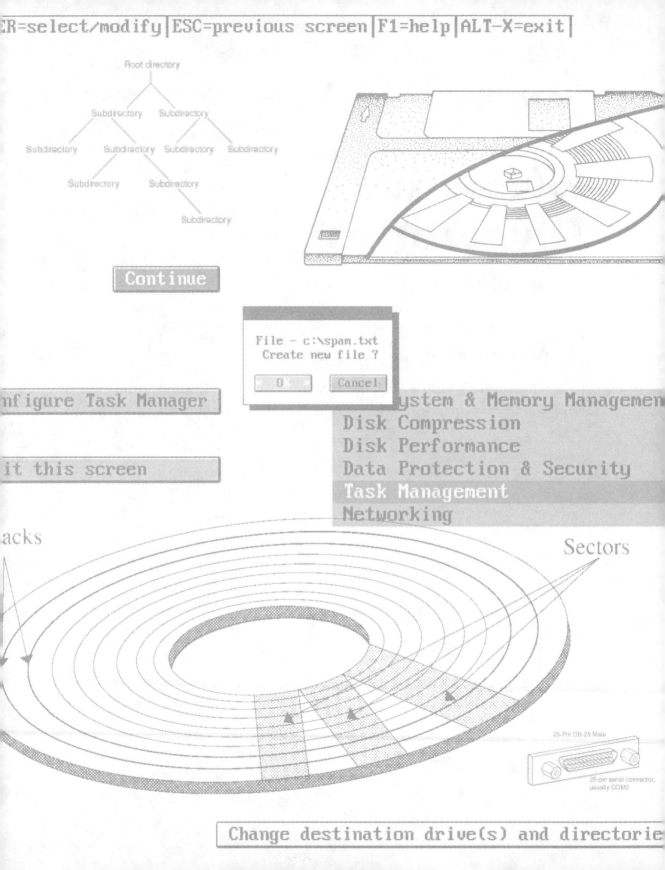

Root directory

Subdirectory   Subdirectory

Subdirectory   Subdirectory   Subdirectory   Subdirectory

Subdirectory   Subdirectory

Subdirectory

Continue

File - c:\spam.txt
Create new file ?

    O   Cancel

nfigure Task Manager   ystem & Memory Managemen
                                        Disk Compression
                                        Disk Performance
it this screen   Data Protection & Security
                                        Task Management
                                        Networking

acks   Sectors

25-Pin DB-25 Male

25-pin serial connector,
usually COM2

Change destination drive(s) and directorie

Chapter 6

Understanding File Storage

Now that (presumably) you have installed Novell DOS 7, you should understand some basics about your computer and its system of file storage structure. This chapter discusses computer disks and their structures and provides an explanation of DOS directories and files.

The following topics are covered:

- Drive and disk structures

- Files and DOS directories

- Directory paths

- DOS files and their attributes

- Wild cards

Drive and Disk Structures

Disk drives are used for the storage of data, such as computer programs, so that the data is available for use when needed. There are two principal types of storage drives: hard drives and floppy drives.

Floppy drives use removable media commonly called disks, floppies, or floppy disks. Floppy disks are broadly categorized by the physical size of their outer covering; although they are made in several sizes, mostly 5 1/4-inch or 3 1/2-inch disks are used with personal computers. A 3 1/2-inch disk has a hard plastic case with a metal slide; a 5 1/4-inch disk has a softer, more flexible outer case. The actual storage media contained in each case is a thin mylar disk with a magnetic oxide coating, similar to the material used in audio cassettes.

Floppies come in various capacities, indicating the amount of data that can be stored on them. The capacity of a disk is measured in kilobytes (abbreviated K or KB) or megabytes (abbreviated M or MB). One *kilobyte* (1K) is equal to 1,024 *bytes*, or units of storage. One *megabyte* (1M) is equal to 1,048,576 bytes. Table 6.1 lists the capacities and sizes of floppy disks you are likely to use with your personal computer.

Table 6.1 Floppy Disk Sizes and Capacities

Size	Capacity	Density
5 1/4 inch	360K	Double
5 1/4 inch	1.2M	High
3 1/2 inch	720K	Double
3 1/2 inch	1.44M	High
3 1/2 inch	2.88M	Extended

You may have noticed that in some places you read that a given disk has two different capacities. For example, a 3 1/2-inch high-density floppy is often marked as capable of containing 1.4M of data; in other places, the capacity is given as 1,457,664 bytes. You may also see the disk as having an unformatted capacity of 2M, or a formatted capacity of 1,474,560 bytes.

Tip
When checking disk capacity ratings, be sure that the measurements are given in the same terms—that you are measuring apples with apples.

The reason for the discrepancy is that each number is a measure of something different. The unformatted capacity—that is, before any format or data location information is applied to the disk—is the full, absolute amount of data that can be stored on the disk. In this example, a 3 1/2-inch high-density floppy has an unformatted capacity of 2M. Once formatted, the full capacity of the floppy is 1,474,560 bytes. At 1,024 bytes per K, that is 1.44M. The difference is the amount of space used for data location markers. When you format this floppy disk, the number of bytes free is somewhat less, or 1,457,664 bytes. The 16,896-byte difference is due to the space used by the disk file allocation table and root directory.

Another less technical reason for the discrepancy in disk capacities, especially with hard disks, is that some people use actual K or M, based on 1,024 bytes per K and 1,048,576 bytes per M, whereas others use 1,000 per K and 1,000,000 per M. Thus, some hard disk manufacturers say that their disk is 40M, and others say that their disk of the same size is 42M.

Hard disk drives, also known as fixed disk drives, are similar to floppy disks except a hard disk's storage platter is made of rigid material. Hard disk drives usually have more than one disk or platter, which cannot be removed, sealed within their outer casing.

Hard disk drives come in a variety of physical sizes and capacities, and despite the very large storage capability of some of these drives, they are built small enough to fit within the personal computer case. The capacity of the hard disk on your computer may fall anywhere in the range from 10 megabytes to more than 2 *gigabytes* (a gigabyte equals roughly one billion characters and is abbreviated G or GB).

Each storage platter, floppy or rigid, is divided into circular rings called *tracks*, the number of which depends on the media and its capacity. The platters are also divided into *sectors*, like slices of a pie. Refer to figure 6.1 for an illustration of tracks and sectors.

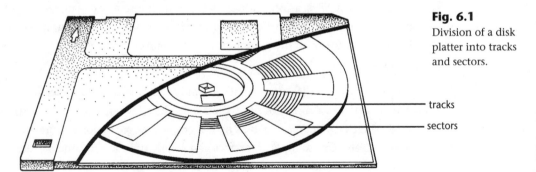

Fig. 6.1
Division of a disk platter into tracks and sectors.

tracks

sectors

III

Files and Directories

The purpose of dividing disks into tracks and sectors is simply to provide storage locations for data. When a disk is formatted (prepared for use), the track and sector locations are marked with addresses. Thus, when data is magnetically recorded on a disk, the data is placed at one or more of these addresses, and a table is maintained so that the computer knows where to find it again.

Storage drives are also divided into *physical drives* and *logical drives*. Physical drives are actual hardware components and may be floppy disks, hard disks, or CD-ROM drives. They may be built-in or added as external devices connected by cables to the computer. A portion of the computer's chip memory also may be set aside as a logical drive, called a RAM disk.

These physical drives can be partitioned into more than one logical drive. Thus, although your computer may have only one physical hard disk drive, it may have been set up so that you have both drive C and drive D installed on that one hard disk. These logical drives are usually referred to as *partitions*.

> **Note**
>
> The designation of logical drives is always that of a letter followed by a colon (:), for purposes of commands and file names. Drives A and C, for example, are respectively known to the computer as A: and C:.

Files and DOS Directories

Almost all software, whether for an operating system such as Novell DOS, or for a program such as a word processor or an electronic spreadsheet, is distributed in files. A *file* is a collection of data grouped into a single unit that can be stored on disk or loaded into memory. *Program* files are, in simple terms, lists of instructions to the computer to do whatever the program is supposed to do.

There are types of files other than program files. This chapter, for example, is being written as a *document file*, which is produced when a word processor is used. There are *data files*, such as lists of employees or friends with related information—for example, addresses and phone numbers, business orders, and inventory or accounting transactions.

In fact, you can think of computer files as paper documents on which you store information such as a name list or a letter. You have to store this information so that it is available to be used when needed. On personal computers, this is normally the purpose of devices called *disks*. Today, most of these computers have hard disks, which can contain many millions of characters of files. Most computers also contain floppy disk drives, which use removable media and are capable of storing only a limited number of files.

To find the information you need on all those pages, you usually keep related data in the same file folder. Then you use a file cabinet to store the file folders. The same analogy applies to hard disks, where large numbers of files can be stored. Disks are divided into areas, called *directories* or *subdirectories* (the file folders), and related files are kept in the same directory. Thus, all files for your word processor are stored in the subdirectory for word processing. Spreadsheet files are stored in the subdirectory for electronic spreadsheet data.

Although all kinds of disks can be so divided, usually hard disks contain a number of directories. A *directory* is a division or compartment of a disk drive where files are stored. Each logical disk drive—whether it's a hard disk, a floppy disk, a CD-ROM drive, or even a RAM disk—has a single main or *root* directory. Other directories may be and usually are created on drives, but they must be subordinate to the root directory in a hierarchical structure, as shown in figure 6.2.

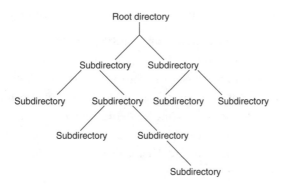

Fig. 6.2
The DOS hierarchical directory structure.

Any directory may have one or more *subdirectories* subordinate to it. The only real limits to the number of directories, and to the number of files they can hold, are limits imposed by the capacity of the disk drive. The root directory, however, is limited because the structure of the root directory and the *file allocation table (FAT)*, which is the *index* of file storage locations on a hard drive, is established when the drive is formatted. Therefore, the total number of entries, for files and subdirectories located in or directly subordinate to the root directory, is limited.

Subdirectories, however, are sized dynamically and may have as many files and subordinate subdirectories as available space permits. Table 6.2 lists the maximum number of entries in the root directory of several types of disk drives.

III

Files and Directories

Table 6.2 Maximum Entries in the Root Directory	
Disk	**Maximum Entries**
360K 5 1/4-inch floppy disk	112
1.2M 5 1/4-inch floppy disk	224
720K 3 1/2-inch floppy disk	112
1.44M 3 1/2-inch floppy disk	224
2.88 3 1/2-inch floppy disk	240
Hard disk drive	512

Generally, you should keep all program files for one application in one
subdirectory. Many programs require multiple subdirectories for their files.
With an application such as a word processor, you may want to establish a
separate directory for the documents you create with the word processor.
That way, you can find them more easily when you need them.

All directories have a name. The name of the root directory is simply the
backslash character (\), so that the root directory of drive C: is named C:\.
The designation of all subdirectories consists of the backslash character (\)
followed by the subdirectory name, as in \NWDOS. Subdirectories, when
created, are generally given a name to identify the type of files stored within
them. The directory name can have as many as eight characters and an optional three-letter extension. Any character that is legal for use in a file name
is legal for use in a directory name.

Whenever you refer to a directory, you should normally use the backslash
character (\) as part of the name. There are exceptions to this guideline,
particularly with regard to some alternative formats of several
directory-management commands discussed in Chapter 7, "Managing Files
and Directories." Specifically, when you mention several levels of directories,
you must include the backslash. For example, C:\WPDOCS\LETTERS\BOB
shows three subdirectories on drive C: \WPDOCS, \LETTERS, and \BOB.
\BOB is subordinate to \LETTERS, and \LETTERS is subordinate to
\WPDOCS.

> **Caution**
>
> Do not confuse the backslash character (\) used for directory names with the forward slash character (/) used for command switches and options.

DOS Files and Attributes

You read previously in this chapter that files are related instructions or information grouped into units. Read this section to learn more about files. In this section, you learn first about file names and file types and then about the attributes of files.

Understanding File Names

DOS files are recognized by their names. *File names* are made up of two parts, the *name* itself and a file *extension* or *type*. The first part, the name, contains up to eight characters. The second part, the extension (generally optional), contains up to three characters. The characters can be alphabetic or numeric, or can be the following:

$ # & @ ! ( ) – { } ' _ ~ ^ '

The characters cannot be a space or any of the following:

$ = / [ ] " : ; , ? * \ < > |

File names should signify what the files do or mean. Most files must include an extension, but some files do not require one. It has become customary on the part of programmers and system designers to use file extensions to distinguish various types of files. It is helpful to do so. For example, when you create documents in a word processor, you might find it handy to use an extension of LTR for all documents that are letters, as in DAVID.LTR (a letter to David). You could call the second letter to David DAVID2.LTR. For facsimile documents, use FAX; for proposals, use PRO; and so on. Most programs use DAT for data files, DBF for database files, TXT for text files, and DOC for document files.

A complete file name has an eight-character name, a period, and an optional three-character extension, as in

GUMSHOE.DOC

III

Files and Directories

Some users improve the readability of file names by separating words. Because the space character is illegal for file names, use the underscore, as in

GUM_SHOE.DOC

If you are consistent in the way you name files, you will make certain file operations more convenient. If all your word processing documents have the DOC extension, you can use the following command to copy them from the current directory to a floppy disk:

```
COPY *.DOC A:
```

Some applications make this easier because they apply default extensions to the files they create.

DOS recognizes three specific file types as commands or instructions: COM, EXE, and BAT. COM (command) and EXE (executable) files are program files. There are technical differences between these two types of files—how they were created and how they work in a computer—but it is not necessary for anyone but programmers to understand the differences. As far as you or your computer is concerned, they are both program files; and when you type the name of either a COM file or an EXE file, you are telling the computer to execute the instructions built into these program files. BAT files are batch files—text files that are simply lists of computer commands exactly the same as those you type at the DOS prompt. You can learn about batch files by reading Chapter 19, "Using Batch Files."

Table 6.3 lists some common file extensions and their meanings. By learning file types, you often can recognize what a file is, or does, without examining its contents.

Table 6.3 Common File Extensions and Their Uses

Extension	Use
BAK	Last version of a data or text file before being changed
BAS	BASIC program file
BAT	DOS batch file
BIN	Binary file, used for program information
BMP	Graphics file
COM	DOS command file

Extension	Use
DAT	Data file
DBF	Database file
DOC	Document file, often used for text editor or word processing
EXE	DOS executable file
GIF	Graphics file
INI	Program or system initialization parameter file
OVL or OVR	Program overlay files (when program is too large to fit all instructions in main program file)
PCX	Graphics file
PIF	Program information file
PRN	Printer file
RPT	Report file
SYS	System file, used for DOS or program configuration
TXT	Text file, often used for text editor or word processing

Note

Although DOS sometimes displays file names on-screen with the file name padded with spaces to fill eight positions, followed by a space and then the extension, such as COMMAND   COM, you should always type a file name by using the name, a period, and the extension (if any) without any spaces. For example, type **COMMAND.COM**.

Understanding File Attributes

When files are stored on disk, you may give them *file attributes*, or they may already have them. These attributes are flags placed in the directory entry of the file to tell DOS how the file is to be handled. By manipulating file attributes, you control whether a file is visible in normal use and whether it can be read, modified, and deleted. Files have four basic attributes: A, R, S, and H.

DOS uses the *A* or *archive* attribute as a flag to indicate that a file has been changed. When some utilities make backups of your files as a safety precaution, for example, Novell DOS normally lists the A attribute for those files.

III

Files and Directories

After a file has been backed up, the A attribute is turned off. If the file is not changed thereafter, you have the option of skipping that file when the next backup occurs.

Any file marked with the *R* attribute is a *read-only* file and cannot be deleted. It can be read and thus can be copied, but it cannot be changed or renamed. Although you have ways around these limitations, you should remember that this attribute is used to protect important files.

> **Note**
>
> When Novell DOS copies a file marked as read-only, the R attribute is also copied.

The *S* attribute stands for *system*. This attribute prevents DIR from displaying the file, COPY from copying the file, and MOVE from moving the file. Although you can get around this limitation, keep in mind that this attribute protects files.

H stands for *hidden*. Hidden files also are not displayed or managed by utilities without special options. You must be careful about hiding files that applications may need to find. Most applications cannot see hidden files.

> **Note**
>
> When you password-protect individual files, they are marked with the H attribute even though they are not really hidden. Refer to Chapter 15, "System Security," for more on password protection.

In addition to these attributes, the *D* attribute is reserved as the only attribute for directories. Refer to Chapter 7, "Managing Files and Directories," to learn more about this flag and the XDIR command.

Using ATTRIB

ATTRIB is the Novell DOS utility that you use to add, change, remove, and display file attributes. By entering **ATTRIB** at the DOS prompt, you tell Novell DOS to display the attributes of all files in the current directory, as shown in figure 6.3.

As you can see in the figure, some files are flagged with no attributes; some are marked as read-only, system, and hidden; and some have only the A attribute, meaning that they have been changed since they were last backed up.

```
[NOVELL DOS] C:\>attrib
--a--- c:nwdos.386
--a--- c:autoexec.bat
------- c:start000.bat
rsa-h- c:stacker.bin
------- c:cdos.com
--a--- c:command.com
rs--h- c:ibmbio.com
rs--h- c:ibmdos.com
------- c:loadsys.com
--a--- c:bootlist.dat
------- c:menu.dat
--a--- c:menu.exe
rsa-h- c:stacker.ini
------- c:drmdos.inp
------- c:ibmbio.ldr
rs--h- c:loader.sav
--a--- c:dconfig.sys
------- c:drmdos.sys
rs--h- c:loader.sys
--a--- c:mconfig.sys
------- c:notes.txt

[NOVELL DOS] C:\>
```

Fig. 6.3
The ATTRIB
command
displaying file
attributes.

Here is the format for the ATTRIB command:

ATTRIB + | *-attribute list* @ **filename.ext** *options*

You use the plus sign (+) to turn on an attribute and the minus sign (–) to turn off an attribute. You can specify more than one attribute, turning some on and others off in the same command line. The + or – has to be typed only once, no matter how many attributes are being set. All attributes must be entered before the file name(s). Consider the following example:

```
ATTRIB +RSH IBM*.COM
```

This command tells Novell DOS that all COM files with IBM as the beginning three characters of their names are to be made read-only, system, and hidden. The operating system is able to read these files for booting, even though most programs cannot.

To remove the same attributes from the same files, enter the following:

```
ATTRIB -RSH IBM*.COM
```

You can list more than one file name on the command line, and you can also tell ATTRIB to execute the command on a list of files. The file list is a single text file and its file name is prefixed with the @ sign on the command line. Refer to the next chapter for more on Novell DOS's file-listing capability.

To enter more than one file on the same command line, follow this example to add the read-only and hidden attributes to two different files:

```
ATTRIB +RH LOGO.WPG TRADE.WPG
```

III

Files and Directories

Two additional options are available with ATTRIB. The first is the pause switch, /P. This switch tells Novell DOS to display only one screen at a time when the file list is longer than one screen. The second switch, /S, causes ATTRIB to operate on files in the current directory and on any subordinate directories.

The example containing IBM*.COM involves a new concept, discussed in the next section. The * is called a *wild-card character* and takes the place of other characters.

Wild Cards

Novell DOS provides a tool that helps you list files and subdirectories easily. The tool is called a *wild card*. In card games, a wild card takes the place of another card. In listing files and directories, wild cards take the place of all or part of file and directory names. Many commands, such as COPY, DIR, and DEL, can operate on files specified by wild cards.

Novell DOS has two wild-card characters: * and ?. The *asterisk* (commonly called a *star*) is used to take the place of one or more characters starting at the position of the *. For example, if you specify the file name as **A***, certain commands will operate on all files starting with A. Specifying **AB*** will operate on all files starting with AB.

As noted, file names have two parts, the name itself and an optional extension. Therefore, to use the asterisk to specify all files, you need to use a wild card for both parts. If you specify **A*.*** to search for all files beginning with A, even those file names that do not have an extension are found with this directive. Characters after the * in the root name are ignored. If you type ***A**, for example, the computer sees only the *. Specifying ***ABC.*** is equivalent to specifying ***.***. To specify all files that have the same name but a different extension, include a wild card only in the extension. **ABCDE.*** specifies all files with the name ABCDE that have any or no file extension.

The second wild-card character, the question mark, is used to take the place of any single character located at the same position as the ?. To specify all files that have mostly the same root name and extension, for example, you can type **?BC.?AT**. Certain DOS commands will operate on all file names with BC as the second and third characters in the name and with AT as the second and third characters of the extension. The first characters can be any alphanumeric characters.

`?AB.?AT` does not return root names more than three characters long. Thus, `?AB.?AT` returns TAB.CAT but not TABBIE.CAT. In this case, you would need to type `DIR ?AB*.?AT` to pick up the file name TABBIE.CAT.

You can use the ? wild card for all positions in a file or directory name instead of using the * character. Thus, typing `????????.???` is equivalent to typing `*.*`. You can type `DIR ?OI???.LTR`, and DOS displays FOIBLE.LTR and COINS.LTR, but not GOINGOUT.LTR.

> ### Note
>
> Use wild-card characters to simplify the search for any subset of files on your system. Thus, if you specify `*.DAT`, Novell searches for all data files with a DAT extension.

Directory Names and Paths

Now that you have a general understanding of disk drives and the storage structure of disks called directories, you can proceed to an understanding of the concept of the *path* and the Novell DOS commands that can be used to change the path.

Naming Directories

Directories are initially named during creation. The MD (MKDIR) command will do nothing if you do not append an appropriate directory name. The following command creates a new directory named TRASH:

```
MD TRASH
```

A directory name can include any character that is legal for file names. For a list of legal characters, see the section "Understanding File Names" earlier in this chapter. Although a complete directory name can consist of only one character, the name can include an eight-character name and an optional three-character extension. The extension is not often used. The following command creates a new directory named TRASH.CAN:

```
MD TRASH.CAN
```

Although Novell DOS allows a directory and a file to have the same name, you should avoid using the same names to prevent confusion when issuing commands that manipulate directories or files.

III

Files and Directories

Combining Directories into a Path

As a term, *path* refers to the location of a file; that is, the logical drive letter and the name of the directory. Software manuals and books often refer to disk files and commands with the term *path* as a placeholder for the file name. When you see this, you should use the drive letter plus the colon plus the backslash character plus the subdirectory name and another backslash character for each subdirectory (if the file is located in a subdirectory) plus the name of the command or file to be operated on, with no spaces.

An example of a path specification for a file in the root directory on drive C is

    C:\AUTOEXEC.BAT

An example of a path specification for a file in a subdirectory named \NWDOS on drive C is

    C:\NWDOS\FORMAT.COM

Specifying the path for a file or command tells DOS exactly where to find it.

The path allows the command processor, the COMMAND.COM file, to search directories other than the current or default directory for a file name that is included in the command line. The device takes the form of a *PATH statement* that consists of the word PATH plus a list of directory names. These directories comprise the *system path*. The PATH statement usually is placed in your system's AUTOEXEC.BAT file.

When you give your computer an instruction to execute, the command processor first checks the list of internal commands. If the instruction is not found among these internal commands, the command processor searches the current directory in the current disk drive for an executable file with the same name as the entered command. If the file is not found in the current directory, the command processor begins checking the PATH statement and searches the first directory listed in the system path. If the file is not found there, the next directory listed in the system path is checked, then the next, and so on, until the file is found. If the entire system path is searched and the file is not found, the search stops, an error message appears: `Command or filename not recognized`.

With the PATH command, therefore, you do not have to be in a subdirectory to execute a program located in that subdirectory. As long as the location of a command file is listed in the PATH statement, you do not have to specify the location of the file when typing the command. Suppose that the file SETUP.EXE is not in the root directory but instead has been placed in the directory C:\NWDOS, and C:\NWDOS has been made part of the PATH command by the Install/Setup utility. When you type **SETUP** and press Enter from the root directory, the PATH statement that includes C:\NWDOS informs the command processor to look in the C:\NWDOS subdirectory, where it finds the file SETUP.EXE and executes the program.

The format for the PATH command is

```
PATH x:path;x:path;...x:path
```

Replace *x* with the drive letter and replace *path* with the directory name, beginning with a backslash. You can add as many directories to the system path as you want, but the number of characters in the command line cannot exceed 128. Each directory listed must be separated from the previous directory by a semicolon (;). If you use the semicolon without any directory names, the system path list is deleted. If you enter only the PATH command at the DOS prompt with nothing following it, DOS displays the current system path.

The following is an example of a PATH command:

```
PATH C:\;C:\NWDOS;C:\NWCLIENT;D:\;D:\TRASH
```

This PATH command tells DOS to search for command files in each subdirectory listed, in the order listed, until the command file is found. If the command file is not found, an error message is displayed. Note that the path may contain root directories and encompass more than one drive.

Typically, the PATH command is issued in the AUTOEXEC.BAT file. The command should be near the front of the file. Any command that precedes the PATH command or is not in the path should have a full path prepended so that the command processor can execute it. If the PATH command within AUTOEXEC.BAT is modified, the new path will not take effect until the computer is rebooted or AUTOEXEC.BAT is executed again.

Because the PATH command is limited to 128 characters, users with many directories may want to execute PATH from a batch file. A typical batch file would set a new path for a specific application and its document files and then execute the application. Use a separate batch file for each of your applications.

To see the current path, enter the PATH command with no parameters. The path is displayed on the command line.

III

Files and Directories

> **Note**
>
> The DOS PATH command is used by DOS to search only for files that contain commands to execute—that is, files with a file extension of COM, EXE, or BAT.

Several commands are provided by Novell DOS, in addition to the PATH command, that pertain to file paths. These commands are APPEND, ASSIGN, JOIN, and SUBST. The next sections discuss these commands.

Using APPEND

The APPEND command is similar to the PATH command. It provides a search list of directories. However, you use APPEND for overlay files and data files that are not found by the DOS path search function. Actually, you do not have to use this command except for older programs that do not use the path. Most new programs are able to determine the location of their files and do not require the APPEND command.

The format for the APPEND command is

> **APPEND** *x:path;x:path;...x:path options*

Replace *x* with the drive letter and replace *path* with the directory name, beginning with a backslash. You can add as many directories to the append search list as you want, but the number of characters in the command line cannot exceed 128. Each directory listed must be separated from the previous one by a semicolon (;). If you use the semicolon without any directory names, the append search list is deleted. If you enter the APPEND command at the DOS prompt without anything following it, DOS displays the current append search list.

Here are the options for the APPEND command:

/X:ON or /X:OFF	Tells APPEND to let a program use its internal functions to search for and execute commands.
/E:ON or /E:OFF	Tells DOS whether to keep the append search path in the DOS environment. The default is /E:OFF.
/PATH:ON or /PATH:OFF	Tells DOS whether the append search list applies to files that have path names. The default is /PATH:ON.

Ordinarily, APPEND will function correctly using its own default. Use its switches only if a program does not function correctly with APPEND.

One popular application that successfully uses the APPEND command is dBASE III+. If you have this program and want to maintain one DBASE subdirectory but several directories of dBASE files, place the location of DBASE in the PATH and APPEND search lists. Then, when you work in any subdirectory where you maintain data files, you can enter **DBASE** and have the program available to work with the local data files. This is necessary because dBASE III+ does not fully support the use of the PATH command.

Caution

Some applications cannot use the APPEND search path for save operations. You may discover that they can find a file in another directory with this command, but can create a file in only the current directory. This may lead to different versions of the same file.

The APPEND command is used in the same manner as the PATH command, but APPEND enables applications to find nonexecutable files. You usually run APPEND from the AUTOEXEC.BAT file. APPEND can also be used in batch files.

Using ASSIGN

Novell DOS provides the ASSIGN command to let you change drive letters "on the fly." ASSIGN allows, for example, drive C to be treated as if it were drive A or drive E. This command comes in handy when programs need to access a particular drive (but you have the information on another drive). Using ASSIGN, you help the program to find the data without having to reconfigure or reinstall the program.

The format for the ASSIGN command is

```
ASSIGN old_drive=new_drive...old_drive=new_drive /S
```

To change drive C to drive A, enter at the DOS prompt the following command:

```
ASSIGN C=A
```

You can enter more than one assignment command at once, separating each set of drive letters with a space. If you enter the ASSIGN command without any drive information, all existing drive assignments are removed. To see a list of all current drive assignments, use the /S switch.

III

Files and Directories

Caution

Be careful when using commands that modify or delete files on reassigned drives. If you don't remember which drive is reassigned, commands like DEL *.* can be disastrous.

Note

You can assign a currently valid drive letter as the new drive letter for another drive, but this denies access to the drive that originally used the letter.

Note

You cannot use a drive letter which is greater than that allowed by the LASTDRIVE command in your CONFIG.SYS or DCONFIG.SYS file. If there is no LASTDRIVE command in your CONFIG.SYS or DCONFIG.SYS file, you cannot use a drive letter outside those actually established on your system. Thus, to use ASSIGN, you may need to insert a LASTDRIVE command in your CONFIG.SYS or DCONFIG.SYS file.

Cancel an ASSIGN command immediately after the assignment is no longer needed. Most commands that refer to an entire drive work improperly when directed to an assigned drive. When you are not sure whether an ASSIGN command has been used, use the ASSIGN command with the /S switch to display all current assignments.

Caution

While you have drive assignments in effect, you should not use the following commands on the affected drives: BACKUP, DISKCOMP, DISKCOPY, DISKOPT, FBX, FORMAT, LABEL, PRINT, RESTORE, SDEFRAG, and SUBST. Do not use the ASSIGN command when running under Task Manager, Desqview, Microsoft Windows, or any other task switcher or multitasking program.

Although you typically run the ASSIGN command from the command line, you may want to run ASSIGN from batch files to change drive assignments to suit the needs of specific applications. The command is sometimes run from the AUTOEXEC.BAT file.

Using JOIN

The JOIN command allows you to add the directory structure, including all the stored files, of one drive to a subdirectory on another drive so that both appear as one drive. After you have joined one drive to another, drive commands like TREE and XDIR work on the combined drive.

The format for the JOIN command is

```
JOIN source_drive: destination_drive:\subdir /D
```

Thus, `JOIN A: C:\TEMP` takes drive A and adds it to the subdirectory \TEMP on drive C. The /D switch is used to disable the JOIN command. The source drive must be specified for the separation to take place. `JOIN A: /D` unjoins the drive joined in the preceding example. If you enter the JOIN command without any drive or switch, DOS displays a list of currently joined drives.

Keep several points in mind when using JOIN:

- The subdirectory on the destination drive must be a directory directly subordinate to the root directory.

- The subdirectory on the destination drive must be empty. If there are files in it, no error is displayed but the files are not available while the join is in effect.

- There can be subordinate directories to the subdirectory on the destination drive, but those directories are not available while the join is in effect.

- The attached drive is no longer a valid drive while the JOIN command is in effect. The destination subdirectory acts as the root directory of the attached drive.

- If the destination subdirectory does not exist, JOIN creates it.

> **Caution**
>
> While you have drives joined, you should not use the following commands on the affected drives: ASSIGN, BACKUP, DISKCOMP, DISKCOPY, DISKOPT, FBX, FORMAT, RESTORE, SDEFRAG, and SUBST. Do not use the JOIN command when running under Task Manager, Desqview, Microsoft Windows, or any other task switcher or multitasking program.

III

Files and Directories

The JOIN command, used similarly to the PATH command, joins drives and subdirectories. You usually run JOIN from the AUTOEXEC.BAT file. JOIN is often used in batch files to run specific applications with their own paths.

Using SUBST

SUBST is a command that substitutes one drive letter for a full path name or substitutes one drive letter for another drive letter. If you want to work with a subdirectory several levels down from the root directory, you can save yourself keystrokes by telling DOS to treat the subdirectory as if it were a drive. SUBST substitutions are useful with programs (usually older ones) that do not recognize subdirectories.

The format for the SUBST command is

> **SUBST** *destination_drive: source_drive:path*

To cancel the substitution, the format is

> **SUBST** *destination_drive:* /D

If no destination drive is specified with the /D switch, all drive substitutions are cancelled.

If, for example, you want to substitute drive F for the subdirectory C:\WPDOCS\LTRS\BOB, you enter the following at the DOS prompt:

> SUBST F: C:\WPDOCS\LTRS\BOB

Then, to access the C:\WPDOCS\LTRS\BOB subdirectory, you just have to type **F:**. To remove the example substitution, enter **SUBST F: /D**.

If you type SUBST without anything following it, DOS displays a list of all current substitutions.

Note

The SUBST command can help you to work around the limitation of 128 characters for the PATH command line. Instead of using many long path names in the PATH command, use SUBST to give a shorter equivalent to some directory names.

> **Note**
>
> You cannot use a drive letter which is greater than that allowed by the LASTDRIVE command in your CONFIG.SYS or DCONFIG.SYS file. If there is no LASTDRIVE command in your CONFIG.SYS or DCONFIG.SYS file, you cannot use a drive letter outside those actually established on your system. Thus, to use SUBST, you may need to insert a LASTDRIVE command in your CONFIG.SYS or DCONFIG.SYS file.

> **Caution**
>
> You should not use the following commands when the target drive is changed with SUBST, because these commands need to work on entire drives: CHKDSK, FORMAT, DISKCOMP, DISKCOPY, DISKOPT, FDISK, LABEL, SDEFRAG, and SYS. Do not use the SUBST command when running under Task Manager, Desqview, Microsoft Windows, or any other task switcher or multitasking program.

You use the SUBST command to enable an application to access a drive other than the drive it is configured to access. This command is typically run from a batch file, but SUBST can be run from the command line or AUTOEXEC.BAT.

From Here...

In this chapter, you learned some basics about hard disks and floppy disks, including how they are structured and how they work as storage for programs and data. You learned some concepts about computer files and about dividing disks with directories and placing related program and data files in the same or related subdirectories.

You can put this knowledge to use in these chapters:

- Chapter 7, "Managing Files and Directories," teaches you how to create, rename, remove, and display directories; list files and directories; and copy, move, compare, and delete files.

- Chapter 8, "Preparing Disks," helps you make your disks ready for use.

- Chapter 10, "Undeleting Files," helps you in protecting your files when they are accidentally deleted.

- Chapter 12, "Backup Utilities," leads you through the process of safeguarding your important files with Fastback Express.

III

Files and Directories

Chapter 7

Managing Files and Directories

Organizing your computer's hard disk is easier if you maintain individual directories for the various applications. As a matter of fact, when you installed some of your applications, their installation procedures probably created one or more subdirectories.

You learned about the concept of files and directories in Chapter 6, along with the commands DOS uses to search directories. In this chapter, you learn how to use the commands that enable you to manage directories and the files they contain.

This chapter covers the following topics:

- Managing directories

- Listing and finding file contents

- Copying, comparing, moving, renaming, and replacing files

- Removing files

- Sorting file contents and changing file date and time stamps

The commands in the first part of this chapter are for creating and deleting subdirectories, changing the default directory, and renaming subdirectories. You then read about other directory-related commands before proceeding to what you need to know to manipulate files.

III

Files and Directories

> **Note**
>
> All the directory commands discussed in this chapter and elsewhere in this book apply to the directory structure, whether on floppy disks, hard disks, or RAM disks.

One thing to remember is that you cannot create a root directory. Root directories are created automatically when a disk drive is formatted. Nor can you change the name of or delete a root directory. These commands are actually for subdirectories.

Managing Directories

Four main commands for managing directories are available: MD (or MKDIR) for creating directories, CD (or CHDIR) for changing to a directory, RD (or RMDIR) for removing directories, and RENDIR for renaming them. A fifth command, TREE, is used for displaying the structure of directories and subdirectories on your disk drives.

Creating a Directory

Whenever you need to create a new directory, use the MD command. With MD, you must specify the name of the subdirectory being created. The name can contain up to eight alphanumeric characters and an optional three-character extension. All alphanumeric characters are allowed, as well as the following characters:

> $ # @ ! ( ) – { } ' _ ~ ^ '

If you don't include the drive letter as part of the command, the current drive is assumed. If you don't include a backslash character (\) as the first character of the directory name, the directory being created is made subordinate to the current directory. But if you include a backslash in front of the subdirectory to be created, then you create a subdirectory subordinate to the root directory. You can specify a complete path for the new directory, including a subdirectory of a subdirectory in the path, but the total command line cannot exceed 63 characters. No spaces are allowed except after the MD command.

If this sounds confusing, several examples may help clear things up. At the root directory, when the `C:\>` prompt is displayed, enter the following command:

```
MD NEWDIR
```

This command creates the subdirectory C:\NEWDIR, which is directly subordinate to the root directory. The same effect can be obtained with this command:

```
MD C:\NEWDIR
```

From the root directory, again at `C:\>`, you can also enter the following:

```
MD C:\NEWDIR\DIR_1
```

This command creates a subdirectory named DIR_1, which is subordinate to the subdirectory NEWDIR. However, if you change to the NEWDIR subdirectory (see the section "Changing the Current Directory" later in this chapter), you can enter the following at the prompt `C:\NEWDIR>` :

```
MD DIR_2
```

This command also creates a subdirectory subordinate to the NEWDIR subdirectory. DIR_2 is the same as DIR_1; both are subdirectories to NEWDIR.

Remember that, as mentioned earlier, if you specifically include a backslash in front of the subdirectory being created, you create a subdirectory subordinate to the root directory. Thus, if you are in the NEWDIR subdirectory and at the prompt `C:\NEWDIR>`, enter the following:

```
MD \OTHERDIR
```

The subdirectory OTHERDIR is then created subordinate to the root directory, not to NEWDIR. Figure 7.1 shows the relationship of the subdirectories you just created with the Novell DOS command MD. (This example uses the TREE command, which is discussed in the section "Using the TREE Command" later in this chapter.)

When you create a new subdirectory, DOS inserts the first two entries into that subdirectory:

.

..

Fig. 7.1
A TREE listing of
directories.

```
[NOUELL DOS] B:\>TREE
     bytes  files  path
         0      0  b:\
         0      0  b:\newdir
         0      0  b:\newdir\dir_1
         0      0  b:\newdir\dir_2
         0      0  b:\otherdir
total files 0    total bytes 0   disk free space 1,455,616

[NOUELL DOS] B:\>
```

These are placeholders to signify the directory to which this subdirectory is subordinate and the subdirectory itself. Without getting too technical, they allow DOS to maintain the entries for the directory files and their locations. These entries cannot be deleted and are removed only when the subdirectory itself is erased.

> **Note**
>
> Name your subdirectories according to the group of files they will contain. For example, you can isolate all your word processing document files in one subdirectory, not cluttered with all the word processing program and auxiliary files. To do this, create \WPDOCS and tell your word processor to look there for the document files.

Changing the Current Directory

One of the Novell DOS commands you may find yourself using quite often is the command to change or display the current or default directory. This command is CD (CHDIR).

CD has two purposes. First, when you enter CD with no other parameters, Novell DOS returns the current drive and directory.

The second form of the command shows the name of the subdirectory to which you want to change. If you want to change to a subdirectory several levels down, you can do so in one step by entering all the levels as part of the command:

```
CD \NEWDIR\DIR_1
```

This command changes the default directory to C:\NEWDIR\DIR_1.

After the default directory is C:\NEWDIR\DIR_1, you move up to the NEWDIR subdirectory by entering the following:

```
CD \NEWDIR
```

To move to the root directory from any subdirectory on the drive, enter this command:

```
CD\
```

This command is valid from any subdirectory level, no matter how far down the directory tree. The lone backslash stands for the root directory.

You can change the current directory to a subdirectory directly subordinate to the current directory by entering the name of the new directory without any backslash, as in this command from the root directory:

```
CD NEWDIR
```

This form of the command is good from any level to the level below it. Thus, if the current directory is NEWDIR, you can change to DIR_1 by entering this:

```
CD DIR_1
```

CHDIR also provides a special character for moving up one level at a time. When you include .. with CD, the current directory moves up one level or changes to the directory to which the current directory is directly subordinate. The .. is the place marker for the directory to which the named or current subdirectory is subordinate, and .. was created by DOS when the subdirectory was created.

Thus, if the current directory is the \NEWDIR\DIR_1 subdirectory and you enter **CD ..**, the current directory is changed to NEWDIR. From NEWDIR, the same command would change the current directory to the root directory.

If you specify a drive other than the current drive when you issue a CD command, the current drive and directory do not change on-screen. However, after you type the command to change to the other drive, the current directory is the one specified with the CD command.

Assume that the current drive and directory is C:\NEWDIR, for example, and you enter the following:

```
CD D:\BATCH
```

The Novell DOS prompt remains C:\NEWDIR> until you enter this:

```
D:
```

Without changing drives, you can access the changed directory on the other drive by just specifying the drive.

To display the list of files in the D:\BATCH directory, you then enter the following command:

```
DIR D:
```

This displays the D:\BATCH directory because that is the current directory on drive D. After you change drives, the Novell DOS prompt displays D:\BATCH >.

Renaming a Directory

After you have subdirectories on your disk, you can rename them to better fit their purpose if you like. At times, you may find it necessary to rename directories. When you want to upgrade an existing application to a new version and retain the old version on your system, for example, you may have to rename the old subdirectory so that there is no confusion with the upgrade to be installed. It is much easier and faster to rename the old subdirectory than to create a new subdirectory (or subdirectories) and copy all the original files to the new location.

Novell DOS does allow you to have multiple subdirectories with the same name, as long as they have different paths. For example, you can have C:\LTRS\BOB, C:\WPDOCS\BOB, C:\FORMS\BOB, and D:\BOB because all the subdirectories named BOB are subordinate to different directories.

The command for renaming directories and subdirectories is RENDIR. This command has no abbreviation.

When you rename a subdirectory, no files are changed, moved, copied, or deleted. The new name is just substituted in place of the old name. You cannot change the relationship of directories by changing the name. When you specify the name and path of the subdirectory to be renamed, you must specify it with both the old name and the new name. You also cannot be in the subdirectory whose name you want to change.

As with creating a new directory, unless you specify the path or use a backslash, the subdirectory being renamed is assumed to be directly subordinate to the current directory.

The following command, for example, changes the name of the subdirectory subordinate to the current directory from NEWDIR to OLDDIR:

```
RENDIR OLDDIR NEWDIR
```

Entering the following has the same effect if you are at the root directory:

```
RENDIR \NEWDIR \OLDDIR
```

> **Note**
>
> Remember that the backslash before a directory name tells the command to look at the root for that directory. If you are not in the root and you issued a RENDIR command with the backslash, the result could be a rename of a duplicate directory name coming off the root, rather than a rename of the subordinate directory.

You can also rename directories by entering the full path and several levels down the tree, as shown in the following example:

```
RENDIR C:\NEWDIR\DIR_1 C:\NEWDIR\DIR_A
```

Removing a Directory

You might want to remove a directory if you move or delete all of its files. Although you can delete a file by entering **DEL** *filename.ext*, this command does not work on directories. To delete a directory, you must use the command RD (RMDIR). You can also delete a subdirectory, but there can be no files in it or subdirectories subordinate to it. And, of course, you cannot delete the root directory.

> **Note**
>
> See the section "Using XDEL" later in this chapter for an explanation of the XDEL command, which can remove all files in a subdirectory and then remove the empty subdirectory with one command.

The normal form of the command specifies the name of the subdirectory you want to delete. If you want to delete a subdirectory several levels down, you can do so in one step by typing all the levels as part of the command.

III

Files and Directories

Entering the following command removes the empty directory
C:\NEWDIR\DIR_1:

```
RD \NEWDIR\DIR_1
```

You can delete a subdirectory directly subordinate to the current directory by
entering the name of the subdirectory without any backslash, as in this command from the NEWDIR directory:

```
RD DIR_1
```

If you specify a drive other than the current drive when you issue an RD
command, the current drive and directory are not changed on-screen; however, the empty subdirectory specified on the other drive is deleted.

Listing Files and Directories

Novell DOS uses three main commands to list file and subdirectory names:
DIR, XDIR, and TREE. The first two are similar in nature; the third shows the
hierarchy of the directory structure on your disk. TREE is also useful for finding the location of a file, in case you forgot where you put it. This section
discusses these three commands.

Using the TREE Command

The TREE command displays directory names and their hierarchical structure.
Figure 7.1, presented earlier, shows the results of entering TREE without any
options, using the subdirectories you created earlier. TREE shows the directory structure on the screen. Each item listed is a directory starting with the
root, then each subdirectory. Also listed are the total number of bytes and
files for all the files in each directory. This default display is called the text
mode for TREE (refer to fig. 7.1).

The basic format of the TREE command is

```
TREE d:pathfilename.ext options
```

Table 7.1 lists the switches you can use with the TREE command.

Table 7.1 TREE Command Switches	
Switch	**Use**
/A	Displays the directory structure in a visual chart format, but using ASCII (or text) characters instead of graphic lines. Use this switch if your monitor does not support graphic characters.
/B	Displays the directory structure in brief format, with only the directory names (without numbers of files and the total directory file sizes).
/G	Displays the directory structure in a graphic chart format, using graphic lines for the structure dependencies (see fig. 7.2).
/F	Lists all files in each directory, including file attributes.
/P	Pauses the display when the listing is too long to fit on-screen in one pass (more than 24 entries). The /P option is another Novell DOS exclusive. When you specify /P, DOS displays up to 24 directories (or files and directories) and then pauses with the message Press Enter to continue.... This allows you to read the screen before continuing.

There are actually two uses for the TREE command. The first use of TREE is to display a directory structure in a graphic manner, as shown in figure 7.2. Seeing this structure on-screen makes it easier to understand.

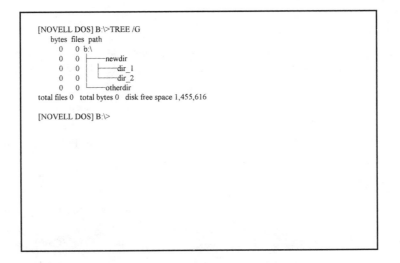

Fig. 7.2
A TREE listing with the /G option.

If you do not specify the drive or path to be listed, TREE displays the current drive starting with the root directory. If you specify a starting path for the directory listing, TREE starts with that subdirectory and displays the subdirectories subordinate to it.

Tip
TREE /B /G produces a listing that resembles the listing produced by MS-DOS's TREE.

You can redirect the output of TREE to a disk file by adding > *filename.ext* to the command, as in

```
TREE /G > DIRLIST.TXT
```

Here a graphic display of the directory listing is output to a disk file named DIRLIST.TXT. You can, of course, specify a complete path for the location of the file.

By adding > PRN to the TREE command, you can send the output to your printer. Make sure that if you use the graphic option (/G), your printer is capable of handling the graphic lines.

The second use of the TREE command is to list files and their locations. There are two ways to list files with TREE:

- Use the /F switch to list all files in each directory that is displayed with the TREE command.

- Enter a file name or wild-card specification in the command line, such as

```
TREE *.DOC
```

Using the DIR Command

The easiest way to list files and directories in your system is to use the Novell DOS command DIR. The simplest use of the command is to type **DIR** and press Enter. Novell DOS responds with a complete listing of all nonsystem, non-read-only, nonhidden files and subdirectories. In one column, Novell DOS displays the complete file name and any extension, the file size, and the last date and time the file was written or updated. A <DIR> in the second column indicates a directory. No size is given for directories.

Figure 7.3 shows a normal (default) directory listing. This listing is the same one you get when you use the /L switch with the command for a long listing.

> **Note**
>
> Remember that every Novell DOS command has its own help screen, which is displayed when you type the command with the /H or /? switch at the Novell DOS prompt. Thus, to see all the options available for the DIR command, enter **DIR /H** or **DIR /?**.

```
        POSTOFFC       <DIR>     5-12-92  10:07p
        RJAMES         <DIR>     5-13-92   9:04a
        RJSCHAMP       <DIR>     5-23-93   2:19p
        RPKACCT        <DIR>     5-15-93   2:44p
        SAYWHAT        <DIR>     5-13-92   9:07a
        SECURITY       <DIR>     5-12-92  10:07p
        TEMP           <DIR>     2-28-93  11:26a
        WPDOCS         <DIR>     5-21-93  10:47a
        NWDOS     386      4778  6-30-93   1:00a
        AUTOEXEC  BAT     1115   8-04-93  12:19p
        START000  BAT      550   5-15-93   5:39p
        CDOS      COM    51792   3-13-92   1:19p
        COMMAND   COM    54503   6-30-93   1:00a
        LOADSYS   COM     4992   7-16-92   9:49p
        BOOTLIST  DAT      143   7-23-93   2:32p
        MENU      DAT     1282   6-14-93  11:20a
        MENU      EXE    15360   4-11-91   6:48p
        DRMDOS    INP      850   6-09-93   4:01p
        DCONFIG   SYS      324   8-04-93  12:19p
        DRMDOS    SYS   252288   6-09-93   4:01p
        MCONFIG   SYS      413   7-23-93   6:07p
        NOTES     TXT    14377   8-10-92  11:48a
               31 File(s)    4909056 bytes free

        [NOVELL DOS] C:\>
```

Fig. 7.3
A directory listing
with the DIR
command.

The full syntax of the DIR command is

DIR *filespec* /L | /2 | /W /P | /N /A | /D | /S /C | /R

If you want, you can look for a specific file or group of files by entering a file
name. The switches that follow the file specification and are separated with
the vertical bar (|) are exclusive of one another. This means that you can use,
for example, /L or /2 or /W as a switch for your DIR command, but only one
of them at a time.

With all uses of the DIR command, you can specify a disk drive and a directory name if you like. If no drive is typed in the command, the current drive
is assumed; if no directory is typed, the current directory is assumed. You can
also specify full or partial file names or directory names by using wild cards.
Thus, if you want to see a listing of all batch files in the current or default
directory, enter the following:

    DIR *.BAT

Table 7.2 gives brief descriptions of all the switches available for the DIR
command. The text that follows explains each switch in detail.

Table 7.2 DIR Command Switches

Switch	Use
/A	All files displayed
/C	Shows no directories and makes other switches the default
/D	Displays files without the system attribute
/L	Shows long format, including date, size, and time
/2	Shows long format in two columns, including date, size, and time
/N	Returns to default and no paging
/P	Pauses at the end of full page (default is no paging)
/R	Other switches become default for this and future directory displays
/S	Displays files with the system attribute
/W	Shows wide format with file and directory names only
none	With no parameters, displays all files using current default switches

As mentioned earlier in the chapter, the periods displayed at the beginning of all subdirectory file listings are place markers to indicate the current subdirectory and the directory to which it is subordinate. The single period stands for the current directory. You can perform a listing of the current directory by entering **DIR**. You can perform a directory listing of the directory to which the current directory is subordinate by entering **DIR...**

Pausing the Directory Listing. The complete listing of a directory is often longer than the number of rows on your screen, so the listing can scroll past too fast to be read easily. To correct this problem, add the /P option to your command. This option makes a list pause after a full screen of files has been displayed. The message `Strike a key when ready...` prompts you to continue to the next full screen until the complete directory listing has been displayed. You can quit this listing by pressing Ctrl-C or Ctrl-Break.

Displaying Multiple Columns. To display the long form of the directory listing in figure 7.3 as two columns, add the /2 switch, as shown in figure 7.4.

```
[NOVELL DOS] C:\>DIR /2

    Volume in drive C is DSK1_DRVC
    Directory of  C:\

CHAMPION     <DIR>        5-12-92 10:07p   CUSTOM       <DIR>        5-13-92  9:10a
DS2          <DIR>        5-15-93  5:50p   FOOD         <DIR>        5-15-93  4:16p
HNCHAMP      <DIR>        5-12-92 10:07p   INDROCK      <DIR>        5-13-92  9:09a
IS           <DIR>        5-12-92 10:07p   ND7          <DIR>        7-19-93  1:54p
NWDOS        <DIR>        7-20-93  9:00a   POSTOFFC     <DIR>        5-12-92 10:07p
RJAMES       <DIR>        5-13-92  9:04a   RJSCHAMP     <DIR>        5-23-93  2:19p
RPKACCT      <DIR>        5-15-93  2:44p   SAYWHAT      <DIR>        5-13-92  9:07a
SECURITY     <DIR>        5-12-92 10:07p   TEMP         <DIR>        2-28-93 11:26a
UPDOCS       <DIR>        5-21-93 10:47a   NWDOS    386     4778     6-30-93  1:00a
AUTOEXEC BAT     1115     8-04-93 12:19p   START000 BAT      550     5-15-93  5:39p
CDOS     COM    51792     3-13-92  1:19p   COMMAND  COM    54503     6-30-93  1:00a
LOADSYS  COM     4992     7-16-92  9:49p   BOOTLIST DAT      143     7-23-93  2:32p
MENU     DAT     1282     6-14-93 11:20a   MENU     EXE    15360     4-11-91  6:48p
DRMDOS   INP      850     6-09-93  4:01p   DCONFIG  SYS      324     8-04-93 12:19p
DRMDOS   SYS   252288     6-09-93  4:01p   MCONFIG  SYS      413     7-23-93  6:07p
NOTES    TXT    14377     8-10-92 11:48a
        31 File(s)    4909056 bytes free

[NOVELL DOS] C:\>
```

Fig. 7.4
A directory listing
with the DIR /2
command.

You can also display the directory list of files as five columns. However, only the file names are used without the size, date, and time stamping so that the five columns can fit on-screen. Subdirectories are indicated with a leading backslash character. To display a five-column list, use the option /W, as in
DIR /W.

Displaying System and Hidden Files. Normal directory listings do not display files marked with the system file attribute or hidden file attribute (or both). The DIR command has no options that work with files marked as hidden; however, DIR has several switches that work with files marked as system files. For more information on attributes, see Chapter 6, "Understanding File Storage."

The file attribute to mark a file as a system file is an old device not used in the same manner today as when it originated. In the days of the original Digital Research operating system, CP/M, a system file was global to all user areas. Today, files are usually marked as system so that certain commands and utilities do not see them. Hidden files are simply marked so that they are not seen. Some commands process files with one attribute but not the other.

The Novell DOS DIR command displays all files including system files when you specify the /A switch, as in DIR /A. Hidden files are not displayed with this switch.

III

Files and Directories

To display files without the system attribute, use /D. To display files with the system attribute, use /S. When you enter **DIR** **/S**, Novell DOS responds with the listing of files marked as system, if there are any. Then Novell DOS informs you that `Directory files exist` (again, if there are any). Conversely, when you enter **DIR**, which uses the default /D switch, you are informed that `System files exist` if files exist with the system attribute.

Repeating the DIR Command. Another useful switch is /C (/R is a duplicate option). When you specify this switch with any form of the DIR command, the instruction is modified to repeat the same form of the command without any switches being specified. Thus, if you have a favorite form of a directory listing, you can enter the full command one time with the /C option and, until the option is countermanded or the computer is rebooted, simply entering **DIR** achieves the same results.

> **Note**
>
> The /C and /R switches do almost the same thing; however, /C just sets the DIR command for the next use and all future uses until you change DIR or reboot your system. /R sets and immediately displays the DIR command format as specified.

> **Note**
>
> Use the /C option for DIR in your AUTOEXEC.BAT file to set the directory display that you prefer. No display is given when the command is executed in the AUTOEXEC.BAT file, but after booting, the format is ready for your use. When working at the Novell DOS prompt, use the /R switch to start the new DIR format immediately.

For example, enter the following command:

```
DIR /2 /P /R
```

This command instructs Novell DOS to provide the long form of file listing—including name, type, size, time, and date stamping—in two columns, and to pause when the listing exceeds the room available on-screen. The new format takes effect immediately and remains in effect until you change it or reboot your system. The /R option tells Novell DOS to remember these settings. DIR then duplicates the previous command without your having to type all the switches. The /N option cancels the page pause for the current command.

Writing the Directory to a File or Printer. You can redirect a listing of any directory to a disk file or printer. For example, enter the following command:

```
DIR /2 > FILENAME.EXT
```

This command places the directory listing in the disk file specified by FILENAME.EXT. To list the directory on your printer, enter this command:

```
DIR /2 > PRN
```

In the preceding two commands, notice that the options or switches for the DIR command are entered after the command. The greater-than sign (>) is used for redirection. PRN is the device name for your printer. You can also use LPT1: or LPT2:. You must have a printer connected to your second parallel printer port for LPT2:.

Using the XDIR Command

In addition to providing the DIR command, Novell DOS 7 supplies an extended file and directory listing command called XDIR. With XDIR, you list files and directories in all kinds of formats. The *X* stands for extended.

As with the DIR command, you can specify a disk drive and a directory name with XDIR if you like. If no drive is typed in the command, the current drive is assumed; if no directory is typed, the current directory is assumed. You can also specify full file or directory names or partial names by using wild cards.

When you enter **XDIR** without any options, Novell DOS responds with a listing as shown in figure 7.5. The first column contains the attributes. As the figure shows, all files are listed, even those set as system, read-only, or hidden. Entries that are subdirectories have DIRECTORY displayed in lieu of attributes.

The second column in figure 7.5 shows the size of each file listed. If the drive is compressed with Stacker, the data-compression ratio is shown next to the file size. The third and fourth columns of the listing display the date and time of the file creation or last update, and the last column shows the file name. At the bottom of the listing is the file count (not including subdirectories), the total bytes in the listed files, and the free disk space. If the drive is compressed by Stacker, the *average compression ratio* is also displayed.

III

Files and Directories

Fig. 7.5

A directory listing
with the XDIR
command.

```
 DIRECTORY             5-12-92   10:07p  c:is
 rs--h-        527     5-13-92   10:35a  c:loader.sav
 rs--h-      5,376     5-13-92   10:35a  c:loader.sys
 ------      4,992     7-16-92    9:49p  c:loadsys.com
 --a---        413     7-23-93    6:07p  c:mconfig.sys
 ------      1,282     6-14-93   11:20a  c:menu.dat
 --a---     15,360     4-11-91    6:48p  c:menu.exe
 DIRECTORY             7-19-93    1:54p  c:nd7
 ------     14,377     8-10-92   11:48a  c:notes.txt
 DIRECTORY             7-20-93    9:00a  c:nwdos
 --a---      4,778     6-30-93    1:00a  c:nwdos.386
 DIRECTORY             5-12-92   10:07p  c:postoffc
 DIRECTORY             5-13-92    9:04a  c:rjames
 DIRECTORY             5-23-93    2:19p  c:rjschamp
 DIRECTORY             5-15-93    2:44p  c:rpkacct
 DIRECTORY             5-13-92    9:07a  c:saywhat
 DIRECTORY             5-12-92   10:07p  c:security
 rsa-h-     51,093     7-24-93    8:24a  c:stacker.bin
 rsa-h-         24     7-23-93    4:51p  c:stacker.ini
 ------        550     5-15-93    5:39p  c:start000.bat
 DIRECTORY             2-28-93   11:26a  c:temp
 DIRECTORY             5-21-93   10:47a  c:wpdocs
 total files 21    total bytes 514,459   disk free space 4,909,056

 [NOVELL DOS] C:\>
```

Novell DOS offers several options for use with XDIR. The first of these selects
files for display based on their file attributes. (For more information on attributes, see Chapter 6, "Understanding File Storage.") To see all files that
have the read-only attribute, for example, enter the following command:

    XDIR +R

To list only directories, enter this command:

    XDIR +D

To list files without any directories, enter the following:

    XDIR -D

Notice that the plus sign signifies to include files with the attribute, and the
minus sign signifies to exclude files with the attribute.

Table 7.3 lists the switches you can use with the XDIR command.

Table 7.3 XDIR Command Switches	
Switch	**Use**
+ I –DAHRS	Includes (+) or excludes (–) directories and files with archive, hidden, read-only, and system attributes.
/B	Suppresses all data other than the file names (B stands for *brief*).

Switch	Use
/C	Displays the file checksums just before the file names. A *checksum* is a binary calculation of all the characters in the file. When these are correctly added together by the algorithm built into the command, the integrity of the file can be confirmed by comparing the checksum with that of the same file on the distribution disk.
/L	Specifies the long format, which is the default with no options used.
/P	Pauses the list when it is too long to fit on-screen.
/S	Displays all files from all subordinate directories that match the file specifications.
/H	Displays all the switches and formats of the XDIR command, in case you forget some of them.
/W	Displays the file listing in the brief format, five columns wide (similar to the same option used with DIR).
/T	Sorts the listing by date and time.
/X	Sorts the listing by file extension.
/Z	Sorts the listing by file size. Directories are listed first.
/R	Reverses the sort order.
/N	Performs no sort at all.
/Y	If the drive has been compressed with Stacker, sorts by the file compression ratio.

In figure 7.5, all files and subdirectories in the listing are sorted by name, which is the default.

Note

Use XDIR /S to look for a file on a drive. If the current directory is the root directory, the search takes place on the entire drive. If you are not in the root directory and want to search the entire drive for a file, use the TREE command.

As with the DIR command, you can use wild-card characters with the XDIR command:

```
XDIR *.BAT /S /P
```

This example tells XDIR to display a list of all batch files in the current and subordinate directories, pausing at each full screen.

III

Files and Directories

Listing File Contents

Now that you know how to list files and directories, you may want to list the contents of files. Listing a file's contents helps remind you of the information the file contains. Furthermore, many software packages are distributed with a file named READ.ME or a similar name. With Novell DOS, you can easily access and read READ.ME files. The two commands that Novell DOS provides for listing file contents are TYPE and FIND.

> **Note**
>
> Both Novell DOS commands discussed in this section operate on text files only (files written in ASCII characters). Binary files cannot be read with either TYPE or FIND.

Displaying File Contents with the TYPE Command

TYPE is a Novell DOS command that displays the contents of ASCII or text files on the screen or printer. Almost all systems contain a number of such files. The DCONFIG.SYS, CONFIG.SYS, and AUTOEXEC.BAT files are text files, for example. Batch files, found on most systems, are also text files.

The following example tells DOS to list on-screen the contents of a file called READ.ME, pausing each time the screen fills:

```
TYPE READ.ME /P
```

Besides the help screen switch (/H), Novell DOS has only one option for the TYPE command: /P. This option pauses the display of the file contents when the screen is filled.

You can use wild cards in the file specification for the TYPE command. For example, you can enter the following command:

```
TYPE *.BAT /P
```

This command tells DOS to display the contents of all batch files in the current directory on the current drive.

> **Note**
>
> The TYPE command is also useful for putting ANSI.SYS codes into effect. For more information, refer to Chapter 14, "Managing the Display and Keyboard," and particularly the section "Controlling Your Display."

Locating Text Strings with the FIND Command

Whereas the Novell DOS TYPE command displays the entire contents of a text file, the FIND command lets you search for the location of a text *search string* in ASCII files. This command usually displays only the lines of the file where the search string is found.

The following example searches the C:\NWDOS\README.TXT file and displays each line containing the word *Novell*:

```
FIND "NOVELL" C:\NWDOS\README.TXT
```

The file names used for the search can be a list of files. You precede the list file with the @ character. Using EDIT, prepare a text file of all the files to be searched, use one file name per line, and include the full path for each file that is not in the current directory. Then, at the Novell DOS prompt, enter the following:

```
FIND "A man called "Joe"" @FILELIST.TXT
```

The search string must be placed within quotation marks. If the text you are looking for contains quotation marks, then double quotation marks must be used. For example, to find the text a `man called "Joe"`, you must specify the search string as `"a man called "Joe""`.

> **Note**
>
> FIND can be very slow when searching a directory with many files. It is faster when you limit the files searched. You can do this by using the file list as shown in the preceding example, or by specifying the files to be searched, such as *.txt:
>
> ```
> FIND "NOVELL" C:\*.TXT
> ```

A number of switches, listed in table 7.4, are available with the FIND command.

Table 7.4 FIND Command Switches	
Switch	**Use**
/B	Shows drive and file name for each line
/C	Shows number of lines that match search string
/F	Shows drive and file name for each file containing the search string

(continues)

III

Files and Directories

Switch	Use
/I	Makes search case-insensitive
/N	Adds line numbers to output
/P	Pauses after each screen
/S	Searches subdirectories
/U	Makes search case-sensitive
/V	Displays only the lines that don't contain search string

Table 7.4 Continued

Alphabetic case (upper- and lowercase letters) is not important unless you specify the /U option with the command. If you do add this switch, *Joe* is not the same as *JOE*. Otherwise, without the option or with the /I switch (the default), they are considered the same. If a match is found, the file name and the full text line are displayed. If no match is found, nothing is displayed, and the Novell DOS prompt is returned without a message. Searching for nonalphanumeric characters may have unpredictable results and is not recommended.

Figure 7.6 shows the results of two searches. The first display is in the default format. The second display is the result of adding the /B switch. This option causes the display format to be changed.

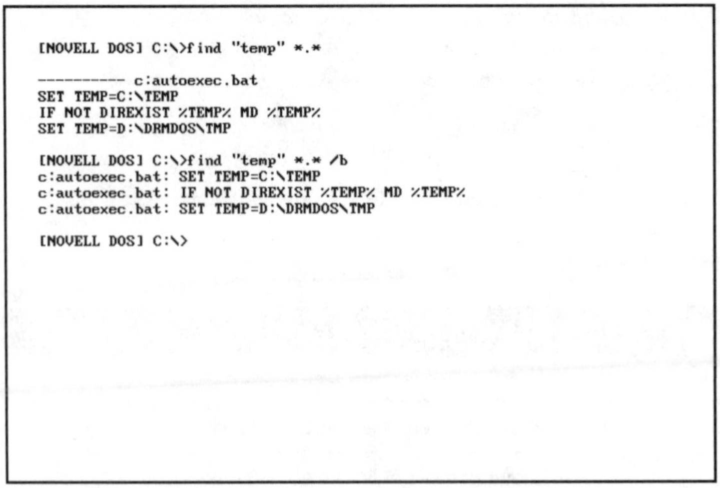

Fig. 7.6
Two examples
of the FIND
command.

```
[NOVELL DOS] C:\>find "temp" *.*

---------- c:autoexec.bat
SET TEMP=C:\TEMP
IF NOT DIREXIST %TEMP% MD %TEMP%
SET TEMP=D:\DRMDOS\TMP

[NOVELL DOS] C:\>find "temp" *.* /b
c:autoexec.bat: SET TEMP=C:\TEMP
c:autoexec.bat: IF NOT DIREXIST %TEMP% MD %TEMP%
c:autoexec.bat: SET TEMP=D:\DRMDOS\TMP

[NOVELL DOS] C:\>
```

The normal display format of the FIND command is to list first the file name in which the search text is found, preceded by 10 hyphens (–), and then each occurrence of the text line with the search text meeting the search specification. With the /B switch, the drive letter and file name are listed, followed by a colon, and then the line with the search text in that file.

Several other options are available for use with the FIND command. For example, /C tells FIND to display only the total number of instances where the search string is found. The /F switch causes FIND to display only the names of the files that contain the string.

When you add the /N option to the command, you can even have Novell DOS display a line number where each search string is found. If you use the /V switch, FIND displays all the lines that do *not* contain the search string (kind of a reverse search).

By using the /S switch, you have an additional option to search files not only in the current directory but also in all directories subordinate to the current directory.

/P is another Novell DOS exclusive that lets you pause the display when the results of the FIND search are too long to fit on-screen in one pass. When you specify this option, DOS displays up to 23 lines and then pauses with the message Press Enter to continue.... You can then read the screen before continuing.

> **Note**
>
> As with almost all Novell DOS commands, you can specify the drive and directory to be searched by the FIND command. If you do not specify the drive, the current drive is used. If you do not specify the directory, the current directory is used.

You can do other tasks with the FIND command. For example, you can redirect the output of the search to a disk file or printer. The following command uses > PRN to send the output to the printer:

```
FIND "A man called "Joe"" *.TXT /S > PRN
```

This command sends the output to the disk file FILENAME.TXT:

```
FIND "A man called "Joe"" *.TXT /S > FILENAME.TXT
```

III

Files and Directories

Copying, Comparing, and Moving Files

Many of the DOS commands for copying, moving, and manipulating files on your computer have become, for many people, part of the mystical computer jargon of the so-called experts. Nevertheless, you may have to perform many of the tasks that we all find necessary, at times, on our computer systems. Don't worry, these commands are not that mysterious or esoteric. Yet they are very powerful and can be quite useful.

This section explains copying and moving files. Novell DOS 7 provides enhanced capabilities with these file management commands, which are quite different from their simple counterparts of the past. Several switches are available for each command that can make your life much easier.

Novell DOS uses several additional commands similar to those discussed in this chapter. However, because those commands are primarily disk utilities, they can be found in Chapter 9, "Copying and Comparing Disks."

Understanding the Copy Process

If there is one most important Novell DOS command, it is the COPY command. When you back up, you copy files. When you move data to another computer, you copy files. When you reorganize your hard disk, you copy files. When you upgrade software on your system, you copy files. The copy process consists of duplicating a file in another location, on another device, or even in the same location but with a different name. The copy process includes a number of different commands that are all forms of copying files.

In this portion of the chapter, you learn about the various Novell DOS copy commands: COPY, XCOPY, MOVE, RENAME, and REPLACE. In Chapter 13, "Controlling System Devices," you learn about FILELINK, which is the utility to copy files to another computer.

Here is the basic format of all Novell DOS copy commands:

```
COMMAND source options destination options
```

If you remember this easy format, you will find that the commands are a lot easier to use. The source file is always mentioned first and may include the path (the drive and/or directory name) if the source file is not located in the current drive and/or directory. The destination is always mentioned second and must include the drive and/or full directory path if the destination is not the current drive and/or directory. If the file name is not changed, the destination does not need to include the file name. If the location is the same as the source, the name of the file must be changed and specified as the destination.

If you want to use options or command switches, you enter them after the file specification, as indicated in the command format.

Using the COPY Command

You can copy files between disk locations, as well as from and to other devices. A device can be the screen, the keyboard, the printer, the null device, or a serial or auxiliary device.

If you attempt to copy a file from any directory or device to the same directory or device with the same name, Novell DOS returns the error message

```
Source and Destination cannot be the same file.
```

Caution

If you copy a file to another directory that already contains a file with the same name, the existing file is replaced with the new file. Novell DOS will not warn you of the replacement.

You can use a number of options with the COPY command, as listed in table 7.5.

Table 7.5 COPY Command Switches

Switch	Use
/A	Assumes that the file is ASCII text; does not copy end-of-file marker from source file; adds end-of-file marker to destination file
/B	Assumes that the file is binary; ignores end-of-file markers
/V	Verifies copy operation by comparing source and destination
/S	Copies hidden and system files
/C	Prompts for confirmation for each file
/Z	Writes a zero to every eighth bit in an ASCII file; used to translate word processor files

For example, to tell COPY that the file being copied is in ASCII format, use the /A source switch. This means that the file will be copied up to but not including the first Ctrl-Z (^Z) found in the file. This character is considered an end-of-file marker. Characters in that file starting with the ^Z are not copied to the new location.

You can also use /A as a destination switch to tell COPY that the destination file is in ASCII format and should be terminated with the end-of-file marker, a ^Z.

Use the /B switch to tell COPY that the file being copied is in binary format and that a ^Z is not an end-of-file marker.

Usually, you don't have to worry about using /A and /B unless you are trying to combine ASCII and binary files. Then these options may have to be placed after the source file name.

You can use the /C switch to have COPY prompt you on whether each file is to be copied. Novell DOS displays each file with (Y/N) ? In response, press Y for yes or N for no. Do not press Enter.

> **Note**
>
> The other copy commands use the /P switch to instruct Novell DOS to request confirmation before copying each file. The basic COPY command uses /C for the same reason.

COPY is allowed to duplicate system or hidden files when you use the /S switch. Otherwise, files with these attributes are ignored. The /S switch does not copy files that have the read-only attribute.

Use the /V option to tell COPY to verify that the new version of the copied file matches the original file. If you have VERIFY=ON in your AUTOEXEC.BAT file, or you have issued this command from the Novell DOS prompt before entering the COPY command, you don't need to use the /V switch. When a file copy is verified, the program is delayed briefly while the comparison is made.

The last option for COPY is /Z. This switch is required only for some ASCII files written by some older word processing programs. The /Z switch causes the top set bit on ASCII characters to be reset to zero in the destination file.

You need to use this switch only when you copy a nondocument file from a word processing program and some weird-looking characters are in the file when you type the file.

Copying to or from Another Location. You can COPY a file to or from another subdirectory by entering this command:

```
COPY FILENAME.EXT C:\NEWDIR
```

You can specify the drive and/or subdirectory as part of FILENAME.EXT. This step is required if the file is not in the current directory. You also need to ensure that the destination actually exists. If the destination directory does not exist, the file is copied to a file with the name of the nonexistent directory.

You can copy a file from another location to the current directory by entering the following:

```
COPY C:\NEWDIR\FILENAME.EXT
```

In this case, you do not need to specify the current location. FILENAME.EXT is copied from the subdirectory NEWDIR located on drive C to the current directory.

> **Note**
>
> After COPY has done its job, Novell DOS reports back on the copy process. If successful, the message 1 File(s) copied appears. If the file is not found for any reason, the message is File not found or 0 File(s) copied.

Of course, you can copy more than one file at a time by using wild cards. To copy all files from one location to another, enter this command:

```
COPY *.* C:\NEWDIR
```

Again, be sure that the destination directory exists. If it does not, the COPY command concatenates all the files that it finds and writes them to a single file called NEWDIR in the root directory of drive C.

To copy all files from a floppy disk to the current directory, enter the following command:

```
COPY A:\*.*
```

III

Files and Directories

This command can also be entered as

```
COPY A:\
```

The last two examples have subtle differences but the same function. In the first instance (A:*.*), the command specifies all files from the root directory of the floppy disk in A. In the second instance, (A:\), the command instructs Novell DOS to copy the entire root directory of drive A.

The command A:*.* is for all files from the current directory on drive A, which may or may not be the root directory.

Note

In all the preceding examples, the files retain their names when they are copied to the new location. The files are also retained in the original location. File attributes are copied with the files, but the archive attribute is set for files in the new location. Refer to Chapter 6, "Understanding File Storage," for more information on file attributes.

Caution

Novell DOS does not warn you when you copy a file to another subdirectory that contains a file with the same name. The original file is overwritten by the copied file.

Remember one other point about COPY. If you specify a different file name as part of the destination, the copied file is renamed in its new location, whether or not it is on the same drive and in the same directory.

Combining Files with COPY. One of the capabilities of the Novell DOS COPY command is to combine files. You can use this feature with either ASCII or binary files, although combining ASCII files is more common. A good use for file combining is copying your AUTOEXEC.BAT and CONFIG.SYS files to a single file to send to the technical support department of a software vendor.

You can combine as many files as you can fit within the maximum length of the command line (128 characters). Remember that the length includes the DOS prompt. Each file to be combined is separated from the other files by a plus sign (+).

The format of the command is

```
COPY FILE1+FILE2+FILE3 NEWFILE
```

Each of the files represented by FILE*n* must include the path if the file is not located on the current drive. The NEWFILE must include the current drive and/or directory.

Caution

Combining binary files usually destroys their usefulness.

Caution

You must also specify the target file name, and this name must be different from any of the source files, unless the newly combined file is in a different location. If no target is named, Novell DOS supplies the name of the first file in the list as the destination file, and that file will be overwritten with the new file and will not have the original contents of the first file.

Copying to or from Another Device. In addition to copying to or from other directories and drives, you can copy files to or from physical and logical devices, as noted earlier. Files can be copied to and from the CON: device (from the keyboard and to the screen). The command COPY CON FILENAME.BAT is a common way to create batch files. Files can be copied to parallel or serial ports for printing and to serial or auxiliary ports for communications.

Note

You should copy only ASCII or text files to the screen or a printer. Any attempt to send a binary file to these devices may have unpredictable results.

Any printer, parallel, serial, or auxiliary device must exist, or the copy will never be completed. For example, if the printer is not turned on and on-line when you issue a command to copy a file to a parallel port (LPT*n*:) or to the Novell DOS print device (PRN), you might suffer a long delay while Novell DOS waits for a response from the printer. Usually, the absence of a device at

III

Files and Directories

a serial or auxiliary port causes one of the following error messages almost immediately:

```
Not ready error writing device COMn
I/O error writing device prn
```

The following message then appears:

```
Abort, Retry, Ignore, Fail?
```

Assuming that an active printer is turned on, on-line, and connected to the primary parallel port, the command to copy a file to your printer is

```
COPY FILENAME.EXT PRN
```

The device name CON stands for *console* and refers to both the keyboard and the video screen. Naturally, you cannot COPY a file *to* the keyboard or *from* the video screen. But the reverse is perfectly normal and legal.

To COPY a file *from* the keyboard, use the command COPY CON and then specify the name of the file. What you are doing with this command is creating a new file. Remember that Novell DOS does not warn you when you are overwriting an existing file with the same name.

The common use of this particular command is to create small batch files. Follow these steps:

1. At the Novell DOS c:\> prompt, enter

```
COPY CON SAMPLE.BAT
```

Novell DOS moves the cursor to the beginning of the next line and waits for your next command.

2. Type the series of commands (one per line) that you want the batch file to execute. Press Enter at the end of each line except the last line.

3. At the end of the last command, press F6 and then Enter. Novell DOS enters a ^Z on the screen and writes the new file to disk with the message 1 file(s) copied....

To display on-screen the contents of a text file, you can use the TYPE command, discussed earlier in this chapter. Or you can use the COPY command in the following manner:

```
COPY FILENAME.EXT CON
```

Files can also be copied to a null device. Generally, a null device is a logical fiction the device really does not exist. (Novell DOS, however, has null device capability.) But this version of the COPY command can be very handy if there are physical problems with the disk and you want to verify that the file can be read. Use the NUL command in the following manner:

```
COPY FILENAME.EXT NUL
```

If the file is read by the COPY command with no errors reported, you should have no problem with it. No copy is created on disk.

Using the XCOPY Command

The Novell DOS XCOPY, or extended copy command, enables you to copy entire subdirectories, with the creation of new subdirectories as needed, to complete the command. This utility is included in the operating system to provide even greater capabilities than those of COPY.

In addition to offering expanded features, XCOPY has another difference from the standard COPY command. COPY performs its operation on one file at a time, displaying the name of each file (if more than one is being copied) in turn as it is read and then copied to the new location. XCOPY, however, reads as many files as can be stored in memory at one time. At this part of the process, it displays Reading source file(s).... When XCOPY has finished reading all the files to be copied or as many as can be read at one time, the message is changed to Writing destination file(s)..., and each file is then listed as it is being written.

Notice that COPY displays the name of the source file with any drive and directory path if specified. XCOPY displays the name of the destination file with the drive and directory even if not specified.

> **Note**
>
> As with the Novell DOS COPY command, you are not warned if XCOPY is going to overwrite a preexisting file with the same name as a file being copied.

XCOPY can also copy a list of files prepared in an ASCII or text file. Refer to Chapter 17, "Using the Novell DOS Text Editor," on how to use Novell DOS EDIT to create such a file. Each file name listed should be on a separate line. When you issue the command, precede the file name on the command line with the @ symbol to indicate that the file name entered contains the list of

III

Files and Directories

files. For example, to copy a list of files contained in a text file to drive A, enter the following command:

```
XCOPY @FILELIST.TXT A:
```

XCOPY has 14 options or switches, listed in table 7.6.

Table 7.6 XCOPY Command Switches

Switch	Use
/A	Copies only those files that have the archive attribute.
/C	Causes XCOPY to pause at each file. After displaying the source file name, the program asks whether the file should be copied with (Y/N) ? Novell added this option to XCOPY because the COPY command also uses the /C switch for the same option. See also /P.
/D	Forces XCOPY to recognize that the destination name specified is that of a directory. Compare this switch with /F.
/D:*mm-dd-yy*	Copies all files with a date stamp of the specified or later date.
/E	Copies an entire directory and any subordinate subdirectories, even if they are empty. This switch must be used with the /S option.
/F	Forces XCOPY to recognize that the destination name specified is that of a file.
/H	Copies files that have the hidden or system attribute.
/L	Copies the disk label to the new disk.
/M	Same as /A and resets the archive attribute on the source file.
/P	Prompts for confirmation before copying.
/R	Overwrites a read-only file when it has the same name as a source file.
/S	Copies all subordinate directories and files in addition to the current directory. Use the /E switch with the /S switch if you have empty subdirectories that should also be copied.
/V	Verifies that the new version of the copied files matches the original files.
/W	Waits for a floppy disk change before the copying of files begins.

Note

You cannot use the DISKCOPY command to duplicate diverse format disks. However, you can use XCOPY. Insert a newly formatted floppy disk in drive A, insert the first installation disk in drive B, log onto B, and enter

```
XCOPY *.* A: /S /H /L
```

This command copies all files in subdirectories, copies all hidden and system files, and duplicates the original disk label on the destination disk.

Caution

Because XCOPY can duplicate many files with one command, make sure that you have enough free space on the floppy disk. If you try to copy files to a floppy disk that does not contain enough free space, the message Disk full appears.

Note

The /L option is handy when you have to duplicate one type of floppy disk on another type of floppy disk. For example, many software distribution disks are supplied on either 3 1/2-inch or 5 1/4-inch disks. Often both formats are not supplied in the same package. The internal disk label is used by some software installation programs to determine which disk is in the drive.

Note

If you have VERIFY=ON in your AUTOEXEC.BAT file, or you have issued this command from the Novell DOS prompt before typing the XCOPY command, you don't need to use the /V switch. When a file copy is verified, the program delays briefly while the comparison is made.

XCOPY can rename files while they are being copied to their new location. The following command copies all data (DAT) files to a backup directory and renames them to DTA so that they can be safeguarded while you are testing some features of an application:

```
XCOPY *.DAT D:\BACKUP\*.DTA /S
```

III

Files and Directories

The /S switch makes sure that any data files in subordinate directories are also copied.

In Chapter 19, "Using Batch Files," you learn about the IF ERRORLEVEL command. XCOPY provides specific error codes for this command when it executes, or tries to execute, your instructions. Table 7.7 lists the ERRORLEVEL codes reported.

Table 7.7 XCOPY Error Codes	
Code	**Meaning**
0	Execution completed or no errors
1	No files found to match the specification
2	Execution aborted with Ctrl-C
3	Error during execution, invalid drive, not enough memory, or not enough disk space
4	Execution ended by disk write error

This feature of XCOPY command (the use of error codes) can be very helpful if you prepare batch files to enhance their operation.

Moving Files

Moving files is a process of taking one or more files from one directory and placing them in another location. When the process is finished, the files no longer exist in the original directory. Unlike the move commands, the copy commands make a duplicate of the source file in the new location. There are three Novell DOS commands for executing a file move: MOVE, RENAME, and REPLACE.

The MOVE command enables you to change the location of a file so that it no longer exists in the original directory. The command combines the actions of the COPY command and the DELETE command into one instruction. MOVE also works on entire subdirectories.

You can use the RENAME command to change the name of a file and to move the file to another location at the same time.

REPLACE is a form of the copy command that replaces existing copies of files with new versions. REPLACE is used most often in upgrading software.

Using the MOVE Command. As noted, you use MOVE to change the location of one or more files to a new location. The new location can be a directory on the same disk or on another disk. The file name specified can refer to one file, to more than one file (with the use of wild cards), or to a list of files. In fact, MOVE can also move an entire subdirectory. MOVE copies the specified files to the new location and then removes them from the original location.

Here is a common use of this command:

```
MOVE FILENAME.EXT D:\SUBDIR
```

The FILENAME.EXT can include the drive and/or the subdirectory where the file is currently located. It must be included if it's not the current drive and/or directory. The D:\SUBDIR is the new location of the moved file and must include the drive letter if it is not the current drive. Because the new location must be another directory, the directory must also be specified, although to move a file to a root directory, all you need is the backslash as the root directory name.

As mentioned, the file name can be a specific file, or you can use wild cards to move a group of files. If you use a list of files, you specify the file name of the list and use the character @ as a prefix to the file name. This measure tells MOVE to move the files listed in the specified file. If you use wild-card characters in your file specification, then you must be moving a group of files.

> **Caution**
>
> Novell DOS does not warn you if a file being moved overwrites a file of the same name in the new location.

A successfully moved file or subdirectory is placed in its new location and removed from the old location. Novell DOS also displays the name and location of all moved files.

Several options, listed in table 7.8, are available to make this command even more powerful.

III

Files and Directories

Table 7.8 MOVE Command Switches

Switch	Use
/A	Moves only those files with the archive attribute, which means that the file has been changed or added after the files were backed up.
/D:*mm-dd-yy*	Moves only the files that have a date stamp equal to or later than the specified date.
/H	Moves files that have the hidden or system attribute.
/M	Moves files that have the archive attribute; resets the archive attribute.
/P	Prompts for confirmation of each file to be moved.
/R	Overwrites read-only files in the new location.
/S	Moves files from subdirectories but does not move directory structure.
/T	Moves an entire subdirectory. The original subdirectories are deleted along with the files from the original location. Can be used only with /P, /V, and /W.
/V	Verifies that the moved files were correctly written in the new location. If you have included VERIFY=ON in your AUTOEXEC.BAT file or typed it at the Novell DOS prompt, this switch is not needed.
/W	Waits for a floppy disk change before the search begins for the files to be moved.

MOVE can also rename files while they are being copied to their new location. Note the following example:

```
MOVE *.DAT C:\BACKUPS\*.BAK
```

This command moves all DAT files to a different directory and renames them with the BAK extension.

Using the REN Command. This section on moving files may seem a strange place to discuss the Novell DOS REN (RENAME) command. This command, however, is very much intertwined with the Novell DOS copy process. Here is the common use of REN:

```
REN OLDFILENAME.EXT NEWFILENAME.EXT
```

This command assigns the new name to the file.

With REN, you can copy files to another location, but only on the same disk, by specifying the destination along with the new name. You can use COPY or XCOPY to rename files during the copy process by specifying a new name along with the location. COPY and XCOPY, however, can rename a file when it is copied to a different drive.

Wild cards are allowed with the RENAME command. The following example takes all files starting with A and renames them as files starting with B:

```
REN A*.* B*.*
```

To rename files and copy them to a different directory (\BACKUP on the same drive) with one command, enter the following:

```
REN *.DAT \BACKUP\*.DTA
```

No switches are available with this command other than the standard /H to display a help screen.

Using the REPLACE Command. The REPLACE command is a special copy command that does selective copying. This command is most often used to update software on your system. You can add files to a directory that do not exist in that directory, skipping the replacement of files that already exist there. Or you can update files that do exist in the target directory. You even have an option to replace files across subdirectories.

REPLACE has the capability to copy files named in a text file. Use Novell DOS EDIT to create the file, with one file name per line. Refer to Chapter 17, "Using the Novell DOS Text Editor," for more on using DOS EDIT. Then specify the file list with the @ character as a prefix to the list file name, as shown in the following command:

```
REPLACE @FILELIST.TXT C:\NEWDIR
```

Several switches, listed in table 7.9, are available that you can use to control the selection process.

III

Files and Directories

Table 7.9 REPLACE Command Switches

Switch	Use
/A	Copies only files that do not exist at the target location.
/H	Includes hidden and system files in the copy process.
/M	Copies files that exist at the destination, but only if the source files have been changed.
/N	Previews the effect of the prospective REPLACE command without actually making any changes or copies. If files would be replaced, the message `The following files would be replaced...` appears. The individual file names are then listed. If the preview shows that no files would be replaced, Novell DOS displays `No files would be added`.
/P	Pauses at each file and prompts on whether each file should be copied.
/R	Allows overwriting of read-only files.
/S	Searches all subdirectories on the destination drive for files that match the source files. When you use this option with REPLACE, you cannot use the /A switch.
/U	Replaces files that are older on the destination disk than those at the source.
/W	Waits for a floppy disk change before searching for the files to be replaced.

The following example instructs Novell DOS to replace all accounting programs on your hard disk from the update floppy disk in drive A, and to replace them on all subdirectories on the hard disk where the files may be found:

```
REPLACE A:\*.* C:\ACCTNG /S
```

Comparing Files

When you begin to duplicate files, chances increase that some files may get updated and others may not. This potential problem is in addition to the possibility of errors caused by any number of other things that happen from time to time on computer systems.

You can use several measures to reduce the number of errors in your files, check the integrity of your files, and ensure that supposedly identical files match.

One measure is to use the command VERIFY. This command works system-wide and is a full-time watchdog if invoked. The other commands are the Novell DOS utilities COMP (compare) and FC. The disk utility DISKCOMP is discussed in Chapter 9, "Copying and Comparing Disks."

Using the VERIFY Command. The Novell DOS VERIFY command tells the operating system to verify that all disk writes were performed without errors. Therefore, after you turn on this option on your system, you will notice a slight delay in disk operations. But the overhead may be worth it if your work is very important to you.

VERIFY has two states: ON and OFF. To find out the status of the command on your system, enter the following command at the Novell DOS prompt:

```
VERIFY
```

Novell DOS responds with either VERIFY=ON or VERIFY=OFF, depending on the current status. You can change the status by entering either

```
VERIFY ON
```

or

```
VERIFY OFF
```

VERIFY does not compare data in source and destination files; VERIFY only confirms that the data was correctly written to the disk. To compare data, use the FC or COMP command.

> **Note**
>
> If you are accustomed to using the /V (verify) option with the various Novell DOS copy commands, you can instead set VERIFY ON in your AUTOEXEC.BAT file.

Using the COMP Command. As mentioned, Novell DOS has two utilities you can use to compare files, COMP and FC. Usually, you use the COMP command to compare ASCII text files that are supposed to be identical. In fact, the first item compared with the two specified files is their length. If the length does not match, you are asked the following:

```
Files are not the same size. Compare them anyway (Y/N) ?
```

You can answer by pressing Y for yes or N for no. Do not press Enter. If you press Y, COMP starts the compare process.

You invoke COMP by typing the command at the Novell DOS prompt. You normally specify the names and, if required, the location of the two files to be compared:

```
COMP C:\ACCTNG\ACCOUNT.DAT A:\ACCOUNT.DAT
```

As with other Novell DOS commands, you do not need to specify the drive or directory if it is the current drive or directory. If the file names are exactly the same at both locations, you do not need to include them at the second location. If the file names don't match, you must specify both file names, including name and extension, if any. Thus, COMP C:\ACCTNG\ACCOUNT.DAT A: is a valid command form because the file name is the same at both locations.

You can use wild cards in the file specifications. This feature is very useful if, for example, you have duplicate files with the same name in two separate directories. COMP matches up files of the same name and compares them, although the files may not be in the same order in each directory. If a file exists in the first directory but not the second, the message No files found to compare appears. To use wild cards, enter the following command:

```
COMP *.* \BACKUP
```

This command instructs Novell DOS to compare all files from the current directory with all files of the same name in the \BACKUP subdirectory.

You don't need to type the name of the files to be compared. If you enter **COMP**, the program prompts you with the following message:

```
Enter source file spec :
```

After you enter the file name, and the location if required, you are prompted with

```
Enter destination file spec :
```

You must then enter the location or the file name. COMP then continues its usual operation.

The switches you can use with COMP are listed in table 7.10.

Table 7.10 COMP Command Switches

Switch	Use
/A	Displays differences in ASCII format instead of the default hexadecimal format
/C	Ignores case
/D	Displays differences in decimal format
/L	Displays differences with line numbers
/P	Pauses after each screen displayed
/M:*nn*	Tells COMP how many mismatches are allowed before ending the comparison (the default number is 10; 0 stands for an unlimited number of differences)

Using the FC Command. FC is an enhanced file-comparison utility provided with Novell DOS 7. It compares both ASCII and binary files and determines from the file type which format to use. Files with an extension of EXE, COM, SYS, OBJ, BIN, or LIB default to a binary comparison. You can force either an ASCII or a binary comparison by using the appropriate switch.

You can specify a list of files to be compared by using a text file with one file name per line. You can create this file with the Novell DOS editor. When you use a file list, the name of the list file is preceded with the @ character. In this case, or whenever wild cards are used, the files being compared must match in name.

The FC utility is rather intelligent. In comparing ASCII files, FC synchronizes the text lines. After it finds a mismatch consisting of a missing or additional line and then finds a match again, FC performs a resynchronization of the files. If there is a difference within a similar line, it shows the difference between those lines in each file.

When you compare the same files with COMP, the output of mismatches starts with the first compare failure. Unless the files themselves become synchronized, the mismatches continue to the end of the file or the end of the compare because of the error count, whichever comes first. Thus, under COMP, one early character mismatch can cause the entire file to show as failing the comparison.

FC does presume to tell you how to make the correction. You may not agree to do it exactly the same way.

III

Files and Directories

Several options or switches, listed in table 7.11, are available that you can use to control the operation of FC.

Table 7.11 FC Command Switches	
Switch	**Use**
/A	Abbreviates the display of the mismatch output. Only the first and last lines of each block are listed.
/B	Forces a comparison of binary files. Use this switch when files are not automatically recognized as such by the file extension.
/C	Ignores any case differences in ASCII files.
/nnn	Controls the number of lines that must match, after which resynchronization occurs. If you do not change the number, 5 is the default.
/L	Forces FC to make an ASCII comparison. You must add this switch if the file extension would cause a binary comparison.
/Mnn	Tells FC how many compare failures or mismatches are allowed before ending the comparison. The default number is 20. Unless you specify 0, which stands for an unlimited number of differences, FC stops the compare after finding nn mismatches.
/T	Does not expand tabs to spaces.
/P	Pauses after each screen.
/W	Treats consecutive tabs and spaces as a single space.

Following are two forms of an AUTOEXEC.BAT file. The only difference is in the first line of file #2. The line is a blank line that is not contained in file #1. Otherwise, both files are identical.

FILE #1 (AUTOEXEC.BAT):

```
@ECHO OFF
CLS
PROMPT [Novell DOS] $P$G
PATH C:\NWDOS;D:\BAT;C:\;C:\VEDIT;D:\PROGRAM
HILOAD APPEND D:\PROGRAM /E
VERIFY OFF
SET TEMP=C:\TEMP
IF NOT "%TEMP%"=="" MD %TEMP% >NUL MEMMAX +U +L >NUL
HILOAD SHARE /L:120
SET CLIPPER=V010;R065;E0;F45
MENU
```

FILE #2 (AUTOEXEC.OLD):

```
<blank line>
@ECHO OFF
CLS
PROMPT [Novell DOS] $P$G
PATH C:\NWDOS;D:\BAT;C:\;C:\VEDIT;D:\PROGRAM
HILOAD APPEND D:\PROGRAM /E
VERIFY OFF
SET TEMP=C:\TEMP
IF NOT "%TEMP%"=="" MD %TEMP% >NUL
MEMMAX +U +L >NUL
HILOAD SHARE /L:120
SET CLIPPER=V010;R065;E0;F45
MENU
```

The following command starts the file comparison:

```
COMP AUTOEXEC.BAT AUTOEXEC.OLD
```

Figure 7.7 shows the output from COMP when comparing these two files. If you look carefully at the source and destination characters, after the first two characters of the destination file, the rest of the file matches, although off by two characters.

If you use the FC command with the same files, figure 7.8 shows the output when you enter the following:

```
FC AUTOEXEC.BAT AUTOEXEC.OLD
```

Fig. 7.7

File comparison with the COMP command.

```
[NOVELL DOS] C:\>COMP AUTOEXEC.BAT AUTOEXEC.OLD

Comparing files in...
C:\
with files in...
C:\

Comparing AUTOEXEC.BAT with AUTOEXEC.OLD
Files are not the same size. Compare them anyway (Y/N) ? Y
Comparing AUTOEXEC.BAT with AUTOEXEC.OLD - Compare failure.
Offset    0h   Source = 40h  Destination =  dh
Offset    1h   Source = 20h  Destination =  ah
Offset    2h   Source = 45h  Destination = 40h
Offset    3h   Source = 43h  Destination = 45h
Offset    4h   Source = 48h  Destination = 43h
Offset    5h   Source = 4fh  Destination = 48h
Offset    6h   Source = 20h  Destination = 4fh
Offset    7h   Source = 4fh  Destination = 20h
Offset    8h   Source = 46h  Destination = 4fh
Offset    ah   Source =  dh  Destination = 46h
10 Mismatches - Reached the specified (or default) number of mismatches.

[NOVELL DOS] C:\>
```

The result of the resynchronization performed by FC is demonstrably clear from this example. After the difference in the first blank line is pointed out, no other mismatches are found in the rest of the files.

Fig. 7.8

File comparison with the FC command.

```
[NOVELL DOS] C:\>FC AUTOEXEC.BAT AUTOEXEC.OLD

ASCII differences between c:\AUTOEXEC.BAT and c:\AUTOEXEC.OLD


Replace line 1 in c:\AUTOEXEC.BAT
< @ ECHO OFF

with lines 1-2 from c:\AUTOEXEC.OLD
>
> @ECHO OFF



[NOVELL DOS] C:\>
```

If mismatches are found when you compare binary files, FC displays the file location offset in hexadecimal (a numerical system based on 16, often called *hex*) and the character in both files at each location. The mismatched characters are displayed in both hex and ASCII format.

You can redirect the output of file comparisons to your printer so that you have a complete printout of all file differences. You can also redirect output to a disk file. The command you use is

```
FC AUTOEXEC.BAT AUTOEXEC.OLD > device
```

The device can be either PRN or the name of a disk file, such as FCREPORT.TXT.

Removing Files

Just as a number of copy commands are provided with Novell DOS 7, a number of powerful file-deletion commands are available. These commands and utilities are just as feature-rich and flexible to make any erasure command easy to use.

Although you have five file-deletion commands, you can actually group them into two sets. The first set includes DEL, ERASE, DELQ, and ERAQ. The other set has just one command—the extended delete command XDEL.

Using DEL, ERASE, DELQ, and ERAQ

First of all, DEL and ERASE (ERA for short) are exactly the same command. They work the same way and have the same options. The other pair of commands, DELQ and ERAQ, are also the same command.

The difference between the two pairs of commands is that both DELQ and ERAQ prompt for approval before deleting any files. This step occurs without any additional switches being used. However, the other two commands, DEL and ERASE (ERA), can also prompt for approval before deleting any files when the /C or /P option is used and when all the files in any directory are to be erased.

All forms of these file-deletion commands have the option of using an /S switch for including any system files that meet the file specification.

To delete any file, enter one of the deletion commands, such as

```
DEL FILENAME.EXT
```

To use wild cards, enter the following:

```
DEL *.DAT
```

This command deletes all files with the DAT file extension. If you enter

```
DEL *.*
```

Novell DOS responds with Are you sure (Y/N) ? You must press Y for yes or N for no without pressing Enter.

When you use the DELQ or ERAQ command, each file name is repeated with a (Y/N) ? prompt. This response occurs whether one particular file is specified or wild cards are used.

You can also delete all the files in a directory with one command by specifying the name of the directory without any file names. The current directory can be emptied if the full path is included.

The following example deletes all files in C:\TEMP even if C:\TEMP is the current directory:

```
DEL C:\TEMP
```

Using XDEL

The Novell DOS XDEL (extended deletion) utility, provides options that make it easy to control file erasures on your system. With one command, you not only can remove files but also can remove the empty subdirectories after the files are gone. This feature is handy if you want to remove one of the newer large applications that create subdirectories under subdirectories.

The normal form of the command is

```
XDEL filename.ext
```

The *filename.ext* specification may contain the drive and directory location of the file if they are not the current drive and/or directory. If the file has an extension, that extension must be entered in the command. The file specification can include wild-card characters.

You can provide an ASCII list of files to the command line. Using Novell DOS EDIT, create the file list, placing each file name on a separate line. Then enter the following command:

```
XDEL @FILELIST.TXT
```

Six optional switches, listed in table 7.12, are available with the XDEL command.

Table 7.12 XDEL Command Switches

Switch	Use
/D	Removes empty subdirectories. This option is usually used with the /S switch.
/N	Deletes files listed without confirmation.
/O	Deletes files permanently. Novell DOS overwrites the full file contents so that the file is permanently erased.

Switch	Use
/P	Prompts for confirmation.
/R	Deletes read-only files.
/S	Deletes files in subordinate directories.

Figure 7.9 shows the messages displayed by XDEL when you specify multiple files to be deleted and when you add the /S switch.

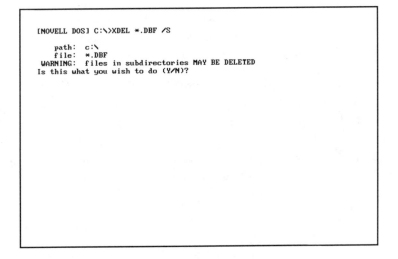

```
[NOVELL DOS] C:\>XDEL *.DBF /S

    path:  c:\
    file:  *.DBF
  WARNING:  files in subdirectories MAY BE DELETED
Is this what you wish to do (Y/N)?
```

Fig. 7.9
Warning messages associated with deleting files.

Other File Commands

Three additional commands need to be discussed: SORT, MORE, and TOUCH. SORT, as the name suggests, sorts data within a text file or from the keyboard. MORE filters screen output a screenful at a time. TOUCH changes the date and time stamp. These utilities often come in handy when you are working with your files.

Using SORT and MORE

The Novell DOS SORT command is a filter utility, which means that it receives input and provides output in a different order than received. By its very name, SORT sorts the specified file or other input. SORT is typically used with ASCII files.

> **Note**
>
> Computer sorting is based on the ASCII code chart, which means that numbers have precedence over alphabetic characters. However, the Novell DOS SORT utility considers upper- and lowercase letters as equal for sorting purposes.

Two sorting options are provided with the SORT utility:

/R	Provides the output in reverse order (for example, Z before A, and 9 before 0).
/+nn	Uses the *nn*th character as the start of the sort string. If no other column is specified with this option, sorting starts with the first character on each line.

The format of the SORT filter must be the command itself with at least an input. If no output is specified, the output is displayed on-screen. You provide input either from a prior command—which is piped, using the pipe character (¦)—to SORT, or from a redirection with the < character. For example, the following command tells Novell DOS to execute the DIR (directory) command, piping the output of that command to the SORT filter and sorting on the ninth column:

```
DIR ¦ SORT /+9
```

When you use this command, a sorted directory is displayed on-screen. To use the same command and to output the results to a disk file or printer instead of to the screen, enter the following:

```
DIR ¦ SORT > device
```

The *device* can be DISKFILE.EXT or PRN.

If you have a text file containing the names of some friends, for example, you can filter that file with SORT (and put it in alphabetic order) to another disk file, the screen, or your printer. At the Novell DOS prompt, enter the following command to SORT the file FRIENDS.TXT and have it output to the disk file SORTED.TXT:

```
SORT < FRIENDS.TXT > SORTED.TXT
```

Use the redirection character < to direct a file to the utility, and use the character > to direct the output.

If you direct the output to the screen and the length of the output exceeds the number of lines on-screen, you can add one other control device, the pipe character. Use the pipe character (¦) and the Novell DOS command MORE to tell SORT to pause at each screenful of output:

```
SORT < FRIENDS.TXT ¦ MORE
```

Novell DOS then prompts you with Strike a key when ready... until the output is completed.

MORE can be used with any commands that produce screen output. Use MORE to view output and pause after each screen. Here is a common example:

```
TYPE README.TXT ¦ MORE
```

The only time that you really need to use MORE, though, is with the SORT command. It is easier to use the /P switch, which is available with all of these commands.

Using TOUCH

Novell DOS provides a unique command that often comes in handy, especially for people who analyze systems and do programming. TOUCH enables you to set and change the date and time stamping of files on your system. Date and time stamping is provided by Novell DOS and many operating systems as an indication of when a file was created, written, or last changed. Whenever you display a listing of the files on your system, you can see the date and time stamps.

Novell's Desktop Systems Group uses date and time stamping to indicate the release date of its software and the version number of the release. If you check your distribution disks for Novell DOS 7, you can see the release date of the specific version you received and the time.

You can specify a single file name for the change, use wild cards to specify multiple files, or use a text file containing a list of files to be changed. In the last case, create an ASCII file with EDIT. Please put each file on a separate line. Then, when you issue the command, type the name of the list file preceded with the @ character on the command line.

III

Files and Directories

> **Note**
>
> Subdirectories are not touched with the TOUCH command. They retain their original creation date and time.

Table 7.13 lists the switches and options available with TOUCH.

Table 7.13 TOUCH Command Switches

Switch	Use
/D:*mm-dd-yy*	Tells TOUCH the date to use for the listed files. If you do not use this option, the current date is used.
/T:*hh:mm:ss*	Tells TOUCH the time to use for the listed files. If you do not use this option, the current time is used. You must use a 24-hour format, which is often called military time. You must include hours and minutes. Seconds are optional.
/F:*x*	Determines the format of the date to be used on the file entry. The three choices, represented by *x*, are E for European format (*dd-mm-yy*), J for Japanese format (*yy-mm-dd*), or U for U.S. format (*mm-dd-yy*). The default for your system depends on the country code specified in your CONFIG.SYS or DCONFIG.SYS file. This switch overrides your system default.
/P	Prompts for confirmation for each file.
/R	Changes the date and time stamping for files marked as read-only.
/S	Operates on all files matching the file specification in the current directory and in all subordinate directories.

> **Note**
>
> Both date and time are changed whether or not you use the switches to indicate to TOUCH what date and time to use. Thus, you may want to add both /D:*mm-dd-yy* and /T:*hh:mm:ss* to your command line so that you control the stamping.

To see which files are changed when you are testing a new application, use the following TOUCH command on all files:

```
TOUCH *.* /T:00:00:00 /R/S
```

This command sets all files in the current and subordinate directories to the current date, but at midnight, and includes files marked as read-only. Then test your application. Any file with a different time stamp was modified by the application.

From Here...

In this chapter, you learned about a number of commands you can use to manipulate files and directories on your disk drives. You may want to turn next to the following chapters:

■ Chapter 6, "Understanding File Storage," explains the basics of computer disks, directories, files, file storage, file attributes, and wild-card characters.

■ Chapter 9, "Copying and Comparing Disks," helps you with the disk versions of the COPY and COMP commands you learned in this chapter.

■ Chapter 10, "Undeleting Files," shows you how to protect your important files from accidental erasure.

■ Chapter 12, "Backup Utilities," discusses Fifth Generation's Fastback Express program for safeguarding your applications and data.

III

Files and Directories

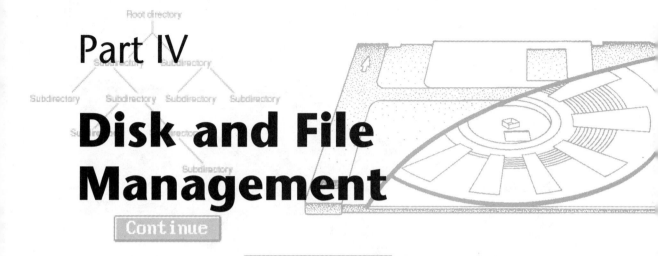

Part IV

Disk and File Management

Continue

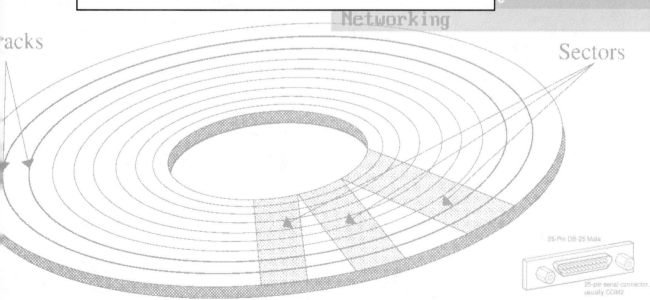

Root directory

Subdirectory   Subdirectory

Subdirectory   Subdirectory   Subdirectory   Subdirectory

Subdirectory   Subdirectory

Subdirectory

Continue

File - c:\spam.txt
Create new file ?

OK   Cancel

nfigure Task Manager

it this screen

ystem & Memory Managemer
Disk Compression
Disk Performance
Data Protection & Security
Task Management
Networking

racks

Sectors

25-Pin DB-25 Male

25-pin serial connector,
usually COM2

Change destination drive(s) and directori

Chapter 8

Preparing Disks

All physical disks, whether floppy disks or hard disks, require preparation before they can be used. This chapter describes the commands used to prepare and maintain disks. The commands do not pertain to RAM disks, which are devices that use chip memory to simulate the action of a physical disk drive.

If your hard disk has already been prepared or is in use, you can skip the next section of this chapter and proceed to the section "Formatting Disks" to learn how to prepare floppies for use on your system. If you have a new system that needs to be prepared to accept Novell DOS 7, or if you are installing a new hard disk or want to change the use of your hard disk (its partitioning), read on to learn about the preparation of hard disks.

This chapter covers the following topics:

- Hard disk structures
- Initializing the hard disk
- Partitioning the hard disk
- Formatting the hard disk
- Transferring the operating system
- Formatting and unformatting floppy disks
- Labeling disks
- Installing multiple versions of DOS

Initializing and Partitioning Hard Disks

Just as operating system technology has progressed over the years for computers, along with the improvements in central processors (8086, 8088, 80286, 80386, 80486, and so on), hard disk technology has progressed also. A number of types of hard disks are in use today, such as MFM, RLL, IDE, ESDI, SCSI, and SCSI-2. Each requires its own hard disk controller or adapter so that it can be used in your computer.

Modern hard disk drives are faster and larger than ever. Only 10 years ago, a 10-megabyte hard disk (capacity of 10 million characters) was considered average. Most hard disks that are available today have a capacity of 80M or more. Novell DOS can handle hard disks up to 2G (gigabytes—thousand million characters) as long as your hardware and system BIOS can handle it. The system BIOS is the Basic Input/Output System software placed on a chip and installed on the motherboard in your computer. (You see the BIOS operating with the sign-on messages and memory test displayed when your system is first powered on.)

As far as speed goes, hard drives a few years ago would take 85 milliseconds to access data. Today's drives usually access data in 8 to 18 milliseconds. That's pretty fast.

Nevertheless, the preparation of a hard disk still takes the same four steps no matter what the drive type: initialization, partitioning, formatting, and operating system transference. The change that affects you is that, unless you have an MFM or RLL type of hard disk, you probably do not have to perform the initialization or low-level formatting of the drive. That is done by the manufacturer in the factory, or requires a special utility most users do not have. In fact, if you perform a low-level format on a drive other than MFM or RLL, you may have to send the drive back to the manufacturer or to a repair facility to correct the damage.

This section describes the processes of initializing and partitioning a hard disk. Later sections of this chapter describe how to format the disk and transfer the operating system.

Understanding Hard Disk Structure

Before you proceed to learn about preparing your hard disk, you should know a few definitions. The basic terms used to describe disk drive hardware are *hard disks*, *heads*, *tracks*, *cylinders*, *sectors*, and *clusters*. Understanding these terms will help you design the best layout for your hard disk (see figs. 8.1 and 8.2).

■ *Hard disks* consist of one of more platters spinning at approximately 3,600 rpm inside a closed container. The platters are connected by a spindle driven by a motor. The surface of each platter is coated with a thin film of material with very precise magnetic properties. Small areas of the coating can be magnetized in specific directions. The magnetic direction determines whether a data bit is a zero or a one. When the direction of the magnetization is detected (read), the data bit state (zero or one) is determined.

■ *Heads* are used to read and write information. Very small read and write heads, similar to those on a tape recorder, are mounted on an arm. This arm can be driven very rapidly back and forth across the disk to position the heads over any part of the disk. The positioning mechanism holds and moves all the arms at the same time.

■ A *track* is the area on one platter surface that passes under one head. After the arm has reached the correct position (after the spinning disk brings the information under the head), the desired information is read. The information on one track is divided into *sectors* (like pie slices) of a fixed size, usually 512 bytes. Performing a low-level format writes these sectors; normal operations rewrite their contents. The number of sectors per track varies, depending on the type and size of the drive.

■ A *cylinder* consists of all the tracks that may be read without moving the access arm. Because the tracks are circular, and the surfaces one above another, the shape created by a stacked series of tracks is a cylinder. The number of cylinders on a disk depends on the disk's capacity. You use cylinder numbers, beginning with zero, to indicate the position and size of a disk partition.

■ A *cluster* is a group of disk sectors that are grouped together as one block. When a file requests disk space, the operating system allocates a cluster of disk space to that file. When that cluster is filled, another cluster is allocated, then another, and so on. The size of the cluster (the number of sectors so grouped) depends on the size of the hard disk partition.

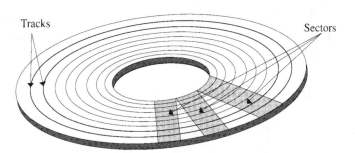

Tracks

Sectors

Fig. 8.1
Concentric tracks
on a disk's surface.

Fig. 8.2
Tracks, platters,
and cylinder.

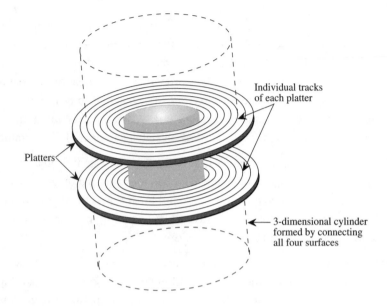

Individual tracks
of each platter

Platters

3-dimensional cylinder
formed by connecting
all four surfaces

Initializing the Hard Disk

The first step in preparing a hard disk is low-level formatting, or initialization—a preparation and test process in which the *disk interleave* is established and information is written onto and then read from each area of the disk. Disk interleave, briefly, establishes how many times the disk has to rotate for one complete track to be read. Each track and sector intersection has a unique address that lets the computer know where data is stored so that it can be found when needed. The more sectors that can be read in one rotation, the faster the data transfer. This process also marks out bad parts of the disk so that they will not be used for your data.

> **Note**
>
> Novell DOS 7 does not provide a utility to low-level format a hard disk. Some system BIOS programs include a utility to do this.

This type of formatting is called low-level because it is the closest to the hardware, or the hard drive. (The use of the FORMAT command is sometimes called high-level formatting.) The purpose of this test is to ensure that each area on the disk can write and read information correctly. Because this procedure requires writing and reading information at every area of the hard drive, the process may take a long time to complete, especially for very large disk drives.

The method of running a low-level format varies, as every disk controller and disk combination uses a different technique to perform a low-level format. Should low-level formatting become necessary, consult your system documentation manuals. If you are required to perform this initialization and were not supplied with the utility to perform it, contact your dealer or the manufacturer.

Caution

When you run a low-level format, all existing information on your hard drive is permanently and irrevocably erased, so make sure that you have good backup before you start.

Creating Partitions with FDISK

The second step in preparation, called *partitioning*, is the process of dividing a hard disk into partitions, or logical pieces. Each hard disk must have at least one partition but may have more than one. Each partition becomes a logical drive. These partitions may be used by one operating system, by different operating systems, or as multiple disks by the same operating system. Even when you run only Novell DOS, you might want more than one partition so that you can divide the disk into smaller logical drives.

Note

As mentioned, Novell DOS 7 is designed to handle hard disk partitions up to 2G in capacity. However, for a number of reasons, for almost all users, this disk size as one partition is unwieldy and wastes file space. Very large hard disks, such as a 2G or 4G disk, should be partitioned into several smaller logical drives.

The FDISK (fixed disk) command is used to create partitions or to change the current partition structure on a hard disk. This command is automatically run during the Novell DOS Install program if you are installing Novell DOS 7 on a new hard disk or new system, but you may need to run FDISK in order to use a newly added hard disk, or to change the structure of your current hard disk.

Note

The Novell DOS 7 FDISK command, after creating a new partition, automatically formats the hard disk.

There are several reasons to divide your disk into multiple partitions. Novell DOS supports partitions up to 2,048 megabytes (2G) in size. When you are using a larger hard disk or you don't want to work with individual drives this large, you need multiple partitions on your hard disk. For instance, you may prefer to store your data on one drive and your programs on another, making data backup easier. Alternatively, you may prefer to use one drive for one application and a different drive for a different application. Don't divide the disk into small pieces, however, as there are other, better ways of dividing the drive into logically related information. For example, using directories and subdirectories to group related information together is an alternative to numerous partitions. However, very large partitions allocate 32K clusters (32,000 characters) for even small files of only a few hundred characters, such as letters, memos, and small data files.

One warning exists with regard to hard disk partitions larger than 32M. Some older hard disk utilities, and perhaps some very old application programs, may not be able to work with your system. If you have any such programs, be careful with their use; and at the first sign of any problems, discontinue their use. You might contact the manufacturer of this older software to see if there is a newer version that works on a larger-size hard disk. It is also wise to make sure that you have a complete current backup of all software and data in case of such a problem.

Do not divide a 32M hard disk (or smaller) into logical drives, because these smaller drives slow down and reduce your computer's efficiency. The reason for the reduced efficiency is the overhead associated with each disk drive:

- Each drive maintains drive status information, which requires some memory in Novell DOS. Additional logical drives increase the amount of memory needed to store this information.

- Each drive needs some free disk space. When you divide your disk into multiple logical disks, the free space on one drive is not available for use with another logical disk.

- For small drives (10M and smaller), Novell DOS uses the same technique for allocating files that earlier DOS versions used. This technique tends to waste more space than later versions of DOS. For this reason, make the partition size 20M or larger.

Unless you have a specific reason to partition your hard disk, create only one large partition for Novell DOS and then subdivide the disk into subdirectories for different kinds of files. Subdirectories are much more flexible than disk partitions. A hard disk of 128M or larger, however, should be divided into a primary partition and at least one logical drive. For large hard drives, DOS uses a larger allocation unit size, and the smaller logical drives reduce wasted space associated with unfilled allocation units.

Note

Plan your disk partitions carefully. Changing the partitioning at a later date, after the disk is filled with files, will be a difficult and time-consuming task. A little time spent for planning will save considerable time later.

Understanding Primary and Extended Partitions. There are two types of partitions: *primary* and *extended*. An extended partition allows you to subdivide a drive into multiple logical drives. Before you can create an extended partition, you must first create a primary partition.

You must create at least one primary partition to use Novell DOS on a hard disk. A primary partition is the drive from which Novell DOS boots and is identified as drive C. You may also create an extended partition and divide the hard disk into additional logical drives. Each of these drives appears as an additional disk, with a unique drive letter. The primary partition is drive C. Additional logical drives, in the extended partition, are drive D, drive E, and so on.

Note

If you have more than one physical hard drive in your computer, the first partition on the first hard disk becomes drive C. The first partition on the second hard drive then becomes drive D. The second and additional partitions of the first hard drive become drive E, F, and so on. The second and additional partitions of the second hard drive then continue the letter designations.

Partitions of other operating systems, which use the hard disk differently than Novell DOS, cannot be used when you are running Novell DOS. Some disk space must be left unassigned when you plan to install another operating system on the hard drive, because this arrangement is the only way in which Novell DOS can share the disk with a non-DOS operating system. You then use the other operating system to create the partition for that operating system.

If you want to use OS/2 with a High Performance File System partition, for example, you need to leave available space and use OS/2 to create the partition. The data on an HPFS partition is not accessible to Novell DOS. When you install the other operating system, you must leave enough space for Novell DOS and your DOS application programs. Novell DOS requires a minimum of 20 cylinders, but you will probably want much more than that. Remember that the size of a cylinder depends on the characteristics of your hard drive.

Using FDISK. Run FDISK by entering the command **FDISK** at the Novell DOS prompt. The initial display of FDISK shows the existing structure of the partitions on your hard disk, including position (starting and ending cylinder numbers), size (in megabytes), status (active or inactive), and type (see fig. 8.3).

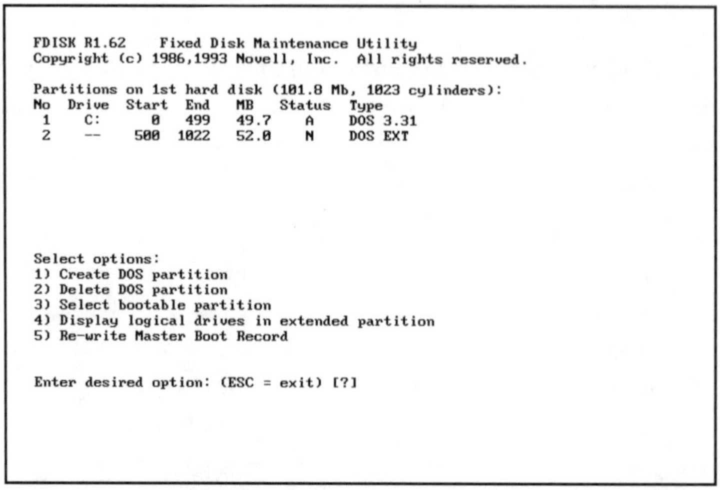

Fig. 8.3
The initial FDISK display.

```
FDISK R1.62     Fixed Disk Maintenance Utility
Copyright (c) 1986,1993 Novell, Inc.  All rights reserved.

Partitions on 1st hard disk (101.8 Mb, 1023 cylinders):
No  Drive  Start  End   MB    Status  Type
 1   C:      0    499   49.7    A     DOS 3.31
 2   --     500   1022  52.0    N     DOS EXT




Select options:
1) Create DOS partition
2) Delete DOS partition
3) Select bootable partition
4) Display logical drives in extended partition
5) Re-write Master Boot Record

Enter desired option: (ESC = exit) [?]
```

The position of the partition on the disk is given by the cylinder numbers at the beginning and end of the partition. The total size of the hard disk, shown on the initial screen, depends on the characteristics of the specific hard disk. The size is calculated by multiplying the number of cylinders by the number of tracks per cylinder by the number of sectors per track by the size of a sector.

The initial screen, as shown in figure 8.3, shows a menu of the available choices. Press the key for the indicated number to move on to the next menu. Press Esc to back up to a previous menu or to exit from FDISK.

FDISK displays a list of available options that apply only to your system. For instance, when you have two hard disks, FDISK provides the option to change to the other hard disk. This option does not appear when you have only one hard disk. Another example is for disks that have previously been prepared with the FDISK command—the Re-write Master Boot Record option. This option does not appear for disks that have not been prepared. After you have created an extended partition, an additional option is provided that enables you to work with logical drives in the extended partitions. Choose the option that describes what you want to do.

When you choose to create a DOS partition, you are asked what kind of partition you want to create. Remember these points:

- You must create a DOS primary partition on a hard disk before creating any extended partitions.

- You may create a DOS primary partition only when a DOS primary partition does not yet exist and sufficient unassigned space is available on the disk.

- When you have a second hard drive, the FDISK command provides the option to choose the second hard drive. The options for a second hard drive are the same as those for the first. Because your second hard drive's partitions may be different in size and number from those of the first drive, the number of cylinders shown may be different from those of the first drive.

- Performing the FDISK command on the second drive does not affect data on the first drive, nor is the reverse true.

- When you have two hard drives, C is usually the primary partition on the first drive, and D is usually the primary partition on the second drive.

- Logical partitions on the first drive are usually designated with the letters in succession beginning with E (or D, when you only have one drive). Logical partitions on the second hard disk will get the next letter in sequence. For instance, when the first drive has partitions C, E, F and G, then the second drive has partitions D, H, I, and so on.

> **Note**
>
> You can change the order of logical drives when you have a second physical drive, by setting the first and all other partitions on the second drive as extended partitions.

When you want to use FDISK to change the partition sizes on your existing hard disk, remember that partitions are deleted before they are reallocated. Make a backup, therefore, because FDISK erases all data from any partitions being changed.

Caution

FDISK deletes all information from the affected partitions on the hard disk when you change the partition sizes!

Creating the Primary Partition. To create a new primary partition, follow these steps:

1. Delete any primary partitions already existing on the disk.

2. From the FDISK display, choose option 1 to create a new primary partition. FDISK displays a message showing how much space is available, in cylinders and megabytes, and asking whether you want to create a partition of that size.

3. Press Y if this is the only operating system used by this disk and you will not be creating any logical disk drives. A single partition that uses all the available space is created.

   Press N if you will be creating logical drives or if another operating system will be installed on this disk drive.

If you answer no to step 3, you are asked to specify the primary partition size by providing starting and ending cylinder numbers for the primary partition. The number of cylinders in a partition is equal to the difference between the starting and ending cylinder numbers, plus one. To determine the partition size, either use a size recommended by FDISK or follow these steps:

1. Use the size information given in cylinders and megabytes from the preceding step 2 to calculate the number of megabytes per cylinder for your system.

2. Use the size information from the preceding step 2 to determine the size of the primary and extended partitions. Typically, a proportion of the total available space is assigned to the primary partition. For instance, to assign half the disk to the primary partition, specify the starting cylinder as 0 and the ending cylinder as one half the total number of cylinders.

The partition must be at least 20 cylinders, and the first few tracks must be error-free. When a problem occurs, a warning message appears, the partition is not created, and a prompt appears for you to provide a different starting cylinder. Enter a different cylinder number, perhaps one cylinder higher, and try again.

Creating the Extended Partition. If you want more than one Novell DOS partition on a hard drive, you need to create an extended partition to hold the second and succeeding logical drives.

A DOS extended partition enables you to divide a hard disk into one or more logical disks. When Novell DOS is the only operating system on the hard disk, assign to the extended partition all space not used by the primary partition. An extended partition is not usable until divided into logical drives. To create an extended partition and divide the partition into logical drives, follow these steps:

1. From the FDISK menu, choose the Create DOS Partition option.

2. Choose the Create Logical Drive option to display a list of currently assigned logical drives, the size of each logical drive, and the default location for a new logical drive. This option is available only for DOS extended partitions.

3. Logical partitions are assigned location by cylinder number, as was the primary partition. The default position of the first logical drive is the first available space within the extended partition. When you want to place the logical drive elsewhere, type the starting cylinder number of the desired location. For the ending cylinder number, use the default ending cylinder number, which is the last contiguous free cylinder in the extended partition; or type a new ending cylinder number. The starting and ending cylinders must be completely within the DOS extended partition, must be free, and must have no assigned space between the first and last cylinder. You may continue to create logical drives in the extended partition as long as free space is available.

> **Note**
>
> If you want to use a Novell DOS extended partition, assign the remaining space to logical partitions. Use all remaining space (up to 512M) for a single drive, use 32M partitions for compatibility with older versions of DOS, or use partitions of up to 128M for most efficient use.

Activating Partitions. If your computer has multiple operating systems installed on the hard drive, only one boots. In general, only one system can be a DOS-type system (see the note at the end of this section for a special technique to get around this restriction).

Your computer boots the operating system stored in the "active" partition. One partition is marked active, which is the partition that boots. Use the FDISK command to see the status of all partitions. The active partition is marked with an A in the status column, and all other partitions are marked with an N in the status column. Only one partition may be active at any one time.

To select the active (bootable) partition, enter the FDISK command. Select the Select Bootable Partition option. Type the number of the partition to be made the active partition, and press Enter.

When you have multiple operating systems installed on your hard disk, use the FDISK command to activate the partition containing another operating system. After you have activated this other partition, you may boot the other operating system. This other operating system should have a program that enables you to activate and return to the DOS partition, after which you may again boot with Novell DOS. Alternatively, you may boot Novell DOS from a floppy disk and then use the FDISK command resident on the floppy disk to activate the DOS partition.

> **Note**
>
> OS/2 is unusual in its partitioning of the hard disk. OS/2 can read and write data in a Novell DOS partition, and can also be installed to allow another operating system to boot from the same hard drive. OS/2 Version 2.1 can even boot from a drive other than C. The command to switch back to Novell DOS depends on the version of OS/2 and the options used for the installation. For more information, consult your OS/2 operating manual or Que's *Using OS/2 2.1*, Special Edition.

You should make an emergency Novell DOS boot floppy disk. With it, you can make the Novell DOS partition active if you cannot do that from the other operating system. An emergency boot disk is also useful whenever Novell DOS becomes unbootable (either from disk corruption or from your error). To create an emergency boot disk, follow these steps:

1. Format a floppy disk, using the /S switch (or use the SYS command).

2. Copy the following files to the floppy disk:

   COMMAND.COM
   FDISK.COM
   RESTORE.COM
   FORMAT.COM
   CHKDSK.EXE
   SYS.COM

3. Copy your favorite text editor to the disk. Or copy EDIT.EXE.

4. If necessary, copy any files installed by your CONFIG.SYS file and set up a corresponding CONFIG.SYS on your floppy disk. This may include Stacker or other disk compression utilities and drivers.

5. Create an appropriate AUTOEXEC.BAT file.

6. Test your emergency floppy disk by rebooting from the floppy. Make sure that you have no errors and that you can edit files successfully.

The Activate Partition menu option on the FDISK menu is not useful when you have only Novell DOS installed on your hard disk. Instead, boot Novell DOS from a floppy and use the FDISK command to make the Novell DOS partition active. This option refers to the same DOS partition even when the partition was created by a different version of DOS (MS-DOS or MultiUser DOS, for example). This is the only option of FDISK that cannot damage data and does not reboot the system on completion.

Note

There is a method for loading more than one DOS operating system version on your hard disk at the same time. Novell's NDSG division has provided a utility called LOADER.COM that performs this task. Read more about LOADER in the section "Installing Multiple Versions of DOS" later in this chapter.

Removing Partitions. Removing partitions is the first step in changing partition sizes. To remove partitions, use the FDISK Delete DOS Partition menu option from the FDISK opening menu.

When your hard disk has a DOS extended partition, you are provided options to delete the DOS extended partition and the logical drives. To remove the DOS extended partition, first remove all the logical drives within that partition and then remove the extended partition. After the extended partition is removed, you may reallocate the partition with a different amount of space.

When you use the Delete Logical option from the FDISK menu, a list of the current logical drives appears. Type the number of the logical drive you want to delete. When you want to delete more than one logical drive at the same time, the order of deletion does not matter.

Caution

Deleting a partition or logical drive deletes all data within that drive. Make sure that you have a good, tested backup of all data on the drive before you delete a partition. When you delete the primary DOS partition on the first hard drive, you need to create a new partition and reinstall Novell DOS before you can boot from the hard drive.

When your hard drive contains a non-DOS partition, you should use the original operating system to remove the partition. When you cannot run the other operating system, you may use the /D switch with the FDISK command to delete non-DOS partitions, as well as DOS partitions. Use this switch only when you must use the FDISK command to delete a non-DOS partition.

Caution

When you use the /D switch to delete a non-DOS partition and later determine that you need the other operating system, you need to reinstall the other operating system. All data in the other operating system's partition is lost.

Formatting Disks

Disks must be formatted before they can be used. This is the third step in preparing hard disks and the primary step in preparing floppy disks. The FORMAT command is used to create the basic DOS structure on both hard disks and floppy disks, but the parameters are slightly different for the two types of media. On a floppy disk, the FORMAT command first tests the surface for bad areas. On a hard disk, however, this test for bad areas is performed by a low-level format program, written to work exclusively with the type of hard drive you are running.

> **Note**
>
> You cannot format a disk over a network. You can only format local drives.

Understanding Basic Disk Structure

The basic areas of an empty disk are created by the FORMAT command. These areas, discussed in this section, are the boot sector, the file allocation table (FAT), the root directory, and an optional disk label.

The Boot Sector. The *boot sector* contains the instructions for your computer to boot from the disk by finding and loading Novell DOS. The boot sector is written even when you don't create a bootable disk. When the disk is not bootable, the boot sector contains instructions to display a message telling you to replace the disk and press any key. When you don't format the disk as a bootable disk, the SYS command can transfer Novell DOS and replace the boot sector. The SYS command is discussed in the section "Transferring the Operating System" later in this chapter.

The Root Directory. The *root directory* contains information about all files not stored in subdirectories and about all subdirectories on the hard drive. The root directory is created by the FORMAT command and is fixed in size. The number of entries is fixed and depends on the type of disk, with more entries possible on a hard disk than on a floppy disk. Because this directory is a fixed size, you may be prevented from creating a file in the root directory, even when space is available on the disk. Filling the root directory, however, requires a very large number of files, especially on hard disks. Table 8.1 lists the number of file entries allowed for the root directory of the major disk sizes.

Table 8.1 Floppy Disk Root Directory File Capacities		
Size	**Capacity**	**Entries**
5 1/4 inch	180K	64
5 1/4 inch	360K	112
5 1/4 inch	1.2M	224
3 1/2 inch	720K	112
3 1/2 inch	1.44M	224
3 1/2 inch	2.88M	240
Fixed	All	512

The File Allocation Table (FAT). The *file allocation table* (abbreviated FAT) describes the status of each *allocation unit*, or cluster, on the disk. The file allocation table has one entry for each cluster, which is either free, bad (contains disk errors), or part of a file. The file allocation table is one of the important areas on the disk because this table contains the location information for files and parts of files on the disk. The directory entry for a file has the cluster number of the first cluster for that file. The file allocation table entry for the first cluster contains the cluster number for the next cluster, and the next, and so on.

The Disk Label. A *disk label*, a special type of zero-length file, is an electronic name applied to the disk and may be up to 11 characters long. You can write a label when you format a disk, or you may decide to omit the label entirely. Some installation programs use a disk label to determine whether you have inserted the correct disk. Use the LABEL command when you want to rewrite the disk label. To determine the label on a disk, use the CHKDSK or DIR command, which displays the disk label as part of its operation. Alternatively, you can use the VOL command to display the current label.

Using the FORMAT Command

The FORMAT command is used to prepare disks for use by creating the basic DOS structure on both hard disks and floppy disks. New disks—both floppy and hard—must be formatted before use.

The syntax of the FORMAT command is

```
FORMAT d: options
```

You must specify the drive letter. If you don't, you will receive the error message You must specify the drive to be formatted. A number of switches are available for use with this command.

> **Caution**
>
> Formatting an existing disk erases the contents of the disk, so be careful not to format anything you might need later without first making a backup.

Table 8.2 lists the available switches for specifying the format requirements.

IV

Table 8.2 FORMAT Command Switches

Switch	Use
A	Makes an audible warning when the format is complete.
/F:*nnn*	Specifies the floppy disk capacity in kilobytes. Table 8.4 lists the allowable entries for *nnn*. This is a valid option only for floppies.
/N:*nn*	Specifies the disk size in number of sectors. This switch must be used together with the /T switch. Replace *nn* with the value for sectors as listed in table 8.3.
/Q	Tells FORMAT to save UNFORMAT information. This option, which is the default, is referred to as the *quick* or *safe* format. You normally do not have to include this switch.
/S	Transfers Novell DOS system files to the boot sector of the new disk. With these system files in the boot sector, Novell DOS loads (boots) when you start your computer from the disk drive. When you omit the /S switch, the boot sector contains a short program that displays a message directing you to change disks and reboot. When you use this switch, the floppy disk has less space available for information files because the system has used some of the disk space.
/T:*nn*	Specifies the disk size in number of tracks. This switch must be used together with the /N switch. Replace *nn* with the value for tracks as listed in table 8.3.
/U	Forces FORMAT to unconditionally prepare the floppy disk—that is, not to perform a quick format.
/V:*xxxx*	Specifies a volume label (*xxxx*) at the command line. If you enter just /V, FORMAT prompts you for the label before it finishes the formatting operation, but this is the default. You really do not need to specify the switch without a label name.

/X	Enables FORMAT to prepare hard disks. When you attempt to format a fixed disk, DOS warns you with this message:
	
	`WARNING: All existing data on non-removable disk C:`
	`will be destroyed! — Continue (Y/N)?`
	
	Enter Y to format the hard disk; enter N not to format the hard disk.

/1	Tells FORMAT to prepare only one side of a floppy disk. This option is valid only for 5 1/4-inch drives and for 320K and 360K floppies. If you are formatting one of these disks in a 1.2M drive, you must also specify the /F:320 or /F:360 parameter.
/4	Used to retain compatibility with earlier versions of DOS, allowing 360K disks to be formatted in a 1.2M drive.
/8	Tells FORMAT to prepare nine sectors but use only eight sectors. This option is valid only for 5 1/4-inch drives and for 320K and 360K floppies. If you are formatting one of these disks in a 1.2M drive, you must also specify the /F:320 or /F:360 parameter.

> **Note**
>
> Save yourself the trouble of remembering all the switches for the floppy disks of different capacities. Use the /F:*nnn* switch when formatting floppies. This option provides the proper information required for the format.

When a floppy disk has been previously formatted to the same capacity, the FORMAT program performs a quick or safe format. This format rewrites the disk as an empty disk without actually rewriting all the data areas. If you want FORMAT to rewrite all areas, use the /U switch. If you force an unconditional rewrite with the /U switch, however, you cannot unformat the disk.

When the format process is completed, a message appears that provides the number of bytes available on the disk, as well as the number of bytes occupied by bad sectors (see fig. 8.4).

Fig. 8.4
A typical FORMAT
operation.

```
[NOVELL DOS] C:\>FORMAT B: /F:1.44
Insert target diskette in drive B:
and press Enter when ready...

Quick formatting disk.
Enter volume label (Max. 11 characters, Enter for none)
Disk formatted successfully.

    1,457,664 bytes total disk space.
    1,457,664 bytes available on disk.

Format another diskette (Y/N)?
```

You are prompted for a disk label. If you don't want a label, you can press Enter. To write a label, type a label containing 1 to 11 characters. You may add, delete, or change a disk label later with the LABEL command.

Safeguarding Data from a Format. Recovering the contents from an accidentally formatted disk may be possible. When you format a disk that has previously been used, the format program attempts to save information needed to recover the old data. This information is saved, however, only when you format the disk with characteristics unchanged from the originally formatted disk and when space is available to save the information.

When you format the disk with different characteristics, the format program is unable to detect any previous information on the disk, and the format program overwrites all old information. If insufficient space is available to save the old information, a message appears asking whether to proceed without saving the old data. If you answer N to prevent formatting without saving the old information, the format program ends. If you answer Y, the disk is formatted without the possibility of recovering any old information. The best practice is to treat formatting as an irreversible process, even though data on formatted disks might be recoverable. Making a backup of important data also prevents the possibility that data might not be recoverable.

Formatting Floppy Disks. On a new floppy disk, the format program writes the basic DOS pattern to all surfaces of the disk and tests to ensure that these areas can be successfully written and read. Areas that cannot be written are marked as bad. The format program then creates the boot sector; an empty root directory; the file allocation table; and, optionally, a label and a copy of the DOS system files. If you used the /S parameter, the disk is made bootable by writing a copy of the Novell DOS system files.

When you format a floppy disk, you need to specify the capacity you want formatted onto the disk and whether you want system files included on the disk. Check to ensure that your drive is capable of formatting to the capacity you want.

Floppy disks are available in two physical sizes, 5 1/4 inch and 3 1/2 inch, and in various capacities for each physical size (see table 8.3).

Table 8.3 DOS Standard Floppy Disk Formats

Disk	Tracks	Sectors	Sides	Capacity
5 1/4 inch	40	8	1	160K
5 1/4 inch	40	9	1	180K
5 1/4 inch	40	8	2	320K
5 1/4 inch	40	9	2	360K
5 1/4 inch	80	15	2	1.2M
3 1/2 inch	80	9	2	720K
3 1/2 inch	80	18	2	1.44M
3 1/2 inch	80	36	2	2.88M

Table 8.4 lists the format switches to use with various disk sizes.

Table 8.4 Valid Format Capacity Entries		
Disk	**Capacity**	**Format Switch**
5 1/4 inch	160K	/F:160
5 1/4 inch	180K	/F:180
5 1/4 inch	320K	/F:320
5 1/4 inch	360K	/F:360
5 1/4 inch	1.2M	/F:1.2
3 1/2 inch	720K	/F:720
3 1/2 inch	1.44M	/F:1.44
3 1/2 inch	1.88M	/F:2.88

If the floppy disk was previously formatted and no format switches are used, the format program defaults to the existing capacity on the disk. Specifying a different capacity, by using the format switches, rewrites the floppy disk at the new capacity and also makes recovery of any old information impossible. For a new floppy disk, the default format capacity is the highest capacity possible with the specified disk drive. Use tables 8.1 and 8.2 to determine which switches to use for what disk capacity.

Floppy disks are manufactured for a specific capacity. Specifying the wrong capacity when formatting may result in a format failure, an excessive number of bad tracks, or a disk that may seem OK initially but later proves to be unreliable. The type of error depends on the computer system's design.

Floppy disks of 5 1/4 inches are available in two density formats: double-density and high-density.

Regular disks, usually labeled double-density, 2D, or DD, are the lower-capacity 5 1/4-inch floppy disks. These disks may be single-sided (abbreviated 1S or SS) with a capacity of 160K or 180K, or double-sided (abbreviated 2S or DS) with a capacity of 320K or 360K. Nearly all 5 1/4-inch disk drives sold today are the double-sided type, meaning that they write information on both sides of the disk.

These disk capacities were used with the early versions of DOS, Versions 1.0 and 1.1. When you format with Novell DOS, you may format disks to these capacities for compatibility with machines still running those DOS versions. Because the most common 5 1/4-inch double-density floppy disk format is 360K, that capacity is sometimes used to refer to this type of drive—a 360K drive.

IBM AT-type computers use high-density (HD) disk drives with a capacity of 1.2M.

Caution

Attempting to format a floppy disk to the wrong capacity usually results in a large number of bad tracks. For instance, the older 360K disk drives have difficulty reading data on floppy disks written on high-density drives, even if the floppy disks were formatted as 360K disks, but especially when the disks are formatted on a high-density drive. Consequently, many computers have both 360K and 1.2M 5 1/4-inch disk drives so that information can be reliably exchanged with computers with either type of 5 1/4-inch drive.

Floppy disks of 3 1/2 inches are available in 720K, 1.44M, and 2.88M capacities, although floppy disk packages are usually labeled with their unformatted capacity of 1M, 2M, and 4M, respectively. All IBM-type computers use 3 1/2-inch double-sided floppy disks; however, some other types of computers use 3 1/2-inch single-sided floppy disks, so single-sided disks are available.

Caution

Some popular computer magazines include advertisements for punches that change a 720K double-density 3 1/2-inch floppy disk into a 1.44M capacity high-density disk. Although to the naked eye, disks of both capacities look the same—except for the special square hole in the corner of the plastic casing—the actual difference is in the electronic properties of the magnetic coating on the internal mylar recording surface. Do not trust your important data on a substandard recording medium.

Formatting Hard Disks. After a hard drive is partitioned with the FDISK command, the formatting is automatically performed, and the disk is ready for use. Thus, using the FORMAT command to format the hard disk is not necessary. You may, however, want to reformat your hard disk if partition sizes were not changed or if the FDISK command was not used.

When you format your hard drive, the /X switch must be used as part of the FORMAT command. This switch is actually a safety feature to prevent you from accidentally issuing the FORMAT command and destroying all the data on your hard disk. When you issue the FORMAT command with the /X switch, a message appears asking whether you are sure you want to format your hard disk. Press Y to proceed with the format process.

Use the /S switch as part of the FORMAT command when formatting the primary partition of your first hard drive. This switch is used to transfer Novell DOS system files to the boot sector of the primary partition. With these system files in the boot sector, Novell DOS is loaded when you start your computer with the primary partition as the active partition. You should include only system files in the primary partition of the first drive because you cannot boot from the other partitions. Putting the system files on other drives does not affect system performance other than the wasted space associated with the unused system files.

> **Caution**
>
> When you format a hard drive, you lose all information on the drive. The information cannot be recovered.

Formatting with a Batch File. In Chapter 19, "Using Batch Files," you learn about the IF ERRORLEVEL command. FORMAT provides specific error codes for this command when it executes, or tries to execute, your instructions from a batch file. The use of this feature can be very useful if you use batch files to format disks. Table 8.5 lists the ERRORLEVEL numbers reported.

Table 8.5 FORMAT ERRORLEVEL Codes

Code	Meaning
0	Execution completed, no errors.
3	Operator aborted execution with Ctrl-C.
4	Error during execution.
5	You entered an N when asked whether to Proceed with Format (Y/N)?

Transferring the Operating System

Use the SYS command if a disk was formatted without the /S switch and you later decide to make the disk bootable. This command writes the boot sector, DOS, and the command processor onto the target disk, enabling your computer to boot Novell DOS. The files are transferred onto the target hard drive from the source drive used to boot Novell DOS. The SYS command replaces any existing operating system with the new system resident on the source drive. The only operand is the target drive.

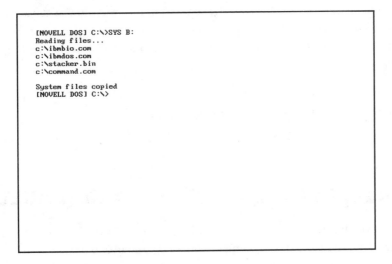

Fig. 8.5
Use the SYS command to make a floppy disk bootable.

Execution of the SYS command requires only that the target disk have enough space available. No particular location is necessary. Executing SYS requires access to COMMAND.COM or whatever is specified by the COMSPEC environment variable. The system is always transferred from the drive used to boot Novell DOS, but the command processor is transferred as the COMSPEC environment indicates. Figure 8.5 shows the results of running the SYS command to make a floppy disk bootable. When you want to boot from this disk, you should also copy any other parts of DOS, such as external commands, that you might need when working with this disk.

Unformatting a Disk with the UNFORMAT Command

You read earlier about the quick or safe format of floppy disks. This is the default method of preparing floppy disks that have been previously used, unless you specified the /U switch. When the quick format is performed, a copy of the system information is stored on an unused area of the disk (as long as there is room). Then, as long as the original files have not been over-written with new data, the UNFORMAT utility can use this information to restore the original files.

You have the best chance of restoring the original data if the reformatted disk has not been used since the quick format. However, if there has been some new data stored, the UNFORMAT command attempts to restore as many of the original files as possible. If the saved system information was replaced with new data, UNFORMAT reports `UNFORMAT information has been over-written`. If UNFORMAT has restored files, it then reports `Disk UNFORMATed successfully`. If you then perform a directory on the restored floppy, you can see the restored files.

The syntax of the UNFORMAT command is simply this:

UNFORMAT *d:*

Changing the Label of a Disk (LABEL)

When you format a disk, you can specify a label for the disk. But what if you didn't specify a label at that point, or you want to change that label later? Use the LABEL command to place an internal label on a disk. This label appears whenever you request a directory of a disk, or when you use the VOL command to display the current label. A label can be added when you format a disk.

To add, change, or delete an existing label, use either of the following procedures:

- Enter the LABEL command with a drive letter, colon, and label. A label can be up to 11 characters long and may include letters, numbers, or spaces, but not these symbols:

    < > = , ; : . * ? [ ] ( ) / \ +

    For example, enter **LABEL B:NEWVOL** to replace the existing label with the new label NEWVOL.

- When you enter the LABEL command with only a drive letter, such as **LABEL B:**, Novell DOS displays the current label and prompts you for a new label (see fig. 8.6). Type the new label and press Enter.

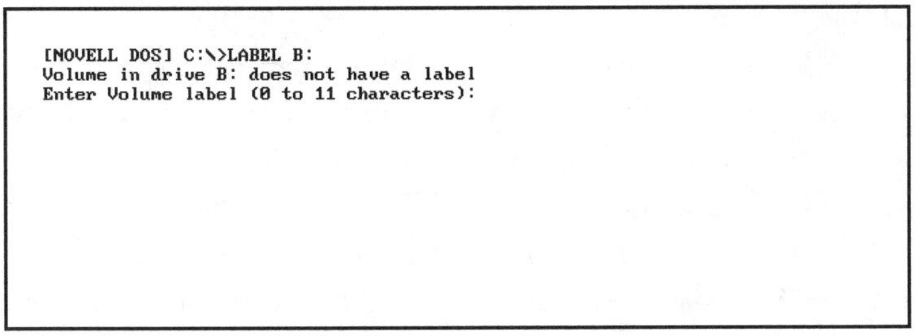

```
[NOVELL DOS] C:\>LABEL B:
Volume in drive B: does not have a label
Enter Volume label (0 to 11 characters):
```

Fig. 8.6
The LABEL com-
mand prompts
you for a new label
if you don't enter
one on the
command line.

To delete the existing label, press Enter at the prompt that asks whether you
want to delete the existing label. Then press Y to delete the label. Figure 8.7
shows the resulting screen when you run LABEL to delete a disk label.

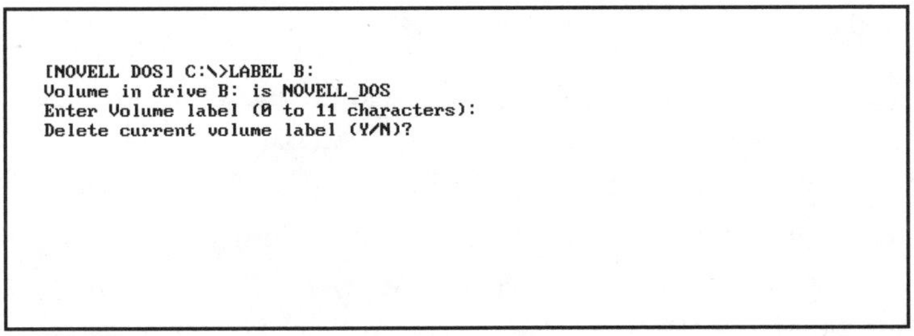

```
[NOVELL DOS] C:\>LABEL B:
Volume in drive B: is NOVELL_DOS
Enter Volume label (0 to 11 characters):
Delete current volume label (Y/N)?
```

Fig. 8.7
The LABEL
command deletes
a label if you press
Enter when
requested to
supply a label.

The internal VOL command displays the current disk volume label of the
default drive or a specified drive.

Installing Multiple Versions of DOS

In the earlier section "Activating Partitions," you learned that you cannot
install more than one active DOS partition on your hard disk, but there is a
way you can install more than one DOS version at the same time. You do this
by using LOADER.COM, a utility originally provided by Digital Research with
its DR MultiUser DOS—a multiuser, multitasking, DOS-compatible operating
system. Novell has made the LOADER.COM utility available to the public on
the CompuServe information and bulletin board service (BBS) for the cost of
the download time.

Briefly, what the LOADER.COM utility does is rewrite the hard disk boot
track with a command to read a special text file that contains the information on multiple DOS versions, and provide a menu for you to choose which
operating system is to be booted with a timeout default if you do not make
another selection within the specified number of seconds.

The first thing you must do is access CompuServe and then enter **GO NOVLIB**. The NOVLIB forum is the Novell library forum where all public files provided by Novell are downloadable. If you are not already a member, you must join (JOIN) the forum. There is no special fee for joining this forum, just the usual CompuServe access and use charges. Once in the forum, you go to the libraries and then to library 12 from the CompuServe menu. Download the file LOADER.ZIP. This file is compressed with PKZIP, which is also available to download if you do not have it. Here is the command to decompress the ZIP file:

```
PKUNZIP LOADER
```

LOADER.ZIP is only 15K and should take a couple of minutes to download at 2400 baud.

After you have downloaded and decompressed the file, four files are available for your use: LOADER.COM, LOADER.DOC, README.1ST, and UNLOAD.EXE. LOADER.COM is the multiboot utility. LOADER.DOC is a text file and contains complete detailed instructions for using the utility with MS-DOS, PC DOS, DR DOS, Novell DOS, DR MultiUser DOS, OS/2, and Interactive UNIX. README.1ST is another document text file with an overview of the utility. UNLOAD.EXE is a utility to remove the multiboot capability of your system if the required multiboot files have been erased or damaged.

If you decide to use this utility, print the entire six-page LOADER.DOC text file with the following command:

```
PRINT LOADER.DOC
```

This document contains detailed instructions on using the utility. Also print README.1ST with this command:

```
PRINT README.1ST
```

From Here...

In this chapter, you learned how to prepare hard disks and floppy disks for use in your computer, and you learned about the command to unformat a disk in case you accidentally formatted over important information.

For more information on disks, read the following chapters:

■ Chapter 9, "Copying and Comparing Disks," teaches you about using other disk commands.

■ Chapter 10, "Undeleting Files," shows you how to protect your information from accidental erasure.

■ Chapter 11, "Disk Optimization Utilities," discusses the ways to improve your computer's hard disk performance.

Chapter 9

Copying and Comparing Disks

To protect your investment, and your sanity if an original disk gets damaged or lost, make a working duplicate of each disk and safely store the original by using the DISKCOPY and DISKCOMP commands. These commands can be good insurance against something happening to your original floppy disks. DISKCOPY duplicates a disk; DISKCOMP ensures that the copy is accurate.

Several methods are available to make copies of floppy disks. DISKCOPY, the most straightforward method, makes an exact copy of a disk onto another disk of the same size and capacity only. The COPY and XCOPY commands make copies onto floppy disks of a different type or size. (See Chapter 7, "Managing Files and Directories," for details on COPY and DISKCOPY.)

In this chapter, you learn to do the following:

- Duplicate floppy disks of the same type and size

- Prepare multiple copies of a disk with DISKCOPY

- Duplicate floppy disks of a different type and size

- Compare two floppy disks to see whether they are identical

Copying Disks (DISKCOPY)

The DISKCOPY command makes identical copies of floppy disks. Use it on floppy disks only, not on hard disks. DISKCOPY can be used to make identical copies only—on a disk of the same size and with the same format.

DISKCOPY can use a single drive to make a copy on the same drive. A special form of DISKCOPY enables you to make multiple copies of the same disk.

> **Caution**
>
> When you use DISKCOPY, any files already on the destination disk are overwritten, and you are not warned!

DISKCOPY works with the contents of tracks rather than the contents of files. Instead of reading and writing files, DISKCOPY reads the contents of each track and writes a matching output track. Because DISKCOPY copies all tracks—including the boot sector, the root directory, and the file allocation table (FAT)—DISKCOPY can make copies on disks of the same type and capacity only.

The *output* disk is a DOS disk because the *input* disk was a DOS disk. If the output disk has not been formatted or has a different format, DISKCOPY attempts to format it to match the input disk.

DISKCOPY has several switches, listed in table 9.1.

Table 9.1 DISKCOPY Command Switches

Switch	Use
/1	Copies only the first side of a double-sided floppy
/A	Creates an audible sound when comparison is complete or when you need to change disks
/M	Prepares multiple copies of a single source disk
/V	Verifies the status of a disk to ensure that there are no errors in copying the disk

The /1 switch tells DISKCOPY to ignore the second side of the original disk. Use this switch if the original disk is single-sided and the disk cannot otherwise be copied. Only 5 1/4-inch disks can be single-sided.

Use /M to make more than one copy from the single source disk. DISKCOPY reads in the first disk and then continues writing copies as long as you continue to answer Y to the prompt. If you need to copy a second input disk with this parameter, use the DISKCOPY command again.

Add /A to have DISKCOPY sound an audible alarm when the copy finishes or when you are prompted to insert a new disk. This feature enables you to work on other tasks without having to monitor the display continually.

To copy a disk onto a different drive, use this command:

```
DISKCOPY A: B:
```

To copy the disk, using the same drive as output, enter the following command:

```
DISKCOPY A: A: /A
```

The /A makes an audible tone when you need to change floppy disks.

If you want to make multiple copies of the same disk, use this command:

```
DISKCOPY A: A: /M
```

Specifying the Source and Destination Disks

DISKCOPY requires that you specify a *source drive* and a *destination drive*. If the destination is omitted, the default is the source drive. If both the source and the destination are omitted, the current drive is both the source and the destination but only if the command is issued from a floppy drive. If you issue the command from a hard drive and do not include at least the source drive, the following error message is issued:

```
Specified drive is invalid, or non-removable media
```

If the same drive is specified (or defaulted to) for both the source and the destination, DISKCOPY reads as much as possible into memory and then prompts you to change disks. DISKCOPY then writes the contents of memory and again prompts you to change back to the source disk. You are prompted to change disks as many times as necessary to perform the copy. Figure 9.1 shows the screen results when you use DISKCOPY to copy a large floppy disk (unformatted) on the same drive.

Fig. 9.1

DISKCOPY of a
1.44M floppy disk
to the same drive.
The floppy was
formatted by
DISKCOPY.

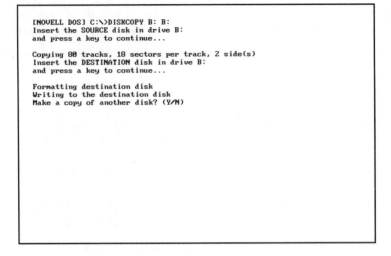

```
[NOVELL DOS] C:\>DISKCOPY B: B:
Insert the SOURCE disk in drive B:
and press a key to continue...

Copying 80 tracks, 18 sectors per track, 2 side(s)
Insert the DESTINATION disk in drive B:
and press a key to continue...

Formatting destination disk
Writing to the destination disk
Make a copy of another disk? (Y/N)
```

Because DISKCOPY uses all available memory of any type, it can use expanded or extended memory to copy a high-density disk (720K, 1.2M, 1.44M,
or 2.88M) with only one change of disks. DISKCOPY can use expanded or
extended memory if you have expanded or extended memory in your computer. You must also be using EMM386.EXE or HIMEM.SYS as your memory
manager. See Chapter 22, "Optimizing Memory," for more information about
expanded and extended memory on your computer.

If you have neither type of memory manager nor enough memory,
DISKCOPY attempts to use space on your hard disk to store an intermediate
copy. To use the hard disk in this manner, make sure that the environment
variable TEMP has a value, a drive letter, and the name of a directory on that
disk. The Novell DOS Install process normally creates your AUTOEXEC.BAT
file with a SET command to define the TEMP variable with the proper value.
To check whether TEMP has been defined, use the SET command by itself
with no operands. Look through the resulting output for a line that begins
with TEMP=. If you see this line, DISKCOPY writes a temporary file to the drive
and directory on the right of that line. If that line is not present, use the following commands to create a directory and set TEMP to point to it:

```
MD C:\TEMP
SET TEMP=C:\TEMP
```

DISKCOPY creates a temporary file on that disk to store the data for the copy
if it doesn't all fit into memory.

Copying Disks with an Image File

If you prefer, the source or the destination may be an *image file*, a file that contains an exact image of a disk. Use the DISKCOPY command with the second parameter specifying a file name instead of a drive letter. The file name usually has an extension of IMG. The image normally is exactly the same capacity as the source disk and is written to a hard disk. After you have created the image file, you can then use DISKCOPY with the image file as input. Only the source or the destination may be an image file, not both.

With image files, DISKCOPY can make multiple copies of a single source file with the minimum amount of disk changing. Figure 9.2 shows a DISKCOPY to an image file on the hard drive.

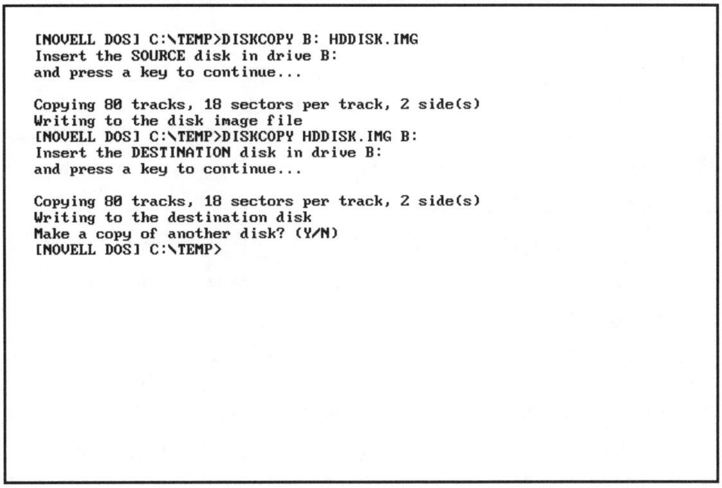

```
[NOVELL DOS] C:\TEMP>DISKCOPY B: HDDISK.IMG
Insert the SOURCE disk in drive B:
and press a key to continue...

Copying 80 tracks, 18 sectors per track, 2 side(s)
Writing to the disk image file
[NOVELL DOS] C:\TEMP>DISKCOPY HDDISK.IMG B:
Insert the DESTINATION disk in drive B:
and press a key to continue...

Copying 80 tracks, 18 sectors per track, 2 side(s)
Writing to the destination disk
Make a copy of another disk? (Y/N)
[NOVELL DOS] C:\TEMP>
```

Fig. 9.2
DISKCOPY of a floppy disk to an image file, and of an image file to a floppy disk.

Dealing with DISKCOPY Errors

The response to an error in DISKCOPY depends on the source of the error. Examine the error message to get a clue about the possible reason. Errors in DISKCOPY can have one of the following causes:

- If DISKCOPY detects a bad area on the output disk, it quits with the message `Bad track detected while formatting`. The destination disk cannot have any bad sectors; although the disk probably could be useful for normal purposes, it cannot be used by DISKCOPY.

- If the disk has only a few errors—just one error causes DISKCOPY to quit—it works fine for normal use, but the DISKCOPY disk must be an *exact* track-for-track copy of the input disk. Try a different output disk.

- DISKCOPY does not write to a different type of disk drive. If DISKCOPY ends with an error message stating that the drives are of different types, try making the copy on a different drive. Because the input drive always is the same type as itself, you can always make the copy on the same drive.

- If, in trying to copy to a different drive, DISKCOPY quits with the Disk type or format error message but you know that the drives are actually the same type, you should check your computer's setup. An incorrect value in the setup information can cause this error.

- An error reading from the input disk can come from several sources, including how the original was created. If the source disk was a single-sided disk and the second side was never formatted, this error may result. In the case of single-sided input, the solution is to use the /1 parameter to force DISKCOPY to read the first side only.

- An input error might result from the method used to create the original disk. Some early machines, used by software manufacturers to replicate their floppy disks, formatted and copied only the tracks that contained data. Because the floppy disks were write-protected and no files referenced the unformatted areas, this feature was invisible to users under most circumstances.

  DISKCOPY attempts to copy all areas, even those that were never formatted. The output probably is OK as long as the DISKCOPY is completed. This problem is most likely to occur with older, original-software floppy disks.

- An error message referring to the output disk often indicates that the disk is write-protected. If it is not write-protected, the message means that there actually was an error—try a different disk.

  If this message recurs, check the type of disk you are using for the output. The disk must have been manufactured for the capacity you are writing. Make sure that it is the correct type. For 5 1/4-inch disks, use HD (high-density) for 1.2M and DSDD (double-sided double-density) for 360K. For 3 1/2-inch disks, use either DSDD (or 1.0M unformatted capacity) floppy disks for 720K, or DSHD floppy disks (labeled as 2.0 for 1.44M or 4.0 for 2.88M). The specific labeling varies by manufacturer.

■ The Destination drive is locked message means that another program is using the drive. You are most likely running DISKCOPY under
Task Manager, Desqview, Windows, or some other multitasking monitor. If another program also is using the drive, DISKCOPY is unable to
have you swap the input disk for the output disk. DISKCOPY cannot
run in this instance unless you end the other program or write the output to a different disk drive.

Copying Disks with Different Capacities

To copy between floppy disks of different types, you must copy the files, not
the disk structure. The XCOPY command, with wild cards, provides a good
method to do this. XCOPY reads a list of files and then writes them to the
output.

Tip
Unlike DISKCOPY,
XCOPY can copy
between a disk
and the hard
drive.

When you use XCOPY, make sure that the destination disk can contain all
the source files. XCOPY leaves any previously existing files unless they are
replaced by files of the same name. XCOPY does not delete system files if the
source disk was not bootable.

To copy all files from the source to a second drive, use the following command:

```
XCOPY A:\*.* B:\ /L /S /E
```

This command copies all files from drive A to drive B. It also copies the disk
label (because the /L parameter is specified). All files in the root directory of
drive A are copied. The /S parameter is used, so all subdirectories and their
contents are copied. Because the /E parameter is used, even empty
subdirectories are copied.

If the drive is omitted, XCOPY defaults to the current drive. If the path name
is omitted, XCOPY defaults to the current directory on that drive. If you use
the same target drive as the source, the output is created on the same disk.

XCOPY does not prompt you to insert a different disk. Most PCs with a single
floppy disk treat drive A as a different drive from B and prompt you to insert
a different disk. You cannot use XCOPY if you have two floppy disk drives.
The alternative is to use a subdirectory on your hard drive.

If you use DISKCOPY to copy a disk, the output is bootable if the source is. If
you use XCOPY, however, you need to use SYS to make the output bootable.
Using /H with XCOPY to copy the hidden files on the source disk does not,

by itself, make the destination bootable. Even if the destination is bootable already, you still may need to use SYS if you want a bootable disk. Using SYS ensures that Novell DOS is on the resulting system and that the boot sector, hidden files, and COMMAND.COM are all the same type (vendor and level).

Caution

Because the allocation units (clusters) and root directories are different sizes on different types of floppy disks, files might not fit even if sufficient space seems to be available. Floppy disks formatted differently have different capacities. If the destination disk has bad tracks, there may not be enough space.

After using XCOPY, check the output carefully to be sure that there were no error messages and that all files were copied.

Comparing Disks

Use the Novell DOS disk-comparison facilities to be absolutely certain that a copy of a disk is identical to the original. If you suspect that your working copy has become corrupted somehow, use these facilities to test that hypothesis. You also can use DISKCOMP after using DISKCOPY to be completely sure that the copy is OK. Another possible use of DISKCOMP is to verify that all tracks of a disk can be read.

If you have copied to a disk of another size or capacity, you must use file-by-file utilities instead of DISKCOMP. In that case, use either FC (file compare) or COMP (compare) to compare the files. These commands are discussed fully in Chapter 7, "Managing Files and Directories."

Comparing Similar Disks (DISKCOMP)

The DISKCOMP utility compares one disk with a second disk. DISKCOMP can also be used to verify that a disk can be read. The two disks must have the same size and format. To be considered identical—containing identical data on every single track—the disks must have been copied with DISKCOPY.

You may compare two disks even if you have only one disk drive of that type. DISKCOMP can also compare a single original disk against multiple copies. A simplified form of DISKCOMP tests a disk to ensure that all parts of the disk can be read.

Use the following command to compare two disks that must be placed in the same floppy drive:

```
DISKCOMP A: A:
```

If you used DISKCOPY to make an image copy of a floppy disk, use the following command to compare the image file with the original disk:

```
DISKCOMP DISK.IMG A:
```

Use the DISKCOMP command with the source drive and the second drive. If you omit one or both, the default is the current drive. The drives can be the same, in which case DISKCOMP prompts you to change disks when necessary. See figure 9.3 for an image of the screen when you compare two disks on the same drive.

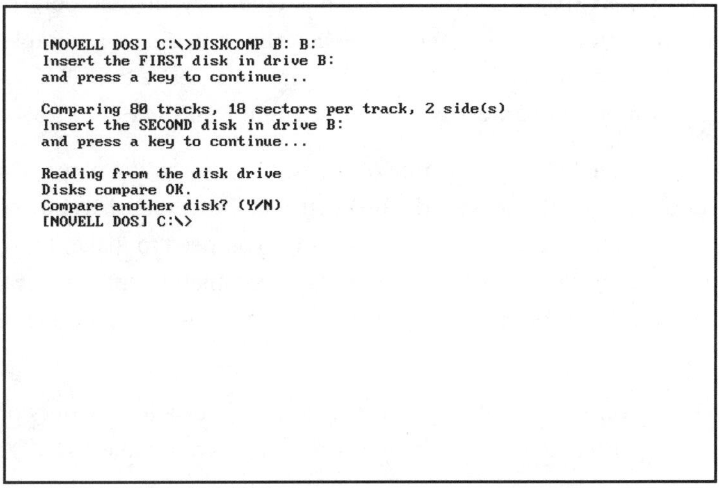

```
[NOVELL DOS] C:\>DISKCOMP B: B:
Insert the FIRST disk in drive B:
and press a key to continue...

Comparing 80 tracks, 18 sectors per track, 2 side(s)
Insert the SECOND disk in drive B:
and press a key to continue...

Reading from the disk drive
Disks compare OK.
Compare another disk? (Y/N)
[NOVELL DOS] C:\>
```

Fig. 9.3
DISKCOMP of two disks on drive A. Both disks are identical.

DISKCOMP reads each track on the first disk and stores the contents in memory. Then the second disk is read in. Every track of the second disk is read and compared with the stored copy of the first disk. If any difference is found—even in an unused area of the disk—DISKCOMP displays the track number where the difference was found. DISKCOMP continues to compare tracks and may report the same track several times. Refer to figure 9.4 to see the results when the two floppy disks are not exactly identical.

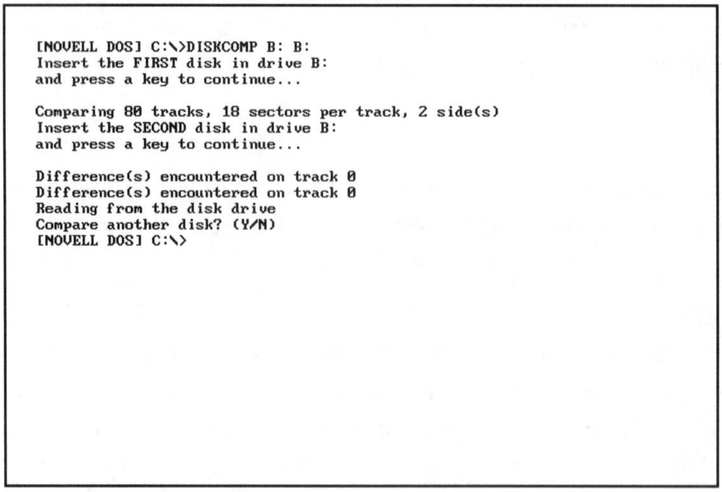

Fig. 9.4

The results of
DISKCOMP when
the disks are
almost, but not
quite, identical.

```
[NOVELL DOS] C:\>DISKCOMP B: B:
Insert the FIRST disk in drive B:
and press a key to continue...

Comparing 80 tracks, 18 sectors per track, 2 side(s)
Insert the SECOND disk in drive B:
and press a key to continue...

Difference(s) encountered on track 0
Difference(s) encountered on track 0
Reading from the disk drive
Compare another disk? (Y/N)
[NOVELL DOS] C:\>
```

DISKCOMP uses expanded memory, extended memory, or a temporary file to minimize the number of disk changes. When the comparison is complete, DISKCOMP asks whether you want to compare more disks. Press Y if you want to continue comparing disks. Press N to end DISKCOMP.

When you use DISKCOMP with one of the two files set to the name of an image file, DISKCOMP can read the image from a faster disk drive. Use this method to minimize the number of disk swaps you need to make. The image file must have been made with the DISKCOPY command. Only one of the two drives can be an image file—you cannot compare an image file to an image file.

Switches can force DISKCOMP to compare a specific disk format only or to operate in a particular way. The switches are described in table 9.2.

Table 9.2 DISKCOMP Command Switches

Switch	Use
/1	Compares just the first side of a disk. Use this switch only if DISKCOMP incorrectly determines that the disk is double-sided when in fact it is single-sided.
/8	Compares the first eight sectors per track. FORMAT can write a disk with nine sectors per track (a 360K disk), but may use only the first eight sectors to make a 320K disk. Use the /8 switch to compare two disks formatted in this fashion. The /8 switch is necessary only if the first disk was formatted with just eight sectors per track and the second disk was formatted with nine sectors per track, but used only eight.

Switch	Use
/A	Makes an audible sound to attract your attention when the comparison is complete or when you need to change disks.
/M	Compares multiple disks. DISKCOMP normally enables you to compare several disks, but it reads the first disk again. The /M switch causes DISKCOMP to compare one disk against several copies. The first disk is not reread. Use this option to ensure that several disks are identical in all respects.
/V	Verifies that there are no errors in reading the data from a disk. When you use /V, DISKCOMP reads the first drive or image file only, but displays the location of any disk errors encountered. Doing a verify does not guarantee that the output disk is correct, but under most circumstances, a disk is read correctly. DISKCOMP used with the /V switch detects read errors. You can use the /V switch to verify the status of a frequently used disk, even if you haven't made a copy of it.

Note

The /1 and /8 switches apply to 5 1/4-inch disks only. You should use them only if you attempt to compare two disks and DISKCOMP reports that they are not the same. A possible cause for the miscomparison is the difference in formatting, so try again. Use CHKDSK to determine the capacity of the first disk, and then use either /8 or /1.

Note

You cannot use DISKCOMP with drives that are networked or with drives that have been changed with ASSIGN, JOIN, or SUBST.

Comparing Dissimilar Disks (FC and COMP)

You must make a file-by-file comparison to compare two disks of unlike capacities. The FC (file compare) program can be used to compare the contents of files. FC verifies only that the contents are the same; the names might be different. Because FC can use wild cards within the same directory only, use FC to compare the contents of each directory. Use the following command:

```
FC A:\*.* B:\*.*
```

You must have an idea of the type of file: binary or text. FC assumes that files with extensions of COM, EXE, LIB, OBJ, SYS, and BIN are binary files. If a binary file has another extension, use /B to indicate binary.

If FC gives the error message File contains a line longer than 256 bytes, the usual cause is that an ASCII (default) comparison was performed between binary files. FC ignores differences in spacing in performing an ASCII comparison. A binary comparison requires every byte to be identical to report identical files.

You can perform a more exact comparison (a byte-for-byte comparison) by using COMP. The files specified to the COMP program can be wild cards, directories (all files in the directory), or disks. To compare all files in the root directory of drive A with those in the drive B, use this command:

```
COMP A: B:
```

Both methods compare the files on drive A only. If the second drive has additional files, you must determine that with directory listings. A wide directory listing—created with the DIR command and the /W parameter—can be useful because it may prevent the screen from scrolling. If you have few enough files, you can see directory listings for both drives at the same time on a wide directory listing. If the file listings don't fit, you may need to redirect the listings to a file, and examine the list of file names. Use the following commands to capture the sorted output of both drives:

```
XDIR A:\*.* /S >C:\FILELIST.TXT
XDIR B:\*.* /S >>C:\FILELIST.TXT
TYPE C:FILELIST.TXT
```

These techniques of comparing files enable you to determine that the files of each disk are identical. To make sure that the disk is bootable, test it by booting from it. If you don't have a disk drive of the proper type, your next best solution is to reissue the SYS command with a target of the desired drive.

From Here...

Now that you have learned how to make copies of disks and compare them, you can turn to the following chapters:

- Chapter 7, "Managing Files and Directories," discusses the commands to copy and compare files.

- Chapter 10, "Undeleting Files," shows you how to protect your information from accidental erasures.

- Chapter 11, "Disk Optimization Utilities," discusses the ways to improve your computer's hard disk performance.

- Chapter 12, "Backup Utilities," shows you how to prepare backup copies of your programs and information.

IV

Disk and File Management

Chapter 10

Undeleting Files

Computers are useful things. They can store huge amounts of data in a way that is easy to retrieve. They can help you do calculations, keep track of birthdays, and make your newsletters look great. But they are also highly susceptible to human error.

Suppose that you have just deleted a file you didn't mean to delete. You are probably not nearly as embarrassed as you are angry. But you realized the error just a little too late, and now you don't know what to do. You look where the file used to be, entering **DIR** again and again in some vain hope that the file might pop in as suddenly as it popped out. But it's gone. Or is it? Before you start cursing the whole technology revolution and kick your computer off the desk, take a minute to calm down. There is probably a good chance you can get your file back, especially if you realized it was gone two seconds after you killed it.

As easy as it is to create files of precious data on the computer, it is far easier to erase them—and to erase the wrong ones. Knowing how to handle that situation if it does happen, as well as which tools to use, can make all the difference in recovering lost data. And even if you cannot get your data back, you can take some measures to make sure that you will get a file back if you make that mistake again.

This chapter covers the following topics:

- Protecting the FAT
- Protecting deleted files
- Recovering deleted files
- Preventing accidental deletions

Understanding the File Allocation Table (FAT)

Your computer keeps track of all files and where they exist on the disk. This information is in the *file allocation table (FAT)*. Whenever an application accesses a file, it looks in the FAT to see where to go on the drive to read the data.

When you delete a file, the operating system does not go to the area of the disk where the file resides and wipe out the bits—the ones and zeros—of data. That would take too long and would be terribly inefficient. Instead, when you delete a file, the operating system goes to the FAT and alters the first byte of the file name entry. This point is important: deleting a file alters only the file's name, not the data the file contains. The data still physically exists on the hard drive in the same space it took up before you "deleted" it. DOS ignores files if the first byte is altered. And it knows that the space taken up by that file is now available for other files. So it is not until other files start writing over the physical space that the data of the "deleted" file get truly erased.

Understanding the Undelete Process

UNDELETE is a Novell DOS 7 program that attempts to recover deleted files. Unless you are using DISKMAP or DELWATCH (two utilities you learn about later in the chapter), UNDELETE tries to perform an unaided recovery of the files. It goes to the FAT and looks for file names that have been altered by the DELETE command. When UNDELETE finds one of those entries, it checks whether the data that took up the physical space is still fully intact. If it is, the program can effectively "undelete" the file. If part of the space has been taken up by another file, or if the FAT entries have been overwritten, the file cannot be recovered. See the section "Recovering Deleted Files with UNDELETE" later in this chapter for more information about the UNDELETE utility.

Your chances of recovering a deleted file, then, are much greater if very little time has passed since you deleted the file. The more time that goes by, the better the chance that some other file is using that space on the hard drive, making your file unrecoverable. This is why you need some of the other utilities Novell DOS 7 provides.

Protecting the FAT with the DISKMAP Utility

DISKMAP is a utility that copies the FAT and saves it to a file on the disk. When you run DISKMAP, it takes a "snapshot" of the FAT as it exists at that moment. DISKMAP is not a TSR (terminate-and-stay-resident) program, so it does not stay in memory. As soon as the FAT is copied, the utility unloads itself. The file that it creates remains unchanged until the next time you run DISKMAP. The next time you run it, whether at boot time or later, the most recent copy of the FAT is read and copied to the file, overwriting the old copy.

The disk map helps UNDELETE recover files because UNDELETE looks at the file that DISKMAP creates to see where on the disk to look for the file. The disk map is especially helpful to UNDELETE if the drive's files are severely fragmented. If the file that you are trying to recover was split into pieces at different locations on the hard drive, your chances of recovering this deleted file are better if you run DISKMAP because the data file will know all the places to find the different sections of the file. And DISKMAP records the number of files contained in a directory. UNDELETE also uses this information to help recover accidentally erased files.

UNDELETE uses the information from the DISKMAP.DAT file to help recover deleted files, but UNDELETE works only if the space the file took on the disk has not been used by another file. If you want a better chance to recover deleted files, you should load DELWATCH in connection with DISKMAP. For more information about DELWATCH, see the section "Installing DELWATCH" later on in this chapter.

You can make DISKMAP run when you first boot your computer by running it from your AUTOEXEC.BAT batch file, as described in the following section.

Enabling DISKMAP

The easiest way to set up DISKMAP in your AUTOEXEC.BAT file is from the Novell DOS 7 Setup utility. To see how it is done, go to the \NWDOS directory and enter **SETUP**. You are probably familiar with this utility by now, so you will recognize the opening screens. You access DISKMAP and DELWATCH (discussed shortly) from the Data Protection & Security screen. To get there, highlight the Data Protection & Security option and press Enter.

Four security options are listed with check boxes next to them. One of these options is DISKMAP File Recovery Utility. To have Novell DOS 7 load this utility for you, highlight the check box next to this option and press the space bar to select it (see fig. 10.1). That's all there is to it. Highlight the Exit This Screen button and press Enter. Then highlight the Save Changes and Exit button, press Enter, and follow the instructions to restart the operating system.

Fig. 10.1

Enabling DISKMAP from the Setup utility.

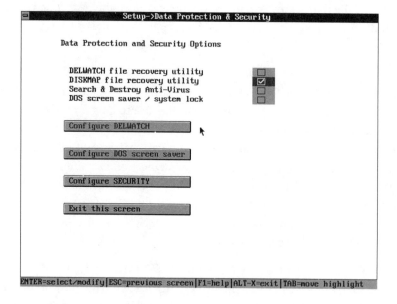

Your new AUTOEXEC.BAT file should include the following line:

```
DISKMAP C:
```

You have learned how to load DISKMAP with the Setup utility, but you can do it yourself by manually editing the AUTOEXEC.BAT file with the Novell DOS 7 text editor. For details, see Chapter 17, "Using the Novell DOS Text Editor."

DISKMAP has a switch that you can use to re-create the DISKMAP.DAT file. DISKMAP /D erases the file and then re-creates it. Without the /D switch, the file is merely updated with any new information. You would need the /D option only if you suspect that the DISKMAP.DAT may be corrupt and you want to wipe it out completely and create another one.

> **Note**
>
> The file that DISKMAP creates on each disk it maps is called DISKMAP.DAT. It is a
> read-only file, so you cannot delete it without removing the read-only attribute. If
> you ever need to delete this file, change the attribute by entering the following:
>
> ```
> ATTRIB -R DISKMAP.DAT
> ```
>
> This removes the read-only attribute of the file so that you can delete it. Note that if
> the file is deleted, the disk is no longer mapped.

Protecting Multiple Drives with DISKMAP

By default, the Setup utility protects only drive C. If you want to make copies
of the FAT of other drives (for example, floppy disks), you can include other
drive letters after, or in place of, C:. Data files on floppy disks are sometimes
just as important as files on your hard drive. If you do want copies of the FAT
of floppy disks, make sure that the disk is inserted in the drive by the time
your system gets to this line in AUTOEXEC.BAT. Unless this disk is also your
system boot disk, you will have to wait for your computer to start loading the
operating system, before you insert the floppy. Once your computer starts
booting, it displays the message `Starting DOS....` If you insert the floppy too
soon, the computer will assume that you want to boot from the floppy disk.
If you insert the floppy too late, Novell DOS 7 will not be able to read the
FAT from your floppy disk and will return the following message:

```
Not ready error reading drive A
Abort, Retry, Fail?
```

If you are unsure about the timing, you can always wait until this message
appears, insert the floppy in the drive, and press R for retry. Although
DOSBook tells you how to do it, mapping floppies at bootup can be trouble-
some. You may prefer to do it from the command line, after bootup.

Understanding DISKMAP Configuration Options

If you like, you can have DISKMAP run every time you return to a system
prompt. If you are in an application that changes data files (such as a word
processor or spreadsheet), when you exit the application and get a prompt
back, the changes to the FAT are automatically recorded. The procedure to
run DISKMAP every time involves two steps, both of which can be included
in the AUTOEXEC.BAT file.

The first step is to set an environment variable that tells the PROMPT command what to do. The environment variable that you need to set is called PEXEC. Somewhere in your AUTOEXEC.BAT file, before the PROMPT command, insert the following line:

```
SET PEXEC=C:\NWDOS\DISKMAP C:
```

This line assumes that the DISKMAP program is in the \NWDOS subdirectory and that the drive you want to run DISKMAP for is drive C.

The second step is to change your PROMPT statement to use the PEXEC environment variable:

```
PROMPT $X$P$G
```

The $X portion tells the prompt to execute whatever command the PEXEC variable is set to.

If you enter both commands and then run a program, when the program is done, you will see a short delay before the command prompt reappears as DISKMAP writes the file. To try it out, enter MEM at the command prompt and notice the pause. It might take you a little while to get used to the wait, but you will be assured that the DISKMAP.DAT file is always current.

If waiting for the prompt to return after you exit a program confuses you, try a new prompt with a reminder. After you set the PEXEC environment variable, enter the following prompt at the command line or in a batch file:

```
PROMPT Wait...$X$H$H$H$H$H$H$H$P$G
```

Now every time you return to a command prompt again, your screen will display the message Wait... while the file is written to disk. When the file has been written, the seven $Hs make the cursor backspace seven characters to erase the Wait... message before your normal prompt (PG) is displayed.

> **Note**
>
> For more information about different PROMPT statements, see the Novell DOS 7 DOSBook on-line documentation program or the Command Reference in Part X of this book.

Handling Deleted Files with DELWATCH and DELPURGE

Another utility provided by Novell DOS 7 to help you recover deleted files is DELWATCH. DELWATCH is a TSR program that automatically saves the files you delete. But if it saves them, how do you delete files? DELWATCH marks them as "pending delete." This means that the files will not show up in a directory if you enter the DIR command, but the space they occupied will not be overwritten with other files either.

If your disk ever gets full of pending-delete files, DELWATCH will remove the oldest files you deleted. The utility really does delete them to make room for new files on your disk. But files you erased last week will disappear before files you erased this morning. DELWATCH assumes that the longer a pending-delete file hangs around without being recovered, chances are that you will not want to recover it. That works pretty well. You usually realize whether or not you deleted the wrong file within a short time anyway.

There is only one problem with DELWATCH saving all your deleted files and removing the oldest ones as new files are created: if your hard drive is full, and DELWATCH has to make room for every new file you create, system performance will be affected. So, in addition to removing files as hard drive space becomes scarce, you can configure DELWATCH to save only a certain number of files (200 is the default). When you delete the 201st file, DELWATCH automatically removes the oldest file it was saving.

There is another way to have DELWATCH remove the files it is saving. You can use DELPURGE to get rid of pending-delete files. DELPURGE is discussed in more detail later in this chapter.

Installing DELWATCH

The easiest way to install and configure DELWATCH is through the Novell DOS 7 Setup utility. To start Setup, go to the \NWDOS directory and enter **SETUP**. DELWATCH configuration is found under the Data Protection & Security option, so highlight that option and press Enter. Next move your cursor to the check box beside the DELWATCH File Recovery Utility option. Press the space bar to select that option (a check mark appears in the box); then move the cursor to the Configure DELWATCH button and press Enter.

Specifying the Number of Files to Save. You should now see the DELWATCH Options screen (see fig. 10.2). In this screen, you can configure three DELWATCH options. You use the first option, Maximum Deleted Files Saved, to enter the number of files that you want DELWATCH to hang onto before it starts removing old pending-delete files. The default value, 200, should be fine, but if you think you may need more or fewer files, go ahead and change this number.

Fig. 10.2
The DELWATCH
Options screen.

Saving Multiple Files with the Same Name. The second configurable option is Files with the Same Name Saved. The default value is 1, which means that if you created a file called MYFILE.DOC, deleted it, created a new file called MYFILE.DOC, and then deleted that one, DELWATCH would save only the last file you deleted; the first MYFILE.DOC would not be protected by DELWATCH. This applies only to files in the same directory. If both of those MYFILE.DOC files were in separate directories, DELWATCH would save both of them. If you use the same file names over and over and would like to increase this number, DELWATCH will save more versions of the file—up to 65,535.

If you have many different files with the same name saved by DELWATCH, the only way of telling the versions apart is by the date and time stamp listed by the file in the UNDELETE screen. If you attempt to undelete a file, and a file with the same name still exists in the directory, UNDELETE will prompt you to rename the file before you undelete it.

Including and Excluding Files. The last option has to do with saving only the specific files you delete. By default, DELWATCH saves only the file types listed, but you may have some files that you don't want DELWATCH to save. Or perhaps you want DELWATCH to save only certain files. If so, you can specify which file types fit your criteria. This feature is helpful if you use Windows on your computer. Windows creates several temporary files as it runs; all have the TMP extension. There is really no point in saving these files, so you could have DELWATCH save all file types *except* ones ending in TMP.

You can enter more than one file type in the list; just separate the extensions with a plus sign (+). For example, you can enter **TMP+BAK+OLD**. Then all files with the extensions TMP, BAK, and OLD would be included or excluded from the list of files that DELWATCH saves.

Completing the Installation. When you have the three options configured the way you want them, press the Accept the Above and Continue button. Then exit the Setup utility and reboot your system. Your AUTOEXEC.BAT file should now include a line like the following:

```
DELWATCH C:  /F:200  /B:5  /E:TMP+BAK+OLD
```

The entry in your AUTOEXEC.BAT may be different, depending on which options you selected. This line tells DELWATCH to save only 200 files and that five deleted files in a directory may have the same name. The line also instructs DELWATCH not to save files with the extensions TMP, BAK, and OLD.

Using Other DELWATCH Options. The three configuration options shown on the preceding AUTOEXEX.BAT line are the most commonly used. Other options, however, are available from the command line. The first thing you should realize as you experiment with DELWATCH is that it has more than one help function. Most of the programs or TSRs display help text when you access the programs with a /? or /H switch from the command line. This approach works with DELWATCH too, but it also has a /HI switch that displays help text about installation options, as well as a /HD switch that displays help text about enabling and disabling options. Keep in mind that, by default, DELWATCH is enabled for all hard disk drives. However, you can enable DELWATCH for floppy drives too.

In addition, DELWATCH has other switches. Entering **DELWATCH /S** displays the current status of DELWATCH, including the drives where it is enabled and the number of files with pending-delete status. Entering **DELWATCH /D** disables it for a specific drive. If you want to disable delete-protection on drive C, for example, you can enter **DELWATCH C: /D**. Entering **DELWATCH /U** uninstalls DELWATCH and removes it from memory, but you must disable all drives before using this option. If you try to uninstall the DELWATCH TSR while some drives are still enabled, you will receive an error. (Enter **DELWATCH /S** to find out for which drives DELWATCH is enabled.)

Because memory usage is a concern with all TSRs, you might be interested in DELWATCH's memory options. DELWATCH, by default, loads into extended memory using DPMS, if DPMS is loaded. If you like, you can make DELWATCH load into other memory locations, such as upper memory or conventional memory. You do this with the following switch:

```
DELWATCH /MPmemtype
```

The *memtype* parameter can be X, U, or L for extended, upper, or lower memory, respectively. However, if you specify a memory type and it is not available, DELWATCH will not install. Conversely, you can specify that DELWATCH not load into a certain memory area. You do this with the /MP*memtype*- switch.

Most of the time, you can stick with the default memory values of DELWATCH and not worry about where it is loading. Because of the Novell DOS 7 DPMS capabilities, you should not have any problems running out of conventional memory. Therefore, unless you really know what you are doing with the memory options, do not worry about changing DELWATCH's load space.

Using DELPURGE

You learned earlier that DELWATCH starts removing pending-delete files under two conditions—if your hard drive runs out of space and if the number of pending-delete files exceeds the configured number that DELWATCH saves (default is 200). Occasionally, though, you might want to remove files regardless of these two conditions. Perhaps you deleted a sensitive document, and you do not want other users to have the opportunity to undelete the file so that they can look at it. Or maybe DELWATCH is removing pending-delete files because the hard drive is full and you are noticing performance degradation on your system; you would rather remove all the pending-delete files.

Whatever your reason for removing pending-delete files, DELPURGE makes the removal easy. The utility has a number of switches that you should learn. (Enter **DELPURGE /?** if you want a quick summary.) To list all the pending-delete files in a directory, you cannot use DIR, but you can use DELPURGE /L instead. If the list gets too large to fit on-screen, add the /P switch to pause the list after a screenful of data is displayed.

If you want to view all the pending-delete files on the hard drive—not just the files in the current directory—add the /S switch. This lists files in the current directory and each subdirectory below it. If you want to remove files deleted before a specific time, use the /T:*hh:mm:ss* switch. Or, if you want to remove files deleted before *and including* a specific date, add the /D:*mm-dd-yy* switch. Finally, if you want to purge files deleted a specific number of days ago as well as before that date, use /D:–*n* where *n* equals the number of days.

When you use DELPURGE to delete files, it will prompt you when it comes to a pending-delete file to make sure that you really want to remove it. If you have a long list of files to purge, this process can get tedious. In that case, you can use the /A switch. When you add /A to DELPURGE, you will not be prompted; the files are simply removed. Use /A with caution, however, because you can easily make a mistake and forget about a file you need, only to learn of it too late. That is how the file was accidentally deleted in the first place, right? So, if you plan to use the /A switch regularly, get in the habit of using /L to list the pending-delete files first, just to be safe.

Recovering Deleted Files with UNDELETE

Now that you know the utilities that help make it possible to recover the files you accidentally deleted, you should know about the utility that actually recovers them, UNDELETE. This utility has two interfaces: a command-line interface, where you use switches and file names to recover files; and a menu-driven interface, where you select options and files from a list. The menu-driven UNDELETE is simpler to use, so you learn about it first. To load the UNDELETE utility, get to a DOS prompt and enter **UNDELETE**. The screen displays directories you can change to, along with files that have been deleted but not completely overwritten by other files (see fig. 10.3).

Fig. 10.3
The UNDELETE
utility.

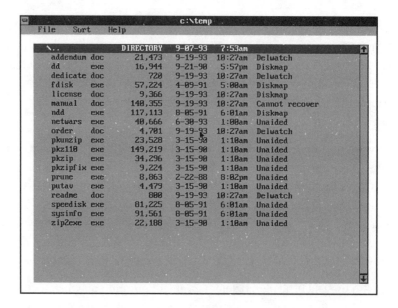

UNDELETE displays the file name, the size of the file, the date and time the
file was last created or modified, and the status of the file or the means that
UNDELETE has of recovering the file. If the file is not protected by either of
those utilities, that information is displayed here. If UNDELETE can recover
the files not protected by either of those utilities, the word Unaided is displayed. If the file is unrecoverable, UNDELETE tells you that the file cannot
be recovered by UNDELETE. You can try a disk editor to recover some data if
it still exists.

To recover a file, simply highlight its name and press Enter. To select more
than one file, highlight the names of the files you want to recover, and press
the space bar to mark them. A single click with the mouse works also. After
the files are selected, press the Enter key to recover them. A dialog box
prompts you for confirmation. Press Enter or choose OK.

To mark a group of similar files, press Alt-F to access the File menu, highlight
Select Group, and press Enter. UNDELETE displays a box asking you to enter
what types of files to recover (see fig. 10.4). You can use wild cards here. For
example, if you want to mark all files with a DOC extension, enter ***.DOC**.
A check mark appears next to all the files with a DOC extension in that
directory.

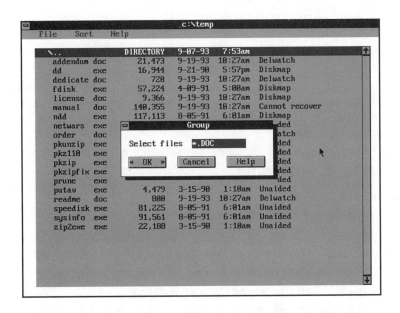

Fig. 10.4
Selecting a group
of files to undelete.

After a file has been successfully undeleted, you see the word RECOVERED next
to the file. A recovered file is now available to applications for reading, writing, or editing—as if that file were never gone.

Using UNDELETE Switches

Recovering files with the UNDELETE utility is easy, but at times, you may
prefer to use UNDELETE from the command line. This method is especially
useful (and faster) if you know the names of the files you want to recover and
where they are located. You will find that the switches are similar to those for
the DELPURGE utility, as discussed earlier in this chapter.

To undelete a file, enter the following at the command prompt:

    UNDELETE *filename*

If you do not know the exact name of the file, wild cards are acceptable. UN-
DELETE pauses as it displays each file that it attempts to recover, unless you
use the /A switch. The /A switch lets UNDELETE do its thing without prompting you for confirmation before every file.

To list deleted files in a directory, enter **UNDELETE** **/L**. If you want to include
files in subdirectories, add the /S switch. If the list is too long and some entries scroll off the top, use the /P switch to pause after each screenful of data.
To recover files that were deleted since a specific time, enter

    UNDELETE /T:*hh:mm:ss*

To recover files deleted since a certain date, enter

    UNDELETE /D:*mm-dd-yy*

or

    UNDELETE /D:*-n*

where *n* represents a maximum number of days. If you ever get stuck and cannot remember all the switches, just enter **UNDELETE /?** for a summary.

Deleting and Restoring a Practice File

Now that you have learned all about deleting and recovering files, it is time to practice what you know. Turn on your computer and get to a DOS prompt. Don't just read over the procedure described here, but perform the steps. When the time comes to recover a file you accidentally deleted, you will be glad you practiced. Of course, you do not want to mess with important files on your system, so the first step is to create a temporary directory where you can practice without worry. Follow these steps:

1. Enter **MD /TEMP**.

   If you already have a TEMP directory, use a different name, such as TMP.

2. To change to that directory, enter **CD /TEMP**.

   You want to copy to this directory some files that you can delete and undelete without worry, so make sure that you are in the TEMP directory.

3. Enter **COPY C:*.***.

   Now you want to load DELWATCH (unless it is already loaded). If you are working from drive C, enable DELWATCH for that drive. If you are working from a different volume, use whatever drive letter applies. Use only volumes that exist on your physical hard drives. UNDELETE works on network drives, but only if DELWATCH was enabled on the server.

4. Enter **DELWATCH C:**.

   One of the files that step 3 copied to your temporary directory was your AUTOEXEC.BAT file. (If you are unsure, enter **DIR** for a list of files in your \TEMP directory.) Now delete that file.

> **Caution**
>
> Remember that you are deleting only the copy of the AUTOEXEC.BAT that resides in your \TEMP directory. If you delete the AUTOEXEC.BAT file in your root directory and you fail to recover it, your computer will not boot properly.

5. Enter `DEL AUTOEXEC.BAT`.

6. Enter `DIR`.

If you followed the steps correctly, you should have no AUTOEXEC.BAT listed. As far as your operating system or any application is concerned, that file no longer exists in that directory. But you can recover it.

7. Enter `UNDELETE`.

This displays the menu-driven version of UNDELETE, and you should see the AUTOEXEC.BAT file listed at the top of the screen. On the right side of the screen, notice that UNDELETE recognized that DELWATCH was loaded, protecting that file. Now recover the file.

8. Highlight the AUTOEXEC.BAT file and press Enter.

A box pops up that asks you to confirm the undelete operation.

9. Press Enter to select the OK button.

Now AUTOEXEC.BAT is still listed, but on the right side of the screen, the word `DELWATCH` is replaced by `RECOVERED`.

10. Press Alt-X to exit the utility.

11. Enter `DIR`.

Do you see the file again? Good. This was just a simple example of deleting and recovering a file. You can see how easy it is, but it is important that you load DELWATCH if you want a good chance at file recovery.

As a final step, you may want to delete the files in the \TEMP directory and remove it.

Preventing Accidental Deletions

Even though the utilities and programs in Novell DOS 7 can do a lot to help you recover from the frustrating mistake of deleting the wrong file again, there are other useful things you can do so that you never have to use those utilities. These are just common-sense rules, not based on a specific technology, that can help you avoid deleting the wrong file in the first place.

Modify the Prompt to Display the Current Directory

Rule Number One: Always make sure that you know which directory you are in before you start deleting files.

Tip
Use the DIR command before deleting with DEL. You want to know where you are and what will be deleted.

First of all, make sure that your command prompt includes the path of the current directory. You should have a statement in your AUTOEXEC.BAT batch file that reads something like PROMPT=PG. When you see a DOS prompt, if it just sits there with a C> and a blinking cursor, chances are that this statement is probably missing. If your prompt looks like that (C>), you have no way of knowing what subdirectory you are in. You could be in the root directory of the hard drive, or in a directory called \APPS\LOTUS123\MYFILES\PROJECT1\WRKSHTS. So what's the big deal? It makes a huge difference which directory you are in when you begin deleting files. Just so you are aware of the current directory before you start typing DEL, let your command prompt help you out. It should look something like C:\APPS>. Entering **DEL *.*** is a lot different in an application directory than it is in the root directory.

Select File Names Carefully

Rule Number Two: Give your documents dissimilar file names.

Second, be thoughtful when assigning file names to documents. Suppose that you have a directory full of office memos you've written, with names like MEMO1.DOC, MEMO2.DOC, MEMO3.DOC, and so on. Altough it might be helpful to see the order in which you wrote the memos, it is easy to mistype a letter (especially numbers) and delete the wrong file. For example, if you wanted to delete MEMO2.DOC but you accidentally typed a 3 instead, you would delete the wrong file! A solution is to give your documents names that are somewhat dissimilar—at least a few characters apart. That way, you can keep from deleting the wrong file because of one stray finger.

Be Careful When You Use Wild Cards

Rule Number Three: Be careful when using wild-card characters (* and ?) with the DEL command.

This rule deals with those oh-so-handy wild-card characters. The wild-card characters are * and ?, which are two of the most helpful tools in command-line computing. If you want to list all the files that start with P, you can just enter `DIR P*.*`. If you want to copy all files with a DOC extension, you can enter `COPY *.DOC`. But these wild cards also work with the DEL command.

Suppose that you are in a directory and want to delete all the office memos you have written. Although you gave the files dissimilar names, you still wanted to be sure that you recognized the files as memos, so you started each file with the letters M-E-M. Now you want to delete all the memo files, so you enter `DEL MEM*.*`, and you think all is well. Unfortunately, you also deleted a personal history document you had been writing called MEMORIES.DOC. This common mistake happens too often. To avoid it, either do not use wild cards when deleting files, or make sure that you know all the files that will be deleted. If you had entered `DIR MEM*.*` and looked at all those files before you deleted them, you probably would have caught the other document.

Make Frequent Backups

Rule Number Four: Back up as if your life depended on it.

Finally, backup, backup, backup! If you have a good backup plan and stick to it religiously, even if you do accidentally delete your precious data, you have the means of getting it back. Using the utilities described in this chapter to recover from a deleted file may be a lot easier than restoring the file from a backup, but there is peace of mind that only a solid backup can give you.

The first reaction when people accidentally delete the wrong file is one of panic. Even if they have used all the precautions discussed in this chapter, they still get a case of the worries. A backup is insurance against that. A backup means that even if you try everything to get your original file back, you know you have a good copy somewhere else. A backup of your data will put your mind at ease in a hundred different situations and is worth every penny and minute spent on it.

Don't Depend on Recovery Utilities
Rule Number Five: Be careful when you use DELWATCH, DISKMAP, and UNDELETE.

It is easy to start relying on these utilities to recover your files and not think twice about deleting files from your hard drive. Just remember that with either DELWATCH or DISKMAP, there is no guarantee that UNDELETE can recover your files. You may have loaded DELWATCH and think you are safe, only to realize that your hard drive is getting full and that a 2M file you just copied to your drive wiped out 50 pending-delete documents. Or you could get carried away with DELPURGE and end up accidentally removing files you thought were protected.

The point is that DISKMAP, DELWATCH, and UNDELETE can get you out of many tough spots. They are very helpful utilities. But do not start depending on them. If you are deleting files, you should still take every measure to make sure that you know you don't want the files before you delete them.

From Here...

Everyone, at some point, deletes a file they wish they hadn't. Often, you can recover from such mistakes, but your chances are much better if you use the utilities provided with Novell DOS 7. DISKMAP makes a copy of a drive's FAT so that UNDELETE has a better chance of recovering the file. DELWATCH actually saves deleted files.

For more information about DOS files and directories, see the following chapters:

- Chapter 6, "Understanding File Storage," covers drive and disk structures, DOS directories, paths, DOS files and their attributes, and the use of wild cards.

- Chapter 7, "Managing Files and Directories," shows you how to create, rename, remove, and display directories; list files and directories; and copy, move, compare, and delete files.

Chapter 11

Disk Optimization Utilities

One feature that makes computers so useful and powerful is their capability to store data. At the touch of a key, you can recall anything that has been entered into the computer. This includes the operating system itself (in this case, Novell DOS 7), applications, and the information that you entered using software, which can include names, addresses, accounting information, letters, and lists.

This storage probably takes place on a *disk*. Quite often, you store information on a *hard disk*, which can retain millions and millions of characters (letters, numbers, and symbols). Novell DOS 7 can work with hard disks with capacities up to 2G (gigabytes or billions of characters).

This chapter is about your hard disk—how to maintain it, improve its speed and performance, and increase its capacity. Novell DOS 7 includes a number of utilities to assist you in getting the most from your computer's disk drives:

- CHKDSK checks your disks and, depending on the errors found, may repair the errors.

- DISKOPT maintains disk files in contiguous storage, which improves disk access and performance.

- NWCACHE maintains the most-used data stored in memory, thus reducing the number of mechanical disk accesses resulting in system speedup.

- SDEFRAG defragments (optimizes) Stacker drives and recompresses Stacker compressed drives. SDEFRAG can be used from either DOS or Windows.

■ Stacker compresses the information stored on your hard disk (or floppy disk), increasing the amount of information that can be stored.

> **Note**
>
> Although this chapter primarily discusses hard disks, much of the information also applies to floppy disks. It is a fact today that most people do not use floppies as a major storage device but rather as a backup, installation, or transfer device.

This chapter covers the following topics:

■ Using CHKDSK to check your computer disks

■ Optimizing disks with DISKOPT

■ Improving performance with NWCACHE

■ Increasing disk space with Stacker

Checking Disks (CHKDSK)

Before you learn about CHKDSK, it might be helpful to learn something about how files are stored on a disk. When a file is created on a disk, the operating system enters the name of the file and the locations of the file. The track and sector are provided from a list of available storage locations, the file allocation table (FAT). The disk operating system (DOS) must make sure that each segment of a file is allocated its proper location entry, that it alone has that location, and that it is no longer available to any other file. Problems arise when sections of the disk are not shown in any directory listing or in the FAT, when more than one file is listed as using the same storage location, or when the listed size of a file does not match the allocated or listed storage capacity.

You use CHKDSK to learn disk status, which includes the amount of total available space, the amount of space used by directories and files, and the amount of free space. CHKDSK can also inform you of any *pending-delete files* (refer to Chapter 10, "Undeleting Files," for information on DELWATCH and pending-delete files). The utility also provides the amount of conventional RAM (random-access memory) and the amount available for running programs. Refer to Chapter 22, "Optimizing Memory," for more information on memory. If there are any errors—such as lost clusters, size errors, or cross-linked files—CHKDSK also informs you of these. CHKDSK can repair most of these errors on floppy, hard, and compressed disks.

The CHKDSK command may be used on a floppy or hard disk. CHKDSK displays messages indicating the total number of bytes used and available on the drive, the number of files and directories, and the status of the drive. The output from this command depends on the type of drive and the options in effect, as well as the types of problems found. Figure 11.1 shows the output of CHKDSK run on a hard drive.

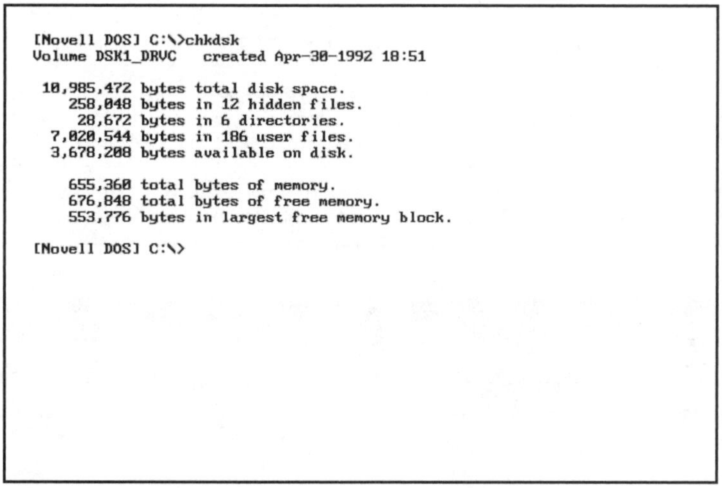

```
[Novell DOS] C:\>chkdsk
Volume DSK1_DRVC    created Apr-30-1992 10:51

10,985,472 bytes total disk space.
   258,048 bytes in 12 hidden files.
    28,672 bytes in 6 directories.
 7,020,544 bytes in 186 user files.
 3,678,208 bytes available on disk.

   655,360 total bytes of memory.
   676,848 total bytes of free memory.
   553,776 bytes in largest free memory block.

[Novell DOS] C:\>
```

Fig. 11.1
Standard output of CHKDSK on a hard disk with no errors.

> **Note**
>
> Although CHKDSK is a very useful utility for repairing those glitches that occur from time to time on any system, be sure to learn how to use Fastback Express and use it regularly to make backup copies of all your important information. Read Chapter 12, "Backup Utilities," to learn about Fastback Express.

Using CHKDSK Switches

The syntax of the CHKDSK command is

CHKDSK *d:path\filename.ext switches*

You enter the CHKDSK command at the DOS prompt. If you do not enter the drive letter (with a colon), the current or default drive is assumed. If you enter a file name, you may use wild-card characters. CHKDSK reports whether the files are contiguous (in one continuous stream). The switches provide various functions, as described in table 11.1.

Table 11.1 CHKDSK Switches	
Switch	**Use**
/B	Allows CHKDSK to be run in a batch file; suppresses pauses for operator input
/D	Displays a detailed error or statistics report for a Stacker compressed drive
/F	Writes any corrections of found errors to the disk
/S	Surface-scans a Stacker compressed drive
/V	Supplies an individual listing of each file checked by the utility
/WP	Tells CHKDSK that it can repair a Stacker compressed drive which has been write-protected because of errors

Note

For more on the Stacker disk compression and the handling of any problems with the utility, refer to the section "Compressing Disks with Stacker" later in this chapter.

To determine whether files are contiguous on the disk, use a file name, including a wild-card character (such as *.DBF), with CHKDSK. Novell DOS can read contiguous files more quickly than files scattered throughout the disk. When many files are scattered throughout the disk, you may notice degraded computer performance. Figure 11.2 shows the output when CHKDSK finds that a matching file is not contiguous. If fragmented or scattered files become a problem with system performance, refer to the discussion of DISKOPT, the utility used to reorganize your files, in the section "Optimizing Disks" later in this chapter.

You use the /V switch with the CHKDSK command to display each file name as the file is tested, as shown in figure 11.3.

When you use this switch, the full path name of every file on your disk appears. On a hard disk, this might be a very long list. You might want to redirect the display output to a file to keep a complete list of current files. For example, enter the following command:

```
CHKDSK C: /V > C:\FILELIST.TXT
```

The redirection symbol (>) with the file name FILELIST.TXT tells CHKDSK to send a complete list of the full path name for every file on disk to the named file.

```
[Novell DOS] C:\ACCTG\DATA>chkdsk *.dbf
Volume DSK1_DRVC   created Feb-28-1993 11:13
Volume Serial Number is 1901-0C44

    52,094,976 bytes total disk space.
       151,552 bytes in 16 hidden files.
        65,536 bytes in 26 directories.
    40,208,384 bytes in 733 user files.
    11,669,504 bytes available on disk.

         2,048 bytes in allocation unit.
        25,437 total allocation units on disk.
         5,698 available allocation units on disk.

       655,360 total bytes of memory.
       585,920 total bytes of free memory.
       552,960 bytes in largest free memory block.


c:\acctg\data\CUSTOMS1.DBF
        2 non-contiguous clusters found.
c:\acctg\data\CUSTOMS6.DBF
        2 non-contiguous clusters found.
c:\acctg\data\MASTER1.DBF
        6 non-contiguous clusters found.
c:\acctg\data\TRANSAC1.DBF
       83 non-contiguous clusters found.
c:\acctg\data\TRANSAC2.DBF
        5 non-contiguous clusters found.
c:\acctg\data\TRANSAC3.DBF
        3 non-contiguous clusters found.
```

Fig. 11.2
Output of CHKDSK with specified file names and a report of noncontiguous files.

```
C:\CONFIG.SYS
C:\DCONFIG.SYS
C:\DRMDOS.SYS
C:\LOADER.SYS
C:\MCONFIG.SYS
C:\STACHIGH.SYS
C:\NOTES.TXT
C:\@AUTOEXE.UI
C:\@COMMAND.UI
C:\@CONFIG.UI
C:\@OLDBDOS.UI
C:\@OLDBIOS.UI
C:\@OLDBOOT.UI

    10,985,472 bytes total disk space.
       258,048 bytes in 12 hidden files.
        28,672 bytes in 6 directories.
     7,036,928 bytes in 187 user files.
     3,661,824 bytes available on disk.

       655,360 total bytes of memory.
       676,848 total bytes of free memory.
       553,776 bytes in largest free memory block.

[Novell DOS] C:\>
```

Fig. 11.3
Output of CHKDSK with the /V option.

> **Caution**
>
> The CHKDSK /F command attempts to fix files that appear incomplete even when the files have not yet been written. When you attempt to fix "errors" in these environments, therefore, you risk introducing actual errors that are extremely difficult to correct.
>
> Using the CHKDSK command when one or more files are being used (even without the /F switch) may damage the logical structure of a disk. Accordingly, do not use the CHKDSK command while running Task Manager, Microsoft Windows, Quarterdeck's Desqview, or any other task switcher or multitasking system. Nor should you use CHKDSK on a network drive.

Finding Disk Problems

The directory entry for a file lists the location for the first cluster of that file. This first cluster in turn points to the next cluster, the next cluster points to the next, and so on, forming a *chain* of clusters. These references are necessary so that the operating system can locate all the information in a file; every cluster must be marked as free, bad, or part of a file.

The CHKDSK program examines the FAT, files, and directories for consistency. Each area is examined to be sure that the information is logically consistent with information found in other areas. No free space should be marked as part of a file. All nonfree space should be marked as part of a file. Each file should contain the exact number of allocation units to match the indicated size of the file.

If you use CHKDSK without the /F switch and the utility uncovers such file errors, it reports the fact and prompts you to write data to the hard disk. Although CHKDSK can write lost allocation units to files, you probably will not be able to use the files, and they take up space on the disk. If CHKDSK reports these types of file errors, reenter the command with the /F switch to free the allocation units.

Lost Clusters. When the FAT entry for a cluster shows it to be part of a file but no directory entry or other cluster refers to this cluster, the cluster is referred to as an *orphan* and has been lost. Orphans do not belong to any file, and therefore, you should mark them as available by using the CHKDSK command. When an orphan refers to other clusters, they are part of the same chain and should also be marked as available. When CHKDSK finds orphans, a message appears asking whether the cluster chains should be converted to files. Select either of the following responses:

- Press Y to make each chain a file named FILE*nnnn*.CHK, where *nnnn* is a sequential number starting with 0000. You can then use the resulting files to attempt reconstruction of the lost information.

- Press N to mark the clusters as available. Reconstruction of lost files is not possible.

> **Note**
>
> Unless you have recently lost extremely valuable information and are willing to attempt reconstruction from the FILE*nnnn*.CHK files, press N to free the orphan chains. You might be able to reconstruct ASCII text files, but other types of files are most likely lost.

Size Errors. The directory entry for a file lists the number of bytes contained in the file, as well as the cluster number of the first cluster of the file. The number of clusters in the cluster chain should be sufficient to contain a file of the size indicated by the directory entry. When the number of clusters is not adequate to hold a file of the indicated size, a portion of the file has been lost. A message appears informing you that the size has been adjusted. You can restore the lost information in one of two ways:

- When the affected file is a text file, the last part of the file has been lost, and you need to reenter the data. The beginning of the file is OK.

- When the affected file is an executable program, you should delete the file and restore the file from another copy. The bad file probably was not run correctly and could lock up your computer, requiring you to reboot your system.

Cross-Linked Files. When the cluster chain of one file refers to a cluster for another file, a portion of both files resides in the same space on the disk, and the files are said to be *cross-linked*. Cross-linked files can cause problems. Use the CHKDSK command to correct cross-linking as soon as the files are found. At least one (and probably both) of the files has been damaged and should be restored from backups.

Optimizing Disks

Every file in DOS has one or more clusters. The size of a cluster varies depending on the size of the disk, but it is often 2K. When the file is created, DOS writes the first cluster and, if another cluster is needed, DOS uses the next free cluster. This process continues until the entire file has been written. When a file is deleted, all of that file's clusters become free.

Suppose that you start with an empty disk and then create two files. If the first file has two clusters and the second has four clusters, the first six clusters are now occupied. If you then delete the first file, the first two clusters become free. However, the second file still occupies the clusters numbered 3, 4, 5, and 6; the second file's location has not moved even though clusters 1 and 2 are now available. If you then create a third file four clusters in size, it uses the clusters numbered 1, 2, 7, and 8. Thus, your third file is a *fragmented file*.

Fragmentation can cause the disk to respond more slowly. When all the clusters of a file are contiguous, the access arm of the drive (the slowest part of the drive, which contains the read/write head) moves once to the beginning of the file and then in very small increments to reach the next cluster. If the file is fragmented, however, the arm must move to reach the first cluster and then move a long distance to reach the next cluster. If the drive is very slow (as a floppy disk drive is) or the file is very large, the additional time can be quite noticeable.

A *disk optimizer program* enhances the performance of a disk drive by moving the files on the disk so that all parts of every file are contiguous. The mechanical arms do not have to travel as much if the files are contiguous as opposed to being stored throughout various parts of the disk. The optimizer program reads those files at the beginning of the disk and rewrites them in free disk space. Then it reads an entire file and rewrites that new file at the beginning of the disk. This process of freeing an area and moving the next file into that area continues throughout the disk. Eventually, the disk has no fragmented files.

Another benefit of disk optimization is reorganization of the files within directories. You can choose the sequence of the file names, so the next time you do a directory list, the names are shown in the sequence you chose. This action can optimize the way you work with directory listings.

You can optimize most kinds of disks that you can use with Novell DOS. Hard drives obviously are good candidates for optimization. You also may want to optimize a floppy disk if you have been replacing many files.

This section describes two optimization programs that come with Novell DOS 7: DISKOPT and SDEFRAG.

> **Caution**
>
> Don't use any reorganization program on a compressed drive unless it is designed to work with compressed disks.

You can use CHKDSK to determine whether you need to optimize your disk. If you use a wild-card character with CHKDSK, the program gives you a message if any matching files are found to be noncontiguous. Figure 11.4 shows the output of CHKDSK if any matching files are not contiguous.

```
[Novell DOS] C:\ACCTG\DATA>chkdsk *.dbf
Volume DSK1_DRVC   created Feb-28-1993 11:13
Volume Serial Number is 1901-0C44

    52,094,976 bytes total disk space.
       151,552 bytes in 16 hidden files.
        65,536 bytes in 26 directories.
    40,208,384 bytes in 733 user files.
    11,669,504 bytes available on disk.

         2,048 bytes in allocation unit.
        25,437 total allocation units on disk.
         5,698 available allocation units on disk.

       655,360 total bytes of memory.
       585,920 total bytes of free memory.
       552,960 bytes in largest free memory block.


c:\acctg\data\CUSTOMS1.DBF
      2 non-contiguous clusters found.
c:\acctg\data\CUSTOMS6.DBF
      2 non-contiguous clusters found.
c:\acctg\data\MASTER1.DBF
      6 non-contiguous clusters found.
c:\acctg\data\TRANSAC1.DBF
     83 non-contiguous clusters found.
c:\acctg\data\TRANSAC2.DBF
      5 non-contiguous clusters found.
c:\acctg\data\TRANSAC3.DBF
      3 non-contiguous clusters found.
```

Fig. 11.4
Output of CHKDSK with noncontiguous files reported.

Precautions for Optimizing

Before you optimize your disk, make sure that you have a good backup. The optimization program is going to move your files around. If it is interrupted, your files may not be usable. Refer to Chapter 12, "Backup Utilities," to learn how to make a backup with Novell DOS 7.

Run CHKDSK before you run an optimization program to make sure that your disk has no problems. Fix any errors displayed first, before you run the optimization program. CHKDSK should not display any error messages; if an error message does appear, try running CHKDSK with the /F parameter to repair the errors. If you have errors, the optimization program should detect them and refuse to reorganize your disk. If you cannot fix the errors, don't try to run DISKOPT or SDEFRAG.

Don't run optimizers under Task Manager, Windows, Desqview, or any other multitasking program. Two problems can arise if you try to reorganize under a multitasking system. The first problem is that any multitasking manager increases the probability of a crash, something you don't want in the middle of a reorganization. The second, and more dangerous, problem is that other programs running would try to access the files on your disk. Be sure that no other program accesses your disk while DISKOPT or SDEFRAG is running.

You should also disable any TSRs that you may have loaded before running an optimizer. A program is a TSR (terminate-and-stay-resident program) if, when you load it, it places at least part of itself in memory and then ends execution. Part of the program remains in memory to intercept keystrokes or watch for other events that cause it to do what it was designed to do. The reason for this is that the TSR could attempt to access a file while the defragmentation is taking place, or it may already have in its possession the location of a file. After the file has been defragmented, it may no longer be where it originally was, thus causing a potential catastrophe. Device drivers, such as a mouse driver, loaded as part of the boot process should not cause a problem. TSRs—for example, electronic notepads and virus detection programs—should be disabled before you attempt the optimization.

Caution

Disk caches, such as NWCACHE, are TSRs and should be either disabled or removed from memory before optimization. See the later section "Improving Disk Performance with a Disk Cache (NWCACHE)" for details.

Optimization programs run for a while. Be sure that you allow time for them. The exact amount of required time depends on the size of the disk as well as the amount of fragmentation. Larger drives take longer. You might want to start the optimization just before you leave your computer.

> **Note**
>
> DISKOPT does not move SYSTEM files (files marked with the system attribute). This feature protects copy-protected software. If you want DISKOPT to be able to move system files, you must first change the attribute. Refer to Chapter 6, "Understanding File Storage," for more on file attributes.

After DISKOPT has completed its work, you may want to reboot your computer to reload any TSRs you normally use.

Reorganizing Disks (DISKOPT)

DISKOPT, the disk optimizer program, is included with Novell DOS 7. DISKOPT reorganizes your drive, rewriting all disk files to put them in contiguous format, thus making access faster to the data on the drive. You can also use DISKOPT to reorganize a drive compressed with Stacker.

DISKOPT can be run in either full-screen mode or command mode from the DOS prompt, which makes it available for use in a batch file without operator intervention.

Starting DISKOPT from the DOS Prompt. Start DISKOPT at the command-line prompt or in a batch file by entering the DISKOPT command followed by any options to tell the utility how you want the defragmentation performed. You must use the /O option to bypass the full-screen version of the utility. DISKOPT has a number of switches, including those that can tell the program how to sort the files and directories.

If you do not specify the drive to be defragmented, DISKOPT operates on the current or default drive. Here is the syntax:

```
DISKOPT d: switches
```

d: is the drive containing the files you want to unfragment.

The /B switch forces DISKOPT to use monochrome instead of color. This switch may be required on a monochrome notebook or laptop computer.

The /M*n* switch tells DISKOPT the disk optimization method to use. Replace *n* with one of the following:

1   Full optimization

2   Full optimization (but files are also reordered)

3   File defragmentation only

4   Free space defragmentation only

5   Sort directories only

6   Full optimization and restack disk

Note

Unless you specify the type of optimization, DISKOPT automatically determines the default optimization method it uses, depending on the type of disk used.

The /O switch tells DISKOPT to start the defragmentation process immediately, without further operator input. This switch is necessary for use without full-screen mode, as in batch files.

The /Sx switch tells DISKOPT what sorting method to use for directories and files. Replace the x with one of the following letters:

a   Sorts alphabetically by name (the default setting for optimization method 5, sorting directories only)

d   Sorts chronologically by creation or last modification date

e   Sorts alphabetically by file extension

n   No sort desired (this is the default if not specified)

s   Sorts by file size (smallest is first)

Note

If you select the /M5 switch and do not specify an /Sx switch, the default for sorting becomes sorting alphabetically by name (the same as /Sa).

Using DISKOPT in Full-Screen Mode. To start the full-screen mode of DISKOPT, enter **DISKOPT** at the DOS prompt. This command has a single switch, /B, for using monochrome mode instead of color (may be required on notebook or laptop computers).

> **Note**
>
> If you want to use DISKOPT in a batch file (for example, after running a full backup at the end of the day) and you don't want to stay around for the utilities to complete their work, use the following command in your batch file:
>
>   DISKOPT *d:* /O /M1 /Sa
>
> This example tells DISKOPT to optimize the specified drive without further operator intervention. The optimization method is to be full, with sorting alphabetical by name. The utility then proceeds through the full process as determined by your instructions, with the full-screen view of the optimization, and returns to the DOS prompt when finished.

The first thing to do when you run DISKOPT is to specify the drive to be reorganized. DISKOPT shows a menu of all available drives. Figure 11.5 shows the DISKOPT Drives dialog box. Use the arrow keys or the mouse to select the drive you want to optimize. Press Enter or double-click the mouse.

Fig. 11.5
The DISKOPT Drives menu.

After you select a drive, DISKOPT analyzes its status (flashing the names of the directories as it performs the analysis) and shows you a statistical display of the drive, including total disk space, allocated space, number of directories and files, fragmentation of files, free space, and available memory. DISKOPT also recommends the optimization method. Press Enter to proceed.

DISKOPT then displays a map of the selected drive, where each block represents one or more clusters. Occupied clusters and free clusters are represented on the map, as shown in figure 11.6. Notice the map legend at the bottom right of the DISKOPT screen.

Before you are ready to proceed, you may want to select the method of optimization and the type of sorting to be performed. At the top of the screen is a menu bar. The Drive option on the Optimize menu enables you to change the drive you want to defragment. You can also use Alt-D and bypass the menu to change drives. The Method menu contains the five optimization methods listed with the /M switch earlier. The current selection is preceded by a check mark.

Fig. 11.6
A DISKOPT map of the selected drive.

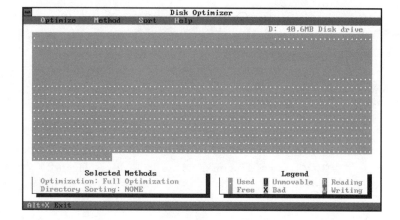

The Sort menu, shown in figure 11.7, enables you to select the sorting order you want used for the directories. Choose No Sort to leave the directory entries as they were. If you choose Names, DISKOPT sorts the directories first, followed by the file names in the selected order. If you choose Date, the files are placed in chronological order. Choose Size to order the files from smallest to largest.

Fig. 11.7
The DISKOPT Sort menu.

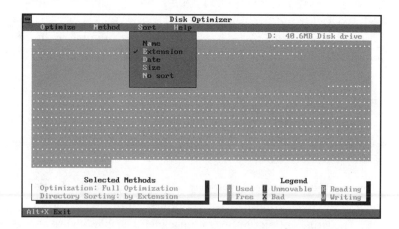

You can begin optimization when you have selected a method and sorting option or taken the defaults as shown at the bottom left of the screen map.

Open the Optimize menu and choose Optimize Disk. You are then required to confirm that you want to optimize the specified drive. Press Enter.

DISKOPT displays the progress, actual elapsed time, and estimated remaining time as optimization continues. The display, shown in figure 11.8, is updated by DISKOPT to show the current location being optimized. If you need to end DISKOPT, press Esc, and the program ends at the next possible opportunity. The program does need to finish writing the file it is processing.

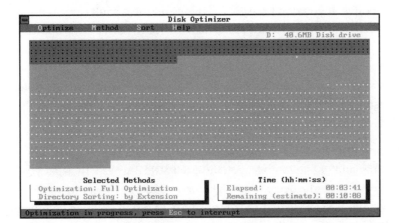

Fig. 11.8
DISKOPT in progress.

Caution

Do not interrupt optimization by powering off or rebooting. You can destroy data.

DISKOPT displays a message when optimization is finished. Press Enter from the dialog box. To end the program, press Alt-X or choose Exit from the Optimize menu. If you want to optimize another drive, choose Drive from the Optimize menu or press Alt-D; then specify the drive you want.

Defragmenting Compressed Disks (SDEFRAG)

SDEFRAG is provided as part of the Stacker disk compression utility. As with DISKOPT, SDEFRAG provides file defragmentation, thus increasing disk access performance. In addition, SDEFRAG can recompress data to minimize the amount of space used by the compressed files on a Stacker compressed drive. DISKOPT does work on Stacker compressed drives; it just does not recompress data. You cannot use SDEFRAG on noncompressed drives.

The precautions you learned about in the earlier section "Precautions for Optimizing" also apply to SDEFRAG.

As with DISKOPT, SDEFRAG can be used either in full-screen mode or in batch or command mode, without any operator intervention. Here is the basic syntax of the SDEFRAG command:

SDEFRAG *d: switches*

If you do not specify the drive to be processed, SDEFRAG uses the current or default drive. If you don't specify the drive and the default drive is not a Stacker compressed drive, SDEFRAG does ask for the drive to be optimized, even in command mode. Several of the option switches for SDEFRAG can be used in either full-screen mode or command mode. SDEFRAG also is used as a utility in command mode to do such tasks as resize the compressed volume. You cannot resize the compressed volume in full-screen mode, which is used only to optimize a drive.

Running SDEFRAG from the DOS Prompt. If you want to use SDEFRAG in the command or batch mode, you must tell SDEFRAG exactly what you want done; otherwise, the defaults are used for all options. However, you must include the /BATCH switch to tell the utility to run in batch or command mode for optimizing a drive if you do not want operator intervention. You must also include a valid Stacker compressed drive letter in the command if the default drive is not compressed. Table 11.2 describes the SDEFRAG switches.

Table 11.2 SDEFRAG Command Switches	
Switch	**Use**
/B	Reboots the computer after it has finished optimizing the drive.
/BATCH	Runs in batch mode or command mode. If the current drive is not a Stacker compressed drive, you must also include the drive letter with the colon.
/BW	Operates in monochrome display mode.
/D	Optimizes only the directories and in the sort order specified. The default sort order is by name and ascending.
/F	Tells SDEFRAG to perform a full optimization.

Switch	Use
/GL	Changes the expected compression ratio. After displaying the current compression ratio, SDEFRAG asks you to specify the ratio you want, which must be within the displayed range.
/GP	Increases the size of the Stacker compressed drive or provides more free, uncompressed space, meaning that you want to resize the compressed drive either larger or smaller. You are first requested to tell SDEFRAG which operation you want to perform and then the amount of the change to be made. Enter a number within the displayed range. (*Note:* You may not be able to resize the compressed drive either larger or smaller. It depends on the amount of data stored on the drive and on the size of the compressed volume within the actual drive.)
/H	Moves hidden or system files; otherwise, they are skipped during defragmentation.
/LCD	Operates in monochrome display mode for LCD video display screens. This switch may be most helpful with notebook or laptop computers.
/P=*n*	Recompresses data; *n* is a compression level, from 1 through 9.
/R	Tells SDEFRAG to recompress the drive while it is being optimized. This option may save some disk space.
/RESTORE=*d*:STACVOL.*ext*	Repairs a Stacker drive if optimization was interrupted by an accidental system reboot or a power failure.
/S*x*	Provides SDEFRAG with the sort order to be used. Replace the *x* with one of the following:
	D Sorts on the file creation or last modification date.
	E Sorts on the file extension.
	N Sorts on the file name; this is the default.
	S Sorts on the file size.
	U Does not sort.
	If you add a minus sign after the sort code, as in /SD–, descending order is used rather than ascending order (which is the default).
/SKIPHIGH	Does not load any data in high memory.

(continues)

Switch	Use
/U	Does not reclaim empty space between files. The quick optimization defragments only those files that are currently fragmented.
/V	Performs verification of all disk writes. This option can slow down the operation, but in cases where your data is extremely valuable, you may want to include it. Of course the best safeguard is a current, good, full backup of your system.

Table 11.2 Continued

Caution

Be careful when you use this switch. You may be affecting some write-protected programs that use hidden or system files as part of their protection scheme.

The following command tells SDEFRAG to optimize the specified drive with full optimization and reordering of all files, to sort files by their extension, to reboot when the process is completed, and to run without further operator intervention:

```
SDEFRAG D: /R /SE /B /BATCH
```

Using SDEFRAG in Full-Screen Mode. When you enter the SDEFRAG command without any options, except possibly one of the video options (/BW or /LCD), SDEFRAG displays the Disk Optimization menu (see fig. 11.9). If you decide not to go through with the optimization, choose Exit to return to the DOS prompt. To specify the drive or drives you want to optimize (if other than the current drive), choose Drive and select the appropriate drives from the displayed list.

Changing the Optimization Method. Before starting the defragmentation process, you may want to override the default methods and sort orders. To change the method, choose Optimization Method. The menu shown in figure 11.10 is displayed, offering the following optimization methods:

■ *Full Optimize.* Optimizes all files on the disk. This includes organizing all files at the beginning of the disk so that all free space is at the end of the disk.

■ *Quick Optimize.* Defragments only fragmented files. The free space between files is left in place. By not reorganizing all files, you save time.

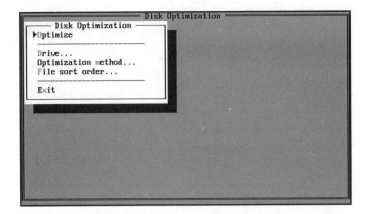

Fig. 11.9
The SDEFRAG Disk
Optimization
menu.

- *Restack*. Recompresses all files on the disk, as well as defragmenting and reorganizing them. This method takes the longest time but often provides more space for more or larger files.

- *Directory Only Optimize*. Optimizes only directories, using the sort order specified. The default sort order is ascending and by alphabetical name.

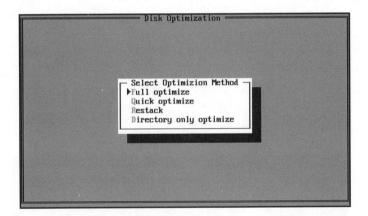

Fig. 11.10
The SDEFRAG
Select Optimiza-
tion Method
menu.

Make your selection by using the up- or down-arrow key and pressing Enter, or by typing the highlighted letter for your selection. You then return to the Disk Optimization menu. You can also press Esc to exit from the Select Optimization Method menu, leaving the selection where it is.

Changing the Sort Order. To change the sort order, choose File Sort Order from the Disk Optimization menu. The Select File Sort Order menu, shown in figure 11.11, gives you two sets of selections: the sort order and whether the sort is to be ascending (A to Z) or descending (Z to A).

Fig. 11.11
The SDEFRAG
Select File Sort
Order menu.

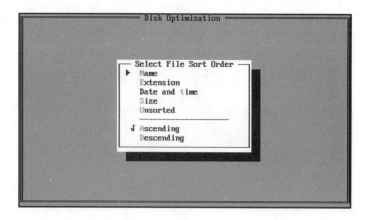

As with other SDEFRAG menus, make your selection here. Choose the Ascending or Descending option first if you want to change the indicated choice. Doing this does not exit the menu. Then specify your choice for the type of sort. You then return to the Disk Optimization menu. Using the Esc key also returns you to the Disk Optimization menu, without making any changes to the file sort order.

Starting the Optimization Process. To begin the optimization, select Optimize from the Disk Optimization menu. If more than one Stacker compressed drive is available on your system, SDEFRAG requests that you indicate the drive to be optimized. All Stacker compressed drives are listed in a dialog box menu, as shown in figure 11.12. Choose your preference and press Enter. If you have already chosen the drive from the Drive option in the Disk Optimization menu, this step is skipped.

Fig. 11.12
Available drives
listed in the
SDEFRAG Select
Drive menu.

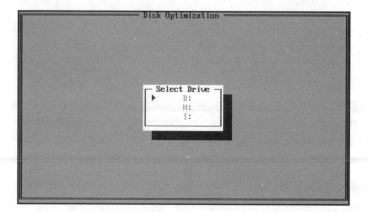

The first thing that SDEFRAG does before performing the optimization is to check the drive. If the fragmentation level percent, which is displayed, is either 0 or very low, SDEFRAG recommends that you do not need to optimize the drive and you should exit. You do not have to follow the program's recommendation, though. A dialog box is then displayed with two choices: Continue and Exit SDEFRAG. If you continue, the method of optimization selected is performed. If the level of fragmentation is sufficient, the recommendation is to perform a full optimization.

Whichever you decide, either press the highlighted letter, or use the up- or down-arrow key to make your selection and press Enter. Choosing Exit SDEFRAG returns you to the DOS prompt.

If the optimization is performed, first the integrity of the directories on the compressed drive is checked, then the integrity of the stored programs and data files. The Disk Optimization screen is then displayed with a map of the selected drive (see fig. 11.13). At the bottom of the screen, the progress is displayed as a percentage of completion and elapsed time, drive information with fragmentation level and method used, and a legend of the disk map.

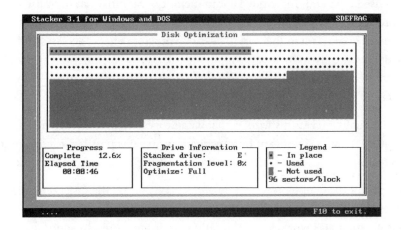

Fig. 11.13
SDEFRAG's Disk Optimization map with optimization in progress.

Each white block with a centered diamond represents a number of disk sectors. (The exact representation is displayed at the bottom right of the screen.) As the optimization progresses, you can watch as files are temporarily moved out of the way. As files are rewritten and completed, the white blocks change to show that.

Tip
R on a diamond indicates that SDEFRAG is reading that sector; W appears when SDEFRAG writes to the sector.

If you have to abort the procedure, press the F10 key. There may be a delay for the program to react, because it must finish writing the current file to disk before it can stop.

When the optimization is finished, SDEFRAG displays a dialog box notifying you of the completion. Press Enter to continue. Depending on the results, SDEFRAG may then display the new statistics as a result of its work. Pressing any key returns you to the Disk Optimization menu. At this point, you can either optimize another drive or exit to DOS.

Improving Disk Performance with a Disk Cache (NWCACHE)

A *cache memory* is a section of random-access memory set aside to store the most frequently accessed information in RAM. A *disk cache* uses memory to speed up access to disks. Because memory is much smaller than disk storage, the cache program cannot put all the data from disk storage into main memory. Instead, some criteria are needed to decide what data is most likely to be used next and, therefore, kept in memory. Data that has been used before is likely to be used again; thus, the cache program stores the most frequently used data in memory. The cache program checks accesses and, if the data is already in memory, supplies the data from memory. If the data is not in memory, the data is read from disk, and a copy placed in the cache. If the cache fills up, the utility removes the oldest data from memory.

What actually makes this work is that data processing is really very repetitive in nature. Thus, a significant improvement in speed is possible, even as much as 5 to 10 times when it comes to software waiting for data from the disk.

This part of the chapter teaches you about NWCACHE, the disk cache that comes with Novell DOS 7. NWCACHE can improve disk performance by consolidating disk writes and eliminating duplicate writes. In addition, NWCACHE can take advantage of the exclusive Novell DOS DPMS (DOS Protected Mode Services) feature, which enables the utility itself to be loaded into extended memory, thus not affecting the amount of lower (conventional) memory you can have to run software applications.

After NWCACHE is installed, it is invisible to the operator and can be used with various types of memory and disk drives, both hard and floppy.

Cache Considerations

As in every performance option, you should test your standard programs before and after installing a cache. Are things running faster? (Less available memory could cause a slowdown.) Do you encounter any problems working with your application? Does it crash now? Did it before? If you don't test your computer after installing a new option, you could find that it doesn't work correctly when you most need it. Finally, installing a cache could cause problems and cannot cure an existing problem.

Disk caches work directly with your PC hardware. Although incompatibilities with software are unlikely, they are possible. Several advanced NWCACHE options provide mechanisms for dealing with this possibility. The use of some options depends on the type of computer you have and the type of processor and type of memory in your computer.

If you need additional help, several resources are available. The commercial on-line services (CompuServe, America On-Line, and BIX) offer forums on Novell DOS. Novell's NDSG division maintains a bulletin board system (BBS), as well as a fax information system.

Disk Caching Terminology

You should be familiar with the following caching terms:

- *Cache buffer.* This is memory allocated to NWCACHE for storage of disk read and write requests.

- *Delayed disk writes.* Write requests are delayed and accumulated before being written to disk. Writing multiple requests as a group speeds up NWCACHE by using fewer disk operations to write larger amounts of data.

- *Flushing.* Flushing immediately completes delayed write requests and clears the cache memory.

- *Lending memory.* This is memory that is shared with applications. If an application requests EMS or XMS memory, NWCACHE reduces its size and lends memory to the application. When the application frees this memory, it is reallocated to NWCACHE.

- *Lookahead buffer.* The lookahead buffer accumulates up to 16K of read and write requests during each disk access. Thus, NWCACHE can fulfill requests and anticipate requests by applications.

- *Write delay.* A write delay is a user-specified period of time to accumulate data to be written to disk. A write request begins the period, and all data in the cache is written to disk at the end of the period.

- *Write-through drive.* This is a drive configured to fulfill all read and write requests immediately. NWCACHE does not delay and accumulate write requests for a write-through drive.

- *Write-through mode.* When a drive is configured to fulfill all read and write requests immediately, the drive is in write-through mode.

You must decide the type of memory where you load NWCACHE: extended or expanded. *Extended memory* refers only to memory accessible when running in 80286 or 80386 mode. If you run Windows in standard or enhanced mode, you should choose extended memory. *Expanded memory* is available if you have an expanded memory card (also known as Lotus-Intel-Microsoft memory, LIM memory, or EMS memory) and the appropriate driver in CONFIG.SYS. Expanded memory may also be available if you are running on an 80386 or 80486 microprocessor and have the appropriate driver installed in CONFIG.SYS. Novell DOS provides a driver to use 80386/80486 memory as expanded memory. Chapter 22, "Optimizing Memory," has more information on expanded and extended memory.

Installing NWCACHE

The easiest way to begin using NWCACHE is to use Install/Setup to turn on disk caching. The program sets the options correctly so that the next time you boot Novell DOS, the disk cache is enabled with the selected values. The Setup program modifies the AUTOEXEC.BAT file to run NWCACHE every time you boot Novell DOS. The parameters used reflect the choices you made in Setup. If you want to change the parameters at any time, rerun Setup and choose Disk Performance. If there is no check mark to show that NWCACHE Disk Cache has been selected, use the up- or down-arrow key to make this selection and press Enter to display the check mark. Then use the down-arrow key to select Configure NWCACHE and press Enter.

Setup then displays the NWCACHE disk configuration screen (see fig. 11.14). This screen shows the NWCACHE parameters to be entered in Setup. The Setup program asks for the size and type of cache to be used. Use Tab or the up- or down-arrow key to move to each of the settings and make your entries. At that point, indicate that you want to make the changes, and then reboot. The changes are in effect after you reboot.

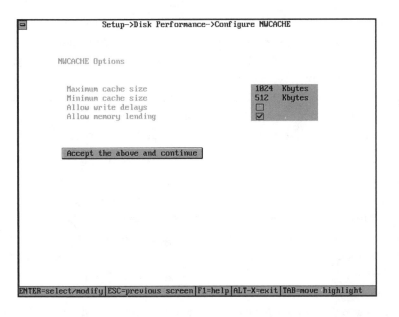

Fig. 11.14
The NWCACHE
disk configuration
screen in Setup.

IV

Disk and File Management

If you run only one application at a time, allocate as much memory as possible to the cache. The practical minimum cache size is usually 512K. If you cannot give NWCACHE at least this amount of memory, don't bother loading the cache, despite the fact that NWCACHE does default to smaller cache sizes if you have less than 1M of RAM in your computer. Table 11.3 lists the default cache size used by NWCACHE if you do not specify the amount of memory to be used as a cache. The maximum size cache supported by NWCACHE is 7670K.

Table 11.3 NWCACHE Default Cache Sizes

Available Memory	Minimum Cache Size
0-384K	0K
385-512K	32K
513-1024K	64K
1-2M	512K
2-4M	1024K
4M	1536K
5M+	2048K

If you are running a multitasking program (Task Manager, Windows, or Desqview, for example) on a computer with less than 2M of extended memory, don't use a cache at all. If you are running a multitasking program other than Windows, reduce the cache size. Windows must have at least 2048K to run in enhanced mode, so be sure to make at least that much available and ensure that the lending option is enabled. If you have 8M or more available, you might turn off lending entirely and set the cache to 2M or larger.

There is no hard-and-fast rule for the best cache size. You need to experiment to find the best value. If you find that your multitasking program continuously runs out of memory, reduce the cache size. If you find that you have plenty of memory, try increasing the cache size slightly. Do you notice an improvement with the larger cache? You have to use your computer for a while before you can tell. If the computer seems to respond faster and have enough memory to perform your normal tasks, leave the cache at the new size. You might try increasing the size later, but don't spend too much time trying to wring the last ounce of performance out of your computer. It is there to help you get your job done, not to take time away from you.

After you enter the cache sizes and decide whether to allow delayed disk writes and lending of memory by the cache to programs that need more memory, choose Accept the Above and Continue.

You can then continue by choosing Exit This Screen and then Save Changes and Exit. Setup writes the command line for NWCACHE in your AUTOEXEC.BAT file, and you can then choose Exit to DOS.

Setup automatically tries to have NWCACHE loaded into the best memory for maximum system performance. For example, if you have a 386 or higher processor with enough RAM and have DPMS turned on, NWCACHE tells NWCACHE to load itself above the 1M area through DPMS.

> **Note**
>
> If you are using a memory manager from another company, such as a 386MAX or QEMM, you may have to modify the load command for NWCACHE provided by Setup. For more information on this, refer to the discussion of the NWCACHE switches in the next section, "Setting Parameters for NWCACHE."

Of course, you can also use the Novell DOS 7 text editor, EDIT, to enter the command for NWCACHE into your AUTOEXEC.BAT file. See Chapter 17, "Using the Novell DOS Text Editor," for more information on EDIT.

Setting Parameters for NWCACHE

The full syntax for using NWCACHE is not actually provided in the Install/Setup utility. Install/Setup sets only the major parameters, with defaults being used for the rest of the possible settings. If you want to change the other settings or want to change how the cache is loaded into memory, you need to understand the command syntax of NWCACHE and use EDIT or another text editor to make the entries in your AUTOEXEC.BAT file or another batch file yourself.

You can use the NWCACHE command to load the cache. With this form of the command, you should specify the memory size settings, the drives to be cached, and the location in memory where you want NWCACHE to load itself. You can also use the NWCACHE command to change several settings or possibly unload the cache.

> **Note**
>
> Although you can enter the cache instructions at the DOS prompt, it can be a little difficult to enter all the parameters manually and be accurate. If you do not want the cache loaded through your AUTOEXEC.BAT file, create a separate batch file for the NWCACHE load statement. You will find it a lot easier and more accurate.

Load Parameters. This section describes the command switches that apply when you load NWCACHE. The syntax of the NWCACHE load command is

```
NWCACHE maxsize minsize d: d:+ d:- /A20 /Bx=size /CHECK /Mx | /MxX
    /W=size /X=address /E /L /LEND=ON | OFF /DELAY=ON | OFF | time
```

When NWCACHE loads, it automatically caches all available drives. Usually, all drives being cached are set with *delayed writes*. This means that when data is to be written to a disk that is cached, the write to disk is held by the cache until more write data is accumulated and all such data is written to disk at the same time.

You turn off delayed writes to any drive by including the parameter *d:*. When there is no delayed write for a drive, it is referred to as *write-through*. You force

NWCACHE to cache a drive and enable delayed writes with *d:+*. You may want to exclude a drive, especially a floppy drive, from being cached at all. You exclude a drive from being cached by using the parameter *d:–*.

> **Note**
>
> You cannot use an NWCACHE control option to reenable caching for a drive disabled at startup.

> **Note**
>
> Notice in the three *d:* parameters that the plus sign, the minus sign, and no sign after the drive letter all mean something different.

You use the *maxsize* setting to tell NWCACHE the maximum size of memory to use for the cache. By default, NWCACHE uses all available expanded or extended memory, up to 7670K (the maximum size of the cache). You learn about the different types of memory in Chapter 22, "Optimizing Memory." The *minsize* setting specifies the minimum size of the cache. The default is based on the amount of RAM in your system, as listed earlier in table 11.2.

The /A20 switch suppresses enhanced A20 mode, which is the gateway to your computer's extended memory (above 1M). Generally, you should not use this option because it degrades cache performance. You may have to use it, though, to fix any unusual compatibility problems with your particular computer. If you do use it, you cannot have XMS memory installed in the system.

You use the /B*x=size* switch to tell NWCACHE where in memory to load the lookahead buffer. Replace *x* with E, L, or U. If you want, you can also specify the buffer size. The range of the buffer must be from 4K to 16K. Note the following descriptions:

/BE   Tells NWCACHE to load the lookahead buffer into EMS memory. If you have installed an add-on memory board in your system, cache performance may be reduced with this switch.

/BL   Tells NWCACHE to load the lookahead buffer into lower (conventional) memory.

/BU   Tells NWCACHE to load the lookahead buffer into upper memory.

The /CHECK option tells NWCACHE to perform a cache memory diagnostic test when the cache is started. This test makes sure that the memory area is available and good.

If /DELAY= is set to OFF, the cache disables write-delay and sets all drives to write-through mode. If /DELAY= is set to ON, the cache enables write-delay, with a default time of 5000 milliseconds. You can specify the time of the delay in milliseconds, with a range of 50 to 5000. If you include *time*, do not use ON.

The /E switch tells NWCACHE to use EMS memory for the cache.

The /L switch tells NWCACHE to use lower memory for the cache.

/LEND=ON | OFF turns on or off the sharing of cache memory with other programs that require and request more XMS or EMS memory. NWCACHE monitors these requests and, if it can, automatically reduces the cache size to honor the requests. When the borrowing program releases the borrowed memory, NWCACHE adds it back to the cache.

The /M*x*X option tells NWCACHE to load itself into lower or upper memory. Replace the *x* with either L for lower memory or U for upper memory. To use extended memory through DPMS, add the X character, as in /MLX or /MUX.

> **Note**
>
> Do not use /MUX if you are using a third-party memory manager, such as 386MAX or QEMM.

The use of the /W=*size* switch sets the delayed write data limit, with a range from 0 to 7670 (the maximum cache size allowed by NWCACHE). If the size is listed as 0, all write requests for all drives are satisfied immediately. If the limit is set to a value greater than zero, a maximum of *size*K is retained in the cache before writing to disk. Note that if you do not set this option, the entire cache area is used for delayed write data.

The /X=*address* switch forces NWCACHE to use extended memory for the cache. If no memory manager is loaded and your computer does have extended memory, you can indicate the location (address) of the cache buffer. If your system has XMS memory, you cannot specify the address.

Use the MEM /A command to display the starting address of XMS memory.

Caution

Be extremely careful in allowing large delay times for disk writes and large cache sizes for write data. If the system is accidentally rebooted or the power to the system is lost before the data write takes place, all the data held in RAM is lost.

Control Parameters. This section describes the switches or parameters used with NWCACHE after it has been loaded. They allow you to change its settings, display the cache status, enable and disable caching, flush the buffers, and quit/unload the cache.

The syntax of the NWCACHE control command is

```
NWCACHE - | + d: d:- d:+ /DELAY=ON | OFF | time /Q | /U /S
    /SIZE=MIN | MAX
```

The – option tells NWCACHE to flush the buffers and disable the cache. This option completes any pending delayed writes, clears all drive data from cache memory, and disables the cache. Note that although NWCACHE is no longer active, it still remains in memory and can be reactivated later if you want.

The + option tells NWCACHE to flush the buffers but stay active. If you have disabled NWCACHE, this option also reenables the cache. The + also resets the cache statistics to zero.

The *d:+* parameter tells NWCACHE to reenable caching of *d:*. Write delay is enabled. The *d:–* parameter tells NWCACHE to exclude *d:* from caching.

The *d:* parameter tells NWCACHE to cache *d:* and treat it as a write-through drive.

Note

Again, notice in the three *d:* parameters that the plus sign, the minus sign, and no sign after the drive letter all mean something different.

Note

You cannot use an NWCACHE control option to reenable caching for a drive disabled at startup.

To enable write delay, set /DELAY= to ON. The default delay is 5000 milliseconds, or you can specify a number (*time*) from 50 to 5000 milliseconds in place of ON. If you use the OFF setting, all drives are set to write-through. Any pending buffers are flushed with this option.

Either /Q or /U tells NWCACHE to end its operation. If the option is successful, all buffers are flushed, and used memory is released. These switches also try to have NWCACHE unload itself from memory. However, this may not be possible if you loaded Task Manager or some other TSR program after the cache was loaded into memory. You first have to remove the latter program from memory, and then you can remove NWCACHE from memory.

The /S switch tells NWCACHE to display cache status, as shown in figure 11.15. This option also flushes any pending data writes before displaying the cache status.

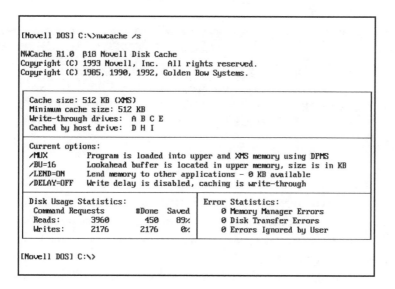

Fig. 11.15
NWCACHE's display of cache status.

The /SIZE= option tells NWCACHE to lower cache size to the minimum when you use MIN, or to raise cache size to the maximum specified (when the cache was loaded) when you use MAX. When you issue this command, the buffers are cleared, and the utility attempts to change cache memory size as requested.

Compressing Disks with Stacker

If you have been purchasing or using software in recent years, you may have noticed that much of that software is distributed on more floppy disks than ever. You may have noticed also that larger and larger drives are being sold with computers. A few years ago, a 20M hard disk (capable of storing 20 million characters of data) was common. Today, you almost cannot find a hard disk smaller than 80M in computer stores or magazine ads.

You may still have a disk that is too small for all the software you want to install on your system, and hard disk drives can be expensive. Novell DOS 7, continuing the heritage from its DR DOS 6 predecessor, includes Stacker, a utility that provides more storage space on your disk by compressing the files to take less room. Now you don't have to spend extra money to get the benefits of this fine utility, which has been sold for a number of years as an add-on for your computer.

> **Note**
>
> If you have a previous version of Stacker or another brand of disk compression program, such as SuperStor or DoubleSpace, do not fret. Novell DOS 7 can convert or use the drives compressed with these programs. Refer to Chapter 4, "Installing Novell DOS 7," for information on converting compressed drives on your system to Stacker 3.1.

Disk compressors access data from the hard drive, decompressing the data as it is read and recompressing it as it is written. The disk drive appears to be a normal disk drive, but the drive capacity is now, in effect, larger than the physical disk capacity. You may have part of your disk compressed while another part remains uncompressed; each part has its own disk drive letter assigned. If you have multiple disk drives or partitions, you may compress some or all of the partitions.

Understanding Disk Compression

Compression works because most files, especially text and data files, have characters repeated in them. Think of how many spaces are in text files, for example, or how much data entered into databases does not fill the entire amount of space allowed for an entry. Compression utilities, including Stacker, work by replacing common character strings with shorter strings. A simple approach might be to replace repeated spaces with a code indicating the number of repetitions; of course, it then becomes necessary to account for an occurrence of the code as part of the text. Modern compression programs, therefore, use a much more elaborate scheme, compressing repeated sequences of characters into one byte or less with algorithms.

The actual compression that you achieve varies, depending on the type of data. The ratio of uncompressed data to compressed data can range from 16 to 1, down to about 1 to 1. Data that has been previously compressed with a regular DOS compression program has the lowest compression ratio, but the compression ratio can, under certain and rare circumstances, reflect an expansion of data. After you have compressed your data, you can display the overall compression ratio, as well as the ratio for specific files. The average ratio is 1.8:1 to 2:1.

Stacker, the data compression program provided with Novell DOS 7, has an advantage over other available programs (such as PKZIP) for data compression. To work with a file compressed by Stacker requires no special action, other than what you do under normal circumstances. The compressed drive appears to be, and is used as, a normal DOS drive.

You accrue an additional space benefit from running Stacker. Novell DOS allocates disk space in units known as clusters. The size of a cluster varies according to the disk capacity, but it is often 2K. With normal Novell DOS files, every file requires a multiple of 2K; therefore, a 1-byte file still requires 2K of disk space. Stacker, however, manages allocations in 512-byte multiples. Thus, the average DOS file loses an average of 1K to round off, whereas Stacker files lose an average of 256 bytes per file (not including any compression). Thus, even if Stacker is unable to compress your files, you still save space.

Compression takes time—time for Stacker to expand data to its original size as the system reads from the disk. Although data expansion increases disk access time, reading compressed data decreases the time: the typical result is that there is no effective change in disk access time. Using NWCACHE can actually reduce disk access time by caching data in larger groups on a host drive.

Special Considerations in Using Stacker

Using compression programs may require other changes in how you use your computer. For example, if you use a disk cache or want to run more than one operating system, you must choose software that is compatible with the disk compression program. Consider the following important points before deciding to compress a disk with Stacker:

- Be prepared to allow your computer to run uninterrupted for a long time during the compression process. The amount of time required depends on the size of your disk, the amount of data on your drive, the speed of your hard drive, and the speed of your computer. The process can take anywhere from 10 or 15 minutes to several hours.

- If you want to defragment your disk at some *later* point, you must use a disk optimizer that was written for use on compressed disks. Disk optimization programs move data to improve the performance of disk drives. Because these programs move data on the drive, they can damage the structure of a compressed drive. DISKOPT, discussed at the beginning of this chapter, is aware of Stacker drives and is able to optimize them. SDEFRAG, also supplied with Novell DOS 7, was created by Stac Electronics especially for its Stacker compression utility. Avoid running other disk optimizing programs on compressed disks.

- You must use compression-compatible operating systems. Compressed drives are accessible from Novell DOS when it is booted from the hard drive. Any operating system that does not have the Stacker drivers installed cannot access compressed drives. Certain operating systems, such as Windows NT, are not compatible with compressed drives. However, many modern operating systems for PCs can use Stacker or have a version of Stacker that can access the same drives. You may want to check with your dealer if you plan to install more than one operating system on your computer.

- Use NWCACHE, SmartDrive, or another disk cache that is able to cache the host drive of a compressed volume. Stacker is compatible with NWCACHE, the disk cache utility provided with Novell DOS 7.

- You can run Stacker only from Novell DOS. If you are using any other environment, such as Task Manager, Windows, or GeoWorks, you must exit from that environment before compressing a drive.

- Be aware that when you install Stacker on a drive and don't compress the entire drive, the drive letters change slightly. Stacker minimizes the changes, but if you have other drives with drive letters higher than the compressed drive, you must be aware of the changes. For example, if you compress part of drive C, the original uncompressed part becomes drive D, while the new compressed drive becomes drive C. If you currently have drive letters D or higher, the compressed disk is assigned the next available letter. Stacker swaps the assigned letter with the old letter; in this manner, the new compressed drive is accessed with the old drive letter, and the uncompressed portion is accessed with the new drive letter. If you are using SUBST, you need to be aware of these additional drive letters. If you compress the entire drive, the drive letters remain unchanged. If you have more than one logical drive on your system before you install Stacker, the swapped drive letters begin after the last drive letter.

Preparing to Use Stacker

Novell DOS does not automatically activate Stacker; before you begin compressing your disk, you must take certain preliminary steps. Read the following sections carefully before starting the Stacker process. You need to understand all this information before attempting to compress your drive.

Caution

After you begin the compression process, the only way back may be to remove the compressed drive and restore the data from a backup. Stacker may not be able to uncompress a drive if the data stored on the drive is larger than the original capacity of the drive, or the actual status of the process may not lend itself to reversal.

Log Off Networks. If you are connected to any network, log off the network before compressing your hard disk. You cannot compress network drives. After the drive or drives have been compressed, you can log back onto the network.

Choose the Drives to Compress. Before using Stacker, you need to decide what drive or drives to compress and how much to leave uncompressed. If you have more than one partition, you may compress any one, some of them, or all of them. You may have up to eight compressed drives. The maximum size of a drive before compression is 512M.

If the drive you choose is not your boot drive and does not have a Windows permanent swap file on it, you may compress the entire drive. If you are going to leave some of the drive uncompressed, you need to decide how much. If this drive is your boot drive, the space required on the uncompressed drive is the space required for the two hidden files of Novell DOS, COMMAND.COM, and several Stacker files. Add the space required for a Windows swap file, if one is needed. A typical Windows installation uses up to 10M of disk space for a permanent swap file. Don't be too close in your space estimate. A little extra can't hurt, but one byte too little can.

Leave enough space on the boot drive for the basic files of Novell DOS, as well as a small amount (at least 10K) extra for editing files. Stacker automatically reserves enough space for the minimum on the boot drive.

Tip
Besides allowing for any special needs, such as the Windows swap file, leave at least 10 percent of the size of the drive to be uncompressed.

The following illustration shows an example of the calculations. Remember that these numbers are only examples; the sizes of files on your disk may be different. The numbers have been rounded to the nearest 4K because files are allocated in 4K units on many noncompressed drives.

Novell DOS hidden files	60K
STACKER.BIN	56K
COMMAND.COM	56K
STACKER.LOG	4K
\NWDOS subdirectory	400K
Subtotal	576K
10M Windows swap file	10240K
Total	10816K

Make sure that you have a minimum of 1M free on the drive before you begin to compress it. Stacker needs at least that much workspace on the drive in order to compress the data. If space is very close to or below the minimum, move some data to another drive temporarily so that Stacker can make more space available. Stacker works by creating a compressed copy of files; after a set of files has been compressed, Stacker can erase the old, uncompressed version of the files. This step makes more space available for repeating the process with another set of files. If this process is interrupted, you may lose your data.

Check for Available Space. Verify that there is sufficient space for Stacker to compress your drive. That may seem contradictory, but Stacker must install some data as well as have free space available for a file to be rewritten in compressed format before removing the original file. A bootable hard disk must have at least 1M of free space. Any other hard disk must have at least 100K of free space. A floppy must have 100K free.

Run CHKDSK. Before you compress your drive, run CHKDSK to verify that the drive has no problems. Any existing problems are only magnified by an attempt to compress a drive. CHKDSK should not show any error messages, but if it does, repeat CHKDSK with the /F parameter. If necessary, tell CHKDSK to write fixes to disk. If you are at all in doubt about how to fix the CHKDSK reported errors, don't compress the drive. Fix the errors and then compress the drive. You may want to refresh your knowledge of CHKDSK by rereading the section "Checking Disks (CHKDSK)" at the beginning of this chapter.

Back Up Existing Files. Before you begin the compression process, be sure to back up important files. Stacker can compress your hard drive without first removing the information. This action means that the disk can be compressed as it stands. During the compression process, however, your disk cannot be used. If the power were to fail during the installation process, you would be left with a hard disk that could not be used until the data was restored. Because of this danger, you should always back up the disk before you begin compressing it. See Chapter 12, "Backup Utilities," for information on how to back up the data on your hard drive before you compress it. Probably nothing will go wrong when you compress your drive, but it is possible, so don't neglect this basic precaution.

At the very least, make backups of files that would otherwise be impossible or difficult to replace. Be sure to back up your CONFIG.SYS and AUTOEXEC.BAT files. CONFIG.SYS is the file Novell DOS uses to load driver programs when the system is booted. AUTOEXEC.BAT runs any programs that need to run when you boot Novell DOS. These two files are modified during the compression process.

Your uncompressed disk contains at least COMMAND.COM and several Stacker files, as well as the two hidden files—IBMBIO.COM and IBMDOS.COM—that are part of Novell DOS 7. Setup also creates a file named STACKER.BIN and places it on the uncompressed boot drive along with STACKER.INI, the initialization file. STACKER.BIN is the device driver for the disk compression and is automatically loaded by Novell DOS without the need for CONFIG.SYS or DCONFIG.SYS. Both STACKER.BIN and STACKER.INI are marked as hidden. The installation process also creates an \NWDOS subdirectory on the uncompressed boot disk and installs several Stacker utilities there.

> **Caution**
>
> If any of the boot or Stacker hidden files are missing or damaged, DOS may fail to boot. Make sure that you have a backup boot floppy disk, just in case. Such a floppy, besides including the normal boot files (the hidden IBMBIO.COM and IBMDOS.COM files and the COMMAND.COM file), should include STACKER.BIN and STACKER.INI so that you can access the compressed drives on your system.

Move Files Incompatible with Stacker. Certain files and configurations are not compatible with Stacker but can be kept on the uncompressed part of the disk. A good example of files that cannot be compressed is Novell DOS itself. Because parts of the operating system may be needed before compression is activated, you cannot compress all of your boot drive. Stacker handles this situation for you. Stacker is also incompatible with some older accounting programs that create constant-size work files.

Uninstall Copy-Protected Software. Copy-protected programs installed on the hard disk are incompatible with the compression process. Usually, these files must reside in specific locations on the hard disk. Because the compression process moves the files to a new location on the (now compressed) drive, you should remove these files first. If you have any copy-protected software installed on the drive, you should run the appropriate uninstall programs. Files of this type can be reinstalled after you compress the drive. The XDIR /S /P command displays all files on a drive with their attributes.

Tip

If you never run Windows, you can ignore this step.

Remove the Windows Swap File. The Windows temporary swap file is among the files that cannot reside on a compressed drive. If you are running Windows, check to see whether you have a permanent swap file. If you do, you should delete it before you compress your hard drive. After you have compressed the hard drive, you can set up a permanent swap file again.

To find out about the Windows swap file, run Windows. The method of determining the swap file information varies, depending on whether you are running Windows 3.0 or 3.1:

■ For Windows 3.0, run the Setup program and choose Help About. The dialog box shows the current state of the Windows swap file. If you have a swap file on the drive you are compressing, add the space required for the swap file to the space to remain uncompressed. If you have a permanent swap file on the drive, you must remove it before you begin the compression. First make sure that you are out of Windows. Then run Windows again in real mode with this command:

```
WIN /R SWAPFILE
```

This command runs Windows in real mode and starts the SWAPFILE program. Select Delete the Permanent Swap File and choose OK. Then you can end Windows, having deleted the permanent swap file and marked Windows so that it uses a temporary swap file the next time you run it. Windows in real mode does not use any swap file, so you have to run in real mode to be able to delete it.

■ For Windows 3.1, open the Control Panel in the Main group and choose the Virtual Memory icon. The resulting dialog box shows the drive and type (permanent or temporary) of swap file. To remove a permanent swap file, choose Change from that dialog box. Select Type, Temporary. When Windows asks whether to restart Windows, you can respond with OK and shut down Windows.

Installing Stacker

Install Stacker from the Novell DOS 7 Setup utility. Do not attempt to install disk compression under Task Manager, Windows, Desqview, or any other multitasking system. There are two reasons for running Stacker alone. First, any interruptions of the compression process may make the partially compressed drive unusable. Second, and more important, the data on the compressed/uncompressed drive is very dynamic and cannot be accessed by any other program while the process is going on.

To begin the process, enter **SETUP**. Use the Tab key or the up- or down-arrow key to select Disk Compression. Press Enter. If it is offered, select the reboot option so that Stacker can disable programs that might interfere with the compression process. After the reboot, the Setup program continues, displaying a list of all system drives (see fig. 11.16). If you have existing Stacker compressed drives, the drive list indicates that with `Stacker host drive`. You cannot select this drive for compression. If you select a Stacker compressed drive, you can choose only Grow/Shrink Stacked Drive (see the later section "Changing the Size of a Stacked Drive" for details).

If the selected hard disk is your only hard disk, be sure to leave space for files besides those that Setup and Stacker automatically leave. If you have more than one hard disk (logical or physical drives), you may want to stack all but one drive, in which case you might leave drive C uncompressed for software that does not like compression. Remember that Stacker allows you to resize a compressed volume at a later date if you want.

Fig. 11.16
Setup's list of system drives for compression.

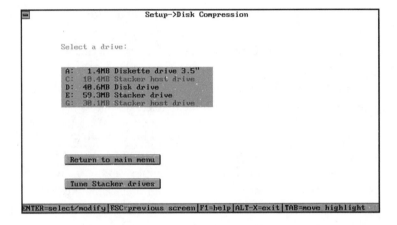

After you select a drive, press Enter to begin the compression process. Because this is a noncompressed drive, you have several options (see fig. 11.17). You can stack the entire drive, or you can create a stacked drive from the free space on the selected drive.

Fig. 11.17
Setup options for compressing a drive.

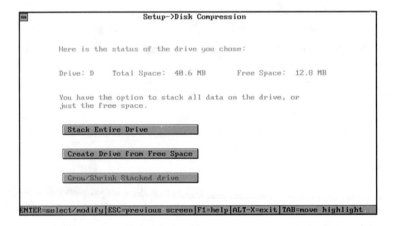

Stack Entire Drive compresses all data and free space into a single volume. Create Drive from Free Space uses only free space to create a new drive. Existing data remains uncompressed on the original drive. Your choice depends on the software you use, the need you have for additional space, and the number of drives in your system. For example, if you have only one drive, are running out of space, and do not use applications that require a non-compressed drive, then you should compress the entire drive. Setup tells Stacker to leave only enough space for the files it requires for booting your computer, and to compress the rest. However, if you have two or more disks, require more space, and use software that does not like disk compression, then you should leave one drive—your boot drive—noncompressed, and compress the other drive(s). You have to make the decision, but you can change it later.

Choose one of these buttons and then select Begin Stacking. Stacker begins to compress the data. The compression process requires anywhere from a few minutes to an hour or more.

When Stacker finishes compressing the data, Setup displays the drive statistics and then a menu giving you the option of rebooting your system or exiting to Novell DOS. You must reboot to be able to read your data from the compressed partition.

Now that you have compressed your data and rebooted the computer, do a directory listing of the new compressed drive by entering **DIR** at the Novell DOS prompt. Notice the amount of space now available.

Displaying the Stacker Drive Map

The Stacker drive map displays all available drives and the swapped drive letter for Stacker compressed drives. At the DOS prompt, enter the following:

    STACKER

Stacker returns with the Stacker drive map, as shown in figure 11.18.

```
[Novell DOS] C:\>STACKER

Stacker 3.10 for Windows and DOS (c) 1990-93 Stac Electronics, Carlsbad, CA

Stacker drive map:
   Drive A: was drive A: at boot time
   Drive B: was drive B: at boot time
   Drive C: was drive C: at boot time
   Drive D: was drive D: at boot time   [ H:\STACVOL.DSK = 40.5MB  ]
   Drive E: was drive E: at boot time   [ G:\STACVOL.DSK = 30.0MB  ]
   Drive F: was drive F: at boot time   [ * -- Not mounted ]
   Drive G: was drive G: at boot time
   Drive H: was drive H: at boot time   [ H:\STACVOL.DSK = 40.5MB  ]
Total of 1 available replaceable drive(s).
[Novell DOS] C:\>
```

Fig. 11.18
The Stacker drive map.

If any drive is marked with an asterisk, the drive is not mounted. This should be taken care of by the Novell DOS Setup utility, which you may have to run to make sure that all drives are mounted so that you can access the data on them.

A stacked (compressed) drive must be mounted. This means that the compressed volume is actually set as a logical drive and becomes accessible. An unmounted drive can be accessed only as the host drive, with the large Stacker file, which is the compressed volume, being seen as a file, not as a drive.

You can mount any stacked drive manually. At the DOS prompt, issue the command

```
STACKER finaldrive:=sourcedrive:\STACVOL.xxx
```

or

```
STACKER finaldrive:\STACVOL.xxx
```

In the first example, from the Stacker drive map, the command reads as

```
STACKER D:=E:\STACVOL.DSK
```

to mount the compressed volume on E: as drive D. In the second example, the command reads as

```
STACKER E:\STACVOL.DSK
```

to mount E: as E:.

You may need to unmount a compressed drive in order to use DISKCOPY or FORMAT on the drive, which essentially makes the drive an empty drive. There is a very large hidden file on the drive, which becomes the compressed volume when mounted, but it is not seen and is treated when unmounted as an ordinary file.

To unmount a compressed drive, use this command:

```
STACKER-d:
```

The minus sign is necessary, and you must specify the drive to unmount.

Displaying Stacker Statistics

You can display the amount of compression by file or drive. Use the Novell DOS CHKDSK command with the /D switch to display information about a compressed drive, including actual bytes used and compressed bytes used, the drive compression ratio, projected drive capacity based on the ratio, and the current fragmentation level. Use the XDIR command to display information about individual files.

To display statistics about compressed drives, enter

    CHKDSK *d:* /D

Figure 11.19 shows a report issued for this command.

```
                        Stacker Drive              STACVOL File
                        Drive D:                   H:\STACVOL.DSK
                        ----------------           -----------------
        Total Bytes:        84,000,768                 42,003,968
        Bytes Used:         30,400,512 ( 36.2%)        17,406,464 ( 41.4%)
        Bytes Free:         53,600,256 ( 63.8%)        24,597,504 ( 58.6%)

        Bytes Per Cluster:       4,096                      2,048

        Stacker Drive Compression Ratio = 1.7:1
        Projected Bytes Free            = 42,938,368
        Fragmentation Level             = 0

     Checking FAT Integrity...

      84,000,768 bytes total disk space.
          65,536 bytes in 14 directories.
      30,334,976 bytes in 833 user files.
      53,600,256 bytes available on disk.

         655,360 total bytes of memory.
         675,856 total bytes of free memory.
         553,728 bytes in largest free memory block.

     [Novell DOS] C:\>
```

Fig. 11.19
A CHKDSK statistics report for a stacked drive.

CHKDSK displays additional information about compressed drives. When you use CHKDSK on a compressed drive, it also tests the integrity of the data and the Stacker information about the drive. CHKDSK displays some information about this additional testing done for Stacker drives, as you can see in figure 11.19. The numbers for bytes available and bytes used will not be exact on a Stacker drive because they are based on a projection from the current compression ratio. The exact capacity depends on the type of files you actually store on the drive.

Use the XDIR command to see information about individual files. Figure 11.20 shows output from the XDIR command, with the compression ratio displayed. XDIR shows the size and compression ratio of files. By default, XDIR displays all files in the current directory, but you can specify different files if you like. You can use wild-card characters to select certain files. XDIR also displays the attributes (read-only, hidden, system, and archive) of files.

To sort the display by compression ratio, use the /Y switch. See Chapter 7, "Managing Files and Directories," for a complete explanation of XDIR.

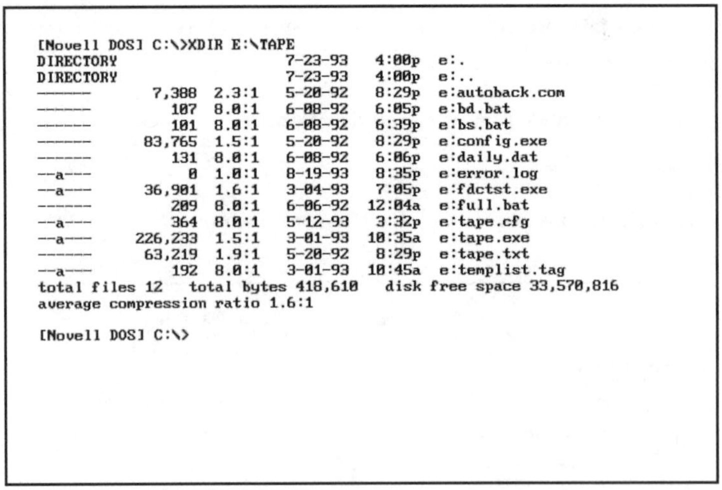

Fig. 11.20

An XDIR file listing for a stacked drive.

```
[Novell DOS] C:\>XDIR E:\TAPE
DIRECTORY                     7-23-93    4:00p   e:.
DIRECTORY                     7-23-93    4:00p   e:..
-------        7,388  2.3:1   5-20-92    8:29p   e:autoback.com
-------          107  8.0:1   6-08-92    6:05p   e:bd.bat
-------          101  8.0:1   6-08-92    6:39p   e:bs.bat
-------       83,765  1.5:1   5-20-92    8:29p   e:config.exe
-------          131  8.0:1   6-08-92    6:06p   e:daily.dat
--a----            0  1.0:1   8-19-93    8:35p   e:error.log
--a----       36,901  1.6:1   3-04-93    7:05p   e:fdctst.exe
-------          209  8.0:1   6-06-92   12:04a   e:full.bat
--a----          364  8.0:1   5-12-93    3:32p   e:tape.cfg
--a----      226,233  1.5:1   3-01-93   10:35a   e:tape.exe
-------       63,219  1.9:1   5-20-92    8:29p   e:tape.txt
--a----          192  8.0:1   3-01-93   10:45a   e:templist.tag
total files 12    total bytes 418,610   disk free space 33,570,816
average compression ratio 1.6:1

[Novell DOS] C:\>
```

Resolving Things That Go Wrong

When you boot your computer, Stacker checks all compressed drives. If Stacker finds a problem with one, it issues a message to you. If there are severe problems, Stacker makes the drive read-only to prevent you from writing to it and causing additional problems.

The first step in case of an error is to back up everything that can be read on the drive that has a problem. Then run CHKDSK with the /F switch on the drive. If Stacker issued a message that the drive is set to read-only, use the CHKDSK /WP command.

If running the CHKDSK /F or CHKDSK /WP command on the compressed drive does not take care of the problem, try running SDEFRAG and tell it to restack the drive. The combination of the two actions can probably fix the problem.

Caution

Make sure that CHKDSK is the Novell DOS CHKDSK program for this version of Novell DOS and is running under Novell DOS. Other versions from other operating systems can cause additional problems. Only the Novell DOS version of CHKDSK is aware of compressed disks and is able to handle them properly. Ensure that MS-DOS or PC DOS programs are in a directory that is not in the path.

> ### Caution
>
> Don't use other third-party disk utilities to attempt to fix problems with compressed drives unless they specifically state that they can work with Stacker compressed disks. Many utilities have been written to deal with uncompressed disks only, not compressed disks. A utility not aware of compressed drives is likely to cause more damage than it fixes.

Changing the Size of a Stacked Drive

You can modify a stacked drive. You may be able to make the compressed portion of a drive larger if there is enough room on the host drive. You can also make the compressed portion of a drive smaller; this may require you to remove some files if the compressed volume is too full. The compressed drive may be optimized for amount of compression or speed of operation.

To resize your stacked drive, you must run the Novell Setup utility. At the DOS prompt, enter SETUP. From the opening menu, select Disk Compression. Setup then asks whether you need to reboot your system to remove any TSRs or other utilities that could interfere with the disk operations to be performed. Choose the appropriate button.

If you choose to reboot, press the F5 key when the message Starting DOS... appears on-screen to bypass loading the CONFIG.SYS or DCONFIG.SYS file and the AUTOEXEC.BAT file. Alternatively, you can press the F8 key when Starting DOS... appears for prompts on the commands in the boot files. Press N at the question for any TSRs or other utilities that affect disk drives. After booting, restart the Setup utility.

If you do not choose to reboot, or after you have rebooted, choose Continue. To optimize speed or compression, choose Tune Stacker Drives. Then select one of the following options: Fastest Speed and Standard Compression, More Compression and a Bit Less Speed, or Best Compression. Choose Accept the Above and Continue to return to the previous screen. To resize, select for resizing only a drive marked as a Stacker drive. When you do so, the display changes to show you the selected drive, total drive space, and free space. Then choose the button labeled Grow/Shrink Stacked Drive.

At this point, Setup loads and executes the SDEFRAG utility from Stacker. Select either Increase Stacker Drive Size or More Uncompressed Space Available, depending on what you want to do. If you choose to shrink the stacked drive and have a Windows permanent swap file on the compressed drive, SDEFRAG informs you that it will delete the swap file. Press Enter, and SDEFRAG starts the disk optimization procedure.

When the drive is ready, you are requested to enter the new size of the compressed drive or the amount of uncompressed space. Enter the number in K (thousands of bytes). SDEFRAG is then ready to perform the modifications. Press Enter to begin. After the resizing is done, SDEFRAG reboots your computer.

Removing Stacker Compression

Novell DOS 7 includes Unstack, the Stacker utility to remove the disk compression from a drive.

Before using Unstack, the first thing you must do is make sure that enough free space is on the drive to hold all the files that are currently compressed on the drive. Suppose that you have a 40M hard disk drive. When wholly compressed, it provides approximately 80M of compressed storage. With all the programs and data stored on the drive, you have about 18M free. With a compression ration of 2 to 1, you must remove more than a third of the files, depending on the mix of data and programs, before you can decompress the drive.

Fortunately, Unstack first checks whether there is enough room to remove the compression, and if there is not, informs you of the problem with a notice of the amount of space you must free up by either deleting or copying files from the drive. Because the Unstack utility requires space to rewrite a file in an uncompressed mode before it can erase the compressed form, Unstack also determines the amount of fragmentation. If there is any, Unstack accesses SDEFRAG to optimize the drive before it can start the decompression. You can read more on SDEFRAG earlier in this chapter.

To start the unstacking process, enter the following command at the Novell DOS prompt:

```
UNSTACK d:
```

Make sure that the specified drive is the compressed drive, not the uncompressed drive.

You cannot remove the current drive. You must change to some other drive before you run Unstack.

Caution

Be sure that you have a good backup before you remove a compressed drive. If you want to remove the compressed disk on the boot drive, make sure that you also have a way to restore or reinstall the operating system. Novell DOS is usually in the directory called \NWDOS on the boot drive; however, if there is a problem such as a power outage while you are removing this compressed drive, you no longer have access to any part of Novell DOS until you restore the data.

Assuming that all is ready, choose Continue or press C. If SDEFRAG is required, that utility is now run without any further action on your part. When SDEFRAG is finished, you are given the following warning:

```
About to unstack ALL DATA on Stacker drive D: Do you wish to
proceed?
```

Press Enter while Exit is highlighted, or use the up-arrow key to choose Unstack and press Enter to begin. Unstack wants to make sure that you are not doing this by mistake, so you are asked Are you SURE ?? Choose No to exit or Yes to proceed. (There are no more confirmations.) Figure 11.21 shows this screen.

Fig. 11.21
Unstack's opening screen asking whether to proceed.

Unstack displays a percentage bar (0% to 100%) showing its progress while decompressing the selected drive. The time required to decompress the drive depends on the size of the drive, the number and size of the files, and the speed of your computer. You can interrupt the process by pressing the F10 key, but this may leave files in a fragmented state, which can be fixed with the SDEFRAG command.

When the decompression has been completed, Unstack informs you of this and instructs you to Press Enter key to restart system. Because of the changes to the system configuration files, this step is necessary, so press Enter and let your system restart.

After your system is up and running, check the directory for the decompressed drive. Notice the vast size difference in the storage capacity of the drive.

From Here...

In this chapter, you learned about several utilities for repairing or improving the performance of your disk drives: CHKDSK, DISKOPT, SDEFRAG, NWCACHE, and Stacker. You may want to turn now to the following chapters:

- Chapter 8, "Preparing Disks," discusses other disk utilities.

- Chapter 12, "Backup Utilities," shows you how to make backups of your data.

- Chapter 16, "Virus Protection," explains how to protect your system from computer viruses.

Chapter 12

Backup Utilities

One of the best measures you have against loss of data is a good backup program. This is the basis for maintaining data integrity in any system. The backup program works in connection with security and antivirus measures to keep your files current and healthy, but also saves you from such accidental disasters as a hard drive crash or corrupted data. Novell DOS 7 includes a program, called Fastback Express, to help you back up your data.

This chapter covers the following topics:

- Backup planning
- Selecting files to back up
- Restoring files
- The Windows backup utility

Planning a Backup Strategy

Many people are hesitant to use backups. It is new territory for many, and they think it is going to be a hassle. It does seem at first to be a minor inconvenience, but all it takes is one incident of lost or damaged data, and you become a backup believer for life. Obviously, you do not have to back up all your files every day. To help you determine how often to back up your files, consider how often your programs change, and how often you make changes to the system files of your operating system. To make the process of backing up your computer's data as painless as possible, you want to spend the least necessary amount of time.

You have some choices to make as you build your backup plan. You can perform a full backup of your system every night, or you can just back up your data files and decide that if your system does crash, you are willing to reinstall and reconfigure applications. As you weigh the pros and cons of various backup approaches, keep in mind that some files almost never change. Your program's executable files change only when an update or upgrade is released. The files that change most often are data files such as spreadsheets, letters, and databases.

Full Backup versus Incremental Backup

The most common approach taken by users is to perform a full backup of every file on their systems once a week. But much can happen in a week, and you would hate to lose a week's worth of work if your system failed. So every day you can back up individual files also, by doing an *incremental backup*. This means that you back up only the files that have changed since the last time your files were backed up.

> **Note**
>
> You can also back up specific individual files. See the section "Specifying Individual Files" later in this chapter for details.

Fastback Express can determine whether a file has changed since the last time a backup of the file occurred. The program maintains an *archive bit*, a file attribute that indicates whether a file has been updated. Fastback Express backs up the file again only if the archive bit is set. The problem with incremental backups is that, if you need to restore your data, you have to rebuild the system by using a combination of full backups and incremental backups. You might perform a full backup on Friday, for example, and incremental backups on Monday, Tuesday, and Wednesday. If your hard drive crashes on Thursday, you must rebuild your system by restoring Friday's full backup, then Monday's incremental backup, then Tuesday's incremental backup, and so on, to bring your system as close as possible to its state at crash time.

Conceivably, you can perform a full backup only once and perform incremental backups thereafter. If your system ever crashes, however, you have to restore months of incremental backups, which is grossly inefficient. Most people prefer to make a full backup about once a week. At worst, then, a data disaster can force them to restore one week's worth of backups.

You may decide, as an extra security precaution for data, to store a copy of your backups off-site. This is a good idea but requires some extra work and planning. What you do is make a full backup of your data on a set day, like Friday. Then make daily incremental backups. When Friday comes, take the complete backup set (the full backup with all incrementals) to an off-site storage facility. This could be the system manager's house or another office. Keep it there while you create another complete backup set the following week. When the new backup is complete, take it off-site and bring the old backup back in to begin copying a new backup set.

This way, you actually have three copies of your data. One is on the hard drive itself; the other is in your office and ready to restore in case your hard drive gets damaged. The third copy is off-site, and therefore safe from damage in the event of a natural disaster or sabotage. Granted, the data may be a week old, but restoring week-old data is preferable to creating the data from scratch.

Choosing the Backup Medium

Now that you know which files to back up and how often to do a backup, you need to decide which backup medium to use. With Fastback Express, you have three basic choices:

- Floppy disks

- Network drives

- Other devices

The most common method is to back up to floppy disks. With only 20-40M of data, this process is not exceedingly difficult or time-consuming. With a higher amount of data, it is more of a hassle to back up to floppy disks—it simply takes too much time and is too tedious a process.

Depending on what type of data is on your hard drive and assuming that you have a backup program with a data compression feature, backing up 20M of data requires at least eight 1.44M floppy disks. Depending on your microprocessor, the process takes at least 15 minutes to accomplish—not too bad if that's all you have to back up. But if you multiply that by five, you can see why backing up to floppy disk is more expensive, in terms of time, than one of the other methods.

Another option is to back up the data that is on your hard drive to another hard drive on your network. The biggest problem with this is that most users do not have enough hard drive space for themselves, let alone for sharing. If you do have the space, however, this is a fast and efficient way of backing up your data.

> **Note**
>
> One way to back up your network is to have all the users copy the files they want backed up to your network hard drive, and then just back up your hard drive.

The final option is to use some other device such as tape or optical storage. Using other devices provides the option (also present when you use floppy disks) of moving the backups to another location where they can remain safe in case a natural disaster affects your work site.

You have many choices of tape devices: quarter-inch cartidge (QIC), quarter-inch minicartridge (Mini), 4-millimeter digital audio tape (DAT), and 8-millimeter video tape (8MM). Capacities vary for each type. Minicartridges can store up to 300M, 8MM can store up to 5G, and new DAT drives are promising 8G. If you are budget-conscious, minicartridges and QICs are probably the best choice.

When choosing a backup medium, keep in mind that the backup becomes useless if the medium is damaged. Tapes and disks must be protected from magnetic devices and extreme temperatures. If your computer equipment is protected by a thermostatically controlled environment, consider extending that environment to include a storage area for backups. If you store backups off-site, be careful that they are not exposed to heat or cold when in transit.

There are potential drawbacks to backing up to other devices. First, you may have to purchase hardware. Depending on your backup needs, though, this is probably still cheaper than hard drive space on a dollar-to-megabyte ratio. Another problem you might face is that Fastback Express needs to recognize this device as a drive letter on your system. This is possible only with certain types of hardware. Some SCSI devices can be recognized as a drive letter if the software that came with the SCSI controller provided that option. Other software choices are available (like SCSI Express from Corel) but work only with specific types of controllers.

Of course, many hardware backup systems also include their own backup software. If this is the case, you might want to use the software included with the system. The software is probably tuned specifically for the hardware; therefore, your backups are more reliable and faster to execute.

Now that you understand the available options, and some pros and cons of each, it is time to develop a plan of your own. If you remember to follow it, a solid backup plan provides enormous peace of mind.

Note a final point about backing up your system's data. You can back up only the files to which you have rights. If you are using Novell DOS 7's peer-to-peer networking capabilities and others are relying on you to make backups of their computers as well, make sure that they give you the rights to all the files they want backed up. Read-only rights are not sufficient. Because the software modifies the archive bit of a file, write privileges are needed as well. You may have to explain this principle to your coworkers. If you fail to do so, they may think you are backing up their files, when in reality, the backup software does not even know those files exist.

Tip
To simplify the rights issue, create a user called BACKUP and give it all rights. When you need to back up, log in as user BACKUP.

Starting the Backup

Fastback Express is loaded by Novell DOS 7 in the NWDOS subdirectory. To start the DOS version, enter **FBX** at the DOS prompt. The program scans the system memory quickly to locate viruses; if none are found, the program is loaded. At the top of the initial screen, you see a menu bar containing the menu options File, Options, and Help (see fig. 12.1). The main part of the screen is separated into five boxes, labeled Operation, Selections, From, To, and Backup Options. Along the bottom is a status bar that displays information about specific options as they are highlighted. Use the Tab key to move from box to box, and the up- and down-arrow keys to move between selections within a box.

To move to a specific box on-screen, press and hold down the Alt key and then press the letter highlighted in the title of each box. For example, to move to the Operation box, press Alt-P; to move to the To box, press Alt-T.

> **Note**
>
> Fastback Express is easier to navigate with the mouse than with the keyboard. If you have a mouse, load its driver in your AUTOEXEC.BAT file so that it is always available.

The Operation list box contains the program functions available to you with this utility. The one you are likely to use most often is at the top of the list: Backup. As you select different operations, the rest of the boxes change to reflect the options available with each one. There is a dot to the left of the choices currently selected.

You can access Fastback Express's help feature through the Help menu or by pressing the F1 key almost anywhere in the program. If you feel stuck somewhere because you do not know what an option means or what you should do next, press F1. Chances are pretty good that you will find the answers you need.

Fig. 12.1
The Fastback
Express utility.

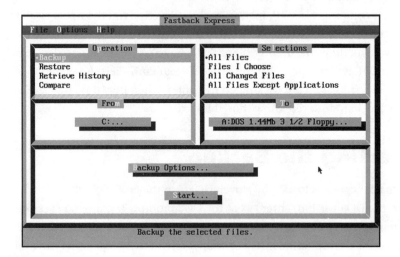

Selecting Files to Back Up

Move the cursor to the Backup operation and take a minute to review the screen. The box directly under Operation is labeled From. This is where you specify which drive volume—either local hard drive or network drive—that you want to back up. Notice that in the Selections box, you have the choice to back up all files in the volume, or just some of them.

Specifying Individual Files. The All Files option in the Selections box performs a full backup of the volume—both data files and program files. You do not want to select this tremendously lengthy option too often. Ordinarily, you might want to use this about once a week.

The Files I Choose option lets you specify exactly which files on the volume you want to back up. With this option, Fastback Express scans all the directories and files on your volume and then displays a directory tree on the left side of the screen, with a list of files on the right (see fig. 12.2). Along the top of the screen is a menu bar with File, View, and Help menus. Under the menu bar, there is a field where you can select which drive you want to view. Under the drive field are four buttons labeled Close, Include, Exclude, and View. Along the bottom of the screen is a status bar. This bar gives you a brief description of what each highlighted item on the screen does. (For more information on exluding files and saving your backup selections, see the sections "Excluding Files with Filters" and "Completing the Backup" later in this chapter.)

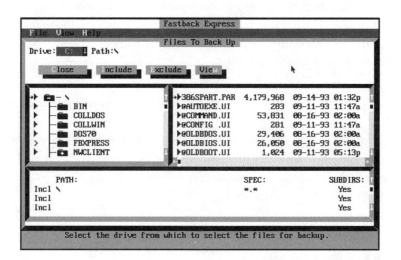

Fig. 12.2
You can specify which files to back up in the Files To Back Up screen.

The Files To Back Up screen can show directories and files for only one drive at a time. To change the drive that is displayed, highlight the drive letter by using the Tab key or mouse, and hold down the Alt key while you press the down-arrow key. A drop-down box appears, allowing you to choose any drive to which you have access. Select the drive that contains your Novell DOS 7 files (probably C:); then press Enter. With the cursor still on the drive letter, press Alt-I to include every file and directory on this drive in the backup. (If you press Alt-E instead, you exclude every file and directory on this drive from the backup.)

Notice in figure 12.2 that every file has a solid triangle (▼) next to it. Whenever a triangle appears beside a file name, the file is selected for backup. Whenever a triangle appears beside a directory name, every file in the directory is selected for backup. If some but not all files in a directory are selected for backup, the triangle beside the directory name changes to a greater than sign (>).

Press Tab to move the cursor to the directory list, and then use the arrow key to highlight the directory that contains your Novell DOS 7 files (probably \NWDOS). It should have a solid triangle next to it. If it does not, press the space bar until one appears.

Press Tab to move to the files list, and select the file ATTRIB.EXE with the arrow key. This program is used to change a file's attributes, but suppose that you don't want to back up this file. Press the space bar to remove the triangle next to the file. Three things happen: the triangle disappears, the triangle next to the \NWDOS directory changes to >, and a line is added to the box below the directories and files (see fig. 12.3). The line reads something like this:

```
Excl \NWDOS                         ATTRIB.EXE    No
```

The third option in the Selections box of the Fastback Express screen is All Changed Files. This selection backs up only the files that have been modified or created since the last backup with Fastback Express was performed. This is what is called an incremental backup.

Fig. 12.3

Deselecting a file for backup.

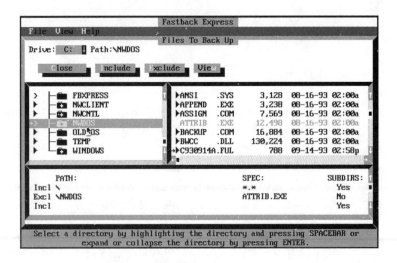

All Files Except Applications is the final option. If you select this option, all files except those with the extensions COM, EXE, and DLL are backed up.

Files with extensions other than these usually come with an application; there are help files, for instance, as well as configuration files, documents, and tutorial files sometimes. If you want to make sure that all of these get backed up, use this option.

Selecting Directories. Notice that some of the icons next to the directories have a plus sign (+) or minus sign (–) in them. If a directory icon has a +, the directory contains subdirectories that are not currently displayed. If it has a –, it has subdirectories that are displayed. To change + to –, or – to +, highlight the directory name and press Enter.

Selecting Groups of Files. Many people are concerned with backing up only their data files. Fastback Express provides a method to do this quickly. If you choose the Groups command from the File menu, the program displays the Groups dialog box, which lists many popular applications and the types of data files they most commonly use (see fig. 12.4). The types of files are identified by extension. Many applications have a specific extension for their data files. Lotus 1-2-3 worksheet files, for example, have a WK? extension (the "?" can be any character).

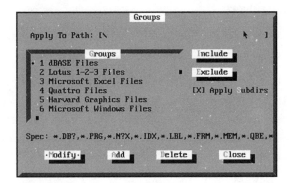

Fig. 12.4
You can back up application-specific files in the Groups dialog box.

Some applications do not work this way. When you save a document in WordPerfect, for example, you can specify any file name you want—WordPerfect does not provide file extensions. If you want to use the Groups command to back up your WordPerfect documents, you have to provide a common file extension yourself. If you look at Group 7 and highlight it, you notice that Fastback Express assumes that you are going to name your files with a WP? extension. If this does not fit your intention, or if you want to add to the list, you can change this definition by choosing the Modify button.

Fastback Express might not know every application you have on your system, so it lets you add application and data file definitions, if you like. Options 26 through 32 are open and available to hold other Groups you define. If you want to free another spot by deleting an application that Fastback Express has defined, simply highlight the name in the Groups list; then choose Delete.

Finding Files Based on Criteria. Another option on the File menu searches for a specific file on your drive. If you select the Find Files option, you can have Fastback Express look for all files that match a certain criteria. For example, if you enter the search criteria SPAM*.DOC, Fastback Express finds all the files on your drive that begin with SPAM and have the extension DOC.

Excluding Files with Filters. The first command on the File menu, Include All, includes all the displayed files in the backup. The next option, Exclude All, excludes all the displayed files and directories. These are simple to deal with, but the next two are trickier.

When you choose Filters, you are prompted to enter more information in the Filters dialog box (see fig. 12.5). In this dialog box, you can specify that any files meeting the criteria you define be excluded from the backup. You can define three filters here:

- The first filter (Exclude Files Dated) excludes files from your backup that were created or modified between the dates you define.

- The second filter (Exclude Files With Sizes) excludes files from your backup that are smaller or larger than a specified value. You might use this option, for example, if you want to back up all the smaller files on your hard drive to floppy disk, and then back up the larger files to a network drive.

- The third filter (Exclude Files With Attributes) excludes files from your backup that meet any of these three attributes: Read-Only, System, or Hidden. This filter comes in handy if you have some files that never change on your system. Because files of these three types are difficult to change, you probably won't need to back them up regularly, so you can use this filter to exclude them from the backup.

Changing the View
If you open the View menu, the Display option should be highlighted. To view the other menu, press the right-arrow key. With these options, you

IV

Disk and File Management

choose which files to view in the files list below. If you want to see both selected and nonselected files, select All (the default). If you want to view only
the files that have changed since the last backup, or only the files that fit
filter criteria you have defined, then this menu is helpful. To see a brief description of each option, highlight it and then look at the status bar.

Highlight the Sort By option in the View menu and press the right-arrow key
to display its menu. This option enables you to customize the file display
further; you can sort the files by size, by date, alphabetically by file name, or
alphabetically by extension. The other commands on the View menu enable
you to expand the directories on your hard drive to display all their
subdirectories.

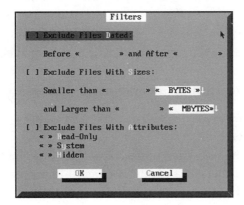

Fig. 12.5
Define filters to
help narrow your
selection of files to
be backed up.

Specifying Backup Options

To specify backup options, choose the Backup Options button at the bottom
of the Fastback Express screen. The Backup Options dialog box appears, as
shown in figure 12.6.

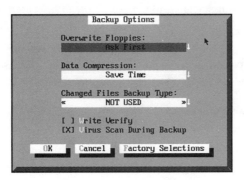

Fig. 12.6
Specifying
preferences in the
Backup Options
dialog box.

Tip
You can restore all options to their default values by choosing the Factory Selections button.

Choosing the Overwrite Option. The first backup option asks whether you want backup data to overwrite the data already contained on floppy disks. If you perform a backup to floppies that have data already on them, Fastback Express asks you, by default, if you want to overwrite the data. You can change the program so that it never overwrites the data, or so that it always overwrites without asking.

Configuring Data Compression. The next option is used to configure data compression. To conserve room on the backup medium, Fastback Express compresses the data it backs up. Depending on what type of data you are backing up, a given file on the target drive might require only 50-75 percent of the space it required on the source drive. If you want to turn this compression off, you can do so here. Compressing data takes time, so Fastback Express lets you choose whether you want compression (to utilize your space on the target volume more efficiently) or do not want compression. The default value is set to save you time, but if extra time is not a problem—for instance, if you perform unattended backups to a network drive—you probably want to change this option so that Fastback Express uses the least space possible.

Verifying the Backup. Write Verify, another option in the Backup Options dialog box, lets you verify that the data you have backed up is identical to the original data. With this option, Fastback Express writes data to the target media and then verifies that the copy is correct. Although this sounds like a great idea, it takes quite a bit of time, so the default is to leave this option unselected. If you suspect that your system might not be reliable when transferring data, you can select this option.

Scanning for Viruses. The last backup option, Virus Scan During Backup, is used to perform a virus scan on the files during the backup procedure. By default, this check box is selected, and you should probably leave it that way. If a virus attacks your system and destroys data and program files, the only means of recovery you have may be to restore those files from your backup. The backup is not going to do you much good if the backup files are infected with a virus. Keeping a clean backup of your files is critical, so unless you have a specific reason for deselecting this option, leave it selected.

Specifying General Options

Fastback Express has some options, more for cosmetic value than for anything else, that are not crucial to the way you perform your work. To see the options that are available, press Alt-O from the main Fastback Express screen to open the Options menu. Press Enter to select the single item on this menu.

The dialog box that appears lets you change the screen colors, configure the mouse pointer, and change the sounds the program makes. Play around with these options as much as you like.

Completing the Backup

Now that all the options are set and all the files are selected as you want them, press Alt-S to start the backup. Fastback Express switches to a new screen that tells you exactly how many files and how many kilobytes of data you have scheduled to back up. When backing up to a floppy, Fastback Exress shows how many floppy disks it thinks you will need, so be sure to have at least that many available. Because this number is just an estimate, have one or two extras available. Another estimate Fastback Express provides is how much time the backup will take. This estimate can help you make sure that you plan enough time to complete the backup without interruption.

Because floppy disks need to be formatted before DOS can write data to them, Fastback Express writes only to formatted floppies. However, if you insert a floppy disk that has not yet been formatted, Fastback Express formats the disk for you.

If the floppy disk is formatted but already contains data, Fastback Express displays a dialog box with some options. The dialog box shows you the files that exist on the floppy disk and asks whether you want to delete files to make room, ignore the files and write over the whole floppy disk, or use the available space on the disk for the backup. You should have a set of disks set aside for backups to avoid any chance of accidentally overwriting them with data from other applications. Keep these disks separate from the other floppies in your files. If you follow your backup plan and perform backups according to a predetermined schedule, you should avoid running into problems that arise from mixing data with your backups.

If, for some reason, your backup medium is faulty, Fastback Express displays a message telling you that it is having problems writing the data and that you need to replace the faulty disk with another one.

The order of the floppy disks is crucial when performing a backup, so make sure that you label the floppy disks accordingly. On each floppy disk, write the date and time of the backup and the number of the floppy disk in the backup order. For example, if your backup requires 10 floppy disks, write

Tip

Label your backup disks clearly and keep them safe from accidental erasure.

IV

Disk and File Management

1/10 on the first disk. This assures that you keep the floppies in order and that you know how many were involved in the backup. If a disk gets misplaced, you know right away.

If something goes wrong during the backup process—for example, the power goes out or you get unavoidably interrupted—you should start the backup process all over again to ensure a reliable backup volume.

When the backup is completed, you can have Fastback Express create a report of the files you backed up, what options were selected during the backup, and the name of the user who performed the backup. To create the report, simply choose the Report button on the Backup screen. It would be a good idea to print out a backup report after each backup session. Keep these reports with your backup disks and you will always be prepared if your data crashes.

Restoring Files

Now that you know how to back up the files on your computer, you had better learn how to get them back when you need them. If you change the operation from Backup to Restore, the screen does not appear to change much, but there are some subtle differences. The From and To boxes switch places, because you are copying data back from the media used to back it up.

Selecting the Files to Restore

For the Restore operation, only two items are in the Selections box: All Files and Files I Choose. If you want to restore all the files on the disks, select the All Files option. If you need to restore only certain files from your backup copy, select the Files I Choose option. Before you select Files I Choose, though, be aware that if you have never performed a backup before, Fastback Express is going to give you an error. Fastback Express keeps track of all the backups you make, and which files are backed up each time. It writes this information in a history file that you can view from Fastback Express. This file is used as an index of all the data that exists in backups. Of course, if your hard drive crashes, you might lose the history file, so Fastback Express can perform a history-unassisted restore.

A backup's history is recorded in the database and remains intact unless that database is damaged or erased. If you try to restore a backup without the history data, Fastback Express tells you that the history data is missing.

Performing a history-unassisted restore shouldn't pose any problems. If you are looking for a particular file in the backup volume, you have to scan through all the floppy disks until you find the file, because Fastback Express no longer knows which disk the file is on. You can restore the history file to your database by selecting the Retrieve History option from the main Fastback Express screen. When you start this operation, Fastback Express asks you for the last disk of the backup volume. A copy of the history file is maintained on the disk, so Fastback Express copies the information from the disk to its history database.

Specifying Restore Options

Just as you were able to configure the backup utility, you can configure the restore utility. Choose the Restore Options button; the Restore Options dialog box appears, offering several options (see fig. 12.7). The first option asks what you want Fastback Express to do if, during the restore process, it tries to restore a file and a file already exists with the same name in the same directory.

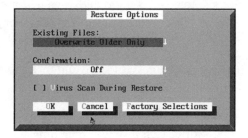

Fig. 12.7
The Restore Options dialog box.

For example, if you are restoring your AUTOEXEC.BAT and CONFIG.SYS files into the root directory of drive C and those files already exist, this option determines how the restore utility acts. The default option is to overwrite the file if the version on the hard drive is older than the version on the backup set. If you want, you can change this so that it overwrites no matter which version is older, or so that it never overwrites a file with the same name.

You can use the Confirmation field to configure the restore utility to ask for confirmation of each directory it restores, only on overwrite, or of each file it restores. The default is to turn off confirmation, which is how you probably want to leave it.

You use the last restore option, the Virus Scan During Restore check box, to instruct Fastback Express to scan files for viruses as they are restored. Presumably, these files were scanned when they were backed up, so you can leave

Tip
If you choose never to overwrite, the file that already exists on the hard drive—regardless of age—is preserved.

this virus scan option deselected. If you are having virus problems, however, and are not sure where they come from, or if you are not sure that the files were scanned during backup, select this option. It might be worth slowing things down a bit to gain greater peace of mind.

Tip
If you've deleted the directory from which the files were backed up, the directory and files are restored to their original locations.

If you have changed the options so much and cannot remember what they were when you started, Fastback Express gives you the option to change the Restore Options to their original settings. To do this, select the Factory Selections button in the Restore Options dialog box. To exit the dialog box, choose OK to save your new option settings or choose Cancel to exit without saving.

Comparing Data

One thing you should check occasionally is the integrity of the backups you are making. Fastback Express helps you to do this with the compare operation. It is important for you to feel comfortable when performing backups, so get a blank floppy disk and practice backing up and comparing files now. Follow these steps:

1. Make sure that Fastback Express is loaded and then move the cursor to highlight the Backup operation.

2. Select Files I Choose. The drive field at the top of the Files to Back Up screen should show drive C. If it shows something else, select C:.

3. Press Alt-E to exclude all files from the backup—you are going to back up only one file.

4. The root directory of drive C should be selected (it should have a small arrow pointing to it). Press the Tab key until the cursor is in the files list. Highlight the file AUTOEXEC.BAT and press the space bar to select it. You know that it is selected when it has a solid triangle beside it. In the bottom box, the following statement should appear:

        Incl \   AUTOEXEC.BAT   No

    This should be the only Incl statement in the box.

5. Press Alt-C to close the Files To Back Up screen and return to the main screen.

6. Make sure that the From box lists only drive C and that the To box lists a floppy drive.

7. Put your blank disk in the floppy drive and then press Alt-S to start the backup.

8. Do not worry about the items that are displayed. The only thing you should care about is a message that says Backup completed. If this appears, you have backed up the file successfully. If the message does not appear, review these steps to see what you may have done incorrectly.

9. Press Alt-C to close this screen.

Backing up more files from your hard drive is just as simple. The only difference between this exercise and an actual backup is that, if you back up many files, you are likely to need more disks.

Now compare your backup with the original to make sure that the backup is correct. Follow these steps:

1. Select Compare from the Operation box and then press Alt-S to start the operation. The Compare Files screen appears.

2. Ignore most of the items displayed on-screen but make sure that Fastback Express returns the message Compare OK! If it does not, you might be using a bad floppy disk, or you might have missed a step. Try the backup and compare operations again from the beginning.

3. Press Alt-C to close this screen and return to the main screen. Then press Ctrl-X to exit Fastback Express.

Tip
If the compares aren't coming out OK, you're probably using bad floppies.

You probably do not need to worry about verifying every backup, but it doesn't hurt to compare backups with originals occasionally to make sure that your hardware is still OK.

Using Fastback Express for Windows

If you have installed Windows utilities when you set up Novell DOS 7, then you also have access to Fastback Express for Windows. You can find the icon for this utility in the Novell DOS 7 program group. You have most of the same options with this Windows utility as with the DOS utility. If you have the Windows utility installed, start Fastback Express for Windows by double-clicking its icon.

The Fastback Express for Windows screen looks different from that for the DOS version, but all the same elements are there (see fig. 12.8).

Fig. 12.8

The main screen of Fastback Express for Windows.

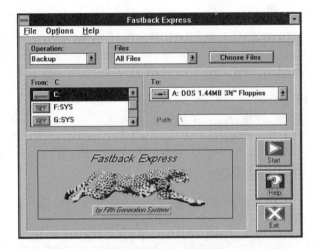

Getting Help

The Windows version includes an excellent help utility. To access it, choose Help, and after a few seconds, the Fastback Express Help screen appears. Click the maximize button in the upper-right corner so that you can view the entire help screen. The help screen displays a duplicate of the main screen of the utility. To learn about any aspect of the program, move your mouse pointer over the section that interests you. The mouse pointer turns into a pointing hand when you reach an item for which help is available. If you move the pointer to the Operation field, for example, and click the mouse button, a window appears that describes the function (see fig. 12.9). To get rid of the information window, click it with the right mouse button.

Spend some time exploring all the functions of the Fastback Express control panel. All the options should be familiar to you because you have already learned the features of the DOS program. Close the Help window after you finish exploring. Notice that many options cannot be completed from the Windows utility, such as whether to overwrite files on the floppy disk and whether to scan files for viruses during backup.

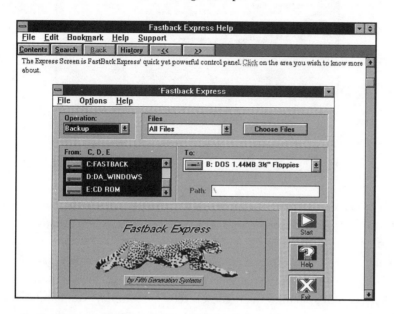

Fig. 12.9
The Fastback Express Help screen.

Testing Your Hardware

One of the utilities you get with the Windows version of Fastback Express tests your computer's hardware to see how fast it can transfer files to floppy drives. This utility, called Hardware Test, is in the same group as Express Backup and uses the same icon. Get a spare floppy disk ready (it should be high-density, if your drive supports this). Make sure that nothing you care about is on the disk because, while the hardware test is running, the data on this scratch disk is at risk. Double-click the icon and look at this utility.

The Hardware Test utility first asks you to remove all disks from the floppy drives, and then asks you to insert the scratch disk. After you insert your spare disk in the floppy drive, press Enter.

Before the test begins, you are advised that the test might make your computer unstable and that you should therefore close all other applications. Do not be alarmed—this is normal. Use Alt-Tab to switch to any application you want to close. When you are ready to begin the test, choose OK. The Test Progress window appears, as shown in figure 12.10.

Tip
You can test your hardware only with the Windows version of Fastback Express, not the DOS version.

Fig. 12.10
The Test Progress
window.

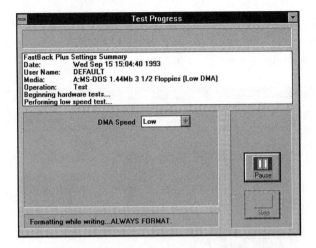

The test takes only about one minute and checks to see whether your hardware can handle fast transfer rates. The test checks transfers first at slow speed, then at medium speed, and finally at high speed. If your system passes the high speed test, Fastback Express backs up your files at high speed from now on. When the test is over, you can see the results. The Hardware Test utility sets your system to the highest level your computer can handle. If a drive does not pass the high speed test, it simply backs up at a slower speed. Virtually every drive can transfer at slow speed.

From Here...

Regularly backing up the data on your computer is the best way to recover from viruses, sabotage, hardware crashes, data corruption, accidents, or natural disasters. There are too many valid reasons to back up your system; no excuse for avoiding a backup is good enough. Now that you know what backing up your computer's information involves, you need to formulate a plan. Make it a policy to do a full backup every x days and incremental backups every y days. Consider this insurance. Perhaps you will never need it, but if you ever do, knowing that you have the means to recover is a tremendous relief.

For more information on working with files and directories, see the following chapters:

■ Chapter 6, "Understanding File Storage," covers drive and disk structures, DOS directories, paths, DOS files and their attributes, and the use of wild cards.

- Chapter 7, "Managing Files and Directories," shows you how to create, rename, remove, and display directories; list files and directories; and copy, move, compare, and delete files.

To learn more about the networking aspects of Novell DOS 7, read the following chapters:

- Chapter 5, "Installing the Network," guides you through the installation process for the Novell DOS network.

- Chapter 23, "Introduction to Networking," shows you how to plan and configure a network.

- Chapter 24, "Network Maintenance," shows you how to tune the network for better performance and how to use the Novell DOS 7 network utilities.

For more information on Using Windows 3.1, read Appendix B, "Installing and Using Windows 3.1."

IV

Disk and File Management

Part V

Device Utilities

Continue

ER=select/modify│ESC=previous screen│F1=help│ALT-X=exit│

Root directory

Subdirectory   Subdirectory

Subdirectory   Subdirectory Subdirectory   Subdirectory

Subdirectory   Subdirectory

Subdirectory

Continue

File - c:\spam.txt
Create new file ?

OK   Cancel

nfigure Task Manager

it this screen

ystem & Memory Managemer
Disk Compression
Disk Performance
Data Protection & Security
Task Management
Networking

acks

Sectors

25-Pin DB-25 Male

25-pin serial connector,
usually COM2

Change destination drive(s) and directorie

Chapter 13

Controlling System Devices

Every time you use your personal computer, you use devices. These devices are an integral part of your computer. Without them, the computer cannot function. Whenever you press a key on the keyboard, look at data on the screen, print a file on the printer, use your mouse, or call another computer by using a cable or a modem, you use a device. These devices, along with other components, make up the structure of the computer. The computer needs all of its devices to function efficiently, just as a car needs all of its parts to run efficiently. Novell DOS provides several commands to control these devices.

The MODE command lets you set the operational modes of the serial and parallel ports and reassign a printer to another device. (MODE can perform some functions relating to the keyboard and display. Those are discussed in Chapter 14, "Managing the Display and Keyboard." MODE can perform internationalizing functions as well, as described in Appendix A.)

Many people believe that PostScript printers (almost all are laser printers) produce output better than any other type of printer. The problem is that any software that communicates with these printers must use the *PostScript printer command language (PCL)*. DOS and most DOS applications do not use this language, but Novell DOS provides the SCRIPT command to let you print from DOS to a PostScript printer.

Novell DOS also provides FILELINK, a utility that lets you transmit files to and receive files from another computer over a cable.

This chapter shows you how to use MODE, SCRIPT, FILELINK and other commands for controlling the devices that constitute your computer system. The following topics are covered in this chapter:

- Using the MODE command to assign printers to a port

- Using the PRINT command

- Using the SCRIPT command to print to PostScript printers

- Sharing files with the SHARE command

- Using FILELINK to transfer files to another computer

Using the MODE Command

The MODE command, very simply, controls the configuration of various system devices: video monitor, keyboard, parallel ports, serial ports, printer, and modem. MODE controls also the use of *code pages*, which are tables used by your computer to display, print, and use national language character sets.

Specifically, you use MODE to do the following tasks:

- Assign a printer to a port

- Set up a printer

- Set up a communications (serial) port

- Set the display type and typematic rate (the speed at which characters are displayed when a key is held down)

- Set up and use code page switching

Read this section to learn about using MODE to control the parallel ports, serial ports, printer, and modem. Read Chapter 14, "Managing the Display and Keyboard," to learn about using MODE to control your keyboard and video display. Refer to Appendix A for information about code page switching.

Parallel ports and serial ports are the system devices used to communicate with external equipment or systems. Your printer is most likely attached to a parallel port on your computer with a cable that has a 25-pin male connector on the computer end and a 36-finger male connector on the printer end.

Some printers work on serial ports. The cable for this type of printer normally has a 9- or 25-pin female connector on the computer end and a 25-pin male connector on the printer end. Modems are serial devices.

Parallel ports send data to another device with a method called *byte-wide*. In addition to having control and ground lines, a parallel cable has eight data lines. Each byte (or character) transmitted through the parallel port is sent at the same time, one bit through each of the eight data lines. (Eight bits make up a byte. These bits are either 1s or 0s, meaning on or off, respectively; and their specific combination indicates a certain character or byte.) Parallel ports are named LPT1, LPT2, and LPT3.

Serial ports send data to another device with a method called *bit-wide*. Serial ports have only one transmit line. Bytes are sent one bit at a time. Serial ports are named COM1, COM2, COM3, and COM4.

Figure 13.1 shows typical IBM-type computer connectors for parallel and serial ports and printers.

9-Pin DB-9 Male

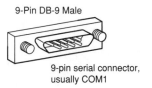

9-pin serial connector,
usually COM1

Fig. 13.1
Typical IBM-type computer parallel and serial connectors.

25-Pin DB-25 Male

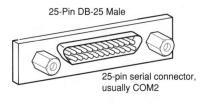

25-pin serial connector,
usually COM2

25-Pin DB-25 Female

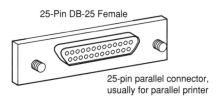

25-pin parallel connector,
usually for parallel printer

Assigning Printers to a Port

Most printers communicate with personal computers through the parallel
port. You may have one, two, or even three (the maximum) parallel ports
built into your specific system. Refer to figure 13.1 for the picture of parallel
connectors you probably have in your computer. You can have as many parallel printers as there are parallel port connectors on your computer (without
using a switch box or network).

Some applications, such as WordPerfect, Windows, and Lotus 1-2-3, have
configuration functions that allow you to set the printer port for the application, but most software sends printer data to only the first printer port
(LPT1). Therefore, you may need to redirect the printer if you need to print
from Novell DOS directly or if you use software that prints only to the default
first parallel port.

To send printer output to another printer port, use the MODE command.
Here is the syntax of MODE:

```
MODE device1:=device2:
```

The first device is the *source*, and the second device is the *destination*. In this
example, all data sent to the printer through port *device1* (for example, LPT1)
is redirected to *device2* (for example, LPT2) and the printer attached to *de-
vice2*. Note that the colon after the device name is optional.

If your parallel port redirection is successful, MODE responds with MODE
resident portion installed. If you attempt to redirect to a port that does
not exist, MODE displays the error message Invalid device.

> **Note**
>
> You do not have to type the MODE commands every time you turn on or reboot
> your computer. These MODE commands can be placed in your AUTOEXEC.BAT file.
> Refer to Chapter 20, "Using HISTORY and DOSKEY," for further information.

Redirecting Parallel to Parallel. You can redirect output from software
configured to use LPT2 or LPT3 and send the data to the printer attached to
LPT1. Use the following command:

```
MODE LPT2:=LPT1:
```

To cancel the redirection, redirect the original parallel port back to itself with this command:

```
MODE LPT1:=LPT1:
```

Redirecting Parallel to Serial. On some occasions, you may need to install a printer that communicates through the computer's serial port—for example, when one printer is already using your only parallel port and you need to install a second printer, or when the printer you have has only a serial interface. You can connect one printer to the parallel port (LPT1) and one to a serial port (COM*n*) only if one of the printers is equipped with a serial interface. To make the serial printer work with the computer, you must initialize the serial port (usually COM1 or COM2) to which the printer is attached (see the section "Initializing Serial Ports" later in this chapter for details). Redirect LPT2 to point to the serial port:

```
MODE LPT2:=COM1:
```

All data sent to parallel port LPT2 is redirected by Novell DOS to serial port COM1. The required data conversion from byte-wide to bit-wide is done by the electronics associated with the port.

Note

If you have a serial printer (and no parallel printer) connected to your computer system, you must use the MODE command to redirect the parallel port LPT1 to the serial port COM1 (or COM*n*). Otherwise, you cannot print from your application programs, because they send data to the parallel port instead of the serial port. If there is no parallel port, the application does not recognize this—it still tries to send information to a nonexistent parallel port.

To cancel the redirection (if you have only a serial port and no parallel port), redirect the first parallel port to the serial port:

```
MODE LPT1:=COM1:
```

To redirect the parallel port to itself, use this command:

```
MODE LPT1:=LPT1:
```

V

Device Utilities

Understanding Redirection Rules. The following rules apply to redirecting ports:

■ Any parallel port can be redirected to any parallel port, as long as the destination port exists in your computer.

■ Any parallel port can be redirected to a serial port, as long as the serial port exists in your computer.

■ Before a parallel port is redirected to a serial port, the serial port must be initialized with its speed and data characteristics (see the section "Initializing Serial Ports" later in this chapter).

■ If a printer is attached to the serial port, the serial port's initialization must include the retry option (P). This option is for handling any timing problems between the computer and the printer.

■ MODE uses 576 bytes of system memory to redirect a parallel port to a serial port.

■ When you redirect the parallel port to the serial port successfully, Novell DOS displays the following message:

```
Printer LPTn: redirected to serial port COMn
```

■ To cancel parallel port redirection, redirect the initial parallel port you redirected back to itself. The following message appears:

```
Output to LPTn: no longer redirected
```

■ Even after you cancel the redirection, MODE remains in memory, using 576 bytes. The only way to remove MODE from memory is to reboot.

Initializing Serial Ports

One of the few times you have to worry about setting the serial port's parameters is when you redirect the parallel port to the *n* serial port. The serial port is most widely used with a modem for communicating to other computers and bulletin board systems (BBSs). To use a modem effectively, computer users obtain communications software, and the software sets all the serial port parameters. You also use the serial port to communicate with another computer, using the FILELINK utility supplied with Novell DOS 7. For more on FILELINK, refer to the section "Sending Files to Another Computer with

FILELINK" later in this chapter. However, FILELINK also requires that you set the serial port to the parameters you intend to use for the file transfer.

Here is the syntax for the MODE command that sets the serial port:

```
MODE COM#: baud rate,parity,databits,stopbits,P
```

The speed at which the serial ports communicate is called the baud rate. A simplified definition of *baud rate* is the bits per second at which information is exchanged. Table 13.1 describes the options available with this form of MODE.

Table 13.1 MODE Command Options for Serial Ports

Option	Use
COM#	Specifies the serial port to set; # can be 1, 2, 3, or 4. The port number must be specified.
baud rate	Specifies the serial port's communication speed: 110, 150, 300, 600, 1200, 2400, 4800, 9600, 19200, 38400, 57600, or 115200. The baud rate must be specified (you can abbreviate with the first two digits of the number).
parity	Specifies the parity at which the serial port operates: N (none), O (odd), or E (even). The default is E.
databits	Specifies the number of data bits at which the serial port operates: 7 or 8. The default is 7.
stopbits	Specifies the number of stop bits at which the serial port operates: 1 or 2. The default is 1, except when the baud rate is 110; then the default is 2.
P	Informs Novell DOS to keep trying to send data to a device that is not responding. There is no default.

Note

For the serial port on your system to be able to handle baud rates greater than 9600, you should check with your hardware documentation or your dealer to see whether you have higher-speed serial chips on your system's I/O board.

V

Device Utilities

For example, to set the second serial port to transmit data at 9600 baud, with 8 data bits, 1 stop bit, and no parity, enter the following:

```
MODE COM2:96,N,8,1
```

To set the first serial port to transmit data at 2400 baud, with 7 data bits, 1 stop bit, and even parity, and to keep retrying to send data if the serial port is not responding, enter the following:

```
MODE COM1:24,E,7,1,P
```

Keep in mind the following details when setting serial ports with Novell DOS:

■ If you specify the retry option (P), a portion of MODE remains in memory, and you see the following Novell DOS message:

```
Infinite retries on serial port COMn:
MODE: Resident portion installed
```

If MODE has been previously installed, the new port setting will be displayed.

■ The MODE command uses 576 bytes of system memory if the retry option is specified.

■ To cancel the retry option, you must issue another MODE command without specifying P.

■ Even after you cancel the retry option, MODE remains in memory, using 576 bytes. The only way to remove MODE from memory is to reboot.

Controlling Parallel Ports

If you connect a new printer to your computer, you probably need to set the parallel port's parameters to reflect the printer's capabilities. For example, if you install a 132-column printer (wide carriage printer, handling paper to 14 7/8 inches), you have to modify the number of characters per line. Otherwise, the printer defaults to 80 characters per line (narrow carriage printer, handling paper to 8 1/2 inches). If you were to print a document with lines more than 80 characters long, each line would take two lines to print. Even if the printer can handle the wider line, the Novell DOS PRINT command defaults to the printer port's default settings.

Here is the syntax for the MODE command that sets the parallel port:

```
MODE LPT#:characters,lpi,P
```

Table 13.2 describes the available options.

Table 13.2 MODE Command Options for Parallel Ports

Option	Use
LPT#	Specifies the parallel port to set; # can be 1, 2, or 3. The port number must be specified.
characters	Specifies the characters per line at which the printer operates, either 80 or 132. The default is 80.
lpi	Specifies the lines per inch at which the printer operates, either 6 or 8. The default is 6.
P	Informs Novell DOS to keep trying to send data to a device that is not responding.

For example, to set LPT1 to 132 characters per line, 6 lines per inch, and to retry sending data if the printer is busy, enter the following command:

```
MODE LPT1:132,6,P
```

To reset the parallel port to the original default settings, enter the following:

```
MODE LPT1
```

Keep in mind the following details when setting parallel ports with Novell DOS:

- If you specify the retry option (P), MODE makes a portion of itself resident. The amount of system memory used by MODE is 576 bytes.

- If you turn off the retry option by issuing another MODE command, MODE retains the 576 bytes of memory allocated for the previous command. The only way to free this memory is to reboot.

- On successful completion of the MODE command, Novell DOS displays the following message:

```
Printer LPTn: 132 columns, 6 lines per inch, infinite
retries
```

V

Device Utilities

Caution

If you try to issue MODE commands to your parallel port and the printer is not attached, not turned on, or not on-line, Novell DOS issues the error message `Printer error`.

Printing Files in the Background with the PRINT Command

Novell DOS provides the capability of printing files in the background while you do other tasks on the computer. With the PRINT command, you can print a large file in the background while you continue working. In contrast, the COPY command ties up the computer until it has finished copying the file to the printer.

With COPY, you can print only one file at a time. With PRINT, you can queue up a maximum of 32 files to print, with a default of 10 files.

Another difference is that the COPY command prints the file and then stops when the file ends. The PRINT command issues a form feed to the printer after the file is printed. Thus, the next print job starts on a new page.

The advantage of using PRINT is clear. However, the major disadvantage of using background printing is that your applications run more slowly. Another disadvantage is that the printer may start and stop, giving you the false indication that it is done printing. By using PRINT's optional parameters, you can alter the way PRINT functions. You can give more or less time to the print function for printing the files. Another disadvantage is that PRINT remains resident, occupying valuable memory.

Note

One useful function of the PRINT command is to print the README.DOC files that come with most software packages. Most of the README.DOC files are longer than one screenful and need to be printed on a printer to be read.

Using PRINT Switches

Here is the syntax of the PRINT command:

```
PRINT /D:device /B:buffsize /U:busyticks /M:maxticks
      /S:timeslice /Q:queuesize drive1:\path1\filename /T /C /P
      drive2:\path2\filename /T /C /P...
```

drive1:\path1\filename is the first drive, path, and file name to be printed, and
drive2:\path2\filename is the second drive, path, and file name to be printed.
The ellipsis indicates that more files can be specified on the command line,
up to a maximum of 128 characters. Wild-card characters are permitted in file
names.

Table 13.3 describes the PRINT command switches.

Table 13.3 PRINT Switches

Switch	Use
/D:*device*	Specifies the device name to which the output is sent. The default is PRN, which is the same as LPT1. Acceptable substitute device names for PRN are LPT1, LPT2, LPT3, COM1, COM2, and AUX. The device name can be specified only the first time the command is used when changing output to another device.
/B:*buffsize*	Specifies the size of the print buffer (in bytes) used in the printing process. The default buffer size, as well as the mininum size, is 512 bytes. A larger buffer size may improve the print speed but requires more of the system's memory. The print process takes blocks of data from the disk that are equal to the size of the print buffer. The buffer size can be set only the first time the PRINT command is executed.
/U:*busyticks*	Specifies how long (in ticks, with a tick equaling 1/18 second) PRINT waits for the printer to be free. The default is 1, but *busyticks* can be set for any value from 1 to 255. If PRINT attempts to send data to the printer and the printer signals that it is busy, PRINT waits the length of time specified by *busyticks* and attempts to resend the data. If the printer is still busy, PRINT transfers control back to Novell DOS before using its allotted *maxticks*.
/M:*maxticks*	Specifies how many ticks PRINT uses when it has control. PRINT waits for the number of ticks specified and returns control to the foreground program. The default is 2, but *maxticks* can be set to any value from 1 and 255.

(continues)

V

Device Utilities

Table 13.3 Continued	
Switch	**Use**
/S:*timeslice*	Specifies how often PRINT controls the system. Too low a number gives the print utility control too often and causes all other applications to run slowly. The range is from 1 to 255, with a default of 8.
/Q:*queuesize*	Specifies the maximum number of files that can be in the print queue at one time. The range of files in the print queue at one time is from 4 to 32; the default is 10.
/T	Deletes the list of waiting files in the print queue and terminates printing of the current file. (*Note:* If the current file has been written to the printer's memory, the file will be printed.)
/C	Deletes a specified file from the print queue—deletes the file name before /C and all file names after /C.
/P	Adds files to the print queue—adds the file name before /P and all file names after /P—and starts the printing process.

When using PRINT, keep in mind the following details:

- After you execute the PRINT command, a portion of PRINT remains in memory. After PRINT has been installed in memory, it cannot be removed or its method of operation changed without rebooting. Therefore, the /D:*device*, /B:*buffsize*, /U:*busyticks*, /M:*maxticks*, /S:*timeslice*, and /Q:*queuesize* switches can be issued only once in each DOS session. You have to reboot to change the settings.

- After you execute the PRINT command and enter **PRINT** at the prompt, Novell DOS displays a list of files in the queue waiting to be printed. The files are displayed in the order in which you issued them for printing. Error messages are displayed also. If you issue the PRINT command but forgot to turn on the printer, the following message appears:

  ```
  Errors on list device indicate that it may be offline.
  Please check.
  ```

- Files in the print queue must remain on the same disk drive and unaltered while they are printing. For this reason, it is a good idea not to run any disk utilities that modify the disk space where the files reside.

- PRINT uses 5,824 bytes of system memory when loaded with default values. Increasing the /B:*buffsize* or /Q:*queuesize* uses more system memory.

- The files are printed in the order in which they were entered.

- Tab characters in the printed file are converted to blanks, up to the next eight-column boundary (the standard length of a tab).

- PRINT cannot be used to send data to a network printer.

- Specifying an invalid device can cause unpredictable behavior by the computer.

- PRINT issues a page-feed command to the printer after the end of each file printed.

- Entering the PRINT command without specifying any options causes PRINT to prompt you for a device name. PRN is the default. Pressing Enter accepts the default PRN, which is usually LPT1.

- Terminating all the files in the print queue does not clear the printer's memory of the data sent to it before the files were terminated. After the printer has printed all the information in its memory, it stops printing. Novell DOS issues the following message when the files are terminated:

```
All files canceled by operator
```

Printing Multiple Files

You do not have to enter at once all the file names that need to be printed. However, the first time you enter the PRINT command is the only time you can change PRINT's operation (without rebooting). If, for example, you have five files to print—REPORT1.TXT, QUARTRLY.TXT, EMPLOYEE.LST, PHONE.TXT, and LETTER5.TXT—and you want to use PRINT's default parameters, enter the following:

```
PRINT /D:LPT1 REPORT1.TXT /P QUARTRLY.TXT EMPLOYEE.LST
    PHONE.TXT LETTER5.TXT
```

If only these files and no others were in the directory, you could enter the following:

```
PRINT /D:LPT1 *.*
```

V

Device Utilities

The order in which the files are printed then depends on their order in the directory.

Alternatively, you could enter the file names one at a time, and they would be printed in the order you requested:

```
PRINT /D:LPT1 REPORT1.TXT

PRINT QUARTRLY.TXT

PRINT EMPLOYEE.LST

PRINT PHONE.TXT

PRINT LETTER5.TXT
```

To remove EMPLOYEE.LST from the print queue, enter the following:

```
PRINT EMPLOYEE.LST /C
```

To cancel all the files being printed, enter this command:

```
PRINT /T
```

After printing the files, if you realize that you need EMPLOYEE.LST before QUARTRLY.TXT, enter the following:

```
PRINT QUARTRLY.TXT /C QUARTRLY.TXT /P
```

This command moves QUARTRLY.TXT from its current place in the queue to the end.

Changing the Printing Speed

By adjusting the default installation, you can have PRINT print faster or slower. Adjusting PRINT to print at a faster rate causes the foreground task to run slower; adjusting PRINT to run slower causes the foreground task to run faster. To adjust PRINT, modify the /B:*buffsize*, /U:*busyticks*, /M:*maxticks*, and /S:*timeslice* parameters.

> **Note**
>
> If you set /M:*maxticks* to a high number, PRINT has almost total control over the system. If /S:*timeslice* is too low, you give the PRINT utility control too often, and the foreground application runs very slowly. You may not even be able to enter a command at the Novell DOS prompt. Try to balance /M:*maxticks* and /S:*timeslice* to allow PRINT enough time to print and the system time to process other requests. Most of the time, the defaults work fine.

Entering the following command increases the print buffer size (/B:*buffsize*) to 8,192 bytes and gives control to PRINT for 6 seconds every 6 ticks (about every 0.3 second):

```
PRINT /D:LPT1 /B:8192 /S:6 /M:108
```

By altering /S:*timeslice* and /M:*maxticks*, you can adjust the print speed in relation to the foreground program you are running. If the foreground program is not keyboard-intensive, you may want to increase the background print parameters for faster printing. Remember, though, that after the parameters are set, the only way to reset them is to restart Novell DOS and reissue the PRINT command with new parameters.

Printing in PostScript with the SCRIPT Command

The SCRIPT command provides PostScript support to Novell DOS and programs running under Novell DOS, and you can use that support if you have a PostScript printer connected to your computer system. You can use SCRIPT also to convert to PostScript all characters in text format, including those that conform to the Hewlett-Packard LaserJet II standard. SCRIPT can take input from a file, system console, or program; convert that input; and send it to a printer or file.

You can use the DOS filter capability to send the output of one command to SCRIPT, as in this example:

```
DIR | SCRIPT
```

V

Device Utilities

This command tells DOS to take the output of the directory command (DIR) and send it to SCRIPT, which then translates it and sends it to the printer.

When issuing the SCRIPT command to print in PostScript format, use the following syntax:

```
SCRIPT /U device | filename device | filename /O=P | L /P=nn
       /TI=nn /T=nn L=nn /R
```

To load SCRIPT as a TSR (terminate-and-stay-resident) program, where the driver intercepts all printer output, including that from application software, issue the following command at the DOS prompt, before running the software:

```
SCRIPT device
```

The *device* is the printer port. Usually, this is the first parallel printer port, LPT1:. You must enter the printer port, even if you used MODE to change the default printer port. After you enter the preceding command, SCRIPT is loaded as a TSR and sends all printer output in PostScript format.

One switch, /U, is used to unload SCRIPT from memory if SCRIPT was installed as a TSR.

Note

SCRIPT must have been the last device driver and TSR loaded in order for it to be removed from memory. This is very important if you intend also to use a PostScript application. You do not want to use a program that outputs data in PostScript format and then have the utility translate those commands from the program as if the commands were data, and then retranslate into PostScript. The results would be less than desirable.

When you invoke SCRIPT as an individual utility or a TSR, you can specify on the command line the parameters that define the output for you. This is especially important when you are printing from DOS. If you do not specify any or all of the parameters, the defaults are assumed.

Table 13.4 describes the optional parameters.

Table 13.4 SCRIPT Options

Option	Use
device | *filename*	Specifies the source and destination device or file name to which PostScript formatting is applied by the SCRIPT command. If the source destination is LPT*n*:, SCRIPT loads itself into memory and stays resident until unloaded.
/L=*nn*	Refers to the margin at the left of the paper, in inches. The default is .25 inch.
/O=P | L	Specifies portrait mode (P) or landscape mode (L). The default is P.
/P=*nn*	Specifies the point size to use in printing the file. The default is 11.
/R	Indicates that the SCRIPT command should generate a software reset to the printer before processing any data.
/TI=*nn*	Specifies the spooler timeout, where the spooler preempts the normal printer timeout and prints any remaining data in the spooler before the printer times out. The default is 10 seconds.
/T=*nn*	Refers to the margin at the top of the paper, in inches. The default is .5 inch.
/U	Removes SCRIPT from memory when it has been loaded as a TSR.

V

Device Utilities

Note

When you specify either of the /T switches, make sure that you use the decimal point and two decimal numbers for inches to refer to the top margin even if the decimal numbers are zeros. Use a whole number, without decimals, for the seconds.

To print REPORT.TXT to LPT2 in portrait mode using 10-point size, enter the following:

```
SCRIPT REPORT.TXT/R LPT2:/O=P/P=10.0
```

When using SCRIPT, remember the following details:

■ To load SCRIPT into system memory, specify the output device: LPT1, LPT2, or LPT3. SCRIPT can be used with both local and remote network printers. To use SCRIPT with a network printer, you must first use the NET CAPTURE command to attach the printer.

- You can change the parameters of the device in the resident part of SCRIPT by issuing another SCRIPT command.

- When SCRIPT is loaded in memory, it uses 19,536 bytes.

- To remove SCRIPT from memory, issue the SCRIPT command with the /U (Uninstall) switch, and Novell DOS displays the following message:

      Script has been uninstalled

- If you issue new parameters to the resident portion of SCRIPT, the following message is displayed:

      Resident parameters updated

- When SCRIPT is loaded successfully as a TSR, Novell DOS displays the following message:

      Script has been installed

- If you issue the SCRIPT command for a device that cannot use PostScript format, Novell DOS displays the following message:

      Invalid device

If you want to have SCRIPT load automatically when you boot your computer, place the command in your AUTOEXEC.BAT file. Do this with the Novell DOS 7 text editor, EDIT. Refer to Chapter 17, "Using the Novell DOS Text Editor," for directions. Make sure that you place the SCRIPT command after any other TSRs if you want to unload it.

Sharing Files with the SHARE Command

Tip
Many Windows applications require the use of SHARE.

If you run several application programs that access the same data files concurrently, you need to share the files by using the SHARE command. If you do not run the SHARE command, one of the programs cannot access files. SHARE is used most commonly when you access network files. Task switching and multitasking through Task Manager and other applications that can run different programs which access the same data files at once also require you to run SHARE.

Here is the syntax of the SHARE command:

SHARE /L:*nnnn* /F:*nnnn* /M*x*

Table 13.5 describes the available switches.

Table 13.5 SHARE Switches

Switch	Use
/L:*nnnn*	Sets up the number of file locks the system uses. The range is from 20 to 1024, and the default is 20.
/F:*nnnn*	Tells DOS how much space to reserve for file information. The *nnnn* is in kilobytes; the default is 1024.
/M*x*	Loads SHARE in a specific area of memory. Use /ML for lower (conventional) memory, /MH for high memory, or /MU for upper memory. (If insufficient upper or high memory is available, SHARE loads into lower memory. Before you can use /MH or /MU, a device driver must be loaded that supports high and upper memory.) The default is /ML.

To load SHARE into high memory and allocate 40 file locks, enter the following command:

    SHARE /L:40 /MH

SHARE provides any file locking required by programs for which the data and files need to be shared at the same time by different programs. Share is most commonly used with networked programs and some TSR programs. After SHARE has been loaded, it cannot be removed from memory except by rebooting.

When using SHARE, keep in mind the following details:

■ Novell DOS has built-in support for large partitions, so you do not need to issue the SHARE command to access these partitions.

Device Utilities

V

Tip
Load SHARE
in your
AUTOEXEC.BAT
file. Refer to Chap-
ter 17, "Using the
Novell DOS Text
Editor," on how to
do this.

- SHARE can be loaded only once after Novell DOS has started. If you attempt to load SHARE again, Novell DOS displays an error message.

- If you do not issue the /L parameter, only 20 files can be open simultaneously.

- When SHARE is loaded, Novell DOS checks each file for file and record locks as it is opened, read, and written.

- The only way to remove SHARE from memory is to reboot.

- With 20 file locks, SHARE uses 1,040 bytes of system memory.

Sending Files to Another Computer with FILELINK

Many people have more than one computer. They may have one at the office and a laptop or notebook computer to use away from the office. They need to track files on both computers. To add to the intricacy, users must ensure, if a file exists on two computers, that they are using the most recent version of the file. Often, you cannot transfer files by using floppy disks because the computers have different floppy drives, or one computer may not have a floppy drive at all. Furthermore, many files may be too large to store on a floppy.

Novell DOS 7 provides the FILELINK utility for transferring files from one computer to another. With FILELINK, you can transfer files without using floppy disks. You simply link two computers together by using a cable, issue a few commands, and sit back and watch the computers work.

FILELINK Basics

FILELINK performs a combination of functions between those of the XCOPY command and a communications program. FILELINK enables you to pass files back and forth between two computers linked by either a parallel or serial cable attached to their parallel or serial communications ports.

To work with FILELINK, you establish communication by setting one computer as a *master computer* or *local computer*, and another computer as a *slave computer* or *remote computer*. When the two computers are linked and FILELINK is active, the computers act as one. The master computer becomes the front end to the slave computer, much like the keyboard and video display are the front end of a computer. The slave computer waits for FILELINK commands from the master computer. FILELINK also has the capability of duplicating itself on the slave computer, and you can tell the utility to run on the slave computer from the master computer.

Because using FILELINK requires hardware connections as well as software commands, this discussion describes both hardware and software requirements. The next few sections explain how to connect the computers together and how to use FILELINK commands to transfer files from one computer to another.

FILELINK Hardware

To hook the computers together, you need to understand the hardware requirements. With FILELINK, two hardware items are needed:

■ One asynchronous communications port (also called a serial port) on each computer or one parallel port on each computer. You cannot communicate between a parallel port and a serial port.

■ One RS232 (serial) null modem cable or a cross-wired parallel cable.

Serial Port. Nearly all computers sold since the IBM PC/XT come with at least one serial port. If the ports on the back of your computer are not labeled, look for a D-shaped connector that contains either 25 pins or 9 pins. The pins in the connector are divided into two rows (refer to fig. 13.1 for a refresher on serial port connectors).

Serial ports are most often used by a mouse, modem, or other serial device. If you have only one serial port and it is being used, you must disconnect whatever device is attached in order to connect the serial cable for FILELINK, or you can purchase a serial port switch box from your dealer. Some computers have more than one serial port. If you have an open serial port, you can leave the FILELINK cable attached to the computer at all times.

Caution

Most manufacturers warn against connecting or disconnecting cables while devices are powered on. Make sure that both computers are turned off before making or breaking cable connections.

V

Device Utilities

> **Caution**
>
> You may have to reboot the computer after connecting the FILELINK cable to a serial port that usually has connected another serial device. A TSR program or a device driver such as a mouse driver may be loaded in memory to control the other serial device. This TSR or device driver could interfere with FILELINK.

All serial ports are named COM#, where # is a number from 1 to 4. Although you can have up to four serial ports in a PC (and even more with special hardware), FILELINK works only with COM1 and COM2. If you have only one serial port, it is called COM1. If you have a second serial port, that port is usually COM2. Make sure that you know the name of the port you plan to use. This knowledge is important when you are configuring FILELINK.

The type of serial cable you use with FILELINK is called a *null modem cable*. This is a cable that you use for communications without using a modem. A null modem cable looks identical to a serial cable on the outside; however, the pin-to-pin connections are different on the inside. If you plan to purchase a cable to use, make sure that you specify a null modem cable.

When getting a cable for use with FILELINK, you must determine the types of connectors you need. For example, if each computer has a 25-pin male connector, you need to get a null modem cable with 25-pin female connectors at each end. Similarly, if one computer has a 9-pin male connector and the other has a 25-pin male connector, you need a null modem cable with a 9-pin female connector at one end and a 25-pin female connector at the other end. Most computer stores have premade cables available for various configurations.

If you want to build your own null modem cable, refer to table 13.6, which shows the pin connections for three possible configurations. For each type of cable, the two columns list pin-to-pin connections.

Table 13.6 Null Modem Cable Connections for Three Cable Types					
Cable 1		**Cable 2**		**Cable 3**	
25-pin	**25-pin**	**9-pin**	**9-pin**	**9-pin**	**25-pin**
2	3	2	3	2	2
3	2	3	2	3	3
4	5	4	6	4	6
5	4	5	5	5	7
6	20	6	4	6	20
7	7	7	8	7	5
20	6	8	7	8	4

One advantage of using a serial cable (and serial ports) with FILELINK is that you can duplicate the utility on the slave computer from the master computer. You cannot do this with a parallel connection between the two computers.

Parallel Port. If either or both of the computers you are trying to bridge do not have a serial port, both have parallel ports. Parallel ports are normally used for printers. FILELINK, however, has the capability of using the printer or parallel ports for transferring files. There is a disadvantage, though, in using these ports in that you cannot use FILELINK to duplicate itself on the slave computer. You must have Novell DOS already installed on this computer, have used a serial port connection previously to duplicate the utility, or have used a floppy disk to make the utility transfer.

The parallel transfer cable must have two male DB25 connectors, one on each end. The parallel connector on the back of almost all IBM-type computers is a female D-type connector with 25 holes to receive the pins. This is not the same cable as used for parallel printers, which have a Centronics-type connector on the printer end. In addition, the parallel cable is a cross-over cable. The pin-outs for the parallel FILELINK cable are listed in table 13.7. Your dealer may be able to provide you with the proper cable, or it may have to be

V

Device Utilities

custom-made. A connector pin at one end of the cable (column one in table 13.7) connects to a specific connector pin at the other end of the cable (column two).

Table 13.7 Parallel Cross-Over Cable Pin-Outs for FILELINK	
DB25	**DB25**
1	1
2	15
3	13
4	12
5	10
6	11
10	5
11	6
12	4
13	3
15	2

Note

If you want to use a parallel cable with FILELINK and do not know how to make one, you can contact the author of this book for such a cable at reasonable cost: Robert P. King & Associates, 4473 Long View Lane, Doylestown, PA 18901, (215) 348-4848.

A common length of a parallel cable is 15 feet. You may have to move one of the computers to be within that distance.

Running FILELINK

Before you can use FILELINK to transfer files from one computer to another, you must complete four basic steps:

1. Configure FILELINK for the master computer.

2. Duplicate FILELINK to the slave computer.

3. Configure FILELINK for the slave computer.

4. Place the slave computer in slave mode.

You need to complete steps 1 through 3 only one time. After you have performed the steps, you do not need to perform them again, unless you delete FILELINK from the slave computer or reconfigure the two computers.

> **Note**
>
> To use FILELINK, it can be on just one of the computers to be connected. You can use the DUPLICATE command to place a copy of FILELINK on the computer that does not contain FILELINK. This means, for example, that if you have Novell DOS 7 on one computer and another version of DOS on another computer, you can make a duplicate copy on the non-Novell DOS computer and use FILELINK without any problems. The duplication can be performed only when you use serial ports, not when you are using parallel ports.

To configure FILELINK, you must specify either the parallel port or the serial port to be used (COM1 or COM2) and, if the port is serial, the speed at which the computers communicate. The earlier section "Initializing Serial Ports" tells you how to configure the serial ports on your computers.

> **Note**
>
> When you are configuring FILELINK, it is possible but unwise to use a baud rate as slow as 110. The lower the baud rate, the longer it takes to transfer files. When you first configure FILELINK, set it up for 9600 baud. This baud rate is supported by many computers. After you have established that you can communicate successfully between the two computers at 9600 baud, set up FILELINK to the fastest baud rate that will make a reliable connection. The best performance comes from using the fastest baud rate. If you have problems with the fastest baud rate, try the next fastest, the next, and so on, until you find the fastest baud rate that works.

You can run FILELINK in one of two ways: as a full-screen utility with menus, or as a command entry at the DOS prompt or in a batch file. If you use the full-screen version, you can use a mouse with FILELINK. However, if you do use a mouse, make sure that you do not select the same serial port for communications to which you have attached the mouse.

V

Device Utilities

Operating the Full-Screen FILELINK Program

This is the easier method of using the FILELINK program. To start FILELINK, enter **FILELINK** at the DOS prompt. If you have a monochrome display and the screen does not look right, use the /B switch (FILELINK /B). This may be required on a monochrome notebook or laptop computer. If you have a small (9-inch) VGA screen, you also may want, for better readability, to use standard screen characters instead of VGA format characters. Use the /N switch (FILELINK /N) to do this.

The opening screen of FILELINK is displayed. You then have the option of pressing Enter or clicking OK, using F1 to read general help for the utility, or pressing Esc to exit FILELINK. If you press Enter, you see FILELINK's initial display, with a menu bar containing two drop-down menus (File and Help) and a menu box in the center of the screen listing the initial options (see fig. 13.2).

Fig. 13.2
The FILELINK
initial display.

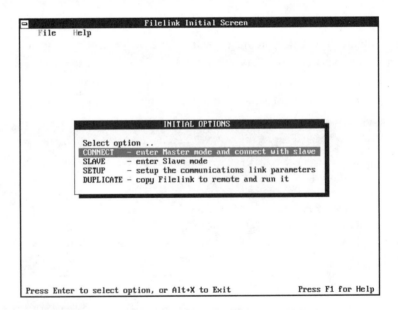

From the Initial Options box, you can access either of the drop-down menus by pressing Alt-F or Alt-H, or by moving the mouse pointer to the top menu bar and choosing one of the menu names. The File menu has only one option: Exit. The options in the Help menu are described in the following section. Pressing Esc returns you to the Initial Options menu.

The Initial Options menu displays four options for configuring and using FILELINK: CONNECT, SLAVE, SETUP, and DUPLICATE. Select the option you want. The first time you use FILELINK, select SETUP. You do not have to use this option again unless you want to change your setup. FILELINK prepares a configuration file (FILELINK.CFG), which is usually placed in the \NWDOS directory and used each time you use the utility.

> **Note**
>
> The same configuration file is used whether you use FILELINK in full-screen mode or command-line mode.

When you select SETUP, a pop-up menu box appears informing you of the current setup and a menu of selections. Figure 13.3 shows the Setup Options menu box. The first time you run FILELINK, the default setup of the first (COM1) serial port at 9600 baud is listed.

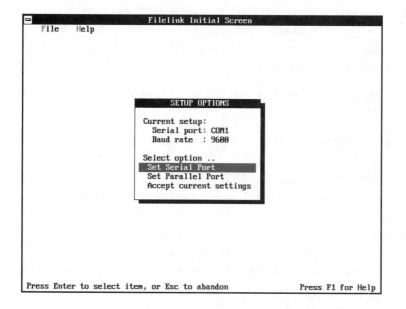

Fig. 13.3
FILELINK Setup Options menu box.

If you want to change the serial port, select Set Serial Port and press Enter. Then select the proper port, either COM1 or COM2. You are then presented with a choice of baud rates (serial port speed). Use the up- or down-arrow key to make your speed selection. For many personal computers, 9600 is the appropriate baud rate. Do not select a faster rate unless your hardware documentation or your dealer informs you that you have a higher-speed serial port. Some computers will need to use 4800 baud or less to enable a connection. Of course, you are free to experiment with faster speeds if you want. Just make sure that the same baud rate is set for both the master computer and the slave computer.

If you select Set Parallel Port, you are presented with the selections LPT1, LPT2, and LPT3. Use the up- or down-arrow key to select your choice; then press Enter. There is no baud rate when you use a parallel port.

Caution

FILELINK does not verify that you have the selected port when you make the selection, but if the port you choose does not exist, you cannot make the communication link.

After you have made your setup selections, you return to the Setup Options menu box where your selections appear. The Accept Current Settings option is highlighted. Press Enter. FILELINK updates its configuration file, and the Initial Options menu appears.

Pressing Esc at the Setup Options menu returns you to the Initial Options menu without changing the default configuration.

If you selected serial communications and do not have Novell DOS 7 on the slave computer, you can tell FILELINK to duplicate itself to that computer. You do this by selecting DUPLICATE from the Initial Options menu. Before proceeding, make sure that you have turned on the slave computer and have installed the appropriate cable. FILELINK then requests the serial port to which the cable is connected on the slave computer (COM1 or COM2). Use the up- or down-arrow key to make the selection. A dialog box appears, telling you to enter several commands at the DOS prompt on the slave PC:

```
MODE COM1:9600,N,8,1,P
CTTY COM1:
```

CTTY is a DOS command covered more fully in Chapter 14, "Managing the Display and Keyboard." These commands set up the slave (remote) computer so that its serial port parameters match those on master (local) computer that FILELINK uses to transfer itself to the slave computer. Refer to the earlier section "Initializing Serial Ports" for information on the command parameters.

After you enter the commands at the DOS prompt on the slave PC, FILELINK displays on the master computer a dialog box reporting that it is Attempting connection.... If it cannot establish a link, an error box appears indicating Cannot maintain link with slave. Try again? Press Y or N. If you press N, the Initial Options menu appears. If the link is successful, you are informed of this, and FILELINK transfers itself to the slave computer. When the transfer is complete, enter **FILELINK** at the DOS prompt and proceed to configure the slave computer as you did for the master computer. After you have done this, select SLAVE in the Initial Options menu to start slave mode on the slave computer. You are then asked whether you want to Allow files on slave to be overwritten? Use the left- or right-arrow key and press Enter, press Y or N, or use your mouse to click the appropriate box.

The FILELINK Slave screen is displayed with a dialog box, as shown in figure 13.4.

The Slave screen dialog box has a rotating bar between the brackets after

Fig. 13.4
The FILELINK
Slave screen.

Waiting.... This bar rotates very slowly when the FILELINK slave computer is waiting for something to do. The bar rotates faster when a file transfer is taking place. The only thing that can now be done on the slave is to exit the

V

Device Utilities

Slave screen. Do this by pressing Ctrl-C on the slave computer. You can also tell the slave to quit with a command from the master computer. Either form of the command returns the slave computer to the Initial Options menu.

You can now return to your master computer where all transfer commands are given.

Navigating the FILELINK Screen. When you have FILELINK working and in slave mode on the remote computer, you can use the local machine as the master and start transferring files. You place your local computer in master mode at the Initial Options menu by selecting CONNECT and pressing Enter. A dialog box with `Trying to connect to slave...` appears, and once the connection is made, the Master screen appears (see fig. 13.5), with another dialog box and the message

`Updating remote directory display....`

Fig. 13.5

The FILELINK Master screen.

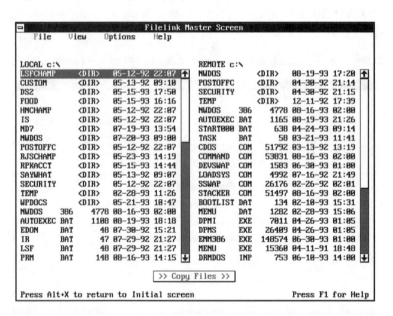

The FILELINK Master screen has two windows plus the top menu bar. Each of the windows displays the directory listing for one of the linked computers: the left side for the master computer, and the right side for the slave computer, as shown at the top of each window. The initial directory displays the default directory when FILELINK was loaded on each computer. Notice that the selected (sending) machine has a highlight bar at the top of the window. To start with, the master computer is the sender. Use Tab to change the sender from master to slave, or slave to master.

The highlight bar tells FILELINK where to perform the instructions you give it. Suppose that you want to change the displayed (and destination) drive or directory on the slave computer. Use Tab to move the highlight bar to the REMOTE window. The current path on the remote computer is displayed after the word REMOTE. Now, when you tell FILELINK to change to the C:\TEMP directory, FILELINK knows that you are referring to the remote (slave) computer.

When you tell FILELINK to send or copy files from one machine to the other, you can select groups of files and then filter this group with *filter options* that specify whether files should be copied with or without the archive attribute set. Refer to Chapter 6, "Understanding File Storage," for information on file attributes. You can also update older copies of files with newer copies (you learn more about this later in this section).

The two ways of giving commands to FILELINK are to use the drop-down menus from the menu bar at the top of the master screen, or the control keys for the menu commands. Table 13.8 describes FILELINK's menu commands, along with their highlighted letters and shortcut keys.

V

Device Utilities

Table 13.8 The FILELINK Menu Commands

Menu	Command and Description	Key to Press	Shortcut
File	*Copy*. Copies the marked files. Copy can be used only when the >> Copy Files >> button is available at the bottom of the screen, which happens when you have selected one or more files.	C	Alt-C
	Filtered Copy. Copies the marked files but only those with the selected filter.	F	Alt-F
	Filter Options. You set these options by using the arrow keys to highlight and the space bar to select any or all of the options. *ARCHIVE* copies only those files that have the archive attribute set. *SINCE* copies only those files	O	

(continues)

Menu	Command and Description	Key to Press	Shortcut
	that have been modified since the date you enter when you select this filter option. *BACKUP* copies only those files that have the archive attribute set and that don't exist on the other computer, or if they do exist there, don't have the archive attribute set. *UPDATE* copies only those files that are newer than those that exist on the other computer. *READONLY* over writes files on the other computer that are read-only, if necessary.		
	Select/Deselect. Selects or deselects an individual file.	S	
	Select Group. Lets you copy all files that match any wild-card specification you enter, such as *.BAT or *.COM.	G	
	Select All. Lets you select all displayed files. You can then use the space bar to individually deselect those files that you don't want copied.	A	
	Deselect Group. Lets you exclude from the copy process any files that match the wild-card specification you enter.	D	
	Deselect All. Lets you deselect all files.	L	
	Exit. Exits from the Master screen to the Initial Options display.	X	Alt-X
View	*Open.* Displays the contents of the subdirectory.	O	
	Close. Closes a displayed subdirectory and changes to the parent directory.	C	Alt-F4
	Drive/Path. Changes to another drive and/or directory. FILELINK displays a dialog box and requests that you enter the desired path.	D	Alt-D
	Display Format. Displays files with their date and time, or their attributes.	F	
	Display Options. Lets you display files that match certain criteria.	P	

Menu	Command and Description	Key to Press	Shortcut
	ARCHIVE displays only those files that have the archive attribute set. *SINCE* displays only those since the date you specify. *HIDDEN* displays those files that have the hidden attribute set (these files are not normally displayed).		
	Sort Options. Tells FILELINK to list files and use any of the following sort orders: No Sort, Sort on Filename, Sort on File Extension, or Sort on File Modification Date.	S	
	Refresh. Reads and refreshes the remote directory window.	R	
	Switch Window. Toggles between directory windows.	W	
Options	**Quit Slave**. Tells the remote computer to exit slave mode and return to the initial Options menu.	Q	
Help	**Help for Help**. Tells you how to navigate the help system.	H	
	Contents. Displays a list of the help system table of contents. You can select any topic.	C	
	Previous Topic. Displays the last help topic accessed.	P	
	About. Displays the current version and copyright information for the FILELINK utility.	A	

Transferring Files. The concept of transferring files between the two connected computers is pretty simple. First, you use the Tab key to select the transmitting machine, placing the highlight bar in the appropriate window. Either the master computer or the slave computer can transfer files to the other. Then select the file(s) you want, and press the space bar. When a file is selected, a check mark is displayed after the file name, as shown in figure 13.6.

V

Device Utilities

Fig. 13.6

Selected files
for transfer.

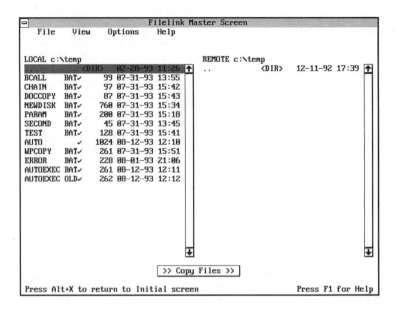

After you have made your selection(s), note that the >> Copy Files >> button
is brightened. Press Alt-C (Copy) or Alt-F (Filtered Copy) if appropriate (you
have filters in operation), and FILELINK goes to work. The utility displays a
dialog box that lists each file one at a time as it is being transferred. Along
with the name in brackets, the number of file bytes (characters) left to be
transferred is displayed, decrementing as the transfer progresses. After all
the selected files are transferred, the message Updating remote directory
listing is briefly displayed. When this dialog box is removed, FILELINK
waits for your next instructions in the Master screen.

> **Note**
>
> Make sure that you select the destination directory before starting the transfer. Oth-
> erwise, the files transmitted may not be in the location you want.

Press Alt-X to return to the Initial Options display, and press Esc to return to
the Novell DOS prompt when you are finished transferring all the files you
want to transfer.

Operating FILELINK from the DOS Prompt. If you decide to use FILELINK
from the DOS prompt or from a batch file, you must give it the correct parameters. FILELINK allows several types of parameters. Here is the syntax of
the FILELINK command:

```
FILELINK command source filename.ext destination filename.ext
        COMn:baud | LPTn switches
```

The *command* tells FILELINK what its action should be. Table 13.9 lists the available commands and their abbreviations.

Table 13.9 FILELINK Commands

Command	Abbrev.	Description
DIRECTORY	DIR	Lists the files on the slave computer
DUPLICATE	DUP	Copies the FILELINK program from the master computer to the slave computer (only through serial cable)
QUIT	QUI	Quits FILELINK on the slave computer, returning the slave to its original condition
RECEIVE	REC	Copies files from the slave computer to the master computer
SETUP	SET	Configures FILELINK for the computer (must be followed by COMn:baud or LPTn)
SLAVE	SLA	Places the computer in slave mode
TRANSMIT	TRA	Copies files from the master computer to the slave computer

Note

As with other Novell DOS 7 commands, FILELINK can use a file list as its file specification.

V

Device Utilities

In addition to the commands, FILELINK has switches to provide flexibility in transferring files. Using switches, you can, for example, specify to transfer only those files modified after a certain date. You can also transfer files that do not exist on the destination drive. Another switch causes FILELINK to prompt you before a file is transferred. The following paragraphs describe the available switches.

The /A switch tells FILELINK to transfer only those files that have the archive attribute set to on—in other words, those files that have been changed since the last backup. Read more on file attributes in Chapter 6, "Understanding File Storage."

The /D:*mm-dd-yy* switch is useful when you are trying to keep files on the slave computer current with files on the master. This switch enables you to transmit files from the master to the slave only if the files meet or exceed a specified date.

Caution

Use care when you are transmitting or receiving files based on a date so that you avoid overwriting files accidentally. If the master and slave computers have different operating systems, you might accidentally replace a utility on the slave computer with a utility of the same name from the master computer. In that case, the utility copied may not work on the slave computer or may work incorrectly.

The /H switch tells FILELINK to transfer hidden or system files.

The /M switch tells FILELINK to transfer files that do not have the archive attribute set on, and then set the archive attribute off for the transferred file.

When used with the TRANSMIT or RECEIVE command, the /P switch tells FILELINK to pause at each file name and request whether it is to be transmitted or received. When used with the DIRECTORY command, this switch tells FILELINK to pause at each screenful of data. Note the different uses of /P for different commands.

You use the /R switch when you want to overwrite files at the destination that are set as read-only. Otherwise, read-only files cannot be overwritten.

The /S switch copies files in subdirectories, creating subdirectories on the destination when necessary. Add this switch to the end of any TRANSMIT or RECEIVE command. Suppose that you want to copy all files in the C:\DATA directory or in subsequent directories changed on August 21, 1993, or later. Use the following command:

```
FILELINK TRA C:\DATA C:\DATA /D:08-21-93 /S
```

In this example, the date is specified with the /D switch, and /S is added to copy files from any subdirectories of \DATA.

The /U switch copies any files from the master computer that do not exist on the slave. /U also updates old files on the slave with newer files from the master.

> **Caution**
>
> When you use the /U switch, be careful to specify exactly the directories you want to
> work with. If you specify an incorrect slave directory, you will transmit files to the
> incorrect slave directory.

The /X switch tells FILELINK not to allow any files on the slave computer to be overwritten.

To configure FILELINK, use the SETUP command along with the parallel port or the serial port and the baud rate. The command to configure FILELINK is

```
FILELINK SETUP COMn:baud | LPTn
```

Suppose that you are configuring FILELINK to work with COM2 at 115200 baud. Here is the command you use:

```
FILELINK SETUP COM2:115
```

To set up FILELINK to work with COM1 at 19200 baud, use this command:

```
FILELINK SETUP COM1:19
```

To set up FILELINK to use the first printer port, use this command:

```
FILELINK LPT1
```

> **Note**
>
> FILELINK must be configured so that both computers operate at the same baud rate.
> If you did not use FILELINK DUPLICATE to send FILELINK to your other computer, use
> FILELINK SETUP to configure FILELINK for the same serial port and baud rate on both
> computers, or use a parallel port on both computers.

If you do not specify the port to use—or, if serial, the baud rate—FILELINK shows the current configuration. For example, entering the command **FILELINK SETUP** might return this message:

```
Current FILELINK is setup for: COM1:9600
```

When you set up FILELINK, the configuration that you specify is stored in a file on disk. The file is called FILELINK.CFG. FILELINK reads this configuration when you use the program. After you configure FILELINK, you never need to use SETUP again, unless you want to change the configuration. This is true even if you have used the full-screen version of FILELINK to configure the utility. FILELINK.CFG is an ASCII text file and may be edited.

After you have configured FILELINK, duplicate FILELINK to the other computer. Reconfigure FILELINK on the slave computer, using the FILELINK SETUP command.

Designating the Slave Computer. As noted, to use FILELINK, one computer must be the slave, and one must be the master. The slave computer must be placed in slave mode. To start slave mode, enter the following command:

    FILELINK SLAVE

When you start slave mode, you see a message on the computer telling you that the computer is in slave mode:

    FILELINK in slave mode. Press Ctrl-C to exit. Waiting...[/]

When starting slave mode, you may include the /X switch. This switch keeps any file on the slave computer from being overwritten. When this switch is in effect, the master computer can copy only those files that do not already exist on the slave computer. Enter the following command to use the /X switch:

    FILELINK SLAVE /X

To quit slave mode, press Ctrl-C on the slave computer. Doing this returns the slave computer to the DOS prompt. Another way to quit slave mode is to issue the QUIT command from the master computer:

    FILELINK QUIT

Displaying Directories. The object of using FILELINK is to transfer files between the master and slave computers. In addition to transferring files, FILELINK enables you to list the files on the slave computer. Before you transfer files from the slave computer to the master computer, if that is what you want to do, you must know the name and location of the files. You can use the DIRECTORY command to list the files on the slave computer. Another reason to use the DIRECTORY command is to see whether a particular file exists on the slave computer. If the file doesn't exist, you might want to transmit the file to the slave computer.

To see a directory, begin by ensuring that the slave computer is in slave mode. Then use the DIRECTORY command from the master computer. For example, to list the files in the current directory on the slave computer, enter the following command on the master computer:

```
FILELINK DIR
```

The result of the directory command is similar to that provided by the Novell DOS XDIR command. You can specify file names and directories to display with FILELINK DIR, and you can use wild cards. For example, to display all the files in the C:\TEMP directory, use this command:

```
FILELINK DIR C:\TEMP\*.*
```

Figure 13.7 shows two FILELINK commands. The first requests a directory of the remote directory C:\TEMP, all files. The second sends the files from the C:\TEMP directory on the master computer to the C:\TEMP directory on the slave.

```
[NOVELL DOS] C:\>filelink dir c:\temp\*.*
Trying to connect to slave ...
Connected to slave.
File not found

[NOVELL DOS] C:\>filelink tra c:\temp c:\temp
Trying to connect to slave ...
Connected to slave.
c:\temp\bcall.bat
c:\temp\chain.bat
c:\temp\doccopy.bat
c:\temp\newdisk.bat
c:\temp\param.bat
c:\temp\second.bat
c:\temp\test.bat
c:\temp\auto
c:\temp\wpcopy.bat
c:\temp\error.bat
c:\temp\autoexec.bat
c:\temp\autoexec.old
        12 File(s) transferred

[NOVELL DOS] C:\>
```

Fig. 13.7

The results of two FILELINK commands.

V

Device Utilities

You can include the /P switch with the FILELINK DIRECTORY command to display one screenful of information at a time. This /P switch works just like the /P switch in DIR and XDIR. Another switch that you can use is /S to display all subsequent subdirectories. If you want to display all files with the extension FAX on the entire hard disk, pausing after each screenful, issue this command:

```
FILELINK DIRECTORY C:\*.FAX /S /P
```

Transmitting Files. Transmitting a file or files is the same as copying a file from one location to another. Use TRANSMIT (TRA) to copy a file from the master computer to the slave computer. To use TRANSMIT, you must specify the file that you want to transmit from the master (including the path to the file if necessary). You can also include the destination path on the slave computer. If you don't specify a destination path, the file or files that you transmit are copied into the current directory on the slave computer.

To transmit the file WORKSHT.WK3 from C:\DATA\SHEET on the master computer to the current directory on the slave computer, use this command:

```
FILELINK TRANSMIT C:\DATA\SHEET\WORKSHT.WK3
```

As a file is transmitted, FILELINK shows the progress of the transmission. FILELINK shows, in square brackets, the number of bytes remaining to be sent.

Suppose that you want to transmit all files in your C:\DATA\WP directory on the master computer to C:\DATA\WP on the slave. Use one of the following commands:

```
FILELINK TRA C:\DATA\WP\*.* C:\DATA\WP
```

```
FILELINK TRA C:\DATA\WP C:\DATA\WP
```

Either command works. All the files are transmitted.

If C:\DATA\WP does not exist on the slave computer, FILELINK creates any specified directory that does not exist on the slave computer.

Receiving Files from the Slave Computer. Receiving files is exactly the opposite of transmitting files. Instead of sending files from the master computer to the slave computer, you are sending files from the slave to the master, and you can perform this task from the master. You do not have to move to the slave computer to transmit files.

Suppose that you want to transfer some files from the slave computer's C:\WORK directory. The names of the files that you want begin with ACCT. You want to place these files on the master in the directory C:\ACCT. Issue the following command:

```
FILELINK RECEIVE C:\WORK\ACCT*.* C:\ACCT
```

Because you are receiving files, the slave computer's directory and file names are the source and are listed first.

You can use any valid switch when receiving files on the master computer. Use the same caution when receiving files as when transmitting files. If you are not careful, you can accidentally overwrite files.

Running FILELINK with a Batch File. If you regularly update files by using FILELINK, creating a batch file is a natural choice. Create any batch files on the computer that you use as the master.

Suppose that you regularly update files on your laptop computer while you are away from the office. When you return to the office, you want to transfer the updated files to your desktop computer. You store all your files in subdirectories of the C:\DATA directory. To achieve the update, create the following batch file, called UPDATE.BAT, on your desktop computer (which you use as the master computer):

```
ECHO OFF
ECHO Ensure that the laptop is in slave mode.
PAUSE
FILELINK RECEIVE C:\DATA C:\DATA /U /S
FILELINK QUIT
```

This batch file, when run, first prompts you to make sure that the laptop is in slave mode and then waits for you to press a key on the master computer. When you press a key, FILELINK begins receiving any updated files. After all files have been transferred, slave mode on the laptop quits. The message `Remote FILELINK terminated` is displayed on the master video screen.

> **Note**
>
> Always test your commands and command sequences before including them in a batch file. Test the batch file on unimportant files and directories. After you are sure that the batch file works as planned, you can substitute real files and directories.

From Here...

This chapter described the ways you can control system devices: using the MODE command to redirect printers to various ports, using the PRINT command to print in the background, using the SHARE command for sharing files, and using FILELINK to transfer files between computers. You may want to turn now to the following chapter and appendix:

- Chapter 14, "Managing the Display and Keyboard," discusses the uses of MODE and other device-specific commands.

- Appendix A, "Internationalizing Your System," explains code page switching and other uses of MODE.

Chapter 14

Managing the Display and Keyboard

The two most important and frequently used devices on your computer are the keyboard and display. Without them, instructing the computer and viewing the results of your instructions would be a very different process. The keyboard takes the information that you type and tells programs what to do. The screen then displays the results of your request.

Suppose that you request the computer to format a floppy disk. The screen displays a message requesting that you insert a floppy disk in the drive and press a key. In this one small event, you have used both the keyboard and the display. The two devices are invaluable.

You can control your video display and keyboard characters by internationalizing your system. Refer to Appendix A for more on the various levels of national custom and language support.

Novell DOS also provides the tools for you to customize your computer display and make it truly yours. All you need to do is read the sections in this chapter on PROMPT and ANSI.SYS and then use your imagination.

This chapter covers the following topics:

- The typematic rate for your keyboard

- Controlling the video display

- Printing graphics

- Switching character tables

- Customizing the DOS prompt

- Using ANSI.SYS to enhance your system

- Using the system clock

Specifying the Typematic Rate

Nearly every time you press a key on the keyboard, a character is displayed on-screen. If you hold down the same key for a period of time, the character begins to repeat on-screen. The number of times per second that a key is repeated is called the *typematic rate.*

Keyboard response time is very important because the quicker the response, the more information you can enter into the computer. Setting the typematic rate won't turn you into a typing wizard, but it can allow you to repeat the same key at an extremely fast rate. How useful this feature is depends on the software you are using.

You may want to adjust the typematic rate if you are typing characters that need to be repeated frequently. To note the current typematic rate of your computer system, create a line of asterisks (*********) on the command line. You may find the default typematic rate slow, but you can adjust it to repeat any character very rapidly.

Use the following MODE command syntax to set the typematic rate:

```
MODE CON: RATE=rate DELAY=delay
```

Table 14.1 describes the options available with this command.

Table 14.1 MODE Typematic Rate Options	
Option	**Use**
CON:	Specifies that you are setting the console's parameters; required for setting typematic rate. The default is none. In this case, CON: refers to the keyboard.
RATE=	Specifies the speed at which characters are repeated on-screen while a key is being held down; required if DELAY= is used. Values range from 1 to 32; the default is none.
DELAY=	Specifies the time it will take, when a key is held down, before the character is repeated (the autorepeat start-delay time). Values range from 1 to 4.

Two adjustments are possible to the typematic rate: the number of times per second a key will repeat (the *rate*), and the length of time you must hold down a key before it starts repeating (the *delay*). You must specify both *rate* and *delay*, or Novell DOS issues the following error message:

```
Rate and delay values must be specified together
```

The *rate* and *delay* values can be specified in any order, as long as both are entered on the same command line. The delay is specified in 1/4-second intervals. The *delay* range is from 1 to 4, for creating delays from 1/4 second to 1 second. The *rate* range is from 1 to 32.

For example, enter the following command to set the keyboard delay rate to 1/4 second before a key is repeated, and to set the typematic rate to 30:

```
MODE CON: RATE=30 DELAY=1
```

> **Note**
>
> Many newer computers have a built-in BIOS setting for the typematic rate. The values mentioned here may or may not be the same as those used by the BIOS manufacturer. Check the computer's manual for any information on the BIOS setting.

Controlling the Display

The display is your view into the computer. Without a display, you would have great difficulty responding to the computer's requests because you couldn't see them. You would also be unable to see what information you were entering into the computer, or what you were instructing the computer to do. If you know how to control the display, you can be more productive and get the information that you require from the computer.

Setting the Display Type (MODE)

Novell DOS provides various choices for setting the display type parameters. Your preference depends on the software you are using. If you are using a spreadsheet and want to put more rows on the screen, you can set the number of lines from the standard 25 to 43 or 50. If you get a new monitor, you will probably need to use the MODE command to inform Novell DOS of the type of monitor it is.

V

Device Utilities

Use the following syntax with the MODE command to set the display type:

MODE *displaymode,*lines

Table 14.2 describes the available parameters. All entries in the Option column (except for *lines*) refer to *displaymode*.

Table 14.2 MODE Display Type Switches	
Option	**Use**
CO40	Sets the display width to 40 characters per line with a color display and makes the graphics display active if more than one adapter is installed.
CO80	Sets the display width to 80 characters per line with a color display and makes the graphics display active if more than one adapter is installed.
BW40	Sets the display width to 40 characters per line with a black-and-white display mode and makes the graphics display active if more than one adapter is installed.
BW80	Sets the display width to 80 characters per line with a black-and-white display mode and makes the graphics display active if more than one adapter is installed.
MONO	Switches to a monochrome display with 80 characters per line.
lines	Sets the number of rows on the screen (25, 43, or 50). This parameter can be used only after the graphics display has been activated. The screen can display 43 lines only if an Enhanced Graphics Adapter (EGA), Video Graphics Adapter (VGA), or Super Video Graphics Adapter (SVGA) is installed. The screen can display 50 lines only if a VGA or SVGA is installed. The default is 25.

If the graphics adapter is already enabled, you can use the following items for *displaymode*:

40	Sets the display width to 40 characters per line (retaining the setting for color or black and white previously established).
80	Sets the display width to 80 characters per line (retaining the setting for color or black and white previously established).

Note

If you issue the MODE command to enable a color display, the screen still displays in black and white. What the command does is enable your application programs to display in color if they are configured to do so.

The following command sets the display type to a color display with 43 lines and 80 columns:

```
MODE CO80,43
```

If the graphics adapter has already been initialized, you can enter the following command and achieve the same results:

```
MODE 80,43
```

Adjusting a CGA Display. Sometimes CGA (Color Graphics Adapter) monitors do not display information correctly on-screen. The information displayed may be cut off on the right or left side of the screen. You can use the MODE command to align the screen for better readability.

The syntax for the MODE command that sets the CGA display type is

```
MODE displaymode,shiftdisplay,testpattern
```

Table 14.3 describes the parameters available with this command.

Table 14.3 MODE CGA Display Type Parameters

Option	Use
displaymode	Specifies how the data will be displayed (refer to table 14.2)
shiftdisplay	Shifts the display left or right by one column (R for right, L for left)
testpattern	Displays a test pattern for screen alignment (T)

To shift the display one column to the left and display a test pattern, enter the following:

```
MODE ,L,T
```

Note

If you are not setting the display type at the same time that you are adjusting the CGA display, you do not have to include *displaymode* on the command line. When you do not use this option, however, you must still include the comma that would follow it if it were there.

V

Device Utilities

After the test pattern is displayed, you are asked whether the alignment is acceptable. If you answer no, the display shifts one column left in this case, or right if you use R in the command line. The process continues until you answer yes to indicate that the display is aligned correctly.

If you issue the CGA MODE command to any display type other than CGA, you get the following error message:

```
Display shift command only available on CGA
```

Adjusting the Cursor (CURSOR). On some displays, the cursor blinks at a faster rate than the display can handle and becomes a dim blur that is hard to locate. LCD displays, in particular, cause the cursor to blink at such a fast rate that the cursor gets lost on-screen. The CURSOR command enables you to slow the rate of the cursor's blinking so that you can locate the cursor on-screen much more easily.

The hardware-generated cursor appears as a single line under the current character being typed. The software-generated cursor produced by the CURSOR command appears as a large block. The software-generated cursor has a variable blink rate, which you can set to suit your own preference, according to the quality of the display you are using.

Here is the syntax of the CURSOR command:

```
CURSOR  /Snn  /C  /B  OFF
```

Table 14.4 describes the switches available with CURSOR.

Table 14.4 CURSOR Command Switches

Switch	Use
/Snn	Sets the cursor blink rate, where nn is a two-digit decimal value giving the blink rate in multiples of 1/20 second. The default is 4/20 (1/5) second.
/C	Turns on CGA compatibility, eliminating the snowlike interference that using a software cursor on a CGA screen can cause.
/B	Enables CGA compatibility with monochrome video; suppresses snow.
OFF	Reenables the hardware cursor and disables the software cursor.

To set the cursor to blink every 3/4 second, enter the following:

```
CURSOR /S15
```

The blink rate is specified in 1/20-second increments. Therefore, setting the /S*nn* switch to 5 makes the cursor blink at 1/4-second intervals. A setting of 10 causes 1/2-second intervals, 15 causes 3/4-second intervals, and 20 causes 1-second intervals. The default rate is 4.

Clearing the Screen (CLS)

Often when you enter a group of commands, you want to begin with a clear screen. When the screen gets cluttered by a program's output, you can clear the screen by using the CLS command.

To clear the screen, just enter the CLS command (the command has no switches):

```
CLS
```

Novell DOS clears the screen and positions the cursor at row 1, column 1.

> **Note**
>
> You can use the CLS command at a system prompt or anywhere in a batch file. CLS is particularly useful in batch files. You can use it to clear the screen before the file issues a group of commands whose output has to be seen clearly, or at the beginning of the file to clear the screen before any of the batch file's commands are executed.

> **Note**
>
> Some versions of MS-DOS do not clear any lines beyond line 25. Therefore, third-party software and patches to device drivers or COMMAND.COM were developed to clear the extra lines from the screen. With Novell DOS, even if you have set the number of lines to 43 or 50, CLS clears all the lines from the screen.

Managing Text Display (MORE)

The MORE command is a filter, just like the SORT and FIND filters. A *filter* takes data in and processes it according to some preset criteria. The MORE filter acts on screenfuls of data, whereas SORT (for sorting data) and FIND (for finding data) work only with ASCII text files and Novell DOS commands that go to the screen. The MORE command causes the display to pause after a screenful of data has been shown.

One use of MORE is to display the README.DOC files that are included with many commercial software packages.

The syntax for the MORE command is

> *command* ¦ **MORE**

or

> **MORE** < *filename*

For example, the TREE command may display information that cannot fit on a single screen. In that case, issue the following command:

> TREE ¦ MORE

MORE collects data, in a temporary file on the disk, that usually goes to the screen. The information can be contained in a file or generated from a program. Using MORE is a more efficient way of viewing data that scrolls by on-screen than using the Pause key.

Keep in mind the following details when you use MORE:

- Press any key at the Strike any key when ready... prompt to view the next screenful of data.

- MORE displays 24 lines of data at a time. With the display set to 43 lines, MORE shows 42. With the display set to 50 lines, MORE shows 48.

- MORE appears to do nothing when issued by itself on the command line. MORE requires input before it does anything.

- Pressing Ctrl-Break or Ctrl-C terminates the MORE command without displaying any more screenfuls of data.

The MORE filter is most commonly used to pause the screen for reading text files. To view the README.DOC file one screen at a time, enter

```
TYPE README.DOC ¦ MORE
```

or

```
MORE < README.DOC
```

Another use of the MORE filter is to stop to read the screen if a program has a large amount of data to display. If you have a directory on your hard disk that has more than 22 files in it, enter the following command:

```
DIR ¦ MORE
```

Note

An alternative to the MORE filter is the /P switch. This switch is available on all Novell DOS commands that scroll text on-screen. Note two examples:

```
DIR /P
```

```
TYPE FILENAME.EXT /P
```

The effects of /P and MORE are identical, but MORE is slower.

Printing Graphics (GRAPHICS)

Sometimes you need to print a copy of what is being displayed on-screen. You can do this by pressing either one key or a couple of keys, depending on your computer. One of the keys that you press is the PrtSc key; the other key (if necessary) may be Shift, Alt, or Ctrl.

The normal print-screen function is an internal function of Novell DOS and is not very sophisticated. When you press the PrtSc key (or press two keys), Novell DOS sends a copy of the screen to the printer, if only text is displayed on-screen. If graphics are displayed on-screen when you press PrtSc, the printer ejects a blank page.

To make the print-screen function complex enough to handle printing graphics, you would have to increase the size of the Novell DOS kernel, allowing less free memory for applications. Accordingly, you cannot print complex graphic information to the printer by using the PRINT command. To print graphics to your printer, you have to load a special printer interface: the GRAPHICS command. This interface takes all information, both text and graphics, from the screen and prints it to your printer. Without using the GRAPHICS command, you are unable to print anything but text information to the printer with the PrtSc key.

The GRAPHICS command is fairly complex; it takes information from the video adapter's buffer and converts it to a printable format. The conversion between the display (video adapter) and the printer is handled by the GRAPHICS command. GRAPHICS is a TSR (terminate-and-stay-resident) program that uses part of your free memory (about 4,448 bytes). GRAPHICS intercepts your print-screen request, grabs the information from the screen, converts it to printable form, and prints it to the printer.

If you have a color printer attached to your computer, you can use the GRAPHICS command to print the colors being displayed. If you don't have a color printer, the printer produces images in black, white, and shades of gray.

Here is the syntax of the GRAPHICS command:

```
GRAPHICS COLOR /R
```

The COLOR parameter enables color printing on an IBM-compatible color graphics printer (in eight colors). The /R switch prints the screen exactly as it appears in black and white. The default is the inverse of screen prints (white on black instead of black on white).

To print graphics images exactly as they are displayed on-screen, enter the following command:

```
GRAPHICS /R
```

To print the graphics as the inverse of how they are displayed, enter this command:

```
GRAPHICS
```

If you have a color printer attached to your system, enter the following:

```
GRAPHICS COLOR
```

Keep in mind the following details when you use GRAPHICS:

- If you specify the GRAPHICS command with no parameters, everything will be printed as the inverse of how it is displayed on-screen.

- The GRAPHICS command loads as a resident program and uses 4,448 bytes of system memory.

- The only way to remove the GRAPHICS command from system memory is to reboot.

- GRAPHICS does not necessarily support EGA and VGA modes. You may need a third-party utility to enable GRAPHICS with these displays.

- After you issue the GRAPHICS command, you cannot change the parameters from the initial parameters loaded with the GRAPHICS command. The only way to change the parameters of the GRAPHICS command after it has been executed is to reboot and reissue the GRAPHICS command with different parameters.

- You must execute the GRAPHICS command before using PrtSc to print a screen with graphics. If you do not run GRAPHICS before printing the screen, the printer may print output that looks like garbage.

- You can print up to eight colors on a color printer.

Tip
If you often use the GRAPHICS command for your work, load it through your AUTOEXEC.BAT file. Then it is always available for use.

V

Device Utilities

Switching Character Tables (GRAFTABL)

The GRAFTABL utility displays extended ASCII characters on your video screen. These characters generally appear in the ASCII code chart from 128 through 255. This command is used only to enable the display of extended ASCII characters when you are using a Color Graphics Adapter (CGA).

The default country setting of the character code page is USA. This setting specifies the appearance of international characters but does not actually change the code page used by your system. You must use the MODE or CHCP command to change the particular code page.

To determine the status of GRAFTABL on your system, type **GRAFTABL /STATUS** and press Enter at the Novell DOS prompt. The message
`No character table is currently loaded` appears.

To load GRAFTABL, enter the following command at the DOS prompt:

```
GRAFTABL
```

Or you can enter this command:

```
GRAFTABL nnn
```

Replace *nnn* with the code page number. When you do not enter the code page or when you use the Setup program to include the GRAFTABL command in your AUTOEXEC.BAT file, the default country is either USA or the country specified in setting up your default code page.

When you require the GRAFTABL utility to be used on your system, you should place it in your AUTOEXEC.BAT file so that GRAFTABL is loaded every time your system is booted.

Refer to Appendix A, "Internationalizing Your System," for more information about code page switching.

Redirecting the Console (CTTY)

The CON (console) device consists of the screen and keyboard. The keyboard is the standard input device, and the screen is the standard output device. The CTTY command enables you to select a different device as the console.

CTTY is a useful command if you need to redirect the console input and output from the standard device CON to an alternative device. One of the undocumented features of CTTY is its capability to direct all screen output and keyboard input to the NUL device. Directing screen output to NUL causes all the program's messages not to be displayed.

Here is the syntax of the CTTY command:

```
CTTY device
```

Replace *device* with one of the following system devices:

CON	Screen output and keyboard input (default)
AUX or COM1	First communications (serial) port
COM2	Second communications (serial) port
NUL	No screen output or keyboard input

CTTY causes all the input and output (I/O) requests issued for the keyboard and screen to be rerouted to the alternative device. The only exception occurs when you set the device to NUL, which allows no keyboard input and no screen output.

> **Note**
>
> Redirecting the CON device to the NUL device can be useful if you are creating batch files that have many steps being executed for which you do not want the program's message displayed. If there is a step where you need to see the program messages, you can redirect the console I/O back to the CON device.

> **Caution**
>
> Do not issue CTTY NUL at the system prompt, because there is no way to get I/O directed back to the CON device without rebooting.

Keep in mind the following details when you use CTTY to redirect the console:

- The following character-based devices can be used as alternative consoles: AUX, COM1, and COM2.

- The physical device that is attached to the relevant AUX, COM1, or COM2 device must be able to accept input and provide output.

- Programs that do not make use of the DOS function calls will not make use of the alternative console.

- NUL cannot be used as an alternative console, even though it is a valid device for redirecting console input and screen output.

One good use of the CTTY NUL line is to place it in your AUTOEXEC.BAT file. After you add this line, no program messages will be displayed during the execution of the AUTOEXEC.BAT file. The following is a sample AUTOEXEC.BAT file:

```
@ECHO OFF
echo LOADING SYSTEM PLEASE WAIT...
CTTY NUL
<programs to run, TSRs to load, and so on>
CTTY CON
```

You can use CTTY NUL to turn off system messages and CTTY CON to turn on system messages whenever you like in a batch file.

Another use of the CTTY command is to place it in batch files to redirect all the output to the NUL device. Suppose that your batch file looks like the following:

V

Device Utilities

```
@ECHO OFF
ECHO Insert blank, formatted floppy in A:
PAUSE
COPY REPORT.DOC A:\REPORT.DOC
COPY LIST.DOC A:\LIST.DOC
XCOPY C:\DATA\*.* A:\*.*
```

If you were to run this batch file, you would see the following messages, along with the copied file names:

```
1 file(s) copied

1 file(s) copied

Reading Source File(s)

(n) File(s) copied

Writing Source File(s)

(n) File(s) copied
```

Suppose that you modify the batch file by adding two CTTY lines:

```
@ECHO OFF
ECHO Insert blank, formatted floppy in A:
PAUSE
Echo Copying Files to Drive A: Please Wait...
CTTY NUL
COPY REPORT.DOC A:\REPORT.DOC
COPY LIST.DOC A:\LIST.DOC
XCOPY C:\DATA\*.* A:\*.*
CTTY CON
Echo Completed Copying Files to Drive A:
```

Then none of the copy messages will be displayed.

Caution

Make sure that a batch file runs correctly before you add the CTTY NUL line. Do not add CTTY NUL before testing the batch file. After you add this line, you will not be able to see whether the file is running correctly.

Note

For some purposes, there is another way of suppressing messages from commands such as COPY. You can use the redirection sign (>) to the NUL device, as in

```
COPY FILENAME.EXT A: > NUL
```

This form of the COPY command does not display file names or 1 file(s) copied when the command finishes executing.

Customizing the DOS Prompt (PROMPT and PEXEC)

You use the PROMPT command to display special text at the DOS prompt. You can be creative with this command because many types of information, including the date and time, can be displayed every time Novell DOS displays the command-line prompt. You do not have to stick with the plain old C> when no PROMPT command has been issued, or the more usual but still boring C:\>.

The Install/Setup program provides several preprogrammed options for your selection, as well as for entry of your own design. From Setup's initial menu, select DOS System & Memory Management and then select DOS System Parameters and PROMPT Command. Using the up- or down-arrow key, highlight the area next to Information to Display. Then press Enter. A pull-down menu presents the options. When you highlight each option in turn, you see at the top of the menu an example of the design. Use Other to design your own.

PROMPT has a number of character codes that tell Novell DOS what to display and how to display it. Table 14.5 lists the various characters to use for creating your PROMPT command design. The $ character must be a prefix for any of the characters.

Table 14.5 PROMPT Character Codes

Character	Purpose
$D	Displays the current system date
$T	Displays the current system time
$N	Displays the current drive letter

(continues)

V

Device Utilities

Table 14.5 Continued	
Character	**Purpose**
$P	Displays the current directory path and drive
$V	Displays the operating system name and version
$B	Displays the ¦ character
$G	Displays the > character
$L	Displays the < character
$Q	Displays the = character
$$	Displays the $ character
$H	Uses the Backspace key to erase the previous character
$E	The escape character
$X	Executes a command every time Novell DOS returns to the prompt
$_ (underline)	Causes the display to move to the next line; supplies a carriage return and line feed (this is the underline character)
$- (minus)	Tells Novell DOS to hide the prompt display (this is the minus character)

Here are some examples of the use of these characters for designing a PROMPT command line:

Command	*Resulting Prompt*
PROMPT [Novell DOS] PG	[Novell DOS] C:\NWDOS>
PROMPT [Novell DOS] NG	[Novell DOS] C>
PROMPT [Novell DOS] DG	[Novell DOS] Mon 04-06-92
PROMPT [Novell DOS] TG	[Novell DOS] 10:20:30.00
PROMPT	C>

Tip
You can begin the statement by just typing **PROMPT** or **SET PROMPT=**.

You can use the [Novell DOS] text or replace it with any personal text you choose. Suppose that you want to use the $T switch to display the time as part of your prompt, but you don't want seconds and hundredths of a second displayed. Use the $H character code to delete the unwanted characters from the prompt. In this instance, type the statement

```
PROMPT $T$H$H$H$H$H$H $P$G
```

to obtain the prompt

```
10:20 C:\>
```

The backspace character code, $H, erases the seconds and hundredths of seconds that would otherwise be displayed.

V

Device Utilities

Another prompt that you might find appealing displays the time and date before displaying the prompt. To create this prompt, enter the statement

```
PROMPT Time: $T$H$H$H$H$H$H$_Date: $D$_[Novell DOS] $P$G
```

and you get the following prompt display:

```
Time: 10:20 Date: Mon 4-06-1992 [Novell DOS] C:\>
```

You can also enhance your system prompt by using ANSI.SYS codes. With a monochrome monitor, for example, you may want to use reverse video for effect. With a color monitor, you can be really imaginative. Refer to the next section on ANSI.SYS for more information about the use of these codes.

You may want to execute a command every time Novell DOS returns to the DOS prompt. To do this, you must first set a special environment variable, PEXEC, by entering a statement with the following command structure:

```
SET PEXEC=command
```

For example, to run DISKMAP every time Novell DOS displays the prompt, add the following statements to your AUTOEXEC.BAT file:

```
SET PEXEC=DISKMAP C:
PROMPT $X$P$G
```

The first statement sets the environment variable, and the second statement includes the $X character code in the PROMPT statement. The path does not need to be specified when the command file is included in your PATH statement.

> **Note**
>
> Executing a command every time Novell DOS returns to the prompt causes a delay in the display of the prompt.

Using ANSI.SYS

You usually communicate with Novell DOS by typing commands at the command prompt. Novell DOS usually communicates with you by displaying messages on the video screen. ANSI.SYS is a screen and keyboard driver that enhances these communications. By using the ANSI codes, you can set screen attributes like blinking, bold, and colors; position the cursor anywhere on-screen; and assign keystrokes to function keys.

Some application programs may require the availability of the ANSI.SYS driver in order for their functions to work correctly. Check the documentation manual for your application programs to see what they need.

The ANSI.SYS driver is loaded through the CONFIG.SYS file. Add this driver with the Setup program or manually place the following statement in your CONFIG.SYS file:

```
DEVICE=C:\NWDOS\ANSI.SYS
```

There are no switches or options to use with this statement.

Using Escape Sequences

To pass commands to the ANSI driver, you must use what are called *escape sequences*, which are strings of codes following the escape character. You can type these escape sequences at the keyboard by using the PROMPT command, or the sequences can be passed from a text file or batch file. The entry of the escape sequences is slightly different depending on the method used:

- When using the PROMPT command, type **$E** as the escape character. The command takes effect when you press Enter.

- When using EDIT to prepare a text or batch file, press Ctrl-P and then press Esc. When your ANSI.SYS codes are in a text file, the command takes effect when you use the TYPE command at the DOS prompt: type **TYPE FILENAME.TXT** and press Enter. When you use a batch file to issue ANSI escape codes, simply execute the batch file.

After supplying the escape character, you then add the [character and one or more code numbers separated by a semicolon (;), plus a command character. EDIT displays Esc as ^[, so you might want to remember that the ANSI string always starts as ^[[.

Tip

Place all your ANSI.SYS commands in text files and name them according to use. Then just issue a TYPE command for them to take effect.

> **Note**
>
> For purposes of clarity, all command examples are listed in uppercase letters except for those that must be in lowercase.

Setting the Screen

Set special screen effects by using the screen character and color codes in tables 14.6 and 14.7. The codes in table 14.6 set the way text is shown, and the codes in table 14.7 set screen colors when you have a color video adapter and monitor. A lowercase m is the screen-mode ANSI code.

Table 14.6 Screen Character Mode Codes

Code	Use
0	Normal display (default)
1	High-intensity text
4	Underline text (monochrome)
5	Blinking text
7	Reverse video (black on white)
8	Hidden text (black on black)

V

Device Utilities

Table 14.7 Screen Color Codes		
Color	**Foreground**	**Background**
Black	30	40
Red	31	41
Green	32	42
Yellow	33	43
Blue	34	44
Magenta	35	45
Cyan	36	46
White	37	47

For example, to set the color screen to blinking characters with white text on a blue background, use the statement

```
PROMPT $E[5;37;44m $P$G
```

when using the PROMPT command.

When using EDIT, press Ctrl-P, press Esc, and enter the following:

```
5;37;44m
```

The m is for setting or changing the display mode.

To set the color screen to normal characters with white text on a blue background, use one of these statements:

```
PROMPT $E[37;44m
```

```
PROMPT $E[0;37;44m
```

When using EDIT, press Ctrl-P, press Esc, and enter one of these statements:

```
37;44m
```

```
0;37;44m
```

Because the code numbers are from different series, the order in which the numbers are specified does not matter.

Earlier in this chapter, you learned how to design a prompt to display the time, date, and current directory with the following statement:

```
PROMPT Time: $T$H$H$H$H$H$H$_Date: $D$_[Novell DOS] $P$G
```

Using the ANSI codes in tables 14.6 and 14.7, along with the PROMPT character codes in table 14.5, you can enhance this prompt for a color monitor by using the following statement:

```
PROMPT $E[1;37;44mTime:
    $T$H$H$H$H$H$H.........$E[40m$E[K$_$E[1;44mDate:
    $D$E[0;30;47m$E[K$_[Novell DOS] $P$G
```

(The nine periods represent nine spaces.)

With this statement, the time and date appear as bright white text on a blue background block, and the prompt appears as normal black text on a white background (see fig. 14.1).

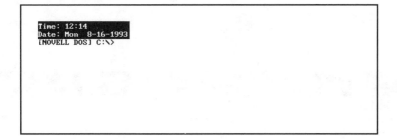

Fig. 14.1
Result of the PROMPT example.

You can enhance the prompt for a monochrome monitor by using the following statement:

```
PROMPT $E[7mTime: $T$H$H$H$H$H$H.........$E[0m$E[K$_$E[7mDate:
    $D$E[0m$E[K$_[Novell DOS] $P$G
```

(The nine periods represent nine spaces.)

With this statement, the time and date appear as black text on a white background, and the prompt appears as normal white text on a black background.

> **Note**
>
> The K of $E[K must be uppercase. The K code erases to the end of the line.

V

Device Utilities

> **Caution**
>
> Do not use ECHO OFF when instructing Novell DOS with the ANSI escape sequences in a text file or batch file.

You can also use ANSI codes to change the screen mode of some video adapters. Just use the ANSI screen mode codes listed in table 14.8 in the following command:

```
PROMPT $E[xh $P$G
```

In this command, you insert the code value in place of the lowercase *x*. The command character is a lowercase h.

> **Note**
>
> You can also use the Novell DOS MODE command to set screen display modes, as described earlier in this chapter.

Table 14.8 Screen Display Mode Codes

Code	Use
0	40 x 25 monochrome
2	80 x 25 monochrome
3	80 x 25 color
4	320 x 200 monochrome
5	320 x 200 color
6	640 x 200 monochrome
7	Turns on word wrap
71	Turns off word wrap

Positioning the Cursor

The ANSI.SYS device driver enables you to place text in specific positions on your display. This comes in handy for messages you want to display and for menus in text files.

The escape sequences are similar to those described earlier for setting screen displays. The command characters are case-sensitive; lowercase *x* stands for the row number from 0 to 24, and lowercase *y* stands for the column number from 0 to 79. Row numbers can be increased to 43 for EGA displays and to 50 for VGA monitors.

For example, when using EDIT in a text file, you place the cursor at row 14 and column 39, press Ctrl-P, press Esc, and then enter the ANSI command

```
14;39H
```

or

```
15;40f
```

Table 14.9 lists the ANSI escape sequences used for positioning the cursor on-screen.

Table 14.9 ANSI.SYS Cursor-Positioning Escape Sequences

Escape Sequence	Use
ESC[*x;y*H	Places cursor at *x,y* position (CUP)
ESC[*x;y*f	Horizontal and vertical position (HVP)
ESC[*x*A	Moves cursor up *x* rows (CUU)
ESC[*x*B	Moves cursor down *x* rows (CUD)
ESC[*y*C	Moves cursor to right *y* columns (CUF)
ESC[*y*D	Moves cursor to left *y* columns (CUB)
ESC[*x;y*R	Cursor position report (CPR)
ESC[6n	Device status report (DSR); instructs ANSI.SYS to issue CPR
ESC[s	Saves current cursor position (SCP)
ESC[u	Restores cursor position from SCP (RCP)

Erasing the Screen

When using ANSI.SYS escape sequences to enhance your screen display, you may also use commands to erase the entire screen and move the cursor to home (row 1, column 1). The erase commands are listed in table 14.10.

V

Device Utilities

Table 14.10 ANSI.SYS Screen-Erasing Escape Sequences	
Escape Sequence	**Use**
ESC[2J	Erases the full screen and homes the cursor (ED)
ESC[K	Erases from the cursor to the end of the line (EL)

To start always with a clean display, use the erase full-screen ANSI.SYS sequence at the beginning of your prompt design. Refer to the multiple-line PROMPT commands in the earlier section "Setting the Screen" for an example that includes the command for erasing to the end of the line.

Assigning Keys

You can assign frequently typed commands to function keys or to other sets of key combinations. You may already be familiar with this concept from word processing or electronic spreadsheets. This key reassignment is usually called a *macro*.

To create a macro, use the following command:

```
ESC[n;xp
```

In this command, you replace the lowercase *n* with the code for the key to be reassigned, and the lowercase *x* with the command to be executed. You may also want to enter the code for a carriage return, code 13, after the command text. For example, type the following command:

```
ESC[0;63;"DIR /W";13p
```

This command assigns the command DIR /W and a keypress of Enter to the F5 key. Table 14.11 provides a list of some key assignment codes. These codes are commonly referred to as *extended character codes* or *scan codes*. These codes are different from ASCII codes, which you can also specify in your reassignment commands.

Note

Many application programs assign their own keyboard macros and override your macro assignments while the application program is running. Usually, when you exit the application program, your macro assignments are restored.

Table 14.11 lists the ANSI extended codes in decimal format. You must notify the ANSI.SYS device driver that these codes are in decimal format by entering the codes in the format 0;*n*. The leading 0; (the zero and semicolon) must be there.

Table 14.11 Selected Extended Character Key Codes

Key	Extended Key Codes
F1 to F10	59 to 68
Shift-F1 to Shift-F10	84 to 93
Ctrl-F1 to Ctrl-F10	94 to 103
Alt-F1 to Alt-F10	104 to 113
Insert	82
Delete	83
Home	71
Ctrl-Home	119
End	79
PgUp	73
Ctrl-PgUp	132
PgDn	81
Ctrl-PgDn	118
left arrow	75
right arrow	77
up arrow	72
down arrow	80

V

Device Utilities

Note

Novell DOS 7 does not support the use of the F11 and F12 keys.

Using Your System Clock

When the first PCs were built, they used a clock (for time and calendar), but no physical clock was built into the computers. Either you had to add a clock board sold by third-party companies; or every time you turned on your computer, you had to enter the date and time. This was not really difficult, but a nuisance. From then on, as long as the power to the computer was not removed, the date and time were maintained. When you turned off the computer, they were lost.

When the AT-type computer was introduced, PCs were delivered with battery-powered clocks that would not lose the date and time when the machine was turned off. And with the PROMPT character codes, you are able to use the date and/or time in your system prompt. Now with Novell DOS 7, you can even translate the date into English (or another language in which Novell DOS 7 is published) with the name of the month and the name of the day of the week. You can also easily translate the time of the day into morning, afternoon, and evening.

Novell DOS 7 provides a neat new set of *system information variables*. You use them as if they were ordinary environment variables. They can be used in your batch files and with ANSI.SYS messages to provide "normal language" displays. You can also get these with your PROMPT command as long as it is issued from a batch file. Table 14.12 lists the system information variables. These variables are also discussed in the section "Understanding Environment Variables" in Chapter 19, "Understanding Batch Files."

Table 14.12 System Information Variables Based on System Clocks	
Variable	**Meaning**
AM_PM	A.M. or P.M. (time of day)
Day	Day number of the month, 01 to 31
Day_of_Week	Sunday to Saturday
Hour	Hour of day, 1 to 12
NDay_of_Week	Day number of the week, 1 = Sunday
Month	Number of month, 01 to 12
Month_name	January to December

Variable	Meaning
Year	1993, 1994, and so on
Short_Year	93, 94, and so on
Hour24	Hour of day (military time), 00 to 23
Minute	00 to 59
Second	00 to 59
Greeting_time	Morning, afternoon, or evening

When you use an environment or system information variable, you place a percentage sign (%) before and after the variable, as in

```
Good %greeting_time%
```

This results in Good morning, Good afternoon, or Good evening, depending on the actual system clock time. If you have installed the Desktop Server or Universal Client (in other words, the network built into Novell DOS 7), you can also use %login_name% to add your name to the greeting.

In the earlier section "Setting the Screen," you learned how to dress up your PROMPT command with color and the date and time. You can enhance the command by adding Good %greeting_time%. The new PROMPT command then is

```
PROMPT $E[1;37;44mGood %greeting_time% $_Time:
    $T$H$H$H$H$H$H.........$E[40m$E[K$_$E[1;44mDate:
    $D$E[0;30;47m$E[K$_[Novell DOS] $P$G
```

(The nine periods represent nine spaces.)

The $_ causes the next part of the prompt display to be placed on the next line. If you are logged into a network, you can add ,%login_name% after %greeting_time to add your name to the prompt. Figure 14.2 displays the results.

Note

Place the PROMPT command in your AUTOEXEC.BAT file. This way, you can use all the PROMPT commands, the ANSI.SYS codes, and the system information variables in your very own custom-designed system display prompt.

V

Device Utilities

Fig. 14.2
Result of the
enhanced
PROMPT
command.

```
Good afternoon, Bob
Time: 14:16
Date: Mon  8-16-1993
[NOVELL DOS] C:\>
```

From Here...

In this chapter, you learned how to set the typematic rate for your keyboard; control your video display; print graphics on your printer with the PrtSc key; and customize your prompt with the MODE command, ANSI.SYS escape sequences, and the new system environment variables. You may also want to refer to the following chapters and appendix:

- Chapter 13, "Controlling System Devices," shows the use of MODE as a device-controlling command.

- Chapter 19, "Using Batch Files," discusses the placing of commands and prompt design in batch files.

- Appendix A, "Internationalizing Your System," explains the use of MODE with code page switching.

Part VI

System Security Utilities

Continue

nfigure   emory Managemer
                                    Disk Compression
                                    Disk Performance
it this screen   Data Protection & Security
                                    Task Management
                                    Networking

racks   Sectors

25-Pin DB-25 Male

25-pin serial connector,
usually COM2

Change destination drive(s) and directorie

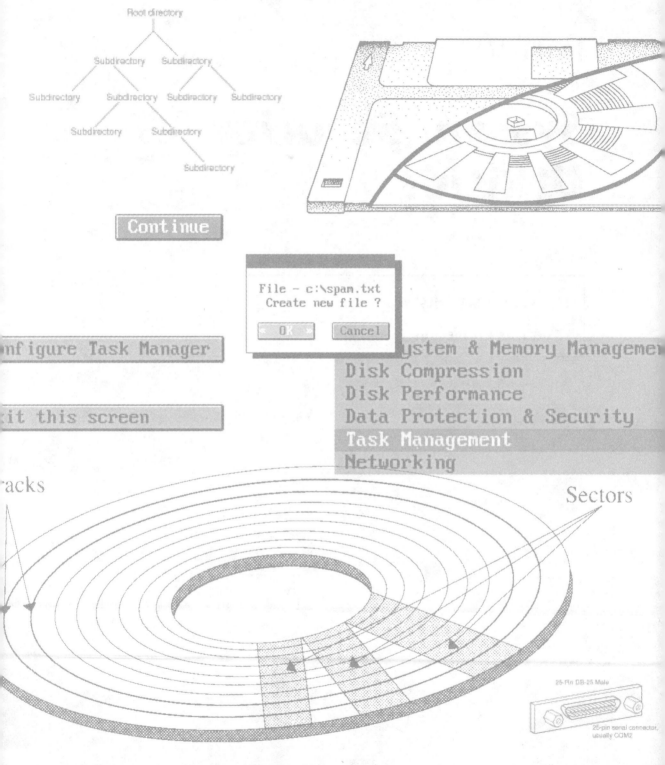

Root directory

Subdirectory Subdirectory

Subdirectory Subdirectory Subdirectory Subdirectory

Subdirectory Subdirectory

Subdirectory

Continue

File - c:\spam.txt
Create new file ?

‹ OK › Cancel

nfigure Task Manager

xit this screen

ystem & Memory Managemer
Disk Compression
Disk Performance
Data Protection & Security
Task Management
Networking

racks

Sectors

25-Pin DB-25 Male

25-pin serial connector,
usually COM2

Change destination drive(s) and directorie

Chapter 15

System Security

If you have used a computer for a while, you have probably heard something about data security. If you have a computer at home, you may not have found any need for security, but the truth is, security is important for every computer user, in any environment. What you need to decide is the level of security you want to implement.

If your computer is not connected to others on a network, some minimum security is appropriate. If, however, you use the networking functions of Novell DOS 7 to connect your computer to others in your office or workgroup, or even in your house, then the need for security grows.

When most people think of security, they imagine crooks sneaking into their offices in the middle of the night, trying to sabotage their operation or steal precious secrets. If your office has a rather open atmosphere, chances are that you aren't worrying too much about maintaining a secure computer system, but remember that security is more than keeping villains from stealing secrets. A well-designed security system also keeps novice users in your office from accidentally deleting all the customer files from your database. A secure system most likely will not fall prey to the careless fingers of a coworker who thought she was erasing her documents, not yours. At home, it can keep your curious three-year-old from changing numbers in your checking account program.

The following topics are covered in this chapter:

- How to secure your computer system at bootup, using Novell DOS 7 utilities

- How to protect your files and directories from unwanted interference

- The special considerations you have to make when you are part of a computer network

Enabling Novell DOS 7 Login Security

Before you can use the security functions of Novell DOS 7, you have to enable them with the Install/Setup utility. This task is relatively easy and painless.

First change to the directory where you installed Novell DOS 7. To do this, enter **CD \NWDOS** at the DOS prompt. If you installed Novell DOS 7 in a directory other than \NWDOS, use that directory's name instead. The reason that you want to change to the directory where you have Novell DOS 7 installed is to make sure that you access the right setup utility. If your PATH statement points to a directory where a different setup utility is located (for instance, your Windows directory), you might run that setup utility accidentally, rather than Novell DOS's Setup utility.

Tip

If you enabled Task Manager, you need to disable it before you can configure security with the Setup utility.

To start Setup, enter **SETUP**. A Setup screen is displayed, containing several menu options. (If the Setup utility does not appear, be sure that drive C is active and you are in the directory that contains the Novell DOS 7 program files.) From the menu choices displayed in the top half of the screen, select the option Data Protection & Security. Then press Enter.

Now a screen titled Data Protection & Security appears. You can see some buttons and check boxes, which you learned about in Chapter 4, "Installing Novell DOS 7." Right now, your concern is the button labeled Configure SECURITY. Use the arrow keys to choose that button and press Enter. If you are using a mouse, just click the button.

The next screen, shown in figure 15.1, informs you that the security feature of Novell DOS 7 prevents unauthorized users from using your computer. The screen also tells you whether security is currently enabled or disabled. If security on your system is currently disabled, enable it now choosing the Enable SECURITY button and pressing Enter.

You are then prompted to enter a password. Selecting the right password is probably the most important step in maintaining a secure computer environment. If the only reason that you want security on your Novell DOS 7 system is to keep curious novices from accidentally doing damage, what you choose for a password is probably not crucial. If, however, you want to keep malicious users from accessing your data, be sure to choose a password that is hard to guess.

Fig. 15.1
Enabling security.

As you type the password, Novell DOS does not display the characters you are typing, but displays asterisks instead. The asterisks prevent someone who might be looking over your shoulder from reading the password you enter.

After you enter the password, the screen prompts you to enter it again to verify what you typed. This helps prevent typographical errors when users enter their passwords. Serious problems could result if you meant to type one password but accidentally keyed in another. You would be in trouble if even *you* did not know what your password was.

Note

See the next section, "Choosing a Login Password," for details on selecting and using login passwords.

After you give Novell DOS 7 your password, a message box displays information about disabling security. Choose OK to continue. Then choose Accept the Above and Continue. This takes you back to the Data Protection & Security screen. Choose Exit This Screen to go back to the Setup screen. If this is all you want to do in Setup right now, choose Save Changes and Exit.

Novell DOS 7 makes some changes to the system configuration files, prompts you to choose OK to continue, and then prompts you to reboot your

VI

System Security Utilities

computer in order for those changes to take place. Press Enter or choose Restart Operating System. Your computer reboots.

When the operating system loads, an entry box asking for your password appears. Simply type what you entered earlier and press Enter. The computer continues booting normally.

To remove security from your Novell DOS 7 system, repeat the procedure just described, but choose the Disable SECURITY button instead of the Enable SECURITY button. You are then asked to enter your password so that your computer knows you have the authority to disable security.

As you experiment with system security, you may have the unfortunate experience of locking yourself completely out of your hard drive (for example, if the file on the drive became corrupted). If you make this mistake, there is a way around it. First, you want to boot from the installation floppy disk. Before the installation program gets anywhere, quit it and exit to a DOS prompt. At the A: prompt, enter **UNSECURE**. At this point, you are asked for the master key password (see fig. 15.2). This is the password you entered when you went through the Setup program and enabled security. After you enter this password, security on your computer is disabled, and you again have access to your files.

Fig. 15.2
The Unsecure
utility.

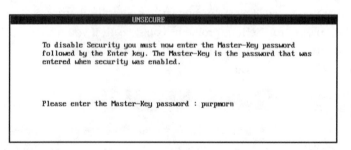

```
╔══════════════════════════════ UNSECURE ══════════════════════════════╗

     To disable Security you must now enter the Master-Key password
     followed by the Enter key. The Master-Key is the password that was
     entered when security was enabled.



     Please enter the Master-Key password : purpmorn

```

Choosing a Login Password

As mentioned, choosing the right password is probably the most important aspect of setting up a secure computer system. Picking the right password is the difference between a would-be thief's succeeding in stealing your data and getting stuck in the process. Most people do not realize what makes a good password, so if you don't know, it is time to learn.

Because people want to make sure that they choose a password they will never forget, they make choices that are obvious to computer thieves. Often users pick the names of their children or spouses. Less-thoughtful users may use their login names to avoid having to remember a password at all. Others choose common nouns like *apple* or *computer*.

Most computer hackers with malicious intent are able to figure out passwords like these. It does not take much effort to do a little research on computer users, find out their interests, learn the names of their children, and subsequently guess their passwords.

Believe it or not, there are programs out there that were designed to figure out passwords. These programs have a built-in dictionary of words, phrases, and names, and they just keep trying until they find the right match. That is why it is so important to have a good password.

Now that you know what constitutes a "bad" password, you need to know what makes a "good" one. The best passwords are words or phrases not found in any name book or even in a dictionary. The advice you receive here applies not just to individual computers but to networked computers as well.

A series of random letters or numbers makes the best password, but such a password is also hard to remember. The next best thing is to take a couple of syllables and put them together in a way that does not make sense. For example, take the letters P-U-R-P from the word *purpose*. Add to it the letters M-O-R-N from the word *morning*. When you put them together, you have *purpmorn*. It sounds silly, but it is a lot easier than trying to remember a series of random letters. If you want to improve on it, add your favorite number to it, so you might have *purpmorn81*. Of course, because this word has appeared in this book, it is no longer a good password. Get creative and have some fun. Just remember, the more random and silly the password, the better.

The best passwords have other characters in them too, of course, but be careful. Novell DOS 7 does not allow certain characters, so you have to stay within the allowable conventions. You can use the letters A to Z, the numbers 0 to 9, the comma (,), the underscore (_), and the hyphen (–).

Tip
The maximum length of a Novell DOS 7 password is 15 characters.

VI

System Security Utilities

Novell DOS 7's passwords are not case-sensitive. This means that if you type them in all uppercase or all lowercase, DOS doesn't know the difference. Some systems, such as UNIX, are case-sensitive and can cause new users some confusion.

Another word of advice about passwords is to change them often. Some system administrators require their users to change their passwords monthly or even weekly. Many people change passwords for a day or two, but soon go back to an old password because it is easier to remember. Do not fall into this habit. Keep your passwords complex and keep them fresh.

Note a final point about passwords: do not tell yours to anyone. The most common way that data thieves break into a system is not through sophisticated equipment or specialized software but through a simple phone call. If you are a user on a computer network and someone claiming to be from the company's computer maintenance department calls to report problems with your user account and to request your password, do not give it to the caller. System administrators keep a master password for the whole system that gives them access to every aspect of the system. It is very doubtful that the caller needs your password when such access is available.

These callers try to confuse people with complex terminology that probably does not mean anything—they sometimes claim to be from Novell. Do not listen to them. Just politely end the conversation, hang up, and immediately notify the system administrator that someone tried to get your password. The administrator can take some action that will foil thieves even if someone else in your organization blows it.

Using File and Directory Security

Often securing your system with a main password is not enough. With Novell DOS 7, you have the ability to secure individual files and directories. You can assign each file or directory its own password, which gives users only the access you allow.

This approach is especially helpful if you share your computer with others. Perhaps you want a directory reserved for all your personal data. Maybe you are working on a report and do not care whether others read it, but you do not want anyone else writing over or accidentally deleting it. This is where file-level security comes into play.

Protecting Files

The PASSWORD.EXE utility is found in the \NWDOS directory and is used to assign passwords to the files and directories on your hard drive. For example, to password-protect a file called FILENAME.EXT, enter the following at the DOS prompt:

```
PASSWORD FILENAME.EXT /R:purpmorn
```

This requires anyone to enter the password *purpmorn* before reading, copying, writing to, deleting, renaming, or changing the attributes of FILENAME.EXT.

You can assign one of three different levels of security to a file:

- The most secure of these is *read inhibit*. If you password-protect a file for read inhibit (as in the preceding example with the /R: switch), you must enter the password every time you want to do anything to the file. If you want to read, copy, update, rename, or delete the file, you must have the password.

- The next level of security is *write inhibit*. You assign it with the /W: switch:

  ```
  PASSWORD FILENAME.EXT /W:purpmorn
  ```

  With /W, you need the password only when you want to change the file. Anyone can read or copy the file, but if you want to write to it, rename it, delete it, or change its attributes, you must have the password.

- The third level of security is *delete inhibit*. To assign it, use the /D: switch:

  ```
  PASSWORD FILENAME.EXT /D:purpmorn
  ```

  Now anyone can read, copy, or write to the file, but if you want to delete the file, rename it, or change its attributes, you are required to enter the password.

Another switch you can use with the PASSWORD program is /G:. Use it when you want to access a group of files with the same password, or when you need to access a file from an application that does not give you a chance to enter the file's password.

This is how the /G: switch works. Assume that you have a directory where you keep your word processing files. All the files have the password *purpmorn* assigned to them, and they are set for read-inhibit password protection. You want to copy those files to a floppy disk to back them up, but copying them one by one, supplying the password each time, would be tedious. With the

/G: switch, you can disable the password protection of every file that matches the global password. To set the global password, enter the following:

```
PASSWORD /G:purpmorn
```

Now every file that is protected with the password *purpmorn* is available without your having to enter the password each time.

Protecting Directories

If you want to password-protect whole directories, you must use the /P: switch. For example, you might have on your hard disk a directory where you keep all your personal letters. Every time you create a new letter, you do not want to have to assign a password to it, so you assign one to the whole directory. Enter the following:

```
PASSWORD C:\LETTERS\PERSONAL /P:purpmorn
```

This automatically assigns read, write, and delete protection to the specified directory so that no one is able to do much with the directory unless that person has the password.

Hiding Your Password

If you are concerned about other people seeing your password when you type it, you can use an asterisk instead of a password, and Novell DOS 7 prompts you for the password. Suppose that you want to assign a password to the file FILENAME.EXT, but you do not want the person next to you to be able to read the password on your screen. Enter the following:

```
PASSWORD FILENAME.EXT /R:*
```

The computer prompts you with the message Please enter the password you wish to set:. Now, as you type the password, the display shows only asterisks. Because you cannot see what you are entering, it is easy to make a typing mistake, so the computer prompts you to enter the password one more time to verify it.

Using Your Protected File or Directory

You have learned how to assign passwords to files, but to gain access to the file, you use the semicolon. Suppose that you want to copy a password-protected file called FILENAME.EXT to the directory C:\DOCS. That file's password is *purpmorn*. To do this, enter the following:

```
COPY FILENAME.EXT;purpmorn C:\DOCS
```

Whenever you want to access a file that has been password-protected, you must type a semicolon and then the file's password. When an application asks for a file name, sometimes it will let you type *filename;password*, and sometimes it won't. It all depends on the application's file-open program. Experiment with the applications on your computer to make sure that you can use the password security of Novell DOS 7.

If you cannot use password protection with a file, you can still protect an application by using directory protection or using the /G: switch before accessing the application.

> **Note**
>
> Novell DOS 7 copies the password attribute with the file when it copies the file. That is, a copy of FILENAME.EXT has the same read protection as the original file you protected. If you are copying the file to give to someone else and you don't want that person to know your password, disable the file's password before copying it.

Removing File Passwords

Even though you have assigned a password to a file or directory, it doesn't mean that you have password protection for life. You can disable passwords with the /N switch. Suppose that you assigned the password *purpmorn* to a file called FILENAME.EXT, but only because you were sharing your computer for a short time. Now you would rather not have to type the password every time you want to access that file. To remove the password, enter

```
PASSWORD FILENAME.EXT;purpmorn /N
```

This command rids the file of security. The method works also for global passwords as well as passwords for directories. To remove the global password, enter

```
PASSWORD /NG
```

To remove a password for a subdirectory, enter

```
PASSWORD c:\LETTERS\PERSONAL /NP
```

This command causes the password security to be removed. After you enter the text as stated, Novell DOS prompts you for the password before it is removed.

Implementing Network Security

Until now, you have learned how to secure your Novell DOS 7 computer in an individual environment. Securing your computer on a network involves much more, because the main reason you have a network is probably to share files. You have to determine which files you want to share with whom and which files you want to keep private. You also have to learn how to access the services provided by other computers.

Before going further, you should understand the four types of access rights. *None* means exactly what it says—no rights to the files in the directory. *All* means just what it says—all rights to the files in the directory. A user with All access rights can create, delete, read, copy, modify, or rename files in the directory. *Read* means that users can read and copy the files, but cannot modify, rename, or delete them. *Write* lets users create, delete, and modify files in the directory, but not read files.

Creating User Accounts

One of the first things to notice as you begin computing over a network is that to access the network services—files, printers, and so on—you must identify yourself. You usually do this through a user name. When you log into the network with your user name, the network gives you access to its services.

A user name can be anything you choose, up to 15 characters long. The most common naming convention in DOS-based networks is to use the first initial of your first name and as many letters of the last name as you can (up to a total of 15 characters).

If your name is Joseph Dallin, for example, your user name would be JDALLIN. Of course, with these conventions, it is possible for you to have the same user name as someone else on the network. In that case, you need to try something else until you come up with a unique name. You could use your whole first name and then the first letter of your last name, such as JOSEPHD. What you enter is not important, as long as it is unique on the network and lets others know that it belongs to you.

To add yourself to the network, use the NET ADMIN command to run the Net utility. Select View Users and File Add to create a new user account. This account is used to keep track of your access rights to services throughout the network.

> **Note**
>
> Depending on the network to which you are attached and the local rules, you may have to contact a system administrator to add you to the network. Refer to Chapter 5, "Installing the Network," for installing the Novell DOS 7 peer-to-peer network, and to Chapter 23, "Introduction to Networking," and Chapter 24, "Network Maintenance," for more on networking.

The only account set up by Novell DOS 7 is the SUPERVISOR account. This account should be carefully password-protected because the SUPERVISOR has rights to just about anything on the network. If you are the system administrator, you may want to set up a separate account for yourself to use daily. If you log into the network as the SUPERVISOR every morning, there is a good chance that someone can come in and make changes to your system. It takes less than a minute for someone to walk up to the system with SUPERVISOR access and create a new account with all sorts of rights to the network. Reserve the SUPERVISOR account for network administration only.

Defining Rights to Network Directories

Now that you have a user account on the network, you are ready to start using the network services. As noted, the main reason that computer users set up networks is to share files. Those files may be programs or documents. If you are going to share your files with other users on the network, you want to make sure that you don't compromise the security of all the other files on your computer.

The best way to maintain security if your computer is a server on the network is through a well-planned directory structure. The way that peer-to-peer networking with Novell DOS 7 works is that if a user has rights to a directory, that user has rights to every subdirectory under that one. Say, for example, that your computer has a directory called APPS and that \WP6, \LOTUS123, and \DBASE are subdirectories of APPS. Now, if you share your APPS directory with everyone, everyone has access to all the files in the APPS directory—as well as all the files in the \WP6, \LOTUS123, and \DBASE subdirectories.

This sounds like an easy way to share lots of programs, and it is. However, this system can get you into trouble too. Suppose that you create a subdirectory under the WordPerfect subdirectory, called WP6\DOCS, and you keep all your WordPerfect documents in that directory, including personal letters. If everyone has access to your WordPerfect directory, everyone can also gain access to your \DOCS directory—and your letters. If you want to keep personal or sensitive documents away from users on the network, put them in their own separate directory.

Setting Up Workgroups and Shared Directories. Setting up file sharing through the network is a three-stage process. First you set up a workgroup. Then you specify which directories you want to share. Finally, you specify the rights for each user in the workgroup. The first two stages are described here. The third stage is covered in the next section.

To set up a workgroup and specify shared directories, follow these steps:

1. Use the NET ADMIN command to access the Net utility of Novell DOS 7.

2. Choose View Shared Directories. You see a list of all the directories shared by network users. To make a new entry, select File Add. You then see a list of workgroup servers. Your server must be on that list so that you can begin sharing your files.

3. Select your server from the list and press Enter.

4. Type a workgroup directory name. This name does not have to be an actual directory name on your computer; just use a name describing what files exist in the directory you plan to share.

   Type **WORDPERFECT**, for example, if you are sharing the WordPerfect program. Or type **OFFICE_MEMOS** if the directory you are sharing has that type of document in it. You can type anything you want, up to 15 characters, but spaces are not allowed. If you include them, the Net utility replaces them with underscores.

5. After you type a directory name, choose OK and begin providing the information for this shared directory (see fig. 15.3). The first field is for the actual directory path of the files you plan to share. Type **C:\DOCS**, for example.

   If you get stuck and cannot remember the path of your files, use the Browse Path command to select a directory from the list.

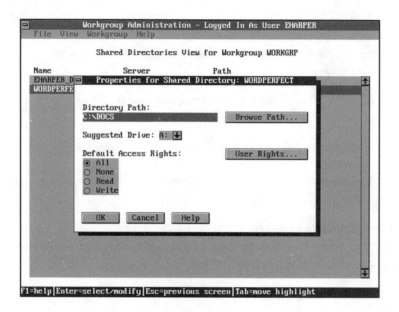

Fig. 15.3
Shared directory
information.

Defining Individual Access Rights. After you set up the workgroup and specify which directory you want to share, you define access rights. This step involves security. You may want only a few individuals to have access to this directory on your hard drive. Or you may want everyone to be able to read the files, with only a few people having the right to edit or delete them. Whatever your needs are, you use two tools to define who has access to what—Default Access Rights and Users with Explicit Rights.

To specify access rights to a shared directory, follow these steps:

1. If the number of people to whom you want to grant access is relatively small—say, 2 or 3 of the 25 people on your network—set Default Access Rights to *None* and then choose the User Rights command.

   The default rights that you decide to grant depend on the number of users you want to access your files. If you want to give many users full access, it is simpler to create the default rights of *All* and then specify those users whom you do not want to have access. Just remember that the fewer user names you have to enter with the User Rights command, the easier your job.

2. When you choose User Rights, you see a box titled Users with Explicit Rights. If this is a new directory you are creating, the box is blank.

3. Choose Add to access the Add User dialog box.

4. In the Username drop-down list, select the people to whom you want to grant access.

5. Specify which type of access (All, None, Read, or Write) to give each person.

6. Choose Close and then choose OK to leave the dialog box.

When all the names have been added to the list, you are finished with configuring your directory for sharing.

Specifying Rights to Printers

Now that you understand how to specify access rights to shared directories, specifying access rights to printers is simple. The steps are similar:

1. Use the NET ADMIN command to run the Net utility.

2. Choose View Shared Printers. If there are any workgroup printers defined on the network, you see a list of them here.

   For this example, choose File Add to create a new one. You then see a list of Personal NetWare servers.

3. Select your server and press Enter.

4. Type a name for the workgroup printer. Because you are not actually creating a network printer in this exercise, enter the name **TEMP**.

5. For the available server port, select LPT1 and press Enter. The box titled Properties for Shared Printer: TEMP appears (see fig. 15.4). The fields in this box should look familiar to you if you have created a network directory. A few differences do exist, though. It would be hard to have read-only rights to a printer, so the access rights option is either All or None.

6. If you want all users to be able to print to a printer, leave Default Access Rights set to All. Then, if you want to exclude a few users from this privilege, use the User Rights command to insert their names in the Users with Explicit Rights list.

If you want only a few people printing to the printer, select None for Default Access Rights. Then, using the User Rights command, insert in the Users with Explicit Rights list the names of those to whom you want to grant access.

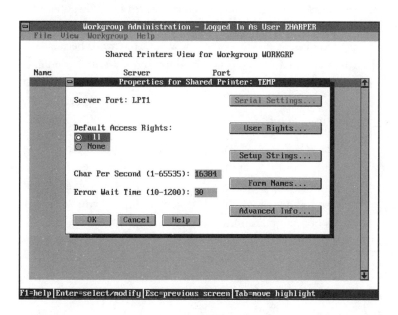

Fig. 15.4
Workgroup printer information.

Locking Your Computer Temporarily

The program LOCK.EXE is installed in your \NWDOS directory and serves two functions: screen protection and security. If you have ever used an Automated Teller Machine at the bank, you probably noticed the darkened shadow of the main screen, created by *screen burn-in*. If a monochrome computer screen displays the exact same output for a prolonged period, the electrons in the tube that cause the image begin destroying that particular area of the display.

To avoid this problem, companies started producing *screen-saver programs*. They are designed so that after a period of inactivity on the computer, they blank the screen and keep that display in memory, often while showing some animated presentation. Because the software either blanks the screen or fills it with images that are always changing, nothing stays on the screen long enough to cause burn-in. To get back to your work, you just press a key or move the mouse.

LOCK.EXE adds a further benefit—keeping thieves from accessing your data. Remember that when you enabled security and assigned the system a password, you had to enter that password when you rebooted your computer. However, if you boot your computer and leave for a 15-minute coffee break, boot security offers nothing. Unless you have security guards policing your office, someone could walk in and start copying files to floppies or deleting files. That person doesn't even have to know your password because you entered it when you first turned on your computer. If security is enabled, the master password you typed when you enabled security is used. If security is not enabled, no password is used. See the section "Using Other LOCK Options" later in this chapter.

When you access LOCK.EXE, it displays an animated line (often called the "worm") bouncing around your monitor. If you press any key, a box appears that prompts you to enter your password (see fig. 15.5). If you enter it correctly, you return to your program or the DOS prompt. If you do not, the worm just keeps bouncing around.

Fig. 15.5
Accessing the password-protected LOCK utility.

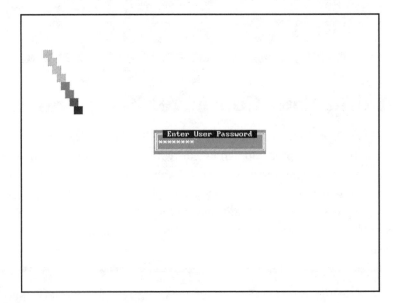

```
Enter User Password
********
```

Using Immediate Screen Lock

To try out the LOCK program, make sure that you are at a DOS prompt. The current directory or subdirectory does not matter as long as \NWDOS is in your PATH statement. From the command line, enter **LOCK**. If you enter the LOCK command without any other parameters, the screen goes immediately blank and displays the worm.

Watch the worm bounce around your screen for as long as you like, but when you get tired of it (eight or nine seconds is usually enough), go ahead and press a key or move the mouse. When you do, the worm stops wandering, and a box appears that prompts you to Enter User Password. Enter the password you defined earlier, and as you type, notice the asterisks as place-holders. The use of asterisks prevents anyone from reading your password by looking at the screen. After you have entered your password, you return to the DOS prompt.

If you enter the password incorrectly or don't enter anything for a few seconds, the box disappears, and the worm starts wandering around again.

Setting Timeout

Because you probably don't want to enter the LOCK command every time you leave your computer idle for a few minutes, LOCK has a timeout feature. You can configure it so that after a specified period of time, LOCK starts automatically. You do this with the /T: switch. Try the following at the command prompt:

```
LOCK /T:10s
```

When you enter this command, nothing seems to have happened. You return to the command prompt, but a message is displayed, telling you that LOCK has been loaded and enabled. If you wait 10 seconds without touching the keyboard or the mouse, the screen goes blank, and the worm wanders again.

The 10 seconds you entered was only an example; you probably do not want to make it that short. Valid times range from 10 seconds (10s) to 60 seconds (60s) and from one minute (1) to one hour (60).

Note

Notice that for the amount to represent seconds, you must enter the s. For the amount to represent minutes, the number alone is sufficient.

VI

System Security Utilities

A good value to enter for the timeout is usually 5 or 10 minutes. With a shorter amount, you have to enter your password every time you turn around. With a longer time, you create too large a window of opportunity for someone to come by while you are away from your desk. You may have to experiment with some numbers to determine which one is right for you, but it is better to be too careful rather than too lenient.

Using Other LOCK Options

In addition to setting the timeout, you can use some parameters to configure LOCK so that it works the way you want. If, for some reason, you want to keep a system password that is different from a screen lock password, you can do so with the LOCK program. Just enter the following:

```
LOCK password
```

Use any word you like in place of the word *password* in this example.

Although keeping two passwords is not recommended, you might find it necessary at times to share your computer with a coworker you trust. Because you don't want that person to have your system password, you can enable LOCK with a different password that you can share for the day.

If you want to disable the password protection of the LOCK utility but continue using the screen-saving function, you can do so with the /N switch. Enter **LOCK** **/N** at the command prompt. The screen blanks, and the worm starts moving. Now press any key to return immediately to the DOS prompt. Use the /N switch if you want to save your screen but are not that concerned about securing your data.

Caution

As you experiment with the switches for the LOCK utility, be sure that you type the slash (/) before a switch. If you forget the slash, LOCK thinks that you are entering an alternative password. For example, if you entered **LOCK** **T:5** instead of **LOCK** **/T:5**, the screen locks up immediately, and your system password ceases to work when you are prompted for a password. To stop the LOCK utility, you then have to enter **T:5** as the password. If you ever enter a password you cannot remember or you mistype your password, you need to reboot your computer to regain access.

If you load the screen-locking utility and later decide that you want to disable it, you can do so by entering **LOCK** **/U** at the DOS prompt. This disables the LOCK TSR (terminate-and-stay-resident) program and removes it from memory.

Installing LOCK from Setup

The best way to use LOCK, from a security standpoint, is to include it in your AUTOEXEC.BAT batch file. This way, you are ensured that your computer's screen and files are protected whenever you boot. You can enter LOCK manually or have the Novell DOS 7 Setup utility do it for you.

To use the Setup utility, enter **SETUP** at the DOS prompt. When the Setup menu appears, select Data Protection & Security and press Enter. Then select the option DOS Screen Saver/System Lock. (The box is selected if it has a check mark in it.) Next select Configure DOS Screen Saver and press Enter to access the options for the screen saver (see fig. 15.6). In the field labeled Time Before Screen Saver Activates, enter the number of minutes you want to wait before the LOCK utility activates. The default value is 1, but you can set it to whatever you want. The command to access the LOCK utility is placed in your AUTOEXEC.BAT batch file so that it loads every time your system boots.

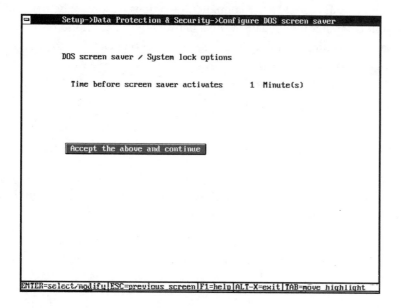

Fig. 15.6
Setting up the LOCK utility.

When you finish entering your specifications, save your Setup changes and either exit to DOS or reboot the computer. The new configuration does not take effect until you reboot your computer.

Using LOCK with Windows

If you set up the LOCK utility to work with Novell DOS 7, LOCK may not necessarily work when you are in Windows. LOCK is pretty much ignored when you are in Windows unless you double-click the LOCK icon in the

VI

System Security Utilities

Novell DOS 7 group. If you load this program in Windows, the screen saver immediately comes on. If system security is enabled, you are required to enter the system password before you can again get control of your computer.

You cannot specify a time period before the Windows LOCK program is enabled, as you can with the DOS version. Nor can you define a different password. If you want to use these features, use the Windows screen saver. You can find it in the Desktop utility of the Control Panel. The only weakness of the Windows screen saver is that it cannot be invoked immediately, as LOCK can. Therefore, if you want to secure your computer instantly while in Windows, use the Novell DOS 7 Windows LOCK utility.

From Here...

Security involves many things, and you may want to implement security features on your Novell DOS 7 computer for various reasons. Whether you use your computer individually or on a network, you can find some use for the security features of this operating system. A good practice is to grant access rights to your computer's services to only those people who need it. Do not forget the most important part of secure computing—choosing a suitable password. If your data is important to you, do not give your password to anyone.

For more information about securing your Novell DOS 7 system, read the following chapters:

- Chapter 10, "Undeleting Files," helps you protect your files when they are accidently deleted.

- Chapter 12, "Backup Utilities," leads you through the process of safeguarding important files with Fastback Express.

- Chapter 16, "Virus Protection," shows you how to protect your system from viruses.

- Chapter 23, "Introduction to Networking," shows you how to plan and configure a network.

- Chapter 24, "Network Maintenance," shows you how to tune the network for best performance and how to use the Novell DOS 7 network utilities.

Chapter 16

Virus Protection

Something computer users keep hearing more and more about is computer viruses. Viruses have the capability to replicate themselves and propagate across a whole computer system. More important, they have the ability to destroy data on your computer system.

One of the biggest problems with computer viruses is that they can stay dormant, hiding in your system for days, weeks, or even years. By the time you notice something wrong, the damage has been done. So it is important to catch viruses as soon as possible.

The best way to combat viruses is to take an aggressive approach and form a protection plan. This usually begins with a good antivirus program, otherwise known as a scanner. A *scanner* compares a list of known virus strings (codes) against the code in a program. If there is a match, the scanner assumes there is a virus and can remove the string. The main problem with scanners is that they are only as good as the virus-string list, which, by definition, is always outdated. A virus has to exist before an antivirus product vendor can dissect the new virus strain and update the virus-string list.

Novell DOS 7 includes two methods to catch viruses. SDRes is a TSR (terminate-and-stay resident) program that checks the programs you execute to look for viruses. SDScan is a utility that you can use to scan files on the hard drives and floppy disks you use in your office. Scanning regularly is important in catching viruses before they have a chance to do much damage.

Although developing virus protection systems and scanning your disks may seem like a hassle, after you have been hit with a virus that destroys or damages a week's worth of work, requires three days to rebuild your system, and costs your company thousands of dollars, you will be a believer for life. Unfortunately, this is a nasty way to learn. Save yourself the grief, and put up with a little inconvenience to avoid these disasters.

This chapter covers the following topics:

- What a virus is and how you catch one

- How to use the Novell DOS antivirus programs

- What you can do if you encounter a virus

What Is a Virus?

A *virus* is a software program that attaches itself to a file on your system; when the file is accessed, the virus is activated. Sometimes viruses act randomly, sometimes continuously, and sometimes they wait for a specific trigger, like a certain date. Files that have been infected with a virus spread the virus to other programs.

Some viruses do not damage files but are just pranks. A virus might pop up a message on your screen at some random point, or it could cause individual characters to start disappearing off the screen. Many viruses are not that harmless; they can destroy your programs and your data.

No one really knows who writes all the viruses. Everyone thinks that it's an underworld group of pale prepubescents with a taste for Twinkies and Jolt Cola. But sometimes it may be a programmer at a respectable company who finds out that he's about to be laid off and wants to get revenge. You never know.

A virus is software. It needs a carrier to get into your system, so it attaches itself to files, boot sectors, or a hard disk partition table. Without a carrier, a virus cannot cause any damage. And it must duplicate itself to cause widespread damage.

Often the code remains dormant until it is set off or triggered. Sometimes the trigger is a date or a counter—that is, when the virus has duplicated itself *x* number of times, it will activate itself. Once it is triggered, it has a better chance of spreading.

Boot sector viruses infect your system only if you boot from an infected floppy disk. They cannot spread across networks but can damage the data on your server if your server boots from an infected disk.

Michelangelo is a boot sector virus. One of the reasons it receives so much publicity is that it has a date trigger—there is a time frame for the media to work in. To get a boot sector virus, you have to boot from an infected floppy. When Michelangelo's birthday (March 6) comes around (the trigger date), the virus will, without warning, begin to format your hard drive.

Types of Viruses

There are different types of computer viruses. Some do more damage than others. Although some viruses can destroy your data, they cannot attach to data. Instead, a virus attaches to an executable program. The virus-infected program accesses and activates the virus, but once the virus loads into memory, it can begin attaching to other executable files. Some viruses, once activated, attack the boot sector of a drive. This prevents the computer from being able to boot again.

Some viruses act in ways that make them hard to detect. *Polymorphic viruses* completely modify their appearance every time they infect a new host program, making them difficult for scanners to identify. *Stealth viruses* use other means to hide their presence.

Polymorphic viruses have an encrypted, self-garbling, "stealth" mechanism that randomly generates different decryptor loaders. The loaders contain a set of instructions in random order. The only way to detect a polymorphic virus is by scanning files one byte at a time.

Stealth viruses are tricky because they know when they are being accessed. Number of the Beast is one of these. It is exactly 512 bytes long, and it conceals itself in memory. When it infects a file, it takes the first 512 bytes of the file and places them at the end. The virus then takes the place of the first 512 bytes at the beginning of the file. When an attempt is made to access the first 512 bytes of an infected file while the virus is in memory, it retrieves the original 512 bytes that it moved to the end of the file and presents those instead.

Catching Viruses

How you share files at work is a good way to see how viruses spread. Like many of your coworkers, you probably take disks home at the end of the day to catch up on some work at your home computer. You put in a floppy disk, copy some files back and forth from the hard drive, and bring that same floppy disk back into work the next day.

Tip
Although, theoretically, a data file virus is possible, none currently exist. Current viruses can ruin data files, but they must be activated by an executable program.

VI

System Security Utilities

What you don't realize is that little Johnny Jr., who uses a computer at school pretty regularly, brings a disk home that a friend gave him. It has the newest, neatest game on it, and he can't wait to try it. So he runs his game, which happens to have a virus on it, and infects your hard drive.

After an hour or two on the game, he decides he better get some of his homework done, so he loads your word processor. Now that is infected. Then he needs to know how much the average yearly rainfall of South Dakota is, so he loads a geography program you have on your system. Now your geography program is infected.

Before too long, Johnny Jr. has roamed around—and consequently infected— your entire system. When you bring spreadsheets home to work on, the virus ends up on your floppy disk, which you take back to work with you in the morning.

As you can see, it is not too difficult to imagine how viruses spread around so quickly. When you take a disk back to work and load a program from it, you have infected your system.

In a peer-to-peer network, any desktop computer that is also a server is, by definition, part of the network. If a file is infected on a PC server and someone accesses that file, the infected file (and hence the virus) now resides in that client's memory and can infect files on that machine.

Sharing Floppy Disks. Be careful when sharing floppy disks with coworkers, your kids, or anyone else. If a floppy disk has a virus on it and you use that disk to boot the computers in your office, all those machines are probably infected. If you take a program off your desktop computer to load on your laptop, your laptop gets infected. Be careful when you share your floppy disks; scan them whenever anyone borrows them and brings them back, and scan every floppy disk you borrow from someone else.

Running Networked Applications. The whole reason that you have a network is to share files, and viruses capitalize on this. When you share programs from the network, each individual computer has a chance of becoming infected. The person who infected the file doesn't have to have the same rights as the person who later accesses that file. But the user (and hence the virus) usually needs write access to a file in order to infect it. If other users later come along with only read access to the file, they can still get the virus in memory and begin infecting other files on their own hard drives. You have to be sure to catch viruses early before they have a chance to spread.

Using Novell DOS Antivirus Programs

Viruses are very difficult to get rid of. Scanning your hard drive every now and then and hoping to catch a virus before it is too late is not enough. You have to be more aggressive, more proactive when it comes to fighting viruses. If you find a virus, kill it and go through all your floppy disks to see whether it made its way to any of those. Then you need to check the network drives to see whether any of the network files was infected. This usually has to be done by a supervisor who is probably the only one with enough access rights to see all the possibly infected files. Then you have to make sure that everyone else in your office checks all hard disks and floppy disks.

Novell, recognizing the increased need for antivirus software, included a virus protector with the DOS 7 operating system. This utility, called Search & Destroy (SDScan), was written by a company with a lot of experience with antivirus utilities—Fifth Generation Systems. The program runs in two different modes—as a loadable scanner and as a terminate-and-stay-resident (TSR) program.

Which one you use depends on how you are planning to nab the viruses that enter your system. When loading, SDRes monitors the amount of installed memory at bootup. A difference indicates that a virus occupies memory space. After you load SDRes, it runs as a TSR in memory watching for viruses. This solves many of your virus problems, but not all. To really be effective, you need the SDScan scanner.

Because SDRes is a small TSR, it's probably not as reliable as the SDScan scanner. The TSR just looks for "virus type" activity, such as writing to the boot sector, writing to an executable program in memory, and so on. The benefit of a TSR like SDRes is that it is always there watching, even though many smart viruses may slip by. SDScan has to be executed by a user to be worthwhile, but as long as the virus signature is in the list, there is a good chance that it will find it.

With SDScan, you actively scan all the files on your disk that may have a virus, whether or not that virus has manifested itself. You learn how to use both tools in this chapter.

Using the Search & Destroy TSR (SDRes)

You can launch SDRes from either your CONFIG.SYS file or your AUTOEXEC.BAT file. This ensures that it is running every time your computer boots. If you would rather not put this program in either of these files, or if you want to add it to another batch file, you can access it from the command line.

> **Note**
>
> To display the help text for SDRes, enter **SDRES** **/?** at the command line. For more information on SDRes, consult DOSBook. See Chapter 3, "Getting Help with DOSBook," for details.

To start SDRes from the command line (or in a batch file), enter

```
SDRES memory
```

You have to know how much memory you have in your system, and then enter that amount (in kilobytes) as part of the command. Whatever your computer counts to when it first boots is the number you enter.

You can also set up SDRes by using the Novell DOS Setup utility. Access Setup from the command line. Select the menu option Data Protection & Security and press Enter. Select Search & Destroy Anti-Virus. If there is a check mark in the box, the SDRes program is already loaded from the AUTOEXEC.BAT file. If the box does not have a check mark, use the space bar to check the box. Exit this screen, then choose Save Changes and Exit at the next screen, and press Enter. A message box appears indicating that Setup is complete and you should press Enter to continue.

You should now be at a screen containing buttons labeled Restart Operating System, Exit to DOS, View CONFIG.SYS (file, View AUTOEXEC.BAT file, and Discard Changes to files (see fig. 16.1). Note that Restart Operating System is available only if changes are made to the configuration files.

To see what changes were made, choose the View AUTOEXEC.BAT file button and press Enter. In the batch file that appears (see fig. 16.2), you should see a line similar to the following:

```
C:\NWDOS\SDRes -m -uC:\NWDOS\SDSCAN.EXE 640
```

The switches are discussed shortly, but basically what the preceding line does is to load the SDRes program from the directory \NWDOS. The command tells the computer that the SDScan utility used to scan memory is also in the

\NWDOS directory. Finally, the command says that the machine has 640K of conventional memory and that the scanner is to scan that memory for the presence of viruses.

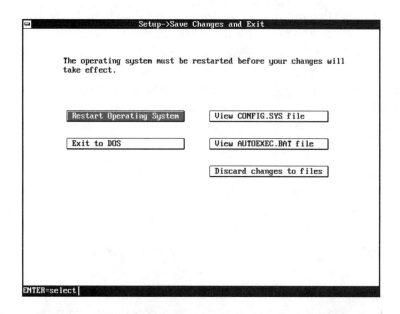

Fig. 16.1
The Setup screen for verifying changes made to the AUTOEXEC.BAT and CONFIG.SYS files.

Fig. 16.2
The SDRes command is added to AUTOEXEC.BAT by the Setup program. If you prefer, you can edit the AUTOEXEC.BAT file to include the SDRes command.

The –u switch informs the SDRes program of the path where the scanner is located. In the preceding example, the SDSCAN.EXE file was in the \NWDOS directory.

The –m switch tells the SDRes program to disable the automatic hooking of interrupt 21. Now this may seem pretty cryptic, but it is not hard to understand. An *interrupt* is simply a signal generated by a program to get the attention of the processor. For example, every time you press the keyboard or move your mouse, you generate an interrupt which tells the processor that something is going on and to pay attention. In other words, you did something that *interrupted* the processor from whatever it was doing (even if it was sitting idle) to tell it to pay attention.

Interrupts work the same way with a piece of software. If your program is supposed to accomplish some task for you, it uses interrupts to notify the processor. Interrupts have different numbers, and many TSRs use interrupt number 21 because, as far as interrupts go, it commands a rather low priority in the processor. Interrupt 21 works perfectly for TSRs that function in the background.

The problems begin if you have other TSRs that want to use interrupt 21 (usually abbreviated as int21), such as network drivers. Sometimes these TSRs disable the int21 hook of SDRes so that they can be first in line to get the attention of the processor. That is fine with SDRes; it can use int21 without being first on the list. Without the –m switch, SDRes tries to be first in line to be processed when the CPU gets to int21; therefore, it might interfere with other programs that use int21 and do like to be first in line.

Other switches that SDRes uses are –n and –e. The –n switch tells SDRes to scan the computer's memory but do not load SDRes permanently. If you use this switch, SDRes is not a TSR program. Use this option if you want memory checked but don't want a TSR taking up memory space.

SDRes uses the expanded memory of your system if it is available. If you would rather that SDRes did not take up expanded memory space, use the –e switch.

Using the Search & Destroy Scanner (SDScan)

One of the most common ways that computer users find viruses on a system is with an antivirus scanner. A scanner searches the files on a floppy disk, hard disk, or network disk to see whether any of the files are infected with a known virus. Using a virus's signature to see what files are infected, the scanner looks at a file and checks whether that file contains a pattern of software code that matches the signature of a virus. If it does, the scanner alerts you that it found a virus and, if possible, tries to eradicate the virus while leaving the host file in tact.

When the scanner runs, the first thing it does is check itself to make sure that it hasn't been infected by a virus. If the scanner is infected, it is not very reliable when scanning or cleaning other infected files on your hard drive.

Running the DOS Scanner. To begin the Search & Destroy scanning program, go to the DOS prompt and enter **SDSCAN**. The opening screen is divided into three sections—Operation, Drive Groups, and a window showing the physical and network drives available (see fig. 16.3).

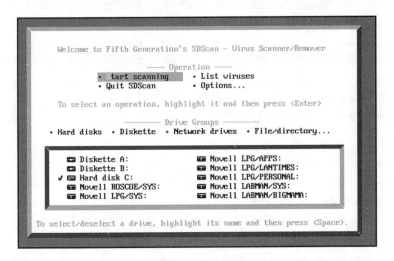

Fig. 16.3
SDScan's main screen.

You use the Operation section to perform actions in the program. Your cursor appears here when you first run the SDScan program.

Displaying Virus Listings. If you want to see what kind of viruses are out there, select List Viruses. SDScan shows you the names of almost 1,800 viruses or strains of viruses it checks for when scanning your system. Some of these are shown in figure 16.4. On the right side of the screen are the types of files each of these viruses infect. Notice that most of them attach to COM and EXE files or attack the boot sector. To return to the main screen, press Esc.

Tip
The scanner finds only those viruses for which it has signatures.

VI

System Security Utilities

Fig. 16.4

A list of some of the viruses that can infect your system.

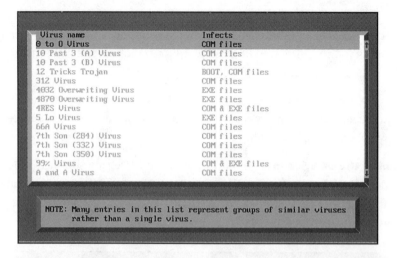

```
 Virus name                        Infects
 0 to 0 Virus                      COM files
 10 Past 3 (A) Virus               COM files
 10 Past 3 (B) Virus               COM files
 12 Tricks Trojan                  BOOT, COM files
 312 Virus                         COM files
 4032 Overwriting Virus            EXE files
 4870 Overwriting Virus            EXE files
 4RES Virus                        COM & EXE files
 5 Lo Virus                        EXE files
 66A Virus                         COM files
 7th Son (284) Virus               COM files
 7th Son (332) Virus               COM files
 7th Son (350) Virus               COM files
 99% Virus                         COM & EXE files
 A and A Virus                     COM files

 NOTE: Many entries in this list represent groups of similar viruses
       rather than a single virus.
```

> **Note**
>
> The *boot sector* on your computer is an area on the disk—usually on the first few sectors—reserved for the operating system. This is where the computer looks for the operating system files when it first boots up.

Specifying Configuration Options. If you select Options, SDScan displays a configuration screen (see fig. 16.5). The first field asks whether you want SDScan to look for boot sector viruses. Because many viruses attack the boot sector, you should leave this set to Yes. This setting also ensures that SDScan looks for viruses in your disk's partition table.

> **Note**
>
> A disk's *partition table* contains information about how your disk is divided into logical drives. If, for example, you had a large hard disk that you divided into two or more logical drives (so that you had both C: and D:), the partition table keeps track of this information for the operating system.

You use the next option, Check, to tell SDScan which types of files you want scanned. You have two options: Program Files and All Files. An asterisk appears next to the option that is currently selected. Use the arrow keys to toggle between the two options; then press the space bar to select one.

Fig. 16.5
SDScan's configu-
ration options.

The default for SDScan is to check only program files—files with an EXE, COM, OVL, OVR, or BIN extension. Scanning all files on your computer takes about five times longer than checking just the program files, and because almost all viruses attach themselves to program files, you are pretty safe leaving this set to Program Files.

Tip
To be extra safe, scan all the files once a month or so.

The next option, Scan, asks whether you want SDScan to check archived and compressed files. These files are really a whole bunch of files compressed into one file so that they take up less room on your hard drive. Most files that you download from a bulletin board system (BBS) with your modem are in compressed format. Because BBSs can be a breeding ground for virus-infected programs, you definitely want to scan these file types; leave both of these fields set to their default values of Yes.

If you think BBSs are clean, think again. Most BBSs check their files regularly and don't have the problem, but not all are like that. Anyone with a modem and an XT can start a BBS, and many don't check uploaded files at all. In fact, some BBSs post the source code for viruses.

If you want to keep track of the results of your scan, SDScan generates a report for you. You can have it either create a text file on your disk or write a report to the printer. If you want SDScan to create a text file with the results of the scan, enter the file name in the Generate Report To box. Be

VI

System Security Utilities

sure to type the drive letter, path, and file name—for example, enter `C:\MYFILES\VIRUS.REP`. If you do not want to create a file but want the results of the scan printed out, enter **PRN** instead of a file name.

Tip
A daily scan makes the report file huge quickly, but the default option is to overwrite the file each time it scans.

The next option, Append to Existing Report, asks whether you want to append this scan report to one that already exists. If you want to create a file that lists the results of the scan—and every scan you do—change this field to Yes. This is a good way to keep a log of the virus scans you perform. The text file that SDScan generates enters the date and time it performs the scan, so if you ever do find a virus, you know exactly the last time your computer was "clean." This can help in finding where the virus came from. If you can pinpoint the time or day the system was last clean, you can begin to investigate what happened since then that may have caused the virus to infect your system.

You may think that by knowing the dates when the system was last clean, you can compare your file dates and times to the clean time and scan those files that have later dates, but a virus can infect a file without changing the date.

If you leave this option at its default of No, SDScan overwrites the text file each time it performs a scan. So you still know when the last scan was, but you have to rely on your memory to know how often you scanned before that date unless you change the name of the report each time.

Tip
If SDScan fixes the virus automatically, it tells you which viruses were found and in which files they were found. You won't get a list of fixed files unless you specify that you want a report.

The next section of the options screen, When a File Is Found to Be Infected, tells SDScan what action to take if it does find an infected file. You have three alternatives: Prompt User, Report Only, and Remove Virus. The default is Prompt User. This means that if SDScan finds a virus, it displays an alert on the screen and asks whether you want to clean the file (see fig 16.6). Unless you have some reason for not doing so, have SDScan clean the file for you. Using this option is a good way of finding out which files on your system are infected.

> **Note**
>
> Knowing which files are infected might help you figure out how the virus got into your system. If, for example, SDScan found a virus on your word processing program and your secretary is the only person that uses that program, chances are pretty good that the virus originated from the machine the secretary uses.

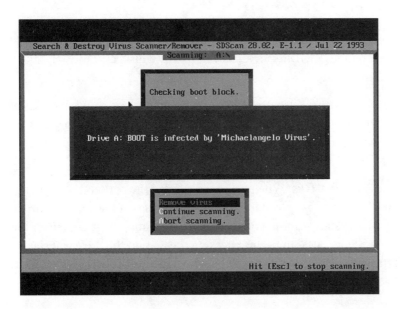

Fig. 16.6
SDScan reporting
a found virus.

If you select the Report Only option, SDScan tells you that it found a virus but takes no further action. If you select the Remove Virus option, SDScan automatically cleans any infected files that it finds during the scan. This option is handy for unattended virus scans. For example, if you were to begin a virus scan before you left the office each night but did not want to hang around until it was finished, Search & Destroy attempts to clean the file.

When you have finished setting all the options you want, press Ctrl-Enter to save the configuration and return to the main screen.

Selecting Drives to Scan. The Drive Groups section of the SDScan main screen specifies what areas you want to scan—hard disks, floppy disks, network disks, or specific files or directories. To make choosing drives easier, you can pick drives two ways: by selecting a drive group or by selecting each drive individually. If you select Hard Disks, for example, a check mark appears in the window next to each icon representing a hard drive. The cursor then jumps to the Start Scanning option near the top of the screen.

If you select the Diskette option, a check mark is placed beside the icons that represent floppy disk drives. If you select Network Drives, all the drives that are mapped to network directories are marked. Remember that if you have a drive letter mapped to a directory on someone else's computer, you must have rights to read and change files on that directory if you plan on scanning and cleaning any of the files that reside there. Note that being mapped to a

Tip
If you have only read access to someone else's computer, not read-write access, you can scan but not fix.

directory on another person's computer does not mean that you can scan the whole hard drive—only the directory and subdirectories you are mapped to. The last option, File/Directory, lets you specify a disk, directory, and file that you want to scan.

If you would rather select the drives to scan one by one, you can do so. Just select the drive you want to scan, and press the space bar to show a check mark next to the drive icon.

Scanning the Disks. When you have selected the options and drives to be scanned, you are ready to start scanning for viruses. If the cursor is not already on the Start Scanning option under Operation, move the cursor there and press Enter. SDScan begins checking the files on the drive you specified. On the left side of the screen, you see the directory tree of the drive. On the right side, you see the files that are being scanned (see fig. 16.7).

Fig. 16.7
A virus scan in progress.

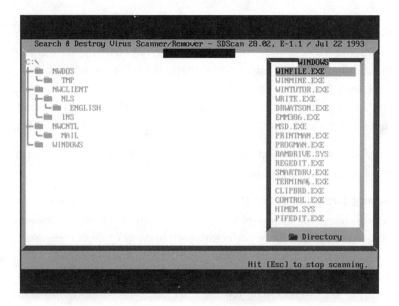

When SDScan has finished scanning all the files on your drive, a message box appears indicating the results of the scan. Press Enter to return to the main screen. When you are through working with SDScan, select the Quit SDScan option and press Enter to return to a DOS prompt.

Running the Windows Scanner. If you elected to install the Windows utilities when you first installed Novell DOS 7, you also have a Windows version of SDScan. This utility, called WSDSCAN.EXE, is in your \NWDOS directory and was probably installed to the Novell DOS 7 Windows group. It looks a little different from the DOS version but serves the same function and has the same configuration options (see fig. 16.8). The main screen lists the drives you can scan; to select one or more, simply click the icon.

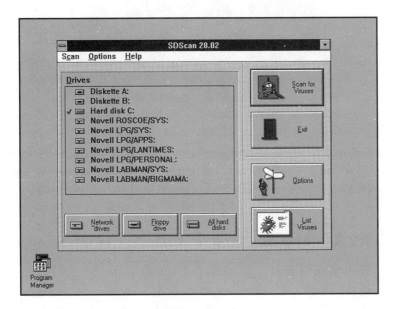

Fig. 16.8
SDScan for
Windows 3.1.

The drive groups are represented by buttons at the bottom of the window. Simply choose the appropriate button to select the drive group.

You have the same configuration options that you had with the DOS version, but with one addition. First choose the Options button to view the SDScan Options dialog box (see fig. 16.9). The new option is shown at the bottom of the window; here you can select the icon that appears as the program checks your drives for viruses. This icon appears only if SDScan is minimized to an icon while it is scanning. You have your choice between a directory tree or an animated icon of a dog sniffing around. Select Sniffy at least once just to see what he does—it is pretty entertaining. If you want the window to minimize as soon as you start scanning, select Scan Iconized. After specifying the options you want, choose OK to return to the SDScan main screen.

Fig. 16.9
SDScan options
in Windows.

When you have finished specifying the drives and options you want, choose the Scan for Viruses button to begin scanning. The computer presents a list of files; each file is highlighted as it is scanned. To exit the utility, choose Exit.

What to Do If You Find a Virus

During the scanning process, suppose that you find a virus but SDScan cleaned it out for you. Now you can relax, right? Wrong. You need a plan to make sure that the virus does not come back. If you never find out where the virus came from, it will probably return. You need to implement strong security measures and go through a thorough cleaning of all computers and floppy disks. If you find an infected machine and fail to conduct an orderly cleanup, including implementing a stronger antivirus plan, experts say that your chances of reinfection within 30 days are 90 percent.

Organize a Cleanup

If you find a virus on your system and are able to clean it up, great. However, that is only the beginning. You need to try to find out where the virus came from. Knowing who in the office regularly brings floppy disks from home and who frequently downloads programs from BBSs is a good place to start. If you found the virus on a program file that only certain people in the office use, that might help. If you have performed regular virus scans and have a log of when the system was clean, you should have a good time frame to work in.

You want to know when the virus entered the system. Knowing when it happened can help you associate events that may have started the virus infection.

If you identify who the virus culprits are, don't hold a grudge or get angry. Such reactions may prevent users from speaking out in the future if they find infected files, and unless they wrote the virus themselves, the infection is probably not their fault. They are victims just as much as you are. The truth is, you need everyone's full cooperation if you are going to scan all computers and floppy disks. You need to ask users to look everywhere—in drawers, under books, in boxes—to find every floppy disk that exists in the office. Then you need to scan each one.

After you have scanned every file and every disk in your office, you need to review prevention procedures again—with everyone. No one wants to go through the hassle of scanning files and floppy disks again and again, but remember the 90 percent reinfection rate mentioned earlier. The first few weeks after you find a virus are your most vulnerable time. So be meticulous, be thorough, be a stickler, and be annoying. You have to be whatever it takes to make sure that you don't get attacked again.

Develop a Protection Plan

The best time to implement a virus protection plan is before you ever get hit. The first thing you want to be sure to do regularly is back up your system. If a virus damages your data, the only way you have of restoring data is from a backup. (Novell DOS 7 includes a backup utility called Fastback Express; see Chapter 12, "Backup Utilities," for details.)

Next, you should review your system's security. Remember that security on a computer system does not exist just to keep out thieves and vandals. Security exists to keep unwitting users from doing completely unintentional damage, so give users rights to only the files and programs they need.

Scan your computer's hard drive regularly—daily is best—and be sure that everyone else on your network does also. Check all incoming floppy disks for viruses. If possible, set up an isolated computer in the corner of your office that users can use anytime to check their disks. On boot disks, use write-protect tabs. Viruses cannot infect a floppy disk that is write-protected. Write-protect all program and boot disks and use separate floppy disks for data files.

VI

System Security Utilities

Use Multiple Scanning Programs

Although the antivirus utilities provided with Novell DOS 7 do a good job at catching the viruses your computer may come in contact with, they may not be enough. New viruses are written every day, and new strains of existing viruses surface with new patterns the scanners do not know to look for. Some viruses are written specifically to avoid certain scanning software.

The best solution for a company that is having frequent virus problems is to use another antivirus package along with Search & Destroy from Novell DOS 7. Experience has shown that if one scanner is good, two are better—and more are even better, if it is feasible.

From Here...

If you think of viruses as just another aspect—albeit an unpleasant one—of computing, you can minimize the damage they cause. If fighting viruses prompts you to conduct regular backups and implement security on your system, maybe you can save yourself some grief when other disasters hit your system, like your hard drive failing.

For more information about virus protection, consult the following chapters:

- Chapter 15, "System Security," discusses the commands that enable you to keep others off your system entirely, or out of specific directories and files on your disks.

- Appendix B, "Installing and Using Windows 3.1," helps you get Novell DOS 7 ready to run the Windows 3.1 operating environment.

Part VII

Advanced Techniques

Continue

Change destination drive(s) and directorie

Root directory

Subdirectory   Subdirectory

Subdirectory   Subdirectory   Subdirectory   Subdirectory

Subdirectory   Subdirectory

Subdirectory

Continue

File - c:\spam.txt
Create new file ?

‹ 0% ›   Cancel

nfigure Task Manager

it this screen

ystem & Memory Managemer
Disk Compression
Disk Performance
Data Protection & Security
Task Management
Networking

racks

Sectors

25-Pin DB-25 Male

25-pin serial connector,
usually COM2

Change destination drive(s) and directori

Chapter 17

Using the Novell DOS Text Editor

One of the unavoidable facts about computing is the need to configure. You have system files, batch files, network configuration files—among others—to worry about. These files need to be modified at times. Fortunately, with the Setup utility, Novell DOS 7 takes away most of the need to edit system files. From Setup, you can configure memory requirements, establish network parameters, load antivirus software, and set up security, to list only a few features. Most of these actions require changes to the CONFIG.SYS, AUTOEXEC.BAT, NET.CFG, or STARTNET.BAT file. When you use the setup utility, necessary changes are written to the appropriate file for you, so you do not have to enter them manually.

At times, however, you may need to edit system files yourself. As you configure your system and try to optimize certain parameters, you might find that it is easier—and faster, if you know what you are doing—to modify these files manually rather than use the Setup utility.

Besides editing system files, you may need to edit other text files. If you use Microsoft Windows on your computer, you may find yourself working with INI files to optimize your system for the applications you use frequently. Some applications, like the Search & Destroy antivirus software, write reports in text format. You can bring these files into a text editor to change their formatting or search for certain text strings.

> **Note**
>
> Text files are files that contain only text characters. Most letters and reports created with your word processor are not straight text files because they include formatting codes that control such elements as margins, fonts, and justification. Text files contain no such formatting specifications.

Fortunately, when you find yourself needing to edit text files, Novell DOS 7 has made the job fairly easy with the program EDIT. Many computer users remember the days of EDLIN, when the task was not so easy. EDLIN was a text file editor, but unlike the word-processor-style editors that are available today, EDLIN used a series of cryptic commands to complete the simplest tasks. Even the act of viewing the whole file on-screen at once took work. To edit individual lines, you had to learn their line numbers; moving lines or words around the file often involved deleting and then retyping them. Such editing was not for the fainthearted.

Modern vendors have realized that editing text files is something with which everyone becomes involved at one time or another, and that providing an easy-to-use editor helps users immensely. In this spirit, Novell has included EDIT. This editor, though small and simple, resembles early word processors and makes it easy to modify text files. In this chapter, you learn how to use EDIT. You learn tricks that make it a snap to work with system text files. You soon should feel very comfortable in creating new files or browsing through existing files.

This chapter covers the following topics:

- Starting the Novell DOS editor

- Loading files into the editor

- Navigating the editor's screen

- Entering and deleting text

■ Manipulating blocks of text

■ Searching for text

■ Saving your text files

Starting the Editor

EDIT is a program just like your separately purchased word processor or spreadsheet package. The only differences are that EDIT is included with your operating system and that it doesn't have the bells and whistles of programs that cost $200 to $500. Unlike a word processor, for instance, EDIT provides neither word wrap nor formatting features such as underline, bold, and font changes. For working with straight text files, however, EDIT is adequate.

As with other programs, you can run EDIT from the command prompt. The program, EDIT.EXE, is installed in the directory that contains DOS programs—usually \NWDOS. This directory should be in the PATH statement in your AUTOEXEC.BAT file so that you can start EDIT no matter which drive and directory are current.

The basic command to start the editor is EDIT. By including a file name when issuing the EDIT command, you can open an existing file or create a new one. The next sections describe these options.

Creating a New File

Although you are most likely to edit existing text files, you can also create files with EDIT, just as you use your word processor sometimes to create documents. To use EDIT to create a new text file, enter **EDIT** without a file name to start the program. When prompted for the name of a file to open, type any unused file name in the File field and then press Enter (see fig. 17.1). The program asks whether you want to create this new file (see fig. 17.2). Because you do, choose OK. You now have a blank workspace where you can create your text file.

Fig. 17.1

The screen that appears when you start EDIT without specifying an existing file to open.

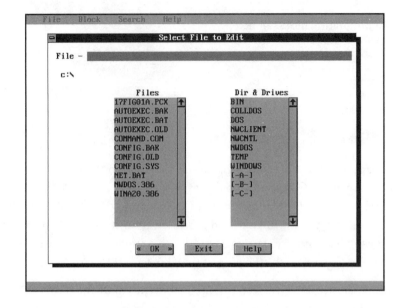

Fig. 17.2

The prompt for creating a new file.

Alternatively, you can type the file name as if you were editing an existing file. For example, if you want to create a new text file called SPAM.TXT, enter **EDIT SPAM.TXT** at the DOS prompt. Novell DOS 7 recognizes that this file does not yet exist and asks whether you want to create the new file. Choose OK, and a blank screen appears, ready for you to create the SPAM.TXT file.

If you are unsure what file you are currently editing, or you cannot remember the name you entered when creating the file, you can check the file name displayed at the bottom-left corner of the screen (see fig. 17.3).

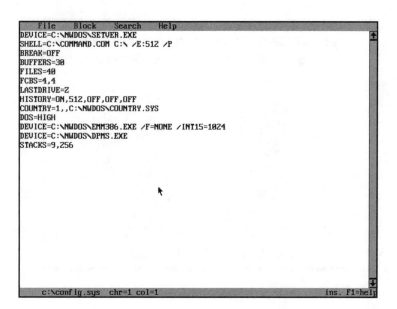

```
    File    Block    Search    Help
DEVICE=C:\NWDOS\SETVER.EXE
SHELL=C:\COMMAND.COM C:\ /E:512 /P
BREAK=OFF
BUFFERS=30
FILES=40
FCBS=4,4
LASTDRIVE=Z
HISTORY=ON,512,OFF,OFF,OFF
COUNTRY=1,,C:\NWDOS\COUNTRY.SYS
DOS=HIGH
DEVICE=C:\NWDOS\EMM386.EXE /F=NONE /INT15=1024
DEVICE=C:\NWDOS\DPMS.EXE
STACKS=9,256




              k




    c:\config.sys   chr=1 col=1                           ins. F1=help
```

Fig. 17.3
The file name—
in this case,
config.sys—is
displayed in the
bottom-left corner
of the screen.

VII

Advanced Techniques

Opening EDIT to Work with an Existing File

When you want to start EDIT and immediately work with an existing text
file, you have two options. First, you can start the program and then load the
text file. Second, you can start EDIT by entering **EDIT** *filename* at the command prompt; when you do, EDIT starts with the file loaded automatically.

If the file you want to work on is in the current directory, all you need to
enter when you start EDIT is the file name. If the file is in a different directory, you need to include its path. EDIT does not use the system's path to
find files. If you want to edit a file called MYFILE.TXT in the \DOCS directory
but you are in the root directory, you must enter **EDIT \DOCS\MYFILE.TXT**. If
you have problems loading the file you want, make sure that you are entering
the correct path and file name. Also remember to enter the entire file name,
including the extension, if there is one.

Opening a File in EDIT

When working in EDIT, you may want to open a file other than the one currently on-screen. Choose File Open; then EDIT asks which file you want to
open (see fig. 17.4). You can press the shortcut Alt-O to accomplish the same
thing. If you have made any unsaved changes to the current file, EDIT
prompts you to save the changes before it opens the new file.

Fig. 17.4

The Select File to Open dialog box.

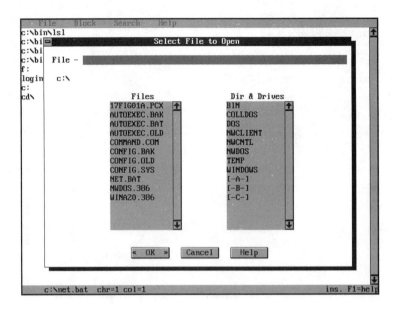

In the Select File to Open dialog box are two list boxes. On the left is the Files list for the current directory. On the right is the Dir & Drives list for the subdirectories of your current directory and the drives to which you have access.

To navigate between these areas on-screen, use either the mouse or the keyboard. The Tab key moves the cursor from section to section, and the up- and down-arrow keys move the cursor to different entries within a section (for example, to specific files within the Files list).

Unless you are working in the root directory of a drive, the top entry in the Dir & Drives list box is the *parent directory symbol* (. .). Selecting this entry takes you to the parent of the current directory. If you start EDIT in a directory called \WORKING\DOCS, for example, and then choose File Open and select the parent directory symbol, the files and directories available in the \WORKING directory are displayed.

When the file you want to edit is highlighted, choose OK or press Enter. The Select File to Open dialog box disappears, the selected file appears, and you can begin editing.

Editing Files

Another way in which EDIT resembles word processing programs is that you need to know how to move the cursor around the screen to reach the section of text you want to edit. You need to know also how to cut, copy, and move text; how to break lines; and how to make other editing changes. Finally, you must be comfortable using menus and commands. The next sections of the chapter describe the parts of the EDIT program that you are most likely to use.

Caution

Examples in the following sections use the CONFIG.SYS file to show editing methods. You should not experiment, however, with your CONFIG.SYS file or other important program files. Use a sample file to work with EDIT until you are familiar with the program.

Navigating the EDIT Screen

If you are going to edit your text files effectively, you have to learn how to move the cursor within the editor. You cannot enter new characters in the middle of text without first placing the cursor there. EDIT has three ways of accomplishing this: using the keyboard, using the mouse, or using a series of commands. You can use any of these methods or a combination of all three, as described in the following sections.

At the bottom of the screen is a status bar. This bar tells you which file is currently being edited. Next is displayed the character position in the file. The value chr=x tells you the row where the cursor is positioned; the value col=x tells you the column where the cursor is positioned.

Moving Around Using the Keyboard. The most common way of using the keyboard to move around in the file is to press the arrow keys. Pressing the right-arrow key moves the cursor one character to the right. Pressing the left-arrow key moves the cursor one character to the left. To move up one line, press the up-arrow key; to move down one line, press the down-arrow key.

In many of the utilities discussed in this book, you press the Tab key to move from section to section on-screen. In EDIT, this is true in dialog boxes. When you work with an open file in the editing screen, however, pressing the Tab key inserts a tab, and the cursor moves to the next tab stop. Tab stops are preset at every eighth column.

To move the cursor one word at a time, press the Ctrl key with an arrow key. To move the cursor one word to the right, press Ctrl-right arrow. To move the cursor one word to the left, press Ctrl-left arrow. If you are editing system files instead of text files, it may be unclear what constitutes a word. When you have a line like

```
DEVICE=C:\NWDOS\EMM386.EXE  /F=NONE
```

you may wonder where a word starts and ends. A *word* is defined by EDIT as a series of characters extending until a blank space. In this example, DEVICE alone is not a word, because it is attached to the equal sign, which in turn is attached to path and file information. Thus, the first word in this line is DEVICE=C:\NWDOS\EMM386.EXE. Although this may seem like three or more words to you, it is considered one word by EDIT. The second word is /F=NONE. If the cursor is at the beginning of this line and you press Ctrl-right arrow, the cursor jumps from the D to the /.

To move to the beginning of a line, regardless of how many words the line contains, press the Home key. To move to the end of a line, press the End key. To move the cursor one page at a time, press the PgUp or PgDn key. To move to the beginning or end of a file, regardless of how long the file is, press the Ctrl key with the Home key or End key, respectively.

Moving Around Using the Mouse. If you have a mouse with the correct driver loaded, you can use the mouse to move within a text file. This may or may not seem easier to you than navigating using the keyboard; some people prefer the keyboard in order to avoid moving one of their hands back and forth so much. If you want to use the mouse to reposition the cursor, simply move the pointer wherever you want the cursor to be, and click once.

You can see a scroll bar along the right side of the screen. At the top of the scroll bar is an arrow pointing upward; at the bottom is an arrow pointing downward. If the text file currently open is too large to display on-screen, you can use the scroll bar to move up and down throughout the file. Clicking the up scroll arrow moves the file up one line; clicking the down scroll arrow moves the file down one line.

Somewhere in the scroll bar is a *slider* (often called a *scroll box*)—you see it only if the file is too large to fit on one screen). To use the slider, position the mouse pointer on the slider, click and hold down the left button, and drag the slider up or down. If you drag it up all the way, you return to the top of the file; if you drag the slider to the bottom of the scroll bar, you reach the bottom of the file. Clicking above or below the slider scrolls the screen 20 lines.

> **Note**
>
> Although not true in most word processing programs, using the scroll bar to change the view in EDIT repositions the cursor.

Using Control Commands. If you have been using computers for a long time, chances are that you have used WordStar at some point. WordStar was the word processor of choice for many people in the early days of personal computing, and several of its elements have carried over to computing today. WordStar did not have menu bars or tool bars to format text. You could not use a mouse to move around because PCs did not have mice yet. WordStar became famous for its *control commands*, so named because they required pressing the Ctrl key with other character keys. Many text editors, including EDIT in Novell DOS 7, still recognize many of these commands because some people prefer them to using the mouse or the arrow keys.

You can try learning WordStar's control commands to see whether they help you work more efficiently. The first thing to learn is the *cursor control diamond*. Look at your keyboard and find the E, S, D, and X keys. Notice that they form an approximate diamond. When you are in EDIT and want to move the cursor one character to the left, press Ctrl-S. To move the cursor one character to the right, press Ctrl-D. If you want to move up one line, press Ctrl-E; to move down one line, press Ctrl-X.

Now find the A and F keys. Imagine that they are extensions of the cursor control diamond. If you want to move the cursor one word to the left, press Ctrl-A; to move one word to the right, press Ctrl-F. Next look at the R and C keys—their respective control commands move the cursor up and down one full page.

Other control commands are more complicated but can handle more complicated tasks. Sometimes, for example, a control command requires you to enter a combination of characters. Press Ctrl-Q and notice that ^Q appears at the bottom-left corner of your screen. Ctrl-Q does nothing by itself, but it is the start of many character combinations. If you press Ctrl-Q and then press S before releasing the Ctrl key, the cursor is moved to the start of the line. Ctrl-Q, D moves the cursor to the end of the line. Notice that you are still using the cursor control diamond. To move the cursor to the beginning of the file, press Ctrl-Q, R. Press Ctrl-Q, C to move to the end of the file.

You learn other control commands later in this chapter. These can be used as shortcuts to move blocks of text or to delete characters, words, and whole lines, among other tasks. A knowledge of these commands may help you work faster in EDIT.

Getting Help

You can use choices from the Help menu to remind you of certain commands or to help you through a process. You can also access Help by pressing the F1 key from anywhere in the program. DOSBook, the on-line documentation for Novell DOS 7, has valuable information about the EDIT program. You can access DOSBook from the Help menu or by entering **DOSBOOK** at any command prompt.

Entering Text

With EDIT, you can do many things—delete text, move blocks of text, and so on. At some point, however, you are likely to enter new text in the files; when you do, keep a few points in mind.

You can use EDIT to create text files of whatever information you want. For example, you can use this program, instead of your word processor, to write small documents, such as to-do lists, phone numbers lists, and short memos. But EDIT does not work the way your word processor works. As mentioned earlier in this chapter, EDIT offers no text-formatting options. You cannot make characters bold or italic. You cannot underline text or center words on the page automatically.

Furthermore, EDIT does not include *word wrap*. With most word processors, as your typing approaches the right margin of the page, words automatically wrap to the next line rather than run off the edge of the page. In EDIT, you must press Enter at the end of each line. If you forget to press Enter, all characters you type continue along the same line.

As you edit files, you can press Enter anytime to insert a new blank line. If you press Enter with the cursor positioned in the middle of an existing line, the character to the right of the cursor moves down to become the first character on the next line, and the cursor moves down also. If you want to move text down to create a new line, yet continue editing the current line, press Ctrl-N. If you do this at the beginning of a line, a blank line is inserted. If you press Ctrl-N in the middle of a line, the text starting at the cursor moves down to the next line, but the cursor remains on the current line.

One of the benefits of working with a computer instead of a typewriter is the ability to combine multiple documents easily into one document. If you want to insert a file existing on disk into the file on which you are currently working (for example, to combine two lists of figures), you *read* the disk file into the current file. To do this, position the cursor wherever you want the disk file's contents to be inserted; then choose File Read, or press Alt-F, R. A dialog box similar to the Select File to Open dialog box appears (see fig. 17.5), and you can select the file to be inserted. Instead of choosing File Read, you can press one of the following key combinations to open the File Read dialog box: Alt-R or Ctrl-K, R.

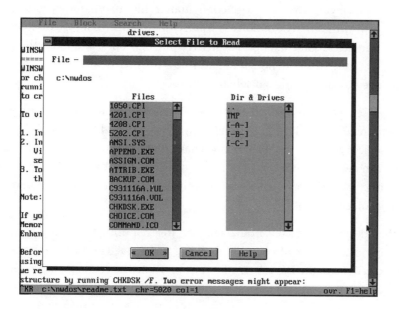

Fig. 17.5
The Select File to Read dialog box.

When you begin entering text, you must pay attention to two modes—Insert and Overwrite. Entering text in Insert mode means that if you position the cursor in the middle of a word or sentence and begin typing, existing characters move to the right to make room for the new text you type. If you enter text in Overwrite mode and the cursor is positioned in the middle of a word or sentence, the new characters that you type delete and replace the existing text.

You can tell which mode you are in by looking at the bottom-right corner of the screen. In Insert mode, ins. is displayed; in Overwrite mode, ovr. is displayed. You can toggle between the two modes by using the Ins key. For instance, if you are in Insert mode (the default) and want to change to Overwrite mode, simply press the Ins key. When you want to return to Insert mode, press the Ins key again.

Another way to tell which mode you are in is to examine the cursor. In Insert mode, the cursor is a small blinking line that you can place under a character. In Overwrite mode, the cursor changes to a large blinking block that completely covers one character.

Deleting Text

When you are editing files, you occasionally may have to delete portions of text. Because no one is a perfect typist, you may have to go back and correct mistakes. Or you may work with configuration files that require you to experiment with different options as you try to optimize your system; to do this, you delete some old options, insert some new ones, and move things around. Thus, it is not enough to know how to enter new text into your files; you need to know how to delete text also.

It may seem obvious how to delete characters. If you have worked with your computer extensively, you are familiar with the Del and Backspace keys. These keys generally delete only one character at a time. In EDIT, however, you can delete an entire word or line at once, as explained in this section. (In the next section, you learn about working with blocks of text; you can delete whole blocks as well.)

When deleting characters from a text file, the first thing you need to know is the cursor's location. If you want to delete the character on which the cursor is located, press the Del key. If you want to delete the character to the left of the cursor, press the Backspace key. If you hold down either of these keys, characters are deleted continuously. This method is easier than pressing the key many times.

If the cursor is at the end of the line, following what appears to be the last character on the line, and you press the Del key, the *newline character* is deleted. This makes the following line "jump up" and become part of the current line. Similarly, if the cursor is at the beginning of the line, and you press the Backspace key, the current line "jumps up" to become part of the preceding line.

Four control commands make it easier to delete sections of text. The T, Y, G, and H keys, which form an approximate square, are the keys to remember when deleting text. If you want to delete the character on which the cursor is located, press Ctrl-G. To delete the character to the left of the cursor, press Ctrl-H.

To delete all or part of a word, press Ctrl-T. To delete the whole word, position the cursor on the first character in the word and press Ctrl-T. If you press Ctrl-T with the cursor positioned in the middle of a word, every character on and to the left of the cursor is deleted in that word. Press Ctrl-Y to delete a whole line of text, no matter where in the line the cursor is located.

As you delete text in a file, remember that EDIT is not exactly like your word processor. Most commercial word processors these days have an *undelete* feature. If you accidentally delete a line of text when using the word processor, it is rather simple to bring the line back again. EDIT does not have such a feature. If you accidentally delete an important line of text, either you have to retype it, or you have to exit the file without saving and then load the file again. Both methods can be a hassle, so be extremely careful. Think twice before you delete a whole line, or even a word. Remember that a *word* in EDIT can be a whole line long, if there are no spaces.

Manipulating Blocks of Text

As you start using EDIT to modify your computer's text files, you may see the need to move whole blocks of text around or to delete them. The order in which you load drivers from your AUTOEXEC.BAT file, for example, helps to determine how much system memory you have left. You may want to move the drivers around in the file to change the order in which they are read and loaded by the computer. In this section, you learn how to work with blocks of text to edit more efficiently.

Using the Block Menu. First, you should familiarize yourself with the Block menu. To access this menu from EDIT, press Alt-B. Notice that the menu is divided into two sections separated by a line (see fig. 17.6). The first two items in the menu are Start and End; you use these items to define the block. The last five items—Hide, Copy, Move, Delete, and Write to File—describe actions you can perform on blocks of data.

Fig. 17.6

The Block menu.

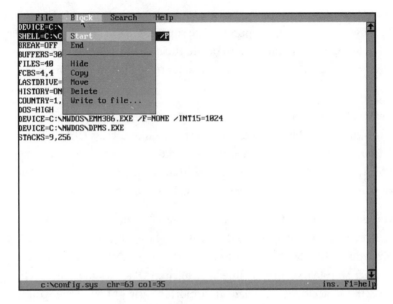

Because you need to define a block before you can do anything with it, you should practice defining blocks. Move the cursor to the first character on the first line of the file. Press Alt-B to access the Block menu. Choose Start. Notice that <B> appears to the left of the cursor. This helps you remember where the block begins. Move the cursor down three lines and then press Alt-B to access the Block menu again. This time, choose End. Notice that the first three lines of the file are highlighted and that the <B> code has disappeared.

Now copy these lines to the bottom of the file. Press Ctrl-End to move the cursor to the end of the file. Choose Block Copy. You should see an exact duplicate of the first three lines at the end of the file.

Delete the three lines at the beginning of the file, because you are going to move the three new lines you just created to take their place. The three lines you copied to the end of the file should still be highlighted. If they are not, mark them by choosing Block Start and Block End. Move the cursor to the top of the file by pressing Ctrl-Home. Then choose Block Move. With the three lines restored at the top of the file, all text should look the same as it did when you started.

If you are working on a large text file and want to hide a block of text from view, use the Hide option in the Block menu. This option is useful if you find yourself moving or copying blocks of text from the beginning to the end of a large file. Moving back and forth can be cumbersome, and it is easier just to hide the middle section from view. To redisplay the block, choose Block Show. (Notice that, unless a block has been hidden, you do not see the Show option.)

You already know how to delete a word or a line of text. You can delete a block of text by choosing Block Delete.

The last choice on the Block menu enables you to write whatever you have blocked to a separate file. If you choose Write to File, you need to give the blocked text a file name (see fig. 17.7). Although you create a new file with the block of data, the block also remains in the current document.

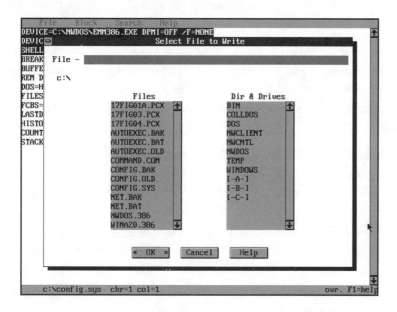

Fig. 17.7
You provide a path and file name for the saved block in the Select File to Write dialog box.

Blocking Text with the Mouse. Some people find it cumbersome having to mark the beginning and end of a block of text by using the keyboard. If you have a mouse, marking a block of text is a simpler process. Place the pointer at the intended beginning of the block; then press and hold down the left mouse button. Drag until you reach the intended end of the block, and then release the button. Highlighting a block takes you only a few seconds with the mouse.

> **Note**
>
> When you use the mouse to mark a block, EDIT does not display the <B> code at the beginning of the block.

Using Block Control Commands. EDIT provides some shortcut keys to perform the same operations as certain menu options. To mark the beginning of a block, press Ctrl-K, B. To mark the end, press Ctrl-K, K. The B and the K form no pattern on the keyboard, but the beginning letter of the word *block* is *b*, and the ending letter is *k*. This should help you remember the keys.

To move a block of text after you have marked it, press Ctrl-K, V. To copy the block, press Ctrl-K, C. To write the block to a file, press Ctrl-K, W. To hide the block, press Ctrl-K, H. To delete the block, press Ctrl-K, Y. (Recall that Ctrl-Y deletes a whole line of text.)

Using Markers

If you become comfortable enough to use EDIT regularly, some other aspects of the program may prove helpful. One is the use of *markers*. Markers are like bookmarks that keep your place in a file. You can set up to 10 markers in each file.

Tip
The only function keys you can use are F1-F10, no matter how many function keys your keyboard has.

To set a marker, position the cursor in the text wherever you want to put the marker. Then press Ctrl-*Fn*, where *Fn* represents a function key. For example, to set marker number one, press Ctrl-F1. When the marker is set, you see the number placed in angle brackets: <1>. You can set a marker for each of the function keys F1-F10. You do not need to use the markers in order; if you want, for example, you can set the first marker with F7, and the second with F3.

Once the markers are set, you can move to them immediately by pressing the Alt-*Fn* key combination. If you set a marker with Ctrl-F7, to get to that marker from anywhere else in the file, you press Alt-F7.

Other similar key combinations are available. To set another type of marker, you can press Ctrl-K, *n* where *n* is a number key (not a function key). To move to one of these markers, press Ctrl-Q, *n*. You can set up to 10 markers using this method, one for each of the keyboard numbers 1-0.

To delete a marker, put the cursor just after the marker and execute the mark procedure again. All markers are lost when you close the file. If you set markers in a file and quit EDIT, and you later return to the file, those markers are gone.

Searching for Text

If you use EDIT to keep track of lists—address lists, for example—you will often use the search feature. You can access the Search menu by pressing Alt-S. The menu has three options: Search for String, Search and Replace, and Repeat Last Search.

Search for String is used to locate a word or entry in your text file. A *string* is a connected series of characters. It can be a letter, a word, a sentence, or a sequence of gobbledygook. After you choose Search for String, a dialog box appears that prompts you for more information (see fig. 17.8).

Fig. 17.8
The Search dialog box.

You enter the *search string*—the string you are trying to locate—in the first field. This dialog box provides three configuration options you can select also. The first is Ignore Case. If you select this option, EDIT looks for any text that matches the string you define, without distinguishing between upper- and lowercase letters. Unless you know the exact case of every character in the search string, you probably do want to select Ignore Case. If you are looking for the word *computer*, for example, and it was typed in your file as *Computer*, EDIT cannot find it without this option selected.

Ignoring case is also useful when you want to see all references to *computer*, regardless of whether they are spelled *Computer* or *COMPUTER*, or some other combination of upper- and lowercase letters.

The second configuration option is Match Whole Words Only. This option is used as a delimiter to keep EDIT from finding extraneous entries. If you are looking for the word *win*, for example, and you neglect to select this option, EDIT locates all text containing *win*—this includes words like *windows*, *wink*, and *throwing*. However, you do not want Match Whole Words Only selected if you are looking for a string and are unsure how it has been entered. Imagine that you have used EDIT to create an address list, and you are trying to find the entry for Peg and Bill Nelson. Unfortunately, you cannot remember if their last name ends in *on* or *en*. When you search for *Nels* without selecting Match Whole Words Only, EDIT locates the entry for you.

The last configuration option in this box is Begin Search at File Start. Usually, EDIT searches for text from the cursor's location down to the end of the file. If the text you are looking for exists before the cursor in the file, you cannot locate the text unless you select Begin Search at File Start.

When you have entered the string and set the configuration options, choose OK to begin the search.

At times, you may want to search for each occurrence of a text string and replace it with another text string (perhaps to correct the misspelling of a name). You can do this by choosing Search and Replace. When you select Search and Replace, a dialog box appears that prompts you for more information (see fig. 17.9). This box is larger than the Search dialog box but contains much of the same information. In the first field, you enter the text string you want to replace. In the second field, you enter the text string with which you want to replace the search string.

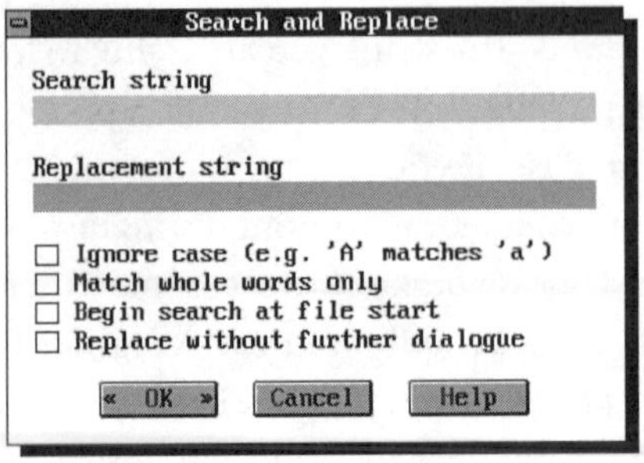

Fig. 17.9

The Search and Replace dialog box.

This box provides four configuration options: Ignore Case, Match Whole Words Only, Begin Search at File Start, and Replace without Further Dialogue. You are already familiar with the first three. You use the last option, Replace without Further Dialogue, when you do not want EDIT to confirm each replacement. When this box is not selected, EDIT asks for confirmation that you want to replace each occurrence of the search string found. This can become tedious, so you may want to select Replace without Further Dialogue. If you want to be cautious, however, do not select this option—let EDIT verify your intention before each replacement.

The last choice on the Search menu is Repeat Last Search. Choosing Repeat Last Search performs a search based on the last set of criteria defined by you, using the most recent search string and configuration options.

Some Search options have shortcut key combinations. Pressing Ctrl-Q, F is the same as choosing Search for String from the Search menu. Pressing Ctrl-Q, A is the same as choosing Search and Replace from the Search menu. Unfortunately, no shortcut exists for Repeat Last Search.

Saving Files

After you make changes to a text file, you most likely want to save the changes. You do this from the File menu. If you have been working on a file, and you try to exit the EDIT program or to open a new file, you are prompted to save the changes that have been made to the file on-screen.

If you want to save your file before you exit the program, or at any time during editing, choose File Save or press Alt-V.

Caution

When you save a file that has been saved in an earlier version, you are overwriting the existing text. EDIT does not warn you to be careful when saving.

Tip
Save your files frequently to prevent loss from a power outage or an equipment failure.

To save changes to the file on which you are currently working, press Ctrl-K, S. To save changes to the current file and then start editing a new file, press Ctrl-K, D. To save changes to the current file and then exit the EDIT program, press Ctrl-K, X. To quit EDIT without saving changes to the current file, press Ctrl-K, Q.

From Here...

EDIT is not a full word processor; it works only with straight text files. For working with certain files—such as your CONFIG.SYS, AUTOEXEC.BAT, STARTNET.BAT, and NET.CFG files—EDIT does a great job.

For more information about Novell DOS 7 files and directories, see the following chapters:

■ Chapter 6, "Understanding File Storage," covers drive and disk structures, DOS directories, paths, DOS files and their attributes, and the use of wild cards.

■ Chapter 7, "Managing Files and Directories," shows you how to create, rename, remove, and display directories; list files and directories; and copy, move, compare, and delete files.

■ Chapter 18, "Configuring Your System," helps you work with the powerful and flexible CONFIG.SYS file used by DOS to configure itself for your computer, its resources, and the features you want to use.

■ Chapter 19, "Using Batch Files," teaches you what a batch file is, how to create a batch file, and the special commands you use with batch files.

Chapter 18

Configuring Your System

Throughout this book you have heard references to your computer's configuration files. When people refer to the configuration files, they are usually talking about the two text files your computer reads when it first boots. Both reside in the root directory. They are your CONFIG.SYS and AUTOEXEC.BAT files. The AUTOEXEC.BAT file is a batch file that loads programs and executes commands. Many lines in your AUTOEXEC.BAT file represent commands that can also be run from the command line. It is from this batch file that you normally run TSRs (terminate-and-stay-resident programs) like DELWATCH, SDRes, or network drivers.

The CONFIG.SYS file is a little different. The lines in a CONFIG.SYS file do not represent commands you can also enter from the command line; they are instructions to the computer on how it should behave. The information, drivers, and specifications you make in the CONFIG.SYS file determine how your computer behaves the whole time it is turned on. From CONFIG.SYS, you can give your computer such capabilities as access to a memory-based disk, support for foreign languages, and access to hardware peripherals.

Depending on what you want to accomplish, you can customize the way your system is configured by using ? prompts, labels, switches, and chains to other configuration files. By using all the tools available, you will be able to optimize your computer so that it works best for you. In this chapter, you learn what goes into a CONFIG.SYS file and what benefits and costs you can incur by including certain options. Many of the options can be configured through Novell DOS 7's Setup utility, but many cannot.

This chapter covers the following topics:

- Specifying system options

- Loading device drivers

- Using labels and chains

Specifying System Options

When you first installed Novell DOS 7 on your computer, a CONFIG.SYS file was created for you. The information in this CONFIG.SYS file depends on what options you chose during the installation process. If you had another DOS operating system on your machine before you installed Novell DOS 7, some of those parameters were saved.

Take a minute to look at your CONFIG.SYS file. You can do this by getting to a command prompt in the root directory and entering **TYPE CONFIG.SYS.** You probably see something like this:

```
DEVICE=C:\NWDOS\SETVER.EXE
SHELL=C:\COMMAND.COM C:\ /E:256 /P
BREAK=ON
BUFFERS=30
FILES=40
FCBS=4,4
LASTDRIVE=Z
HISTORY=ON,512,OFF,OFF,OFF
COUNTRY=1,,C:\NWDOS\CONTRY.SYS
DOS=HIGH
DEVICE=C:\NWDOS\EMM386.EXE /F=NONE
DEVICE=C:\NWDOS\DPMS.EXE
```

If you have lines in your CONFIG.SYS file that are not listed here, or if you are missing some of the lines shown, do not worry. Again, the information in your CONFIG.SYS file depends on what options you selected when you first set up your system. The following sections describe each of the typical commands in the CONFIG.SYS file. For more details on these commands, see the Command Reference in Part X of this book.

BREAK

If BREAK is set to ON, you can stop a program while it is running by pressing Ctrl-Break or Ctrl-C. This is often helpful if you have problems with a program and it seems to run on and on without relinquishing control back to you. If BREAK is OFF, you can still press Ctrl-Break or Ctrl-C to stop a program, but only while it is performing standard input or output (I/O) operations. An I/O operation interacts with other parts of your computer, such as printing, displaying data on the screen, reading from the keyboard, writing to disk, and so on. (Some programs trap Ctrl-Break so that the application doesn't see it.) This is the syntax for the BREAK command:

    BREAK=ON | OFF

Some programs have moments when they do not use I/O very often. If a program is performing complicated calculations before displaying any output, you would not be able to interrupt it with Ctrl-Break if the BREAK statement in your CONFIG.SYS were set to OFF.

The default value for BREAK is OFF. If this statement is missing from your CONFIG.SYS file, BREAK is set off. But Setup probably put in a BREAK=ON statement when you installed Novell DOS 7 on your system. Many programs disable this feature; they don't want you interrupting them. But they often provide another means of interrupting them that is a little more friendly to the application. Check your program's documentation for more details.

BUFFERS

Buffers are blocks of memory that the operating system uses to temporarily save information it is writing to or reading from disk. Because applications can access data in memory much faster than straight from disk, if an application finds the data in a buffer, performance greatly increases. But buffers can take up memory normally used for applications, so if you configure too many buffers, your application can actually run slower than without the buffers at all. Here is the syntax of BUFFERS:

    BUFFERS=*nn*

You can set the BUFFERS value to any number from 3 to 99, but the default is 15. Many disk-caching programs serve the same function as buffers, but a lot more effectively. So if you are using a disk-caching program, you might want to decrease the number of BUFFERS to 10. Check the cache program's documentation for recommendations. Also keep in mind that some applications have their own recommendations for BUFFERS. They might automatically increase the value in your CONFIG.SYS file when you install them. Generally, you should stick to what the program recommends, but it won't hurt to play around with this number a little to see whether you notice any performance gains.

For more information on setting BUFFERS, refer to the Command Reference in Part X.

CLS

Adding this line to your CONFIG.SYS simply clears the screen of all characters before it displays any more information regarding the files or drivers it loads. You can add the CLS line to CONFIG.SYS before an important line loads so that the line remains on-screen for a second or two. You can also add CLS before a ? prompt or SWITCH statement so that the user has a clear view of what is being asked.

COUNTRY

The COUNTRY command configures the date and time format for your country, the currency symbol of your country, and the code page to use. You must provide the country code (*nnn*)—a number that identifies any of 25 countries recognized by Novell DOS 7. The country code for the United States is 1. Following is the syntax:

```
COUNTRY=nnn,cp,d:\path\COUNTRY.SYS
```

The code page (*cp*) refers to a table that sets up the keyboard and displays characters for various foreign languages. If you neglect to specify a code page, Novell DOS 7 uses the default code page for the country code you listed. The default code page for the United States is 437.

You also have to specify the drive and path where COUNTRY can find the COUNTRY.SYS file. Usually, it's in the \NWDOS directory of drive C. Because it would be unreasonable to memorize the country code and code page for every country, the easiest way to configure the COUNTRY entry is through Novell DOS 7's Setup utility. This provides a list of all the countries supported; you can access it through the DOS System & Memory Management menu option and the Country and Keyboard menu option. For more details on setting up keyboard, monitor, and printer formats and changing code pages, see Appendix A, "Internationalizing Your System."

CPOS

CPOS stands for *character position*. This statement defines where the cursor is displayed on-screen. The first number specifies the row (or vertical position); any number from 1 to 25 is allowed. The second number specifies the column (or horizontal position); any number from 1 to 80 is valid. Both numbers and the comma are required. Here is the syntax:

```
CPOS nn,nn
```

You cannot change modes until the CONFIG.SYS file has finished executing. Therefore, CPOS is best used from the command line or in batch files.

DOS

Use the DOS statement to specify where in memory the operating system software loads. The three options you have are high memory, upper memory, or conventional memory. High memory is the first 64K block of extended memory. This is the default area for the operating system. Here is the syntax you use:

```
DOS=HIGH | UMB | LOW
```

Upper memory (UMB) is the 384K of memory above conventional memory. This memory area is used by system hardware (like your video or network adapters), terminate-and-stay-resident software (TSRs), and drivers. 384K sounds like a lot of space for all these things, but it fills up quickly. You should put the DOS files here only if high memory is unavailable.

Conventional memory (LOW) is the first 640K of system memory. This is the memory area where most DOS programs have to load, so you want to keep as much of it as free as possible.

ECHO

The ECHO command causes your computer to display any message you want. Whatever you enter for the message shows on your screen when your system gets to that line in your CONFIG.SYS. Here is the syntax:

```
ECHO=message
```

Note an example of ECHO:

```
ECHO=The following lines load the memory management software.
```

> **Note**
>
> ECHO=ON | OFF is not an option when you use ECHO in the CONFIG.SYS file. This command works only in batch files.

EXIT

The EXIT command in a CONFIG.SYS file causes the system to immediately quit executing any more lines. This is most often used with labels and GOTO statements, which are discussed later in the chapter. Here is the syntax:

    EXIT

EXIT has no switches or arguments.

FASTOPEN

FASTOPEN records, in memory, the locations of files. You specify the number of files it tracks (*nnnnn*). The default value is 512 entries, but any number from 128 to 32768 is valid. When an application needs to open a file, normally it has to read the file allocation table (FAT) on the disk to determine where the file is located. If the application can get this information from a FASTOPEN table stored in memory, it can access the file more quickly. Use the following syntax:

    FASTOPEN=*nnnnn*

> **Note**
>
> The equal sign is mandatory when options are included. For commands that have no options, such as EXIT, the equal sign should not be included.

The benefits of the FASTOPEN command are obvious, so why not max out FASTOPEN? The reason is that each entry takes up two bytes of precious memory. If less memory is available to an application, the advantages are outweighed by the cost. Unless your applications suggest that you raise this number, you probably should just leave it at the default value.

FCBS

The FCBS entry configures the number of files that can be opened at the same time by applications that use file control blocks (FCBs). The first number (*m*) specifies the number of files you can open by FCBs; any value from 1 to 255 is valid. The second number (*n*) specifies the number of files opened by FCBs that are protected from automatic closure.

For example, if your program attempts to open a fifth file and you have configured *m* for 4, the operating system tries to close one of the files already opened. The *n* value protects those files from being closed. If the *n* value is only 3, the operating system automatically closes one of the files and protects the other three. If the *n* value is also 4, the operating system can't automatically close any of the *m* files. Note the syntax of FCBS:

> **FCBS=*m*,*n***

Most programs, however, do not use FCBs to open files. Instead, they use the FILES statement in CONFIG.SYS to control the number of files that may be opened. The installation program normally adds an FCBS=4,4 line to CONFIG.SYS, but it might not be necessary if none of your applications requires it. Note that FCBS cannot be set to zero. For applications that don't use FCBS, set FCBS=1,1.

FILES

This number configures the number of files that can be simultaneously opened by programs. It reserves space in memory for your operating system to track the number of open files. The default value is 20, but any number from 20 to 255 is valid. Many database programs open a large number of files and might suggest that you increase this number so they run properly. Other applications might not check the FILES statement in your CONFIG.SYS file when they are installed, but if you try to access certain features, they return an Insufficient file handles error message. If you get this error, try increasing this value until your program runs satisfactorily. Here is the syntax of FILES:

> **FILES=*nnn***

If you have enabled the network features of Novell DOS 7 and have configured your computer as a peer server, you might have to increase this number. Because many applications might be opened at once by other users, your operating system has to allocate more memory to control the open files. The number you use depends on your memory needs. Usually, 20-40 files are sufficient.

HISTORY

Use HISTORY to have the operating system remember commands that you type at the DOS prompt. You can set HISTORY either on or off. If you set it to ON, you must specify the number of bytes (*nnnn*) to reserve in memory for the buffer. The default value is 512 bytes, which is enough to remember about the last 10 commands you issued. Valid values range from 128 to 4096 bytes of memory. Use the following syntax:

```
HISTORY=ON[,nnnn,ON | OFF] | OFF
```

Note that if you set HISTORY to ON, you must add the comma, indicate the number of bytes, and then specify the insert mode (ON or OFF). If you set HISTORY to OFF, none of these options are necessary.

If HISTORY is turned on, you can use the up-arrow key to scroll through previous commands you have entered at the DOS prompt. After you specify the number of bytes for HISTORY to allocate in memory, you must specify whether you want "insert mode" turned ON or OFF. If insert mode is turned on, the cursor changes to a small block character; if insert mode is off, the cursor is a blinking underscore. With insert mode turned on, you can edit command-line entries by inserting new characters. If it is turned off, you can still turn it on with the Ins (Insert) key on your keyboard.

If you do not want to use the HISTORY options, simply insert the line `HISTORY=OFF` in your CONFIG.SYS. A typical use of HISTORY looks like this:

```
HISTORY=ON,512,ON
```

INSTALL and HIINSTALL

Although most "programs" are loaded from the AUTOEXEC.BAT file rather than from the CONFIG.SYS file, some applications have the capability to be loaded in either place. The DOS programs you can load from the CONFIG.SYS file are these:

CURSOR.EXE
GRAFTABL.COM
GRAPHICS.COM
KEYB.COM
NLSFUNC.EXE
PRINT.COM
SHARE.EXE

For more information about these programs, refer to the Command Reference in Part X.

An advantage of loading programs from CONFIG.SYS is that if you were loading programs based on a user-specified configuration—for example, if you were using GOTOs and LABELs with the ? prompt—you might want these programs included in one configuration and not in another.

Simply add the name of the program and the path where it can be found after the INSTALL statement in your CONFIG.SYS file. If you would like to load the program into upper memory, substitute INSTALL for HIINSTALL. The syntax for this command is

```
[HI]INSTALL=filespec options
```

Do not confuse the INSTALL statement, which is used to load programs, with the DEVICE statement, which is used to load device drivers. You learn more about the DEVICE statement later in this chapter.

LASTDRIVE

Usually, the operating system assumes that you have only enough drives for drive letters A through E. A: is used for your first floppy drive, B: for a second floppy drive (if one exists), and C: for your first hard drive. You might have more hard drives, or you might have to use other drive letters for mapped Novell DOS 7 network drives. Set the LASTDRIVE value to accommodate as many drive letters as you think you might need. LASTDRIVE has this syntax:

```
LASTDRIVE=drive_letter
```

When a network is enabled, the last drive is generally specified as Z. There are no disadvantages to specifying Z as the last drive with the VLM architecture used with Novell DOS 7.

REM

Use the REM command for nonexecuting lines in your CONFIG.SYS file. You can insert REM (or a semicolon) before a comment in the file or before a command you want to disable temporarily. When the operating system comes to a CONFIG.SYS line that starts with REM, it simply ignores any characters in the rest of the line. Here is the syntax of REM:

```
REM | ; comment
```

SHELL

The SHELL statement is most likely the first line in your CONFIG.SYS file. It serves a number of functions. You can use it to specify where the operating system should look for the command processor (COMMAND.COM). Usually, this file is in the root directory, but you might elect to move it to your \NWDOS directory so you do not accidentally delete it. If you did this, your SHELL statement would read

```
SHELL=C:\NWDOS\COMMAND.COM C:\NWDOS
```

Notice that this statement displays an additional path after the path to COMMAND.COM. The first path tells the computer what file to use. The second path tells it where the file is located.

Or you might want to load a command processor other than the default file that came with Novell DOS 7. In that case, you specify with SHELL the name of that processor and where it is located. SHELL has the following syntax:

```
SHELL=filespec dirpath /P:filename E:nnnnn Mx
```

The /P switch serves two purposes. When entered by itself, /P makes the command processor permanent in memory. If followed by a batch file name, /P tells the operating system to look for a batch file other than AUTOEXEC.BAT to execute when the system boots. By default, the operating system looks first at the CONFIG.SYS file and then at the AUTOEXEC.BAT file and executes commands from each. If you would rather use a file other than AUTOEXEC.BAT, you specify it with the /P:*filename* switch. This can be helpful if you want to use your computer with different configurations.

The /E:*nnnnn* switch specifies the amount of memory reserved by the operating system for environment variables. The default size is 256 bytes, but you can specify a value from 129 to 32751. Environment variables are often defined by SET commands. PATH, PEXEC, and PROMPT are examples of environment variables. If you have a long PATH statement, a complex system PROMPT, and a number of other environment variables defined, you might need to increase the /E value. The Setup program normally specifies 512, but if the line were missing from the CONFIG.SYS file, the system would default to 256.

Use the /M*x* switch to load the command processor in a specific memory area. Valid values for *x* are L for conventional memory, H for high memory, and U for upper memory. The default value is L and should be sufficient for most systems.

Loading Device Drivers

Device drivers are pieces of software that allow the operating system and its programs to communicate with the hardware that makes up your computer. Many basic drivers are built into the operating system and do not require any special attention or configuration. But other drivers let you configure your system to accommodate certain tasks or functions. For example, to access high memory areas of your system, you must have a memory manager. To use a mouse, you must load the driver that interprets what the mouse actions mean.

Other drivers are used to extend the basic capabilities of your computer's hardware. You do not have to load a special device driver to see visual images on your monitor, for example, but if you want to customize those images with color or graphics, you might have to use the ANSI.SYS device driver.

Whatever device driver you load, the syntax for the DEVICE entry in your CONFIG.SYS file is

```
[HI]DEVICE=filespec options
```

To load drivers in conventional memory, use DEVICE=. To load the driver into upper memory, use HIDEVICE= or DEVICEHIGH=.

The following sections describe some of the optional device drivers included with Novell DOS 7 and what they do. You learn ways to have the operating system prompt you before it loads a driver, as well as what to do with drivers provided by other vendors.

ANSI.SYS

The ANSI.SYS driver lets you configure your keyboard and display. With the ANSI.SYS driver loaded, you can use escape sequences (commands that start with the escape character) to position the cursor, erase displayed characters, change display modes, or program keys to execute commands. Some programs that perform these functions require that ANSI.SYS be loaded so that they can operate normally.

DISPLAY.SYS

Use DISPLAY.SYS if you plan to use code page switching. A *code page* is a table that sets up the keyboard and display characters for various foreign languages. If you're going to use your computer to compose documents in a foreign language or to read foreign language documents, you should probably have code page switching. (See Appendix A for details.)

PRINTER.SYS

Use PRINTER.SYS if you need code page switching for your printer. You should have this driver enabled if you plan to print documents in a foreign language. (See Appendix A for details.) The PRINTER.SYS driver doesn't depend on the use of a predefined code page.

VDISK.SYS

VDISK.SYS lets you allocate a portion of memory to be used like a disk (creating a *virtual disk*). This "disk" is very fast because a program can access its files without relying on the relatively slow speeds of a hard drive. There are two problems with setting up a virtual disk. First, it is only temporary. When you turn off your computer, all the data saved in the memory of the disk is lost and must be re-created. The second drawback is that if you lose power to your computer unexpectedly, the data in the virtual disk is gone and cannot be recovered.

Your virtual disk can use expanded memory, if available on your system. A virtual disk using expanded memory can be up to 32M—similar to the size of many hard drives. You could install whole programs to a virtual disk of this size; that program would run very fast, but when the power to the system is turned off, the virtual disk would be lost. Some people load small programs into the VDISK for maximum performance.

DRIVER.SYS

DRIVER.SYS is used to define the parameters of a disk not otherwise supported by the ROM BIOS of your computer's hardware. If the BIOS did not recognize 3 1/2-inch floppy drives and you wanted to use one, you could load DRIVER.SYS and force your computer to recognize it. Because the BIOS on most computers built in the last few years supports most floppy drive types, the need for this device driver is waning.

Third-Party Device Drivers

There are many possibilities for device drivers. If you added a scanner to your system, for example, you would need a device driver in order for your applications to recognize and use the scanner. Just remember that each device driver takes up space in memory. And each driver has its own set of configuration options. If you buy and install a new piece of hardware for your system, consult the documentation for information on how best to optimize the accompanying driver with your system.

Using the ? Prompt

At times, you may want to load a device driver, and at other times, you may not. Novell DOS 7 recognizes this possibility and provides the means for the operating system to prompt you before it proceeds to load the driver. You arrange for the prompting by inserting a question mark in the line where you are loading the driver.

If you wanted the operating system to ask you whether to load the VDISK.SYS driver, you would insert the following line in your CONFIG.SYS file:

```
?DEVICE=C:\NWDOS\VDISK.SYS 200 256 32
```

When the operating system arrived at this line in the CONFIG.SYS file, it would display the following message:

```
DEVICE=C:\NWDOS\VDISK.SYS 200 256 32 (Y/N) ?
```

If you press Y, the operating system would create the virtual disk of 200K with a sector size of 256 bytes and a maximum of 32 files. If you press N instead, the line would be ignored.

You also have the option of inserting your own text as a prompt. (The prompt must appear in quotation marks.) For example, if you entered in your CONFIG.SYS file the line

```
?"Create Virtual Disk?"DEVICE=C:\NWDOS\VDISK.SYS 200 256 32
```

the operating system would pause and ask

```
Create Virtual Disk?
```

If you press Y, the virtual disk would be created; press N, and the line would be ignored. Just remember that the whole line of a CONFIG.SYS statement cannot be longer than 128 characters. So, if you are asking long questions and loading drivers with many parameters, any characters beyond the first 128 are ignored by the operating system. Because the screen is normally 80 characters wide, 128 characters fill about 1 1/2 lines on the screen.

You can set a TIMEOUT value when using the ? prompt. If you add the line TIMEOUT=*n* in your CONFIG.SYS file (where *n* is a number in seconds), any line after it in the file will wait the specified number of seconds before automatically ignoring the command. In the preceding example, if you enter the line

```
TIMEOUT=10
```

before the line that prompts you to create the virtual disk, and you fail to respond with a Y or N within 10 seconds, the line will automatically be ignored. In fact, the TIMEOUT setting applies to all ? prompts that follow it in the CONFIG.SYS file (but not ? prompts in the AUTOEXEC.BAT file).

Using Labels

There are so many options available for a CONFIG.SYS file, and so many ways of configuring your system, that some people think of a CONFIG.SYS file as a program in itself. If you want to get fancy and configure your system for many different options, you should familiarize yourself with labels. A *label* is simply a line in your CONFIG.SYS file that identifies a specific section of the file. You can label a section that loads all the drivers you might need if you are code page switching. You can create another label for a section that loads your mouse and scanner drivers.

The syntax for adding a label is simply to add a colon:

```
:label
```

A label is different from a REM statement because you can use other commands to automatically jump to labeled sections. The normal process for reading a CONFIG.SYS file is to start at the top and work your way down. But with statements like GOSUB, GOTO, RETURN, and SWITCH, you can configure the order so that only the lines you want for a specific configuration are read. The following sections describe these commands.

GOTO

GOTO is probably the simplest command for jumping to a label. If you use it with a ? prompt, you can change the order in which commands are executed based on questions you answer at boot time. Use this syntax:

```
GOTO label
```

For example, if you entered in CONFIG.SYS the lines

```
?"Load Mouse Driver?" GOTO MOUSE
.
.
:MOUSE
DEVICE=MOUSE.SYS
```

when the operating system came to the ? line, you would be prompted to enter a Y or N. If you press Y, every line below the :MOUSE label would be executed; anything between the ? prompt and the :MOUSE label would be ignored. If you want the operating system to jump to a label and then jump back, use GOSUB and RETURN commands instead of GOTO.

GOSUB and RETURN

GOSUB works much like the GOTO statement, but when the operating system encounters a RETURN command, execution jumps back to the line immediately following the GOSUB command. If you entered in CONFIG.SYS the lines

```
?"Load Mouse Driver?" GOSUB MOUSE
.
.
EXIT
:MOUSE
DEVICE=MOUSE.SYS
.
.
RETURN
```

the operating system would prompt for execution of the GOSUB routine. If your response was Y, execution would jump to the :MOUSE label, and every line below it would be executed until the RETURN. When the RETURN was encountered, execution would jump back to the line immediately after the GOSUB command. The EXIT command is there to avoid executing the commands under the :MOUSE label again. When the operating system encounters an EXIT command, it immediately stops executing any more lines of the CONFIG.SYS file.

SWITCH

The SWITCH command introduces another level of complexity. Instead of asking yes or no questions to determine execution order, SWITCH lets you choose up to nine different options. When the operating system encounters a SWITCH command in your CONFIG.SYS file, it prompts you to enter a number that corresponds to a specific subroutine. Each subroutine starts with its own label and, like the GOSUB command, ends with a RETURN command. Here is the syntax:

```
SWITCH label1, label2, labeln
```

If you entered in CONFIG.SYS the lines

```
ECHO=Subroutine 1
ECHO=Subroutine 2
ECHO=Subroutine 3
ECHO=Please select Subroutine 1, 2, or 3
SWITCH SUB1, SUB2, SUB3
ECHO=Finished
EXIT
:SUB1
ECHO=Subroutine 1 selected
RETURN
:SUB2
ECHO=Subroutine 2 selected
RETURN
:SUB3
ECHO=Subroutine 3 selected
RETURN
```

the computer would display

```
Subroutine 1
Subroutine 2
Subroutine 3
Please select Subroutine 1, 2, or 3 ?
```

You could then enter the number 1, 2, or 3 from your keyboard. Whatever subroutine you selected would then execute. For example, if you pressed 3 and then pressed Enter, the computer would display

```
Subroutine 3 selected
Finished
```

If you press Enter without making a numerical selection, number 1 is automatically chosen. You can use the TIMEOUT command as you did with the ? prompt. When the specified time expires, number 1 is automatically selected.

Using CHAIN

So far, you have learned about many things you can do with a CONFIG.SYS file. But that was all under the assumption that there was only one CONFIG.SYS file. Actually, you can have more than one file with the same commands and parameters you use in your CONFIG.SYS file. To jump from one configuration file to another, use the CHAIN command. The syntax is

CHAIN=*filespec*

When the operating system encounters the CHAIN command, it jumps to the file specified and starts executing the commands in that file. The other file can have any name you choose—from CONFIG2.SYS to SPAM—and can exist on any drive that you can access. CHAIN is useful if, for some reason, you wanted to have many small configuration files rather than one large CONFIG.SYS file.

Note

If you use CHAIN to jump to a configuration file on another drive, you must specify the full path of all commands in that second file. This is required because the operating system expects to find the DOS files (even DEVICE and INSTALL) in the same drive as the CONFIG.SYS file. As that is no longer the case, you have to show the operating system where to find these files by including their path.

After you have jumped to another configuration file, you can use CHAIN to jump to yet another. Using CHAIN with ? and SWITCH prompts allows unlimited configuration possibilities. As you experiment, you will find you can use CONFIG.SYS to load any number of configuration options. You can customize your computer to load whatever is needed based on what tasks you plan to accomplish. Do not hesitate to take advantage of that capability.

A Point of Order

Now that you have learned about all the elements that go into your
CONFIG.SYS file, you might be wondering whether the order in which you
place these elements matters to your system. The answer is sometimes yes,
usually no. Your main concern when ordering the commands in CONFIG.SYS
is one of memory. As your computer reads down the CONFIG.SYS file one
line at a time, it may load programs, drivers, or other items into memory
space. If you want to make the most of this space, here are some considerations:

- If you want to use the Novell DOS memory manager to load device
  drivers into high, upper, or extended memory, make sure that the
  memory manager is one of the first lines in your CONFIG.SYS file.
  It should precede any other drivers. The next line should be your
  DPMS.SYS driver. Placing this at the beginning of the file ensures that
  all the drivers and TSRs that follow the DPMS specification do not take
  up precious conventional memory space.

- If you have several device drivers that are loaded into high memory,
  you may want to load the largest drivers first. The largest drivers have
  the largest file size on disk, so do a directory of your drivers to see how
  big or small they are. The reason that you want to load the largest drivers first is the way DOS uses memory space.

- When the operating system encounters a driver to be loaded into upper
  memory, it looks for an empty block big enough to hold the driver.
  When the system finds one, it places the driver there. It does the same
  with the next driver, but it doesn't bother to put the drivers next to
  each other necessarily. Often there is a small gap between drivers in
  memory. When you load large drivers first, sometimes small drivers will
  fit in the gaps. If you load the small drivers first, often the area has so
  many small drivers that the only spaces left are the gaps between them,
  and large drivers just will not fit and must load into conventional
  memory. Of course, the same goes for TSRs you would load from a
  batch file.

Luckily, Novell DOS 7 uses DPMS to avoid most memory problems, so this is
fortunately becoming less of an issue. But if memory space is important and
you are still having problems, try rearranging the load order of your files, and
you may free up all the memory you need.

From Here...

When you turn your computer on, the first file it looks for to determine its configuration is the CONFIG.SYS file. The information, drivers, and specifications you make in this file determine how your computer behaves the whole time it is turned on. From the CONFIG.SYS, you can give your computer such capabilities as access to a memory-based disk, support for foreign languages, and access to hardware peripherals.

For more information about your computer's configuration files, see the following chapters:

- Chapter 1, "Understanding DOS," provides information about the concept and history of DOS and the development of Novell DOS, as well as the components of the computer and how Novell DOS functions with each component.

- Chapter 13, "Controlling System Devices," shows you how to manage your printer, print in PostScript from DOS, set up printer ports, transfer files between computers without a network, and use the SHARE utility for disk management.

- Chapter 19, "Using Batch Files," teaches you what a batch file is, how to create a batch file, and the special commands you use with batch files.

- Chapter 22, "Optimizing Memory," guides you through the powerful memory management features of Novell DOS.

- Chapter 23, "Introduction to Networking," provides information for understanding DPMI and DPMS advanced memory features.

- The Command Reference in Part X contains the Novell DOS 7 commands, shown with syntax, applicable rules, and examples where needed.

Chapter 19

Using Batch Files

Every time you enter a command at the Novell DOS prompt, you are pro-gramming your computer to execute that instruction. That is exactly what software is—a more or less permanent file that includes a list of commands for the computer to execute. Of course, most programs are quite complicated and need experienced programmers to prepare the instructions.

Batch files are also programs for your computer. Although they usually per-form simple tasks and might be less sophisticated than most professional software, batch files can be complicated. You can even find commercial soft-ware that uses a batch file to install the application.

This chapter explains the issues regarding naming, creating, and running batch files and describes each of the commands and statements used in batch files. The chapter also provides some batch file examples that you can use on your own system.

In this chapter, the following topics are covered:

- The basics of batch files

- How DOS executes commands

- The AUTOEXEC.BAT file

- How to create, run, and chain batch files

- What you can do in batch files

Understanding Batch Files

A *batch file*, at minimum, is a file that contains a list of commands usually typed at the DOS prompt. Novell DOS, however, provides additional and enhanced capabilities for batch files. You can make them work like "real" programs with labels, subroutines with returns, process loops, and even menus. (Later sections of this chapter describe all these possibilities.)

The operating system provides batch processing so that you don't have to manually type every individual command that you require in order to use your system regularly. For example, you probably run your word processing program everyday. To do so, several steps are required, as outlined in the following example:

1. Switch to the proper drive.

   ```
   D:
   ```

2. Change to the subdirectory for word processing.

   ```
   CD\WORDPROC
   ```

3. Start the word processing program.

   ```
   WP
   ```

4. After you finish your word processing session and exit the program, return to the root directory in the boot drive.

   ```
   C:
   CD\
   ```

5. Run your computer menu.

   ```
   MENU
   ```

You can type each command manually every time you want to edit a document, or you can prepare a batch file that contains all these commands and then let the computer perform the steps for you. If you include all these commands in a batch file named WP.BAT, for example, you can just enter **WP** at the Novell DOS prompt to have all the individual commands executed automatically. This approach is not only easier but also much faster. Novell DOS's batch files, therefore, can make you more productive.

Understanding How DOS Executes Commands

Computers that run Novell DOS execute only three kinds of files in addition to internal commands (those that are built into DOS and don't require or use separate files): files with the extension COM, EXE, or BAT. The first two file types are command (COM) and executable (EXE) files, in binary format, that have been assembled or compiled and linked. The third file type is the batch (BAT) file.

To use batch files, you need to understand how Novell DOS executes commands. Suppose that you type a command at the DOS prompt. The operating system first checks to see whether what you typed is an internal command. If not, DOS searches the current directory, first for a COM file with the specified name, second for an EXE file, and third for a BAT file.

If Novell DOS finds no file that it can execute, the system then proceeds along the search path (specified by the PATH statement in the AUTOEXEC.BAT file) to the first specified directory. The operating system starts looking there for a COM file, an EXE file, and then a BAT file. If unsuccessful, Novell DOS continues to the next directory in the search path and starts all over again.

If a batch file and a command or executable file with the same name exist in a directory, the batch file is not executed because Novell DOS always finds the COM or EXE file first. You can bypass this convention, however, by typing the file name and the extension name. If you create a batch file with the name of FORMAT.BAT, for example, it conflicts with the Novell DOS utility named FORMAT.COM. To force the execution of the batch file instead of the command file, enter `FORMAT.BAT`.

Keep in mind that this technique does not work, however, when the batch file has the same name as a Novell DOS internal command. DIR.BAT does not work because as soon as Novell DOS sees the DIR command, which is an internal command, it executes the directory listing and ignores the BAT file extension.

Tip
You can save yourself some grief by never naming a batch file with the same name as a Novell DOS command, whether external or internal.

Understanding the AUTOEXEC.BAT File

AUTOEXEC.BAT is the batch file for use in booting your system. The file name AUTOEXEC.BAT is reserved for this specific use. The purpose of this file is to automatically load and/or execute any desired programs and set the environment each time you boot your computer. AUTOEXEC.BAT must be located in the root directory of the boot drive. The Novell DOS Install utility created this file for you if your system did not already have one, or modified the file if it did. All batch commands discussed in this chapter are valid for the AUTOEXEC.BAT file.

The AUTOEXEC.BAT file is usually where you set the system search path, load the cache, set environment variables, load Task Manager, and perhaps load the Desktop Server and network client drivers. The following is a simple AUTOEXEC.BAT file created by the Novell DOS 7 Install/Setup utility:

```
@ECHO Off
PATH C:\NWDOS
VERIFY OFF
PROMPT [Novell DOS] $P$G
SET TEMP=C:\TEMP
IF NOT DIREXIST %TEMP% MD %TEMP%
SET NWDOSCFG=C:\NWDOS
```

Creating Batch Files

You have two methods for writing batch files. The first is to use EDIT, a word processing program in ASCII or text mode, or another text editor. (In the instructions for creating the sample batch files in this chapter, it is assumed that you are using EDIT to create and edit batch files.) For information on EDIT, see Chapter 17, "Using the Novell DOS Text Editor."

The second method is to write the batch file directly in the Novell DOS environment with the COPY command. Follow these steps to use COPY CON (COPY to the *con*sole) to create a batch file:

1. At the Novell DOS prompt, enter the following command:

   ```
   COPY CON filename.BAT
   ```

Tip
Batch file names follow the usual DOS-naming conventions but must have the BAT extension.

   Substitute your batch file name, such as SAMPLE, for *filename*. Novell DOS moves the cursor to the beginning of the next line and awaits your next command.

2. Type the series of commands you want the batch file to execute, with one command per line. This batch file displays a directory in two different formats. Press Enter at the end of each line except the last line. For SAMPLE.BAT, type these command lines:

   ```
   CLS
   DIR/P
   PAUSE
   DIR/W
   ```

3. At the end of the last command entered, press either the F6 key or Ctrl-Z. In either case, Novell DOS enters a ^Z on-screen. Press Enter, and DOS writes the new file to disk with the message 1 file(s) copied.

You have just created a batch file. The process is rather simple, but nonetheless it works. This method of writing batch files is useful only for short files. You have no way to fix a typing mistake or change a command without completely rewriting the file after you have pressed Enter. The EDIT program is more useful because it enables you to edit the contents of your batch file.

Caution

When you use COPY CON to create a batch file, be careful not to name the batch file with the name of an existing file in the same directory. If you do, you overwrite the existing file, and Novell DOS does not issue a warning.

You can enter up to 128 characters in one batch file command or statement. Only one command or statement can be on each line.

Running Batch Files

After you have created your batch file, running it is simple. At the Novell DOS prompt, just type the name of the batch file and press Enter. You don't need to type the period and the file extension (.BAT) unless you have used the same name for your batch file as that of a COM or EXE file.

Note

Create a subdirectory on your system (MD \BAT) and copy all your batch files into that subdirectory (COPY *.BAT C:\BAT). Make C:\BAT the first directory in your PATH statement (PATH C:\BAT;...). Then, to execute any batch file, you just have to type its name from any directory in your system.

Using Batch Commands

You can use several types of statements and commands in batch files. This section explores the following batch commands and processes:

- Chaining from one batch file to another

- Running a batch file from another batch file (CALL)

- Commands that stop batch files (PAUSE and EXIT)

- Commands that pertain to screen operations (@, ECHO, and REM)

- Commands used for the processing of parameters (%1 through %9, SHIFT, and FOR)

- Commands that customize batch execution, depending on the results of conditional testing (IF, ERRORLEVEL, EXIST, DIREXIST, and ENVIRONMENT)

- Commands for branching with batch files (:*label*, GOTO, GOSUB with RETURN, CHOICE, and SWITCH)

Novell DOS gives you two ways to run another batch file from inside your batch file: direct changing of execution to the second batch file (*chaining*) and running the second batch file as a subroutine (*calling* the second batch file). The following sections describe these options. Later sections describe the other batch commands.

Chaining to a Second Batch File

When you want to run a second batch file from within your batch file, just type the name of the batch file as a command in your batch file. When Novell DOS executes your first batch file and reaches the command that names the second batch file, the operating system immediately chains to the other file and starts executing that set of instructions.

No other command or statement is required. Keep in mind, however, that when Novell DOS passes control to the other file, execution does not return to the original batch file.

Caution

Because DOS doesn't return to the first batch file after chaining to the second, any commands in the first file that come after the chaining instruction are not executed.

To see how the chaining process works, use EDIT to prepare two sample batch files. To begin the first file, enter the following at the Novell DOS prompt:

```
EDIT CHAIN.BAT
```

EDIT asks whether you want to create CHAIN.BAT. Press Enter or choose OK. In the editing screen, type the following, remembering to press Enter after each line:

```
@ECHO OFF
ECHO This is the First Batch File
SECOND
ECHO This is the First Batch File again!
```

The first line is discussed in the section "Suppressing the Display of Text (@) " later in this chapter.

Save this first batch file by choosing File Save. Choose File Open, type **SECOND.BAT** as the name for the file you want to open, and choose OK or press Enter when EDIT asks whether you want to create the SECOND.BAT file. In the editing screen, type the following:

```
@ECHO OFF
ECHO This is the Second Batch File
```

Save this second batch file and exit to DOS. Now execute the first batch file by typing **CHAIN** and pressing Enter at the DOS prompt. Figure 19.1 shows Novell DOS's response.

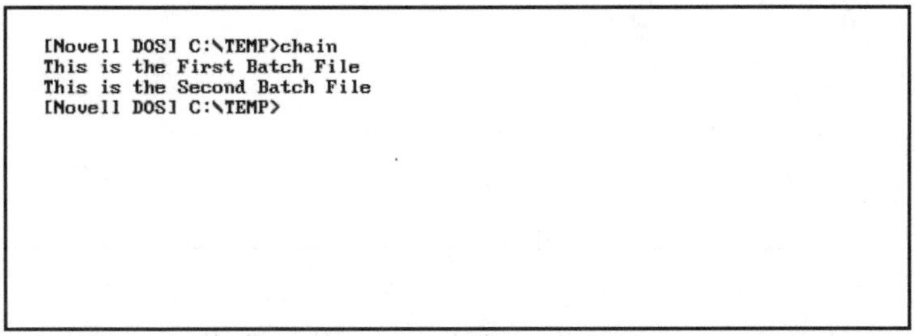

Fig. 19.1
Chaining to a second batch file.

Calling a Second Batch File (CALL)

You can also run a second batch file from within your batch file and have control passed back to the original file. The second batch file acts as a *subroutine*.

To see how this process works, use EDIT to create a new sample batch file named BCALL.BAT. (CALL.BAT does not work because CALL is an internal batch file command.) Type the following command to create the file in EDIT:

```
EDIT BCALL.BAT
```

Press Enter or choose OK to create the new file. At the editing screen, choose File Read to load CHAIN.BAT. When EDIT asks for the name of the file to read in, type **CHAIN.BAT** and press Enter. This step saves you from having to type the entire text of this batch file. The text of CHAIN.BAT appears in the editing screen as the following:

```
@ECHO OFF
ECHO This is the First Batch File
SECOND
ECHO This is the First Batch File again!
```

Move the cursor to the third line, on the S of SECOND. Press Ins (if necessary) to display the ins. indicator on the status line at the bottom right of the screen. Type **CALL** and press the space bar. Then save the new batch file and return to DOS.

Now execute the second batch file by entering **BCALL** at the DOS prompt. Figure 19.2 shows Novell DOS's response.

Fig. 19.2
Calling a second
batch file.

```
[Novell DOS] C:\TEMP>BCALL
This is the First Batch File
This is the Second Batch File
This is the First Batch File again!
[Novell DOS] C:\TEMP>
```

Notice the difference between figures 19.1 and 19.2. In the first instance, when you just chained to the second batch file, the message This is the First Batch File again! did not appear. In the second instance, when you called the second batch file as a subroutine, the message appeared, indicating that execution returned to the first file.

Interrupting Batch Files

A batch file can end in one of three ways. First, it can run out of commands to execute. Second, you can interrupt a batch file by pressing Ctrl-C. Third, you can program the file to use the EXIT command. See the section "Exiting the Batch File (EXIT)" later in this chapter.

If you interrupt a batch file by pressing Ctrl-C, Novell DOS stops the execution and displays the question Halt Batch Process (Y/N) ? Press Y or N. If you answer yes to halt the batch process, Novell DOS returns to the DOS prompt. If you answer no, indicating that you want to continue the batch process, Novell DOS continues executing the instructions from where you interrupted the batch file.

You can also tell a batch file to interrupt its processing and wait for you to signal it to continue. To do so, you use the PAUSE command, as described in the next section.

Pausing the Batch File for a Response (PAUSE)

At times in the execution of batch files, you need to have Novell DOS halt the operation of the batch commands until some event has occurred. In a batch file controlling the copying of documents to a floppy disk, for example, you want execution to stop until the floppy disk has been inserted in the drive. PAUSE enables you to pause execution in this manner.

To see how PAUSE works, create a sample batch file to copy word processing documents to a floppy disk. First enter the following command at the Novell DOS prompt:

```
EDIT DOCCOPY.BAT
```

Tell EDIT that you want to create a new file. In the editing screen, type these lines:

```
@ECHO OFF
CLS
ECHO Insert the Backup Floppy Disk and
PAUSE
COPY C:\WPDOCS\*.DOC A:
```

Then save the batch file and return to DOS by choosing File Exit. At the Novell DOS prompt, execute the batch file by typing **DOCCOPY** and pressing Enter. As shown in figure 19.3, Novell DOS displays the first request you entered in the batch file (Insert the Backup Floppy Disk and) and then displays the message from PAUSE (Strike a key when ready...), asking you to tell the system when the disk has been inserted.

Fig. 19.3
Using the PAUSE
command to halt
execution.

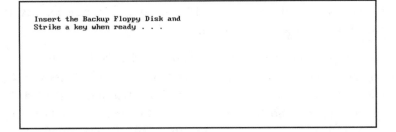

```
    Insert the Backup Floppy Disk and
    Strike a key when ready . . .
```

You can use Ctrl-C to cancel a batch file when the execution of the batch
commands has been halted and is waiting for the PAUSE response.

Exiting the Batch File (EXIT)

EXIT causes termination of the batch file execution and an immediate
return to Novell DOS without any message. You don't need to use the EXIT
command as the last statement in your batch file. That step would be redundant because the batch file terminates there anyway.

> **Note**
>
> You can enter your own pause message by putting the complete text of the message
> on lines starting with ECHO, and adding the redirection sign and the NUL device
> name (> NUL) to your PAUSE command. This step prevents the display of the stan-
> dard PAUSE message on-screen. It is sent to the NUL device. Here is an example:
>
> ```
> ECHO Insert the Backup Floppy Disk and
> ECHO Press Enter when ready
> PAUSE >NUL
> ```

In a batch file that you have divided into sections, you can use the EXIT command to end batch processing at any one of the sections without processing
any other section. This is most often used with batch file labels. See a discussion on labels in the section "Using Labels" later in this chapter.

Controlling the Screen

You have several ways to control the screen's appearance during batch file
processing. You can use the symbol @ to suppress the display of individual
lines, ECHO to control the display of all lines or to include instructions to the
operator, or REM to add comments and remarks for your own use.

Suppressing the Display of Text (@). Use the symbol @ to indicate
to Novell DOS that the command which follows on the same line is not to
appear on-screen. The @ is often combined with the ECHO command to

prevent that command and all the commands that follow in the file from being displayed, as in this example:

```
@ECHO OFF
```

> **Caution**
>
> Although batch file commands can be indented, the @ symbol cannot be indented. If @ is not in the first position on its line, Novell DOS displays the command as it executes and continues to execute the rest of the batch file normally.

Displaying and Suppressing Screen Prompts (ECHO)

The ECHO command, which you can also use at the Novell DOS prompt, has two options: ON (the default) and OFF. You use ECHO to tell Novell DOS to display or not to display on-screen the commands that follow it. For example, if you create a custom menu, you want the users to see the menu only, not the underlying commands that create the menu.

You can use ECHO also to display comments and messages during the execution of your batch files. This feature makes the on-screen appearance of your batch files more professional and can help the user know what to do. Even if you have specified ECHO OFF, you can send a message to the operator, as in this command line:

```
ECHO This function prepares new floppy disks for use.
```

To avoid an error message, make sure that you enter a space between the ECHO command and the start of the message.

Combine ECHO with @ as a prefix to keep the ECHO command itself from displaying on your video monitor unless ECHO is off.

Annotating the Batch File with Remarks (REM). You can use the REM command to add remarks or comments to your batch files. This feature is especially helpful in a complicated batch file. When you want to modify the file at a future date, the remark may remind you why you did what you did in the batch file—and maybe when you did it. The REM command can be used also to disable commands that are not operating correctly. This is a rudimentary form of program debugging. The following lines show one way you might want to use REM:

Tip
To display a blank line on-screen in your batch file, add a period to the end of the ECHO command, without including any spaces (ECHO.).

```
@ECHO OFF
REM   Created by me, 12/01/93
REM   Floppy formats presume 1.2M A: and 1.44M B: drives
```

> **Caution**
>
> If you have inserted remarks in your batch file but have not specified ECHO OFF, your comments appear on-screen.

Processing Parameters

The passing of parameters to batch files is how Novell DOS gives you the ability to affect the execution of your batch processing. You can create a general-use batch file and make it specific each time you use it. You can use up to nine parameters, can use SHIFT to provide a parameter loop and access more than nine, and can use FOR to perform multiple executions of a command sequence. The next sections describe all these options.

Passing Parameters (%1 through %9). You can pass up to nine parameters to your batch file. With parameters, you can change the operation of the file and its instructions. Thus, you can create a batch file for general use and, depending on the parameter, execute the file for a specific use. The parameters take the variable names %1 through %9.

When you have a batch file statement referencing the parameters %1 through %9 and you type the name of the batch file as a command for execution, the parameters that follow the command replace the %1..%9 variables.

> **Note**
>
> The parameter %0 always stands for the batch file's name entered at the command line, including the BAT extension if typed as part of the command.

At the Novell DOS prompt, you enter the name of the batch file followed by up to nine elements in the command tail. Novell DOS executes the batch file and replaces the %1 parameter with the first parameter passed, the %2 parameter with the second parameter passed, and so on.

To help you understand the concept of parameter passing, note the following batch files, named MCD.BAT and MOVE.BAT:

MCD.BAT	MOVE.BAT
@ECHO OFF	@ECHO OFF
MD %1	COPY %1 %2
CD %1	DEL %1
^Z	^Z

The first example, MCD.BAT, creates a directory and then makes it the current directory. For example, if you enter **MCD BLORP** on the command line, the batch file creates and changes to a directory named \BLORP. The second example, MOVE.BAT, "moves" files by copying them to a destination and then deleting the source files. For instance, if you enter **MOVE A:*.* B:**, the batch file copies all files from drive A to drive B and then deletes all files from drive A.

Note

Although Novell DOS usually does not care whether you type a command in upper- or lowercase letters, parameters are passed to batch files without translation.

Note

When testing for the existence of parameters, place quotation marks before and after the parameter number. This step ensures that you get the response you are expecting. An incorrect or missing parameter generates an error message or may cause execution to fail.

Passing Multiple Parameters (SHIFT). You can process batch file parameters in another way, by providing a loop for parameters and allowing more than nine in the command tail. In fact, you can enter as many as you can fit within the command-line limit of 128 characters.

With the SHIFT command, only one parameter is processed at a time. Then the parameter list is shifted to the left one place, the command is reexecuted for the second parameter, and so on. Executed parameters are lost. To see exactly how the SHIFT command works, create a batch file called TEST.BAT with the following statements:

```
@ECHO OFF
ECHO This batch file demonstrates the use of SHIFT
:START
IF "%1"=="" GOTO DONE
ECHO %1
SHIFT
GOTO START
:DONE
```

After you type these lines, save and exit. At the Novell DOS prompt, enter the following command:

```
TEST 1 2 3 4 5 6 7 8 9 10 11 12
```

Novell DOS responds with the display shown in figure 19.4. Notice that each parameter is executed only when it is shifted to become %1. Notice also that when all parameters which have been typed into the command tail have been processed, the conditional statement checking for their existence changes the operational flow to the ending label (:DONE).

Fig. 19.4
Using SHIFT to loop through more than nine parameters.

```
[Novell DOS] C:\TEMP>TEST 1 2 3 4 5 6 7 8 9 10 11 12
This batch file demonstrates the use of SHIFT
1
2
3
4
5
6
7
8
9
10
11
12
[Novell DOS] C:\TEMP>
```

> **Note**
>
> You must include both :START and :DONE labels when using SHIFT. :START marks the beginning of the command loop, and :DONE ends the execution when all the entered parameters have been processed. Of course, you can name the labels anything you want, but there must be at least two labels.

Now create another batch file called WPCOPY.BAT. Enter the following statements:

```
@ECHO OFF
CLS
ECHO This procedure copies various document types to backup
ECHO floppy disks.
ECHO.
:START
IF "%1"=="" GOTO DONE
ECHO Insert the Backup Floppy Disk for %1 files and
PAUSE
COPY C:\WPDOCS\*.%1 A:
SHIFT
GOTO START
:DONE
ECHO Done.
```

After you type these lines, save the file and exit. At the Novell DOS prompt, execute the batch file by entering the following command:

    WPCOPY PRO LTR MEM FAX

The use of SHIFT in this batch file enables you to easily copy proposals (PRO), letters (LTR), memos (MEM), and faxes (FAX) onto individual backup floppy disks. Novell DOS responds with the display shown in figure 19.5.

```
[Novell DOS] C:\TEMP>WPCOPY PRO LTR MEM FAX
This procedure copies various document types to backup
floppy disks.

Insert the Backup Floppy Disk for PRO files and
Strike a key when ready . . .
```

Fig. 19.5
Using the SHIFT command to perform multiple copies.

Repeating a Command (FOR). FOR is an iterative processor for batch files, which means that with one statement in your batch file, you can execute a command several times. The FOR statement is made up of three parts. The first part specifies a variable to be used for processing the second part, which is the list of items to be processed. The third part is the command to be executed on the list.

The variable can be any alphanumeric character preceded by two percent signs (%%). However, when you use this statement from the Novell DOS prompt rather than from inside a batch file, use only one percent sign in front of the variable character.

The target list on which the command is to be executed can be made up of specific file names, file names with wild-card characters (* or ?), or even disk drive letters. Or you simply can use parameters for the list (%1 through %9) and then specify the file names on the command line when running the batch file. The list can be as long as you can fit within the maximum line length of 128 characters. The list must be surrounded by parentheses.

Caution

If you decide to write your batch file with the FOR statement and the %1 through %9 parameter variables, use an alphabetic character rather than a numeric character as the loop variable in the command statement to avoid confusion.

The third part of the FOR statement consists of DO plus the command to be executed followed by the variable target of the command. Make sure that the variable is specified with two percent signs.

You can specify only one command in your FOR statement. You cannot nest FOR statements, which means that you cannot run FOR statements within FOR statements. However, you can call another batch file that contains multiple commands.

For a demonstration of FOR, write another batch file to copy word processing documents to a floppy disk. Call this file ONECOPY.BAT. Type the following lines:

```
@ECHO OFF
CLS
ECHO This function copies word processing documents to a
ECHO floppy disk in drive A:
PAUSE
FOR %%A IN (PRO LTR MEM FAX) DO COPY C:\WPDOCS\*.%%A A:
```

After typing these lines, save and exit to Novell DOS.

When you type the name of this batch file at the command line, Novell DOS executes the FOR statement four times. At each repetition, the variable %%A in the COPY command is substituted with each of the list items (PRO, LTR, MEM, and FAX).

Using Conditional Processing

One of the most important features that you can use in a batch file is the verification of conditions. Depending on a variety of circumstances, you can change the execution of the batch file and control branching. (For more on branching, see the section "Branching in Batch Files" later in this chapter.)

All conditional processing starts with the use of IF. You use IF to determine whether certain conditions are met—whether a passed parameter provides a match, a file or directory exists, the execution of a command causes a DOS ERRORLEVEL number to be set, or an environment variable has been established.

In this section, you learn how to implement conditional processing with IF, ERRORLEVEL, EXIST, and DIREXIST.

Note

Double equal signs are required in all conditional statements.

Checking for True or False Conditions (IF and IF NOT). The sample batch file you created previously in this chapter, WPCOPY.BAT, uses this line to check whether the parameter %1 exists:

```
IF "%1"=="" GOTO DONE
```

If the condition is true—in other words, if "%1" is empty ("")—Novell DOS is instructed to jump to the label :DONE. If the condition is not met, the parameter %1 is not empty and execution continues with the statement on the next line.

The use of the quotation marks is for readability in the batch file. You should use them especially when testing for the absence of a parameter; otherwise, the test fails.

You can also make the condition negative by using IF NOT. By verifying that parameters are passed in the first place when the command is typed, you can bypass the display of an error message. You can change the sample batch file to read as follows:

```
@ECHO OFF
CLS
ECHO This procedure copies various document types to backup
ECHO floppy disks.
ECHO.
IF NOT "%1"=="" GOTO START
ECHO.
ECHO Specify document file types on the command line.
ECHO.
ECHO USAGE: WPCOPY xxx xxx xxx xxx <Enter>
ECHO where xxx stands for PRO MEM DOC FAX or other
ECHO document type.
ECHO.
EXIT
:START
IF "%1"=="" GOTO DONE
ECHO Insert the Backup Floppy Disk for %1 files and
PAUSE
COPY C:\WPDOCS\*.%1 A:
SHIFT
GOTO START
:DONE
ECHO Done.
```

Using Environment Variables

Another feature of Novell DOS's batch file processing is the capability to access the Novell DOS environment. *Environment variables* are settings made in the AUTOEXEC.BAT file, in the CONFIG.SYS file, or at the command line. They are a source of information that can be accessed to indicate various things. Some application programs require environment variables to know where to access their auxiliary files.

All Novell/DR operating systems automatically set several environment variables when they boot. In the case of Novell DOS 7, OS is set as NWDOS, and VER is set as 7. The system search PATH is another environment variable, as is COMSPEC, which tells Novell DOS and any inquiring application software where to find COMMAND.COM. Table 19.1 lists the standard environment variables used by Novell DOS 7.

Table 19.1 Standard Environment Variables

Variable	Meaning
APPEND	The list of the current APPEND search path
COMSPEC	The location and name of the command processor (COMMAND.COM)
NWDOSCFG	The location of Novell DOS configuration files
OS	The name of the operating system in use
PATH	The list of the current search path
PEXEC	The name of the command file to be executed by the PROMPT command
PROMPT	The current design of the system prompt
TEMP	The name of the subdirectory to hold temporary files
VER	The version of the operating system in use

You can have your batch file access the variables listed in this table. You must place a percent sign on both sides of the variable.

> **Note**
>
> When testing for an environment variable, place quotation marks before the leading percent sign and after the ending percent sign. Note an example:
>
> ```
> IF "%TEMP%"=="C:\TEMP" CD \TEMP
> ```
>
> The percent signs are required. The quotation marks are not necessary, but they do ensure the proper error processing if the test fails.

The programmers at the NDSG division of Novell implemented additional environment variables in Novell DOS 7 called *system information variables*. They are quite similar to standard environment variables but are set by the operating system when it is booted. You are free, however, to use them as you like in your batch files. Table 19.2 lists the system information variables.

Table 19.2 System Information Variables	
Variable	**Meaning**
AM_PM	A.M. or P.M. (time of day)
Day	Day number of the month, 01 to 31
Day_of_Week	Sunday to Saturday
Hour	Hour of day, 1 to 12
NDay_of_Week	Day number of the week, 1 = Sunday
Month	Number of month, 01 to 12
Month_name	January to December
Year	1993, 1994, and so on
Short_Year	93, 94, and so on
Hour24	Hour of day (military time), 00 to 23
Minute	00 to 59
Second	00 to 59
Greeting_time	Morning, afternoon, or evening
Errorlevel	Error return code
OS	Operating system in use
OS_Version	Operating system version number

If you have the NetWare drivers and shell loaded, the following system information variables are also available:

P_Station   Physical station number on the network

Station   Station number on the network

Testing for Error Codes (IF ERRORLEVEL). Many application programs and utilities provide a code to Novell DOS when they finish executing. This code usually indicates whether the program functioned properly. Possible codes range from 0 to 255. The operating system receives these codes but does not display them. You can access these codes in your batch file by testing for the ERRORLEVEL.

An ERRORLEVEL of 0 usually means that no error occurred, or it could mean that no error code was passed to the operating system. In some circumstances, ERRORLEVEL codes are used specifically as flags or indicators for something else. You can use third-party utilities to generate an ERRORLEVEL code so that you can create a menu in a batch file. Depending on the ERRORLEVEL code issued, another batch file is run to execute an application. In Novell DOS, you can use the CHOICE and SWITCH commands to do the same thing. See the following sections on how to use CHOICE and SWITCH.

> **Note**
>
> No standard list of ERRORLEVEL codes exists. The code passed depends on the program returning the code and may vary from program to program. Check the manual for the specific program to see whether ERRORLEVEL codes are passed and, if so, their meanings.

To test for the ERRORLEVEL, you cannot just request that the code be provided. You must test for its existence. In testing for the validity of an ERRORLEVEL code, you must test the higher level first. All ERRORLEVEL codes of a number equal to or lower than the returned code test as true.

Thus, if the ERRORLEVEL passed is 255, all codes from 255 to 0 test as true. If the ERRORLEVEL passed is 4, codes above 4 test as false, but codes from 0 to 4 test as true.

> **Note**
>
> Novell DOS stores only one ERRORLEVEL at a time. The completion of the next pro-
> gram changes any previous code passed.

The following is a sample batch file that demonstrates the use of IF (the batch
file also includes the CHOICE command, which is explained later in this
chapter):

```
:START
@ECHO OFF
CLS
ECHO SDEFRAG
ECHO DISKOPT
CHOICE /C:SDQ Select an option or Q to quit
IF ERRORLEVEL 3 GOTO BAILOUT
IF ERRORLEVEL 2 GOTO OPT
IF ERRORLEVEL 1 GOTO FRAG
:FRAG
SDEFREG D:
CLS
GOTO START
:OPT
DISKOPT C:
CLS
GOTO START
:BAILOUT
CLS
```

Testing for Files (IF EXIST and IF NOT EXIST). You can make your batch
file test for the existence of a file in the default directory or in the directory
specified with the file name. Make sure that you test for files with the complete file name, including the file extension if one exists. You can also specify
wild cards in the file specification. The negative version, IF NOT EXIST, tests
for the absence of the named file.

To see how IF EXIST and IF NOT EXIST work, again edit the sample batch
file WPCOPY.BAT, which you previously created in this chapter, so that it
includes the following line immediately above the message line telling you
to insert the correct floppy disk:

```
IF NOT EXIST C:\WPCOPY\ *.%1 GOTO NEXT
```

Then add the label :NEXT in a line just above the SHIFT command. After these changes, the batch file should read as follows:

```
@ECHO OFF
CLS
ECHO This procedure copies various document types to backup
ECHO floppy disks.
ECHO.
IF NOT "%1"=="" GOTO START
ECHO.
ECHO Specify document file types on the command line.
ECHO.
ECHO USAGE: WPCOPY xxx xxx xxx xxx <Enter>
ECHO where xxx stands for PRO MEM DOC FAX or other
ECHO document type.
ECHO.
EXIT
:START
IF "%1"=="" GOTO DONE
IF NOT EXIST C:\WPCOPY\*.%1 GOTO NEXT
ECHO Insert the Backup Floppy Disk for %1 files and
PAUSE
COPY C:\WPDOCS\*.%1 A:
:NEXT
SHIFT
GOTO START
:DONE
ECHO Done.
```

Save the batch file and exit to Novell DOS. Now run the batch file and specify files that do not exist. For example, enter this command:

```
WPCOPY XXX YYY ZZZ
```

The batch file returns to the Novell DOS prompt without any prompting for disks to be inserted, because the file checked and saw that no files with the extensions XXX, YYY, or ZZZ exist.

In this example, you checked for the nonexistence of files, using the * wildcard character. Many batch files check for the existence of a specific file to see whether the current disk or directory is the correct one.

Checking for Directories (IF DIREXIST and IF NOT DIREXIST). Corresponding to the file-checker command IF EXIST is the IF DIREXIST command, which checks for the existence of a directory. This command often is used in batch files that install software. To avoid error messages, you can find out whether the directory exists, and if not, create one, as in this example:

```
IF NOT DIREXIST C:\WPDOCS MD C:\WPDOCS
```

Branching in Batch Files

When you enter commands individually at the Novell DOS prompt, you make adjustments according to the results of your instructions and the returns that Novell DOS makes. In a batch file, you have no way to make such judgments and the required adjustments. Thus, Novell DOS provides another tool.

You can plan for possible obstacles in completing the tasks you want your batch files to do. Set up multiple sections of your batch files, and start each section with an appropriate label. Then check for the possible error conditions that might occur and, depending on the result of the test, jump to the section to handle the obstacle.

Each referenced section of a batch file starts with a *label*, which must begin with a colon. The commands to move execution to the lines following the label are GOTO, GOSUB with RETURN, and SWITCH.

Using Labels. Labels delineate the various sections of your batch files. Several of the batch files you have already written contain labels. Look, for example, at WPCOPY.BAT.

Always signal a label by the use of the colon when it indicates the beginning of the referenced section. Never use the colon in the referencing statement (GOTO, GOSUB, or SWITCH).

> **Note**
>
> Labels never appear on-screen, even with ECHO ON, and never execute. They are not commands but act only as place markers.

Look at part of the batch file WPCOPY.BAT listed next. The file contains three labels: :START, :NEXT, and :DONE. The second, third, and ninth lines of the file include the commands for execution to jump to the appropriate labeled sections:

```
:START
IF "%1"=="" GOTO DONE
IF NOT EXIST C:\WPCOPY\*.%1 GOTO NEXT
ECHO Insert the Backup Floppy Disk for %1 files and
PAUSE
COPY C:\WPDOCS\*.%1 A:
:NEXT
SHIFT
GOTO START
:DONE
ECHO Done.
```

You can continue batch operations at another section by jumping there with GOTO; temporarily pass operation to another section with GOSUB and then return to the line following the jump command; or select a section of the batch file to execute, depending on the answer to a parameter, a condition, or the SWITCH command. Each of these commands works with a referenced label.

Jumping to Another Part of the Batch File (GOTO). Use GOTO to jump unconditionally and directly to another section of the batch file. You tell Novell DOS to continue to process the commands after the label referenced in the GOTO statement. Do not use the colon in the GOTO statement. WPCOPY.BAT provides a typical example of the GOTO command:

```
IF "%1"=="" GOTO DONE
```

In this case, if no parameter is passed from the user, the batch file jumps to the DONE section of the batch file and executes the commands in that section.

Executing a Subroutine (GOSUB and RETURN). With this pair of commands, you have the ability to jump to what is called a subroutine. A *subroutine* is a self-contained set of commands that you can execute more than once in a batch file without having to include the commands more than once. Whenever your program flow needs to have these commands processed, use a GOSUB to the label defined for the subroutine. When Novell DOS reaches the RETURN command, control returns to the line immediately following the GOSUB command.

Using EDIT, edit the batch file WPCOPY.BAT, changing the file to use a subroutine with GOSUB and RETURN with the following instructions. Line 17 of the batch file currently looks like this:

```
IF NOT EXIST C:\WPCOPY\*.%1 GOTO NEXT
```

Delete the word NOT in this command, and change GOTO NEXT to GOSUB PROCESS. Then insert the following two lines after line 17, as lines 18 and 19:

```
GOTO START
:PROCESS
```

Notice that a line following SHIFT also includes a GOTO START label; delete that line. Delete the line with the :NEXT label and insert the following line after the SHIFT command:

```
RETURN
```

WPCOPY.BAT now should look like this:

```
@ECHO OFF
CLS
ECHO This procedure copies various document types to backup
ECHO floppy disks.
ECHO.
IF NOT "%1"=="" GOTO START
ECHO.
ECHO Specify document file types on the command line.
ECHO.
ECHO USAGE: WPCOPY xxx xxx xxx xxx <Enter>
ECHO where xxx stands for PRO MEM DOC MEM FAX or other
ECHO document type.
ECHO.
EXIT
:START
IF "%1"=="" GOTO DONE
IF EXIST C:\WPCOPY\*.%1 GOSUB PROCESS
GOTO START
:PROCESS
ECHO Insert the Backup Floppy Disk for %1 files and
PAUSE
COPY C:\WPDOCS\*.%1 A:
SHIFT
RETURN
:DONE
ECHO Done.
```

This batch file now uses a subroutine with the flow controlled by the GOSUB and RETURN commands.

To execute this batch file, enter **WPCOPY** followed by one or more document file extensions, such as PRO, MEM, DOC, and FAX used in the example. Novell DOS executes the batch commands and jumps to the :START label when the test for the first parameter in line 6 returns a TRUE value.

In the section with the label :START, the first statement checks to see whether the first parameter exists. If not, execution jumps to the label :DONE. Otherwise, line 17 of the batch file is processed. The statement first checks for the existence of the specified document type and, if true, calls the subroutine :PROCESS, using the GOSUB command.

The section labeled :PROCESS performs the actual copy command. When all documents with the particular extension type are copied, the parameters are shifted to the left one position, and the RETURN command returns to line 18, the line after the calling subroutine. This line sends execution back to the :START label. Thus, the :PROCESS subroutine is executed as many times as necessary to fulfill all the document types passed as parameters to the batch file.

Creating a Simple Menu (SWITCH). Novell DOS gives you the ability to build menus in batch files. The command that provides this feature is SWITCH. In your batch file, you can provide the operator with a selection of as many as nine choices. You begin by preparing a section referenced by a label for each menu selection. Each section must start with the normal label structure and end with a RETURN, EXIT, or GOTO command. Immediately following the menu of choices, you enter the SWITCH command followed by each of the labels for the menu selections, separated by commas and spaces.

> **Note**
>
> SWITCH responds only to the number keys, from 1 to 9, on the standard keyboard or the numeric keypad. Therefore, the maximum number of labels handled in a SWITCH command is nine.

To see how the SWITCH command works, create a sample batch file called SMENU.BAT with the following commands (replace the italicized lines with the commands to run your particular applications):

```
@ECHO OFF
CLS
ECHO.
ECHO     *** SELECTION OF APPLICATIONS ***
ECHO.
ECHO     1.  Accounting System
ECHO     2.  Inventory System
ECHO     3.  Electronic Spreadsheet
ECHO     4.  Word Processing
ECHO     5.  Format Disks
ECHO     6.  Back Up Data Files
ECHO.
ECHO          Make your selection (1-6)
SWITCH ACCTG, INVENT, SPRDSHT, WORDPROC, FORMAT, BACKUP EXIT
:ACCTG
<include here the lines for running your accounting system>
RETURN
:INVENT
<include here the lines for running your inventory system>
```

```
RETURN
:SPRDSHT
<include here the lines for running your spreadsheet program>
RETURN
:WORDPROC
<include here the lines for running your word processing
program>
RETURN
:FORMAT
<include here the lines for running the format utility>
RETURN
:BACKUP
<include here the lines for running the backup utility>
RETURN
```

When you run the batch file, just press the number of the menu selection you want.

Creating a Menu with More than Nine Selections (CHOICE). Novell DOS gives you the ability to build menus in batch files with an alternative to SWITCH. This method uses the external DOS file CHOICE.COM. In your batch file, you can provide the operator with a selection of as many as 62 choices. You begin this process by preparing a section referenced by a label for each menu selection. Each section must start with the normal label structure and end with either an EXIT command or a GOTO command. Immediately following the menu of choices, enter the CHOICE command followed by /C: with each of the selection keys for the menu items, and then any switches or command options allowed, followed by the prompt text for the selection.

Here is an example of the command format for CHOICE:

```
CHOICE /C:YNE Yes, No, or Exit
```

After you issue this command, Novell DOS displays the following:

```
Yes, No, or Exit [Y,N,E]
```

After the operator answers this query, Novell DOS returns an ERRORLEVEL (see the earlier section "Testing for Error Codes" for more on ERRORLEVEL). The first supplied key for a possible response, if pressed, returns ERRORLEVEL 1; the second supplied key, if pressed, returns ERRORLEVEL 2; and so on. If the user interrupts the batch file by pressing Ctrl-C, ERRORLEVEL 0 is returned. If the user presses an invalid key—a key that is not in the list after /C:—ERRORLEVEL 255 is returned.

Tip

Remember that some applications are launched from batch files. To run them from MENU.BAT, you need to use the CALL command.

As mentioned, several options or switches may be used with the CHOICE command. These are described in table 19.3.

Table 19.3 CHOICE Command Switches	
Switch	**Use**
/C:*xxx*	Lists allowable selection keys. You can use numbers and alphabetic keys. If you omit this list, [Y,N] is displayed by default.
/N	Disables the display of the choice keys within the brackets and the question mark after the prompt text.
/S	Indicates that the choice keys must be upper- or lower-case as displayed.
/T:*x,nn*	Tells CHOICE to default to response *x* if no key is pressed within *nn* seconds.
/? or /H	When following the CHOICE command, displays the help screen for CHOICE.

To see how the CHOICE command works, create another sample batch file that provides a menu, using the name CMENU.BAT and the following statements (again, adjust the menu and the commands to run your particular applications):

```
:START
@ECHO OFF
CLS
ECHO.
ECHO      *** SELECTION OF APPLICATIONS ***
ECHO.
ECHO    A   Accounting System
ECHO    I   Inventory System
ECHO    S   Electronic Spreadsheet
ECHO    W   Word Processing
ECHO    F   Format Disks
ECHO    B   Back Up Data Files
ECHO.
CHOICE /C:AISWFBQ Make your selection or Q to Quit /T:A,15
IF ERRORLEVEL 255 GOTO START
IF ERRORLEVEL 7 EXIT
IF ERRORLEVEL 6 GOTO BACKUP
IF ERRORLEVEL 5 GOTO FORMAT
IF ERRORLEVEL 4 GOTO WORDPROC
IF ERRORLEVEL 3 GOTO SPRDSHT
IF ERRORLEVEL 2 GOTO INVENT
IF ERRORLEVEL 1 GOTO ACCTG
GOTO START
:ACCTG
```

```
<include here the lines for running your accounting system>
GOTO START
:INVENT
<include here the lines for running your inventory system>
GOTO START
:SPRDSHT
<include here the lines for running your spreadsheet program>
GOTO START
:WORDPROC
<include here the lines for running your word processing
program>
GOTO START
:FORMAT
<include here the lines for running the format utility>
GOTO START
:BACKUP
<include here the lines for running the backup utility>
GOTO START
```

When you run the batch file, just press the letter of the menu selection you want. If you don't make a selection within 15 seconds, the batch file automatically executes the commands to run your accounting system.

From Here...

Batch files are text files created to program repetitive tasks for your computer so that you do not have to type a string of individual commands every time you want to perform certain tasks. Batch files can be simple or complex and can change their operation, depending on conditions tested within the batch file or on parameters you enter when you run the batch file. For more information on batch files, refer to the following chapters:

- Chapter 17, "Using the Novell DOS Text Editor," shows you how to use the editor to create and modify batch files.

- Chapter 18, "Configuring Your System," discusses the AUTOEXEC.BAT file as it relates to system configuration.

- Chapter 20, "Using HISTORY and DOSKEY," shows you how to use DOSKEY in place of some batch files.

Chapter 20

Using HISTORY and DOSKEY

As you become more proficient in the use of your computer, you will look for more and more ways to save time. Two features provided by Novell DOS 7 that directly help you do this are HISTORY and DOSKEY. These features work together and were designed to help you make the best use of your time. You use HISTORY to have the operating system remember the commands typed at the DOS prompt. Of all the commands you enter, you probably use the same 10 to 15 (with minor variations) 90 percent of the time. Would it not be helpful to have the operating system remember those for you so that all you had to do was press a key or two to recall them? That is what HISTORY provides.

DOSKEY takes automation a step further by enabling you to save a whole set of instructions as one command or macro. Unlike batch files, DOSKEY macros are faster because they reside in memory; the operating system does not need to go to disk to read the commands. The only drawback to this approach is that you lose those macros when you turn off your computer. In this chapter, you learn how to save those macros and reinstall them whenever you need them. Remember, the more work the computer does for you, the more work you can do on the computer.

The following topics are covered in this chapter:

■ How to use HISTORY to recall the commands you enter with just a few keystrokes

■ How to use DOSKEY to create macros (memory-resident batch files) to speed up your work

Configuring the HISTORY Utility

You may not realize the benefits of the HISTORY feature unless you have used it. Do you have some data files in a directory that take about 30 characters to get to? All you have to do is type the command once and then, if you have to get there again, simply recall the command you typed the first time. Do you set macros with DOSKEY? (If you do not yet know how, you learn later in this chapter.) HISTORY is perfect for resetting and editing DOSKEY macros. In fact, the practical uses of HISTORY are limitless.

You can set up your computer to use HISTORY two ways—from the Novell DOS 7 Setup utility or by manually editing your CONFIG.SYS file. In this section, you learn how to use both methods.

Configuring HISTORY with the Setup Utility

To use the Setup utility to install and configure HISTORY, you must first get to a command prompt and enter **SETUP**. The first screen shows a list of configuration features you can access from the Setup utility (see fig. 20.1). Select the DOS System & Memory Management option.

Fig. 20.1
Setup's main menu.

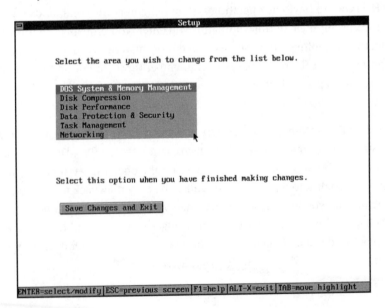

The next screen lists options for configuring your system (see fig. 20.2). There are options regarding memory management, language and keyboard, and so on. The menu option that you want right now is DOS System Parameters. Highlight it and press Enter.

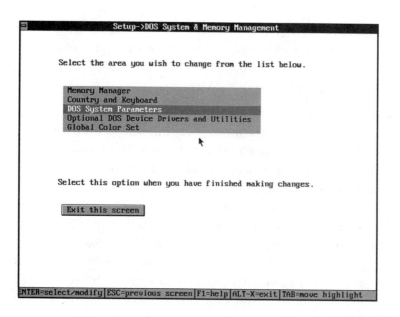

Fig. 20.2
The system
configuration
menu.

VII

Advanced Techniques

The next screen displays a menu for configuring different aspects of your computer's environment settings (see fig. 20.3). The third option is Configure Keyboard HISTORY. Select this option and press Enter.

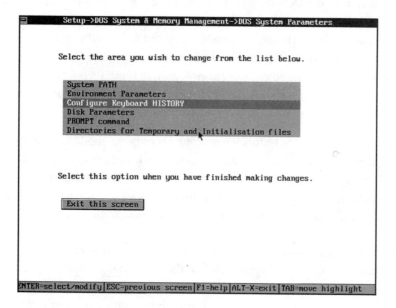

Fig. 20.3
The DOS system
parameters menu.

You may have encountered the next Setup screen, shown in figure 20.4, when you first installed your system. You use three fields here to install and configure HISTORY:

- *HISTORY*. This option controls whether you want to turn HISTORY on. Because you will be using it extensively, set this option to ON. Move the highlight to the HISTORY line; then press the space bar or the Enter key to toggle between ON and OFF.

- *Buffer Size*. Old commands that you type are saved in an area of memory called the *HISTORY buffer*. In this field, you configure the size of that buffer. The default value is 512 bytes. This is enough memory space to hold from 10 to 20 commands, depending on the length of the commands you are typing. If you use DOSKEY to create many macros and you find yourself editing these macros regularly, you may want to increase this value. Of course, the more you increase it, the more memory is used. But if your DOS program files are loaded into the high memory area, the HISTORY buffer will load high as well. How much memory you need depends on how you use HISTORY. You will not know until you spend some time with it, so just leave this value at 512 bytes for now.

- *Insert Mode*. This option controls whether the computer is in Insert mode when it boots. If Insert mode is turned on, when you edit commands at the DOS prompt, the original text makes room for new characters you type. If Insert mode is turned off, new characters that you type overwrite the old commands. You can tell whether you are in Insert mode by the way the cursor looks at the command prompt. If Insert mode is turned on, the cursor is a small blinking block that covers part of the characters it is over. If Insert mode is off, the cursor is a blinking line that rests beneath the characters.

  What you choose in this screen controls only the mode your computer is in when it boots. You can still toggle back and forth at the command line by pressing the Ins key on your keyboard. When you configure HISTORY, Setup will turn this setting to ON by default; leave the setting as is, or change it to OFF. You can always change your mind later.

After you have everything configured the way you want it, choose the Accept the Above and Continue button, choose the Save Changes and Exit button to save changes you made while in Setup, and choose the Restart Operating System option as you exit. When your system boots back up, you will have a line in your CONFIG.SYS file similar to this:

```
HISTORY=ON,512,OFF
```

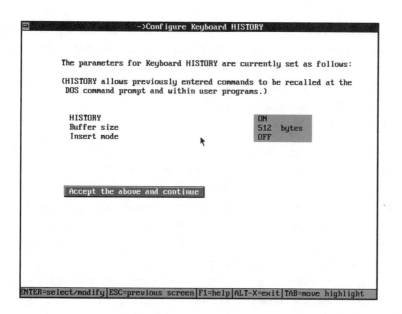

Fig. 20.4
Configuring
Keyboard
HISTORY.

Your entry may be different, based on the options you chose in the Setup
utility.

Running HISTORY from CONFIG.SYS

You may want to edit your CONFIG.SYS file manually to set up the HISTORY
command or modify the HISTORY settings. The options for the HISTORY
command when run from CONFIG.SYS are the same as those specified with
the Setup utility. The complete syntax for the HISTORY command in
CONFIG.SYS is

```
HISTORY=ON[,nnnn,ON | OFF] | OFF
```

You can set HISTORY to either ON or OFF. If you set it to ON, you must
specify the number of bytes (*nnnn*) to reserve in memory for the buffer. Valid
values range from 128 to 4096 bytes of memory. Finally, you must specify
whether you want Insert mode turned ON or OFF.

Using the HISTORY Utility

If HISTORY is turned on, you will be able to use the up- and down-arrow keys
to scroll through commands you have previously entered at the DOS prompt.
Depending on the size of the buffer you configured when you installed HIS-
TORY and how long the commands are, you will be able to recall the last 10
or more lines of text you entered at the command line.

For example, if you change to the \NWDOS directory by entering **CD** **\NWDOS**, and then do a directory listing of the contents by entering **DIR**, you can use the arrow keys to recall those commands without typing them again. If you press the up-arrow key once, DIR appears again next to the prompt because that was the last command entered. If you press the up-arrow key again, CD \NWDOS appears because that was the command you entered before DIR.

When you cycle to a command you want to repeat, simply press Enter, and it will be the same as if you had retyped the command. Often, though, you will want to edit previously typed commands so that you can do something else. In that case, use the left- and right-arrow keys to move through the command. Use the Del and Backspace keys to erase characters; enter new characters by simply typing them. When the line reads the way you want it, press the Enter key. For example, to change a directory such as \NWCLIENT, press the up-arrow key twice so that CD\NWDOS appears. Use the Del key to delete the characters DOS, type **CLIENT**, and press Enter to change to the \NWCLIENT directory.

Using DOSKEY to Create Macros

One of the greatest uses you will get from the HISTORY capability of Novell DOS 7 is to edit DOSKEY macros. A *macro* is a series of commands executed in sequence. Macros are similar to batch files, with a few exceptions:

- Batch files are files saved to disk. Macros are stored in memory, which means that they cease to exist when the power to the system is shut down. In fact, they use the memory allocated for HISTORY buffers.

- Batch files can be very long; their commands can take up several lines. The maximum length for macros is 127 characters because that is the maximum length for a command at the DOS prompt. When you reach the end of the 127-character limit, the computer will alert you with a beep.

- Batch files let you add labels and GOTO, GOSUB, and RETURN statements to configure the execution order of the commands. These options are not available for macros. You can, however, call from within a macro a batch file that has these options. In a batch file, each line represents a different command; in macros, commands are separated by a $t (or $T).

You can use replacement variables in both batch files and macros. (A replacement variable is what you assign the command to.) In batch files, replacement variables can be %1 through %9. In macros, $1 through $9 are valid replacement variables. For a detailed discussion of batch files, refer to Chapter 19, "Using Batch Files."

You do not have to set up anything in order for DOSKEY to work; you simply begin using the command. Creating a macro is easy. Just use the following syntax:

```
DOSKEY macroname=command $t command $t command...
```

A macro can be one command in length, or as many as you like (as long as the total line does not exceed 127 characters).

Understanding How DOSKEY Macros Work

You can use macros to do anything you would normally do with commands. If you usually copy new documents from a directory called \DOCS to a floppy disk and then delete all documents with the OLD extension, you probably type something like this:

```
CD \DOCS
COPY *.NEW A:
DEL *.OLD
CD\
```

Instead, you can create a macro to do all these steps for you. Enter the following:

```
DOSKEY TEST=CD \DOCS $t COPY *.NEW A: $t DEL *.OLD $t CD \
```

From now on, to accomplish those steps, you just type the macro's name—in this case, TEST.

As mentioned, you can use replacement variables in macros. For example, you could specify which files to copy to the floppy disk and which files to delete by adding replacement variables. Edit the macro to look like this:

```
DOSKEY TEST2=CD \DOCS $t COPY $1 A: $t DEL $2 $T CD\
```

Now, to obtain the same results, you would enter **TEST2 *.NEW *.OLD** at the command line. Of course, you could substitute *.NEW and *.OLD with whatever file specifications you choose.

If you ever need to stop a macro from executing its current command, press Ctrl-C. If you need to stop the macro from executing every command, keep pressing Ctrl-C until you have stopped every command in the macro.

Using DOSKEY Command Options

DOSKEY has several options that let you configure its features. To clear the memory of all defined macros, enter the following command:

```
DOSKEY /REINSTALL
```

To get a list of all macros currently defined, enter this command:

```
DOSKEY /MACROS
```

You can also use the /MACROS switch to create a batch file that will load the macros for you the next time you boot. Because macros are lost when the computer is turned off, typing the same macros can become tedious. You can enter the macros in your AUTOEXEC.BAT file, or you can create a batch file specifically to load the macros. To do this, you first enter all the macros you want to save. Then you enter a list of the macros, but redirect the output to a batch file:

```
DOSKEY /MACROS > MACROS.BAT
```

Now you can use the batch file to save your macros. When you reboot your computer, they are still saved.

Here is another command switch for DOSKEY:

```
DOSKEY /HISTORY
```

This switch lists the contents of the HISTORY buffer. If you are wondering how many commands are actually saved, or if you want to review a command you typed earlier, you can use this switch to list all the commands in the buffer.

To change the HISTORY buffer size, use the following command:

```
DOSKEY /BUFSIZE=size
```

Of course, when you reboot your computer, the size you specified in CONFIG.SYS will take precedence. If you find yourself changing the size of the buffer often, it is best to reconfigure the HISTORY statement in your CONFIG.SYS file.

Normally, you would change the Insert mode while editing the command line with the Ins key. Press it once to turn Insert on; press it again to turn Insert off. But if you ever want to change the mode from a batch file or macro, it is possible with DOSKEY. To turn Insert mode on, enter the following command:

```
DOSKEY /INSERT
```

To turn Insert mode off, enter this command:

```
DOSKEY /OVERSTRIKE
```

From Here...

Two features of Novell DOS 7 that you will want to become familiar with are HISTORY and DOSKEY. Because there are probably only 10 to 15 commands that make up 90 percent of the work you do, the HISTORY feature has great benefits. But it really shines when you add its complement, DOSKEY. DOSKEY enables you to save a series of commands to a macro. Macros execute these commands in a defined order and work much like batch files.

For more information about batch files and Novell 7 DOS commands, refer to the following chapters:

■ Chapter 19, "Using Batch Files," teaches you what a batch file is, how to create a batch file, and the special commands you use with batch files.

■ The Command Reference in Part X contains the Novell DOS 7 commands, arranged in alphabetical order and shown with syntax, applicable rules, and examples where needed.

Part VIII

Maximizing Your System

Continue

Change destination drive(s) and directorie

Root directory

Subdirectory Subdirectory

Subdirectory Subdirectory Subdirectory Subdirectory

Subdirectory Subdirectory

Subdirectory

Continue

File – c:\spam.txt
Create new file ?

< OK >   Cancel

nfigure Task Manager

it this screen

System & Memory Managemen
Disk Compression
Disk Performance
Data Protection & Security
Task Management
Networking

acks

Sectors

25-Pin DB-25 Male

25-pin serial connector,
usually COM2

Change destination drive(s) and directorie

Chapter 21

Multitasking and Task Switching

One of the goals that computer hardware and software manufacturers have strived to attain is to make their products work more like you do. Novell DOS 7 has moved one step closer to this goal by enabling your computer to perform more than one task at a time. This seemingly small feat of magic is accomplished by a component of Novell DOS called the Task Manager. With Task Manager, you can load up to 20 tasks in your computer and move easily from one to another. Task Manager even permits you to configure your computer to run all 20 tasks concurrently. Using the options made available by Novell DOS and Task Manager, you can markedly increase your productivity. With a little practice, you will find that using Task Manager is a simple process that quickly becomes an extension of the way you work. The use of Task Manager is entirely optional, so you may choose to use it or leave it out of your system.

This chapter covers the following topics:

- The concepts of task switching and multitasking

- Configuring Task Manager

- Using Task Manager

- Troubleshooting Task Manager

Understanding Task Switching

Novell DOS supports two types of task management. One type is called *task switching*. The task-switching mode of Novell DOS permits you to load many programs at the same time, yet only one is active. You access other tasks by switching among them. When you switch tasks, Novell DOS suspends the application you were working with and activates the task you want to work with. During the time a task is inactive, it may remain in your computer's memory or be copied to a *swap file* on disk if available memory is insufficient. This process is called *swapping out*. When you return to the suspended application, the computer copies the application back into your computer's memory. This process is called *swapping in*. The swapping process is very fast, and the time to activate a swapped-out task is very short.

Understanding Multitasking

If your computer has at least an 80386 microprocessor installed, you can make use of the multitasking mode of Task Manager. As with the task-switching mode, Novell DOS is able to run up to 20 applications in your computer at one time, but unlike task switching, multitasking mode enables all the applications to run at the same time—each one competing for a slice of your computer's resources. The Novell DOS Task Manager software ensures that one task does not interfere with any other task. You still can work with only a single task at a time, but the tasks you are not working with continue to run. The multitasking mode of Task Manager does not use a swap file, so all tasks must fit into the available memory installed in your computer; however, moving between tasks is nearly instantaneous.

Configuring Task Manager

Before you can make use of Task Manager, you must let Novell DOS know how you want to use it. This is the configuration process, performed with the Novell DOS Setup program. To begin this process, open Setup from the DOS prompt and select Task Management (see fig. 21.1).

After you select Task Management, you must decide whether you want to use Task Manager in multitasking mode or task-switching mode. You can choose task switching or multitasking, or neither. In fact, you can remove Task Manager capabilities from your system by turning off both multitasking and task switching. The selection buttons are toggles; to select or deselect the option, move the cursor to the option and press either the space bar or the Enter key.

The options are exclusive—you may select only one. If you have selected to use task switching or multitasking, choose Configure Task Manager and press Enter. The screen appears as shown in figure 21.2.

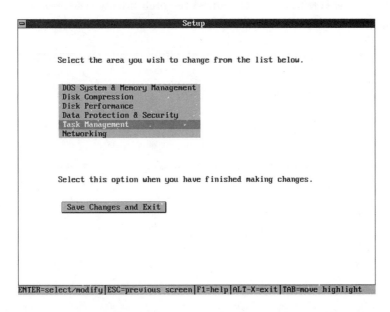

Fig. 21.1
Selecting Task Management from the Setup menu.

Fig. 21.2
The Task Management screen.

Configuring for Multitasking

The configuration options for multitasking and task switching differ slightly. The items that you need for configuring the multitasking mode of Task Manager are covered first. Figure 21.3 shows the multitasking version of the Task Manager configuration screen.

Fig. 21.3
Options for multitasking.

The first option is the designation for Shift Key(s). Task Manager maintains a pop-up type interface that you can activate from the keyboard at any time. You signal your wish to communicate with Task Manager by pressing a combination of primary keys. The default combination is Ctrl-Esc. You can change the keys to some other combination by moving the cursor to the Shift Key(s) option and pressing Enter. Or you can click the down-arrow icon at the right; a drop-down list displays available key combinations (see fig. 21.4). Choose a key combination that isn't used by an application you want to multitask.

As you can see, quite a collection of single- and multiple-key combinations are available. After you have made your selection, press Enter to confirm your choice. Next, you need to select the second key of the key combination to access the Task Manager menu. If you would like to change the default value, move to the Menu 'Hot Key' option and press Enter or click the down-arrow icon. You can use the Esc key, the Enter key, or the space bar. Select the key you want. Then press Enter or click your selection with the mouse. You return to the previous menu.

Fig. 21.4
A list of available
primary keys.

The Foreground/Background Ratio option controls how Novell DOS divides
the power of your computer system among the various tasks you may have
loaded. The default value of 5 indicates that the process currently connected
to your computer's console—that is, the task in the foreground—gets five
times as much of your computer's time as all the programs in the background. The assumption is that you want the application you are currently
working with to be the most responsive, so it requires the most processor
power. You can change this value to a larger or smaller number by moving
the cursor to this item, pressing Enter, and changing it. The higher the value,
the more time the foreground task gets at the expense of the background
tasks. To make all tasks equal in priority so that each gets the same share of
processor time, use the value 1.

Notice in figure 21.3 that Global Drives & Paths is selected. This is the default
setting for this option, which means that changes to network mappings will
be visible in all tasks.

Some applications, if given the opportunity, attempt to allocate all the
memory and resources that are available in your computer. The Novell DOS
Task Manager permits you to place a cap on the amount of extended memory
allocated by an individual task. If you want to limit the amount of memory
any single process can have, move the cursor to the Maximum Extended/
Expanded Memory per Task option and press Enter. Don't enter more
memory than you have in your computer, of course.

VIII

Maximizing Your System

The dialog box shown in figure 21.5 appears, and you can enter the value you want. You will need to experiment with this value if your applications use their normal operations. Start with the default value that Novell DOS determines and decrease it if your applications produce memory error messages. When you are finished, press Enter to return to the Task Management screen.

Fig. 21.5
Maximum
memory
per task.

Configuring for Task Switching

If you do not have a need for multitasking but want to have multiple applications loaded at the same time, you should elect to use the task-switching capability of Task Manager. You can make this choice by selecting Load Task-Switching Software from the Task Management screen. Then move on to configure the task-switching mode of Task Manager by choosing Configure Task Manager and pressing Enter.

The next menu, shown in figure 21.6, is slightly different from the one displayed when multitasking was selected. The Shift Key(s) and Menu 'Hot Key' options are the same and are configured exactly like the multitasking selections. The Foreground/Background Ratio, however, has been replaced by Directory for Swap File.

A task switcher does not divide computer time among loaded processes; thus, the task in the foreground always gets 100 percent of your computer's capabilities. To ensure that as much of your system's resources are available as possible, Task Manager swaps out inactive tasks. The default location on your hard disk to be used for this swapping procedure is C:\NWDOS\TMP. If you would like to use a different location, such as a virtual (or RAM) disk, you should enter the full path name of the new area in the Directory for Swap File entry box. You may also instruct Task Manager to use extended memory (XMS), expanded memory (EMS), or a combination of the two for task switching, in addition to using the hard disk. The use of XMS or EMS decreases the time to switch between tasks. If you have sufficient XMS memory and want to use it for task switching, select that option. XMS is preferable to EMS, as EMS may be a bit slower in operation.

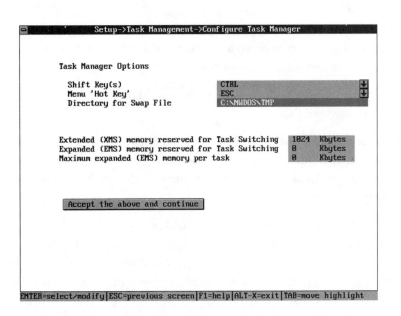

Fig. 21.6
Options for task
switching.

A dialog box like that in figure 21.7 appears, and you have the opportunity to enter a new value. You may also enter zero to disable the use of XMS memory for task switching. Again, you will need to experiment with the value if your applications use extended or expanded memory for their normal operations. Start with the default value that Novell DOS determines and decrease it if your applications produce memory error messages.

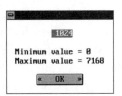

Fig. 21.7
Maximum
memory
per task.

You can use EMS memory instead of, or in addition to, XMS memory. Select the option Expanded (EMS) Memory Reserved for Task Switching and press Enter. A dialog box appears in which you can enter the amount of memory to be used. Again, you may disable the use of EMS memory for task switching by entering a value of zero.

You can elect to restrict the amount of expanded memory (EMS) that may be allocated to any individual task. If you want to restrict EMS memory usage, select Maximum Expanded (EMS) Memory per Task and press Enter. To disable the use of EMS memory by the application, enter a value of zero here.

Note that you can use EMS memory only if the memory manager for your computer has been configured to support it. For information on Novell DOS memory management tools, see Chapter 22, "Optimizing Memory."

To leave Setup, choose Accept the Above and Continue, Exit This Screen, and Save Changes and Exit.

Understanding Changes Made to System Files by Setup

When you configure Task Manager, the Setup program makes changes to several system files to reflect your configuration choices. This section briefly describes the files that are modified.

CONFIG.SYS. Setup manipulates the /MULTI switch on the DEVICE=EMM386.SYS entry in CONFIG.SYS. Setup makes this modification only if you are running on an 80386 or higher microprocessor, you have elected to use multitasking, and you did not previously elect to load the DPMI software when configuring the memory manager. The /MULTI switch enables the use of the DOS protected mode interface (DPMI), which is required by the multitasking mode of Task Manager. Chapter 18, "Configuring Your System," provides information on using the CONFIG.SYS file.

AUTOEXEC.BAT. When Task Manager is configured with the Setup program, it is configured to load from within the AUTOEXEC.BAT file. Setup adds the TASKMGR command to AUTOEXEC.BAT, along with the appropriate switches that determine its initial operating characteristics. If you edit AUTOEXEC.BAT, you must be sure that anything which affects the global environment of your computer system—such as print spoolers, network software, mouse drivers, MEMMAX, sound card drivers, and disk cache programs—must be loaded before the execution of the TASKMGR command. Anything that is executed after TASKMGR is loaded applies only to the environment of a single Task Manager task. The SHARE command must be run before Task Manager.

TASKMGR.INI. The TASKMGR.INI file is usually located in the directory C:\NWDOS. This file contains parameters that define the overall operating characteristics of Task Manager. You can look at this file with the TYPE command from the DOS prompt or with the text editor (EDIT). Although experienced users can edit this file, it typically is modified by the Setup program.

Loading Task Manager

The preferred way to load Task Manager is to allow Setup to insert the appropriate statements in the AUTOEXEC.BAT file. You can initially execute Task Manager from the DOS prompt. You load Task Manager in multitasking mode with the TASKMGR command, using this format:

```
TASKMGR /? | H /D=dirpath /E=nnnn /F /M /S V:1 /X=nnnn
```

If you are already in multitasking mode, you can repeat the command, adding the /S switch, to switch to task-switching mode.

You use /? or /H to request help on the use of the TASKMGR command. If you use these switches, all others that you enter from the DOS prompt are ignored. You can also use DOSBook for more information on the TASKMGR command.

The /D=*dirpath* switch indicates the directory where the swap file may be found. By default, it is C:\NWDOS\TMP.

/E or /E=*nnnn* tells Task Manager how much extended memory should be used to swap tasks. If you use /E=0, no extended memory is allocated. If you do not specify a value or if the value you indicate is more than the amount of extended memory available, all available extended memory is used.

The /F switch causes any fonts and code pages that are loaded or modified by an application to be saved across a task switch. This allows each application to use its own screen fonts and code pages.

The /M switch enables you to use the number keys at the top of your keyboard to switch tasks, rather than those on the numeric keypad.

/S tells Novell DOS to use task-switching mode or to replace the multitasking mode of Task Manager with the task-switching mode.

/V or /V:1 provides support for task switching with a VGA display. This switch forces the VGA display to emulate an EGA display in certain ways. You should try /V:1 first, and if problems arise, use /V. Use this switch only to correct problems with the display.

/X or /X=*nnnn* is similar to the /E switch but references expanded memory (EMS). You specify a value the same way as for /E.

Understanding the Task Manager Environment

When you first start DOS, certain values and conditions define the system *environment*. The settings for various system components are stored here. Some of these items are your current search path, the settings for the DOS prompt, the last drive accessible by DOS, the operating system version number, and more. Either you or your applications may add items to the environment. Applications can add items as a reminder of where files may be found or of the default values to be used for certain functions. You can view the contents of your environment by entering **SET** at the DOS prompt and pressing Enter. Figure 21.8 shows a sample of the output of the SET command.

Fig. 21.8
Displaying the environment with the SET command.

```
[Novell DOS] C:\>set
COMSPEC=C:\COMMAND.COM
OS=NWDOS
VER=7
PATH=C:\NWDOS;C:\;C:\NWCLIENT;C:\TSE;C:\WINDOWS
PROMPT=[Novell DOS] $P$G
NWDOSCFG=C:\NWDOS
NWLANGUAGE=ENGLISH
TEMP=C:\temp

[Novell DOS] C:\>
```

When Task Manager is active on your system, multiple environments are created: a *global environment* that includes the environment before Task Manager is loaded, and a *local environment* created for each task as Task Manager starts it.

Using Task Manager

Task Manager is always accessible from your keyboard. You can activate the Task Manager menu by pressing the Shift/Hot Key(s) combination, usually Ctrl-Esc, at any time. From this menu, you can add a new task, remove a task, copy data between tasks when you are using the task switcher, and obtain information about Task Manager. You can also perform some of these operations from the DOS prompt, using the TASKMGR command.

Adding New Tasks

To add a task to the task list, you activate the menu with the Shift/Hot Key(s) combination. The menu shown in figure 21.9 appears on-screen. To add a task, press Insert. A new local environment is created, and the DOS prompt appears. Now you may start your application. You can verify that you have in fact started a new task by displaying the Task Manager menu again and looking in the task list. The new task appears in this list.

 NovDOS7 C:\>

Fig. 21.9
The task list after a second task has been added.

If you want to add a new task from the DOS prompt, you can use the TASKMGR command. Here is the command syntax:

```
TASKMGR /C command parameters
```

You can verify that the application started by activating the Task Manager menu and looking at the task list. The new task appears in this list. You can add up to 20 tasks by using the Task Manager menu or typing the command at the DOS prompt. The actual number of tasks that you can start depends on the memory and disk resources of your computer.

Switching between Tasks

Switching between loaded tasks is a simple matter. You can call up the Task Manager menu, choose the task you want, and press Enter. Or you can press Ctrl and the number key on your numeric keypad that represents the task you want to switch to. You obtain the task number from the task list. If you have redefined the Shift key in Setup to be a key other than Ctrl, you must use that key with the number key to switch tasks. Also, if you are not using an Enhanced keyboard or you started Task Manager manually with the /M switch, you should use the number keys at the top of your keyboard.

Removing Tasks

To remove or delete a task, simply open the Task Manager menu and choose the task. To terminate the task, press the Del key. If an application is running, a dialog box will prompt for confirmation.

VIII

Maximizing Your System

To remove a task at the DOS prompt, enter the following:

```
TASKMGR  /K:nn
```

The value for *nn* is the task number of the task to be deleted. Obtain this number from the task list.

Rebooting under Task Manager

If you attempt to reboot your computer by pressing Ctrl-Alt-Del while Task Manager is active, the task that you are currently working with is terminated. If there are no more active tasks, you are asked whether you want to terminate Task Manager. If you answer yes to terminate and then issue a Ctrl-Alt-Del, your computer reboots.

Removing Task Manager

To remove Task Manager, bring up the Task Manager menu and delete all the tasks until the following message appears:

```
Remove TaskMgr
Are you sure (Y/N)?
```

If you press Y, Task Manager is removed from the system. With any other reply, Task Manager remains active with one active task. You can also remove Task Manager by using Ctrl-Alt-Del until the Remove Task Manager message appears, but this approach is not recommended.

Troubleshooting Task Manager

Although Task Manager is simple to use and reliable in operation, some circumstances may present problems for the user, as discussed in this section.

Task-Switching Key Conflicts

Sometimes the task-switching key combination may conflict with keys used by the applications you are running. If you have this problem, you can use the Setup program to change the keys that Task Manager uses to switch tasks. Try different combinations until the conflict is resolved.

Running Windows as a Task

You can run Microsoft Windows 3.1 as a task under Task Manager in standard mode. You use the WIN /S command to invoke Windows in this manner. Task Manager does not support Windows in enhanced mode, nor does it support versions other than 3.1. To run in enhanced mode or other versions of Windows, terminate Task Manager first.

The Ctrl-Esc key combination is used by Windows, so the Task Manager must be configured with another combination.

If Windows is running as a task, you will not be able to switch to other tasks. Windows must be terminated in order to resume task switching.

Exceeding the Open File Limit

You will probably find that, while multitasking, you can exceed the number of permissible open files because of the number of applications that are running concurrently. To correct this problem, use Setup or EDIT to increase the value of the FILES= statement in the CONFIG.SYS file.

Running Multiple Copies of the Same Application

If you attempt to run more than one copy of an application that was not designed to run in a multiuser or multitasking environment, you may get error messages, the application may terminate abnormally, or you may get unexpected results or corrupted files. You can circumvent some of these problems by duplicating your data files into separate subdirectories and by marking shared files as read-only with the ATTRIB +R command. Be sure to set any overlay files for the application to read-only to prevent file-sharing conflicts when the overlay is loaded.

Note

Some applications have license restrictions that prohibit the concurrent execution of the same copy of the software. Check your license agreement before running multiple copies of the same application.

File-Sharing Conflicts

If you have applications that report a file-sharing conflict, you may have to reorder how you run the applications. In other words, try to avoid loading applications that open the same files in read/write mode. If your applications can be configured for use across a network, try configuring them for this type of operation. In addition, you may be able to use the ATTRIB +R command to set as read-only any shared file used only for lookup. Setting a file as read-only may relieve the file-sharing problem. Your applications naturally cannot write to the file while the read-only attribute is set.

From Here...

Task Manager is a powerful addition to the Novell DOS operating system. The Task Manager pop-up interface makes multitasking and task switching easy and enables you to effectively increase the usability and availability of your computer system. You may want to turn next to the following chapters:

- Chapter 18, "Configuring Your System," helps you work with the powerful and flexible CONFIG.SYS file, which is used by DOS to configure itself for your computer, its resources, and the features you want to use.

- Chapter 22, "Optimizing Memory," covers the memory management features of Novell DOS.

Chapter 22

Optimizing Memory

The personal computer, like many other things in this world, has continued to evolve. Software packages have become increasingly more sophisticated as developers strive to produce applications that enable us to explore our own creativity. The price of this increased functionality has been the growing demand for system resources such as microprocessor power and memory. With Novell DOS MEMMAX, you can optimize the use of your computer's memory. This chapter shows you how.

This chapter covers the following topics:

- Novell DOS system memory

- Novell DOS memory management tools

- Configuring and fine-tuning your system's memory

The History of Memory

The era of IBM-compatible personal computing began with the introduction of the 8086 microprocessor by Intel. This new device was a significant step forward from the 8-bit Intel-compatible chips that were being used. This new processor offered up to 1 million bytes of memory (see fig. 22.1), a major increase from the 64,000 bytes previously available. Intel attempted to maintain an architectural similarity between this new processor and its 8-bit predecessors, a practice that continues today with the company's newest devices. IBM designed its personal computer to use the new Intel chip, but limited the usable memory to 640,000 bytes—assuming that this amount would more than satisfy the needs of personal computer users for some time to come. It was logical for IBM to have made this decision; after all, their mainframe systems of the period did not often exceed 8 million bytes of memory. Little did Intel and IBM know the impact that this new processor and the machine built around it would have on the computing industry!

Fig. 22.1
The 8086 memory map.

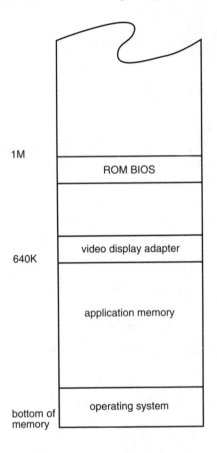

It did not take very long for software developers to find themselves cramped by the memory restrictions imposed by the personal computer's architecture. To circumvent these problems, designers became intent on providing creative hardware and software solutions to give applications access to ever-increasing amounts of memory.

Intel was not resting on its laurels either. The next-generation 80286 microprocessors provided access to even greater amounts of memory. Unfortunately, accessing this memory was complicated by the chip design and required sophisticated programming techniques. With the introduction of the 80386 processor, Intel at last provided a mechanism where reliable access to vast amounts of memory could be easily and reliably obtained. Gone was the requirement to install special hardware devices to access additional memory. You could now purchase a simple software driver and additional memory chips to provide the working room that the new applications required. The software driver and the new microprocessor chips would work together to simulate the old hardware devices used previously, thereby preserving compatibility with software written to the old standards.

Now Novell DOS has all but eliminated the need to purchase additional software or hardware to perform sophisticated memory management. With MEMMAX, a standard component of Novell DOS, you can make use of almost any microprocessor or additional hardware that you might have in order to effectively gain access to greater amounts of application memory.

The Novell DOS Memory System

Novell DOS provides you with the tools necessary to manage all the memory in your computer and provides the mechanisms with which to access it. Memory is classified by Novell DOS into several types: lower (conventional), upper, high, expanded, and extended (see fig. 22.2). Not all types of memory may be present in a computer. The MEM command will display the types of memory available in your computer.

Lower or Conventional Memory

In Novell DOS, the term *lower memory* describes the first 640K of program memory or RAM installed in your computer. If you have less than this amount installed, lower memory describes only the amount of RAM you actually have in your computer. Novell DOS further divides this area into two subareas. The first part, or *bottom of memory*, is typically where the operating system is loaded, as well as some device drivers. The rest is where Novell DOS loads your applications. Lower memory is sometimes called *conventional memory*. All microprocessors have some lower memory, and it has become rare to find one that has less than the full 640,000 bytes.

Upper Memory

Any memory installed in your computer that is addressed from the 640K line upward to 1M is defined as *upper memory*. Computers that are most likely to have memory installed in this area are based on an 80286, 80386, 80486, Pentium, or compatible microprocessor. Some 8086-based computers may have special hardware that adds upper memory. Unlike lower memory, the upper memory address range, or *memory space*, generally has gaps in it. This is due to the presence of software to operate devices such as video adapters, some disk controller cards, and network cards. You may have other specialty cards installed in your computer that occupy upper memory addresses. Taking an inventory of these items and recording their memory address settings are good ideas. If upper memory is available, Novell DOS may be able to make use of it by loading parts of the operating system, buffers, and device drivers into this area. The more software installed in upper memory, the less lower memory is required; thus, more lower memory area is available for use by your applications.

Fig. 22.2
The Novell DOS
memory map.

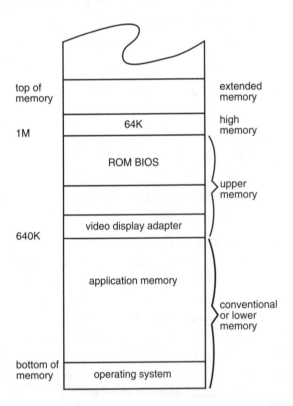

Note

In computer terminology, the abbreviations K and M stand for kilobyte and megabyte, respectively. The values they represent are rounded up to the nearest power of 16, so 1K is 1,024 bytes, and 1M is 1,024 kilobytes.

Extended Memory

Some computers have the capability to address memory in excess of 1M. This area is called *extended memory*. If you have more than 1M of memory installed and your computer contains an 80286, 80386, 80486, Pentium, or compatible microprocessor, you can use extended memory. Your processor must enter a special mode of operation that enables the features needed to address this memory. In its normal or real mode, your computer functions just like an 8086 processor and is limited to addressing only 1M. Protected mode, available on an 80286, 80386, 80486, Pentium, or compatible processor, provides addressing above 1M. The environment created by protected mode is not entirely compatible with the 8086 environment expected by most applications, so certain programs are written specifically to use this mode of operation. Novell DOS allows most applications that conform to the DOS Protected Mode Interface (DPMI) to access the protected mode of these advanced processors and to directly address any installed extended memory. Virtual 8086 mode allows your computer to function as though it contains multiple 8086 processors. This mode, available only on an 80386, 80486, Pentium, or compatible processor, appears as a real mode to your applications but provides many protected mode features, such as memory paging. Special software provided with Novell DOS can make use of extended memory to provide such features as high-speed memory disks (VDISK.SYS) and disk caches (NWCACHE.EXE).

High Memory

If your computer is equipped with extended memory, you have the option of using *high memory*. High memory occupies 64,000 bytes of memory at the bottom of extended memory. In some cases, you can run some of your applications, device drivers, or TSRs (terminate-and-stay-resident programs) in this area. Novell DOS can also be instructed to relocate part of its kernel to this area, instead of or in combination with upper memory, providing you with a larger lower memory area.

XMS

The *extended memory specification*, or XMS, is a relatively new standard developed by Lotus, Intel, and Microsoft to take advantage of the capabilities of an 80286, 80386, 80486, Pentium, or compatible microprocessor. The new XMS is a software driver that can provide your XMS-aware 8086 applications with a standard mechanism for accessing all the new memory addressing modes introduced by these processors. With XMS, you can gain access to as much as

16 million bytes of installed memory in an 80286 processor. On an 80386 or higher processor, you can access up to 1 billion bytes of installed memory.

Expanded Memory

The *expanded memory specification*, or EMS, was developed by Lotus, Intel, and Microsoft to provide a standard method that your applications may use to gain access of up to 32M of memory. EMS memory, or LIM as it is sometimes called, maps up to four 16K blocks of memory into an otherwise empty area that exists in the high memory area. An 8086 microprocessor requires that this memory be resident on a special adapter called an EMS or LIM card. 80386 or higher processors can simulate the capabilities of these cards by using the addressing capabilities of virtual 8086 mode. Only a maximum of 64K of EMS memory is accessible to you at any given time. To access memory that is not in the current EMS memory page, one of the existing 16K page frames must be exchanged for a new one. This technique is sometimes called *paging* or *bank switching* and requires the use of a special device driver called an *enhanced memory manager*. EMS memory cards are typically supplied with a driver that is specific to the card. Novell DOS supplies device drivers that work with the enhanced memory mode of the 80386 or higher processors and IBM XMA cards. Although EMS is a mature standard that has been abandoned by some developers, much software has been developed over the years that can make use of the additional storage provided with EMS. As with XMS, your application must be aware of the EMS installed in your computer and have routines included in it to access the additional expanded memory.

DOS Protected Mode Services (DPMS)

DOS Protected Mode Services (DPMS) is a standard supported by Novell. This standard provides access to extended memory for programs and data that know how to use it. Several components of Novell DOS make use of DPMS to reduce their consumption of lower memory. Examples are Stacker, DELWATCH, NWCACHE, and the Desktop Server.

Novell DOS Memory Management Tools (MEMMAX)

The memory management tools provided with your copy of Novell DOS are collectively known as MEMMAX. This section describes the tools built into MEMMAX.

Drivers

A *device driver* is software that manages memory and controls the operation of a physical or virtual device. This software is customized to the particular hardware environment in which it operates.

EMM386.SYS. EMM386.SYS is an extended memory manager driver that is supplied with your Novell DOS system. It is intended to provide support for 80386 or higher microprocessors. EMM386 can be configured to provide you with the following:

- Expanded memory support conforming to the LIM 4.0 specification without additional hardware

- The ability to relocate parts of Novell DOS to high or upper memory

- The ability to load device drivers, TSRs, and some operating system components into upper memory

- The ability to use some video memory as lower memory

- Relocation of slower ROM code and data to faster RAM

- 256K of extended memory on COMPAQ or COMPAQ-compatible computers

- Support for XMS and DPMS

- Support for Task Manager software in multitasking and task-switching modes

- Support for Microsoft Windows through Version 3.1 in real, standard, and enhanced modes

- Support for applications that access extended memory directly, with the DOS Protected Mode Interface (DPMI) standard

EMM386.SYS enables certain applications to run in the virtual 8086 mode of your 80386 or higher microprocessor. This mode normally causes a program that attempts to enter protected mode to fail with a protection fault. The exception is the application that conforms to the DOS Protected Mode Interface (DPMI) standard. EMM386.SYS has been designed to permit applications that are DPMI-compliant to operate correctly while EMM386.SYS is loaded.

VIII

Maximizing Your System

HIMEM.SYS. If your computer contains an 80286 or higher microprocessor, Novell DOS provides a driver, HIMEM.SYS, that can make use of any extended memory installed in your computer by relocating the DOS kernel to high memory. HIMEM.SYS can also provide you with application access to your extended memory.

If your computer has ROM relocation or is designed around the Chips & Technologies' NeAT, NeATsx, LeAPSet, LeAPSetsx, or SCAT chipset, HIMEM.SYS can often relocate the DOS kernel, certain system data structures, some device drivers, and TSRs into upper memory.

EMMXMA.SYS. Many IBM PS/2 computers contain memory that conforms to the Extended Memory Architecture (XMA) standard. If your computer is an IBM PS/2 with XMA memory, the driver EMMXMA.SYS can be used to convert all or part of this memory to expanded memory that meets the LIM 4.0 specification.

Commands

MEMMAX contains several commands to control how Novell DOS uses the memory made available to it by the drivers. The commands are of two types: those placed in the CONFIG.SYS file and those executed from the command line.

HIDEVICE and HIINSTALL attempt to load drivers and TSRs into upper memory. Another CONFIG.SYS directive, DOS=HIGH, relocates as much of the operating system as possible into high memory. DOS=UMB, like DOS=HIGH, attempts to relocate the operating system but uses upper memory if it is available. With DOS relocated to upper memory, more lower memory is available for you to use.

HILOAD, like HIINSTALL, attempts to load a TSR program into upper memory. The difference between the two is that HILOAD is executed from the DOS prompt. This command is useful for TSRs that are run only occasionally or run from AUTOEXEC.BAT. Like all other MEMMAX commands, HILOAD loads a program in lower memory if upper or high memory is not available.

The MEMMAX command permits you to turn selected MEMMAX features on or off. It is used to compensate for programs that fail to operate when loaded into the 64K lower memory region created when the operating system is relocated to upper memory. MEMMAX can also disable access to upper memory or to the areas of memory adjacent to your video display adapters.

You can use the MEMMAX command also to display the status of upper, lower, or video memory. The video adapter card contains video memory that can sometimes be partially used as lower memory.

Selecting the Proper Hardware/ Software Combination

The features that are provided to you by MEMMAX depend on the type of computer you have as well as the drivers and commands you use to configure MEMMAX.

If you have an 80386 or higher microprocessor, you have the full range of features available to you. Your computer can make use of the EMM386.SYS driver and all MEMMAX commands.

Your 80286-based computer with extended memory alone can relocate the operating system to high memory, using HIMEM.SYS. If your 80286 computer was constructed using specific Chips & Technologies chipsets, HIMEM.SYS can provide most of the facilities available to 80386-based computers.

If your 80286 computer has permanently installed and enabled RAM in upper memory, HIMEM.SYS can make use of RAM to provide upper memory reloca- tion. HIMEM.SYS also enables your 80286-based computer with a LIM 4.0- compliant EMS card and its companion driver to provide upper memory service and relocation of the operating system.

Finally, EMMXMA.SYS can give your IBM PS/2 with XMA memory the capa- bility to provide LIM 4.0-compatible access to expanded memory.

Setting Up Your System's Memory Usage

You can configure your computer's memory in one of two ways: by using the Novell DOS Setup utility or by directly editing CONFIG.SYS and AUTOEXEC.BAT. If you are using a third-party memory manager, you may have to edit CONFIG.SYS directly in order to configure it. The memory man- agers provided with Novell DOS, however, have been designed to be config- ured through the Setup program. Although you can configure the Novell DOS memory manager by directly editing the configuration files, it is an involved process that should be avoided if at all possible. Novell DOS Setup has been designed to be a comprehensive, easy-to-use tool. The Novell DOS Setup program looks at your system environment to make sure that you do not specify incompatible configuration options, and provides you with the necessary information to configure your system for optimum performance.

Starting the Setup Process

The Setup program finds your microprocessor type, installed memory and device drivers, and the presence of Windows. The selections that it subsequently provides depends on the information it has found about your system. For instance, EMM386.SYS configuration options are provided only if your computer has an 80386 or higher processor installed.

To start the Setup program, simply enter **SETUP** at the Novell DOS prompt. You are presented with the screen shown in figure 22.3. You should select DOS System & Memory Management, using the up- or down-arrow key, and then press Enter. The System & Memory Management menu appears, as shown in figure 22.4. Select Memory Manager.

Fig. 22.3
Setup's main menu.

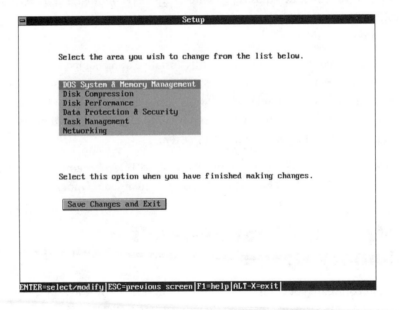

After you select one of the options, you are given the opportunity to configure one or more of the major system components of Novell DOS. If you have
a computer capable of supporting the facilities of MEMMAX, it is the first
item in the list.

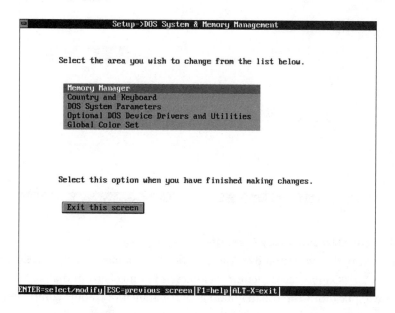

Fig. 22.4
The DOS System &
Memory Manage-
ment menu.

The Memory Manager Options menu has several options preselected by the
Setup program. These selections are based on what the Setup program was
able to determine about your computer system and any settings that you may
have changed during a previous execution of Setup. Looking at figure 22.5,
you can see that the i386/486/586 Memory Manager option is selected. (If
your computer is based on an 80286 processor, the 80286 Memory Manager
option is selected instead.)

Notice also that the Configure option is not selectable for the 80286 memory
manager. You can manually choose the 80286 memory manager by moving
the highlight to the 80286 Memory Manager option in the menu and pressing Enter. If you do this, notice that the Configure option becomes selectable
and that the Configure option for the i386/486/586 memory manager is no
longer selectable.

Fig. 22.5
The Memory
Manager Options
menu.

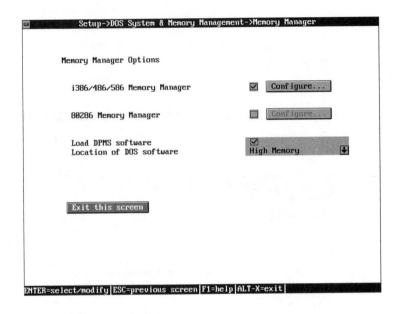

Using the DPMS Memory Manager

The next option you should consider is the DPMS memory manager. DPMS stands for DOS Protected Memory Services. It is a mechanism that DPMS-aware applications can use to obtain additional memory. Some components of Novell DOS, such as NWCACHE, make use of the DPMS server if it is loaded, and greatly reduce their lower memory requirements. Setup enables DPMS by default; to disable it, select the Load DPMS Software option and press Enter.

Relocating the Operating System

Novell DOS has the capability to relocate much of the operating system away from the lower memory area. You direct the operating system to do this through the Location of DOS Software option. If you select this option, you are presented with a drop-down menu (see fig. 22.6).

If you choose Upper Memory, Novell DOS attempts to relocate itself to the memory area that lies above the 640K line and below the 1M line. If you choose High Memory, Novell DOS attempts to relocate itself to the 64K region that exists just above the 1M line.

Configuring the Memory Manager

You may now select the memory manager configuration that is appropriate for your computer, either the 80286 memory manager or the i386/486/586 memory manager. Select the appropriate option and press Enter.

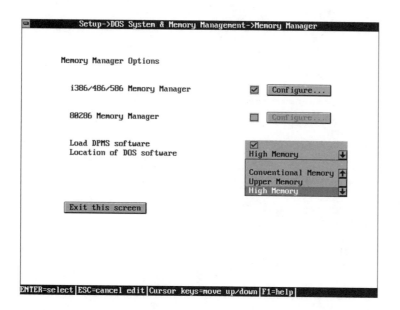

Fig. 22.6
The DOS reloca-
tion options.

Basic 80286 Options. The options for the i386/486/586 and 80286 memory managers differ at this point; the 80286 memory manager configuration options are presented first. You configure the memory manager by selecting the Configure option for the 80286 memory manager.

The 80286 Memory Manager Options menu is shown in figure 22.7. As you can see, the only option is to decide whether you want to make any excess memory in the video adapter address range available to applications. Selecting this option does not directly make this memory available but instead enables the MEMMAX +V switch. This option should not be enabled if Microsoft Windows is used.

Advanced 80286 Options. You should now be finished with memory management configuration. In some cases, however, you may need to fine-tune the way Novell DOS allocates upper memory. To do this, choose the Advanced Options Screen button below the 80286 Memory Manager Options menu, shown in figure 22.7. Then press Enter.

Figure 22.8 shows what Setup displays when you access the Advanced Options screen. If you are not very familiar with your hardware layout and are confident in the selections presented here, you should accept these settings and allow Setup to perform this configuration for you.

VIII

Maximizing Your System

Fig. 22.7
The 80286
Memory Manager
Options menu.

Fig. 22.8
The default
settings in the
Advanced Options
screen.

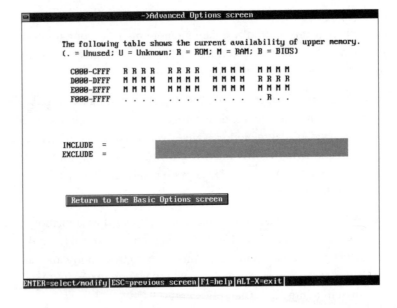

The 80286 memory manager attempts to create as large an upper memory
area as possible. It does this by scanning the area of memory between 640K
and 1M for installed ROM and available RAM in this region. The memory
manager attempts to use these areas as appropriate for upper memory. You
can manually include areas that Setup has not selected by placing the appropriate addresses in the INCLUDE= item on-screen. You can also exclude areas

from use, such as the memory area occupied by network adapter cards, by placing the addresses in the EXCLUDE= item. Both the INCLUDE= and EXCLUDE= entries have the same format; they are groups of address ranges separated by commas. To enter an INCLUDE or EXCLUDE address range, select the appropriate item and press Enter. Figure 22.9 shows the INCLUDE= dialog box presented by Setup and how address ranges are entered. When you are finished, accept the settings by choosing OK or pressing Enter.

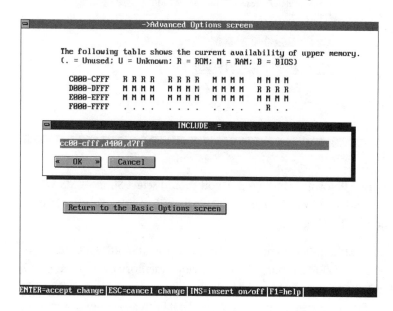

Fig. 22.9
Including memory.

VIII

Maximizing Your System

Basic Options for 80386 and Higher Systems

If your computer contains an 80386, 80486, Pentium, or compatible micro-processor, use the i386/486/586 memory manager. Looking at figure 22.10, you can see that this memory manager has four more selections than the 80286 memory manager.

One of the selections is Copy Slow ROM into Fast RAM. If you choose this option, Novell DOS copies ROM into extended memory, reducing the amount of extended memory available to your applications. If your computer's ROM BIOS setup also copies ROM to RAM, a process called *ROM shadowing*, you may want to skip this option.

If you have DOS applications that use expanded memory or EMS, Novell DOS can simulate this for you. To do so, select Provide LIM 4.0 EMS Support and press Enter.

Fig. 22.10
i386/486/586
memory manager
configuration.

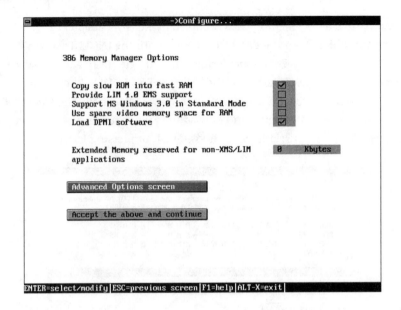

If you use Microsoft Windows 3.0, you should select Support MS Windows 3.0 in Standard Mode. Do *not* select this item if you are running Microsoft Windows 3.1 or higher.

Like the 80286 memory manager (HIMEM), the i386/486/586 memory manager (EMS386) supports the use of video memory by applications. As with the 80286 memory manager, the same cautions apply, and some applications may experience difficulty if you enable the use of excess video memory. Do not enable this option if you are using Microsoft Windows.

The DOS Protected Mode Interface permits you to run applications that require the 32-bit protected mode of 80386 or higher microprocessors. If you have applications that require the use of the protected mode of the microprocessor, you should enable the DPMI software in the 386 memory manager by selecting Load DPMI Software. If you are unsure whether you have any applications that require DPMI, you may safely enable it. There is no memory penalty experienced by the use of DPMI.

The last option to consider is Extended Memory Reserved for Non-XMS/LIM Applications. If you need to reserve extended memory for applications that cannot use XMS or LIM, select this option. If you have such an application that you must execute, enter the amount of memory to reserve for it from the extended memory pool. Note that this memory is not available for XMS or LIM applications.

Advanced Options for 80386 and Higher Systems

You access the Advanced Options screen for the i386/486/586 memory manager by selecting the Advanced Options Screen button and pressing Enter.
The obvious difference between the i386/486/586 Advanced Options screen,
shown in figure 22.11, and the 80286 Advanced Options screen is the addition of the FRAME and ROM items.

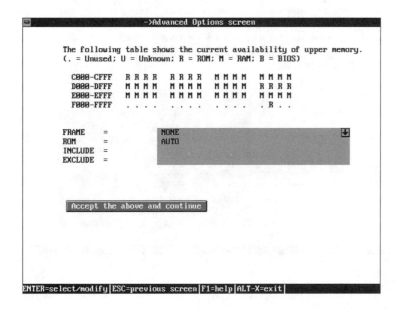

Fig. 22.11
The i386/486/586
Advanced Options
screen.

If you selected the LIM 4.0 support in the previous screen, you have the option of specifying the address in upper memory where the LIM frame is to be
addressed. By default, Novell DOS automatically determines the frame address when the operating system is loaded; this should be sufficient in most
cases. Some applications expect the LIM frame address to be at a specific
location and do not function if Novell DOS should select a different frame
address. If this is the case, you can select a different address by moving the
cursor bar to the FRAME= item and pressing Enter. A submenu like the one in
figure 22.12 appears; you can choose the appropriate address from the list
presented.

The ROM= entry corresponds to the Copy Slow ROM into Fast RAM option in
the previous menu. By default, the entry for this item is NONE if you did not
select the ROM copy option, and AUTO if you did. AUTO allows Novell DOS
to determine the location of all ROM addresses in your system and to copy
automatically the contents to RAM during Novell DOS startup. If your system

does not run correctly using the AUTO parameter, you may want to specify directly each ROM address by moving the cursor to the ROM= item and pressing Enter; the dialog box and format are similar to those for the INCLUDE= item. Supply each address range and press Enter when you are finished.

Fig. 22.12
LIM 4.0 frame address options.

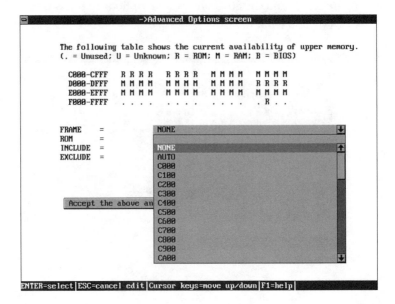

The INCLUDE= and EXCLUDE= options are identical to those in the Advanced Options screen for the 80286 memory manager and are manipulated in exactly the same way.

After selecting memory options, choose command buttons as they are presented to accept options, exit screens, save changes, and exit. Most changes will not take effect until the computer is rebooted.

Fine-Tuning Your Computer's Memory

Fine-tuning the memory configuration in your computer is a matter of managing the use of the various types of memory that may be installed in your computer—that is, lower (conventional), upper, high, expanded, and extended. Remember that not all memory types may be enabled in your configuration.

Using the MEM Command to Manage Memory

The MEM command is a utility that provides you with a picture of memory usage in your computer. With the MEM command, you can determine exactly how much of each type of memory is in use and what is using it. Look at figure 22.13; this screen was generated by the MEM /B command and shows the general layout of the lower memory area. In this display, you can see the various operating system components, programs, and drivers that are loaded in the lower memory area. Similarly, the MEM /U and the MEM /F commands show the area usage for upper and high memory, as depicted in figures 22.14 and 22.15, respectively.

```
┌─ Address ─┬─ Name ──┬─ Size ──────┬─ Type ──────────────────────────────┐
│  0:0000   │ -------- │  400h,  1,024 │ Interrupt vectors                   │
│ 40:0000   │ -------- │  100h,    256 │ ROM BIOS data area                  │
│ 50:0000   │ DOS     │  200h,    512 │ DOS data area                       │
│ 70:0000   │ BIOS    │  900h,  2,304 │ Device drivers                      │
│ 100:0000  │ DOS     │ 13F0h,  5,104 │ System                              │
│ 23F:0000  │ DOS     │ 4470h, 17,520 │ System                              │
│ 24D:0000  │ SETVERXX │ 1F0h,    496 │ DEVICE = installed device driver    │
│ 26D:0000  │ VCPIXXX0 │ D50h,  3,408 │ DEVICE = installed device driver    │
│ 2C8:0000  │ EMMXXXX0 │   8h,      0 │ DEVICE = installed device driver    │
│ 2DE:0000  │ VMXXXXX0 │   8h,      0 │ DEVICE = installed device driver    │
│ 32D:0000  │ DPMIXXX0 │   8h,      0 │ DEVICE = installed device driver    │
│ 343:0000  │ DPMSXXX0 │  400h,  1,024 │ DEVICE = installed device driver    │
│ 384:0000  │ SCSIMGR$ │ 2240h,  8,768 │ DEVICE = installed device driver    │
│ 686:0000  │ COMMAND │  210h,    528 │ Program                             │
│ 6A7:0000  │ COMMAND │  210h,    528 │ Environment                         │
│ 6C8:0000  │ MEM     │   F0h,    240 │ Environment                         │
│ 6D7:0000  │ MEM     │ 15940h, 88,384 │ Program                            │
│ 1C6B:0000 │ -------- │ 83940h, 538,944 │ FREE                             │
│ 9FFF:0000 │ DOS     │ 38010h, 229,392 │ System                            │
└───────────┴─────────┴───────────────┴─────────────────────────────────────┘
```

Fig. 22.13
Displaying lower memory with MEM /B.

VIII

Maximizing Your System

```
┌─ Address ─┬─ Name ──┬─ Size ──────┬─ Type ──────────────────────────────┐
│ C800:0000 │ -------- │ 8000h, 32,768 │ ------------- ROM ---------------  │
│ C800:0000 │ EMS     │ 10000h, 65,536 │ ---------- EMS memory -----------  │
│ D800:0000 │ -------- │ 4000h, 16,384 │ ---------- Upper RAM -----------  │
├───────────┼─────────┼───────────────┼─────────────────────────────────────┤
│ D800:0000 │ EMM386  │  100h,    384 │ XMS Upper Memory Block              │
│ D818:0000 │ DOS     │ 2910h, 10,512 │ System                              │
│ DAA9:0000 │ -------- │ 1560h,  5,472 │ FREE                              │
│ DBFF:0000 │ DOS     │ 4010h, 16,400 │ System                              │
├───────────┼─────────┼───────────────┼─────────────────────────────────────┤
│ DC00:0000 │ -------- │ 4000h, 16,384 │ ------------- ROM ---------------  │
│ E000:0000 │ -------- │ 10000h, 65,536 │ ---------- Upper RAM -----------  │
├───────────┼─────────┼───────────────┼─────────────────────────────────────┤
│ E000:0000 │ XMS     │  410h,  1,040 │ XMS Upper Memory Block              │
│ E041:0000 │ DOS     │ 2A40h, 10,816 │ System                              │
│ E043:0000 │ MVPROAS │ 2A20h, 10,784 │ DEVICE = installed device driver    │
│ E2E5:0000 │ -------- │ 4010h, 16,400 │ FREE                             │
│ E6E6:0000 │ 7410    │ 71A0h, 29,088 │ Data                                │
├───────────┼─────────┼───────────────┼─────────────────────────────────────┤
│ F800:0000 │ -------- │ 1000h,  4,096 │ ---------- Shadow ROM ----------  │
└───────────┴─────────┴───────────────┴─────────────────────────────────────┘
```

Fig. 22.14
Displaying upper memory with MEM /U.

You can obtain a consolidated display of lower, upper, and high memory usage in your computer system by entering **MEM /PROGRAM** (see fig. 22.16). In general, fine-tuning memory is an attempt to obtain the largest possible lower memory area. You accomplish this task by maximizing the use of upper, high, and extended memory. The MEM command can be used to monitor your progress in this effort.

Fig. 22.15

Displaying high memory with MEM /F.

```
┌─ Address ─┬─ Name ─┬─ Size ──────────┬─ Type ───────────────────
│ FFFF:1590 │   DOS  │ FA0h,    4,000  │ DOS BIOS code
│ FFFF:2530 │   DOS  │ 6C80h,  27,776  │ DOS kernel code
│ FFFF:91B0 │   DOS  │ 3E58h,  15,960  │ BUFFERS=  30 disk buffers
│ FFFF:D008 │ ────── │ 1A65h,   6,757  │ FREE
│ FFFF:EA6D │  SHARE │ 1173h,   4,467  │ Program
└───────────┴────────┴─────────────────┴──────────────────────────
```

Fig. 22.16

Displaying all memory types with MEM / PROGRAM.

```
┌─────────────────────────────────────────────────────────────────────┐
│ 23F7:0000    MEM    15810h,  88,080   Program                         │
│ 3978:0000  ──────   66870h, 419,952   FREE                            │
│ 9FFF:0000    DOS    28010h, 163,856   System                          │
│                                                                       │
│ C800:0000  EMM386    1C0h,      448   XMS Upper Memory Block          │
│ C81C:0000    DOS     1B0h,      432   XMS Upper Memory Block          │
│ C837:0000    DOS     510h,    1,296   XMS Upper Memory Block          │
│ C888:0000    DOS    10B0h,    4,272   System                          │
│ C88A:0000    CON    1090h,    4,240     DEVICE = installed device driver│
│ C993:0000    DOS    4350h,   17,232   System                          │
│ C995:0000 _STAC_HI  4330h,   17,200     DEVICE = installed device driver│
│ CDC8:0000    DOS     C90h,    3,216   System                          │
│ CE91:0000   SAVE     F0h,      240    Environment                     │
│ CEA0:0000  SHARE    3840h,   14,400   XMS Upper Memory Block          │
│ D224:0000    MEM     E0h,      224    Environment                     │
│ D232:0000  ──────   1ACE0h, 109,792   FREE                            │
│                                                                       │
│ FFFF:00E0  COMMAND  1480h,    5,248   Program                         │
│ FFFF:1590    DOS     FA0h,    4,000   DOS BIOS code                   │
│ FFFF:2530    DOS    6CA0h,   27,808   DOS kernel code                 │
│ FFFF:91D0    DOS    3E58h,   15,960     BUFFERS=  30 disk buffers     │
│ FFFF:D028  ──────    ED8h,    3,800   FREE                            │
│                                                                       │
│ Press Enter to continue...                                            │
└───────────────────────────────────────────────────────────────────────┘
```

In this particular configuration, part of NWCACHE is loaded in upper memory. The NWCACHE disk-caching program can be configured to run in several types of memory. If you load NWCACHE into high memory by using the program's /BH and /MUX switches, there is no decrease in lower memory usage.

Using Other Utilities That Affect Memory

You can experiment with other utilities that have similar switches to maximize your lower memory area. You can also use the HIDEVICE command in CONFIG.SYS to load device drivers into upper memory. Likewise, you can use HIINSTALL in CONFIG.SYS to load TSRs into upper memory, thus reducing the demand for lower memory space. Be sure to review all the available documentation for the drivers or TSRs you plan to load into high memory; some drivers or TSRs do not function properly in upper memory. Measure your progress by using the MEM command; it is your best gauge of memory usage. If you do not run or infrequently run programs that use LIM 4.0 EMS memory, you may want to disable this option in Setup. If you do so, the base frame used for LIM 4.0 is released, and additional upper memory is made available for use by the operating system and applications that are able to use upper memory. When loading device drivers and TSRs in CONFIG.SYS, try to load the largest ones first. If you do this, the operating system is able to allocate memory more efficiently. Be sure to review your documentation, though, because some drivers and TSRs—memory management and network drivers in particular—are very sensitive to the order in which they are loaded.

Using MEMMAX to Optimize Memory

MEMMAX is a command-line interface to the Novell DOS resident memory managers. You use MEMMAX to selectively enable or disable access to upper, video, and lower memory. Remember that these options were set in the memory manager configuration screens of the Setup program.

If you enabled the use of excess video memory, you now can enable its use with the MEMMAX +V command. Using this command increases the lower memory area by 96K! You can also run programs in upper memory by using the LOADHIGH or LH command. Some programs, such as MS-Windows, do not run when program memory is mapped into display memory. For these programs, first use MEMMAX -V to shut down access to excess video memory space. Background FAX programs are good choices for the LOADHIGH command. To use the LOADHIGH command, just prefix with LH the command line that you normally use to execute the program. As with device drivers and TSRs, check to see whether there are any cautions against running the program in high memory. You may also specify the LOADHIGH command as HILOAD. Novell recommends that these programs be loaded high: CURSOR.EXE, GRAPHICS.COM, GRAFTABL.COM, and JOIN.EXE. Naturally, you should not load them if you do not need the functionality they provide.

If you have an application that does not run in lower memory—some TSRs, for example—you can disable lower memory with the MEMMAX -L command. Use MEMMAX +L to enable it again.

You can request the status of lower, upper, and video memory at any time with the MEMMAX /L, MEMMAX /U, and MEMMAX /V commands, respectively.

From Here...

Novell DOS has gone a long way to provide the most versatile operating environment available for your applications today. The memory management functions available with the operating system are superb and easy to work with. After taking some time to familiarize yourself with Novell DOS memory management, you will find that you are rewarded with an application environment that provides you with plenty of room to grow. You may want to turn next to these chapters:

- Chapter 6, "Understanding File Storage," covers drive and disk structures, DOS directories, paths, DOS files and their attributes, and the use of wild cards.

- Chapter 8, "Preparing Disks," helps you make your disks ready for use.

- Chapter 11, "Disk Optimization Utilities," discusses ways to improve your computer's hard disk performance.

Part IX

Using the Network

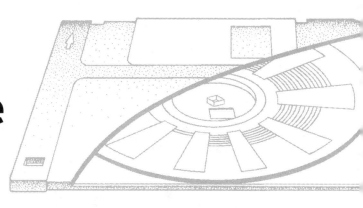

Continue

| 23 | Introduction to Networking |
| 24 | Network Maintenance |

nfigure   emory Managemen

Disk Compression
Disk Performance
Data Protection & Security
Task Management
Networking

it this screen

acks

Sectors

Change destination drive(s) and directorie

Root directory

Subdirectory Subdirectory

Subdirectory Subdirectory Subdirectory Subdirectory

Subdirectory Subdirectory

Subdirectory

Continue

File – c:\spam.txt
Create new file ?

« OK »   Cancel

nfigure Task Manager

it this screen

ystem & Memory Managemen
Disk Compression
Disk Performance
Data Protection & Security
Task Management
Networking

acks

Sectors

25-Pin DB-25 Male

25-pin serial connector,
usually COM2

Change destination drive(s) and directorie

Chapter 23

Introduction to Networking

Local area networking is a term used in the personal computer universe to describe the capability to share the resources of one computer with other computers. Many types of networks have come and gone over the years, but by far the most widely used networking software has been NetWare by Novell. Naturally, when the decision was made to make networking a standard component of Novell DOS, Novell chose to use networking software derived from its flagship NetWare product.

NetWare, like many of its contemporaries, is a *client/server* type of network. In networking terms, a *server* is any system that makes its resources—that is, printers and disks—available for use by other computer users (*clients*). Only servers can make their resources available for sharing; clients cannot share the resources of other clients. If you want to share a copy of a file on your computer with a coworker who is using another computer, you must first copy the file to the server, and the other user must access the data on the server or copy the data to her machine. Novell DOS 7 has provided you with another option, however, by creating a version of NetWare that will permit one or more computers both to share their own resources and to share the resources of any of the other computers participating in the network. This is called *peer-to-peer networking*. With peer-to-peer networking, you can configure any network computer to be a client, server, or both.

This chapter covers the following topics:

■ How to plan and configure a network

■ How to add users

■ How to share disks and printers with other users

Planning the Network

One thing that you may be asking yourself right now is, Do I really need to use a network? The answer is a very definite maybe. If you have more than one IBM-compatible computer at your location and you routinely need to share information or printers among the computers, you would probably benefit from using a network environment. With a network, only one copy of your files needs to be maintained because they may be shared with your co-workers who use the network. In some cases, you may even share a single copy of your software, eliminating the need to purchase multiple copies of the same product. (But see the next section for some important details on sharing software.)

Sharing Software

Many software vendors are very specific about how their software may be used in a networking environment. Running software on multiple computers from a single copy installed on the network may be in violation of your license agreement for the program, and in some cases, may also be illegal. Be sure to read your license agreement before attempting to share software through the network. If you have any questions, contact the software vendor before using the software on the network.

You may experience difficulty if you attempt to run software concurrently on several computers in the network that was not designed for a networking environment. Typically, the problem arises when more than one user attempts to access the same information. If you experience this problem, try running the software on a single computer at a time. If the problem persists, contact the software vendor for more information. A special version of the software may be required to operate properly with networking.

Organizing Resources

The options and configuration possibilities for setting up a network are so varied that they cannot all be presented in the scope of one chapter. For any setup, however, you should begin by answering these general questions:

■ How many computers are to participate in the network?

■ What type of network interface adapters will be used to connect the computers to the network?

■ Should the different computer users be segregated into work groups, or is a single work group for all users sufficient?

■ What files must be shared by users, and where are the files located?

■ Will you be using a common device to back up all your disks?

■ Are there printers that you will want to share?

■ Do you need to secure access to the network or any of its resources?

After you have answered these questions, draw a diagram of your planned network configuration, as described in the next section.

Designing Workgroups

NetWare groups network users into clusters called *workgroups*, and, consequently, every network user is a member of one or more workgroups. Workgroups are generally used to define network users with common characteristics. A small network may consist of one workgroup. A large company may define a network with several workgroups based on the operational units that exist within the company, such as payroll and manufacturing.

Figure 23.1 is a sample of a single workgroup network. In this layout, the network designer has elected to define a single server. Both of the network users can be given permission to share the files and printer of the server. Notice that Kimberly's workstation has a printer attached to it. Her workstation is defined as a client only. Pam's workstation, which is defined as both a client and the workgroup server, cannot access Kimberly's printer because Kimberly is not a server. Typically, Kimberly will use her own printer to print draft copies of documents, continuous-form labels, and multipart forms, and she will use Pam's printer to print word processing documents or computer-generated graphics. This arrangement permits both Pam and Kimberly to have access to the types of equipment they require to perform their jobs without duplicating expensive equipment.

Figure 23.2 shows how SuperDooper Software, a fictitious company, has organized its network. It consists of five workgroups: ADMINISTRATION, SALES, TECHSUPPORT, DEVELOPMENT, and DISTRIBUTION. All the workgroups are

Tip
To keep the setup on the diagram in perspective, place the names of users next to the equipment they will be using.

IX

Using the Network

connected together as a single network. What you must remember is that a client may be logged into only one workgroup at a time; if you try to log into a different workgroup, you will first be automatically logged out of the workgroup you are currently logged into.

Fig. 23.1
Network configu-
ration with a
single workgroup.

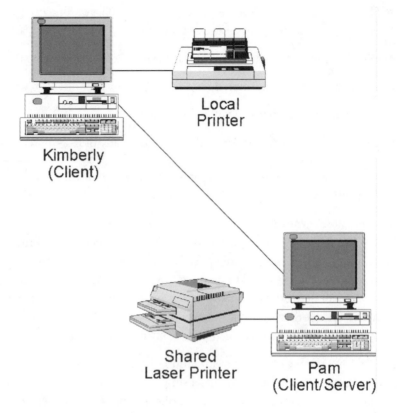

Kimberly
(Client)

Local
Printer

Shared
Laser Printer

Pam
(Client/Server)

Installing the Network

In this section, you define and configure a sample network so that you can build on it to create your own environment. Figure 23.3 depicts a fictitious home-based business called Aesop's Typesetting. This company performs computerized typesetting and document processing for low- and medium-volume customers. Aesop's consists of three individuals—Martha, Carl, and Reynolds—who perform all the administrative functions necessary to operate the business.

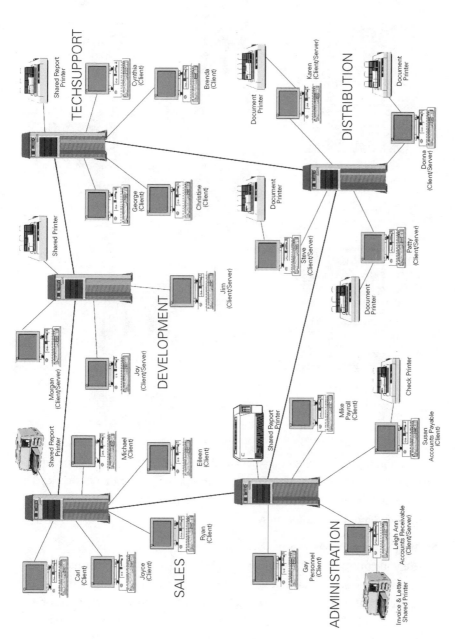

Fig. 23.2
Network
configuration
with multiple
workgroups.

Fig. 23.3
Network configu-
ration for Aesop's
Typesetting.

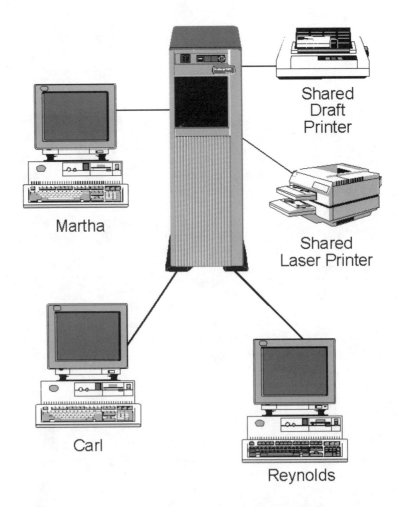

The configuration consists of a server and three workstations. (A *workstation* is
just another name used to define a computer participating in a network.) The
server provides all data storage, tape backup facilities, a high-resolution laser
printer, and a dot-matrix printer.

Setting Up the Hardware

Before you configure the Novell DOS 7 Desktop Server, you must have installed the necessary local area network hardware used to connect the various
computers that make up the network. Novell DOS 7 provides support for a
wide variety of network adapters, including ARCnet, EtherNet, and Token
Ring, to name a few. Installation instructions are usually provided with the
equipment. If not, contact the company or individual from which you obtained it.

Aesop's has decided to use EtherNet, a type of network hardware, to tie the server and workstations together. After the hardware arrived, it was installed and tested by the vendor. The hardware vendor has subcontracted the software configuration to you, so now it is your opportunity to finish the installation. The rest of this chapter focuses on the network software installation and configuration.

Installing the Network Software

You must first install Novell DOS 7, the networking software, and interface card on the server and each workstation in the network. Remember, you must purchase one copy of Novell DOS 7 for each computer. Chapter 5, "Installing the Network," details the basic steps required to install the network software; this section provides additional suggestions on configuring the setup. The choice of interface card is largely a personal one. Some types may have a cost advantage over others, and some may have speed advantages. In addition, you may be restricted by distances the network must run or by the types of cable you must use. If you are installing Novell DOS 7 networking into an existing network, you will naturally have to select the same type of card that is used in the rest of the network.

The name for the server in this example is SERVER_PC. The name of the server is generated automatically by the Setup program when _PC is appended to the name placed in the User of This Computer field. To ensure that this server's name is SERVER_PC, place the name SERVER in that field in Setup's Networking screen (see fig. 23.4).

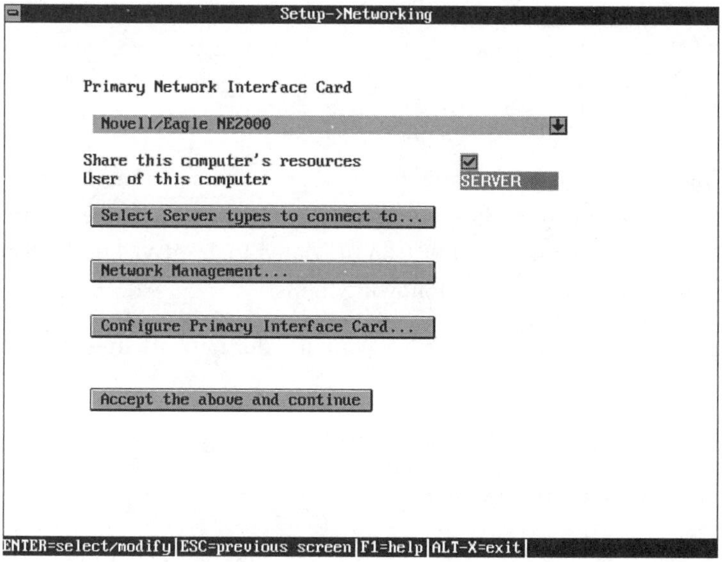

Fig. 23.4
Creating the server name.

IX

Using the Network

Notice that the Share This Computer's Resources option has been checked in this figure. Unless you select this option, the network will contain only client support—that is, it will be able to communicate with a server but not be able to share any of its own resources.

After specifying the name for the server, choose Select Server Types to Connect To. On the screen that appears, indicate that you want connectivity to Personal NetWare Desktop Servers, as shown in figure 23.5.

Fig. 23.5
Selecting server connectivity.

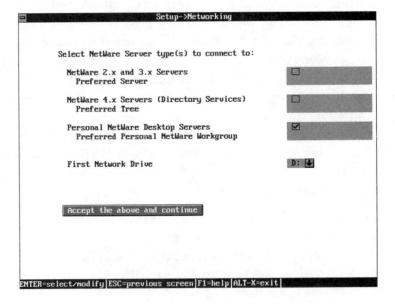

Finally, using Setup's Network Management option, enable the network to load the Network Management Responder (NMR), as shown in figure 23.6. Unless you select this item, you will not be able to run Novell DOS 7 network diagnostics.

After you have installed the network, reboot the server so that the changes take effect. If the network does not automatically start, enter the command **STARTNET** to run the file STARTNET.BAT (located in C:\NWCLIENT). The STARTNET batch file loads the following items:

- Device drivers that connect NetWare to your network interface card

- A component of NetWare called IPXODI that serves as an intermediary between the device driver and NetWare

- The network software itself

You will see a number of messages displayed on your screen as NetWare initializes itself. No responses are required from you if errors are not encountered during startup. If errors are encountered and a reply is requested, you should reply as indicated. Unless the network software indicates that an error condition has been successfully recovered, you should assume that the network did not start. If no errors are found, the network will start, and the program returns to the DOS prompt.

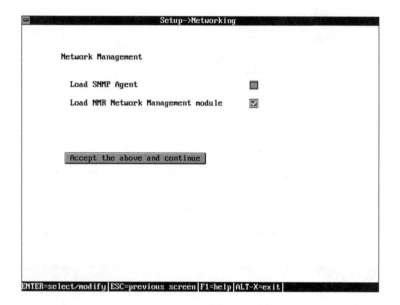

Fig. 23.6
Setting up network management options.

Configuring the Network

When you are finally returned to the DOS prompt after initializing the network, enter the command **NET LOGIN SUPERVISOR**. This command is used to attach you to the network as the system administrator, which is necessary to configure the network. Because you have not created a workgroup yet, LOGIN asks whether you want to connect to the SYSTEM workgroup (see fig. 23.7). You should enter **1** here, and LOGIN will continue. You are authenticated to the SERVER_PC server and then logged into the workgroup SYSTEM as the user SUPERVISOR.

IX

Using the Network

Now you will use the Net utility to create the workgroup. To begin network configuration, enter **NET ADMIN**. This command is used to enter the administrative mode of the configurator. Because you have logged in as SUPERVISOR, you have the required privileges to use this command. The initial menu is displayed as shown in figure 23.8. You can see that SERVER_PC is not associated with a workgroup.

Fig. 23.7
Logging into the network for the first time.

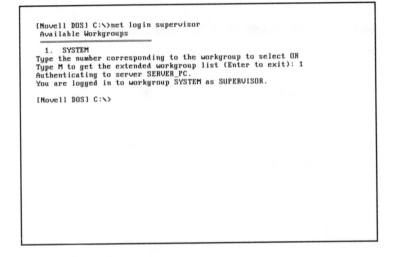

```
[Novell DOS] C:\>net login supervisor
 Available Workgroups

   1.  SYSTEM
Type the number corresponding to the workgroup to select OR
Type M to get the extended workgroup list (Enter to exit): 1
Authenticating to server SERVER_PC.
You are logged in to workgroup SYSTEM as SUPERVISOR.

[Novell DOS] C:\>
```

Fig. 23.8
Network administration initial menu.

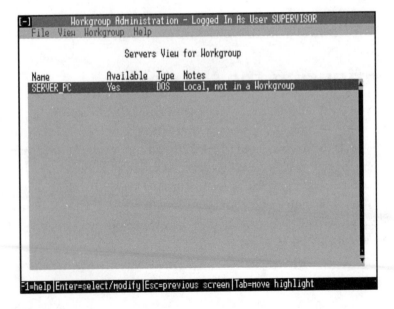

```
[-]       Workgroup Administration - Logged In As User SUPERVISOR
   File  View  Workgroup  Help

                    Servers View for Workgroup

   Name            Available  Type  Notes
   SERVER_PC       Yes        DOS   Local, not in a Workgroup




F1=help│Enter=select/modify│Esc=previous screen│Tab=move highlight
```

If you look back at the hardware configuration for the sample network shown in figure 23.3, you will see that the plan is to have two printers attached to the server—a laser printer for high-quality output and a dot-matrix printer for draft copy and utility printing. By default, the network supports only a single shared printer. You must inform the network that you will be sharing two printers on this server. You do this by modifying the definition of SERVER_PC. Just press Enter, and a configuration menu is displayed. Move the cursor to Advanced Settings and press Enter. The dialog box shown in figure 23.9 then appears.

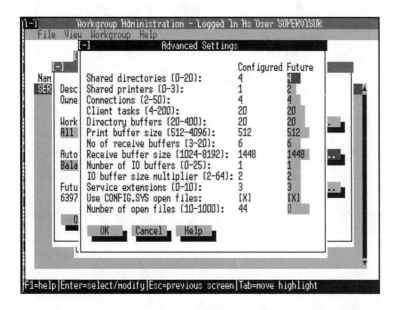

Fig. 23.9
Server Advanced Settings.

Tab down to the Shared Printers item and change the Future setting to 2, as shown in the figure. Then choose OK. Likewise, choose OK on the next menu to return to the Servers View screen.

Creating the Workgroups

To enable clients to use the network, you have to create workgroups for them. To do this, open the Workgroup menu and choose Create a Workgroup. The utility displays the dialog box shown in figure 23.10.

To create the workgroup, you have to give it a name. For this example, use AESOP, the name of the client's company. Type **AESOP** in the Workgroup Name text box. Then choose OK. The workgroup AESOP will be created, and SERVER_PC, your server, will be moved into it. Now log into the new workgroup by choosing Workgroup and then Login. The dialog box shown in figure 23.11 is displayed. Only one workgroup will be in the list, so you just need to press the Enter key to select it.

Fig. 23.10
Creating a
workgroup.

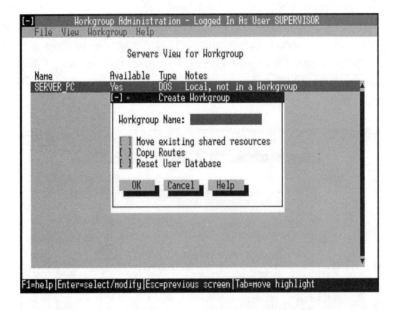

Fig. 23.11
Workgroup
selection dialog
box.

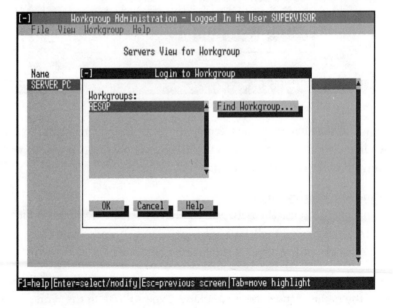

The dialog box shown in fig. 23.12 is displayed next. Type **SUPERVISOR** for Username and then press Enter three times. You will now be logged into workgroup AESOP as the system administrator.

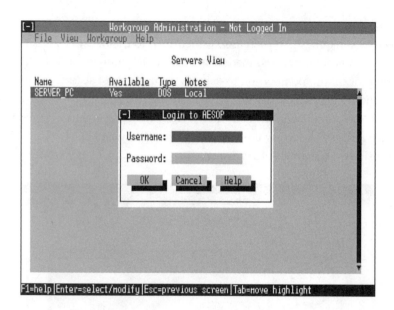

Fig. 23.12
Login from Servers
View.

When asked whether you want to update NET.CFG with the new workgroup, choose OK. This permits you to be automatically attached to this workgroup when the server is restarted. Now that you are logged into the workgroup as shown in figure 23.13, you can proceed to add users.

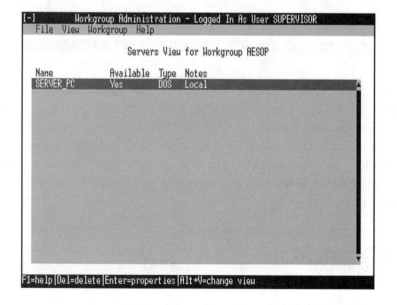

Fig. 23.13
Workgroup login.

IX

Using the Network

Adding Users to the Network

Novell DOS requires that each user be identified to the network so that re-sources can be allocated and made available to each individual. The identification process also permits you to define various levels of access security to meet different demands. As you recall, there are three users of this network—Martha, Carl, and Reynolds. You will use these names as the user names for the network. To add a new user, open the View menu and choose Users. The screen shown in figure 23.14 is displayed.

Fig. 23.14
Workgroup
user list.

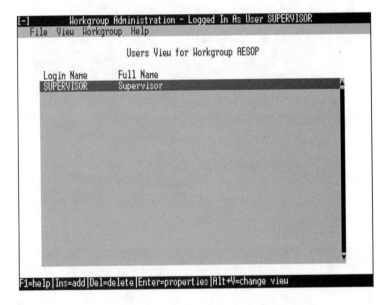

The list presented in this screen contains all the users defined for this workgroup. As you can see, only a single user, SUPERVISOR, has been defined in the workgroup. This was done automatically for you when you created the workgroup. Now press the Ins key, and the Add User dialog box appears (see fig. 23.15). Enter **Martha** for the first user and press Enter. You then see the dialog box shown in figure 23.16. You may enter the user's full name in the first text box.

By default, the utility assumes that this user is to have administrator privileges for the AESOP workgroup. Select Workgroup Administrator and press the space bar. The X in this field will be replaced by a blank. You will not be using passwords for this example, so after ensuring that Password Required is not checked, choose OK and press Enter. Martha will be added, and her name will appear in the Users View screen.

Repeat this process for Reynolds and Carl. When you are finished, the Users
View screen should look similar to that in figure 23.17.

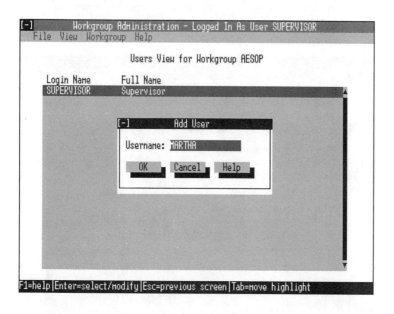

Fig. 23.15
Adding a user to a
workgroup.

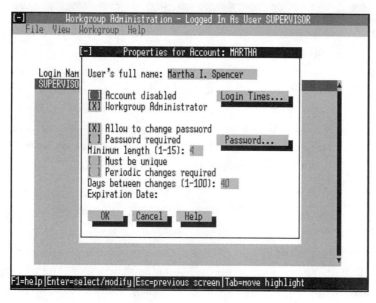

Fig. 23.16
Entering user
properties.

IX

Using the Network

Defining Shared Directories

The next task is to define the disk resources that will be made available to the users of the workgroup. Novell uses the term *shared directories*, rather than shared disks, to refer to disk-based shared resources.

Fig. 23.17
List of configured users.

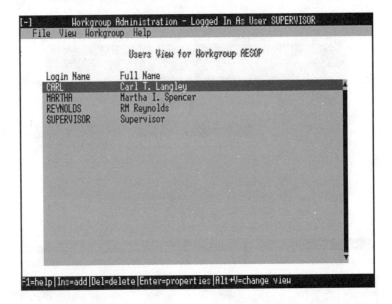

The server in this example contains a single hard disk partitioned as a single logical drive, drive C:. There will be a subdirectory called C:\SHARED that all the network users must be able to access. In addition, each user will have a private area on the disk. These subdirectories are to be called C:\MARTHA, C:\REYNOLDS, and C:\CARL for the user's Martha, Reynolds, and Carl, respectively. To create these subdirectories, exit the Net utility and enter the following commands from the operating system C:\ prompt:

```
MD \SHARED
MD \MARTHA
MD \REYNOLDS
MD \CARL
```

Now restart the Net utility and configure the network to access the new directories. To begin this process, open the View menu and choose Shared Directories. Press the Ins key, and you then see the dialog box shown in figure 23.18.

Type **SHARED** for the directory name and choose OK. The dialog box shown in figure 23.19 is displayed.

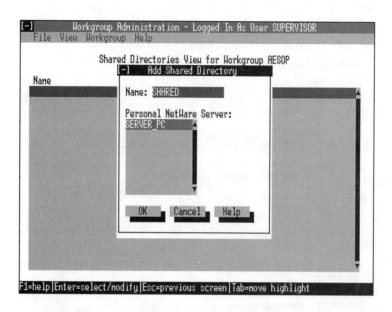

Fig. 23.18
Defining shared
directories.

Fig. 23.19
Entering properties
for shared
directories.

IX

Using the Network

Enter **C:\SHARED** in the Directory Path text box. Select Suggested Drive and
press Enter. A drop-down list of drive letters appears. Select D: and press Enter. You use D: because there is only a single drive C: on each of the workstations in this example.

You are now positioned at the Default Access Rights section. Select All and
press Enter. This gives all network users full access to this directory by default.

Repeat this process for the next user, using MARTHA for the directory name. This time, specify None for Default Access Rights and then choose User Rights. The dialog box shown in figure 23.20 appears.

Fig. 23.20
Adding specific
user rights.

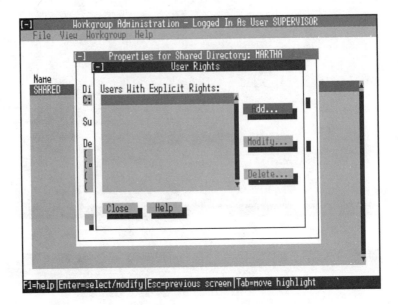

Choose Add, and the Add User dialog box is displayed (see fig. 23.21). Pick MARTHA from the list and press Enter.

Fig. 23.21
Updating user
directory access
rights.

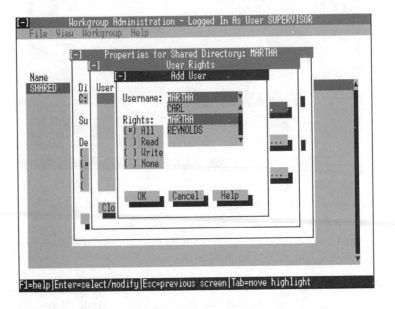

Select All and press Enter or the space bar. This gives user MARTHA full access to the directory C:\MARTHA. Choose OK. Add CARL and REYNOLDS, giving them None for access rights to the directory C:\MARTHA. When you are through, the dialog box for the shared directory C:\MARTHA should look like that in figure 23.22.

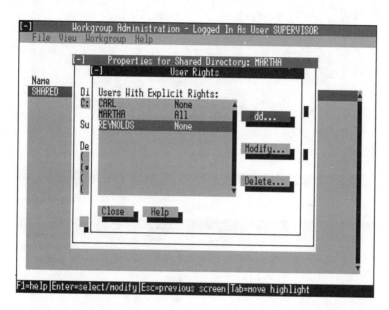

Fig. 23.22
User rights for
C:\MARTHA.

You must repeat this process to give full rights for CARL to the shared directory C:\CARL and full rights for REYNOLDS to C:\REYNOLDS. As with the shared directory C:\MARTHA, other users should have no access rights to directories other than their own private directories and the shared directory C:\SHARED. When you are through, the workgroup directory list should look like that in figure 23.23.

Defining Shared Printers

Now you will define the two printers to the network so that they can be accessed by all users. Novell DOS enables you to define access controls like those used for shared directories; however, you have no need to use such controls at Aesop's. To begin the definition process, open the View menu and choose Shared Printers. The display shown in figure 23.24 appears.

As you can see, no printers are defined for the network. Press the Ins key, and the Add Shared Printer dialog box is displayed (see fig. 23.25).

You will define the laser printer first, so enter **LASER** for the printer name.

Fig. 23.23
Final shared
directory list.

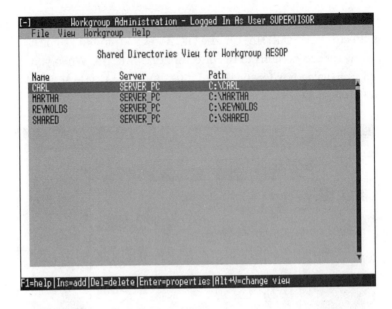

Fig. 23.24
Initial shared
printer list.

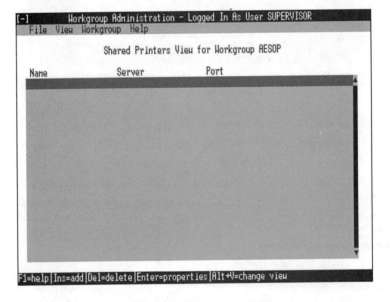

Position the cursor at the Port text box and press Enter. A list of available
ports is displayed. In this example, the printer is connected to LPT1, so position the cursor at LPT1 and press Enter. Then choose OK. You next see the
Properties for Shared Printer dialog box (see fig. 23.26).

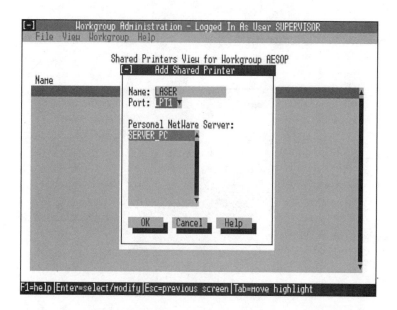

Fig. 23.25
Defining a shared printer.

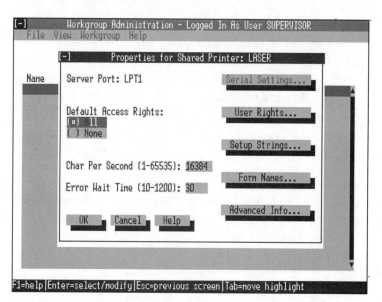

Fig. 23.26
Defining shared printer properties.

You do not need to change any of the settings for the printer in this example, but you may review the settings if you like. If you want a description of any of the fields shown, just position the cursor on the field and press the F1 key. When you are through, exit this dialog box by choosing OK.

Repeat the process for the DRAFT printer that is attached to LPT2. When you are done, the shared printer list will look like the one shown in figure 23.27.

Fig. 23.27
Updated shared
printer list.

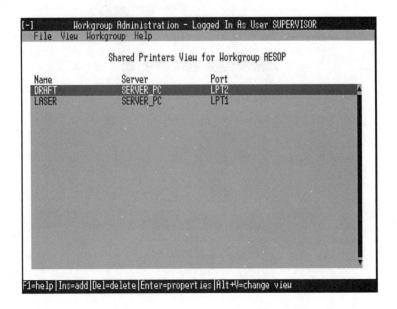

Setting Up the Workstations

To complete your installation, you have to prepare the network for the user workstations (clients)—that is, the computers that Martha, Carl, and Reynolds will use to access the network. You must first install the operating system and the networking software as you did for the server. Be sure that you do not choose to share the computer's resources and that the user's name appears in the user area as you defined it for the network. Look at figure 23.28 to see how this setup should appear for user MARTHA.

You should also select the Personal NetWare Desktop Servers option as shown previously in figure 23.5, and enter the workgroup name where indicated. However, you do not need to select a network management module. The definition should look like that in figure 23.29.

When you complete this process, Setup will build the batch file STARTNET.BAT in the C:\NWCLIENT directory on the workstation and place a call to STARTNET.BAT in C:\AUTOEXEC.BAT. The line looks like this:

```
?"Load Network Software (Y/N) ?"CALL C:\NWCLIENT\STARTNET.BAT
```

Add the following commands to AUTOEXEC.BAT after the call to STARTNET.BAT:

```
NET LOGIN MARTHA
NET MAP D: SHARED
```

```
NET  MAP  E:  MARTHA
NET  CAPTURE  LPT1  LASER
NET  CAPTURE  LPT2  DRAFT
```

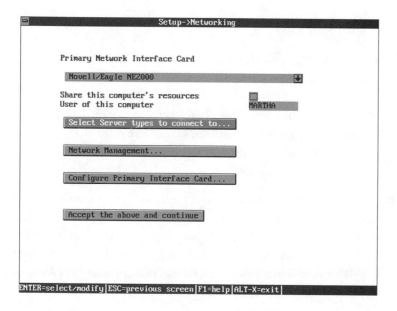

Fig. 23.28
Setup workstation
network selections.

Fig. 23.29
Setup worksta-
tion network
management.

Note the descriptions of these commands:

- The first line logs the user into the network. Naturally, you should replace the user name MARTHA with the name of the appropriate user for that workstation.

- The NET MAP D: and NET MAP E: commands make the shared directories C:\SHARED and C:\MARTHA appear as drives D: and E: on the workstation. Again, replace MARTHA with the shared directory names of the appropriate user. Remember that these are the directory names as known to the network and not the actual disk paths that exist on the server's hard disk. The path name and shared directory names are the same to prevent confusion.

- The two CAPTURE commands are like the MAP commands except that they make the shared printers LASER and DRAFT appear on the workstation as LPT1 and LPT2. Note that if a printer is later attached to the LPT1 or LPT2 port on the workstation, it will not be accessible after the CAPTURE command is executed. In this case, try using LPT3 for the CAPTURE command that is in conflict.

When you are finished, save your changes and reboot the workstation. Your workstation should reboot and log into the network if the server is in operation.

From Here...

In this chapter, you learned how Novell DOS has provided an efficient, easy-to-use networking system. You learned about networking concepts and how you plan for a network installation. You also installed a sample network, from the planning stages to network startup. There are many variations on how to install a Novell network—so many, in fact, that volumes have been written on the subject. If you have a need for a greater understanding of the NetWare environment, you should consult one of these sources. For more information about networking, refer to the following chapters:

- Chapter 5, "Installing the Network," guides you through the installation process for your new operating system.

■ Chapter 24, " Network Maintenance," shows you how to tune the network for best performance and how to use the Novell DOS 7 network utilities.

IX

Using the Network

Chapter 24

Network Maintenance

In Chapter 23, you learned how to plan and install a basic Novell DOS network. You assumed that the network consisted only of workstations that used Novell DOS 7 and the networking software provided with this operating system. The network consisted of a server, called the Desktop Server by Novell, and one or more users or clients. The client component of Novell DOS 7 networking is called the Universal Client. Novell chose this name because, unlike other NetWare client software, the version supplied with Novell DOS 7 is able to connect not only to Novell DOS 7 networks but also to NetWare Versions 2, 3, and 4. In fact, you can configure the client software to enable connectivity to any combination of NetWare 2, 3, 4, or Personal NetWare. Personal NetWare, by the way, is another term used by Novell to describe the new networking architecture provided with Novell DOS 7 and soon to be offered as a separate product for use with other DOS-compatible operating systems.

This chapter covers the following topics:

- How to improve network performance

- How to use network diagnostics

- How to use the Net and Personal NetWare utilities

Setting Up the Universal Client

To use the Universal Client with other versions of NetWare, you must first install the operating system and networking software, as described in Chapter 5, "Installing the Network." You indicate within the Setup utility the type of network you want to connect to, using the menu shown in figure 24.1.

In this figure, the Universal Client is configured to communicate with networks using NetWare Version 3 and Personal NetWare.

Fig. 24.1

SETUP's network connectivity options.

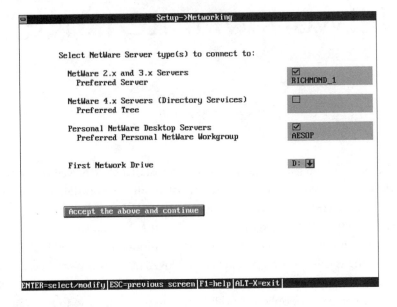

Naturally, you must be physically connected to the network to which you want to communicate. The selection shown in figure 24.1, however, is the only operating system change required to support NetWare Version 2, 3, or 4. After you have made the changes you want with the Setup utility, you must contact your network administrator to ensure that you have proper access authority for the NetWare network.

It is important to note that Novell DOS 7 networking provides all the required software to support connectivity to other versions of NetWare. You should remember also that, as with NetWare Versions 2, 3, and 4, no connectivity is possible with NetWare Lite. Novell DOS 7 is the designated replacement for NetWare Lite and, consequently, you should upgrade these networks to the new product as soon as it is practical. Chapter 5 details the conversion aids provided with Novell DOS 7 for this purpose. Your network administrator will have to provide you with any additional software, batch files, or instructions required to access specific applications or features of your network.

Tuning the Network

When you installed the sample network described in the previous chapter, you permitted Novell DOS to make certain assumptions about your environment and how you would use the network. In general, the setup process does a good job in the choices it makes. There are some things that you can do, however, based on your knowledge of how your configuration is used, to make network operation more efficient. This process is called *tuning*. The following sections describe how you can improve network performance by changing the software setup and the hardware setup.

Changing the Network Setup

To change the network's setup, you first have to log into the network. Using the sample network from the preceding chapter, enter the command **NET LOGIN SUPERVISOR** to log into the workgroup AESOP as the supervisor. Now enter the Net utility by issuing the command **NET ADMIN**. You will see that SERVER_PC is displayed on-screen as the only server available. If there were more servers in the network, they would appear also in this list. The cursor bar is already positioned on SERVER_PC, so just press Enter to select this server. The dialog box shown in figure 24.2 appears next.

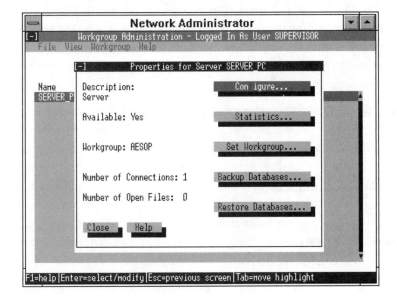

Fig. 24.2
The Properties for Server dialog box.

IX

Using the Network

Choose the Configure button to bring up the Server Configuration dialog box shown in figure 24.3.

Fig. 24.3

The Server Configuration dialog box.

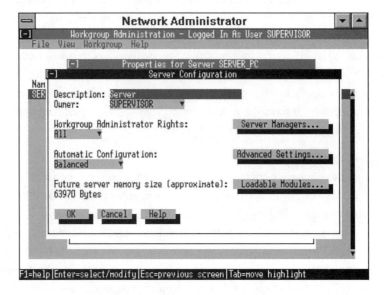

The item labeled Automatic Configuration is currently set at Balanced. Move the cursor to this field and press Enter. You are presented with three choices: Balanced, Max Performance, and Min Memory. These choices enable you to increase or decrease the amount of memory used by the network for buffering data for printers, disks, and traffic between the server and workstations, as well as for other internal uses.

Generally, the more memory the network has to work with, the faster the throughput. Any increase in memory usage by the network, however, comes at the expense of other applications. If your server is also functioning as a user workstation—that is, as a client—you may want to leave the setting at Balanced. If your workstation is a server and client, but shares few of its re-sources, change this setting to Min Memory. In this example, your server functions only as a server and shares all its resources. You will want the great-est possible performance, so change this setting to Max Performance. Then choose Advanced Settings to access the dialog box shown in figure 24.4.

This dialog box shows two columns labeled Configured and Future. The val-ues in the Configured column are for the running network software. The Future column displays the values that will be used the next time you start the network, assuming you save the new configuration.

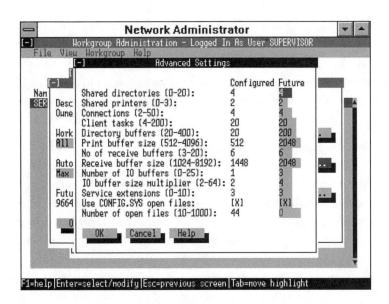

Fig. 24.4
The Advanced Settings dialog box.

Notice that the values for Directory Buffers, Print Buffer Size, No of Receive Buffers, Number of IO Buffers, and IO Buffer Size Multiplier have all increased. These values mean a substantial increase in the amount of memory the network will use during its operation. The advantage is that data will move in and out of the server, and between its components, at a much higher rate.

Changing the Hardware

You can also increase the performance of your network by the type of hardware you use. The first item to consider is the network interface card. The network at Aesop's uses an Ethernet adapter that is capable of transmitting data at a rate of 10 million bits per second (megabits/sec). At first glance, this may seem like a great deal of information moving across the network cable. In reality, a combination of factors contributes to an actual throughput that is only a fraction of the expected data rate.

First of all, the network itself imposes an *overhead*—that is, extra work devoted to the operation of the network itself and not on behalf of any user. This overhead is greater for this particular type of Ethernet card, the NE2000, than for other types. If you change to a more advanced card, more of the effort to support the network connections can be performed by the interface itself, reducing the burden placed on the server processor and resulting in an increase in throughput.

IX

Using the Network

Other network interfaces, such as Token Ring, support speeds in excess of 10 megabits/sec. Typically, Token Ring cards are available in speeds up to 16 megabits/sec. There are other technologies, including a very advanced Ethernet and fiber-optic-based devices, that support rates in excess of 100 megabits/sec. The cost of these newer interface cards may be prohibitive, though.

Changing the Equipment Configuration

In very large network configurations, it may be advantageous to configure multiple interconnected, physical networks. LANs or networks are like highways: the more traffic, the greater the potential for traffic jams. Decreasing the amount of traffic on any given LAN or highway by using multiple data paths can result in a reduction in the potential for data traffic jams. Probably the most significant thing that you can do is plan how you are going to use network resources. If you have one user that uses an application which performs a great deal of disk reads and writes, and the data is not shared, it would be to your advantage to place the data on a local disk, thereby keeping the activity off the shared network disk.

On the subject of disks, the network can access data only as quickly as the server processor can provide it. That seems obvious enough, so the faster your disks, the more quickly data can be made available to network users. Faster drives, faster controllers, and disk caching will all contribute to greater availability of disk information to your network users. Furthermore, periodically compressing or defragmenting your disks with DISKOPT will go a long way in improving your disk access times.

Many other items can also be investigated. Consult a NetWare engineer or Novell technical support for answers to your more sophisticated requirements.

Using Novell DOS 7 Diagnostics

Networking utilities such as those provided with Novell DOS 7 are very complex creations. As such, the potential exists, although not very great, for things to go wrong.

If a problem does surface, the one thing that you will want to know is where to look. Of course, you should ask individuals questions to try to narrow down the problem. In most cases, it will be obvious, such as a disconnected cable, a powered-off PC, or a full disk. On other occasions, the problem may seem elusive, such as a general sluggishness in the system. Well, Novell has provided you with some help. Although not comprehensive, it can point the finger at the source of some network-related problems. The Novell Network Diagnostics program is a Microsoft Windows application that provides a real-time monitor for the following:

- Data traffic to and from each PC participating in the network

- Data traffic between the server and workstations

- Total data traffic within the workgroup over time

- Disk space utilization

To use the network diagnostics, start Windows and choose the Novell DOS 7 group. This group was created for you when you installed Novell DOS 7. If you installed Windows after Novell DOS 7 was installed and you have not subsequently run the Novell DOS Setup utility, run that utility now. All the required support software for Windows will be installed for you. Be sure that you run Setup from the \NWDOS directory, as the Windows Setup utility has the same name. Figure 24.5 shows the Novell DOS 7 program group; choose the Network Diagnostics icon by clicking it with your pointing device.

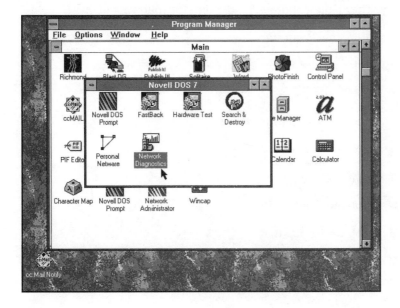

Fig. 24.5
The Windows program group for Novell DOS 7.

IX

Using the Network

When the diagnostics application is initialized, the Personal NetWare Diagnostics screen is displayed, as shown in figure 24.6.

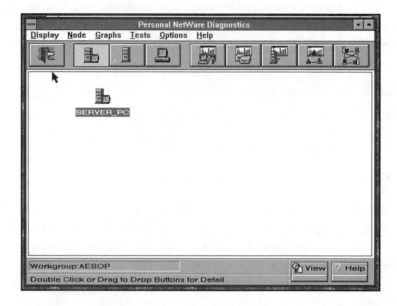

The first thing that you will want to do is take a look around to see that everything is functioning properly. Notice a row of icons across the top of the screen. They represent, from left to right, the following items:

- Exiting the diagnostic
- Displaying all connections
- Limiting the display to servers
- Limiting the display to clients
- Graph node traffic
- Graph disk utilization
- Graph server utilization
- Graph workgroup traffic
- Running all points test

Checking Server Traffic

First click the third icon from the left, the Server icon. Now look at some traffic. Click the Graph Node Traffic icon to display a graph like that in figure 24.7.

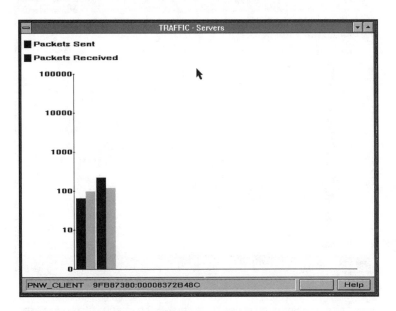

Fig. 24.7
Node traffic graph.

This graph shows a pair of vertical bars, one red and one blue, for each node (PC) connected to the network. The blue bar, or the one on the left, is the traffic sent to the network by this node. The red bar, or the one on the right, is the traffic received by this node from the network. Generally, you would not expect to see one node with data traffic that is disproportional to the other nodes.

Terminate this display and click the Server Utilization icon. Figure 24.8 shows the server utilization graph.

In this figure, the display is limited to clients. You can also select all nodes (connections) or just servers for this or any other graph at any time. For now, this graph shows the real-time traffic between each client and the server. If any single client is consuming a large amount of the network, this graph will make that situation obvious.

Tip
To limit the display to logged-on clients, click the terminate button (to the left of the Help button), click the Client icon, and restart the node traffic graph.

IX

Using the Network

You can also get a historical view of the total traffic in the workgroup by clicking the Work Group Traffic Graph icon (the eighth icon from the left). The graph that appears is shown in figure 24.9.

Fig. 24.8
Server utilization graph.

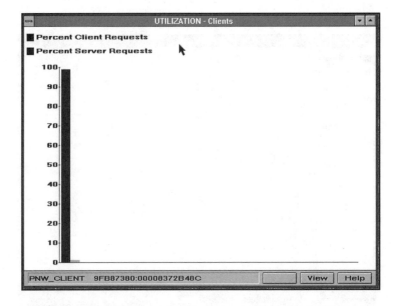

Fig. 24.9
Workgroup traffic graph.

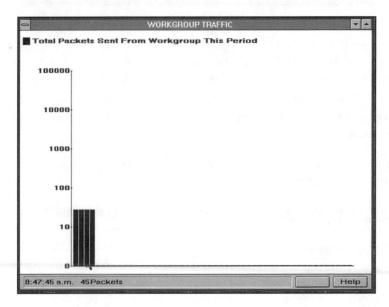

A vertical bar shows the total traffic in the workgroup. A snapshot is taken every five seconds. To see the actual number of packets sent, click any vertical bar, and a display will show the actual number of packets sent and the time the snapshot was taken.

Checking Disk Space

To see a graph of available disk space on the servers or workstations, click the Disk Space Graph icon. A sample of this display is shown in figure 24.10.

Depending on the display you have selected—all nodes, server, or client—two bars will be displayed for each node. The first shows the total disk space for this node, and the second shows available space.

Running the All Points Test

You may also run an all points test. This test, started when you click the All Points Test icon, sends packets to each node and counts the number of packets returned (see fig. 24.11). The counts should be equal. Any disparity may indicate a problem with the corresponding network PC.

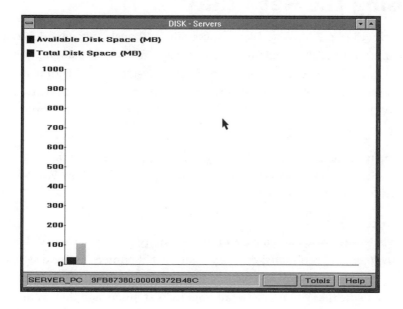

Fig. 24.10
Available disk space graph.

IX

Using the Network

Fig. 24.11
All points test.

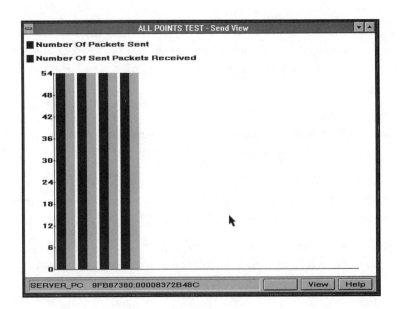

Using the Net Utility

The Novell DOS 7 Network Diagnostics utility, although quite useful, is not comprehensive. Additional utilities are available for NetWare and may be helpful. They will not point out problems, however, that exist with items unique to the Novell DOS 7 networking environment. Additional help can always be obtained from your local NetWare engineer or Novell technical support.

The network utilities provided with Novell DOS, in addition to the diagnostics program, are the Net utility, which runs under DOS, and the Windows-based Personal NetWare application.

Restricting Access Times

You have already made some use of the Net utility when you created the workgroups, defined shared directories and shared printers, and added users. You elected not to add security for the users for the AESOP project. Now suppose that you receive a call from users at Aesop, and they want to restrict access to their system. The Net utility permits security features to be associated with each user. To see how this is done, start the utility by entering **NET ADMIN** and logging into the workgroup as SUPERVISOR, as explained in Chapter 23. Open the View menu and choose Users. The Net utility displays the screen shown in figure 24.12.

The first item that AESOP would like is to permit access to the system only between 8 a.m. and 6:30 p.m. on Monday through Friday. To do this, first select the user—in this case, Martha—by highlighting the entry and pressing Enter. The Properties for Account dialog box appears, as shown in figure 24.13.

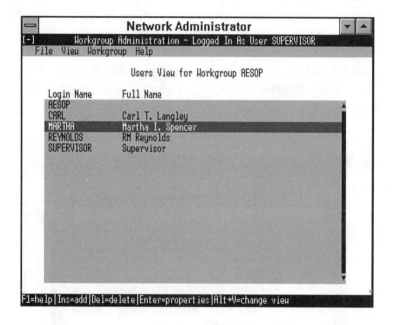

Fig. 24.12
The Users View screen.

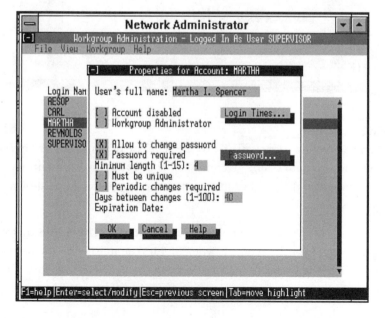

Fig. 24.13
The Properties for Account dialog box.

Now choose the Login Times button and press Enter. The Login Time Restrictions dialog box appears (see fig. 24.14).

This dialog box shows that a login is permitted for Martha during each half-hour time period where an asterisk is present. To change the default—which is 24 hours per day, 7 days per week—to the new requirement, move the cursor to the time period to be changed and press the space bar. The space bar serves as a toggle: press it once, and the asterisk changes to a space; press it again, and the space changes back to an asterisk. Now disable all the time periods except for 8 a.m. to 6:30 p.m. on Monday through Friday. The display should now look like that in figure 24.15. choose OK, and the Properties for Account dialog box is redisplayed (refer to fig. 23.13).

Fig. 24.14
Default login times.

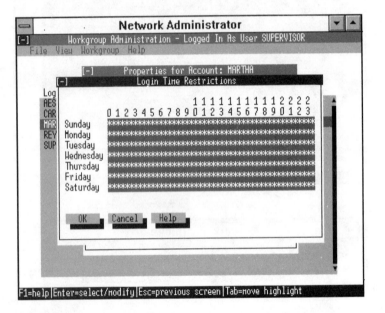

Setting Passwords

You can also require passwords. To do this, check Password Required in the Properties for Account dialog box and then choose the Password button. You are now given the opportunity to enter the new password, as shown in figure 24.16.

The Password and Verification fields are data-protected. This means that you will not see what you are typing as you enter it. You must enter the password twice—once in the Password field and once in the Verification field. For the passwords to be accepted, you must enter them identically. Then choose OK

to return to the previous screen. To require that the password be changed
periodically, you can check Periodic Changes Required and indicate the number of days between changes. When you are through, choose OK to accept
your changes.

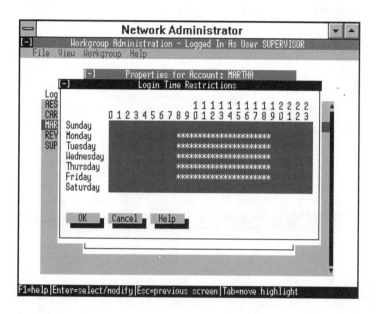

Fig. 24.15
Restricted login
times.

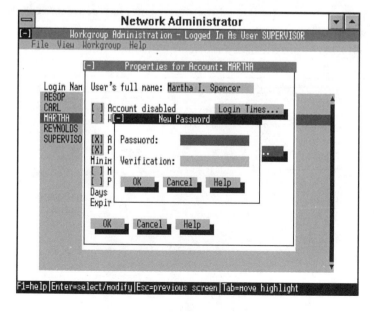

Fig. 24.16
Entering a
password.

IX

Using the Network

Getting Help with the Net Utility

The Net utility is a general-purpose network utility. In addition to providing the administrative functions you have used, it can perform various general-purpose functions. To see the functions that the utility can perform, enter **NET HELP** or **NET ?** from the DOS prompt. The screen shown in figure 24.17 appears.

Fig. 24.17
The NET help screen.

```
 NET                          NET Command-line Help                    1.00

    Purpose: To display online help for commands.
    Syntax:  NET [command] /?

    Commands:
        ADMIN        INFO         RECEIVE       TIME
        AUDIT        JOIN         RIGHTS        ULIST
        CAPTURE      LINK         SAVE          USER
        CONNECT      LOGIN        SEND          VLIST
        CONSOLE      LOGOUT       SETDOG        WAIT
        CONTEXT      MAP          SETPASS       WGFIND
        DIAGS        NTIME        SHARE         WGLIST
        DOWN         PLIST        SLIST         XLIST
        HELP         PRINT        SYNC

    For example, to:                         Type:
      Display help for NET MAP                 NET MAP /?


 [Novell DOS] C:\>
```

To request help on an individual command, enter **NET command HELP**. For instance, if you would like to learn about the NET LOGIN command, enter **NET LOGIN HELP**. You then see the screen shown in figure 24.18.

Fig. 24.18
The LOGIN help screen.

```
 NET                              Login Help                            1.00

    Purpose: To log in to a workgroup user account.
    Syntax:  NET LOGIN [[workgroup/][username]]|[@batfile]

    To:                                      Use:
      Log in to a specific workgroup           workgroup name
      Log in as a specific user                username
      Log in using a batch file created using
        the NET SAVE command                   @batfile name

    For example, to:                         Type:
      Log in as KIM to workgroup SALES         NET LOGIN SALES/KIM

      Use MYLOGIN.BAT batch file               NET LOGIN MYLOGIN.BAT


 [Novell DOS] C:\>
```

You can also use the DOSBook utility to view the networking commands. If you enter **NET** by itself, a full-screen display similar to that you saw with NET ADMIN is provided for you. An example of this screen is shown in figure 24.19.

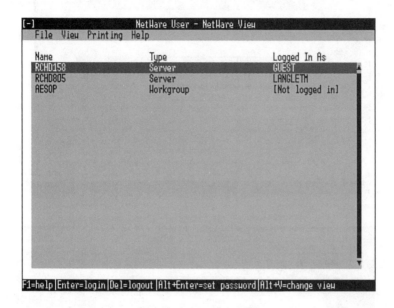

Fig. 24.19
A NET user
display.

To perform a login by using the user display, move the cursor to the entry you want to log into—in this case, AESOP—and press Enter. The login screen shown in figure 24.20 appears. This is the same screen that you used with NET ADMIN.

Experiment with the other features of NET while you are in the full-screen utility. You may always press the F1 key to obtain help.

Using the Personal NetWare Utilities

Novell has also provided a Windows version of the Net utility. It is in the Novell DOS 7 group and is called Personal NetWare. Choose this item by clicking the associated icon. The screen shown in figure 24.21 appears.

If you would like to log in with this utility, highlight the workgroup or server and then press Enter. A new dialog box is displayed (see fig. 24.22). Enter your name and click OK. As before, you can press the F1 key or click the Help button for additional help.

IX

Using the Network

Fig. 24.20
The NET login
dialog box.

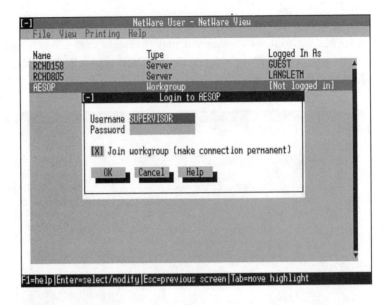

Fig. 24.21
The Personal
NetWare applica-
tion screen.

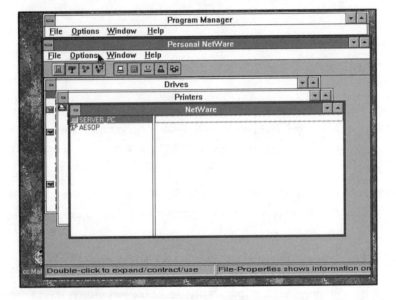

From Here...

In this chapter, you learned about connecting to other versions of NetWare.
You learned how you can adjust parameters within the network setup to
improve the performance of your network. The diagnostic utilities covered

can provide you with the tools necessary to identify and correct common problems. The Net and Windows-based Personal NetWare utilities are the key utilities for access and modification with the Novell DOS 7 networking software.

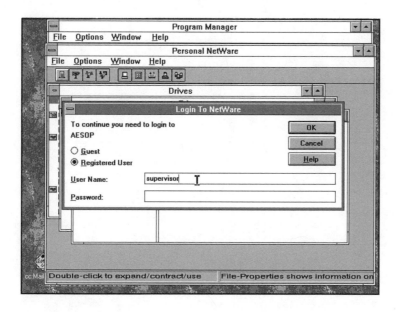

Fig. 24.22
The Login To NetWare dialog box.

For more information on networking, turn to the following chapters:

- Chapter 5, "Installing the Network," guides you through the installation process for the Novell DOS network.

- Chapter 23, "Introduction to Networking," shows you how to plan and configure a network.

IX

Using the Network

Part X

Command
Reference

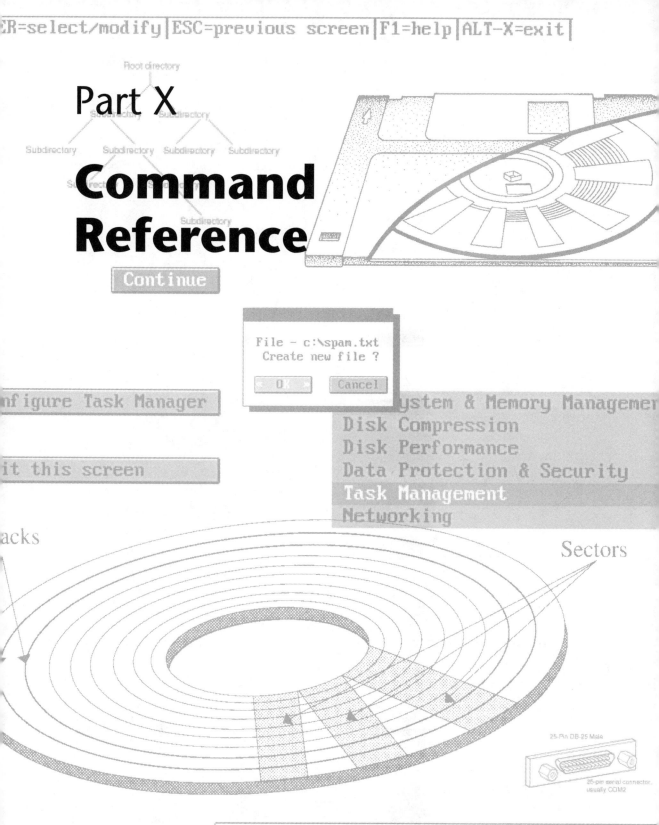

Continue

```
File - c:\spam.txt
Create new file ?

  <  O K  >     Cancel
```

nfigure Task Manager

it this screen

ystem & Memory Managemer
Disk Compression
Disk Performance
Data Protection & Security
Task Management
Networking

acks

Sectors

Change destination drive(s) and directorie

Root directory

Subdirectory   Subdirectory

Subdirectory   Subdirectory   Subdirectory   Subdirectory

Subdirectory   Subdirectory

Subdirectory

Continue

File - c:\spam.txt
Create new file ?

< O >   Cancel

nfigure Task Manager

it this screen

ystem & Memory Managemer
Disk Compression
Disk Performance
Data Protection & Security
Task Management
Networking

racks   Sectors

25-Pin DB-25 Male

25-pin serial connector
usually COM2

Change destination drive(s) and directori

Command Reference

The entries in this Command Reference include all commands that you can issue in the CONFIG.SYS file, DCONFIG.SYS file, AUTOEXEC.BAT file, and other batch files, as well as from the DOS command line. For your convenience, the Command Reference is divided into three sections: "Commands for CONFIG.SYS or DCONFIG.SYS," "Commands for Batch Files," and "Commands for the DOS Prompt."

Commands for CONFIG.SYS or DCONFIG.SYS

The commands described in this section may be issued in the CONFIG.SYS or DCONFIG.SYS file.

\<F5\>   Internal

Strictly speaking, the pressing of the F5 key is not part of the CONFIG.SYS or DCONFIG.SYS file. You press this key when, on booting your system, you see the message Starting DOS... on-screen to tell DOS not to process the CONFIG.SYS, DCONFIG.SYS, or AUTOEXEC.BAT file at all. You have about five seconds to press the key before any other messages appear; otherwise, it is too late.

\<F8\>   Internal

As with the F5 key, the pressing of the F8 key is not part of the CONFIG.SYS or DCONFIG.SYS file. You press this key when, on booting your system, you see the message Starting DOS... on-screen to tell DOS to process the CONFIG.SYS or DCONFIG.SYS file and the AUTOEXEC.BAT file but to request confirmation for executing each statement or command in each file. You have about five seconds to press the key before any other messages appear; otherwise, it is too late.

Note

You cannot press both the F5 key and the F8 key in the same boot process. You can press only one key.

?   Internal

When you place a question mark at the beginning of a statement in the AUTOEXEC.BAT, CONFIG.SYS, or DCONFIG.SYS file, DOS asks whether you want the command to be executed when the file is read during booting. You can enter a message to appear in place of the command if you like.

Syntax

```
? "message" command
```

The optional *message* must be enclosed in double quotation marks. This command is useful if you want to change settings, depending on the applications you want to run. You can use the CONFIG.SYS or DCONFIG.SYS TIMEOUT command (see the section on TIMEOUT) to set a time limit for DOS to wait for an answer. Otherwise, you cannot proceed until you answer the question. You can answer by pressing either Y for yes or N for no, and you do not press Enter afterward.

Notice that the maximum length allowed for a command statement, including ? and a message string, is 128 characters. Any statement longer than that is ignored.

Examples

1. The command

   ```
   ?DEVICE=EMM386.EXE MULTI DPMI=ON /F=AUTO
   ```

   in your CONFIG.SYS or DCONFIG.SYS file causes DOS to ask

   ```
   DEVICE=EMM386.EXE MULTI DPMI=ON /F=AUTO (Y/N) ?
   ```

2. The command

   ```
   ?"Do you wish to set up the multi-tasker (Y/N)
   "DEVICE=EMM386.EXE MULTI DPMI=ON /F=AUTO
   ```

   causes DOS to ask

   ```
   Do you wish to set up the multi-tasker (Y/N) ?
   ```

:*label*   **Internal**

You can define sections of your CONFIG.SYS or DCONFIG.SYS file by heading any section with a label. Later, you can use GOSUB, GOTO, or SWITCH to jump to that section.

Syntax

    :*label*

The ***label*** must be alphanumeric (up to eight characters) and must be preceded with a colon. The label must be on a line by itself. Place the commands to be executed when the label is read on the next and following lines. A jump to a section is made in a CONFIG.SYS or DCONFIG.SYS file from a GOSUB, GOTO, or SWITCH command.

Example

```
?"Do you want a memory disk (Y/N) ?"GOTO MEMDISK
        .
        .
        .
        :MEMDISK
        DEVICE=VDISK.SYS
        .
```

This example allows you to choose whether you want to load the virtual (RAM) disk.

BREAK   **Internal**

BREAK determines whether you can press Ctrl-Break or Ctrl-C to stop a program while it is running.

Syntax

    BREAK=*xxx*

xxx is either ON or OFF. If you set BREAK=ON, DOS checks for the abort keys (Ctrl-Break or Ctrl-C) when a program is running, and aborts the program. If you set BREAK=OFF, DOS checks only when the running program reads from the keyboard, writes to the screen, or sends data to a printer. Entering this command without any parameter at the DOS prompt informs you of the current status of BREAK.

Note

Some application programs disable the use of BREAK to abort them.

BUFFERS   Internal

The BUFFERS command tells DOS how many small memory blocks to use for disk read and write operations. Generally, the more buffers, the faster DOS accesses files.

Note the recommended number of buffers for the amount of memory installed in your computer:

Less than 640K	Use 10 buffers
640K	Use 20 buffers
More than 1M	Use 20-30 buffers

When using a disk-caching utility, such as NWCACHE, reduce the number of buffers to 3 or 4. Too many buffers will slow the operation of the cache. Follow the recommendations of the manufacturer of your caching utility.

Syntax

    BUFFERS=*nn*

Replace *nn* with the number of memory blocks. The range is from 3 to 99. The default for Novell DOS is 20. These buffers do use memory that is not then used for the program and the data. Thus, too many buffers can slow your application. Many software programs indicate in their documentation or installation utilities the number of buffers to use for optimum performance.

CHAIN   Internal

The CHAIN command enables you to transfer execution from the CONFIG.SYS or DCONFIG.SYS file to another named configuration file when your system is booting. You can invoke CHAIN with the ? command to use different configurations while booting.

Syntax

    CHAIN=*filename.ext*

The *filename.ext* must include the file location path if the specified file is not in the default directory. You must also include the file extension if there is one. The chained file must follow the rules of the CONFIG.SYS or DCONFIG.SYS file, even though the name might not match.

CHAIN verifies that the specified file exists. If the file is found, CHAIN closes the current file and begins to process the chained file. If the file does not exist, processing continues in the original file.

CLS   Internal

CLS is the same as the DOS command-line CLS command and is used to clear the screen and move the cursor to the upper-left corner.

Syntax

```
CLS
```

Place this command on a line by itself. It is quite helpful when you want to ask questions (as in using ?). However, the on-screen messages obscure what you want, so clear the screen first.

COUNTRY   Internal

The COUNTRY command loads the DOS COUNTRY.SYS file, which provides the national date and time format, the national currency symbol, and optionally, the code page to use for national characters for the specified country.

Syntax

```
COUNTRY=nnn,cp,COUNTRY.SYS
```

Although most people using this book are probably following the U.S. national customs for date, time, and currency, many people still may want to use other national formats. The *nnn* refers to the country code number, as used with the international telephone convention. Appendix A contains the country code table for Novell DOS 7.

The code page number, which is different from the country code and is referenced in the preceding format by *cp*, does not have to be specified unless you want to enable code page switching. (Refer to Appendix A for more about code page switching.) If you do not specify the code page, you still must enter the second comma (,). You cannot mix page codes with country codes. If you use the country code 001 (United States), you cannot use the code page code 863 (French Canada).

You must specify the location of the file COUNTRY.SYS if it is not in the current directory.

Examples

1. The following line is the default entry for most U.S. systems, containing the country code 1 (for USA) and no code page entry:

```
COUNTRY=1,,C:\NWDOS\COUNTRY.SYS
```

2. The following line identifies that the users want to use the date and time formats and currency symbol for Italy:

```
COUNTRY=039, 437, C:\NWDOS\COUNTRY.SYS
```

CPOS   Internal

This command enables you to place the cursor at any valid location on-screen. CPOS is quite useful if you want to design a menu system within your CONFIG.SYS or DCONFIG.SYS file.

Syntax

```
CPOS nn,nn
```

The first parameter (*nn*) is for the row, with a range of 1 to 25. The second parameter (*nn*) is for the column, with a range of 1 to 80. The two parameters must be separated by a comma.

Example

```
CPOS 10,20
```

This command tells DOS to place the cursor on-screen in row 10, column 20.

DEVICE   Internal

You use this command to tell DOS to install device drivers. Depending on the driver, you may be able to specify configuration switches.

Syntax

```
DEVICE=filename.ext options
```

You need device drivers to load and operate certain devices on your system when they are not recognized by DOS as default parts of your computer. These drivers may be for hardware devices such as a mouse or CD-ROM drive, or for software devices such as a memory manager or RAM disk.

The following device drivers are included with Novell DOS 7:

ANSI.SYS	Auxiliary device driver for your keyboard and screen. Provides extra features for handling these devices. You can use ANSI codes with your PROMPT commands and in batch files.
DISPLAY.SYS	Driver to enable code page switching for EGA and VGA screen displays.
DPMS.EXE	Memory manager for loading DPMS client drivers and TSRs above the 1M memory area on 386 and higher systems.
DRIVER.SYS	Defines the characteristics of a physical disk drive that the operating system does not see automatically.
EMM386.EXE	Memory manager for 386 and higher computers.
EMMXMA.SYS	Memory manager for converting extended memory on XMS memory cards to expanded memory.
HIMEM.SYS	Memory manager for 286 computers.
PRINTER.SYS	Driver to enable code page switching for printers that have code page switching.
VDISK.SYS	Driver that allows you to establish a disk drive in RAM instead of using an actual physical drive.

If you obtain hardware that does not have a device driver included in this list—for example, a mouse driver—you must receive the driver for that device from the manufacturer with the device and then manually add it to your CONFIG.SYS or DCONFIG.SYS file. Some items have an install procedure that does this for you.

The related command, HIDEVICE or DEVICEHIGH, is listed later in this Command Reference.

Example

```
DEVICE=C:\NWDOS\ANSI.SYS
```

This command tells DOS to load ANSI.SYS every time you start your computer.

DOS   Internal

This command tells the operating system where to load DOS in memory.

Syntax

```
DOS=xxx
```

In place of **xxx**, use HIGH, LOW, or UMB. If your computer includes extended memory, with this command, DOS can be loaded in high memory or in upper memory blocks. Without this command or with the LOW parameter, DOS is automatically loaded at the bottom of lower (conventional) memory. You can increase memory for applications if you can load DOS high.

To load DOS high, you must first have installed a memory manager (EMM386.EXE, HIMEM.SYS, or EMMXMA.SYS).

Example

```
DOS=HIGH
```

This is the default installation for Novell DOS 7 if you have an 80386SX or higher computer and you do not tell DOS to load itself in another location.

DRIVPARM   Internal

The DRIVPARM command is used to describe to DOS the characteristics of a drive that exists but is not recognized correctly by DOS. For example, if a computer recognizes a second floppy drive but sees it as a 5 1/4-inch drive rather than as a 3 1/2-inch drive, use the DRIVPARM command to redefine the drive parameters to match the actual drive.

Syntax

```
DRIVPARM=/D:n /C /F:n /H:nn /I /N /S:ss /T:nn
```

Switches

/D:*n*	Specifies a number (0 to 25) that corresponds to the logical drive for which you are defining characteristics.
/C	Specifies that the drive is able to detect when a disk is changed.
/F:*n*	Specifies the drive type. Use one of the following number codes: 0 = 360K, 1 = 1.2M, 5 = hard disk, 6 = tape, 7 = 1.44M, 8 = read/write optical disk, and 9 = 2.88M
/H:*nn*	Specifies the maximum number of drive heads (from 1 to 99). The default depends on the value specified for /F:*n*.
/I	Specifies a 3 1/2-inch floppy disk drive that is installed on your computer and uses the existing floppy disk drive controller. Use this switch when your computer does not support 3 1/2-inch floppy disk drives.
/N	Specifies that the drive is for permanent media.
/S:*nn*	The number of sectors (from 1 to 99) supported by the drive. The default depends on the value specified for /F:*n*.
/T:*nn*	The number of tracks supported by the drive. The default depends on the value specified for /F:*n*.

ECHO   Internal

The ECHO command tells DOS to display messages when it processes your CONFIG.SYS or DCONFIG.SYS file. This command is quite handy for setting up menus and system configuration choices.

Syntax

ECHO *message*

When DOS processes CONFIG.SYS or DCONFIG.SYS, it usually displays only those messages caused by any drivers or other utilities loading. With this command, you can display your own messages. Do not use any quotation marks for your message.

The ECHO command may be used to document your CONFIG.SYS or DCONFIG.SYS file. ECHO is often used to display a message indicating that a specific command is being executed.

EXIT   Internal

This command tells DOS to end processing of the CONFIG.SYS or DCONFIG.SYS file at the current statement.

Syntax

```
EXIT
```

FASTOPEN   External

This command tells DOS to set up a special memory area to store the names and locations of the most frequently used files. FASTOPEN can speed up your system so that it does not have to search for the files every time they are accessed.

Syntax

```
FASTOPEN=nnnnn
```

You specify the number of entries (*nnnnn*) for the table. The range is 128 to 32768, and the default is 512. The table for FASTOPEN uses two bytes of memory for each entry. Thus, do not specify more than you need.

FCBS   Internal

The FCBS command provides data structures called File Control Blocks (FCBs) for those older application programs that use them rather than the newer FILES command to keep track of open files.

Syntax

```
FCBS=mm,nn
```

The first parameter, *mm*, specifies the number of FCBs (from 1 to 255) that can be open at one time. The second parameter, *nn*, specifies the number of files (from 1 to 255) opened with FCBs that are protected from automatic closure by the system. The second parameter protects files so that when an application tries to open more files than are indicated by *mm*, all files except the first *nn* files may be closed. Both parameters must be specified.

Example

```
FCBS=8,4
```

This command sets the allowed maximum number of open files to eight, and the number of protected files to four.

Note

Most users should set FCBS=1,1 to minimize memory usage. Increase the parameters only if DOS 1.0 applications are used. FCBS cannot be set to zero.

FILES   Internal

This command specifies the number of files that can be opened simultaneously by all operating software. DOS uses this command to determine how much memory to use for controlling open files.

Syntax

```
FILES=nn
```

The range you can enter in place of **nn** is from 20 to 255. Do not enter a number smaller than the default of 20. The documentation for your applications should tell you whether more file handles are required so that the software can run properly. You also may receive an error message indicating that the number of open files allowed is not enough for a program. Don't forget that when you change any CONFIG.SYS or DCONFIG.SYS statement, you must reboot your system for the changes to take effect.

GOSUB   Internal

This command tells DOS to continue processing the CONFIG.SYS or DCONFIG.SYS file at the statement following the location of the label in the file and then return to the next command when a RETURN command is encountered after the label.

Syntax

```
GOSUB label
```

You must specify the label for the jump. The **label** in the command does not have a leading colon. The label, as the header for the section of the CONFIG.SYS or DCONFIG.SYS file, must have the leading colon. Sections referenced by a GOSUB command must finish with a RETURN command. In programming, such a section is referred to as a *subroutine*.

Example

```
GOSUB MEMDISK
EXIT
:MEMDISK
DEVICE=VDISK.SYS
RETURN
```

In this example, you see the GOSUB command executing the MEMDISK subroutine and then returning to execute the EXIT command.

GOTO   Internal

Use this command to change the order in which statements in the CONFIG.SYS or DCONFIG.SYS file are executed. The execution continues with the statement following the label referenced by the GOTO command.

Syntax

```
GOTO label
```

You must specify the label for the jump. The *label* in the command does not have a leading colon. The label, as the header for the section of the CONFIG.SYS or DCONFIG.SYS file, must have the leading colon. Sections referenced by a GOTO command do not have to jump elsewhere in the file, but they may.

An excellent use for GOTO is with the ?. Thus, depending on the response, a different part of the file can be executed.

Example

```
?"Do you want to optimize the disks (Y/N) ?"GOTO OPT
CHKDSK /F
EXIT
:OPT
CHKDISK /F
DISKOPT C:
SDEFRAG D:
EXIT
```

This example gives you the option of checking and optimizing the disks, or bypassing the optimization and just checking.

HIDEVICE or DEVICEHIGH   Internal

This version of the DEVICE command (refer to the earlier section on DEVICE) loads a device driver into upper memory. Both forms of this command name have the same effect.

Syntax

```
HIDEVICE | DEVICEHIGH size=nnnn filename.ext
```

You must include the name of the file and its extension. Some device drivers, when loaded high, require more memory to initially load than they require once installed, and they are unable to determine the memory requirements. You can specify the `size=` parameter to assist the driver.

For you to determine the memory requirements of any such driver, before placing the driver in the CONFIG.SYS or DCONFIG.SYS file, boot your system and run the MEM command. Then load the driver into lower memory and again run the MEM command. The difference between the two numbers is the number to use with `size=`.

Example

```
HIDEVICE=C:\NWDOS\ANSI.SYS
```

This command loads the ANSI.SYS driver into upper memory; the similar command, using `DEVICE=`, loads ANSI.SYS into lower memory.

HIINSTALL or INSTALLHIGH   Internal

This command enables you to load a program or TSR into upper memory from the CONFIG.SYS or DCONFIG.SYS file rather than from the command line or a batch file. This command is different from the HIDEVICE and DEVICEHIGH commands, which load device drivers, not programs. The INSTALL command loads these programs into lower memory. Both forms of the command name have the same effect.

Syntax

```
HIINSTALL | INSTALLHIGH=filename.ext options
```

You must enter the full name and extension of the program file to be loaded high. You may also include any parameters required by the program. A memory manager must be enabled in order for the command to have effect. Options are any command-line parameters that are passed to the program being loaded.

For you to determine the memory requirements of any such program, before placing the command in the CONFIG.SYS or DCONFIG.SYS file, boot your system and run the MEM command. Then load the program into lower memory and again run the MEM command. The difference between the two numbers is the amount of memory required in upper memory to load it high.

You can load the following Novell DOS utilities with HIINSTALL/INSTALLHIGH:

> CURSOR.EXE
> GRAFTABL.COM
> GRAPHICS.COM
> KEYB.COM
> NLSFUNC.EXE
> PRINT.COM
> SHARE.EXE

Example

```
HIINSTALL=C:\NWDOS\CURSOR.EXE
```

This command installs the CURSOR program in upper memory.

HISTORY   Internal

The HISTORY command lets you enable or disable the command-line recall and edit feature of Novell DOS. Commands entered at the DOS prompt are stored in a special buffer for recall and editing.

Syntax

```
HISTORY=xxx,nnnn,yyy
```

Replace *xxx* with ON, which enables HISTORY, or OFF, which disables HISTORY. You can also specify the size of the buffer that DOS uses for command-line storage. Replace *nnnn* with a number in a range of 128 to 4096 bytes. The size of the buffer determines the number of commands that can be stored. A buffer size of 512 bytes, the default, holds approximately 10 commands, depending on the length of the commands.

Replace *yyy* with ON, which toggles the insert mode on, or OFF, which toggles the insert mode off. The insert mode determines whether characters you enter while editing a command line overwrite the characters at the cursor or are inserted in the line.

Example

```
HISTORY=ON,512,OFF
```

This command enables the feature, sets the storage buffer at 512 bytes, and turns off the insert mode.

INSTALL   Internal

Use this command to load a program into lower memory from the CONFIG.SYS or DCONFIG.SYS file every time you start your computer. You can specify any parameters the program requires or can use. Typically, less memory is required when a command is loaded by INSTALL.

Syntax

```
INSTALL=filename.ext options
```

You must include the path of the file if the location is not in the current directory. Additionally, you must include the complete file name, with extension. Use the DEVICE= command to load device drivers into lower memory.

You can load the following Novell DOS utilities with INSTALL:

CURSOR.EXE
GRAFTABL.COM
GRAPHICS.COM
KEYB.COM
NLSFUNC.EXE
PRINT.COM
SHARE.EXE

Example

```
INSTALL=C:\NWDOS\GRAPHICS.COM
```

This command loads the GRAPHICS utility for using the PrtSc key to print a graphics display on your graphics-capable printer.

LASTDRIVE   Internal

This command tells DOS to set a different last drive letter from that which is automatically determined at boot time. The operating system assigns a drive letter to each logical drive found during system startup. The letter for the last drive found is the last drive letter unless changed with this command.

Syntax

```
LASTDRIVE=x
```

Replace the *x* with an appropriate drive letter. Be sure to allow for use of the ASSIGN and SUBST commands and any devices that may require an extra drive letter.

REM   Internal

Use this command to add comments to your CONFIG.SYS or DCONFIG.SYS file or to tell DOS not to execute any line that starts with REM. You can also use a semicolon to disable the execution of a statement.

Syntax

```
REM comment
```

The *comment* is optional, in case you want to use REM to provide a line of space in the CONFIG.SYS or DCONFIG.SYS file. Otherwise, it can be a comment or note to remind you of the reason for a command, or a statement you do not want executed.

RETURN   Internal

This command is used with a GOSUB or SWITCH command to end execution of a subroutine within CONFIG.SYS or DCONFIG.SYS and to return processing to the line following the GOSUB or SWITCH. For more information on those commands, refer to GOSUB and SWITCH in this section of the Command Reference.

Syntax

```
RETURN
```

This command appears on a line by itself.

Example

```
GOSUB MEMDISK
EXIT
:MEMDISK
DEVICE=VDISK.SYS
RETURN
```

This example executes the MEMDISK subroutine before returning to the EXIT command.

SET   Internal

You can use the SET command to add variables to the main environment, which can then be tested by programs and by AUTOEXEC.BAT or other batch files to direct execution.

Syntax

```
SET envvar=value
```

Replace *envvar* with the environment variable being established; replace *value* with what you want the variable to represent. Then any program or batch file, which wants to test for this environment variable to see what it represents, can change actions depending on the result of the test.

Example

```
SET VDISK="FALSE"
?"Do you want a memory disk (Y/N) ?"GOTO MEMDISK
EXIT
:MEMDISK
DEVICE=VDISK.SYS
SET VDISK="TRUE"
EXIT
```

In this example, the memory disk is loaded only if you answer Y to the question. Before you answer the question, the environment variable is established with a value of "FALSE". If you answer the question with N, the execution ends, and any test of the variable VDISK returns a FALSE value. If you answer Y to the question, however, the execution proceeds to the section labeled :MEMDISK, and after the device driver VDISK.SYS is loaded, the environment variable VDISK is reset to "TRUE".

The next group of commands in the AUTOEXEC.BAT file can now determine what action to take, depending on the value of VDISK:

```
IF "%VDISK%"=="FALSE" GOTO NORAMDSK
IF "%VDISK%"=="TRUE" GOTO ISRAMDSK
```

SHELL   Internal

This command is used to tell DOS the name and location of the command processor being used by the operating system.

Syntax

```
SHELL=filename.ext path /P:filename /E:nnnnn /Mx
```

DOS, by default, loads COMMAND.COM from the root directory of the boot drive, C:. You can use the SHELL command to change the name of the command processor as well as the location of the file. You must specify the full name and extension of the command processor file, and the path must include the drive and directory where it is located. The Novell DOS Install utility automatically places COMMAND.COM in C: and sets the SHELL statement in CONFIG.SYS or DCONFIG.SYS.

The *path* parameter is the "reload" path when you use COMMAND to run programs. This establishes a path back to the initial command processor.

Switches

/P:*filename*	The /P (permanent) switch is required with the SHELL command to fix the specified command processor in memory. You should always use this option for the main or primary command processor. If not, you can exit from the command processor and can continue to use the computer only by rebooting it. On loading secondary command processors, you usually do not include this switch so that you can return to the primary environment.
	The *filename*, if included, allows you to change the name of the AUTOEXEC.BAT file to whatever batch file you specify. Otherwise, AUTOEXEC.BAT is the default name of the boot batch file for DOS.
/E:*nnnnn*	This switch specifies the size of the command processing environment in bytes. For *nnnnn*, use a number from 129 to 32751. The default size is 256 bytes. Increase the size if you get an Out of Environment error.
/M*x*	Use this switch to force the command processor to load into a specific memory area, where *x* is L (lower), H (high), or U (upper). The default is L for lower memory. To load the command processor into upper or high memory, you must have a memory manager that supports high or upper memory.

The SHELL command in your CONFIG.SYS or DCONFIG.SYS file automatically sets the environment variable COMSPEC with the name and location of the command processor as defined with SHELL.

Example

```
SHELL=C:\NWDOS\COMMAND.COM C:\NWDOS /P /E:512
```

This command loads COMMAND.COM from the C:\NWDOS subdirectory rather than from the root directory.

STACKS   Internal

The STACKS command supports the use of data stacks for hardware interrupts.

Syntax

STACKS=*nnn*,*mmm*

Some applications require the use of the STACKS command so that they can interface correctly with hardware. The *nnn* parameter is for the number of stacks, with a range of 8 to 64, or you can specify 0 and not use any stacks. The *mmm* parameter is for the size of each stack, with a range of 32 to 512. You should specify a size of 0 when you set 0 stacks.

The default STACKS setting is 0,0 for IBM PCs and PC/XTs and is 9,128 for other computers.

SWITCH   Internal

You use the SWITCH command to cause execution of different labeled sections of your CONFIG.SYS or DCONFIG.SYS file. SWITCH tells DOS to prompt you to make a selection, presumably of various system configurations, and then jumps to the selected subroutine.

Syntax

SWITCH *label1*, *label2*, *label3*,..., *label9*

Each section of the file must have a unique label, and each subroutine must end with a RETURN command. You must use at least two labels and can use a maximum of nine. You enter your selection by typing from 1 through the number of subroutines you have configured. By pressing the Enter key alone, the first selection is chosen. If you use the TIMEOUT command, the default selection is the first configuration listed if the TIMEOUT period passes without a keystroke.

Example

```
CLS
ECHO Menu Option #1
ECHO Menu Option #2
ECHO Menu Option #3
ECHO Please select Menu Option #1, #2, or #3:
SWITCH LABEL1, LABEL2, LABEL3
ECHO SYSTEM CONFIGURATION COMPLETE
EXIT
:LABEL1
ECHO Configuration #1 selected
RETURN
:LABEL2
ECHO Configuration #2 selected
RETURN
:LABEL3
ECHO Configuration #3 selected
RETURN
```

When your system reboots with the preceding menu in your CONFIG.SYS or DCONFIG.SYS file, the following display appears on your monitor:

```
Menu Option #1
Menu Option #2
Menu Option #3
Please select Menu Option #1, #2, or #3:
```

You can press Enter to select the first option, or enter 1, 2, or 3 to make your selection. If you have TIMEOUT active and the specified number of seconds passes, option 1 is automatically selected. After the message for the selected option, `Configuration #n selected`, execution continues with the statement after the SWITCH command. The final display is `SYSTEM CONFIGURATION COMPLETE`, and execution of CONFIG.SYS or DCONFIG.SYS ends.

TIMEOUT   Internal

Use this command in your CONFIG.SYS or DCONFIG.SYS file to set a time limit for the processing of the file to continue when DOS encounters a ? or SWITCH statement and no key is entered within the specified time period.

Syntax

```
TIMEOUT=nn
TIMEOUT nn
```

Both forms of the command are valid. You must have TIMEOUT execute in CONFIG.SYS or DCONFIG.SYS before the ? or SWITCH command if you want it to affect those commands. The *nn* denotes the number of seconds for ? or

SWITCH to wait. The default value is 0, causing TIMEOUT to wait indefi-
nitely for a keystroke. All commands starting with ? are ignored when the
specified TIMEOUT period expires. All commands starting with SWITCH
execute the first selection when the specified TIMEOUT period expires.

Commands for Batch Files

The commands described in this section may be used in batch files.

Batch Command   Internal

A batch command executes one or more commands contained in an ASCII
text file that has a BAT extension.

Syntax

```
filename.ext parameters
```

filename.ext is the root name of the batch file.

parameters are those used by the batch file.

Rules for Batch Files

1. A batch file must use the extension BAT.

2. To invoke a batch file, type the name. For example, to invoke the batch
   file OFTEN.BAT, type **OFTEN** and press Enter.

3. DOS executes each command one line at a time. The specified parameters are substituted for the command placeholders (%0-%9) when the
   command is used.

4. DOS recognizes a maximum of 10 parameters. You can use the SHIFT
   subcommand to get around this limitation.

5. You can stop a running batch file by pressing Ctrl-Break or Ctrl-C. DOS
   displays the following message:

   ```
   Halt batch process (Y/N) ?
   ```

   If you press Y for yes, all subsequent commands are ignored and the
   system prompt appears. If you press N for no, DOS skips the current
   command but continues to process the other commands in the file.

6. You can make DOS execute a second batch file immediately after the first is finished. Enter the name of the second batch file as the last command in the first file. You can also execute a second batch file within the first and return to the first file by using the CALL subcommand.

Rules for the AUTOEXEC.BAT File

1. If you do not specify a batch file to be executed in the SHELL command in your CONFIG.SYS file, the file must be named AUTOEXEC.BAT.

2. AUTOEXEC.BAT must reside in the root directory of the boot disk, unless you are using Superstor (SSTORDRV.SYS and DEVSWAP.COM). If you are, AUTOEXEC.BAT must reside in the root directory of the drive that becomes logical drive C.

3. DOS, when booted, automatically executes the AUTOEXEC.BAT file or the alternative file named in the SHELL statement.

Rules for Creating Batch Files

1. A batch file contains ASCII text.

2. You can include any valid DOS system-level command in a batch file.

3. You can enter any valid batch subcommand. (The batch subcommands are included in this Command Reference.) You also can use replaceable parameters (%0-%9). You can use environment variables by enclosing the name of the variable in percent signs (such as %COMSPEC%).

4. To designate a file name that contains a percent symbol as part of the file name, enter the percent symbol twice. For example, to use a file called A100%.TXT, you enter **A100%%.TXT**. This rule differs from the one for parameter markers, where percent symbols precede the parameter markers, and for environment variables, which are enclosed in percent symbols.

5. You can prevent the display of any line from the batch file if @ is the first character on the line.

6. Do not name a batch file by using the same name as a DOS command or program. Typically, the DOS command or program will be involved, and the batch file will be ignored.

@   **Internal**

This command tells DOS not to display a command in a batch file when it
executes the command and ECHO is turned on.

@ must be the first character in the command line. There can be a space after
@, but not before @.

@ normally is used with ECHO (as in @ECHO OFF), which tells DOS not to
display the following batch file instructions and not to display the ECHO OFF
command either.

CALL   **Internal**

This subcommand runs a second batch file and returns control to the first
batch file.

Syntax

```
CALL filename.ext parameters
```

filename.ext is the name of the called batch file.

parameters are those used by the batch file.

Rule

The batch file is run and parameters are passed to the called batch file as if it
were being run by the user.

CHOICE   **External**

CHOICE is a batch file subcommand that provides the user with displayed
options. The user makes a selection by pressing a key, and CHOICE returns
an ERRORLEVEL depending on the key pressed. By reading the ERRORLEVEL,
the execution of the batch file is altered. This command is similar to the
SWITCH command.

Syntax

```
CHOICE /C:choices /N /S /T:key,nn text
```

Parameters or Switches

/C:*choices*   This switch lists the keys from which the user makes the
                  selection. The selection can be any key you can enter at a

DOS prompt, except the space bar, the Tab key, and the slash keys (\ and /). If no key choices are entered, CHOICE displays [Y,N] ? If a prompt text is supplied, the choices are displayed after the text.

/N   This option disables the display of the options and the question mark.

/S   This switch tells CHOICE that the options are case-sensitive, meaning that if a selection is shown as a, you must press lowercase *a* to make the selection.

/T:*key*,*nn*   This switch tells CHOICE to default to choice *key* after *nn* seconds passes and no key is pressed. Note that *key* must be one of the characters specified in the /C switch. *nn* has a range of 0 to 99 seconds. If you enter 0, the /T switch is effectively ignored.

text   This is the prompt text you want displayed for the user. The key selections included in the /C:*choices* switch appear after this text. This text may not include a slash (/).

Examples

1. The following command requests a selection from the user, with a text prompt:

```
CHOICE /C:yne Yes, No, or Exit
```

When this line is executed in a batch file, the following is displayed on-screen:

```
Yes, No, or Exit [Y,N,E]
```

If the user presses Y, the ERRORLEVEL is set to 1. If the user presses N, the ERRORLEVEL is set to 2. If the user presses E, the ERRORLEVEL is set to 3.

2. The following command requests a selection from the user, with a text prompt, but has a default answer of N after 10 seconds if no key has been pressed:

```
CHOICE /C:yne /T:n,10 Yes, No, or Exit
```

When this line is executed in a batch file, the same message appears on-screen, but if no key is pressed within 10 seconds, CHOICE sets the ERRORLEVEL to 2 for the default N. Here is how the message looks:

```
Yes, No, or Exit [Y,N,E] ?
```

If the user presses Y, the ERRORLEVEL is set to 1. If the user presses N, the ERRORLEVEL is set to 2. If the user presses E, the ERRORLEVEL is set to 3.

3. The following is a sample batch file demonstrating the use of CHOICE with the selection of two Novell DOS utilities:

```
:START
@ECHO OFF
CLS
ECHO SDEFRAG
ECHO DISKOPT
CHOICE /C:SDQ Select an option or Q to quit
IF ERRORLEVEL 3 GOTO BAILOUT
IF ERRORLEVEL 2 GOTO OPT
IF ERRORLEVEL 1 GOTO FRAG
:FRAG
SDEFREG D:
CLS
GOTO START
:OPT
DISKOPT C:
CLS
GOTO START
:BAILOUT
CLS
```

Notes

1. CHOICE enters an ERRORLEVEL of 1 if the user presses the key corresponding to the first option, an ERRORLEVEL of 2 if the user presses the key for the second option, and so on. If the user presses Ctrl-C instead of the options in /C:*choices*, the ERRORLEVEL is set to 0. If the user enters any other invalid key, the ERRORLEVEL is set to 255.

2. You must then, in the batch file, test for the ERRORLEVEL. You always check the highest ERRORLEVEL first, because IF ERRORLEVEL always returns a TRUE if the ERRORLEVEL found is equal to or greater than that for which the IF ERRORLEVEL statement tests.

ECHO   Internal

Displays a message and enables or prevents the display of batch commands and other messages as DOS executes batch subcommands.

Syntax

To display a message, use the following form:

ECHO *message*

To turn off the display of commands and other batch command messages, use the following form:

ECHO OFF

To turn on the display of commands and messages, use this form:

ECHO ON

To see the status of ECHO, use the following form:

ECHO

message is the text of the message to appear on-screen.

To place a blank line between ECHO statements that display text, use

ECHO*p*

where *p* is one of the following punctuation marks:

. , : ; " / \ * ?

Rules

1. For unconditional display of a message on-screen, use the command ECHO *message*. The *message* you designate appears whether ECHO is turned on or off.

2. When ECHO is turned on, the batch file displays commands as DOS executes each line. The batch file also displays any messages from the batch subcommands.

3. When ECHO is turned off, the batch file does not display the commands as DOS executes them. Additionally, the batch file displays no messages produced by other batch subcommands. Exceptions to this

rule are the Strike a key when ready message generated by the PAUSE subcommand and any ECHO *message* command.

4. DOS starts the system with ECHO on.

5. An ECHO OFF command is active until batch processing is complete or until an ECHO ON command is encountered. If one batch file invokes another, ECHO remains off until the final batch file is processed.

6. ECHO affects messages produced only by batch subcommands. The command does not affect messages from other DOS commands or programs.

Note

You can suppress the display of a single batch file line by using @ as the first character in a line. When you use the line @ECHO OFF, the command ECHO OFF does not appear. To suppress the output of a command, use I/O redirection to the null device (NUL). For example, to suppress a copied file message when you are using COPY, use the following form:

```
COPY file1.ext file2.ext >NUL
```

The command output is sent to the null device and does not appear on-screen.

FOR..IN..DO   Internal

This commmand repeats the processing of a DOS command.

Syntax

```
FOR %%variable IN (set) DO command
```

variable is a single letter.

set is one or more words or file specifications. Each file specification is in the form *d:path\filename.ext*. Wild cards are allowed.

command is the DOS command to be performed for each word or file in the set.

Rules

1. You can use more than one word or full file specification in the set. You must separate words or file specifications by spaces or commas.

2. **%%variable** becomes each literal word or full file specification in the set. If you use wild-card characters, FOR..IN..DO executes once for each file that matches the wild-card file specification.

3. You can use path names with FOR..IN..DO.

4. You cannot nest FOR..IN..DO subcommands (put two of these commands on the same line). You can use other batch subcommands with FOR..IN..DO, including CALL, if you want to execute more than one command on the items in the set.

5. Two percent signs (%) are needed if the command is used in a batch file; one percent sign is needed if the command is entered from the command line.

GOSUB   Internal

The GOSUB subcommand transfers control to the line following a label in a batch file and continues execution until a RETURN command is encountered. At that point, batch file execution continues on the line after the GOSUB.

Syntax

    GOSUB *label*

label is the name of the subroutine, consisting of one or more characters. Only the first eight characters of the label name are significant.

Rules

1. After the command GOSUB *label* executes, DOS jumps to the line following :*label* in the subroutine and continues execution of the batch file.

2. After the RETURN command is reached, DOS jumps to the line following the command GOSUB *label* and continues execution of the batch file.

Example

```
GOSUB CACHE
EXIT
:CACHE
NWCACHE 1024 512
RETURN
```

This example uses a subroutine to load a disk cache.

GOTO   Internal

The GOTO command transfers control to the line following the label in a
batch file and continues execution from that line.

Syntax

```
GOTO label
```

label is the name used for the subroutine, consisting of one or more characters. Only the first eight characters of the label name are significant.

Rule

Afer the command GOTO *label* is executed, DOS jumps to the line following
:*label* in the subroutine and continues execution of the batch file.

Example

```
?"LOAD CACHE (Y/N) ?"GOTO CACHE
EXIT
:CACHE
NWCACHE 1024 512
EXIT
```

This example gives you the option of loading the cache or not. It exits in
either case.

IF   Internal

The IF command enables the conditional execution of a command.

Syntax

```
IF NOT condition command
```

condition is what is being tested and can be any of the following:

ERRORLEVEL *number*   DOS tests the exit code (0 to 255) of the program. If the exit code is greater than or equal to the number, the condition is true.

string1==string2   DOS compares these two alphanumeric strings to find whether they are identical.

EXIST *d:path\filename.ext*   DOS tests whether *d:path\filename.ext* is in the specified drive or path (if you give a drive name or path name) or is in the current disk drive and directory.
A command is any valid DOS batch file command.

Rules

1. For the IF subcommand, if the condition is true, the command is executed. If the condition is false, the command is skipped, and the next line of the batch file is immediately executed.

2. For the IF NOT subcommand, if the condition is false, the command is executed. If the condition is true, the command is skipped, and the next line of the batch file is immediately executed.

3. The only DOS programs that produce exit codes are BACKUP, CHOICE, FORMAT, RESTORE, and XCOPY. Using an ERRORLEVEL condition with a program that does not leave an exit code is meaningless.

4. For *string1==string2*, DOS makes a literal, character-by-character comparison of the two strings. The comparison is based on the ASCII character set and is case-sensitive.

Examples

1. The following batch file runs the COPY command and then tests for error 2 (file not found). If the command runs successfully, the batch file ends. If the command returns error 2, the batch file displays an error message.

```
@ECHO OFF
CLS
COPY A:*.* B:
```

```
IF ERRORLEVEL 2 GOTO errmess
GOTO EXIT
:errmess
ECHO Files not found
GOTO EXIT
:EXIT
```

2. The following batch file, ARETHERE.BAT, tests for a string. The %1 is
   the parameter that holds the string. Entering the command

   ```
   ARETHERE FLEAS
   ```

   produces a message. Notice that the batch file tests for the string in
   both upper- and lowercase because the test is case-sensitive.

   ```
   @ECHO OFF
   CLS
   IF '%1'=='FLEAS' GOTO alert
   IF '%1'=='fleas' GOTO alert
   GOTO EXIT
   :alert
   ECHO Look out...fleas!
   :EXIT
   ```

3. The following batch file tests for the existence of AUTOEXEC.BAT in
   the root directory and displays it. If it is not found, the batch file
   displays a message.

   ```
   @ECHO OFF
   CLS
   IF EXIST C:\AUTOEXEC.BAT TYPE /P C:\AUTOEXEC.BAT
   IF NOT EXIST C:\AUTOEXEC.BAT ECHO Where is your
        AUTOEXEC.BAT file?
   ```

   The optional literal NOT tests for the opposite of the condition and
   executes the command if the condition is false.

PAUSE   Internal

The PAUSE command suspends batch file processing until a key is pressed.

Syntax

PAUSE *message*

Rules

1. The optional *message*, a maximum of 122 characters, must be on the same line with PAUSE in the batch file.

2. When DOS encounters a PAUSE in a batch file, DOS displays the optional message even if ECHO is turned off.

3. Regardless of the ECHO setting, DOS displays the following message:

```
Strike a key when ready...
```

REM   Internal

The REM command places a comment within a batch file.

Syntax

```
REM message
```

Rules

1. The optional *message* can contain up to 122 characters and must immediately follow the command REM.

2. When DOS encounters a REM in a batch file, DOS displays the message if ECHO is turned on. If ECHO is turned off, DOS does not display the message.

RETURN   Internal

When used with a GOSUB label command or a SWITCH structure, the RETURN command returns execution to the line following the GOSUB label command or SWITCH structure.

Syntax

```
RETURN
```

Rule

RETURN must appear after the lines following the label(s) referred to in a GOSUB label command or a SWITCH structure. Otherwise, the commands between the one that transferred control to the label and the label itself are not executed.

SHIFT   Internal

SHIFT enables a batch file to use more than 10 parameters by shifting them one parameter to the left. For example, %2 becomes %1, %1 becomes %0, and the content of %0 is deleted.

Syntax

```
SHIFT
```

Rules

1. When you use SHIFT, DOS moves the command-line parameters one position to the left.

2. DOS discards the former first parameter (%0).

Example

The following batch file, MOVIT.BAT, "moves" files by copying them to a target location and then deleting the source files. Use the command with the form

```
MOVIT FILE1 FILE2 FILE3...FILEn
```

The batch file copies the first file to a target location and deletes its source file. Then the SHIFT command makes the replaceable parameter contain the next file name to be copied and deleted. This subroutine loops as many times as necessary to process each file on the command line:

```
ECHO OFF
CLS
:sub
COPY %1 A:
DEL %1
SHIFT
IF "%1"=="" GOTO EXIT
IF NOT "%1"=="" GOTO sub
:EXIT
```

SWITCH   Internal

SWITCH pauses for a numeric key to be pressed and transfers control to any of several points in a batch file, depending on which numeric key is pressed. Chapter 19, "Using Batch Files," presents a menu batch file that uses SWITCH.

Syntax

```
SWITCH label1, label2, label3, ..., label9
```

Rules

1. The labels following SWITCH must be separated by commas and optionally by spaces.

2. You can use up to nine labels in a SWITCH command.

3. If the reader presses 1, control is transferred to the line following the first label in the SWITCH statement; if the reader presses 2, control is transferred to the line following the second label; and so on.

4. When DOS encounters a RETURN command, control is transferred to the line following the SWITCH command.

Commands for the DOS Prompt

The commands described in this section may be issued from the DOS command line.

APPEND   External

The APPEND command instructs DOS to search the specified directories on the specified disks for nonprogram and nonbatch files called by a program.

Syntax

To establish the data file search path the first time, use the following form:

```
APPEND d1:path1;d2:path2;d3:path3;...;dn:pathn
```

d1:, *d2:*, and *d3:* are valid disk drive names.

path1, *path2*, and *path3* are valid paths to the directories you want DOS to search for nonprogram or nonbatch files.

The ellipsis represents additional disk drive and path names, up to 128 characters.

To use any of the APPEND switches, use the following form:

```
APPEND /X:ON /E:ON /PATH:ON
```

To change the data file search path, use the following form:

APPEND *d1:path1,d2:path2;d3:path3;...*

The default state for a search for files that have the drive or path specified is

APPEND /PATH:ON /E:OFF /X:OFF

These are the defaults, so this command is equivalent to using APPEND.

To turn off a search for files that have the drive or path specified, use the following form:

APPEND /PATH:OFF

To see the search path, use the following form:

APPEND

To disconnect the data file search, use the following form:

APPEND;

Switches

/X:ON	Redirects programs that use the DOS function calls SEARCH FIRST ENTRY and EXECUTE
/X:OFF	Turns this feature off
/E:ON	Places the disk drive paths in the environment
/E:OFF	Does not keep the disk drive append path in the environment
/PATH:ON	Turns on the search for files that have drive or path specified
/PATH:OFF	Turns off the search for files that have drive or path specified

Rules

1. The first time you execute APPEND, the program loads from the disk and installs itself in DOS. APPEND then becomes an internal command and is not reloaded from the disk until you restart DOS.

2. You can use the /X and /E switches only when you first invoke APPEND. You can include path names on the same line as these two switches.

3. If you specify more than one set of paths, the following rules apply:

   ■ The path sets must be separated by semicolons.

   ■ The search for the nonprogram files is made in the order in which you gave the path sets. The specified directory (or current directory if none is specified) is first searched. *d1:path1* is then searched, followed by *d2:path2*, and so on, until either the file is found or APPEND exhausts the list of directory paths.

4. The length of the paths given for APPEND cannot exceed 127 characters; this limit includes the six letters in APPEND.

5. If an invalid path is encountered, such as a misspelled path or a path that no longer exists, DOS skips the path and doesn't display a message.

6. If you use the /X:ON switch, APPEND processes the DOS function calls SEARCH FIRST, FIND FIRST, and EXEC.

7. You can disable the /X:ON switch by using /X:OFF.

8. Don't use RESTORE while using the /X switch.

9. Don't use BACKUP while using APPEND.

10. To disable APPEND, give the command followed by a semicolon. APPEND remains resident but inactive until you issue another APPEND command with path names.

11. If you use the /E:ON switch, DOS establishes an environment variable named APPEND. The variable holds the current paths that APPEND uses.

12. If you use the /E:OFF switch with a new path, the old path remains in the environment; however, only the new path is searched. To clear the path from the environment use SET APPEND=.

13. A file found by APPEND can be safely read by the program. However, any changes to the file are saved in a copy of the file placed in the current directory. The original file remains intact.

14. If you're using the ASSIGN command with APPEND, you must issue the APPEND command before you use ASSIGN.

Examples

1. The following command loads the APPEND command and establishes APPEND to intercept the DOS function calls SEARCH FIRST ENTRY and EXECUTE (the /X:ON switch). DOS places in the environment the paths you give to APPEND (the /E:ON switch). DOS also instructs APPEND to search the specified or current directory for nonprogram files and then the directories C:\BIN and C:\BIN\OVR. This command assumes that APPEND is in the current directory or in the PATH:

```
APPEND /X:ON /E:ON C:\BIN;C:\BIN\OVR
```

2. The following command instructs APPEND to ignore invalid drive or path designations and to search the APPEND path for the file:

```
APPEND /PATH:ON
```

If you enter **TYPE C:\TEMP\DOCUMENT.TXT**, but the directory C:\TEMP doesn't exist, the APPEND paths are searched for DOCUMENT.TXT.

3. The following command disables APPEND (otherwise, the APPEND command stays in memory until you restart DOS):

```
APPEND;
```

To reactivate APPEND, use the APPEND command with a set of path names.

Notes

1. APPEND is the counterpart of the PATH command, which works with program files. APPEND is the PATH command for data and other nonprogram files. The command is especially useful if you run programs that don't support hierarchical directories. With the APPEND command, you can place additional program files (such as those used with dBASE III+) or data files in any directory. The command is even more useful for programs that may load properly but can't locate files such as drivers, overlays, or configuration files unless you are in their home directory.

2. You can use APPEND /X:ON to trick programs at three levels. First, when a program attempts to open a file to read, APPEND enables the program to find the file to be opened. Second, when a program searches for a file name, APPEND enables the program to find the file name. Third, when a program attempts to execute another program, APPEND helps find and execute the program.

3. The /E:ON switch places the paths fed to APPEND in the environment, under the variable named APPEND. If you use /E:ON, programs can examine the environment for the APPEND variable and use the contents to find their files. However, do not use APPEND from within a program if you use /E:ON. The changes that APPEND makes to the environment are temporary, and the copy of COMMAND.COM used to run APPEND is temporary. When you return to the program, changes made by APPEND are lost.

4. Be cautious if you write to files that APPEND finds. APPEND tricks programs into reading files from any location. APPEND doesn't trick programs when the programs write files. DOS saves changes you make to a file in a copy of that file, which DOS then places in the current directory. The original file in the directory on which you used APPEND remains unchanged. This file duplication can be confusing when you use a file in one directory, save the new version, and then move to another directory to attempt to reuse the file. You are working with the original file without the changes, while the altered file remains in the directory from which you made the changes.

For more information, see the PATH command in this Command Reference.

Messages

1. `Incorrect APPEND Version`

   ERROR: You used a version of APPEND from a different version of DOS. Make sure that you do not use an APPEND version from the IBM Local Area Network (LAN) program. The problem can be that the wrong version of APPEND is loading first from a pathed directory.

2. `No APPEND Path`

   INFORMATION: You typed **APPEND** to see the current path, and APPEND is currently inactive.

ASSIGN   External

ASSIGN instructs DOS to use a disk drive other than the one specified by a program or command.

Syntax

To reroute drive activity, use the following form:

```
ASSIGN d1=d2 d3=d4...dm=dn /S
```

d1 is the letter of the disk drive the program or DOS normally uses.

d2 is the letter of the disk drive that you want the program or DOS to use instead of the usual drive.

The ellipsis represents additional disk drive assignments.

To clear the reassignment, use the following form:

```
ASSIGN
```

Switch

/S   Displays all current drive assignments

Rules

1. You can reassign any valid DOS drive to any other drive, but not to itself.

2. Do not use a colon after the disk drive letter for *d1* or *d2*. You can use a space on either side of the equal sign.

3. You can give more than one assignment on the same line. Use a space between each set of assignments, as in the following example:

   ```
   ASSIGN B=C A=C
   ```

4. Do not ASSIGN a disk drive to a drive not on your system. If you make this mistake, DOS returns this error message:

   ```
   Invalid directory specified
   ```

5. Don't use the following commands when you have used ASSIGN to assign a disk: BACKUP, DISKCOMP, DISKCOPY, FORMAT, LABEL, PRINT, RESTORE, and SUBST.

X

Command Reference

Examples

1. The following command reroutes any activity from drive A to drive C:

```
ASSIGN A=C
```

You can use a space on either side of the equal sign if you want.

2. The following command reroutes any activity from drives A and B to drive C:

```
ASSIGN A=C B=C
```

3. The following command displays the current drive assignments:

```
ASSIGN /S
```

4. The following command clears any previous drive assignment:

```
ASSIGN
```

Note

An alternative to ASSIGN is SUBST, which assigns a disk drive letter to a subdirectory (see the SUBST command). For compatibility with future versions of DOS, consider using SUBST rather than ASSIGN.

ATTRIB   External

ATTRIB displays, sets, or clears a file's read-only, hidden, system, or archive attributes.

Syntax

```
ATTRIB +| -RASH @filename.ext| @filelist.ext /S /P
```

@filename.ext is the name of the file(s) for which the attribute is displayed or changed. Wild cards are permitted.

@filelist.ext is the name of the file containing the list of files you want to affect.

Parameters or Switches

+ | -RASH	Sets on (+) or off (-) a file's read-only (R), archive (A), system (S), and hidden (H) attributes
/S	Sets or clears the attributes of the specified files in the specified directory and all subdirectories to that directory
/P	Pauses the screen when it becomes full

Rules

1. If you don't include a file name, DOS assumes *.*. If you give an incorrect file name, DOS displays this error message:

```
"FILENAME.EXT"...file not found
```

2. You can use R, A, S, and H together or individually in the command. You can mix the plus and minus attributes of the commands (for example, +R -A), but you cannot use plus and minus for the same character in the command (for example, +R -R).

Examples

1. To set the file's attributes, use the following form:

```
ATTRIB +RASH FILENAME.EXT /S
```

2. To clear the file's attributes, use the following form:

```
ATTRIB -RASH FILENAME.EXT /S
```

3. To display a file's attribute status, use the following form:

```
ATTRIB FILENAME.EXT /S /P
```

4. To set, clear, or display the attributes of the files named in a list file, use the following form with the appropriate switches from the previous forms:

```
ATTRIB @FILELIST.EXT
```

Message

```
File not erased: FILENAME.EXT -- Access denied
```

X

Command Reference

ERROR: You are attempting to delete a read-only file, perhaps included in a wild-card pattern. To delete the file, use ATTRIB with the -R parameter to remove the read-only attribute. Then use DEL to delete the file.

BACKUP   External

The BACKUP command backs up one or more files from a hard disk or a floppy disk to another disk.

Syntax

```
BACKUP d1:path\filename.ext d2: /S /M /A /D:date /T:time
       /F:size /L:filename1.ext1
```

d1: is the hard disk or floppy disk drive to be backed up.

path is the starting directory path for the backup.

filename.ext specifies the name(s) of the file(s) you want to back up. Wild cards are allowed.

d2: is the floppy disk drive that receives the backup files.

Switches

/S	Backs up all subdirectories, starting with the specified or current directory on the source disk and working downward.
/M	Backs up all files modified since the last backup.
/A	Adds the file(s) to be backed up to the files already on the specified floppy disk drive.
/D:date	Backs up any file that you create or change on or after the specified date, using the *mm-dd-yy* format.
/T:time	Backs up any file that you create or change on or after the specified time on the specified date (given with the /D switch), using the *hh-mm-ss* format.
/F	Formats the destination floppy disk to the maximum capacity of the drive if the disk is not formatted. If the disk is formatted, performs a quick format.

/F:*size*   Formats the destination floppy disk according to the size specified. If you have a 1.2M disk drive, but only 360K disks, you can specify /F:360 to format the 360K disk in the 1.2M drive. If the disk is already formatted, performs a quick format.

/L:*filename1.ext1*   Creates a log file.

Exit Codes

The following are the ERRORLEVEL exit codes supplied when BACKUP ends operation:

0	Successful backup
1	No files found to be backed up
2	Some files not backed up because of sharing problems
3	Aborted by the user (Ctrl-Break or Ctrl-C)
4	Aborted because of an error

BATCH FILES can be used to read these codes and display appropriate messages to the user.

Rules

1. Give both a source and a destination for BACKUP. Neither disk can be a networked disk, and neither disk can be used in an ASSIGN, SUBST, or JOIN command.

2. The source name must specify the valid name of the disk drive to be backed up. The source name can also include either or both of the following:

   ■ A valid directory path that contains the files to be backed up.

   ■ A file name with appropriate extensions, if desired. Wild cards are allowed.

3. The destination is any valid name for a floppy disk drive.

4. To keep the files on a previously used backup disk, use the /A option. If you do not use this switch, all files previously stored on the receiving disk are destroyed.

To use the /A option with floppy disks, you must start with a disk that contains the special files created by BACKUP, named CONTROL.*nnn* and BACKUP.*nnn* (*nnn* is the number of the disk). Otherwise, BACKUP displays the message No backup files present on destination disk and aborts the process.

5. All files are placed in the root directory of the backup floppy disk.

6. To create a log of the files that BACKUP processed, use the /L switch. If you do not specify a full file name, BACKUP creates the log file under the name BACKUP.LOG in the source disk's root directory. If you give a log file name, you must use a colon between the L and the first character in the name. Do not use spaces from the beginning of the switch to the end of the log file name. If you do not give a log file name, do not use a colon after the L.

If a log file already exists, BACKUP adds to the log file. If a file does not exist, a new file is created. You cannot place the log file on the destination disk (the disk used to store the backup files).

Examples

For the following examples, assume that the hard disk is C and that the following subdirectories exist:

```
C:\;C:\DOS;C:\WP;C:\DATA;C:\DATA\LETTERS;C:\DATA\MEMOS
```

1. *Backing up the entire hard disk.* In the following command, the source to back up is specified as C:\, and the /S switch instructs BACKUP to back up all subdirectories of the root directory:

```
BACKUP C:\ A: /S
```

2. *Backing up a specific subdirectory.* To back up only a single subdirectory, you do not need to use any switches. The subdirectory LETTERS is backed up in the following command:

```
BACKUP C:\DATA\LETTERS A:
```

3. *Backing up several subdirectories.* In the following command, because of the /S switch, all subdirectories of the source directory (\DATA) are backed up:

```
BACKUP C:\DATA A: /S
```

4. *Backing up all files as of a specified date.* In the following command, all files created or modified on or after July 21, 1992, are backed up. The /S switch is given to back up all subdirectories of the source directory (in this case, the root).

```
BACKUP C:\ A: /S /D:07/21/92
```

5. *Backing up modified files on entire disk.* The /M switch tells BACKUP to back up all files with the archive bit set. When you create or modify a file, the archive bit is set. When you back up a file, BACKUP resets the archive bit. The following command uses the /M switch:

```
BACKUP C:\ A: /S /M
```

6. *Adding modified files from entire disk to the current backup disks.* In the following command, not only is the backup limited to modified files, but BACKUP also does not overwrite files on the backup disk:

```
BACKUP C:\ A: /S /M /A
```

Instead, you see the message

```
Insert last backup disk in drive A: Strike a key when
ready
```

After you press a key, BACKUP begins to add modified files to the backup disks because of the /A switch.

Notes

1. A file on the target floppy disk, called CONTROL.*nnn*, holds the directory, file names, and other housekeeping information. All backup files are placed in one large file called BACKUP.*nnn*. (For both files, the *nnn* represents the number of the backup disk.) The two files are marked as read-only, so that you do not inadvertently erase or alter them.

2. You cannot determine which disk holds a given file. The log file is the only method for locating a backup file.

Messages

1. Could not load FORMAT

ERROR: While running BACKUP, you provided an unformatted floppy disk, and BACKUP could not find the FORMAT command.

2. `Destination must be a valid disk drive`

ERROR: The destination disk is a hard disk or networked disk. When you see this message, BACKUP aborts. To recover from this error, issue the BACKUP command again without the /F switch and/or use a floppy disk drive as the destination.

3. `Insert disk number` *nn* `in drive` *d:*

All files in the root directory of the destination disk are deleted. Strike a key when ready.

INFORMATION and WARNING: This message appears during the backup process when you back up to floppy disks. When you use the /A switch, the message does not appear for the first target disk but does appear for subsequent disks. This message appears for all disks when you do not use /A.

The message instructs you to put the first or next backup disk (disk number *nn* in the series) into drive *d:* and press any key to continue. The message also warns that BACKUP deletes all existing files in the root directory of the receiving disk before files are transferred. Make sure that the proper disk is in the disk drive and press any key to start.

4. `Insert last backup disk in drive` *d:* `Strike any key when ready`

INFORMATION: This message appears only when you use the /A switch and invoke BACKUP without placing the final disk for the backup set in the correct disk drive. Put the correct disk into the disk drive and press any key to start.

5. `No backup files present on destination disk`

WARNING or ERROR: This message appears when you use the /A switch and the disk in the disk drive is not the part of a previous series.

6. `Destination disk is full -- Use a new disk`

WARNING or ERROR: This message appears when you use the /A switch and when the disk in the disk drive is not the last disk of a previous series. If you used a disk previously processed by BACKUP, BACKUP aborts.

7. `Log file path not found`

ERROR: This message appears when you specify an invalid or nonexistent drive or path for the log file.

BREAK   Internal

BREAK determines when DOS looks for a Ctrl-Break sequence to stop a
program.

Syntax

To turn on BREAK, use the following form:

    BREAK ON

To turn off BREAK, use this form:

    BREAK OFF

To determine whether BREAK is on or off, use this form:

    BREAK

CD or CHDIR   Internal

This command changes or shows the path of the current directory.

Syntax

To change the current directory, use the following form:

    CD *d:path*

To show the current directory path on a disk drive, use this form:

    CD *d:*

d: is a valid disk drive name.

path is a valid directory path.

Rule

To start the move with the disk's root directory, use the backslash as the
path's first character. Otherwise, DOS assumes that the path starts with the
current directory.

Notes

1. To move through more than one directory at a time, separate each
directory name with the backslash. You can chain together as many
directories as you want, provided that the total number of characters for
the path does not exceed 63.

2. You are not restricted to changing directories on the current disk. For example, if the current drive is drive A and the disk with the sample directory is in drive B, you can type **B:** before each path name, and your commands work the same.

3. To move to the directory one level above the current directory, enter the shorthand form **CHDIR...**

CHCP   Internal

This command changes or displays the code page (character set) used by DOS.

Syntax

To change the current code page, use the following form:

    CHCP *codepage*

codepage is a valid three-digit code page number.

To display the current code page, use this form:

    CHCP

Refer to Appendix A for a list of countries and their code page numbers.

Rule

You must use NLSFUNC before issuing the CHCP command.

Notes

1. CHCP is a system-wide code page (character set) changer. CHCP simultaneously resets all affected devices to the changed character set. MODE works similarly but changes only one device at a time. When you successfully select a code page, the new code page becomes the specified code. If you include CONFIG.SYS directives for devices that use code pages, such as DEVICE=PRINTER.SYS or DEVICE=DISPLAY.SYS, CHCP loads the correct code pages for the devices.

2. You can access the COUNTRY.SYS file to get new country information. If you do not specify the location of COUNTRY.SYS when you use NLSFUNC, COUNTRY.SYS must exist in the current disk's root directory, or DOS returns a File not found message.

3. Installing code pages is easiest when you use the Novell DOS Install program. You can select the code pages to be used and the devices to be supported from a menu. Install modifies your AUTOEXEC.BAT and CONFIG.SYS files appropriately.

Messages

1. `Code page nnn not prepared for all devices`

ERROR: CHCP could not select the code page *nnn* because of one of the following errors: (a) you did not use MODE to prepare a code page for this device; (b) an I/O error occurred while DOS was sending the new font information to the device; the device is busy—for example, a printer is in use or off-line; or (c) the device does not support code page switching.

Check to make sure that the command MODE CODEPAGE PREPARE was issued for the appropriate devices and that the devices are on-line and ready. Try CHCP again.

2. `Invalid Code Page, NLSFUNC not loaded, or COUNTRY.SYS not found`

ERROR: CHCP could not select the code page *nnn* because of one of the following errors: (a) you did not run NLSFUNC, (b) you specified an invalid code page (*nnn*), or you did not prepare a code page using the MODE command. Be sure that you run NLSFUNC and that you use the command MODE CODEPAGE PREPARE to prepare the code page for the appropriate devices.

CHKDSK   External

CHKDSK checks the directory and file allocation table (FAT) of the disk and reports the status of the disk and memory. CHKDSK can also repair errors in the directories or FAT. CHKDSK supports STACKER compressed drives.

Syntax

CHKDSK *d:path\filename.ext* /B /D /F /S /V /WP

d: is the disk drive to be analyzed.

path is the directory path to the files to be analyzed.

filename.ext is a valid DOS file name. Wild cards are permitted.

Switches

/B	Runs CHKDSK in batch mode, without any pauses.
/D	Tells CHKDSK to display detailed statistics on STACKER compressed drives.
/F	Fixes errors and saves lost clusters to files.
/S	Performs a surface scan of STACKER drives.
/V	Shows CHKDSK's progress and displays more detailed information about the errors the program finds. This switch is known as the verbose switch.
/WP	Checks and repairs STACKER compressed drives that are write-protected.

Rules

1. You must direct CHKDSK to make repairs to the disk by giving the /F switch. Unless you do, CHKDSK displays only information messages. When you do give this switch, CHKDSK asks you to confirm that you want the repairs made before the program proceeds.

2. CHKDSK cannot process a directory on which you used the JOIN command—that is, a second disk joined to a subdirectory.

3. CHKDSK cannot process a disk on which you used a SUBST or ASSIGN command or a networked disk.

4. CHKDSK cannot repair a drive while Task Manager or Windows is running.

Notes

CHKDSK shows you the following items of information for all drives:

1. Volume name and creation date (only disks with volume names), and serial number if there is one.

2. Total disk space.

3. Number of files and bytes used for hidden or system files.

4. Number of files and bytes used for directories.

5. Number of files and bytes used for user (normal) files.

6. Number of files and bytes used for files that have been deleted with the delete commands but are still being protected by DELWATCH.

7. Bytes used by bad sectors (flawed disk space).

8. Bytes available (free space) on disk.

9. Bytes of total memory (RAM).

10. Bytes of free memory.

11. Bytes of free memory in the largest available block. CHKDSK checks a disk's directories and the FAT. The command also checks the amount of memory in the system and determines how much of that memory is free. If errors are found, CHKDSK reports them on-screen before making a status report.

CHKDSK /D shows you the following additional information for STACKER compressed drives:

1. Volume name and creation date (for disks with volume names).

2. Cluster integrity.

3. Total bytes on drive—compressed and noncompressed.

4. Bytes used—compressed and noncompressed.

5. Bytes free—compressed and noncompressed.

6. Bytes per cluster.

7. Compression ratio.

8. Projected bytes free—based on current compression ratio.

9. Fragmentation level.

The following command checks to see whether the specified files are stored contiguously on the disk:

```
CHKDSK filename.ext
```

DOS reports any noncontiguously stored programs and how many different sections store the file(s). If CHKDSK reports many noncontiguous files on a floppy disk, format a new disk. Use the command COPY *.* (not DISKCOPY) to consolidate files from the old to the new disk.

Messages

1. `All specified files are contiguous`

INFORMATION: The files you specified are stored in contiguous sectors on the disk, and the performance from this disk or disk subdirectory is optimal.

2. *Filename* `contains` *n* `non-contiguous blocks`

INFORMATION and WARNING: The file is not stored contiguously on the floppy disk or hard disk but is stored in *n* number of pieces. This leads to less than optimal disk performance. If you find that many files on a floppy disk are stored in noncontiguous pieces, copy the files to another disk to increase performance. If you use a hard disk, you should back up, format, and restore the hard disk. (Use the COPY, BACKUP, FORMAT, and RESTORE commands.)

3. *Filename* `has an incorrect length`

WARNING: The file has an invalid sector number in the file allocation table (FAT). The file was truncated by CHKDSK at the end of the last valid sector. Check this file to verify that all information in the file is correct. If you find a problem, use your backup copy of the file. This message usually appears when the problem is in the FAT, not in the file. Your file probably is still good.

4. *Filename* `contains an invalid cluster`

WARNING: The file has a bad pointer to a section in the FAT on the disk. If you give the /F switch, DOS truncates the file at the last valid sector. Otherwise, no action is taken.

Check this file to see whether all information is intact. If the file is intact, CHKDSK usually can correct the problem with no loss of file information. Alternatively, part of the chain of FAT entries for the file name points to a nonexistent part of the disk. The /F switch truncates the file at its last valid sector. If you do not give /F, DOS takes no corrective action. Try to copy this file to a different disk; then rerun CHKDSK with /F. Part of the file may be lost.

5. *Filename1* is cross-linked at unit *x. filename2* is cross linked
at unit *x*

WARNING: Two files, *filename1* and *filename2*, have an entry in the
FAT that points to the same area (cluster) of the disk. In other words,
the two files believe they own the same piece of the disk. CHKDSK takes
no action. To handle the problem, copy both files to another floppy
disk, delete the files from the original disk, and edit the files as necessary. The files may contain garbage.

6. Errors detected, /F option required to update disk

INFORMATION and WARNING: CHKDSK has found errors, but you did
not use the /F switch. CHKDSK takes no action unless you use the /F
switch. Repeat the CHKDSK command using the /F switch.

7. *directoryname* is an invalid subdirectory

WARNING: *directoryname* contains so much bad information that the
directory is no longer usable. Rerun CHKDSK with the /F switch.

8. *directoryname* is an invalid subdirectory -- Convert to file
(Y/N) ?

INFORMATION and WARNING: You have run CHKDSK with the /F
switch. If you press Y, CHKDSK converts the directory to a file so that
you can use DEBUG or another tool to repair the directory. If you press
N, no action is taken. Pressing Y is a last resort (not for novices)!

Respond with N the first time you see this message. Try to copy any
files you can from this directory to another disk. Check the copied files
to see whether they are usable. Then rerun CHKDSK to convert the
directory into a file, and try to recover the rest of the files.

9. Cannot use CHKDSK on a NETWORK, ASSIGNed, JOINed or SUBSTed
drive

WARNING: CHKDSK encountered a directory that is actually a virtual
disk created by a network or by one of the commands mentioned.
CHKDSK aborts.

10. Insufficient room in root directory. Erase files from root and
repeat CHKDSK

ERROR: CHKDSK recovered so many "lost" cluster chains from the disk that the root directory is full. CHKDSK aborts at this point. Examine the FILE*xxxx*.CHK files. If you find nothing useful, delete them. Rerun CHKDSK with the /F switch to continue recovering lost clusters.

11. *xxx* `lost clusters found in` *yyy* `chains`

    INFORMATION: Although CHKDSK found *xxx* blocks of data allocated in the FAT, no file on the disk is using these blocks. They are lost clusters, which normally can be freed by CHKDSK /F if no other error or warning message appears.

12. `Convert lost allocation units to FILE`*nnnn*`.CHK files (Y/N) ?`

    INFORMATION: CHKDSK has found blocks of data allocated on the disk that are not being used by any file. If you give the /F switch and answer Y now, CHKDSK joins each chain of lost clusters into a file placed in the root directory of the disk, called FILE*nnnn*.CHK, in which *nnnn* is a number between 0000 and 9999. Examine and delete those files that contain no useful information.

    If you answer N, CHKDSK simply frees the lost chains so that the disk space can be reused by other files. No files are created. If you have omitted /F, CHKDSK displays the actions you can take, but does not take any action.

CLS   **Internal**

CLS erases the display screen.

Syntax

```
CLS
```

Note

This command clears all information on the screen and places the cursor at the home position in the upper-left corner. This command affects only the active video display, not memory. If you used the ANSI control codes to set the foreground and background, the color settings remain in effect. If you have not set the colors, the screen typically reverts to light characters on a dark background.

COMMAND   External

The COMMAND command invokes another copy of COMMAND.COM, the command processor.

Syntax

    COMMAND d:path\ cttydevice /E:size /P:filename.ext /C string
        /Mlocation

d:path is the drive and directory location of COMMAND.COM. This path is assigned to the COMSPEC environment table.

cttydevice is the device used for input and output. The default is CON:.

string is the set of characters you pass to the new copy of the command interpreter.

Switches

/E:*size*	Sets the size of the environment. Size is a decimal number from 160 to 32768 bytes, rounded up to the nearest multiple of 16 (refer to the SHELL command). The default environment size is 512 bytes.
/P:*filename.ext*	Keeps this copy permanently in memory (until the next system reset). If you specify a file name, that file is executed in place of AUTOEXEC.BAT. The /P switch is to be used only with SHELL= in CONFIG.SYS.
/C	Passes a string of commands to the new copy of COMMAND.COM and returns to the primary processor.
/M*location*	Tells which part of memory in which to place COMMAND.COM. For *location*, use L for lower memory, H for high memory, and U for upper memory.

Rules

1. The string in the /C option is interpreted by the additional copy of COMMAND.COM, just as though you had typed the string at the system level. /C must be the last switch used on the line. Do not use the form COMMAND /C *string* /P.

2. You can exit from the second copy of the command processor by issuing the command EXIT.

3. If you issue the /P and /C switches together, /P is ignored.

4. If you specify a file name with the /P switch, place a colon before it. Otherwise, don't use a colon.

Note

COMMAND is often used with the SHELL directive. This combination enables you to relocate COMMAND.COM from the root directory of a disk to a subdirectory. You can use COMMAND in place of CALL to call a second batch file from an originating batch file. For example, suppose that a batch file called BATCH1.BAT contains the following line:

```
COMMAND /C BATCH2
```

BATCH1 calls BATCH2.BAT. BATCH2.BAT executes and, after completing the last line of the batch file, returns to BATCH1 to complete the originating batch file. The difference is that anything placed in the environment by the second batch file is lost when you return to the originating batch file. Use CALL if you want the second batch file to place information in the environment that should remain there when the first batch file finishes.

COMP   External

COMP compares two sets of disk files of the same name and length. This command is not available with some DOS versions. If COMP is not available on your version of DOS, see the FC command.

Syntax

```
COMP filename1.ext1 filename2.ext2 /M:n /A /C /D /L /N:n /P
```

filename1.ext1 is the file name for the first set of files. Wild cards are allowed.

filename2.ext2 is the file name for the second set of files. Wild cards are allowed.

Switches

/M:*n*	Tells COMP to terminate after *n* mismatches. The default is 10. Specify 0 to continue without terminating regardless of the number of mismatches.
/A	Displays differences as text characters. By default, they are displayed in hexadecimal format.
/C	Tells COMP to disregard case differences (lower- versus uppercase).
/D	Displays mismatches in decimal format instead of hexadecimal format.
/L	Displays the number of lines that mismatch.
/N:*n*	Compares the first *n* number of lines in the files.
/P	Tells COMP to pause after each screenful of data.

Special Terms

d1:path1\filename1.ext1 is the *primary file set.*

d2:path2\filename2.ext2 is the *secondary file set.*

The primary set file and the secondary file set may be the same.

Rules

1. If you do not enter a file name, all files for that set, whether primary or secondary, are compared, which is the same as entering *.*. However, only the files in the secondary set with names that match file names in the primary set are compared.

2. If you do not enter a drive, path, or file name, COMP prompts you for the primary and secondary file sets to compare. Otherwise, the correct disks must be in the correct drives if you are comparing files on disks. COMP does not wait for you to insert disks if you give both primary and secondary file names.

3. The paths are optional and are not needed if the files are unique and are in the default path.

Note

A more versatile utility for file comparison is FC, also discussed in this command reference.

Messages

1. `Offset xx Source = yyy Destination - zzz`

   INFORMATION: The files you are comparing show differences. At *xx* (hex) bytes from the beginning, the primary file set contains a byte with the hex value *yyy*, whereas the secondary file set contains a byte with the hex value *zzz*.

2. `Files are not the same size. Compare them anyway (Y/N) ?`

   WARNING: You asked COMP to compare two files of different lengths.

3. `nn Mismatches -- ending comparison`

   WARNING: COMP found 10 mismatches (or the number you have specified with the /M switch) between the two files you compared. COMP therefore assumes that no reason exists to continue, and the comparison is aborted.

COPY   Internal

The COPY command copies files between disk drives or between drives and devices, and enables you either to keep or to change the file names.

Syntax

To copy a file, use the following form:

```
COPY /A /B filename1.ext /A /B /C /Z filename2.ext /A /B /S /V
```

To join several files into one, use the following form:

```
COPY /A /B filename1.ext /A /B /C /Z + filename2.ext /A
       /B +...
```

filename1.ext and *filename2.ext* are valid file names. Wild cards are allowed.

The ellipsis represents additional files in the form `filenamex.ext`.

Switches

/C	Prompts you before copying the file with the message `filename.ext` (Y/N) ?
/Z	Zeros the eighth bit of the destination file. Use only with ASCII files.
/S	Includes files with the system and/or hidden attributes.
/V	Verifies that the copy was written to a readable sector and matches the source copy.

The following switches create different effects on the source and the destination.

For the source file:

/A	Treats the file as an ASCII (text) file. The command copies all the information in the file up to, but not including, the end-of-file marker (Ctrl-Z). Data after the end-of-file marker is ignored.
/B	Copies the entire file (based on size, as listed in the directory) as if the file were a program file (*binary1*). All end-of-file markers (Ctrl-Z) are treated as normal characters, and EOF characters are copied.

For the destination file:

/A	Adds an end-of-file marker (Ctrl-Z) to the end of the ASCII text file at the end of the copying process.
/B	Does not add the end-of-file marker to this binary file.

X

Command Reference

Special Terms

The file copied *from* is the *source file*. The names that contain *1* and *2* indicate source files.

The file copied *to* is the *destination file*. This file is indicated by *0*.

Rules

1. You must give either a path name or a file name. Wild cards are allowed in the source file name.

   If you do not give a destination file name, the copied file has the same name as the source file.

2. You can substitute a device name for the complete source or destination name.

3. When you copy between disk drives, COPY assumes that binary files are copied (as though the /B switch were given).

4. When you copy to or from a device other than a disk drive, COPY assumes that ASCII files are copied (as though the /A switch were given).

5. An /A or /B switch overrides the default settings for COPY (see rules 3 and 4).

6. You can specify several different files or wild cards in the source file name if you separate them with a plus sign (+).

Note

The meanings of the /A and /B switches depend on their positions in the line. The /A or /B switch affects the file that immediately precedes the switch and all files that follow the switch until another /A or /B is encountered. When you use one of these switches before a file name, the switch affects all following files until contradicted by another /A or /B.

Messages

1. `Destination file contents lost before copy`

   WARNING: A destination file was not the first source file. The previous contents were destroyed. COPY continues to concatenate any remaining files.

2. Source and destination cannot be the same file

ERROR: You attempted to COPY a file back to the same disk and directory that contains the same file name. This error usually occurs when you misspell or omit parts of the source or destination drive, path, or file name. Check your spelling and the source and destination names. Try the command again.

CREATE   External

You use the CREATE utility to create a STACKER compressed drive from the available space on a removable disk, such as a floppy disk.

Syntax

CREATE *d:\xxx.yyy* /S=*sss.sx* /R=*n.n* /C=*n* /M

d: is the drive letter of the host drive.

xxx.yyy specifies the name of the STACVOL file to create. If this is not specified, STACVOL.DSK is used.

If no other options are used, STACVOL.DSK is the STACVOL file name, and /S=0 is used to allocate all available space on *d:* for the file.

Switches

/S=*sss.sx*	Amount of space in *sss.s* to allocate for the STACVOL file. The *x* is either K for kilobytes or M for megabytes.
/R=*n.n*	Sets maximum size of the Stacker drive by specifying an anticipated compression ratio of *n.n*:1.
/C=*n*	Sets cluster size, in K, for Stacker drive; *n* = 4, 8, 16, or 32.
/M	Uses monochrome display mode.

Example

CREATE B:

This command tells STACKER to CREATE a stacked floppy on drive B, using all available disk space.

CTTY   **Internal**

The CTTY command changes the standard input and output device to an auxiliary console, or changes the input and output device back from an auxiliary console to the keyboard and video display.

Syntax

    CTTY *device*

device is the device you want to use as the new standard input and output device. This name must be a valid DOS device name.

Valid devices are the following:

CON:	Keyboard input, screen output, and default
AUX: or COM1:	First serial communications port
COM*n*:	The second, third, or fourth serial port (*n* = 2, 3, or 4)
PRN:	Printer port
LPT*n*:	The first, second, or third parallel printer port (*n* = 1, 2, or 3)
NUL:	The null device that accepts no input and produces no output

Rules

1. The device is typically a character-oriented device capable of both input and output.

2. Typing a colon after the device name is optional.

3. CTTY does not affect any other form of redirected I/O or piping. For example, <(redirect to), and ¦ (pipe between programs) work as usual.

X

4. Before using CTTY on a serial or parallel port, you may have to use the MODE command to set the port with the proper parameters.

Notes

1. The CTTY command was originally designed so that a terminal or tele-printer, rather than the normal keyboard and video display, can be used for console input and output. This capability has little use for most personal computer users.

2. The CTTY NUL: command is used to mask an operation from view and from interruption by the user. Typically, a batch file runs the CTTY NUL: command, another command is run, and then the CTTY CON: command is run to return control to the console. Choose the second command carefully; it must be able to perform its operations and then return control to the operating system without user input. If errors occur or if the command cannot return control to the operating system, the hardware is left in a state that cannot process input or output. The computer needs to be turned off and then on to reboot.

CURSOR   Internal

This command enables you to change the cursor to a block and control the blink rate.

Syntax

> **CURSOR** /C /S*nn* OFF

Switches

/C	Prevents "snow" on CGA screens
/S*nn*	Sets the blink rate to *nn*/20 of a second
OFF	Turns off the software-generated cursor, restoring the hardware cursor

Notes

1. The default blink rate is 4/20 of a second.

2. This command is most useful on LCD screens, where a small cursor is difficult to see.

DATE   Internal

The DATE command displays or changes the system date.

Syntax

> **DATE** *date_string*

date_string is a date in one of the following forms:

> *mm/dd/yy, mm/dd/yyyy, mm-dd-yy, mm-dd-yyyy, mm.dd.yy,* or *mm.dd.yyyy*
> for North America
>
> *dd-mm-yy* or *dd-mm-yyyy* for Europe
>
> *yy-mm-dd* or *yyyy-mm-dd* for East Asia

In the date string, *mm* is a one- or two-digit number for the month (1 to 12), *dd* is a one- or two-digit number for the day (1 to 31), and *yy* is a one- or two-digit number for the year (80 to 99). The 19 is assumed. *yyyy* is a four-digit number for the year (1980 to 2099).

The delimiters between the day, month, and year can be hyphens, periods, or slashes. The result that can be displayed varies, depending on the country code set in the CONFIG.SYS or DCONFIG.SYS file.

Rule

Date entry and display must correspond to the country setting in your CONFIG.SYS file.

Notes

1. When you boot the computer, DOS issues the DATE and TIME commands to set the system clock. If you placed an AUTOEXEC.BAT file on the boot disk, DOS does not automatically display a prompt for the date or time. If you have an older computer without a battery-maintained clock, you can include the DATE or TIME command in the AUTOEXEC.BAT file to have these functions set when DOS boots.

2. When you create or update a file, DOS updates the directory with the system date. This date shows which copy is the latest revision of the file. The DOS BACKUP command uses the date in selecting files to back up.

X

3. The day-of-year calendar uses the time-of-day clock. If you leave your system on overnight, the day advances by one at midnight. DOS also makes appropriate calendar adjustments for leap years. With some systems, however, you must boot the system each day so that DOS advances the date properly. If your computer is left on but not used during the weekend, DOS may be two days behind when you return Monday.

DEBUG   External

The Novell DOS DEBUG program is a testing and editing tool.

Syntax

        DEBUG *path\filename.ext test-params*

path is the location of the file to be edited, if it is not current.

filename.ext is the full name and extension of the file to debug.

test-params are the parameters for the program to be debugged.

After DEBUG starts, type **?** to display a list of debugging commands. Appendix D lists the valid DEBUG commands.

DEL   Internal

DEL removes one or more files from a directory.

Syntax

        DEL *filename.ext* /C /P /S

filename.ext is the name of the file(s) to be erased. Wild cards are allowed.

Switches

/C	Prompts you before erasing the file with the message *filename.ext* (Y/N) ?
/P	Same as /C (do not use with /C)
/S	Deletes system files

Rules

1. If you do not give a disk drive name, the current disk drive is used.

2. If you do not give a path name, the current directory is used.

3. If you give a disk drive name or path name (or both) but no file name, DOS assumes that the file name is *.* (all files). DOS will prompt for confirmation.

4. If you specify *.*—or no name—for the file name, DOS displays the following prompt:

   ```
   Are you sure (Y/N) ?
   ```

   If you answer Y, all files in the specified directory are erased. If you answer N, no files are erased.

Note

As long as no file modifications take place on the disk, you can recover the erased file with the utility program UNDELETE. The DOS utility RECOVER does not recover erased files, as you might expect. RECOVER is designed only to repair a file that contains bad sectors or has a bad directory entry.

Message

```
File not erased: filename.ext -- Access denied
```

ERROR: You attempted to erase a file that is marked as read-only or is in use by another program or computer and is temporarily marked as read-only. If the file you intend to erase has the read-only attribute set, use the ATTRIB command to turn off the read-only flag.

DELPURGE   External

If you have DELWATCH installed, deleted files are saved until a specified number of files are stored pending actual deletion. DELPURGE deletes all files that are pending deletion, prompting you to confirm each file to delete.

Syntax

```
DELPURGE filename.ext /D:date | /D:-nn /T:time /A /L /S /P
```

filename.ext is the name of the file(s) to be erased. Wild cards are allowed.

Switches

/D:*date*	Purges files deleted before the specified date
/D:*-nn*	Purges files deleted more than *nn* days ago
/T:*time*	Purges files deleted before the specified time
/A	Purges files without prompting
/L	Lists the files pending deletion but does not purge them
/S	Purges files in subdirectories of the specified directory
/P	Pauses after each screen

DELQ   Internal

This command removes one or more files from the directory, prompting you first for permission.

Syntax

```
DELQ filename.ext /S
```

filename.ext is the name of the file to be erased. Wild cards are allowed.

Switch

/S	Deletes system files

Note

DELQ is exactly the same as DEL with the /C switch and follows the same rules (see the earlier section on DEL).

DELWATCH   External

The DELWATCH command saves a specified number of deleted files so that they can be undeleted.

Syntax

```
DELWATCH d1:... /S /D /B:nnnnn /O:ext... /E:ext... /F:nnnnn |
         /F:ALL /MU /ML /MRmemtype /MRmemtype /MBmemtype
         /MPmemtype /MPmemtype- /U
```

d1: is the drive on which to save deleted files.

The ellipses represent additional drives separated by spaces on the command line.

Switches

/S   Displays the current status of DELWATCH.

/D   Disables DELWATCH for a specific drive, without unloading it from memory.

/B:*nnnnn* Specifies how many copies of the same file in the same directory should be saved. *nnnnn* is the maximum number of copies of one file.

/O:*ext*... Tells DELWATCH to protect only those files with the extension *ext*. The ellipsis represents additional extensions to protect. Wild cards may be used.

/E:*ext*... Tells DELWATCH to protect all files except those with the extension *ext*. The ellipsis represents additional extensions not to protect. Wild cards may be used.

/F:*nnnnn* Tells DELWATCH how many files to protect. When the number *nnnnn* is reached, the file least recently deleted is purged. The default is 200 for hard drives and 20 for floppy drives. Specifying 65535 enables unlimited files up to the disk capacity.

/F:ALL   Tells DELWATCH not to purge any files automatically. Ignores /B.

/MU   Prevents DELWATCH from being installed unless there is a device driver providing reserved memory and enough memory to hold the device driver.

/ML   Loads DELWATCH into lower memory whether or not reserved memory is available.

/MR*memtype* Loads real mode code into specified memory; *memtype* = X (extended), U (upper), or C (conventional).

/MR*memtype*- Excludes real mode code from specified memory; *memtype* = X (extended), U (upper), or C (conventional).

/MB*memtype* Loads data buffers into specified memory; *memtype* = X (extended), U (upper), or C (conventional).

/MB*memtype* -	Excludes data buffers from specified memory; *memtype* = X (extended), U (upper), or C (conventional).
/MP*memtype*	Loads TSR code into specified memory; *memtype* = X (extended), U (upper), or L (conventional).
/MP*memtype* -	Excludes TSR code from specified memory; *memtype* = X (extended), U (upper), or L (conventional).
/U	Removes DELWATCH from memory if there are no drives enabled.

Rules

1. DELWATCH protects files on all the drives you specify on the command line. You must separate drive names with spaces.

2. By default, DELWATCH protects only one copy of a file with a given name in a given directory. You can change this number to any value up to 65535 with the /B switch.

3. You can specify up to 10 extensions to protect by using the /O switch. The extensions must be separated by plus signs. No spaces are allowed between the extensions and the plus signs.

4. Unless you restrict the files to be protected with the /O switch, DELWATCH protects all files.

5. You can specify up to 10 extensions for DELWATCH to ignore using the /E switch. The extensions must be separated by plus signs. No spaces are allowed between the extensions and the plus signs.

Note

Deleted files still take up space in the directory. If the root directory becomes full and you don't use the /F:ALL switch, deleted files are purged from the root directory as needed to make room.

DIR   Internal

DIR lists all files and subdirectories in a disk directory.

Syntax

```
DIR filename.ext /P /W /2 /L /D /S /A /N /R /C
```

filename.ext is a valid file name. Wild cards are permitted.

Switches

/P	Pauses when the screen is full and waits for you to press any key.
/W	Gives a wide display of the file names. Information about file size, date, and time is not displayed.
/2	Displays the long form of directory entries in a two-column format.
/L	Gives the long form of directory entries, including file size, date, and time.
/D	Displays all files except system files.
/S	Displays only system files.
/A	Displays all files.
/N	Forces DIR to revert to default paging.
/R	Makes the form of the display that is determined by the other switches on the command line the default for future directory displays. Displays the directory.
/C	Makes the form of the display that is determined by the other switches on the command line the default for future directory displays. Does not display the directory.
No switches	Displays all files except system and hidden files, in long form, in a single column, without pausing.

Rule

You cannot use the DIR command on a disk drive on which you used the ASSIGN or JOIN command. You must break the assignment before you view the directory. You can use the DIR command on the host disk drive involved in a JOIN command.

Notes

1. DIR does not report statistics for disk drives on which you used the ASSIGN or JOIN command. For disk drives on which you used JOIN, DIR reports the free space of the host disk drive (the disk drive to which

the second disk drive is joined). DIR does not, however, report the total of the two disk drives on which you use the JOIN command. In the case of ASSIGN, first remove it from the drive to find its amount of free space.

2. You can set DIR switches in the AUTOEXEC.BAT file with this command:

```
DIR /C switches
```

DISKCOMP   External

Use the DISKCOMP command to see whether the contents of two floppy disks are identical. DISKCOMP compares two floppy disks on a track-for-track, sector-for-sector basis, or compares a floppy disk with an image file of the contents of a floppy disk.

Syntax

```
DISKCOMP d1: d2:\pathi\filenamei.exti /1 /8 /A /M /V
```

d1: and *d2:* are the disk drives that hold the disks to be compared. These drives can be the same or different.

pathi is the path to an image file to be compared with a floppy disk.

filenamei.exti is the name of the image file.

Switches

/1	Compares only the first side of the floppy disk, even if the disk or disk drive is double-sided
/8	Compares only eight sectors per track, even if the first disk has a different number of sectors per track
/A	Causes a beep to sound when the comparison is complete or when you must change disks
/M	Allows you to compare one floppy disk or image file with a number of others
/V	Verifies that the floppy disk or image file is readable

Rules

1. If you give only one valid floppy disk drive name, that drive is used for the comparison.

2. Only compatible floppy disks, or a floppy disk and an image file made from the type of floppy disk you are comparing, should be compared. The two disks must be formatted with the same number of tracks, sectors, and sides.

3. Do not use DISKCOMP with a disk drive on which you used the ASSIGN, JOIN, or SUBST command.

Note

Disks duplicated with the COPY command may have the same files, but the disks are not true duplicates. Compare only floppy disks that were duplicated with DISKCOPY, or compare floppy disks with an image file created with DISKCOPY.

Messages

1. `Difference(s) encountered on track` *tt*

   WARNING: The disks you are comparing are different at track number *tt*. DISKCOMP does not specify which sectors are different, only that one or more sectors are. If you just used DISKCOPY on these disks and no problem was reported, the second disk probably has a flaw. Reformat the disk and try DISKCOPY again. Otherwise, assume that the disks are different.

2. `Disks compare OK`

   INFORMATION: DISKCOMP compared the two floppy disks and found that they match.

3. `Disk type or format error. Insert a replacement disk (Y/N) ?`

   ERROR: The disk drives or floppy disks are different. The first disk was successfully read on both sides. However, the second disk or disk drive is not identical to the first disk or drive. You may insert a different disk and continue the comparison after pressing Y. If you press N, the program terminates.

4. `Physical media error`

WARNING: Four attempts were made to read the data from the floppy disk. If the disk in the drive is the destination (copied) disk, the copy is probably bad. (The disk has a "hard" read error.) If the disk is the original disk, a flaw existed when the disk was formatted, or a flaw developed during use.

Run CHKDSK on the original disk and look for the line that indicates bytes in bad sectors. If this line is displayed, the original disk and the copy may be good. When you format a disk, FORMAT detects bad sectors and "hides" them. However, DISKCOMP does not check for bad sectors and attempts to compare the tracks, even if bad sectors are present. Although CHKDSK shows that the original disk has bad sectors, the destination disk may be good. Either way, it is preferable to destroy a flawed disk and use another.

DISKCOPY   External

DISKCOPY copies the entire contents of one floppy disk to another on a track-for-track basis, making a "carbon copy." It can be used also to make an "image file" of a floppy disk on another disk. The image file can be used to create identical copies of the original floppy disk.

Syntax

```
DISKCOPY d1: d2:\pathi\filenamei.exti /1 /A /M /V
```

d1: is the floppy disk drive that holds the source (original) disk or image file.

d2: is the disk drive that holds the destination disk (disk to be copied to) or image file.

pathi is the path to the location where an image file is to be created.

filenamei.exti is the name of the image file.

Switches

/1	Copies only the first side of the disk
/A	Causes a beep to sound when the copy is complete or when you must change disks

/M   Allows you to copy one floppy disk or image file to a number
                      of others

/V   Verifies that the disk is copied correctly

Special Terms

The floppy disk you are copying *from* is the *source* floppy disk.

The floppy disk you are copying *to* is the *destination* floppy disk.

An *image file* is a file that contains information needed to reconstruct an
exact copy of the source floppy disk. The image file may be on a disk of a
different type. An image file may be used as the source or created as the
destination.

Rules

1. The source disk drive must be a real floppy disk drive. It cannot be a
   hard or networked disk drive, a RAM disk, or a disk drive on which you
   used the JOIN or SUBST command. The destination disk drive must be a
   real floppy drive of the same type, unless the destination is an image
   file. Defaulting to or giving a nonreal source or destination disk drive
   causes DOS to return an error message and abort the disk copy.

2. If you do not give a source disk drive name, DISKCOPY uses the default
   disk drive. If you give an invalid source disk drive, DISKCOPY issues an
   error message and aborts. In other instances, DISKCOPY uses the current disk drive as the source disk drive.

3. DISKCOPY destroys any information recorded previously on the destination disk. Do not use a destination disk that contains information
   you want to keep.

4. To ensure that the copy is correct, run DISKCOMP on the two disks.

5. DISKCOPY ignores the effects of an ASSIGN command.

6. If your system has two floppy disk drives of the same size, but one is a
   high-density or extended-density drive, you can copy a normal-capacity
   floppy disk by placing the source floppy disk in the high-density or
   extended-density drive and the destination floppy disk in the normal-
   capacity drive.

Note

If enough memory is available, DOS reads the entire source disk before prompting you to switch to the destination floppy disk. DOS uses expanded memory, extended memory, or temporary files to store any information that won't fit into lower memory. If you have no memory other than lower memory and no hard disk, you may be prompted to switch disks several times. If so, you should write-protect the source disk so that you don't inadvertently copy over part of it.

Messages

1. `Specified drive is invalid, or non-removable media`

ERROR: The drive types or disk capacities you tried to use are different and cannot handle the operation, or the destination disk is the wrong capacity. The first disk was successfully read, but the drive specified to receive the copy was not the right type. You cannot DISKCOPY high-density disks in lower-density disk drives or copy double-sided disks in single-sided disk drives. See the identical message under DISKCOMP for remedial action.

2. `Error reading from the disk`

WARNING: DISKCOPY cannot accurately read or write to the disk. The disk is not properly inserted, the source disk is not formatted or is a non-DOS disk, or the drive door is open. Check these possibilities and try again.

3. `Disk type or format error. Insert a replacement disk (Y/N) ?`

ERROR: The disk drives or floppy disks are different. The first disk was successfully read on both sides. However, the second disk or disk drive is not identical to the first disk or drive. You may insert a different disk and continue the copy after pressing Y. If you press N, the program terminates.

4. `Invalid drive specification error`

ERROR: If your system has a single floppy disk drive and you give only one valid floppy disk drive name, the name is used as both the source and destination disk drive for the copy. If your system uses two floppy disk drives, giving only one valid disk drive name results in this error message.

DISKMAP   External

This command records information about the file allocation table (FAT) to help you use the UNDELETE command.

Syntax

```
DISKMAP d1: d2:...dn: /D
```

d1:, *d2:*, and *dn:* are the disk drives you track with DISKMAP.

Switch

/D   Deletes the file containing the information about deleted files and writes a new one

Rules

1. If you use ASSIGN, you must place this command before the DISKMAP command.

2. Information about deleted files is saved in the file DISKMAP.DAT. This file is used by the UNDELETE command.

Note

DISKMAP helps you track deleted files by making a copy of the FAT, which shows the location of each file. If the information in this file is current, UNDELETE can probably find all the parts of a deleted file and recover it accurately. But this method of protecting deleted files is not as effective as the one provided by DELWATCH, which actually saves the deleted files in a hidden form. However, DISKMAP is not a memory-resident program, and therefore won't reduce your available memory. It also won't take up disk space with deleted files that have not been purged.

Caution

The DISKMAP and UNDELETE commands are not a replacement for proper backups of your hard disk!

DISKOPT   External

The DISKOPT command defragments files on a disk, moving free space to the end; optionally, it sorts directories. This command can be used as a full-screen utility or from the command line.

Syntax

    DISKOPT *d:* /B /M*x* /O /S*x*

d: is the drive having files you want to unfragment.

Switches

/B   Displays in monochrome

/M*x*   Specifies the optimization method, where *x* is one of the following:

> 1   Full optimization
>
> 2   Full optimization with file reorder
>
> 3   File defragment only
>
> 4   Free space defragment only
>
> 5   Sorts directories only

/O   Optimizes immediately without prompts

/S*x*   Sorts by directory, where *x* is one of the following:

> A   Sorts on name
>
> E   Sorts on extension
>
> D   Sorts on date
>
> S   Sorts on size
>
> N   Leaves directory unsorted

Notes

1. You can run DISKOPT from the command line or as a full-screen program.

2. You should always run CHKDSK and back up the disk to be optimized before running DISKOPT.

3. DISKOPT may take quite a while to complete its task. You might want to run DISKOPT during your lunch hour or at the end of the work day.

DOSBOOK   External

DOSBOOK is the complete Novell DOS 7 on-line documentation and reference utility.

Syntax

        DOSBOOK *topic* /B /N

topic is the topic or command about which you want information.

Switch

/B	Displays in monochrome
/N	Forces the use of standard EGA/VGA font; needed with video adapters that do not display correctly

Note

When no topic is specified on the command line, DOSBook runs in full-screen mode with a menu-driven interface. You can use the Search Text command to open the Text Search dialog box. When you type a topic name in the text box and press Enter, DOSBook displays information about the topic.

Chapter 3, "Getting Help with DOSBook," gives you a complete explanation of this utility.

DOSKEY   External

DOSKEY is the Novell DOS macro utility for increasing productivity at the command line.

Macros are similar to batch files, except that macros are temporary and are stored in RAM, whereas batch files are stored on disk. When you create a long or complicated command, you have to type it every time you want to use it. If you attach a brief name to the command keystrokes, you create a macro. You can type the macro name, and the full command is executed. Because you create the macro at the command line, you can edit the macro by using command-line HISTORY to recall and edit the macro.

You can create a macro file, store it on disk, and load it into memory for easy recall. You can also create a single batch file to contain all your normal macros. By just running the batch file, you can re-create your macros and make them available for use every time you reboot your computer.

Syntax

```
DOSKEY /mname=text /REINSTALL /BUFSIZE=nnn /MACROS /HISTORY
       /INSERT | /OVERSTRIKE
```

Switches

/mname=text	mname is the name of the new macro. text specifies the commands you want the macro to execute. This switch deletes the macro when you do not specify any text.
/R or /REINSTALL	Clears all macros from the command-line buffer and installs a new version of DOSKEY.
/B or /BUFSIZE=nnn	Changes the size of the macro and command-line history buffer, where nnn is the number of bytes. The default size is 512 bytes.
/M or /MACROS	Lists all the DOSKEY macros currently stored in the buffer.
/H or /HISTORY	Lists the contents of the command-line history buffer.
/I or /INSERT	Sets the default editing mode to Insert.
/O or /OVERSTRIKE	Sets the default editing mode to Overstrike.

Example

```
DOSKEY /M1=DIR /W /P
```

This example creates a macro named M1. The full instruction executed by the macro tells DOS to display a directory in wide format and to pause for each full screen.

To execute the macro, enter **M1** at the DOS prompt.

EDIT   External

This command loads the Novell DOS text editor, EDIT, and optionally loads a file at the same time.

Syntax

```
EDIT filename.ext /D /N
```

filename.ext is the name of the file to be edited.

Switches

/D   Uses BIOS for screen writes; suppresses "snow" with CGA adapters

/N   Forces the use of standard EGA/VGA font; needed with video adapters that do not display correctly

Rules

1. If you run EDIT without a file name parameter, the Select File to Open dialog box appears.

2. EDIT creates and edits ASCII text files.

Notes

1. If you specify a nonexistent file to be edited, you are asked whether you want to create the file.

2. You can get help with EDIT commands by pressing F1.

ERA or ERASE   Internal

The ERA command deletes files from the disk. ERA is an alternative command for DEL and performs the same functions. See DEL for a complete description.

ERAQ   Internal

This command deletes files from the disk, prompting for permission before deleting each file. ERAQ is an alternative command for DELQ and performs the same functions. See DELQ for a complete description.

EXE2BIN   External

The EXE2BIN command changes specially formatted EXE files into BIN or COM files.

Syntax

    EXE2BIN *filename1.ext1* filename2.ext2 /Shhhh

filename1.ext1 is the name of the file to be converted.

filename2.ext2 is the name of the output file.

Switch

/*Shhhh*   The base segment value to use for segment fix-ups, expressed as a four-digit hexadecimal number

Special Terms

The file to be converted is the *source* file.

The output file is the *destination* file.

Rules

1. You must specify a name for the source file (the file to be converted).

2. If you do not specify a name for the destination file, EXE2BIN uses the name of the source file.

3. If you do not specify an extension for the source file, EXE2BIN uses the extension EXE.

4. If you do not specify an extension for the destination file, EXE2BIN assumes an extension of BIN or COM, depending on the header of the source file.

5. The EXE file must be in the correct format (following Microsoft conventions).

Note

EXE2BIN is a programming utility that converts EXE (executable) program files to COM or BIN (binary image) files. The resulting program takes less disk space and loads more quickly. Unless you use a compiler-based programming language, you probably won't use this command.

EXIT   Internal

The EXIT command quits COMMAND.COM and returns to the program that started COMMAND.COM.

Syntax

```
EXIT
```

Rule

This command has no effect if COMMAND.COM is loaded with the
/P switch.

FBX   External

This command loads Fifth Generation's Fastback Express backup and restore
utility, which comes with Novell DOS 7. With this program, you don't have
to dread protecting your system with backups, because it does the job of restoring and backing up quickly and easily.

Syntax

```
FBX /A /B /F /M /3
```

Switches

/A	Forces the use of a graphics mouse cursor
/B	Disables the use of a graphics mouse cursor
/F	Disables the 3-D screen display
/M	Changes the screen display to monochrome
/3	Enables the 3-D screen display

FC   External

The FC command compares two sets of disk files.

Syntax

```
FC @d1:path1\filename1.ext1 d2:path2\filename2.ext2 /A /B /C
   /L /Mx /W /T /N /P /nnnn
```

d1: is the drive that holds the first set of files to compare.

path1 is the path to the first set of files.

filename1.ext1 is the file name for the first set of files. Wild cards are
allowed.

d2: is the drive that contains the second set of files to compare.

path2 is the path to the second set of files.

filename2.ext2 is the file name for the second set of files. Wild cards are allowed.

@ specifies that the names of the files in the first set are contained in a list in the file *filename1.ext1*.

Switches

/A	Abbreviates ASCII comparison displays; shows first and last lines of each block
/B	Forces a binary file comparison
/C	Causes DOS to ignore case-sensitivity
/L	Compares files in ASCII mode
/M*x*	Sets the maximum number of mismatches in a binary comparison to *x*
/W	Treats consecutive spaces and tabs as a single space
/T	Does not expand tabs
/N	Displays line numbers
/P	Pauses after each screen
/*nnnn*	Sets maximum number of lines that must match before files are resynchronized

Special Terms

d1:path1\filename1.ext1 is the *primary file set.*

d2:path2\filename2.ext2 is the *secondary file set.*

Notes

1. FC is a file-comparison program similar to COMP but more powerful (see the section on COMP in this Command Reference). With FC, in addition to comparing binary files byte by byte, you can compare ASCII files of different lengths.

2. The default number of lines before resynchronization is 2. This means that if FC finds a mismatch when comparing ASCII files, it scans the next line in the second file for a matching line. If it finds one, it continues the comparison from that line. You can increase the number of lines before a mismatch by using the /*nnnn* switch. FC stops if it doesn't find a match.

FDISK   External

FDISK readies a hard disk to accept an operating system such as Novell DOS.

Syntax

    FDISK /D

Switch

/D   Deletes unknown partition types

Example

    FDISK

This command starts FDISK from a floppy disk in any drive, as long as that drive is the current drive.

Notes

1. You must use FDISK to create a partition on a hard disk before you can use FORMAT to format the hard disk.

2. If you plan to use more than one operating system, use FDISK to partition part of the hard disk for DOS and another part of the hard disk for the other operating system.

> **Caution**
>
> Do not use FDISK to remove or change a partition unless you have all data on the partition safely backed up. Removing or changing a partition causes all data on that partition to be lost.

FILELINK   External

The FILELINK program transfers files to another computer via a serial port or parallel port connection. This program can be run in full-screen mode or from the command line.

Syntax

```
FILELINK command @source filespec destination filespec
        COMn:b | LPTn switches
```

source filespec is the source file specification.

destination filespec is the destination file specification.

Entering **FILELINK** starts the full-screen interface for the utility.

The following commands may be used for the command-line version:

SETUP	Displays current configuration.
SETUP and COMn:b	Configures FILELINK to use COM port *n* at baud rate *b*.
SETUP and LPTn	Configures FILELINK to use LPT port *n*.
DUPLICATE	Transfers FILELINK to the slave computer through the COM port.
SLAVE	Enters slave mode (run from the master computer).
SLAVE /X	Causes slave to enter slave mode (run from the slave computer).
DIRECTORY *filespec*	Shows directory of the slave computer; shows full directory if no *filespec* is included. Wild cards are allowed.

All commands may include port setup parameters (COMn:b or LPTn) to override the current configuration.

Switches

/A	Displays or copies only the files that have the archive attribute set.
/B	Uses a monochrome, full-screen menu.

/D:*mm-dd-yy*	Copies only files created or modified since the specified date.
/H	Displays or copies hidden or system files.
/M	Copies only files that have the archive attribute set and that don't exist on the destination directory or don't have the archive attribute set on the destination directory. This switch resets attribute.
/N	Do *not* redefine the font in EGA/VGA—full-screen mode.
/P	When transmitting or receiving, prompts for permission before copying each file.
	Displays one screen of files at one time (when the DIRECTORY comand is used).
/R	Allows read-only files on the destination directory to be overwritten.
/S	Displays or copies files in subdirectories of the specified directory.
/U	Copies only files that do not exist in the destination directory or have an earlier date stamp in the destination directory.
/X	Prevents files in the destination directory from being overwritten. This switch is used with the FILELINK SLAVE command.

Special Terms

The computer in control is the *master* or *local* computer.

The computer being controlled is the *slave* or *remote* computer.

The file being copied from is the *source file*.

The file being copied to is the *destination file*.

A file containing a list of file names to be acted on is a *list file*.

Rules

For using FILELINK in the command-line mode:

1. You must first enter the command **FILELINK SETUP** COM*n*:*baud* | LPT*n* on each computer.

2. You must next enter the command **FILELINK SLAVE** on the slave computer.

3. Thereafter, you enter all commands on the master computer.

4. The location of the source and destination depends on whether you are receiving or transmitting. However, drive names on each computer do not change. Drive C on the slave computer remains drive C, and drive D on the master computer remains drive D, regardless of the direction in which the files are sent.

5. If you don't specify a source drive, the default drive is assumed.

6. If you don't specify a source directory, the default directory is assumed.

7. You must specify a source file name or a list file. The list file must contain complete path information for all listed files.

8. If you don't specify a destination drive, the default drive is assumed.

9. If you don't specify a destination directory, the default directory is assumed.

10. You do not have to specify a destination file name. If you don't, the files have the same name on the destination as on the source.

11. The /S switch doesn't work when transmitting.

Note

You can use the /A, /D:*date*, /H, /S, and /P switches with the DIRECTORY command.

FIND   External

FIND displays from the designated files all the lines that match (or do not match, depending on the switches used) the specified string. This command can also display the line numbers.

Syntax

```
FIND /B /V /C /N /F /I /U /S /P "string" @filename.ext...
```

string is the set of characters you want to find. As indicated in the syntax line, the string must be enclosed in quotation marks.

filename.ext is the file you want to search. Wild cards or a list file may be used.

@ indicates that the file is a list file, containing the names of the files to be searched.

Switches

/B	Displays the matches for each file under a header showing the file name.
/V	Displays lines that do not contain the string.
/C	Displays the total number of lines that contain the string.
/N	Displays lines that contain the string, preceded by the line number in the file.
/F	Shows only the names of the files that contain the string.
/I	Ignores case-sensitivity in the search. This is the default.
/U	Specifies that the search is case-sensitive.
/S	Searches files in subdirectories of the current directory.
/P	Pauses after each screen.

Rules

1. If you do not give any file specifications, FIND expects information from the keyboard (standard input).

2. You must enclose the string in double quotation marks. To use the double quotation mark character in the string, use two consecutive double quotation mark characters.

Notes

1. FIND is one of several filters provided with DOS. The command can find lines that contain strings and those that do not. FIND can also number and count—rather than simply display—lines of text.

2. This filter is useful when combined with DOS I/O redirection. You can redirect FIND's output to a file by using >, the redirection symbol. Because FIND accepts a sequence of files to search, you do not need to redirect the input to FIND.

FORMAT   External

This command initializes a disk to accept DOS information and files. FORMAT also checks the disk for defective tracks and optionally puts DOS on the floppy disk or hard disk.

Syntax

> **FORMAT** *d:* /S /1 /4 /8 /A /B /Q /U /X /N:*ss* /T:*ttt* /V:*label*
>   /F:*size*

d: is a valid disk drive name.

Switches

/S	Places a copy of the operating system on a disk so that DOS can boot from the disk.
/1	Formats only the first side of the floppy disk. Use only with 5 1/4-inch drives.
/4	Formats a floppy disk in a 1.2M disk drive for double-density use. Use only with 320K and 360K 5 1/4-inch disks.
/8	Formats a nine-sector floppy disk but uses only eight sectors.
/A	Sounds a beep when the format is finished.
/B	Formats an eight-sector floppy disk, leaving the proper places in the directory for any operating system version, but does not place the operating system on the disk.
/Q	Forces a quick format for previously formatted disks. Information for an UNFORMAT is preserved. This is the default.
/U	Specifies an unconditional format for a floppy disk. Unconditional formatting destroys all data on a floppy disk, which prevents you from unformatting the disk. For information about unformatting, see the UNFORMAT command.
/X	Specifies that you are formatting a hard disk.

/N:ss   Formats the disk with ss number of sectors, where ss is a
                 number from 1 to 99. Use with /T:ttt.

T:ttt   Formats the disk with ttt number of tracks per side, where
                 ttt is a number from 1 to 999. Use with /N:ss.

/V:label   Transfers the volume label to the formatted disk. Replaces
                 the label with an 11-character name for the new disk.

/F:size   Formats the disk to equal or be less than the disk drive's
                 maximum capacity, with size designating one of the
                 following values:

Drive	Capacity	Size
5 1/4 inch	160K	160
5 1/4 inch	180K	180
5 1/4 inch	320K	320
5 1/4 inch	360K	360
5 1/4 inch	1.2M	1.2
3 1/2 inch	720K	720
3 1/2 inch	1.44M	1.44
3 1/2 inch	2.88M	2.88

Rules

1. If you do not give a disk drive name, the current disk drive is used.

2. Unless otherwise directed through a switch, DOS formats the disk to the
   DOS maximum capacity for the drive.

3. Some switches do not work together. For example, you cannot use the
   following switch combinations:

   /S with /B

   /1, /4, /8, or /B with a hard disk drive

   /F with /N and /T

   /Q with /U

4. If you are formatting a hard disk, FORMAT displays the following message:

```
WARNING, ALL existing data on non-removable disk d: will be
destroyed! -- Continue (Y/N) ?
```

Press Y to format the hard disk, or press N to abort formatting the hard disk.

Notes

1. Do not try to format any type of virtual disk; a disk that is part of an ASSIGN, SUBST, or JOIN command; or a networked disk. FORMAT usually gives an error message and aborts the operation.

2. Never try to format a RAM disk. Under some circumstances, FORMAT acts erratically when formatting a RAM disk, particularly VDISK (the DOS RAM disk program). The responses can range from a DOS display of a `Divide overflow` message to a lockup of your computer. If the computer locks up, first turn off the system and then turn it on again. You lose the RAM disk's contents, but no hard disks or floppy disks are damaged.

3. Unless you use the /U switch, FORMAT performs a safe format. When you use the command to format a previously formatted disk, the file allocation table and root directory are copied before they are cleared, and the disk is checked. The existing data is not cleared. If you accidentally format a safely formatted disk, you can unformat the disk. To erase all data from a previously used floppy disk, include the /U switch. An unconditional format takes about 27 percent longer than the default safe format.

Messages

1. `Existing disk format is different -- Continue (Y/N) ?`

INFORMATION and WARNING: FORMAT has checked the disk to see whether it has been formatted previously. It has been formatted to a capacity other than the one you specified.

2. `Quick formatting disk`

INFORMATION: The disk has been previously formatted. The directory and FAT are being saved on the disk, and a safe format is performed. A safely formatted disk can be unformatted.

3. Insufficient space to save UNFORMAT information without
destroying some data -- Continue (Y/N) ?

WARNING: The previously formatted disk doesn't have room for the
mirror-image file, the file that contains a copy of the FAT and root
directory. The disk doesn't have enough room to save a copy of the
root directory and FAT, or you are changing the contents of the disk
by using the /B or /S switch. Be sure that you want to format the disk
located in the drive. You cannot unformat this disk after it has been
formatted.

4. Invalid format for target drive

WARNING and ERROR: You have specified a combination of switches
that cannot be used on the drive in which you are trying to format the
disk.

5. Disk failure, or write protected

WARNING: Track 0 holds the boot record, the FAT, and the directory.
This track is bad and the floppy disk is unusable, you are trying to format a write-protected disk, or you have specified an invalid size for the
type of disk you are formatting.

This error can occur when you format 720K floppy disks as 1.44M
floppy disks (if you forget to give the /F:720 switch when you formatted on a 1.44M disk drive), or when you format 360K floppy disks as
1.2M floppy disks (if you forget the /4 switch).

This error can also occur when you format 1.2M floppy disks at lower
capacities, such as 360K, and give the /4 switch. In this case, try using
a floppy disk rated for double-sided, double-density use.

6. WARNING, All existing data on non-removable disk drive d: will
be destroyed! -- Continue (Y/N) ?

WARNING: FORMAT issues this warning when you are about to format
a hard disk. Answer Y to format the hard disk. If you do not want to
format the hard disk, answer N.

GRAFTABL   External

GRAFTABL loads into memory the tables of additional character sets to be
displayed on the Color Graphics Adapter (CGA).

Syntax

To install or change the table used by the CGA, use the following form:

> GRAFTABL *codepage*

codepage is the three-digit number of the code page for the display.

To display the number of the current table, use this form:

> GRAFTABL /STATUS

Switch

/STATUS   Displays the selected code page

Rules

1. To display legible characters in the ASCII range of 128 to 255 when you are in APA (all-points-addressable) mode on the Color Graphics Adapter, load GRAFTABL.

2. GRAFTABL increases the size of DOS by 1,664 bytes.

3. For the code page, use any of the following codes:

437	United States
850	Multilingual
852	Slavic
860	Portugal
863	Canadian-French
865	Norway and Denmark

   If no page is specified, the code 437 is assumed.

4. After you invoke GRAFTABL, the only way to deactivate the command is to reboot.

Note

The IBM Color Graphics Adapter in graphics mode produces low-quality ASCII characters in the range of 128 to 255. GRAFTABL is useful only when your system is equipped with the Color Graphics Adapter and when you use the Adapter in medium- or high-resolution graphics mode.

GRAPHICS   External

The GRAPHICS command prints the graphics-screen contents on a suitable
printer when you press the Print Screen key.

Syntax

```
GRAPHICS COLOR /R
```

Switches

COLOR   Produces a color printout on an IBM-compatible color
                printer with a color ribbon

/R   Reverses colors so that the image on the paper matches the
                screen—a white image on a black background

HILOAD or LOADHIGH   Internal

HILOAD loads memory-resident programs into high memory, beyond lower
memory.

Syntax

```
HILOAD | LOADHIGH filename.ext prog_options
```

filename.ext is the name of the device driver or memory-resident program
to load high.

prog_options are any options required by *filename.ext*.

Rules

1. You must use a computer equipped with an Intel 80286, 80386SX,
   80386, 80486, or Pentium microprocessor and at least 1M of RAM.

2. If you have an 80386SX, 80386, 80486, or Pentium microprocessor,
   your CONFIG.SYS file must load EMM386.EXE.

3. If you have an 80286 microprocessor, you must have a NeAT, SCAT,
   or LeAP chipset. You must have also a shadow RAM memory area or
   expanded memory provided by a LIM 4.0 driver. Your CONFIG.SYS
   or DCONFIG.SYS file must contain the line DEVICE=HIMEM.SYS.

4. You must have sufficient reserved memory available. Determine
   available memory by using MEM /U.

5. You must execute MEMMAX +U before you attempt to use HILOAD. The MEMMAX +U command can be executed by your AUTOEXEC.BAT file.

6. If not enough reserved memory is available to accommodate the program, it is loaded in lower memory without warning.

7. If you prefer to use LOADHIGH, you can abbreviate it as LH.

JOIN   External

The JOIN command produces a directory structure by connecting one disk drive to a subdirectory of another disk drive.

Syntax

```
JOIN d1: d2:\dirname /D
```

d1: is the disk drive to be connected.

d2: is the disk drive to which *d1:* is to be connected.

\dirname is a subdirectory in the root directory of *d2:*, the host drive.

Switch

/D   Disconnects the specified disk drive from the host drive

Rules

1. You must specify the disk drive to connect.

2. If you do not name a host disk drive, DOS uses the current disk drive.

3. You must specify the subdirectory name on the host drive. If the subdirectory does not exist, DOS creates it.

4. The host subdirectory, if it exists, should be empty (DIR should show only the . and .. entries). If it isn't empty, you lose access to the files in that directory until you disconnect the connected drive.

5. The host and connected disk drives must not be networked disk drives or part of a SUBST and ASSIGN command.

6. You cannot use the current disk drive as the connected disk drive.

7. When the disk drives are joined, the connected disk drive's root directory and entire directory tree are added to the host subdirectory.

All subdirectories of the connected drive's root directory become subdirectories of the host drive's subdirectory.

8. A connected disk drive, when joined, appears to be part of the host subdirectory. You can access this disk drive only through the host disk drive and subdirectory.

9. To break the connection, specify the connected drive's normal name with the /D switch. You can use the connected drive's normal name only when you disconnect the drives.

10. To see all the current disk drive connections, enter **JOIN** with no parameters. If no connections exist, JOIN does not display any message, and the system prompt appears.

11. Do not use the BACKUP, DISKCOMP, DISKOPT, DISKCOPY, FDISK, RESTORE, SDEFRAG, SUBST, and FORMAT commands on the guest or host disk drive.

12. When JOIN is in effect, the DIR command works normally but reports the bytes free only for the host disk drive.

Notes

1. You can use JOIN to connect a RAM disk to a real disk, enabling the RAM disk to be used as if it were part of a floppy disk or hard disk drive. You can also use JOIN to connect two hard disk drives.

2. JOIN does not affect the guest disk drive. Instead, JOIN affects only the way you access the files on that disk drive. You cannot exceed the maximum number of files in the guest disk's root directory. In the host subdirectory, a file's size cannot exceed the guest disk's size.

KEYB   External

This command changes the keyboard layout and characters to languages other than American English.

Syntax

```
KEYB countrycode+ | -, codepage /Mx
```

countrycode is the two-character keyboard code for your location. + signifies an enhanced keyboard. - signifies a standard (83/84-key) keyboard.

codepage is the three-digit code page that you want to use. These codes are listed in Appendix A.

Switch

/M*x*   Tells which part of memory KEYB should be placed in. In place of *x*, use L for lower (conventional) memory, H for high memory, and U for upper memory.

Rules

1. To use one of the language character sets, load the KEYB program and type the appropriate two-letter code for the country.

2. If you do not specify a code page, DOS uses the default code page for your country. The default code page is established by the COUNTRY directive in CONFIG.SYS or, if the COUNTRY directive is not used, the DOS default code page.

3. You must specify a code page that is compatible with your keyboard code selection.

4. To use the /MH or /MU switch, you must have loaded a device driver that makes high or upper memory available.

5. After loading, the program reconfigures the keyboard into the appropriate layout for the specified language.

6. To use the American English layout after you issue the KEYB command, press Ctrl-Alt-F1. To return to the foreign-language layout, press Ctrl-Alt-F2.

7. When used the first time, the KEYB command increases the size of DOS by 4,640K. After that, you can use KEYB as often as you want without further enlarging DOS.

8. To display the active keyboard and the code pages, use the KEYB command without any parameters.

Messages

1. `Keyboard program not loaded`

INFORMATION: You issued the KEYB command to display the current setting but have not previously loaded a keyboard layout.

2. Requested code page not valid for this country

ERROR: You gave a keyboard code to KEYB, but you did not give a code page, or you gave a code page that did not match the keyboard code. The specified keyboard code does not match the currently active code page for the console. KEYB does not alter the current keyboard or code page. Reissue the KEYB command and specify the appropriate matching code page.

3. Keyboard program currently loaded for keycode, code page *nnn*

INFORMATION: The current keyboard code is a two-character keycode, and the code page used by the keyboard is a three-digit code page.

LABEL   External

The LABEL command creates, changes, or deletes a volume label for a disk.

Syntax

LABEL *d:volume_label*

d: is the disk drive whose label you want to change.

volume_label is the disk's new volume label.

Rules

1. When given, a valid 11-character volume label immediately becomes the volume label for the specified disk drive.

2. If you do not specify a volume label, DOS prompts you to enter a new volume label. You can do one of the following:

   ■ Enter a valid 11-character volume label and press Enter. DOS makes this name the new volume label. If a volume label already exists, DOS replaces the old volume label with the new label.

   ■ Press Enter to delete the current label without specifying a replacement label. DOS asks you to confirm the deletion.

3. If you enter an invalid volume label, DOS responds with a warning message and asks again for the new volume label.

4. Do not use LABEL on a networked disk drive (one that belongs to an-other computer). If you try to use LABEL on a networked drive, DOS displays an error message and ignores the command.

5. Do not use LABEL on a disk in any drive affected by the ASSIGN or SUBST command, because DOS labels the "real" disk in the disk drive instead. Suppose that you use the command ASSIGN A=C. If you then use the command LABEL A:, DOS actually changes the volume label of the disk in drive C.

Notes

1. When you format a disk, you are prompted to enter a volume label. Any characters that you can use in a file name are valid in a volume label.

2. Remember that a space is a valid character in a volume label. Spaces and underscores can increase the readability of a volume label.

Messages

1. `Delete current volume label (Y/N) ?`

INFORMATION and WARNING: You did not enter a volume label when requested. DOS is asking whether to delete or leave the current label unaltered. You can delete the current label by pressing Y or keep the label intact by pressing N.

2. `Illegal characters in label`

INFORMATION and ERROR: The label you entered contains characters that are DOS command characters. The program aborts without enter-ing or changing the volume label.

LOCK   External

This command locks your keyboard so that you can leave your computer unattended without fear of interference or snooping. The command provides a screen-saver for DOS and Windows.

Syntax

    LOCK *password switches*

password is the password used to unlock the computer.

Switches

/N	Does not prompt for password if user is logged in.
/U	Unloads lock from memory.
/D:*path*	Sets path for file creation.
/F	Does not save/restore screen font.
/S	Saves video memory.
/B	Color scheme for VGA gas plasma display.
/T:*nn*	Sets timeout in minutes (maximum of 60). Append an s for seconds (for example, /T:30s).

Rules

1. If you have installed system security through the Install or Setup program, you must enter either the master or user password to regain system control from LOCK.

2. If you enter a password with the LOCK command, you must enter the password to regain system control from LOCK.

3. The password can contain up to 12 alphanumeric characters and is not case-sensitive.

Notes

1. If you type a password on the command line, it remains on-screen—so that anyone can copy it—unless you press another key. At this point, the LOCK screen appears with an error message. Strike a key to display the password-entry screen.

2. If you load LOCK as a task within Task Manager (see the section on TASKMGR in the Command Reference), you can switch to that task without exiting from the program you're currently using.

LOGIN   External

This command displays the LOGIN screen and prompts for a password.

Syntax

LOGIN *df:pathf*

df: is the drive containing LOGIN.TXT.

pathf is the directory containing LOGIN.TXT.

Notes

1. LOGIN does nothing unless you have installed system security through the Install or Setup program.

2. If you have installed system security, the CONFIG.SYS file runs LOGIN automatically, displaying the LOGIN screen and prompting you for your password. Your system cannot finish booting until you enter a correct password.

MD or MKDIR   Internal

MD creates a subdirectory.

Syntax

> **MD** *d:path****dirname**

d: is the disk drive for the subdirectory.

path indicates the path to the directory to hold the subdirectory.

dirname is the subdirectory you are creating.

Rules

1. If you do not specify a path name but give a disk drive name, the subdirectory is created in the current directory of the specified drive. If you do not specify a path name or a disk drive name, the subdirectory is created in the current directory of the current disk drive.

2. If you use a path name, separate the path name from the directory name with the path character, the backslash (\).

3. You must specify the new subdirectory name, which uses one to eight characters, and an optional extension. The name must conform to the rules for creating directory names.

4. You cannot use a directory name that is identical to a file name in the parent directory. For example, if you have a file named MYFILE in the current directory, you cannot create the subdirectory MYFILE in this directory. If the file is named MYFILE.TXT, however, the names do not conflict, and you can create the MYFILE subdirectory.

Note

You are not restricted to creating subdirectories in the current directory.
If you add a path, DOS establishes a new subdirectory in the directory
you specify.

Messages

1. Unable to create directory

ERROR: One of the following errors occurred: (1) you tried to create a
directory that already exists, (2) you gave an incorrect path name, (3)
the disk's root directory is full, (4) the disk is full, or (5) a file by the
same name already exists.

Check the directory in which the new subdirectory was to be created.
If a conflicting name exists, either change the file name or use a new
directory name. If the disk or the root directory is full, delete some files,
create the subdirectory in a different directory, or use a different disk.

2. Path not found

ERROR: You attempted to create a subdirectory of an existing directory,
but either you mistyped the name of the existing directory or it doesn't
exist.

MEM   External

The MEM command displays the amount of used and unused memory, allocated and open memory areas, and all programs currently in the system.

Syntax

    MEM /A /B /F /S /P /M /U /CLASSIFY /DEBUG /PROGRAM

Switches

/A	Displays all information
/B	Displays areas of lower memory only
/F	Displays memory usage only in segment FFFF (high memory)
/S	Displays the memory addresses and sizes of disk buffers, file handles, and file control blocks (FCBs)

/P	Pauses and waits for a keypress when the screen fills up
/M	Displays the locations of RAM, ROM, UMBs, and EMS memory, along with a graph of the same information
/U	Displays the areas of upper memory in use
/CLASSIFY	Displays programs loaded into lower memory
/DEBUG	Displays programs and drivers (don't use /DEBUG with /PROGRAM)
/PROGRAM	Displays loaded programs
No switches	Displays a table showing the areas of memory available and in use

Note

If you use an 80386 or higher PC or an 80286-based PC with shadow RAM, an advanced chipset, or LIM 4.0 memory, you can use MEM /U extensively as you begin loading device drivers and TSRs in reserved memory. MEM gives the location and size of each program in memory. This information can help you determine the order that device drivers and TSRs load for best use of the reserved memory space.

MEMMAX   External

MEMMAX displays the status of your memory-management utilities or selectively enables and disables them.

Syntax

```
MEMMAX + | -L + | -U + | -V /L /U /V
```

Switches and Parameters

+ | -L	Enables or disables access to lower memory.
+ | -U	Enables or disables access to upper memory.
+ | -V	If you have used the /VIDEO option of EMM386.SYS or HIDOS.SYS, +V enables the use of video graphics memory by programs. Otherwise, -V disables access to video memory.
/L	Tells whether access to lower memory is enabled.

/U   Tells whether access to upper memory is enabled.

/V   Tells whether access to video memory is enabled.

No switches   Tells MEMMAX to display the status of upper, lower, and video memory.

Rules

1. To use upper memory, you must have a device driver installed that makes reserved memory available.

2. To use video memory, you must have either EMM386.EXE or HIMEM.SYS installed with the /V option.

3. If you have enabled access to video memory, you cannot use programs that display graphics.

Note

By default, INSTALL places the command MEMMAX -U in your AUTOEXEC.BAT file. You must change it to MEMMAX +U if you want to use the HILOAD command or if you have TSRs that load themselves into reserved memory automatically when available.

Message

`Packed file is corrupt`

INFORMATION: If, when loading a program, you see this message, you must disable access to lower memory by using the command MEMMAX -L. This allows the program to load normally. After you exit the program, you can reenable access to lower memory with the command MEMMAX +L.

MODE CODEPAGE PREPARE   External

This command prepares the code pages to be used with a device.

Syntax

```
MODE device CODEPAGE PREPARE = ((codepage,
    codepage,...)pagefile.ext)
```

device is the device for which the code page(s) is chosen. You can select one of the following devices:

CON: The console

PRN: The first parallel printer

LPTx: The first, second, or third parallel printer (x = 1, 2, or 3)

codepage is the number of the code page(s) to be used with the device. The ellipsis represents additional code pages.

pagefile.ext is the file that holds the code page (character set) information.

The following hardware is explicitly supported by the MODE CODEPAGE PREPARE command:

pagefile.ext	**Description**
EGA.CPI	Enhanced Graphics Adapter (EGA) or Video Graphics Array (VGA)
4201.CPI	IBM ProPrinter, ProPrinter XL, and compatibles
4208.CPI	IBM ProPrinter X24, ProPrinter XL24, and compatibles
5202.CPI	IBM QuietWriter III
1050.CPI	Epson FX 850, FX 1050, and compatibles

Rules

1. You must specify a valid device, as listed here. The colon after the device name is optional.

2. You can use CODEPAGE or CP, and PREPARE or PREP.

3. You must specify one or more code pages. You must separate the numbers with a comma if you give more than one code page. You must enclose the entire list of code pages in parentheses.

4. When you add or replace code pages, enter a comma for any code page that you do not want to change.

5. Do not use a hardware code page (the code page given to DISPLAY.SYS for the console or to PRINTER.SYS for printers).

Notes

1. MODE CODEPAGE PREPARE is used to prepare code pages (character sets) for the console (keyboard and display) and the printers. Issue this command before issuing the MODE CODEPAGE SELECT command, unless you use the IBM QuietWriter III printer, which holds its character set information in cartridges. If the needed code page is in a cartridge and the code page was specified to the PRINTER.SYS driver, no PREPARE command is needed.

2. You can load a code page for the screen without first preparing it—without even loading NLSFUNC—by using the KEYB command and specifying a keyboard layout at the same time.

MODE CODEPAGE REFRESH   External

This command reloads and reactivates the code page used with a device.

Syntax

```
MODE device CODEPAGE REFRESH
```

device is the device for which you choose the code page(s). You can use one of the following devices:

CON: The console

PRN: The first parallel printer

LPT*x*:   The first, second, or third parallel printer (*x* = 1, 2, or 3)

Rules

1. You must specify one of the valid devices in the preceding list. The colon after the device name is optional.

2. You can use CODEPAGE or CP, and REFRESH or REF.

Note

MODE CODEPAGE REFRESH reactivates the currently selected code page on a device. Use this command after you turn on your printer or after a program crashes.

MODE CODEPAGE SELECT   External

This command activates the code page used with a device.

Syntax

```
MODE device CODEPAGE SELECT = codepage
```

device is the device for which a code page(s) is chosen. You can use one of the following devices:

CON:	The console
PRN:	The first parallel printer
LPTx:	The first, second, or third parallel printer (*x* = 1, 2, or 3)

codepage represents the number(s) of the code page(s) to be used with the device.

Rules

1. You must specify one of the valid devices in the preceding list. The colon after the device name is optional.

2. You can use CODEPAGE or CP, and SELECT or SEL.

3. You must specify the code page. The code page must be either part of a MODE CODEPAGE PREPARE command for the device or the hardware code page specified to the appropriate device driver.

Notes

1. MODE CODEPAGE SELECT activates a currently prepared code page or reactivates a hardware code page. You can use MODE CODEPAGE SELECT only on these two types of code pages. MODE CODEPAGE SELECT usually downloads any software character set to the device, except for the QuietWriter III printer, which uses cartridges.

2. MODE CODEPAGE SELECT activates code pages for individual devices. You can use the CHCP command to activate the code pages for all available devices.

MODE CODEPAGE STATUS   External

This command displays a device's code page status.

Syntax

```
MODE device CODEPAGE /STATUS
```

device is the device for which a code page is chosen. You can select one of the following devices:

CON: The console

PRN: The first parallel printer

LPTx: The first, second, or third parallel printer (*x* = 1, 2, or 3)

Switch

/STATUS or **/STA**   Displays the status of the device's code pages

Rules

1. You must specify one of the valid devices listed here. The colon after the device name is optional.

2. You can use either CODEPAGE or CP.

3. The MODE command, with no switches, is the same as MODE /STATUS.

4. MODE /STATUS displays the following information about the device:

   ■ The selected (active) code page, if one is selected

   ■ The hardware code page(s)

   ■ Any prepared code page(s)

   ■ Any available positions for additional prepared code pages

Note

MODE CODEPAGE /STATUS shows the device's current code page status.

MODE COM (Port)   External

This command controls the protocol characteristics of the Asynchronous Communications Adapter or any other serial port.

Syntax

    MODE COM*y*: *baud*,*parity*,*databits*,*stopbits*,P

y: is the adapter number (1, 2, 3, or 4); the colon after the number is optional.

baud is the baud rate (110, 150, 300, 600, 1200, 2400, 4800, 9600, or 19200).

parity is the parity checking (N for none, O for odd, or E for even). The default is E (even).

databits is the number of data bits (7 or 8). The default is 7.

stopbits is the number of stop bits (1 or 2). The default is 1, but 2 is the default for 110 baud.

P specifies continuous retries on timeout errors.

Rules

1. You must enter the adapter's number and a baud rate, separated by a colon, a colon and a space, or a space.

2. If you do not want to change a parameter, you must enter a comma for that value.

3. If you enter an invalid parameter, DOS responds with an Invalid parameter message and takes no further action.

4. You may enter only the first two digits of the baud rate (for example, 11 for 110 baud and 96 for 9600 baud).

5. The 19200 baud rate is valid only for PS/2 computers. If you try to use the 19200 baud rate on a PC or compatible, DOS displays the message Communication port does not support requested baud rate and takes no further action.

6. If you want continuous retries after a timeout, you must enter the P whenever you use the MODE COM*n*: command. If you do, DOS displays the message Infinite retries on serial port COM*n*.

7. If the adapter is set for continuous retries (P) and the device is not ready, the computer appears to be locked up. You can abort this loop by pressing Ctrl-Break.

MODE (Display)   External

This command switches the active display adapter between the monochrome display and a graphics display (Color Graphics Adapter, Enhanced Graphics Adapter, or Video Graphics Adapter) on a two-display system and sets the graphics adapter's characteristics.

Syntax

> MODE *dt*,*s*,*T*

dt is the display type, which can be one of the following:

40	Sets the display to 40 characters per line for the graphics display
80	Sets the display to 80 characters per line for the graphics display
BW40	Makes the graphics display the active display and sets the mode to 40 characters per line, black and white (color disabled)
BW80	Makes the graphics display the active display and sets the mode to 80 characters per line, black and white (color disabled)
CO40	Makes the graphics display the active display and sets the mode to 40 characters per line (color enabled)
CO80	Makes the graphics display the active display and sets the mode to 80 characters per line (color enabled)
MONO	Makes the monochrome display the active display

s shifts the display right (R) or left (L) one character.

T requests alignment of the graphics display screen with a one-line test pattern.

Rules

1. The *s* parameter (R or L) works only with the Color Graphics Adapter. The display does not shift if you use this command with any other adapter.

2. The *T* parameter displays the test pattern only on a Color Graphics Adapter.

Note

Sometimes CGA (Color Graphics Adapter) monitors do not display information correctly on-screen. The information displayed may be cut off on the right or left side of the screen. You can use the MODE command to align the screen for better readability.

The syntax for the external MODE command that sets the CGA display type is

```
MODE displaymode,shiftdisplay,testpattern
```

To shift the display one column to the left and then display a test pattern, enter the following:

```
MODE ,L,T
```

If you are not setting the display type at the same time that you are adjusting the CGA display, you do not have to include the display mode on the command line. When you do not include the display mode, however, you must still include the comma that would follow it if it were there.

After the test pattern is displayed, you are asked whether the alignment is acceptable. If you answer no, the display shifts one column left (in this case, or right if you use R in the command line). The process continues until you answer yes to indicate that the display is aligned correctly.

If you issue the CGA MODE command to any display type other than CGA, you get the following error message:

```
Display shift command only available on CGA
```

MODE (Lines and Columns)   External

This command sets the number of lines and columns on the console.

Syntax

```
MODE CON: LINES=x COL=y
```

x specifies the number of columns to display; 40 or 80 columns are possible.

y specifies the number of lines on the display; *y* can have the value 25, 43, or 50. (Your display adapter may not support all three values.)

Rules

1. You can specify lines, columns, or both.

2. If you specify a value for *x* or *y* that your adapter doesn't support, DOS displays the message `Unrecognized display mode`.

MODE (Key Repeat) External

This command adjusts the keyboard repeat rate of the console.

Syntax

```
MODE CON: RATE=x DELAY=y
```

x is a value that specifies the character-repeat rate. You can select a value from 1 to 32.

y is a value that specifies the length of delay between the initial pressing of the key and the start of automatic character repetition. This value can be 1, 2, 3, or 4, which represent delays of 1/4 second, 1/2 second, 3/4 second, and 1 second, respectively.

MODE (Printer Port) External

This command sets the parallel printer characteristics.

Syntax

```
MODE LPTx:cpl,lpi,P
```

`x:` is the printer number (1, 2, or 3). The colon is optional.

cpl is the number of characters per line (80 or 132).

lpi is the number of lines per inch (six or eight).

P specifies continuous retries on timeout errors.

Rules

1. You must specify a printer number, but all other parameters are optional, including the colon after the printer number.

2. If you do not want to change a parameter, enter a comma for that parameter.

3. This command cancels the effect of `MODE LPTx:=COMy:`.

4. A parameter does not change if you skip that parameter or instead use an invalid parameter. This is not true of the printer number, however, which you must enter correctly.

5. If you specify P for continuous retries, you can cancel the request only by reentering the MODE command without P.

6. The *cpl* and *lpi* portions of the command affect only IBM printers, Epson printers, and other printers that use Epson-compatible control codes.

Notes

1. This command controls the IBM Matrix and Graphics Printers, all Epson printers, and Epson-compatible printers. The command may work partially or not at all on other printers.

2. When you change the column width, MODE sends the special printer-control code that specifies the normal font (80) or the condensed font (132). When you change the lines-per-inch setting, MODE sends the correct printer-control code for printing 6 or 8 lines per inch. MODE also sets the printer to 88 lines per page for an 8-lines-per-inch setting and to 66 lines per page for a 6-lines-per-inch setting.

3. If you give the option P and attempt to print on a deselected printer, the computer does not issue a timeout error. Instead, the computer internally loops until the printer is ready (turned on, connected to the PC, and selected). For about a minute, the computer appears to be locked up. To abort the continuous retry, press Ctrl-Break.

MODE (Redirection)   External

This command forces DOS to print to a serial printer rather than a parallel printer.

Syntax

```
MODE LPTx:=COMy:
```

x: is the parallel printer number (1, 2, or 3). The colon is optional.

y: is the Asynchronous Communications Adapter number (1, 2, 3, or 4).

Rules

1. You must give a valid number for both the parallel printer and the serial printer.

2. After you give the command, all printing that normally goes to the parallel printer goes to the designated serial printer.

3. This command can be canceled by the **MODE LPT***x***:** command.

Notes

1. This form of MODE is useful for systems connected to a serial printer. When you type the following command, the serial printer receives all the output that usually is sent to the system printer (assuming that the serial printer is connected to the first Asynchronous Communications Adapter):

   ```
   MODE LPT1:=COM1:
   ```

2. This output includes the print-screen (Shift-PrtSc) function. Before you issue the **MODE LPT=COM***y* command, use the **MODE COM***n***:** command to set up the serial adapter used for the printer.

MODE STATUS   External

The MODE STATUS command displays the status of a specified device or of all devices that can be set by MODE.

Syntax

MODE *device* **/STATUS**

device is the optional device to be checked by MODE.

Switch

/STATUS or **/STA**   Checks the status of a device or devices

Note

This command enables you to see the status of any device that you normally set with MODE. Entering **MODE LPT1 /STA**, for example, displays the status of the first parallel port.

MORE   Internal

MORE displays one screen of information from the standard input device and then pauses and displays the message More. When you press any key, MORE displays the next screen of information.

Syntax

```
command ¦ MORE

MORE < filename.ext
```

command is the command that has output you want to pause.

filename.ext is a text file that you want to display in pages.

Rules

1. MORE displays one screen of information on the standard output (display).

2. After displaying a screen of information, MORE waits for a keystroke before filling the screen with new information. This process repeats until all output appears.

3. MORE is useless without I/O redirection or piping.

Using MORE without redirection or piping may have unpredictable results and leave the hardware in an unstable condition. A reboot may be required for you to continue.

Notes

1. MORE is a DOS filter that enables you to display information without manually pausing the screen.

2. MORE, when used with redirection or piping on a text file, is similar to the TYPE command; however, MORE pauses after each screen of information.

3. One screen of information is based on 40 or 80 characters per line, and 23 lines per screen. MORE, however, does not always display 23 lines from the file. Instead, the command acts intelligently with long lines, wrapping those that exceed the display width (40 or 80 characters). If one of the file's lines takes three lines to display, MORE displays a maximum of 21 lines from the file, pauses, and shows the next screenful of lines.

4. When used with a command, entering **MORE** prevents the display generated by the command from scrolling off the screen before you can read it.

5. Often there is a delay before screen output begins, as MORE builds temporary files.

MOVE   External

MOVE moves files or subdirectories from one location to another.

Syntax

    MOVE @*filename1.ext1 filename2.ext2* /A /D:*date* /H /M /P /R /S
         /T /V /W

filename1.ext1 and *filename2.ext2* are valid file names. Wild cards are allowed.

@ signifies that *filename1.ext1* is a list file.

Switches

/A	Moves only those files that have the archive attribute set; does not clear the archive attribute on the destination
/D:*date*	Moves only files created or modified on or after *date*
/H	Moves hidden and system files
/M	Moves only files that have the archive attribute set; clears the archive attribute on the destination
/P	Prompts you before moving each file with the message filename.ext (Y/N) ?
/R	Overwrites read-only files on the destination that have the same name as the source file
/S	Moves files from subdirectories of the source but does not move subdirectory structure
/T	Moves the entire branch of the subdirectory tree, including all files and subdirectories subordinate to the source
/V	Verifies that the destination files are readable
/W	Waits for a floppy disk to be inserted before moving files

Special Terms

The file being moved is the *source file*. The items in the syntax line that contain 1 relate to the source file. Wild cards are allowed.

The file that is moved to is the *destination file*. The items in the syntax line that contain 2 relate to the destination file. Wild cards are not allowed.

A *list file* is a text file containing a list of file names with complete path specifications.

Rules

To copy files with both source and destination given:

1. The following rules apply to the file name:

■ You must give either a path name or a file name. Wild cards are allowed in the source file name. If you do not give a file name but give a path name for the source, DOS assumes *.*.

■ If you do not give a destination file name, the copied file has the same name as the source file.

2. If the source drive is not specified, the current drive is assumed.

3. If the source directory is not specified, the current directory is assumed.

4. If the destination drive is not specified, the current drive is assumed.

To move files with only one file specified:

1. The file specification you give, *filename1.ext1*, is the source. This specification needs one or both of the following:

■ A valid file name. Wild cards are allowed.

■ A drive name, a path name, or both. If you give only one name, that name must be different from the current drive name or path name. If both names are given, at least one name must differ from the current drive name or path name.

2. The destination is the current drive and current directory.

3. Moved files have the same name as the source files.

NLSFUNC   External

The NLSFUNC command supports extended country information in DOS and enables use of the CHCP command. This command is used for code page switching.

Syntax

```
NLSFUNC filename.ext /Mlocation
```

filename.ext is the country information file. This information is contained in the file COUNTRY.SYS.

Switch

/Mlocation   Tells in which part of memory KEYB should be placed. For *location*, use L for lower (conventional) memory, H for high memory, and U for upper memory.

Rules

1. If you give a drive or path name, you must give also the name of the information file, which usually is COUNTRY.SYS.

2. If you omit the full file name, DOS searches for the file COUNTRY.SYS in the current disk's root directory.

3. Once loaded, NLSFUNC remains active until you restart DOS.

4. NLSFUNC must be loaded before you use the CHCP command.

5. When you use the /MH or /MU switch, if there is insufficient memory of the correct type, the NLSFUNC program will load into lower memory.

Note

You can use the INSTALL command to activate the NLSFUNC command from CONFIG.SYS. After specifying the COUNTRY line in CONFIG.SYS, use the following form:

```
INSTALL=NLSFUNC filename.ext
```

This method uses less memory than if you start NLSFUNC from the DOS prompt.

NWCACHE   External

Novell DOS includes disk caching software that takes advantage of the high degree of repetition in DOS disk operations. The software, NWCACHE, reduces the frequency of disk access by storing data in a special memory area (a *cache*) that contains a copy of the data read from and written to your disk. When data is requested that already exists in the cache, a slower hardware access of the disk is avoided. This provides significant improvement in the time needed to access data. When the cache is full, the least recently used data is discarded.

Syntax

Use the following format for loading the cache into memory:

```
NWCACHE d: | d:+ | d:- maxsize | minsize /A20 /Bx=size /CHECK
        /DELAY=nnnn /Mxx /W=size /X=address /E /L /LEND=xxx
```

Use the following format when the cache is already loaded into memory:

```
NWCACHE - | + d: | d:- | d:+ /DELAY=nnnn /Q | /U /S /SIZE=MIN | MAX
```

Parameters or Switches

Use the following when you are loading the NWCACHE command into memory:

d:+	Forces caching of drive *d*. Write delay is enabled by default.
d:-	Excludes drive *d* from caching.
d:	Identifies drive as a write-through drive.
maxsize	Maximum size of the cache. By default, all available expanded or extended memory up to 7670K (the maximum size of the cache) is used.
minsize	Minimum size of the cache. The default is based on the amount of available memory.
/A20	Suppresses enhanced A20 mode, if you are using the extended memory cache. This option degrades cache performance and should be used only when required to resolve unusual compatibility problems. You can also use it only if an XMS memory manager is not loaded.

/BE=*size*	Loads the lookahead buffer into EMS memory. If you include the =*size* parameter, you can specify the buffer size in a range of 4K to 16K. Note that some LIM memory boards are slow and can reduce performance of the cache. Use this switch as a last resort.
/BL=*size*	Loads the lookahead buffer into lower (conventional) memory. If you include the =*size* parameter, you can specify the buffer size in a range of 4K to 16K.
/BU=*size*	Loads the lookahead buffer into upper memory. If you include the =*size* parameter, you can specify the buffer size in a range of 4K to 16K.
/CHECK	Enables a diagnostic test when the cache is loaded.
/DELAY=OFF	Disables write delay and sets all drives to write-through.
/DELAY=ON	Enables write-delay of 5,000 milliseconds.
/DELAY=*nnnn*	Specifies the write-delay value (*nnnn*) with a range of 50 to 5000 milliseconds.
/E	Uses EMS memory for the cache (may not be the fastest memory for the cache).
/L	Uses lower memory for the cache.
/LEND=*xxx*	Where *xxx* is ON or OFF, enables the sharing of cache memory with programs that require more EMS or XMS memory than is otherwise available. When a program that borrows cache memory ends, NWCACHE takes the memory back for the cache.
/ML	Loads NWCACHE into lower memory, overriding the default use of DPMS.
/MLX	Loads NWCACHE into lower memory and extended memory through DPMS.

/W=*size*	Sets the delayed write data limit with a range of 0 to 7670K. This option limits the amount of delayed write data that can be accumulated in the cache. If the limit is set to 0, no write delay exists.
/X	Forces the use of extended memory for the cache.
/X=*address*	Forces the use of extended memory for the cache when no memory is enabled but extended memory is available. The *address* is the location of the cache memory for non-XMS extended memory.

Use the following after the cache is already loaded:

	Flushes and disables the cache. Use this option to complete any pending delayed writes and clear all data from cache memory. The cache is temporarily disabled but remains loaded in memory. Use this switch to disable the cache before defragmenting your hard disk, for example.
+	Flushes and reenables the cache. Use this option to complete any pending delayed writes and clear all drive data from cache memory. The cache is not disabled, but if it was previously disabled with the - option, this option reenables it. The cache statistics are reset to zero.
d:+	Reenables caching of drive *d* with write delay.
d:-	Excludes DOS drive *d* from caching.
d:	Identifies DOS drive *d* as a write-through drive.
/DELAY=ON	Enables write-delay. The default delay is 5,000 milliseconds.
/DELAY=OFF	Sets all drives to write-through. This option completes any pending delayed writes as well as sets all drives to write-through.

/DELAY=*nnnn*	Specifies the write-delay (*nnnn*) with a range of 50 to 5000 milliseconds. If the delay is set to 0, there is no write delay.
/Q or /U	Quits the cache and tries to unload it from memory. Also completes any pending delayed writes and permanently releases all buffer, cache, and control table memory. The cache may not be able to unload from memory because another program is controlling the system interrupt vectors.
/S	Displays cache status and completes any pending delayed writes before displaying the status report.
/SIZE=MIN | MAX	Sets the cache size to the minimum or maximum startup size. This option also completes any pending delayed writes and clears all drive data from cache memory. If the startup cache size cannot be attained, the highest possible amount of memory is set.

Notes

1. NWCACHE works with STACKER, SuperStor, and DoubleSpace by caching the host drive.

2. NWCACHE automatically loads itself into XMS memory through DPMS if DPMS is enabled.

3. If your machine has a 80286 microprocessor and has extended memory, be sure to use HIMEM.SYS or the /X=*address* switch.

4. If your machine has a 80386 or higher microprocessor, use the EMM386.EXE memory manager.

5. NWCACHE automatically caches all disk drives unless you specify otherwise on loading. RAM disks and remote network drives are not cached.

6. The easiest way to configure NWCACHE is to use the Novell DOS Setup utility.

7. You cannot enable caching of a drive for which caching was disabled at startup.

8. The maximum size of the cache is 7670K.

PASSWORD   External

The PASSWORD command establishes or removes various levels of password protection for files and directory paths.

Syntax

PASSWORD *d:path\filename.ext* /R:*pwd* /W:*pwd* /D:*pwd* /P:*pwd*
        /G:*pwd* /N /NP /NG /S

d: is the drive containing the file to be password-protected or unprotected.

path is the directory containing the file to be password-protected or unprotected.

filename.ext is the file to be password-protected or unprotected. Wild cards are allowed.

pwd is a password of up to eight characters.

Switches

/R:*pwd*   Establishes a password for reading, writing, copying, deleting, renaming, or changing the attributes of a file; creates the password attributes RWD.

/W:*pwd*   Establishes a password for writing, deleting, renaming, or changing the attributes of a file; creates the password attributes WD.

/D:*pwd*   Establishes a password for deleting, renaming, or changing the attributes of a file; creates the password attribute D.

/P:*pwd*   Establishes a password for a directory. A password is then required in any command including the directory path name. This switch does not protect the files in the directory.

/G:*pwd*	Establishes a global password, which remains in effect until you change it or reboot the computer.
/N	Removes a password, prompting you for it first.
/NP	Removes a password from a directory, prompting you for it first.
/NG	Removes a global password.
/S	Applies the password to the specified directory, as well as those in the specified directory.
No switches	Displays a list of files in the specified directory, with their password attributes.

Rules

1. A password may contain any characters that are legal in file names. Passwords are not case-sensitive.

2. If you do not specify a drive, the current drive is assumed.

3. If you do not specify a directory, the current directory is assumed.

4. If you do not specify a file name, *.* is assumed.

5. To access a password-protected file, enter the file name, followed by a semicolon and then the password. Do not put spaces around the semicolon.

6. If you attempt to remove a password from multiple files, you are prompted with `filename.ext...file password?` for each file. You must then type the password for each successive file. The password does not appear on the screen; instead, each character is represented by an asterisk.

Note

Do not password-protect files that are used by an executable file (for example, overlays, printer drivers, and secondary executable files). If you do, you cannot run the program that uses them, because you cannot enter a password when the application calls the subsidiary files.

PATH   Internal

The PATH command tells DOS to search specific directories on the specified drives if a program or batch file is not found in the current directory.

Syntax

> **PATH** *d1:path1*;*d2:path2*;*d3:path3*;...

d1:, *d2:*, and *d3:* are valid disk drive names.

path1, *path2*, and *path3* are valid path names to the commands you want to run while in any directory.

The ellipsis represents additional disk drives and path names.

Rules

If you specify more than one set of paths, the following rules apply:

1. The path sets must be separated by semicolons.

2. The search for the programs or batch files is made in the order in which you give the path sets. First, the current directory is searched. *d1:path1* is searched, then *d2:path2*, then *d3:path3*, and so on, until the command or batch file is found.

Notes

1. The PATH command establishes the value of an environment variable named PATH. To view the current value of PATH, use the PATH or SET command with no arguments.

2. When you type the name of a program or batch file, the current directory is searched. If the program or batch file is not found, DOS searches each path in sequence. If the program or batch file is not found in any of the paths, DOS displays the error message `Command or filename not recognized`.

PRINT   External

The PRINT command allows the printer to print a list of files while the computer performs other tasks.

Syntax

PRINT /D:*device* /B:*bufsize* /M:*maxtick* /Q:*maxfiles* /S:*timeslice*
/U:*busytick* *filename1.ext1* /P /T /C *filename2.ext2* /P /T
/C...

filename1.ext1 and *filename2.ext2* are the files you want to print. Wild cards are allowed.

The ellipsis represents additional file names in the form *dx:pathx\filenamex.extx*.

Switches

You can specify any of the following switches, but only when initially running the PRINT command:

/D:*device*	Specifies the device to be used for printing. *device* is any valid DOS device name. (You must list this switch first whenever you use it.)
/B:*bufsize*	Specifies the size of the memory buffer to be used while the files are printing. *bufsize* can be any number from 1 to 16386. The default is 512 bytes.
/M:*maxtick*	Specifies in ticks the maximum amount of time that PRINT uses to send characters to the printer every time PRINT gets a turn. (A tick is the smallest measure of time used on PCs. A tick happens every 0.0549 seconds.) *maxtick* can be any number from 1 to 255. The default is 2.
/S:*timeslice*	Specifies the number of slices in each second. *timeslice* can be any number from 1 to 255. The default is 8.
/U:*busytick*	Specifies in ticks the maximum amount of time for the program to wait for a busy or unavailable printer. *busytick* can be any number from 1 to 255. The default value is 1.

You can specify any of the following switches whenever you use PRINT:

/Q:*maxfiles*	Specifies the number of files that can be in the queue (line) for printing. *maxfiles* can be any number from 4 to 32. The default is 10.
/P	Queues the file(s) for printing.
/T	Terminates the background printing of all files, including any file currently printing.
/C	Deletes file(s) from the queue.

Rules

1. If you do not give a file name, the background printing status is displayed.

2. You can specify any of the switches from the first set (/D, /B, /M, /S, and /U) only when you first use PRINT. If you give the /D switch, you must type this switch first on the line. You can give the group's remaining switches in any order before you specify a file name.

3. The /D switch specifies the print device you want to use. If you omit /D the first time you use PRINT, DOS displays the following prompt:

```
List device? [PRN]:
```

You can respond in one of two ways:

- Press Enter to send the files to PRN (normally LPT1:). If LPT1: is redirected (see the MODE command), the files are rerouted.

- Enter a valid DOS device name. Printing is directed to this device. If you enter a device that is not connected to your system, PRINT accepts files in the queue. The files are not processed, however, and you lose processing speed. You cannot change the assignment for background printing until you restart DOS.

4. If you name a file with no switch, DOS assumes that the /P switch is given.

5. Files print in the order in which you give their names. If wild cards are used, the files are printed in the order in which they are listed in the directory.

6. The command PRINT /C has no effect if no file name is specified.

7. The first time you use PRINT, DOS increases in size by approximately 5,500 bytes. When you increase or decrease certain default settings, you proportionally change the size of DOS. To regain this memory space, however, you must restart DOS.

Notes

1. The /B switch acts as a disk buffer. PRINT reads into memory a portion of the document to print. As you increase the value of *bufsize*, you decrease the number of times that PRINT must read the file from the disk, thereby increasing printing throughput. You should always use a multiple of 512 as the value of *bufsize*. The default size (512 bytes) is adequate for most uses, but using /B:4096 increases performance for most documents of two pages or fewer.

2. For the /M or /S switch, the following formula determines how much CPU time PRINT gets per second:

   PRINT's % of CPU time = *maxtick* * 100 (1 + *timeslice*)

3. When the default values are assumed, PRINT gets 22 percent of the computer's time. Increasing *maxtick* gives PRINT more time; increasing *timeslice* gives PRINT less time. Because keyboard action becomes sluggish as PRINT uses more time, the default values for PRINT usually work well.

4. The positions of the /P, /C, and /T switches on the command line are important. Each switch affects the immediately preceding file and all following files until DOS encounters another switch.

5. If you use the /T switch, background printing is canceled for all files in the queue, including the file currently printing. You do not need to give a file name with /T because the switch terminates printing for all files.

6. If a disk error occurs during background printing, DOS cancels the current file and places a disk-error message on the printout. The printer then performs a form feed, the bell rings, and DOS prints all files remaining in the queue.

Messages

1. `filename is currently printing/filename is on queue`

   INFORMATION: This message tells you which file is printing and names the files that are in line to be printed. The message appears when you use PRINT with no parameters or when you queue additional files.

2. `No files in Print queue`

   INFORMATION: No files are in line to be printed by PRINT.

3. `Print queue full`

   WARNING: You attempted to place too many files in the PRINT queue. The request to add more files fails for each file past the limit. You must wait until PRINT processes a file before you can add another file to the queue.

PROMPT   Internal

This command customizes the DOS system prompt.

Syntax

PROMPT *promptstring*

promptstring is the text to be used for the new system prompt.

Meta-Strings

A *meta-string* is a group of characters transformed into another character or group of characters. All meta-strings consist of a dollar sign and one additional character. The following list contains meta-strings and their meanings:

Meta-String	What the Meta-String Produces
$$	$
$_ (underscore)	New line (moves to the first position of the next line)
$b	¦
$e	The escape character, CHR$(27)
$d	The date (as for the DATE command)
$h	The backspace character, CHR$(8), which erases the previous character
$g	>
$1	<
$n	The current disk drive
$p	The current disk drive and path, including the current directory
$q	=
$t	The time (as for the TIME command)
$v	The DOS version number
$(any other)	Nothing or null (the character is ignored)

Rules

1. If you do not enter *promptstring*, the standard system prompt reappears (*drive>*).

2. Any text entered for *promptstring* becomes the new system prompt. You can enter special characters by using meta-strings.

3. The new system prompt stays in effect until you restart DOS or reissue the PROMPT command.

4. The PROMPT command creates an environment variable named PROMPT. You can use the SET command to set the value of the PROMPT variable.

RD or RMDIR   **Internal**

This command removes a directory or subdirectory.

Syntax

> RD *d:path*

d:path is the path to the subdirectory. The last path name is the subdirectory you want to delete.

Rules

1. You must name the subdirectory to be deleted.

2. The subdirectory to be deleted must be empty, including no hidden files.

3. You cannot delete the current directory.

Messages

1. Directory not empty or in use

ERROR: RMDIR did not remove the specified directory because one of the following errors occurred:

- Files still exist in the directory.

- You entered a file name rather than a directory to be removed.

Check each possibility and try again.

2. Invalid directory specified

ERROR: RMDIR did not remove the specified directory because one of the following errors occurred:

- You gave an invalid directory in the path.

- You tried to remove the current directory.

Check each possibility and try again.

RECOVER   External

The RECOVER command recovers a file with bad sectors or a file from a disk
with a damaged directory.

Syntax

```
RECOVER d: | d:path\filename.ext
```

d: is the disk drive that holds the damaged file or floppy disk.

path is the path to the directory that holds the file to be recovered.

filename.ext is the file you want to recover.

Rules

1. If you give only a drive name, DOS attempts to recover the disk's
   directory.

2. RECOVER does not restore erased files.

3. Do not use RECOVER with ASSIGN, SUBST, or JOIN.

Notes

1. RECOVER attempts to recover either a file with a bad sector or a disk
   with a directory that contains a bad sector. To recover a file that holds
   one or more bad sectors, enter **RECOVER d:filename.ext**. (DOS tells you
   whether a file has bad sectors, by displaying a disk-error message when
   you try to use the file.)

   When RECOVER works on a file, DOS attempts to read the file's sectors
   one at a time. After RECOVER successfully reads a sector, the information is placed in a temporary file. RECOVER skips any sectors that
   cannot be read successfully, but the FAT is marked so that no other
   program can use the bad sector. This process continues until the entire
   file is read. RECOVER then erases the old file and gives the file's name
   to the temporary file, which becomes a new replacement file. This new
   file is placed in the directory where the old file resided.

2. If the damaged file is a program file, the program probably cannot be
   used. If the file is a data or text file, some information can be recovered.
   Because RECOVER reads the entire file, make sure that you use a text
   editor or word processor to eliminate any formatting or unwanted
   characters in the file.

3. Do not use RECOVER to recover an entire disk. DOS creates a new root directory and recovers each file and subdirectory. The system names the recovered files FILE*nnnn*.REC (*nnnn* is a four-digit number). Even good files are placed in FILE*nnnn*.REC files. To determine which original file corresponds to a FILE*nnnn*.REC file, you must use the TYPE command to view each file, print each file and use the last printed directory of the disk, or have a good memory.

4. RECOVER does not recover erased files. Use the UNDELETE command to recover erased files.

REN or RENAME   Internal

This command changes the name of the disk file(s).

Syntax

```
REN filename1.ext1 filename2.ext2
```

filename1.ext1 is the file's current name. Wild cards are allowed.

filename2.ext2 is the file's new name. Wild cards are allowed.

Rules

1. You can give a disk name and path name only for the first file name.

2. You must give both the old and the new file names and all appropriate extensions. Wild-card characters are permitted in the file names.

Note

REN, or the long form RENAME, changes the name of a file on the disk.

Messages

1. `File already exists`

    ERROR: You attempted to change a file name to a name that already exists. Check the directory for conflicting names. Make sure that the file name exists and that you spelled the name correctly. Reissue the command.

2. `File not found`

ERROR: You asked DOS to rename a file that does not exist in the directory. Make sure that the file exists and that you spelled the name correctly. Reissue the command.

REPLACE   External

REPLACE replaces files on one disk with files of the same name from another disk, and adds files to a disk by copying the files from another disk.

Syntax

```
REPLACE ds:paths\filenames.exts dd:pathd /A /M /P /R /S /W /U
        /N /H
```

ds: is the disk drive that holds the replacement file(s).

paths is the path to the replacement file(s).

filenames.exts is the name of the replacement file(s). Wild cards are permitted.

dd: is the disk drive that contains the file(s) you want to replace.

pathd is the directory to receive the replacement file(s).

Switches

/A	Adds files from the source disk that do not exist on the destination disk.
/M	Merges only modified files on the source to the destination, whether or not they exist on the destination; resets the archive attribute on the source. This switch does not copy read-only, hidden, or system files.
/P	Prompts whether you want the file replaced or added to the destination.
/R	Replaces files on the destination disk, although the read-only attribute for the files is on.
/S	Replaces all files with matching names in the current directory and the subordinate subdirectories.
/W	Causes REPLACE to prompt and wait for the source floppy disk to be inserted.

| /U | Replaces only files having a date and time earlier than the source file's date and time. |

/N   Shows you which files will be replaced, without actually replacing them.

/H   Replaces hidden or system files.

X

Command Reference

Rules

1. If you do not name the source disk drive, DOS uses the current disk drive.

2. If you do not name the source path, DOS uses the current directory.

3. You must specify a source file name. Wild cards are allowed.

4. If you do not name the destination disk drive, DOS adds files to—or replaces files on—the current drive.

5. If you do not name the destination path, DOS adds files to—or replaces files in—the current directory.

6. /S does not work with the /A switch.

Notes

1. If you do not use REPLACE with caution, this command's speedy "find and replace" capability can have the effect of an unrelenting "search and destroy" mission on your data. Be careful when you unleash RE-PLACE on several subdirectories at a time, particularly when you use REPLACE /S on the entire disk. Because REPLACE updates the file based on the file name alone, you could replace a file that you want to save somewhere on the disk. To prevent such unwanted replacements, limit the destination path name to cover only the directories that hold the files you want replaced. Check the source and destination directories for matching file names. If you find conflicts or have doubts, use the /P switch; REPLACE asks for approval before replacing files. Alternatively, add the /N switch to your command to see a list of every file that would be replaced if you actually carried out the command.

2. The /U switch can help you avoid replacing the wrong files. /U compares the files' date and time stamp. The destination file is replaced only if the file is older than the source file.

Messages

1. *filename*...cannot be copied onto itself

WARNING: The source and destination disk and directories are identical. You probably did not specify a destination, so the source disk and directory are the current disk and directory. Otherwise, you specified the same disk drive and directory twice. REPLACE does not process *filename*.

Check the command line to ensure that you specified the correct source and destination for REPLACE; then try the command again.

2. *nnn* File(s) added

or

nnn File(s) replaced

INFORMATION: REPLACE indicates how many files are successfully added or replaced. The first message appears when you use the /A switch; the second message appears if /A is not used. These messages do not indicate that potential files are added or replaced successfully. Instead, the message appears when at least one file is added or replaced successfully, regardless of errors that occur later.

3. "*filename*"...file not found

ERROR: REPLACE could not find any files that matched the source file name *filename*. One of the following errors probably occurred:

- You misspelled the source file name.

- You gave the disk drive and directory name but omitted the file name.

- You gave the wrong disk drive or directory name for the source.

- You put the wrong floppy disk in the disk drive.

Check the command line to ensure that the correct disk is in the disk drive; then try the command again.

4. Invalid combination of options A and S

ERROR: You gave both the /A and /S switches, which cannot be used together in the same REPLACE command. To replace files, omit /A.

Remember that, because you cannot add files to more than one directory at a time, you cannot give /S along with /A. To add files to more than one directory, issue separate REPLACE commands, each time specifying a different directory to which files are to be added.

RESTORE   External

This command restores one or more backup files from one disk to another disk. RESTORE complements the BACKUP command.

Syntax

```
RESTORE d1: d2:path\filename.ext /S /P /M /N /B:date /A:date
        /L:time /E:time
```

d1: is the disk drive that holds the backup files.

d2: is the disk drive to receive the restored files.

path is the path to the directory to receive the restored files.

filename.ext is the file you want to restore. Wild cards are allowed.

Switches

/S   Restores files in the current directory and all subordinate subdirectories. When this switch is given, RESTORE re-creates all necessary subdirectories that were removed and restores the files in the re-created subdirectories.

/P   Causes RESTORE to prompt for your approval before restoring read-only files or files that have changes since the last backup.

/M   Restores files that were modified or deleted since the last backup.

/N   Restores files that do not exist on the destination.

/B:*date*   Restores all files that were created or modified on or before the date you specify.

/A:*date*   Restores all files that were created or modified on or after the date you specify.

/L:*time*   Restores all files that were created or modified at or later than the time you specify.

/E:*time*   Restores all files that were created or modified at or earlier than the time you specify.

Exit Codes

0   Normal completion

1   No files were found to restore

2   Some files not restored because of a file-sharing conflict

3   Terminated by the operator (through a Ctrl-Break or Esc)

4   Terminated by an encountered error

Rules

1. You must give the name of the drive that holds the backup files. If the current disk is the one to receive the restored files, you do not need to specify the destination disk drive.

2. If you do not name a path, RESTORE uses the current directory of the receiving disk.

3. If you do not give a file name, RESTORE restores all backup files from the directory. Giving no file name is the same as using *.*.

4. RESTORE prompts you to insert the backup disks in order. If you insert a disk out of order, RESTORE prompts you to insert the correct disk.

5. Do not combine the /B, /A, and /N switches in the same RESTORE command.

6. Be cautious when you restore files that were backed up while an APPEND, ASSIGN, SUBST, or JOIN command was in effect. When you use RESTORE, clear any existing APPEND, ASSIGN, SUBST, or JOIN commands. Do not use RESTORE /M or RESTORE /N while APPEND /X:ON is in effect. RESTORE attempts to search the directories for modified or missing files. APPEND tricks RESTORE into finding files in the paths specified to the APPEND command. RESTORE may then restore files that should not be restored, and not restore files that should be restored. Use APPEND; to disable APPEND.

Messages

1. `Insert disk number nnn in drive d: Strike a key to continue`

INFORMATION: RESTORE wants the next disk in sequence. This message appears when you are restoring files that were backed up to floppy disks. Insert the next floppy disk (in the proper sequence) in drive *d:* and press any key.

2. `No backup files present on source disk`

ERROR: RESTORE found no files that were backed up with the BACKUP command. BACKUP may have malfunctioned when backing up files, or you inserted the wrong disk. You also see this message if you insert backup disks out of sequence.

3. `Destination and source drives are the same`

ERROR: RESTORE determined that the disk drive holding the backup files is the same as the drive you designated to receive the restored files. You may have forgotten to specify the disk drive that holds the backup files or the target disk.

4. `BACKUP file sequence error`

WARNING: You inserted a backup floppy disk out of order or from the wrong backup series. Place the correct disk in the drive and continue.

SCRIPT   External

The SCRIPT command allows you to print files on a PostScript printer that have not been formatted for such a printer, or to translate printer output into PostScript format and save it in a file.

Syntax

```
SCRIPT device1 | filename1.ext1 device2 | filename2.ext2 /O=P |
L
     /P=nn /TI=yy /R /U /T=nn /L=nn
```

device1 is a device from which input should be taken.

filename1.ext1 is the file to be printed.

device2 is the device to which the PostScript output should be sent.

filename2.ext2 is the file to which PostScript output should be sent.

Switches

/O=P | L	Specifies the page orientation; use P for portrait (vertical) and L for landscape (horizontal). The default is portrait.
/P=*nn*	Specifies a size of *nn* points for the output. The default is 11.
/TI=*yy*	Specifies the number of seconds to wait before emptying the spool to the printer.
/R	Resets the printer before printing.
/U	Unloads SCRIPT if it is loaded as a TSR.
/T=nn	Top page margin (in inches).
/L=nn	Left page margin (in inches).

Rules

1. If you enter SCRIPT with no file or device names, a help screen appears.

2. If you enter a non-PostScript printer as the source and a PostScript printer as the destination, SCRIPT becomes a TSR and intercepts all output bound for the non-PostScript printer, redirecting it to the PostScript printer and translating it.

3. Specify a file as the source and a different file as the destination to create the file in PostScript-ready format.

4. Output, or files, in HP LaserJet II format can be translated to PostScript format.

5. When loaded as a TSR, SCRIPT enlarges DOS by about 19K.

SDRES   **External**

The SDRES command executes SDRes, the memory-resident antivirus software that tests your system's RAM for viruses every time you reboot your computer. This utility runs under DOS and Windows.

Syntax

SDRES /N /E /U*path* /M *avail-mem-in-K*

avail-mem-in-K is the physical memory in your computer. SDRes examines this amount of memory for viruses.

Switches

/N	Executes the memory scan without installing as memory-resident.
/E	Does not install the memory-resident part of SDRes in expanded memory.
/U*path*	Specifies the location of SDScan, the scanner program. If SDSCAN.EXE is not located in the same directory as SDRes, you must inform SDRes where to find the scanner.
/M	Disables the automatic rehooking of INT21. Use this switch if you have problems with other TSRs such as network drivers or redirectors.

SDSCAN   External

The SDSCAN command executes SDScan, the antivirus Search & Destroy scan program. This utility runs under both Novell DOS and Windows. Under DOS, you can use the full-screen mode, or you can use the command line.

Refer to Chapter 16, "Virus Protection," for a complete understanding of SDScan and SDRes.

Syntax

```
SDSCAN /H /B /A /Vx /N /R:filename.ext /R+filename.ext /SA+ | -
      /SC+ | - filespec
```

Switches

Use the following switches to execute SDScan from the command line:

/H	Scans all hard disk drives. Otherwise, the default is drive C.
/B	Tells SDScan not to scan for viruses in the boot block, which is the default.
/A	Tells SDScan to scan all the files on the disk, including data files. The default is for the scanner to scan only program files.

/Vx	Tells SDScan to prompt (*x* = P) the user when it finds a virus, report when it finds a virus (*x* = R), or destroy (*x* = D) any virus it finds without prompting.
/N	Tells SDScan not to scan memory, but only the disk drive(s). You can use SDRes to scan just memory if you want.
/R:*filename.ext*	Generates a report.
/R+*filename.ext*	Generates a report and appends to existing report.
/SA+	Checks archive files.
/SA-	Skips archive files.
/SC+	Checks compressed executables.
/SC-	Skips compressed executables.
No switches	Starts the full-screen mode.

Rules

1. You can configure SCScan to scan either program files or all files.

2. Compressed files may be scanned by SDScan.

3. If a virus is detected, be sure to follow all directions given in screen messages.

SET   Internal

The SET command sets or shows the system environment.

Syntax

```
SET name=string
```

name is the string you want to add to the environment.

string is the information to be stored in the environment.

The environment is the portion of RAM reserved for alphanumeric information that can be examined and used by DOS commands or user programs. For example, the environment usually contains COMSPEC, the location of COMMAND.COM; PATH, the additional paths for finding programs and batch files; and PROMPT, the string defining the DOS system prompt.

Rules

1. To delete a name, enter **SET** *name*= without specifying a string.

2. Any lowercase letters in *name* are changed to uppercase letters when placed in the environment. The characters in *string* are not changed.

3. You can use the SET command rather than PROMPT or PATH to set the system prompt and the information for the PATH command.

4. Use the SET command with no parameters to display several environment settings.

5. Valid SET strings are COMSPEC, NWDOSCFG, OS, PEXEC, and TEMP.

SETUP   External

SETUP is the Novell DOS 7 configuration utility. Refer to Chapter 4, "Installing Novell DOS 7," and Chapter 5, "Installing the Network," for everything you need to know about this program.

SETVER   External

SETVER allows you to change the operating system version number that DOS returns to an application. By default, when a program requests the operating system to return its version, Novell DOS 7 returns a 6.00, meaning that it is compatible with MS-DOS 6.00.

Syntax

```
SETVER filename.ext n.nn /P /DELETE /QUIET
```

filename.ext is the name of the application that seeks the DOS version.

n.nn is number of the version that DOS returns to the application.

Switches

/P	Tells SETVER to pause after each full screen
/DELETE	Tells SETVER to delete the entry for the named application
/QUIET	Tells SETVER to delete the named application without displaying information about the deletion
No switches	Displays the current list of applications and version numbers

Examples

1. When you type the following line, you get a display of the current list of applications and DOS version numbers that have been set for each application, in two columns, with the display pausing at the end of each full screen:

```
SETVER C:\NWDOS /P
```

2. The following example either modifies a program already in the list or adds a new program to the list:

```
SETVER C:\NWDOS D:\TAPE\TAPE.EXE 5.00
```

3. The following example deletes an entry from the list:

```
SETVER C:\NWDOS D:\TAPE\TAPE.EXE /DELETE
```

Notes

1. Make sure that you specify the location of the SETVER.EXE utility if you are not in that directory or if the \NWDOS directory is not in the path.

2. Make sure that you use the two decimal places for the version number. SETVER lists 3.3 as 3.03, not as 3.30.

3. Even though you tell DOS to return the proper version number to an application that requests it, the application may not run properly.

4. Changes to SETVER do not take effect until you reboot the computer.

SHARE   External

The SHARE command enables DOS support for file and record locking.

Syntax

SHARE   /L:*nnnn* /X /M*location*

Switches

/L:*nnnn*   Sets the maximum number (*nnnn*) of file or record locks to use. The default, and the minimum, is 20. The maximum is 1024.

/X   Unloads SHARE.

/M*location*   Tells in which part of memory SHARE should be placed. For *location*, use L for lower (conventional) memory, H for high memory, and U for upper memory.

Rules

1. When SHARE is loaded, DOS checks for file and record locks as each file is opened, read, and written.

2. When loaded in lower memory, SHARE normally enlarges DOS by approximately 4,816 bytes. If *nnnn* is increased or decreased, DOS also increases or decreases proportionately in size.

3. To load SHARE into upper memory or high memory, you must have a device driver loaded that makes this type of memory available. By default, SHARE is loaded into high memory if it is available, or into upper memory if it is available but high memory is not.

4. Task Manager requires that SHARE be installed.

5. You can load SHARE with Install in your CONFIG.SYS or DCONFIG.SYS file.

Notes

1. You use SHARE when two or more programs or processes share a single computer's files. After SHARE is loaded, DOS checks each file for locks whenever the file is opened, read, or written. If a file is open for exclusive use, an error message results from subsequent attempts to open the file. If one program locks a portion of a file, an error message results if another program tries to read or write the locked portion.

2. SHARE is most effective when all file-sharing programs can handle the DOS functions for locking files and records. SHARE is either partially or completely ineffective with programs that do not use the DOS file- and record-locking features.

3. SHARE affects two or more programs running on the same computer—not two or more computers using the same file (networked computers). For networks, record and file locking are made possible by software provided with the network. However, some networks, including the Desktop Server, require that SHARE be loaded.

SORT   External

The SORT command reads lines from the standard input device, performs an ASCII sort of the lines, and then writes the lines to the standard output device. The sorting can be in ascending or descending order and can start at any column in the line.

Syntax

    SORT /R /+c

Switches

/R   Sorts in reverse order. Thus, the letter Z comes first, and the letter A comes last. The default sort order is ascending.

/+c   Starts sorting with column number c, which is a positive integer.

Rules

1. If you do not specify the /+c switch, sorting starts with the first column (first character on the line).

2. If you do not redirect the input or output, all input is from the keyboard (standard input), and all output is to the video display (standard output). If you redirect input and output, use different names for the input and output files.

3. SORT can handle a maximum file size of 63K (64,512 characters).

4. SORT sorts text files and discards any information after—and including—the end-of-file marker.

Examples

1. The following example sorts the lines in the file WORDS.TXT and then displays the sorted lines on-screen:

```
SORT < WORDS.TXT
```

2. The following example sorts in reverse order the lines in the file WORDS.TXT and then displays the sorted lines on-screen:

```
SORT < WORDS.TXT /R
```

3. The following example sorts the lines in WORDS.TXT, beginning at the eighth character in each line, and then displays the sorted lines on-screen:

```
SORT /+8 < WORDS.TXT
```

4. The following example displays the directory information sorted by file size (the file size starts in the 14th column). Unfortunately, other lines—such as the volume label—are also sorted starting at the 14th column.

```
DIR ¦ SORT /+14
```

SUBST   External

The SUBST command creates an alias disk drive name for a subdirectory. SUBST is used principally with programs that do not use path names.

Syntax

SUBST *d1: d2:pathname* /D

d1: is a valid disk drive name that becomes the alias. *d1:* may be a non-existent disk drive.

d2:pathname is the valid disk drive name and directory path that will be named *d1:*.

Switch

/D   Deletes the alias, or substitution

Example

    SUBST

This example displays the current aliases.

Rules

1. Use the SUBST command with no parameters to see a display of the current substitutions.

2. While SUBST is in effect, CHKDSK works only on the real disk drive name and path name. Avoid using ASSIGN, JOIN, or LABEL. Do not use BACKUP, DISKCOPY, DISKCOMP, FDISK, FORMAT, or RESTORE with the SUBST disk drive name.

Messages

1. `Cannot SUBST a network drive`

   ERROR: You tried to use another computer's disk drive (that is, a networked disk drive) as the alias or nicknamed disk drive. You cannot use a networked disk drive with SUBST, nor can you "cover" a network disk drive with a SUBST command.

2. `Invalid directory specified`

   ERROR: You specified a directory that doesn't exist, mistyped the name of a directory that does exist, or specified a drive name for the alias that isn't available. DOS normally provides drive letters A through E, unless you allow for a higher drive letter by using a LASTDRIVE command in the CONFIG.SYS file. If you have verified that the directory exists and its name has been typed correctly, use a different drive letter as an alias, or edit your CONFIG.SYS to provide for a higher last drive letter. Then reboot the computer.

SYS   External

The SYS command puts a copy of IBMBIO.COM, IBMDOS.COM, and COMMAND.COM on the specified disk so that it can boot the computer.

Syntax

> **SYS** *d1:* *d2:*

d1: is the source drive for the system files.

d2: is the disk drive to receive the copy of DOS.

Rules

1. You must specify the disk drive to receive a copy of DOS.

2. The disk to receive the copy of DOS must be formatted and have enough room for the three required files.

3. A copy of DOS (the IBMBIO.COM, IBMDOS.COM, and COMMAND.COM files) should reside on the current disk. Otherwise, you are shown a message describing the correct syntax and procedure.

4. You cannot use SYS on a networked disk drive.

5. If *d1:* is not specified, the source system files must be in the system path.

Messages

1. `Error writing system files`

   ERROR: Either the destination disk didn't have enough room for the system files, or another error occurred.

2. `System files copied`

   INFORMATION: DOS successfully placed IBMBIO.COM, IBMDOS.COM, and COMMAND.COM on the destination disk.

TASKMGR   External

Task Manager enables you to load more than one application as a task and switch among tasks quickly. It can be run as a multitasker or task switcher on a 386 or higher computer with at least 2M of RAM, or as a task switcher on a 286 or lower computer.

Task Manager, as a multitasker, runs multiple programs simultaneously. You switch among them by using either the Task Manager menu or the "hot keys." A hot key usually consists of the Ctrl key plus a numeric key on the numeric keypad. When you switch a program to the background (not currently on the video screen), the program keeps running.

Task Manager, as a task switcher, loads multiple programs but runs only the foreground task. You switch among tasks by using either the Task Manager menu or the hot keys. When you switch a program to the background (not currently on the video screen), the program is suspended. When you switch a task to the foreground (currently on the video screen), the program resumes.

Syntax

Use the following form for Task Manager as a task switcher:

> **TASKMGR** /C *command* /D=*dirpath* /E=*nnnn* /F /K:*nn* /L=*nnnn* /M
> /N:*nn* *name* /V:1 /X=*nnnn*

Use this form for Task Manager as a multitasker:

> **TASKMGR** /C *command* /M /K:*nn* /S

command is the program to be run as a task.

Switches

Use the following switches to load Task Manager as a task switcher:

/D=*dirpath*	Tells Task Manager the location (*dirpath*) of the swap file. Task Manager uses the swap file to store suspended applications when there is not enough RAM available. Unless you change it, the default location is C:\NWDOS\TMP.
/E=*nnnn*	Allocates the specified amount *nnnn* (K) of extended memory for Task Manager to use. The default amount, without =*nnnn*, is all available extended memory. To disable the use of extended memory, use 0 for the amount.
/F	Saves user-defined fonts and code pages when you switch tasks.

X

/M	Allows you to switch tasks using the numeric keys on the main keyboard instead of on the numeric keypad. This is very useful when you are using a keyboard that does not have a separate numeric keypad, as on a notebook computer.
/V:1 or /V	Supports task switching on some VGA monitors/adapters that are not fully compatible. Try /V:1 first to see whether the display works better; then try /V if necessary.
/X=*nnnn*	Allocates the specified amount *nnnn* (K) of expanded memory for Task Manager to use. The default amount, without =*nnnn*, is all available expanded memory. To disable the use of expanded memory, use 0 for the amount.

Use the following switches when loading Task Manager as a multitasker:

/M	Allows you to switch tasks by using the numeric keys on the main keyboard rather than on the numeric keypad. This switch is useful when you are using a keyboard that does not have a separate numeric keypad, as on a notebook computer.
/S	Tells Task Manager, although configured to run as a multitasker, to load as a task switcher.

Use the following switches after Task Manager is already loaded as a task switcher:

/C *command*	Adds a new task. Use this switch from the DOS prompt or within a batch file. *command* is the normal command you use to run a program, and can be the actual executable program or a batch file.
/K:*nn*	Removes the task indicated by *nn*. You cannot use this option to delete the current task.

/L=*nnnn*   When Task Manager is loaded and configured to use
                   expanded memory, this switch limits the amount of
                   expanded memory (to *nnnn* K) that any task can use.

/N:*nn name*   Lets you change the name of the current task (no *nn*
                   included) or the numbered task (*nn* included) to the
                   new *name*. Task Manager supplies the name of the
                   running program as the default name for each task. If
                   you rename a task and reissue the TASKMGR com-
                   mand with the /N switch and no name, the original
                   task name is restored.

Use the following switches after Task Manager is already loaded as a
multitasker or a task switcher:

/C *command*   Adds a new task. Use this switch from the DOS prompt
                   or within a batch file. *command* is the normal command
                   you use to run a program, and can be the actual ex-
                   ecutable program or a batch file.

/K:*nn*   Removes the task indicated by *nn*. You cannot use the
                   option to delete the current session.

Rules

1. SHARE must be loaded before you can run Task Manager. For
   information about switches, see the section on SHARE in this
   Command Reference.

2. The /D, /E, /F, /M, /V, and /X switches may be used only when you
   initially load Task Manager as a task switcher.

3. /M and /S are the only switches you can use when you initially load
   Task Manager as a multitasker.

4. If the amount of memory specified by the /X and /E switches exceeds
   the available memory, only the available memory is allocated.

5. Use the Novell DOS 7 Setup utility to configure Task Manager and set
   the hot keys.

Notes

1. After Task Manager is loaded, it is run from either a menu or the command line. To display the menu, press Ctrl-Esc. To run Task Manager from the command line, use the /C, /K, and /N switches with appropriate information.

2. Tasks are given numbers based on the order in which they are started. To switch to another task, press Ctrl plus the number of the task.

3. If Task Manager is loaded, pressing Ctrl-Alt-Del does not reboot the computer. Instead, it deletes the current task or DOS session. When you press these keys at the last running task or session, Task Manager is removed from memory, after you are asked you to confirm that is what you want to do.

TIME   Internal

The TIME command sets and shows the system time.

Syntax

    TIME *hh:mm:ss.xx* /C

hh is the one- or two-digit number for hours (0 to 23).

mm is the one- or two-digit number for minutes (0 to 59).

ss is the one- or two-digit number for seconds (0 to 59).

xx is the one- or two-digit number for hundredths of a second (0 to 99).

Switch

/C   Displays the time until a key is pressed

Notes

1. Depending on the country code's setting in your CONFIG.SYS or CONFIG.SYS file, a comma may be required between seconds and hundredths of seconds.

2. The TIME command sets the computer's internal 24-hour clock. The time and date are recorded in the directory when you create or change a file. This information can help you find the most recent version of a file when you check your directory.

   Personal computers sold in the United States use a software clock based on the 60 Hz power supply. This kind of clock usually loses or gains several seconds a day. The inaccuracy is not the computer's fault, but a normal problem with the AC power provided by your power company.

3. If you do not enter the time when starting up many PCs and PC/XTs, the time defaults to 00:00:00.00. If you want your system to use the correct time, you must set the time manually.

4. Many computers retain the time of day through a battery-backed circuit. The real-time clock is read and displayed when you start the computer. Such clocks usually are accurate to within one minute a month, which is about the same accuracy as a digital watch. After you boot your computer, DOS uses the software time clock, which suffers from the same inaccuracies as the PC clock.

5. Your computer clock uses a 24-hour format; thus, 1 a.m. is 01:00, but 1 p.m. is 13:00.

TOUCH   External

This command changes the time and date stamp on one or more files. TOUCH optionally changes the date format to conform to a different country's style.

Syntax

    TOUCH @*filename.ext* /T:*time* /D:*date* /F:*country* /P /R /S

filename.ext is the file that has a date or time to be changed. Wild cards are allowed.

@ signifies that *filename.ext* may be a list file, containing the full path specifications of the files to be changed.

Switches

/T:*time*	Specifies the time the file should have, expressed in your country's time format.
/D:*date*	Specifies the date the file should have, expressed in your country's time format.
/F:*country*	Specifies the country format to be used. *country* may be E for European formats, J for Japanese format, or U for U.S. format.
/P	Prompts for permission to make changes with a message in the form *filename.ext* (Y/N) ?
/R	Changes dates or times on read-only files included in the file specification.
/S	Includes files in subdirectories of the specified subdirectory.

Rules

1. If no drive is specified, the current drive is assumed.

2. If no directory is specified, the current directory is assumed.

3. A file name must be given, but wild cards are acceptable.

Note

The country format specified by the /F switch overrides the one established in CONFIG.SYS.

TREE   External

The TREE command displays all the subdirectories on a disk and optionally displays the number of files in each directory and the bytes used by each file in each directory.

Syntax

TREE *d:* /A /F /G /P /B

d: is the disk drive holding the disk you want to examine.

Switches

/A	Displays the tree in text format rather than graphical format. Use this option when your video display or printer does not support graphics.
/F	Displays the names of all files in the directories.
/G	Graphically displays the tree structure.
/P	Pauses when the screen is full and waits for a press of the Enter key.
/B	Omits the number and total size of the files in each directory.

Note

The /F switch cancels the effect of the /G switch when both are used.

TYPE   Internal

The TYPE command displays a file's contents on the monitor.

Syntax

```
TYPE filename.ext /P
```

filename.ext is the file to be displayed. Wild cards are not permitted.

Switch

/P	Waits for a key to be pressed when the screen becomes full

Notes

1. The TYPE command displays a file's characters on the video screen. Strange characters appear on-screen when you use TYPE on some data files and program files, because TYPE tries to display the machine-language instructions as ASCII characters. Batch files and other text files composed only of ASCII text are the real targets of the TYPE command.

2. The output of TYPE, like most other DOS commands, can be redirected to the printer by adding >PRN to the command line or by pressing Ctrl-PrtSc after you display the contents. You can also use the toggle Ctrl-P and the TYPE command to send the output to both the screen and the printer. Don't forget to toggle Ctrl-P off again when you are finished.

UNDELETE   External

UNDELETE recovers files you deleted with the DEL command. When available, UNDELETE uses DELWATCH's pending-delete files or DISKMAP's delete-tracking file to restore a deleted file. UNDELETE can be run from either the command line or its full-screen interface.

Syntax

```
UNDELETE filename.ext /B /A /D:date | -dd /T:time /L /P
        /R:protection_method /S
```

filename.ext is the file to be undeleted. Wild cards are permitted.

Switches

/B	Displays the menu in black and white; no other switches are permitted with this switch. Runs in full-screen mode.
/A	Undeletes all files matching *filename.ext* but does not prompt before each one.
/D:*date*	Undeletes or lists deleted files saved by DELWATCH that were created or modified since the specified date.
/D:*-dd*	Undeletes or lists deleted files saved by DELWATCH during the last *dd* days.
/T:*time*	Undeletes or lists deleted files saved by DELWATCH that were created or modified since the specified time.
/L	Lists all files matching *filename.ext* but does not undelete them.
/P	Pauses for a keypress when the screen is full.
/R:*protection_method*	Undeletes only files protected by *protection_method*. *protection_method* may be DISKMAP, DISKWATCH, or UNAIDED.
/S	Undeletes files in subdirectories of the specified directory as well as the specified directory.
No switches	Starts the full-screen interface version of UNDELETE.

X

Command Reference

Rules

1. If you specify any switches except /B and do not enter a drive name, the current drive is assumed.

2. If you specify any switches except /B and do not enter a path name, the current directory is assumed.

3. If you specify any switches except /B and do not enter a file name, *.* is assumed.

4. If you do not use the /A switch, the name, attributes, size, date, and time of each matching file is displayed, along with the message Recover (Y/N) ?

5. If you want to undelete a file in a subdirectory that has been removed, you must first undelete the subdirectory.

Examples

For these examples, assume that the DOS commands are stored in C:\DRDOS, which is on the search path.

1. The following command restores all deleted files on drive C:

    UNDELETE /S /A

2. The following command provides a listing of all presently deleted files:

    UNDELETE /L

Notes

1. When you specify any switches, UNDELETE displays each file that matches the criteria you specified and asks whether you want to undelete it. Unless you used the /R switch, UNDELETE tells you which method is used to undelete the file and the chances of successful recovery.

2. If you load the UNDELETE menu, the current directory shows a list of deleted files and information about the protection method used and chances of successful recovery. You can move to other directories either by selecting them by name or by selecting the .. directory. You can change to another drive by using a menu selection.

3. Although UNDELETE enables you to recover files that have been de-leted accidentally, do not use this command as a substitute for backing up data. Be sure to keep up-to-date backups of your data.

UNFORMAT

This command recovers disks inadvertently reformatted with the Novell DOS FORMAT command. The UNFORMAT command works on hard disks and floppy disks.

Syntax

```
UNFORMAT d:
```

d: is the disk drive to be unformatted.

Rules

1. To unformat your hard disk, you first must reboot from drive A.

2. If you format a floppy disk by using the /U switch, UNFORMAT cannot restore the disk.

Messages

1. `UNFORMAT information has been overwritten`

   INFORMATION: UNFORMAT cannot unformat the disk because you have written files to it since you formatted it.

2. `Disk UNFORMATted successfully`

   INFORMATION: The disk has been restored to its condition before formatting.

UNINSTAL   External

The UNINSTAL command removes all Novell DOS files from the hard disk.

Syntax

```
UNINSTAL /C
```

Switch

/C   Removes operating system files from the previous
                            installation of DOS

Rules

1. For UNINSTAL to successfully restore your previous operating system,
   you must have chosen to save it while running the Install program.

2. Be sure that all your programs are compatible with Novell DOS 7 before
   you delete the old version of DOS with UNINSTAL /C.

Note

When you upgrade to Novell DOS 7, the old version of DOS is usually preserved on your hard disk. After you are sure that the upgrade works correctly
and that you find no incompatibility with programs that you normally use,
you can delete the old DOS from the hard disk by using the /C switch, thus
freeing additional storage space. If, in fact, you discover that your old programs do not work with Novell DOS 7, you can restore your previous operating system, deleting your new one. This also frees additional storage space.

UNSECURE   External

If you have installed login security on your hard disk and cannot access the
hard disk, UNSECURE lets you disable security, but only if you know the
master password. UNSECURE is not a tool for bypassing your login security.

Syntax

UNSECURE

Note

You must boot your system from the first installation floppy disk for Novell
DOS 7, exit the Install program, and enter **UNSECURE** at the system prompt.
You are then prompted for the master password. If you enter the correct
password, UNSECURE disables security.

UNSTACK   External

This utility removes the Stacker disk compression for any Stacker-compressed
drive.

Syntax

> UNSTACK *d:*

You must specify *d:*, the drive letter. The drive must be a Stacker-compressed drive, and it must be mounted as the specified drive. If the drive letter entered is an acceptable drive, UNSTACK loads as a full-screen utility.

UNSTACK then verifies the size of the files on the compressed drive. If there is not enough room to place the files in uncompressed format on the drive without Stacker, you are warned of the amount of space that must be freed, and you are requested to press Enter to return to the DOS prompt so that you can free the space.

VER   Internal

The VER command displays the DOS version number on-screen.

Syntax

> VER

Note

The VER command displays the DOS version number and copyright information, reminding you which DOS version the computer is using, currently Novell DOS 7.

VERIFY   Internal

The VERIFY command sets the computer to check the accuracy of data written to a disk to ensure that the information was recorded correctly. VERIFY then shows whether the data was checked.

Syntax

> VERIFY ON | OFF

Rules

1. VERIFY accepts only the parameter ON or OFF.

2. When on, VERIFY remains on until one of the following events occurs:

   ■ A VERIFY OFF is issued.

■ A SET VERIFY system call turns off the command.

■ DOS is restarted.

3. By default, VERIFY is off.

Note

If VERIFY is on, data integrity is assured. If VERIFY is off, you can write to the disk more quickly. You are usually safe to leave VERIFY off if you are not working with critical information, such as a company's accounting figures. You are wise to turn VERIFY on, however, when backing up your hard disk or making important copies on floppy disks.

VOL   Internal

The VOL command displays the disk's volume label, if one exists.

Syntax

```
VOL d:
```

d: is the disk drive whose label you want to display.

XCOPY   External

XCOPY copies groups of files from one or more subdirectories.

Syntax

```
XCOPY @ds:paths\filenames.exts dd:pathd\filenamed.extd /A /C /D
       /D:date /E /F /H /L /M /P /R /S /V /W
```

ds: is the source disk drive, which holds the files to be copied.

paths is the starting directory path to the files you want to copy.

filenames.exts is the file to be copied. Wild cards are allowed.

@ signifies that the names of the files to be copied may be contained in a list file.

dd: is the destination disk drive, which receives the copied files. DOS refers to the destination drive as the target.

pathd is the starting directory to receive the copied files.

filenamed.extd is the new name of the file that is copied. Wild cards are allowed.

Switches

/A	Copies files that have the archive flag on, but does not turn off the archive flag (similar to the /M switch).
/C	Prompts you for approval before copying a file. This swtich has the same effect as /P.
/D	Tells XCOPY that the destination is a directory rather than a file.
/D:*date*	Copies files that were changed or created on or after the date you specify. The date's form depends on the setting of the COUNTRY directive in CONFIG.SYS or DCONFIG.SYS.
/E	Creates parallel subdirectories on the destination disk, even if the original subdirectory is empty.
/F	Tells XCOPY that the destination is a file, not a directory.
/H	Copies hidden and system files.
/L	Copies the disk label as well as the files.
/M	Copies files that have the archive flag on (modified files) and turns off the archive flag (similar to the /A switch).
/P	Causes XCOPY to prompt for approval before copying a file.
/R	Overwrites read-only files in the destination directory.
/S	Copies files from this directory and all subsequent subdirectories.
/V	Verifies that the copy was recorded correctly.
/W	Causes XCOPY to prompt and wait for the correct source floppy disk to be inserted.

Error Codes

0	Command was completed normally.
1	No files matched the criteria.
2	User interrupted with Ctrl-Break or Ctrl-C.
4	Not enough space on the destination, not enough RAM, or an invalid destination was specified.
5	Command was terminated because of an error writing to the destination disk.

Rules

1. You must specify the source drive, path, and file name first, and then the destination drive, path, and file name.

2. Do not use a device name other than a disk drive for the source or destination name. For example, you cannot use LPT1: or COM1:.

3. The source file specification (*ds:paths\filenames.exts*) must have one or both of the following:

    ■ A valid file name (wild cards are permitted)

    ■ A drive name, a path name, or both

4. If you do not specify the source drive name, DOS uses the current drive.

5. If you do not specify the source path, DOS uses the disk drive's current directory.

6. If you specify a disk drive or path for the source but do not specify a source file name (*filenames.exts*), DOS assumes *.*.

7. If you omit a new file name for the destination file, the copied file uses the same name as the source file.

8. If you do not give the destination file specification, the source file specification must have either or both of the following:

    ■ A disk drive name other than the current disk drive

    ■ A path name other than the current disk's current directory

9. Do not use the source disk in an APPEND /X:ON command. If the

source disk is part of an APPEND command, disconnect the command by using APPEND before you use XCOPY.

Notes

1. To use XCOPY to copy more files than can fit on one destination disk, make sure that each file's archive attribute is on. You can perform this step with the ATTRIB command. Then use the XCOPY command repeatedly with the /M switch or the /M and /S switches.

When the destination floppy disk is full, change floppy disks and reissue the same command. The files that were copied now have their archive attribute off, so XCOPY skips these files. XCOPY copies the files that were not yet copied—those files that have the archive attribute on.

2. If you specify a file name as the destination and there is no file or directory by that name, XCOPY creates a directory by that name. If there is a file by that name, XCOPY copies every selected file to that file. The result is a file that has a copy of the last file copied.

3. To use XCOPY to copy from the current directory, you may specify the source as a period.

Messages

1. Cyclic copy not allowed

ERROR: You used the /S switch, and one or more of the destination directories are subdirectories of the source directories. When /S is used, XCOPY cannot copy to destination directories that are part of the source directories. If you must copy files from more than one directory, issue individual XCOPY commands to copy the directories one at a time.

2. Cannot XCOPY to/from a reserved device

ERROR: The source or destination file name is a device name. XCOPY cannot copy to or from devices. You may have misspelled one of the file names.

3. Reading source file(s)

INFORMATION: XCOPY is reading the source directories for file names.

4. *nnn* File(s) copied

INFORMATION: XCOPY copied *nnn* files to the destination disk. This message appears regardless of errors that occur.

5. Not enough disk space

ERROR: The destination disk is full. The file that you were copying when the error occurred is erased from the destination disk. Either delete any unneeded files from the destination disk, or use a different disk and run the command again.

XDEL   External

XDEL deletes multiple files in subdirectories and removes subdirectories containing files.

Syntax

XDEL *@d:path\filename.ext* /D /N /O /P /R /S

d: is the disk drive that holds the files to be deleted.

path is the starting directory path to the files you want to delete.

filename.ext is the file to be deleted. Wild cards are allowed.

@ signifies that the names of the files to be deleted may be contained in a list file.

Switches

/D	Deletes empty subdirectories
/N	Deletes all specified files without prompting for permission
/O	Overwrites the specified files with other data before deleting them, ensuring that they cannot be undeleted
/P	Prompts you by displaying each file name, with the message (Y/N) ?
/R	Deletes read-only files
/S	Deletes files in subdirectories of the specified directory

Rules

1. If you do not enter a drive name, the current drive is assumed.

2. If you do not enter a directory name, the current directory is assumed.

3. If you do not enter a file name, *.* is assumed. DOS displays a message in this form:

```
path: d:\pathfile:  *.* Is this what you wish to do (Y/N)
      ?
```

You can terminate the process by pressing N or continue it by pressing Y.

4. To delete all files in a subdirectory and the subdirectory as well, use the /D and /S switches together.

Messages

1. `path: d:\path file: filename.ext Is this what you wish to do (Y/N) ?`

INFORMATION and WARNING: You have specified only a path name as the file name to be deleted, or have specified multiple files and have not asked that each file name be presented for permission individually.

2. `path: d:\path file: filename.ext Warning: FILES IN SUBDIRECTORIES MAY BE DELETED. Is this what you wish to do (Y/ N) ?`

INFORMATION and WARNING: You have used the /S switch and have not used the /P switch. If you proceed, all files matching the specification in all subdirectories of the specified directory are deleted.

XDIR   External

XDIR is the extended directory command for Novell DOS. A number of

options are available with XDIR that are not available with DIR.

Syntax

```
XDIR +| -ADHRS @filespec... /B /C /L /N /P /R /S /T /W /X /Y
      /Z
```

filespec specifies multiple files, directories, or file lists on a single command line. You can also specify file names enclosed by double quotation marks, if you want to include the file list symbol (@) as part of a file name.

Parameters or Switches

+ | -ADHRS	Includes (+) or excludes (-) files with attributes (A, D, H, R, and S) in the listing. For example, -HS tells XDIR not to display files that are either hidden or system (or both). The default for XDIR is to display all files, regardless of the attribute.
/B	Displays the files in "brief" mode, showing only file names and paths.
/C	Computes and includes a checksum for each file in the display. A checksum is a four-digit hexadecimal number calculated from the bytes within the file. This is quite handy, for example, in verifying that files are identical to the original.
/L	Forces the default "long" format.
/N	Forces XDIR not to sort the directory listings alphabetically, which is the default. Instead, they are displayed in their order on the disk.
/P	Pauses after each full screen of the listing.
/R	Reverses the sort order you specified, either by accepting the default (alphabetical by file name) or by using another switch: alphabetical by file extension (/X), chronology (/T), size (/Z), or compression ratio (/Y).
/S	Includes files in subdirectories below the specified directory.
/T	Sorts the contents of the directory by date and time, from earliest to latest (unless you also use /R).
/W	Causes the listing to display in a wide, abbreviated format. This switch is useful if the listing consists of more than one full screen. Can be combined with /P, as in /WP.

/X	Sorts the contents of the directory alphabetically by file extension. See also /R.
/Y	Sorts the contents of the directory by Stacker compression ratio. See also /R.
/Z	Sorts the contents of the directory by size, from largest to smallest, unless you use /R with /Z.

Note

Note that the order in which you specify the sort switches (/R, /T, /X, /Y, and /Z) is significant with XDIR. If, for example, you specify /Z before /X, the directory is sorted by file size first and then alphabetically by file extension (if two files of the same name are found). If you specify /X before /Z, however, the directory is sorted so that all files with the same file extension are grouped together and then listed according to size.

X

Command Reference

Appendix A

Internationalizing Your System

The world we live in is made up of a rather large number of countries with a varied group of national languages and customs. As of this writing, Novell has published Novell DOS 7 in English, French, and German. Other national versions are also planned, including Italian, Spanish, and Japanese.

You might consider that your standard version of Novell DOS is perfect for most uses but that you want another national format for expressing time, date, and/or currency. Novell DOS makes this task easy to accomplish. You can use COUNTRY.SYS to provide national formats, but this works only for currency, date, and time. With the KEYB.COM utility, however, you can "nationalize" your keyboard.

> **Note**
>
> You place the device driver COUNTRY.SYS in your CONFIG.SYS file. You enter the KEYB.COM command in the AUTOEXEC.BAT file or at the Novell DOS prompt.

In addition, Novell DOS gives you the capability to internationalize (use other languages) the character set displayed on your computer's video screen and possibly even your printer. This feature is called *code page switching*. With this method, you can use foreign language character sets on your EGA or VGA monitor, keyboard, and certain printers that support this feature.

To enable code page switching, you must first set aside memory for the language tables by using DISPLAY.SYS and PRINTER.SYS statements in the CONFIG.SYS file. In the AUTOEXEC.BAT file or at the Novell DOS prompt, you then enter the NLSFUNC command to enable national language support,

> **Tip**
>
> The easiest way to enable both internationalization features is to use the Novell DOS Setup utility.

Appendixes

specifying the COUNTRY.SYS file. To load the code page tables, you use the MODE DEVICE CODEPAGE PREPARE command once for your video display and once for your printer. After you have made all these preparations, you change your system to use the new language character set by issuing the CHCP command for the appropriate code page number or by using the MODE DEVICE CODEPAGE SELECT command.

This appendix shows you how to use these capabilities so that you can make the adjustments to your system's configuration files and customize your computer to "go international."

Using Alternative Country Formats

You use the device driver COUNTRY.SYS to display alternative currency, date, and time formats on your system without using other language characters. When you perform a disk directory (DIR) command, the date and time stamps for disk files are displayed in the current national format as set with COUNTRY.SYS.

You can display dates in the USA format as MM-DD-YY or in alternative formats such as YY-MM-DD (French Canadian), DD-MM-YY (United Kingdom), or DD/MM/YY (Italian), among others.

You can display time formats with colons (:) to separate hours, minutes, seconds, and hundredths of a second, as in HH:MM:SS:HS. Or you can use periods (.) or commas (,), as in HH.MM.SS.HS and HH:MM:SS,HS.

In addition to such currency symbols as $, £, and f, some customs dictate that the decimal characters or the thousands separators in currency amounts be either periods (.) or commas (,).

Each country is identified by a country code, which is the code given by international convention for telephone usage. Table A.1 lists some country codes that are supported by the Novell DOS COUNTRY.SYS device driver.

Table A.1 International Country Codes	
Country	**Code**
USA	001
Canada	002

Country	Code
Latin America	003
Russia	007
Netherlands	031
Belgium	032
France	033
Spain	034
Hungary	036
Italy	039
Switzerland	041
Austria	043
United Kingdom	044
Denmark	045
Sweden	046
Norway	047
Germany	049
Australia	061
Japan	081
Korea	082
Turkey	090
Portugal	351
Finland	358
Middle East	785
Israel	972

COUNTRY.SYS contains information only for the video display and nothing for the keyboard. To provide keyboard support, you must use the KEYB command in your AUTOEXEC.BAT file or from the Novell DOS prompt. In the following sections, you learn about using both COUNTRY.SYS and KEYB.

Appendixes

Specifying the Country Format (COUNTRY.SYS)

Novell DOS gives you two methods for enabling the COUNTRY.SYS device driver. You have a choice of using the Novell DOS Setup utility or the EDIT text-editing utility to add the following statement to your CONFIG.SYS file:

```
COUNTRY=xxx,yyy,COUNTRY.SYS
```

> **Note**
>
> If you don't have COUNTRY.SYS in the root directory of your boot drive, you must specify the location of the file as in C:\NWDOS\COUNTRY.SYS. The file usually is the \NWDOS subdirectory.

The three-character numeric country code (refer to table A.1) must be the first parameter, as indicated by *xxx* in the preceding statement. This code cannot be omitted. The second parameter, as represented by *yyy*, is the code page number for the country. If you omit this code, Novell DOS uses the default code page number for the country specified by the country code. You cannot omit the comma.

> **Note**
>
> The international country code is *not* the same code number as the country code page number. Table A.1 lists supported country codes. Table A.4 in this appendix's section on "Understanding Code Page Switching" lists some supported country code page numbers. See that section for more information.

Here is the default statement for the U.S. version:

```
COUNTRY=001,,COUNTRY.SYS
```

If you want to use the United Kingdom currency, date, and time formats, the statement should read as

```
COUNTRY=044,,COUNTRY.SYS
```

If you choose to use Setup, select DOS System and Memory Management and then Country and Keyboard from the configuration area list; then press Enter. The currently selected country, keyboard, and keyboard type are displayed. Highlight the line to change the country and/or keyboard, and then press Enter.

Setup then presents the list of international country codes. Move the highlight bar to the country code of your choice and press Enter. Setup rewrites the CONFIG.SYS file for you with the correct statement to match your selection.

The next step is to select the keyboard you want to use. You do that by using KEYB. The next section describes this process.

Chapter 4, "Installing Novell DOS 7," has complete instructions for using the Install/Setup utility.

Specifying the Keyboard Format (KEYB.COM)

Whereas the COUNTRY.SYS driver provides nondefault formats on the display screen, KEYB.COM provides compatible keyboard characters for the selected nationality. Table A.2 lists the supported international keyboard codes, alphabetically by country.

Table A.2 International Keyboard Codes

Country	Code
Belgium	BE
French Canada	CF
Denmark	DK
Finland	SU
France	FR
Germany	GR
Hungary	HU
Italy	IT
Latin America	LA
Netherlands	NL
Norway	NO
Portugal	PO
Russia	RU
Spain	SP

(continues)

Appendixes

Table A.2 Continued	
Code	**Country**
Sweden	SV
French Switzerland	SF
German Switzerland	SG
Turkey, type F	TF
Turkey, type Q	TQ
English, United Kingdom	UK
English, USA	US

KEYB.COM is usually placed in the AUTOEXEC.BAT file, but you can type the command at the Novell DOS prompt. If you use Setup to provide a national selection, Novell DOS places the command in the AUTOEXEC.BAT file for you. If you use EDIT, then enter the command manually in AUTOEXEC.BAT. The format of this command is

KEYB *xx*+ | -,*yyy* /ML /MH /MU

The following paragraphs explain each of these components.

The first parameter, *xx*, is the two-letter international keyboard code (see table A.2). Use a plus sign (+) if the keyboard is a 101-key or 102-key Enhanced keyboard, and a minus sign (–) if the keyboard is the 84-key type.

You can add several options to the KEYB command. After the keyboard national code and type, you can add the country code page number if you enable code page switching. Add a comma and the code page number as indicated by the *yyy* in the format line. (For more information, see the section "Switching Code Pages" later in this appendix.)

You can also specify the location in memory where Novell DOS should locate the KEYB program. Use /ML to force KEYB.COM to load in lower or conventional memory, /MH to force KEYB.COM to load in high memory, and /MU to force KEYB.COM to load in upper memory. (Refer to Chapter 22, "Optimizing Memory," for an understanding of the different types of memory.)

Coping with the Changed Keyboard

When you change the default country and keyboard codes on your computer system, you will find that certain keys no longer work as labeled. The following information pertains to standard U.S. keyboards, but changing the country code also may affect the various national keyboard designs.

To see an example of how the keyboard changes, change your country code to 044, United Kingdom, by using Setup or EDIT. The line in your CONFIG.SYS file should read as the following:

```
COUNTRY=044,,COUNTRY.SYS
```

In your AUTOEXEC.BAT file, enter this line, or use Setup to do this for you:

```
KEYB UK+
```

This command assumes that you have an Enhanced (101-key) keyboard with the plus sign (+). Use a minus sign (–) if you have an 84-key keyboard.

Because you changed your CONFIG.SYS file, you need to reboot your system. After your system reboots, press the backslash key (\). Notice that your system displays a pound sign, #, rather than a backslash. The pound sign key (Shift-3) now displays the British currency symbol, £. A few other key remappings are required to use the United Kingdom country and keyboard codes on a standard American keyboard with the American default version of Novell DOS 7. Table A.3 lists the remapping for this configuration.

Tip
To keep from having to remember the key changes, you can print the changed characters, cut them out, and paste them on your keyboard in the remapped position.

Tip
Press Alt-92 (using the numeric keypad) to enter the backslash. You need it when working with subdirectories.

Table A.3 Using UK Country and Keyboard Codes on a U.S. Default System

Standard	Remapped
~	¬
@	"

(continues)

Table A.3 Continued	
Standard	**Remapped**
#	£
¦	~
\	#
"	@

Switching Code Pages

Code page switching sounds much more formidable than it really is. The term refers to the areas of memory in your system that store the character tables for your video screen and keyboard. These tables are called *code pages*. By switching the tables, you can configure Novell DOS 7 to use alternative character tables to suit your national language and customs. That is, you can use other alphabetic characters. COUNTRY.SYS does not affect character tables.

You can set your system to use an alternative code page permanently, or you can enable several code pages and switch between them depending on your current needs. These are software-prepared code pages. Your system already has a built-in hardware code page.

In the earlier section "Using Alternative Country Formats," you learned that each country or area of the world has a unique country code number borrowed from the international telephone convention. Each country, group of countries, or even a part of a country also has a code page number. (Several countries share a single code page number.) Table A.4 lists the code pages supported by Novell DOS 7.

Table A.4 National Code Page Numbers	
Country	**Code**
Austria, Australia, Belgium, English Canada, Finland, France, Germany, Italy, Latin America, the Netherlands, Spain, Sweden, Switzerland, the United Kingdom, and the United States	437
International	850

Country	Code
Hungary	852
Turkey	857
Portugal	860
Israel	862
French Canada	863
Middle East	864
Denmark, Norway	865
Russia	866

Note

Note that code page number 850 is an international code page that you can use for a number of national language characters. This common code may simplify international communications so that documents prepared with this character table can be processed by people in different countries using different languages, with all characters appearing the same to all concerned.

The international code page 850 has some graphic limitations in order to provide room for additional language characters required by some countries. After all, only a total of 255 codes are available. If you normally use the United States code page 437, for example, you may find that boxes under 850 lose their graphic corners, which are replaced with other characters.

Appendixes

Hardware Requirements for Code Page Switching

You do need the proper hardware in order to use software code page switching. You must have an EGA or VGA video display. Hercules-type monographic and CGA screens do not support this feature. Your printer must be an IBM Proprinter, Proprinter XL, Proprinter X24, Proprinter XL24, or Quietwriter III. The Epson FX850 and FX1050 models also support code page switching. If your printer emulates one of these printers, it must also have the capability of accepting code page switching. Some printers emulate but do not have code page support. Check your printer's manual to find out if your printer has this support.

Installing Code Page Switching

You need to take a number of steps and load a number of programs before you can enable code page switching for both your video screen and printer. You can do all the preparation with the Novell DOS Setup utility, but you may prefer to use EDIT or another text editor. Setup does all the work for you.

To begin the installation procedure, type **SETUP** and press Enter to load the Setup utility. Highlight the DOS System and Memory Management option and press Enter. Select Country and Keyboard, move the highlight to Country, and press Enter. Finally, select the proper country and country code from the displayed list. Do the same with Keyboard and Keyboard Type. Exit the screen.

Next proceed to Optional Device Drivers and Utilities, and use the arrow keys to highlight the brackets for code page switching. Press Enter or the space bar to place an X within the brackets if there is none. Then, using the down-arrow key, highlight Select Default Code Page and press Enter. You have the choice of using either the selected country page code or the international code page as the default on booting.

If you have one of the printers listed earlier or one that is 100 percent compatible, highlight Configure Printers for Code Page Switching and press Enter. Select the port to which the printer is attached (usually LPT1), and press Enter. Select the printer type or None.

IBM 4201 refers to the code page file (4201.CPI) for IBM Proprinter and IBM Proprinter XL. IBM 4200 refers to the code page file (4200.CPI) for IBM Proprinter X24 and IBM Proprinter XL24. IBM 5202 refers to the code page file (5202.CPI) for IBM Quietwriter III. Epson 850/1050 refers to the code page file (1050.CPI) for Epson FX850 and Epson FX1050 printers.

Tip
If you select Other, keep in mind that the printer must support the selected code page.

If you do not have one of these printers, select Other. If you do not have a printer attached to LPT1, select None. If you intend to use another printer port or code pages different from those listed by Setup, you must make the changes in your CONFIG.SYS and AUTOEXEC.BAT files with EDIT. To make the process easier for yourself, select a printer here and use EDIT to change what needs to be changed.

Press Esc to return to the opening Setup screen and highlight the Save Changes and Exit box. Setup then rewrites the CONFIG.SYS and AUTOEXEC.BAT files with all the COUNTRY.SYS, KEYB.COM, and code page switching commands entered for you. You have nothing more to do except to exit to DOS or reboot the computer so that the new entries take effect.

> **Note**
>
> With code page switching enabled for a printer, you must have your printer turned on and on-line when you boot your computer so that the proper signals can be downloaded to the printer.

Specifying the Monitor Code Page (DISPLAY.SYS). Use the device driver DISPLAY.SYS to enable code page switching for your video display. You can use this driver only if you have an EGA or VGA monitor and adapter. The monitor type must be entered as the first parameter for the CON (console) device.

You can use either of the following command formats:

```
DEVICE=\DISPLAY.SYS CON=(mon,hdwre,xx)

DEVICE=\DISPLAY.SYS CON=(mon,hdwre,(xx,y))
```

Use either DEVICE or HIDEVICE depending on the memory configuration of your computer. DISPLAY.SYS is a device driver that can be loaded high if you have the memory available and the configuration to use high memory. Unless you move the DISPLAY.SYS file to the root directory of your boot drive, you must specify the location of the file, which is normally C:\NWDOS. Replace *mon* with either EGA or VGA, whichever is appropriate. EGA, which saves memory, can be used for both EGA and VGA.

The second parameter, *hdwre*, refers to the built-in hardware code page number. In the U.S., this number is 437, but do not specify it if you are not certain of your system. The variable *xx* refers to the number of code pages you want enabled in your system. The maximum number is 12. This parameter tells Novell DOS to set aside memory for the number of additional character tables to be installed in the AUTOEXEC.BAT file or at the Novell DOS prompt.

With the variable *y*, you can specify the number of fonts that Novell DOS stores in memory. EGA displays can have two fonts, and VGA displays can have three. Normally all are stored. You can lower the number stored and thus save the memory used by reducing the number of fonts. If you specify this variable, you must place a pair of parentheses around the number of code pages and the number of fonts, as shown in the second DISPLAY.SYS example.

EGA screens can display two different font sizes: one consisting of characters constructed from 8 x 14 pixels, and one from 8 x 8 pixels. (Pixels are the little dots that actually make up your display screen.) If you specify only one font for your EGA monitor, only the 8 x 14 font is retained.

VGA screens can display three different font sizes: one consisting of characters constructed from 8 x 16 pixels, one from 8 x 14 pixels, and one from 8 x 8 pixels. If you specify two fonts for your VGA monitor, the 8 x 16 and the 8 x 8 characters are retained. If you specify only one font, the 8 x 16 is used.

To enable code page switching for your display for French Canada and to allow for the use of the international code, enter the following statement in your CONFIG.SYS file:

```
DEVICE=\DISPLAY.SYS CON=(VGA,,2)
```

No default hardware code page is declared, and Novell DOS is instructed to set aside memory for two code pages for a VGA adapter and monitor, and the default number of fonts.

Besides the hardware code page, you can specify up to 12 additional code page tables to be prepared in memory. Just remember that code pages take up RAM and may lower the amount of conventional memory available for your applications.

Caution

Don't set aside more memory than is required for your needs. Each code page takes up 5,632 bytes of RAM for EGA or VGA.

Specifying the Printer Code Page (PRINTER.SYS). Use the device driver PRINTER.SYS to enable code page switching for your printer (if you have one of the supported printers or a compatible). A supported printer can be attached to any or all of the three allowed parallel printer ports: LPT1, LPT2, and LPT3.

The format of the command is

```
DEVICE=PRINTER.SYS LPTx=(print,hdwre,yyy)
```

Use either DEVICE or HIDEVICE depending on the memory configuration of your computer. Unless you move the PRINTER.SYS file to the root directory of your boot drive, you must specify the location of the file, which normally is C:\NWDOS. Replace the *x* in LPTx with the proper parallel port number—1, 2, or 3.

Replace *print* with 4201, 4200, 5202, or 1050, whichever is appropriate for your printer. The next parameter, *hdwre*, refers to the built-in hardware code page. In the U.S., this number is 437, but do not specify it if you are not certain of your printer. The variable *yyy* refers to the number of code pages you want enabled in your system. This parameter tells Novell DOS to set aside memory for the number of additional character tables to be installed in the AUTOEXEC.BAT file or at the Novell DOS prompt.

The following statement entered in your CONFIG.SYS file does not declare a default hardware code page and instructs Novell DOS to set aside memory for two code pages for an Epson FX1050 or compatible printer attached to LPT1:

```
DEVICE=PRINTER.SYS LPT1=(1050,,2)
```

You can specify up to 12 code page tables to be prepared in memory. As mentioned in the preceding section, however, do not set aside more memory than is required for your needs because these tables consume memory.

Note

To enable code page switching on your printer, make sure that your printer is turned on and is on-line when your system is booted. Otherwise, the control signals cannot be downloaded into the printer.

To set up more than one printer for code page switching, place additional code page information for each printer port, as in this example:

```
DEVICE=PRINTER.SYS LPT1=(1050,,2) LPT2=(4201,,2)
    LPT3=(5202,,2)
```

Appendixes

Adding NLSFUNC.EXE to the AUTOEXEC.BAT. After you have the required statements for COUNTRY.SYS, DISPLAY.SYS, and PRINTER.SYS taken care of in your CONFIG.SYS file, move your attention to AUTOEXEC.BAT. Make sure that your keyboard is specified for the appropriate national keyboard and code page number. See the earlier section "Specifying the Keyboard Format" for details.

You then must include NLSFUNC as the next command for providing the national language support for the code page switching that was prepared in the CONFIG.SYS file. NLSFUNC.EXE is the National Language Support Function utility provided for code page activation. You can type this command at the Novell DOS prompt or place it in your AUTOEXEC.BAT file for automatic loading each time your computer boots.

The command tail for NLSFUNC includes the COUNTRY.SYS file previously listed in CONFIG.SYS, and you must specify the location of the file, as shown in the following command:

```
NLSFUNC COUNTRY.SYS
```

You can also add a switch to tell Novell DOS to load this function in lower (/ML), high (/MH, the default), or upper memory (/MU).

Up till now, you have specified your country code and prepared your system to use code page switching. The following paragraphs explain how you load the specified code pages into the prepared memory areas.

Using the MODE Command to Load Code Page Tables

Use the MODE CON: command to load the code page information for your video display. With this command, you specify the code pages to be prepared and the code page file to use for the tables. You can list as additional code pages as many code pages as you specified in the CONFIG.SYS file. Do not specify the hardware default code page number because this table is already built in.

The format of the MODE CON: command is

```
MODE CON: CODEPAGE PREPARE=((xxx,yyy,zzz)EGA.CPI)
```

MODE CON: is the command and the target of the command. CODEPAGE (or CP for short) is the command for code page switching, and PREPARE (or PREP for short) is the function to perform. You must then enter all the code pages you want loaded into memory. *xxx* is for the first additional code page number, followed by a comma and a second code page number (*yyy*), followed by another comma and a third code page number (*zzz*), and so on. The file EGA.CPI is used for both EGA and VGA monitors.

The following command, for example, uses MODE to prepare (PREP) the console (CON:) for code pages (CP), with code pages 863 for French Canada and 850 for the international code page:

```
MODE CON: CP PREP=((863,850)EGA.CPI)
```

EGA.CPI is listed as the table file for EGA and VGA monitors. The location of this file is in C:\NWDOS.

For your printer, use the MODE command for each parallel printer port listed in the PRINTER.SYS statement of the CONFIG.SYS file. Use this command to load the code page information for each printer and download it to the printer. Make sure that your printers are turned on and on-line to receive the downloaded data. Following are two examples:

```
MODE LPT1: CODEPAGE PREP=((863,850)1050.CPI)

MODE LPT2: CP PREP=((863,850)4201.CPI)
```

As with the other AUTOEXEC.BAT commands for code page switching, you can also enter the MODE commands at the Novell DOS prompt.

Completing the Code Page Switch

After you have completed all the preparation work—specifying the nationality and code page numbers to be used, setting aside the memory for the language tables, and loading the character tables—you want to use your "new" tables.

In these examples, you prepared your system to use the French Canadian character set. To put it in use, you must issue the CHCP (change code page) command. For the French Canadian character set, the command is

```
CHCP 863
```

Enter this command either in your AUTOEXEC.BAT file or at the Novell DOS prompt. The application of this instruction tells Novell DOS to change the current code page to the new code page specified in the command on all devices prepared, including the printer if you have included it in the

CONFIG.SYS and AUTOEXEC.BAT files. Make certain that the printer is on and on-line so that the new code page can take effect.

You can also change the code pages of individual devices. You use MODE SELECT instead of CHCP. The full format of the command is

MODE device CODEPAGE SELECT=xxx

For *device*, use either CON, PRN (which is the same as LPT1), or LPT*y* where *y* is 1, 2, or 3. Then you must indicate the word CODEPAGE or the initials CP, and the word SELECT or SEL. After the equal sign (=), enter the code page number (*xxx*).

To change the code page so that you can print a document on your Epson FX1050 printer, which is attached to LPT1, and use the French Canadian character set without displaying it on your monitor, type the following command and press Enter:

```
MODE LPT1 CP SEL=863
```

Exploring More Uses for MODE

To determine the currently active code page for any device, issue this command:

MODE device CODEPAGE /STATUS

Again, you can abbreviate CODEPAGE as CP. This command works the same with or without the /STATUS option on the command tail. Novell DOS returns the status of the active code page and all prepared code pages for the specified device, including the hardware code page. At the Novell DOS prompt, for example, enter this command:

```
MODE CON CP
```

At times you may need to refresh the code page for a particular device. This requirement is especially true of code page printers. The printers do not store the code page fonts when they are turned off and on again. You should also use the following command if the printer was not both on and on-line when you enabled code page switching for the printer:

MODE device CODEPAGE REFRESH

In addition to abbreviating CODEPAGE as CP, you can shorten REFRESH to REF. At the Novell DOS prompt, for instance, type this command and press Enter to refresh the printer attached to LPT1:

```
MODE LPT1 CP REF
```

If you issue a code page command for your printer, through CHCP, MODE SELECT, or MODE REFRESH, and your printer does not accept code pages or is not both on and on-line, you receive an error message when you attempt to print something. You may experience a delay before receiving the error message, depending on the length of the time-out period.

Using Dead Keys

When you tell Novell DOS to use a different keyboard or character set, your keyboard gives you different results, as you learned in the earlier section "Coping with the Changed Keyboard." In addition to the remapped keyboard, a new device with the keyboard enables you to enter special language characters. This device is called a *dead key*.

Usually, when you type an alphabetic character on your keyboard, the letter appears without any accents. The use of a dead key enables you to enter acute (´), grave (`), and circumflex (^) accent characters and umlauts (¨) with certain vowels and other keys. Table A.5, for example, lists the remapped U.S. keyboard with code page 863.

Table A.5 Remapping a U.S. Keyboard with French Canadian Language Support

Standard	Remapped
`	#
~	¦
@	"
#	/
^	?
\	<
¦	>
/	é
?	É

When you press the dead key, nothing appears on-screen. When you type the next appropriate letter, the character appears with an accent. If you type an inappropriate letter, Novell DOS causes your computer to beep. Table A.6 lists the dead key keyboard mappings for French Canada.

Table A.6 Dead Keys for French Canadian Language Support		
Dead Key	**Character**	**Remapped As**
]	c	ç
Shift–]	C	Ç
Shift–]	e	ë
Shift–]	i	ï
Shift–]	u	ü
Shift–]	E	Ë
Shift–]	I	Ï
Shift–]	U	Ü
[	a	â
[	e	ê
[	i	î
[	o	ô
[	u	û
Shift–[	A	Â
Shift–[	E	Ê
Shift–[	I	Î
Shift–[	O	Ô
Shift–[	U	Û
'	a	à
'	e	è
'	u	ù

Dead Key	Character	Remapped As
'	A	À
'	E	È
'	U	Ù
'	'	`

By experimenting with the *dead keys* and the same second characters on your own system when a different code page in effect, you can prepare your own table of characters for your use.

Appendix B

Installing and Using Windows 3.1

Computer users differ greatly in their opinions concerning the general worth of the traditional DOS prompt that greets them when they start their computers. Many users swear by the DOS prompt, saying that it is the easiest and most direct way to use DOS. Other users, however, swear at the DOS prompt, saying that it is neither intuitive nor easy to use.

The most popular alternative to working with the DOS prompt is a *graphical user interface (GUI)* by the name of Microsoft Windows, whose current version is 3.1. Novell DOS 7 works with Windows and even provides many Windows utilities both for DOS and for the network. If you have at least a 386 microprocessor in your computer, you can use either the standard mode or the 386 enhanced mode of Windows. You can also use Windows as a task if you are running Task Manager as either a multitasker or a task switcher.

This appendix helps you integrate the GUI with Novell DOS 7 so that, as a Windows user, you can get the best of both worlds—the graphical interface you want with the best DOS available today. The following sections deal with installing Novell DOS 7 when Windows is already installed on your system, installing Windows after Novell DOS is installed on your system, using Windows with Task Manager, using Windows with your Novell DOS network, and using Windows with Stacker disk compression.

Installing Novell DOS 7 after Windows

When you install Novell DOS 7 and if Windows 3.1 already exists on your computer, there is an option in Install to place the Novell DOS Windows utilities on your hard drive. Figure B.1 shows the Install display where you can enable or disable the installation of parts of Novell DOS. One of the components is for the MS Windows utilities.

Fig. B.1

The Novell DOS 7 Install component installation screen.

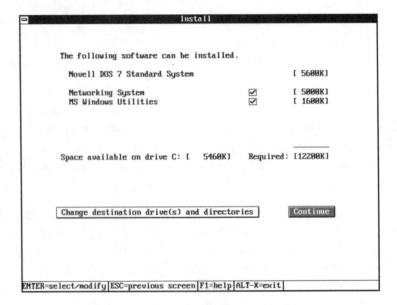

If Windows is on your system and Install detects it, the default for the installation is to place the Windows utilities on your hard disk. If you do not disable this option, the installation process not only places the files on your hard disk but also tells Windows that the utilities are available for use.

Install creates a Windows group called Novell DOS 7 and places in the group window the icons for the Novell DOS prompt, the Fastback Express backup utility, the Fastback Hardware Test utility, the Search & Destroy virus scanner, and the screen saver and temporary security utility LOCK. If you install the network, icons are included for Personal NetWare and Network Diagnostics. Figure B.2 shows the Novell DOS 7 group in Windows.

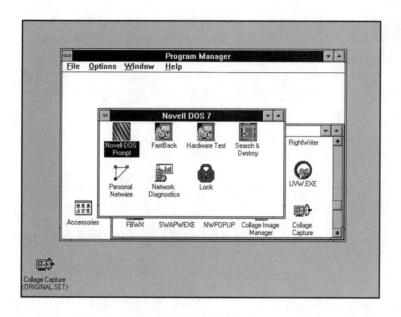

Fig. B.2
The Novell DOS 7
Windows group.

When you complete the installation of Novell DOS 7 and reboot your system, before running Windows, you must take one step. You must close software access to upper memory on your system, as Windows wants this area all to itself. You do this by entering the following command:

```
MEMMAX  -U
```

If you have a 386 or higher system, the normal way to get the most conventional memory for application software is to open up both upper and lower memory. If you check your AUTOEXEC.BAT file with the Novell DOS text editor, EDIT, you should see the following statement:

```
MEMMAX  +U  +L  >NUL
```

This command opens up access to upper and lower memory. You can read more about EDIT in Chapter 17, "Using the Novell DOS Text Editor." You can read more about memory and MEMMAX in Chapter 22, "Optimizing Memory," but before you can run Windows, you must close upper memory with MEMMAX -U. Only then you can run Windows by executing the normal WIN command.

> **Note**
>
> You can close off upper memory by adding MEMMAX -U at the end of your
> AUTOEXEC.BAT file (before any menu). You can also set up a batch file for running
> Windows. A sample batch file, called WIN.BAT, would have the following lines:
>
> ```
> MEMMAX -U
> CD\WINDOWS
> WIN
> CD\
> MEMMAX +U
> ```
>
> The commands in this batch file close upper memory access, change to the
> \WINDOWS subdirectory and run the GUI, return to the root directory, and reopen
> access to upper memory. If you have a menu on your system, this batch file can be
> incorporated with the menu. You can call your batch file WIN.BAT and place it in the
> root directory of your boot drive.

After executing the batch file, you should see the Novell DOS 7 icon in the
Program Manager window. Double-click the icon, and you'll see the programs
that Novell DOS Install grouped for you. If you installed the Novell DOS
network on your system, those icons are also there.

If you have, and intend to use, the Novell DOS 7 network on your computer
with Windows, other issues must be handled. Read in a later section of this
appendix, "Using Windows with the Novell DOS Network," about these network issues with Windows 3.1.

Installing Windows after Novell DOS 7

If you have already installed Novell DOS 7 on your computer and decide to
add Windows 3.1, the Novell utilities for MS Windows probably have not
been copied to your hard disk. You may have told Install to copy the files,
but the process is not finished. This poses a minor dilemma because the work
that the Novell Install utility performs to integrate the two packages has not
been completed.

An easy way around the problem exists so that you can enjoy the advantages
of Novell DOS and Windows without having to work directly with DOS.

The first step is to install Windows 3.1 in the usual way. Before you do this, however, you must not be using Task Manager in either multitasking or task-switching mode. If you are not sure how to remove Task Manager from memory on your system, refer to Chapter 21, "Multitasking and Task Switching." After you have unloaded Task Manager, be sure to turn off software access to upper memory, as Windows wants this area all to itself. You do this by entering the following command:

```
MEMMAX -U
```

If you have a 386 or higher system, the normal way to get the most conventional memory is to open both upper and lower memory. If you check your AUTOEXEC.BAT file with the Novell DOS text editor, EDIT, you should see this statement:

```
MEMMAX +U +L >NUL
```

This command opens up access to upper and lower memory. You can read more about EDIT in Chapter 17, "Using the Novell DOS Text Editor." You can read more about memory and MEMMAX in Chapter 22, "Optimizing Memory," but before you can run the Windows installation program, Setup, you must close upper memory with the preceding command. Then insert Windows' first installation disk in the appropriate floppy drive and log onto that drive by entering either **A:** or **B:**, depending on the drive. Install Windows following the normal directions as displayed on your video screen and in the Windows documentation.

When you have finished installing Windows, do not restart your computer as recommended by the Windows installation program. Exit to Novell DOS. Windows placed some commands in your system configuration files that you must remove.

Use the Novell DOS editor in the root directory of your boot drive, usually C:\. Enter **EDIT CONFIG.SYS** or **EDIT DCONFIG.SYS**, depending on which file your system is using. Note that Novell DOS prefers the DCONFIG.SYS file to the CONFIG.SYS file if both are present on your system, whereas the Windows installation program recognizes only CONFIG.SYS. In the CONFIG.SYS file, two lines were added by Windows. The first is

```
DEVICE=C:\WINDOWS\HIMEM.SYS
```

Appendixes

Delete this line. Novell DOS has its own, better memory manager. The second line is

```
STACKS=9,256
```

You can keep this line in your configuration file. Also make sure that the Windows installation program did not change the location of the EMM386.EXE file to that supplied with Windows, as in `DEVICE=C:\WINDOWS\EMM386.EXE`. If it did, change the location back to `C:\NWDOS\EMM386.EXE`. Now save the modified file and exit to the DOS prompt.

You must also modify the AUTOEXEC.BAT file. Using the Novell DOS text editor, type **EDIT AUTOEXEC.BAT**. The first line is

```
C:\WINDOWS\SMARTDRIVE.EXE
```

Delete this line. Novell DOS has its own, better disk cache. Save the modified file and exit to the DOS prompt. You may also notice that the Windows installation program placed the \WINDOWS subdirectory as the first item of your system PATH command. This is fine unless you have some other idea and want to change it. You might just want to place C:\WINDOWS at the end of the PATH statement. Do not forget to place a semicolon (;) to separate it from the rest of the line.

Part of the installation process is for Windows to search all drives and directories for any applications that it recognizes as programs. Any programs found are candidates for addition to your Windows Applications Group window so that you can run those applications from within Windows. But Windows cannot find all the Novell DOS Windows utilities and provide icons for them if you do not have Novell DOS Install copy the files to your hard disk. You have another step.

This may sound a little redundant, but what you must do now is to *reinstall* NOVELL DOS 7. Install the first installation disk in the appropriate floppy drive, log onto the proper drive, and enter the following command:

```
INSTALL
```

Now that Install sees Windows on your system, it automatically sets itself to copy the Windows utilities. However, during the installation process, you are asked whether the utility should overwrite certain INI files. Do not let the installation process do this after you have already configured your system. Cancel the overwriting when prompted with the dialog boxes. Otherwise, follow the normal installation process you performed previously.

Once Install finishes the copying of all the files and doing its Windows integration work, the final screen is displayed. At this point, use the Tab key to highlight the Discard Changes to Files button; then press Enter. This keeps your configuration files exactly as you had them, while not affecting the Windows integration performed by the installation process.

Now you can choose Exit to DOS or reboot your system to run Windows. Before you can run Windows, though, you must close upper memory with the MEMMAX -U command. Then you can run Windows by executing the normal WIN command.

Note

You can set up a batch file for running Windows, containing the following lines:

```
MEMMAX -U
CD\WINDOWS
WIN
CD\
MEMMAX +U
```

The commands in this batch file close upper memory access, change to the \WINDOWS subdirectory, run the GUI, return to the root directory, and reopen access to upper memory. If you have a menu on your system, this batch file can be incorporated with the menu. You can call your batch file WIN.BAT and place it in the root directory of your boot drive.

If you have, and intend to use, the Novell DOS 7 network on your computer with Windows, other issues must be handled. Read in a later section of this appendix, "Using Windows with the Novell DOS Network," about these network issues with Windows 3.1.

Using Windows with Task Manager

You can run Windows with Task Manager. Task Manager can be in either multitasking mode or task-switching mode. Windows under Task Manager in multitasking mode runs only in standard mode. Windows under Task Manager in task-switching mode can run in either standard mode or enhanced mode. If Windows is in enhanced mode, however, you cannot switch out of Windows to another task unless you first exit Windows. If Windows is in enhanced mode, Windows can multitask its own applications in the usual way.

Of course, without Task Manager, on a 386 or higher computer with enough memory, you can run Windows in 386 enhanced mode. On a 386 computer with less than 2M of memory, or on a 286 or lower computer, you can run Windows only in standard mode.

You might consider running Windows in enhanced mode, which can multitask, instead of loading Windows as a task under Task Manager. The advantages of running Windows with Task Manager are improved speed and conventional memory available for using DOS application software as other tasks (instead of trying to use this software under Windows). If you are using Windows applications only, there might not be any advantage for you.

If you are running Task Manager as a multitasker or as a task switcher, you can run Windows as a task. Make sure that you follow these steps:

1. Load Task Manager in the normal way.

2. Add a task for Windows, or switch to the DOS session you will use for Windows. At the DOS prompt, enter the command MEMMAX -U if required (if it is not in a batch file for loading Windows as outlined earlier).

3. Run Windows with the normal WIN command. Windows automatically recognizes that it must run in standard mode under either version of Task Manager.

> **Note**
>
> When Windows runs in standard mode, you cannot use the multitasking capability of Windows, but you have the multitasking capability of Task Manager on 386 or higher machines. The task-switching capability of Task Manager is available on lower machines.

Now that you are operating Windows under Task Manager, you need to be able to switch to other tasks or other DOS sessions.

If you are in Windows, to access Task Manager, press the Ctrl-Esc hot key combination for the Windows version of the Task Manager control panel, the Task List. Figure B.3 displays the Task List.

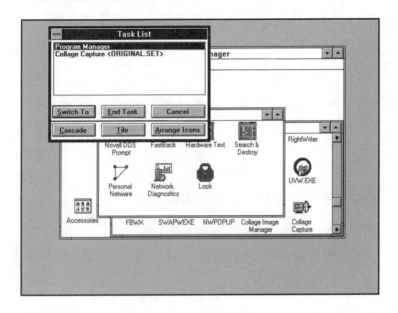

Fig. B.3
Windows Task List
for Task Manager.

Use the up- or down-arrow key to highlight your selection from the list of displayed tasks and then press Enter, or double-click your selection. Task Manager now places Windows in the background and displays the selected task on your screen.

When you are in a non-Windows task, you can access the Windows session through the Task Manager menu, by pressing the Ctrl-Esc hot key combination and selecting the Windows task. You can also use the Ctrl-*n* combination, where *n* is the keypad number of the session for Windows.

Using Windows with the Novell DOS Network

You can run Windows with Novell DOS 7, with the Novell network, and with or without Task Manager.

If you installed Novell DOS 7 after Windows is already on your hard disk, you can skip the following steps, as Novell DOS 7's installation procedure does this work for you. But if you installed Windows after you installed Novell

Appendixes

DOS, before you run your Novell DOS network with Windows, you must follow these steps:

1. Boot your system without Task Manager or the network.

2. Change to the \WINDOWS subdirectory and edit the SYSTEM.INI file. Use the Novell DOS EDIT text editor. At the DOS prompt, enter

   ```
   EDIT SYSTEM.INI
   ```

3. Scroll the file one page, to a section with the title [386Enh]. Move the cursor to the space immediately after this title. Press the Enter key, which opens up a blank line. Now type the following text:

   ```
   TimerCriticalSection=10000
   ```

   Be sure to type the line exactly as shown.

4. Press Enter to open a second line, and type

   ```
   ReflectDOSInt2A=TRUE
   ```

   Be sure to type the line exactly as shown.

5. Press Enter to open a third line, and type

   ```
   OverLappedIO=OFF
   ```

   Again, be sure to type the line exactly as shown. You are now finished with the changes you must make. Do not press Enter; choose File Save to save the modified file and then File Exit to return to the DOS prompt.

You can now run Windows with the network. The order of the steps must be the following:

1. Load the network with STARTNET.BAT. If Novell DOS displays a prompt asking whether you want to load the network, answer Y.

2. Load Task Manager—as either a multitasker or a task switcher—depending on how you told the Novell DOS Install or Setup utility the mode you wanted for Task Manager.

3. If necessary on your system, execute

   ```
   MEMMAX -U
   ```

4. Load Windows.

> ### Note
>
> If you run Windows 3.1 on a computer with a 386 or higher processor with enough memory, without Task Manager (either mode), and with the network loaded, you can run Windows in either the standard mode by starting it with **WIN /S** or in the 386 enhanced mode by starting it with **WIN**. The network does not affect the mode of Windows.

Besides the NetWare icons for Personal NetWare and Network Diagnostics being placed in the Novell DOS 7 grouping within Windows, other network changes have been made to Windows by the Novell DOS installation program.

From the Main group in Windows, choose Window Setup, Options, and then Change System Settings. The fourth item in the box on-screen is for the network. The setting should be for Personal NetWare (v1.0). If you click the down arrow to the right of this entry, you see a complete list of the networks that Windows 3.1 supports.

Also from the Main group in Windows, choose File Manager, and then from the menu list across the top of the screen, choose Disk. From the pull-down menu, choose Network Connections. The NetWare Drive Connections dialog box is displayed (see fig. B.4).

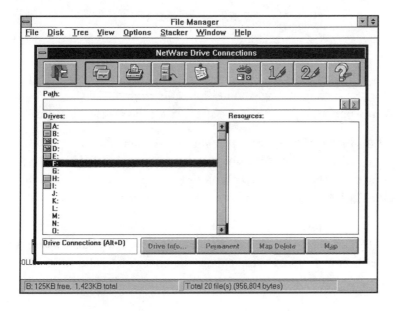

Fig. B.4
The NetWare Drive Connections dialog box.

Appendixes

Across the top of this dialog box is a series of buttons for exiting the window; displaying and setting drive connections, printer connections, and NetWare connections; sending messages, and displaying and establishing NetWare settings. There are also two user-defined buttons and one for NetWare Help. Of course, for these areas to be active for you, you must be part of a network.

Using Windows with Stacker Disk Compression

If you have installed Stacker disk compression—or converted your old Stacker, SuperStor, or Double Space disk compression to the Stacker version that came with your Novell DOS 7 package—and you have Windows 3.1 installed, there is a modification of the Windows File Manager group for Stacker.

From the Main group in Windows, choose File Manager. Across the top of the File Manager window is a list of pull-down menus. The sixth menu item should be Stacker. Click this menu title, and a pull-down menu displays two options: File Info and Disk Info.

> **Note**
>
> Before you can access either menu option, you must have selected a Stacker com-
> pressed drive from the Disk pull-down menu, the Select Drive option, and made that
> drive active in the display.

You can then select a directory on the left and a file on the right to display the file statistics, including compression ratio, from the File Info option. The Disk Info option displays the drive statistics for the selected disk drive.

You can also create a Windows permanent swap file on a Stacker compressed drive if you run Windows in enhanced mode. Enhanced mode allows Windows to switch tasks to a swap file on disk, which can only be done without loading Task Manager or by running Task Manager as a task switcher.

From the Main program group, click the Control Panel icon. Then choose the Virtual Memory icon to open the Virtual Memory dialog box. Choose the Change button so that you can change the drive to a Stacker drive.

> **Note**
>
> A Windows temporary swap file cannot be stored on a Stacker compressed disk.

Your Windows 3.1 documentation contains more information on the size and use of a permanent swap file.

Appendix C

Installing and Using GeoWorks

If you are using the graphical user interface GeoWorks Ensemble Version 1.1 or 1.2, or Geoworks Pro Version 1.2 or 2.0, you will find that GeoWorks works quite well with Novell DOS 7. In fact, you can run GeoWorks both as a stand-alone program under Novell DOS itself and as a task under Task Manager in task-switching mode. If you have GeoWorks Ensemble 1.0, you do need to upgrade the software.

The advantage of using GeoWorks with Task Manager and Novell DOS 7 is that under GeoWorks alone, you can shell to DOS and run non-GeoWorks applications. This takes time and costs some memory overhead so that you can return to GeoWorks when you are finished. Under Task Manager, you can run multiple applications at the same time and still run GeoWorks and switch between them. This saves a lot of time, better utilizing your system resources.

Installing GeoWorks

If GeoWorks is already on your system when you install Novell DOS 7, and you are not upgrading from DR DOS 6, you should let GeoWorks know that you are using a different operating system. Do this by changing to the Geoworks directory. This is normally \GEOWORKS for the earlier versions and \GEOS20 for the new Version 2.0. In this directory, enter the following command:

    SETUP

Appendixes

You want to be in the GeoWorks subdirectory so that you do not run the Novell DOS Setup utility. Just follow the directions in Setup. You do not have to make any changes. Follow the directions on-screen to save the settings and exit normally. Then run GEOS or GEOS20 as usual. GeoWorks now knows that it is working with DR DOS UNKNOWN VERSION, which is how it reports Novell DOS 7.

If GeoWorks is not on your system, all you have to do is install GeoWorks normally as an application in the Novell DOS 7 environment. Just follow the directions for the GeoWorks installation. Then run GEOS or GEOS20 as explained in the GeoWorks documentation.

Using Task Manager with GeoWorks 1.2

Before running GeoWorks, start Task Manager either by having the command TASKMGR in your AUTOEXEC.BAT file or by entering the command at the Novell DOS prompt. Then start GeoWorks with the usual GEOS command, or from whatever system menu you use on your computer. From the GeoWorks Welcome screen, select Advanced Workplace or Professional Workplace. This is the only area of GeoWorks where you can access Task Manager.

You should now be seeing the GeoManager screen. With your mouse, click the Express button near the top left of the screen. In the Express menu, you should see a selection (second from the bottom) called TaskMax Control. The DR DOS 6 Task Manager was called TaskMax, so while in GeoWorks, be prepared to use the term *TaskMax* instead of *Task Manager*. Either press the T key or click the TaskMax Control option.

GeoWorks then displays the TaskMax (Task Manager) control panel. If there are any active tasks in addition to GeoWorks, they are listed in the Active Tasks window. If you want to add a new task, press A or click the Add button. Task Manager adds a new task and switches to it, at the DOS prompt. Tasks at the DOS prompt show the name Command both in the Task Manager menu and in the GeoWorks active task list. To return to GeoWorks, press Ctrl-1, assuming that GeoWorks is the first task. You can also activate the Task Manager menu by pressing Ctrl-Esc, using the up- or down-arrow key to highlight the GeoWorks entry, and pressing Enter. You cannot access the normal Task Manager menu while within GeoWorks. You must use the GeoWorks TaskMax control panel.

From the GeoWorks TaskMax control panel, to switch to or delete another task, use your mouse to click the selected task. The Run and Delete buttons are activated. Click the Run button (or press R) to switch to the selected task. Click Delete (or press D) to delete the selected task.

The TaskMax control panel also displays the amount of free swap space available for additional tasks, measured in kilobytes. There is also a Clipboard Support selection that you can turn on or off. If it is on, the GeoWorks Clipboard works with the TaskMax cut-and-paste feature. You can click the Clipboard Support selection off if you want.

Note

In this version of Novell DOS 7, Task Manager does not currently include a cut-and-paste feature. It may be added in a future release.

To return to GeoWorks, click the Close button (or press C).

When additional tasks are active under Task Manager, you can access these tasks from within the Express menu while in the Advanced Workplace or Professional Workplace. Open this menu, and under the Welcome option, there are options for the other active tasks. Click one of the active tasks, and you can switch to that task. You do not have to use the TaskMax control panel.

Using Task Manager with GeoWorks 2.0

Before running GeoWorks, start Task Manager either by having the command TASKMGR in your AUTOEXEC.BAT file or by entering the command at the Novell DOS prompt. Then start GeoWorks with the usual GEOS20 command, or from whatever system menu you use on your computer.

Using your mouse, click the Preferences icon. In the bottom right of the Preferences menu is a merry-go-round icon called Task Switch. Select this icon. A list of available task switchers that work with GeoWorks is displayed. Click the DR DOS 6.0 TaskMAX option. The DR DOS 6 Task Manager was called TaskMax, so while in GeoWorks, be prepared to use the term *TaskMax* instead of *Task Manager*. Then click OK to return to the Preferences menu. Now click the minus (–) button at the top-left corner of this menu and click Close.

You should now see the GeoManager screen. With your mouse, click the Express button near the top left of the screen. In the Express menu, you should now see a selection (about the third line) called TaskMax Control. Either press the T key or click the TaskMax Control option.

GeoWorks then displays the TaskMax (Task Manager) control panel. If there are any active tasks in addition to GeoWorks, they are listed in the Active Tasks window. If you want to add a new task, press A or click the Add button. Task Manager adds a new task and switches to it, at the DOS prompt. Tasks at the DOS prompt show the name Command both in the Task Manager menu and in the GeoWorks active task list. To return to GeoWorks, press Ctrl-1, assuming that GeoWorks is the first task. You can also activate the Task Manager menu by pressing Ctrl-Esc, using the up- or down- arrow key to highlight the GeoWorks entry, and pressing Enter. You cannot access the normal Task Manager menu while within GeoWorks. You must use the GeoWorks TaskMax control panel.

From the GeoWorks TaskMax control panel, to switch to or delete another task, use your mouse to click the selected task. The Run and Delete buttons are activated. Click the Run button (or press R) to switch to the selected task. Click Delete (or press D) to delete the selected task.

The TaskMax control panel also displays the amount of free swap space available for additional tasks, measured in kilobytes. There is also a Clipboard Support selection that you can turn on or off. If it is on, the GeoWorks Clipboard works with the TaskMax cut-and-paste feature. You can click the Clipboard Support selection off if you like.

> **Note**
>
> In this version of Novell DOS 7, Task Manager does not currently include a cut-and-paste feature. It may be added in a future release.

To return to GeoWorks, click the OK button.

When there are additional tasks active under Task Manager, you can access these tasks from within the Express menu. Open this menu, and under the TaskMax Control option, there are options for the other active tasks. Click one of the active tasks, and you can switch to that task. You do not have to use the TaskMax control panel.

Appendix D

Using DEBUG

DEBUG, a programming debugger, is a useful utility that comes with Novell DOS 7. You can use DEBUG to test and debug programs. Of course, debugging programs is not the normal task of most users. However, if you do need to test or debug a program interactively, you will be glad that DEBUG is available. DR DOS 5.0 and DR DOS 6.0 included SID, or Symbolic Instruction Debugger. The programmers at Novell changed the name to match other DOS debugger utilities and modified the more powerful SID commands so that the new version is now compatible, although a superset, of the MS version. The Novell DOS DEBUG utility works with all PC processors from the 8086 through the Pentium (586) chips.

You may find DEBUG useful in other ways also. Some popular computer magazines provide DEBUG scripts that you can use to create some neat little utilities for your system.

This appendix is not designed to give you a grueling step-by-step tutorial of DEBUG. Instead, it shows you how to start and quit DEBUG, gives you some of the characteristics of DEBUG, and provides a list of commands you can use with DEBUG.

Running DEBUG

There are several ways to start and use DEBUG. The simplest method is to start the utility by just entering the following at the DOS prompt:

    DEBUG

The DEBUG prompt, a hyphen (–), appears after the version and copyright information. You enter all commands for DEBUG from this hyphen prompt.

Enter a question mark (?) for a list of commands available to you within DE-
BUG.

Often, when you use DEBUG, you will want to load a program. When you
issue the command to start DEBUG, you can enter the name of the program
and any arguments or switches required by the program being loaded. The
syntax for starting DEBUG in this way is

```
DEBUG path:filename.ext parameters
```

The *filename.ext* is the program to load. You must supply the full file name,
and if the location of the target file is not in the system path, you must include that with the file name. If you want to use any parameters required by
the test program, you can specify them on the command line.

The third method for starting DEBUG is for creating command files (COM)
from scripts you find in computer books or magazines. The first step is to
create the ASCII text script file. You do this with a text editor, such as EDIT
provided with Novell DOS 7. After you prepare the script, enter the following
command:

```
DEBUG < scriptfil.ext
```

The redirection symbol (<) tells DOS to supply the script file (*scriptfil.ext*) to
DEBUG, which then processes the script into the command file.

To quit DEBUG and return to the DOS prompt, enter **Q** (or **q**) at the hyphen
prompt.

DEBUG Command Conventions

Each command is entered with the first character. This determines the action
you want taken, and you can place one or more arguments after the command. The arguments are the values required for specific actions.

All numeric values must be expressed in hexadecimal notation, and you must
separate such values by a comma or space. You can also use a comma or space
to separate other arguments.

If the first character of a DEBUG command line is a semicolon (;), DEBUG
regards that line as a comment and ignores it.

Most DEBUG commands require one or more addresses as operands. An *address* consists of an optional segment register or four-digit segment address, plus an offset value. These must be separated by a colon (:). If you omit the required segment register or segment address, DEBUG supplies a default value, depending on the command entered. The default segment for the A, G, L, T, U, and W commands is CS:. The default segment for all other commands is DS:.

Some DEBUG commands, by their nature, require you to specify a range of memory for the operation to be performed. You must specify both the *start_address* and *end_address*, or the *start_address* and the length of the range, preceded with an L.

DEBUG Commands

Table D.1 lists the commands you can use in DEBUG.

Command	Format	Description
?	?	Lists available DEBUG commands
A	A *address*	Assembles 8086-Pentium mnemonics
C	C *range address*	Compares two blocks of memory
D	D *range*	Displays the contents of a block of memory
E	E *address data*	Enters data into memory starting at a specified address
F	F *range data*	Fills a block of memory with specified values
G	G =*address breakpoints*	Runs the executable file currently in memory
H	H *value1 value2*	Performs hexadecimal arithmetic
I	I	Displays a one-byte value from a specified port
L	L *address*	Loads either the contents of a file or the contents of disk sectors into memory

Command	Format	Description
M	M *range address*	Moves the contents of a block of memory
N	N *path:filename.ext*	Specifies a file for an L or W command, or specifies the parameters for the file being tested
O	O *port value*	Sends a one-byte value to an output port
P	P *=address number*	Executes instructions from the specified address in the test program
Q	Q	Quits from the DEBUG utility
R	R *register*	Displays or alters the contents of one or more registers
S	S *range data*	Searches a block of memory for a specified sequence of one or more byte values
T	T *=address number*	Trace-executes one instruction and then displays the status of all flags, the contents of all registers, and the decoded form of the instruction that DEBUG executes next
U	U *range*	Disassembles bytes and displays the corresponding source statements
W	W *address*	Writes the file currently being tested to a disk

Index

Symbols

GO AHEAD. PLUG YOURSELF INTO PRENTICE HALL COMPUTER PUBLISHING.

Introducing the PHCP Forum on CompuServe®

Yes, it's true. Now, you can have CompuServe access to the same professional, friendly folks who have made computers easier for years. On the PHCP Forum, you'll find additional information on the topics covered by every PHCP imprint—including Que, Sams Publishing, New Riders Publishing, Alpha Books, Brady Books, Hayden Books, and Adobe Press. In addition, you'll be able to receive technical support and disk updates for the software produced by Que Software and Paramount Interactive, a division of the Paramount Technology Group. It's a great way to supplement the best information in the business.

WHAT CAN YOU DO ON THE PHCP FORUM?

Play an important role in the publishing process—and make our books better while you make your work easier:

- Leave messages and ask questions about PHCP books and software—you're guaranteed a response within 24 hours

- Download helpful tips and software to help you get the most out of your computer

- Contact authors of your favorite PHCP books through electronic mail

- Present your own book ideas

- Keep up to date on all the latest books available from each of PHCP's exciting imprints

JOIN NOW AND GET A FREE COMPUSERVE STARTER KIT!

To receive your free CompuServe Introductory Membership, call toll-free, **1-800-848-8199** and ask for representative **#597**. The Starter Kit Includes:

- Personal ID number and password

- $15 credit on the system

- Subscription to CompuServe Magazine

HERE'S HOW TO PLUG INTO PHCP:

Once on the CompuServe System, type any of these phrases to access the PHCP Forum:

GO PHCP   **GO BRADY**
GO QUEBOOKS   **GO HAYDEN**
GO SAMS   **GO QUESOFT**
GO NEWRIDERS   **GO PARAMOUNTINTER**
GO ALPHA

Once you're on the CompuServe Information Service, be sure to take advantage of all of CompuServe's resources. CompuServe is home to more than 1,700 products and services—plus it has over 1.5 million members worldwide. You'll find valuable online reference materials, travel and investor services, electronic mail, weather updates, leisure-time games and hassle-free shopping (no jam-packed parking lots or crowded stores).

Seek out the hundreds of other forums that populate CompuServe. Covering diverse topics such as pet care, rock music, cooking, and political issues, you're sure to find others with the sames concerns as you—and expand your knowledge at the same time.

Complete Computer Coverage

Que's 1994 Computer Hardware Buyer's Guide

Que Development Group

This absolute must-have guide packed with comparisons, recommendations, and tips for asking all the right questions familiarizes the reader with terms they will need to know. This book offers a complete analysis of both hardware and software products, and it's loaded with charts and tables of product comparisons.

IBM-compatibles, Apple, & Macintosh

$16.95 USA

1-56529-281-2, 480 pp., 8 x 10

Que's Computer User's Dictionary, 4th Edition

Bryan Pfaffenberger

This compact, practical reference contains hundreds of definitions, explanations, examples, and illustrations on topics from programming to desktop publishing. You can master the "language" of computers and learn how to make your personal computer more efficient and more powerful. Filled with tips and cautions, *Que's Computer User's Dictionary* is the perfect resource for anyone who uses a computer.

IBM, Macintosh, Apple, & Programming

$12.95 USA

1-56529-604-4, 650 pp., 4³/₄ x 8

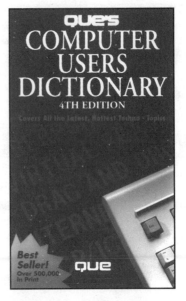

To Order, Call: (800) 428-5331

Que—The World's Leading 1-2-3 Experts!

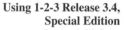
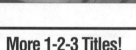
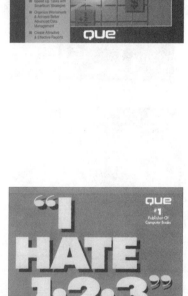